The Anthology of Social Studies

Volume 1
Issues and Strategies for Elementary Teachers

The Anthology

of Social Studies

Volume 1

Issues and Strategies for Elementary Teachers

Roland Case
Penney Clark
Editors

Pacific Educational Press
Vancouver, Canada

Copyright 2008 Roland Case and Penney Clark
ISBN 978-1-895766-80-6

Published by Pacific Educational Press
Faculty of Education
University of British Columbia
6365 Biological Sciences Rd.
Vancouver, Canada V6T 1Z4
Telephone: 604-822-5385
Fax: 604-822-6603
E-mail: pep@interchange.ubc.ca

Library and Archives Canada Cataloguing in Publication Data

The anthology of social studies/edited by Roland Case and Penney Clark.

Includes bibliographical references and index.
Contents: v.1. Issues and strategies for elementary teachers.
ISBN 978-1-895766-80-6 (v.1)

1. Social sciences—Study and teaching (Elementary).   2. Education, Elementary—Curricula.

I. Case, Roland, 1951–   II. Clark, Penney

LB1584.A54 2008   372.83'044   C2006-903469-9

Cover Illustration: Genie Macleod
Cover Design: Warren Clark
Editing: James Allen, Merrill Fearon, Tanya Howe

Printed in Canada
6   5   4   3   2   10   11   12   13

In memory of our parents
Warren and Mary Case
Hugh and Mildred Clark

Contents

Preface

Encouraged by the enduring regard for *The Canadian Anthology of Social Studies* published in 1997, we decided to extend the scope of this work by creating two volumes—an elementary and a secondary book—and to renew its focus by creating new emphases and topics. This collection is compiled from revised and updated versions of chapters published in the original anthology and eleven newly commissioned pieces. The salient changes include the following:

- There are now two volumes, one for each of elementary and secondary schools, to better focus the text for our two audiences. This has allowed us to add more chapters dealing with primary and upper elementary issues to this volume.
- There are new topics. We have added a number of chapters on topics such as First Nations, reading instruction in content areas, historical thinking, ways of engaging students, planning for inquiry teaching, use of artifacts, creating a community of thinkers, and enhancing critical thinking.
- This volume has nine fewer chapters than the previous single-volume anthology had. We removed chapters that seemed least current and, where possible, shortened the existing chapters by eliminating irrelevant examples.
- The discussions have been updated. Many of the chapters are revisions to those in the original volume. Where substantive changes have been made, we have slightly modified the chapter title so as not to mislead readers into thinking the original and current chapters are identical.
- A new query feature provides questions for readers to consider while they read the chapters and at the end of each chapter.
- The new book title reflects the division between elementary and secondary students and the word "Canadian" has been removed. Although all of the chapters have been written by Canadian educators, the previous edition aroused interest among American and British teachers.

Notwithstanding the changes reflected in this new volume, we have retained, in fact enhanced, what we and others saw to be the strengths of its predecessor.

This work is in a true sense an anthology that marries the best of theory and practice in social studies. The word "anthology" originally meant a collection of flowers. It subsequently came to refer to a collection of the "flowers" of verse and, by extension, to the "flowers" of professional and scholarly thinking. Like a bouquet, this anthology of thirty-two chapters by twenty-eight teachers and teacher educators from across Canada has the diversity and richness that comes only from a multiplicity of viewpoints and experiences. Like a carefully arranged bouquet, the different perspectives—rather than competing with others in the volume—complement and accentuate the features of the other chapters. In this respect, we are especially proud of both the harmony and the diversity of ideas in this volume. Collectively, they speak of a powerful and exciting vision of social studies. As well, they blend in countless very specific, practical suggestions with important discussions of the foundational issues at the heart of social studies teaching. We believe this new book will be of even greater value as a methods text for beginning teachers in teacher education programs and as a professional resource for experienced teachers and other educators working in social studies.

In a project of this undertaking, many individuals deserve thanks for the crucial contributions they have made. We especially appreciate the authors of the works found in this anthology. We believe they are among the finest educators and teacher educators in Canadian social studies and their writings reflect this expertise. The guidance and editorial support from our publisher, Catherine Edwards, and her editors, Laraine Coates, Merrill Fearon, and Tanya Howe, have greatly enhanced the book.

We are grateful to The Critical Thinking Consortium for granting permission to reproduce or adapt many teaching ideas found in its award-winning series, Critical Challenges Across the Curriculum. For more information about this international, non-profit group, and to view the many social studies resources they have developed, consult its website at www.tc2.ca.

Roland Case
Penney Clark

PART 1 Foundations

1

Challenges and Choices Facing Elementary Social Studies Teachers

Neil Smith

The challenges and choices facing social studies teachers are neither new nor simple. What goals should we emphasize? What methods could we employ to achieve these goals? How might we engage students in their own learning? This chapter invites social studies teachers to think in broad terms about what is needed to make social studies a valuable and interesting educational experience for students.

Whether we love social studies or reluctantly teach this subject, all of us can benefit from looking afresh at what social studies means to us and to our students. We may need to reconcile our personal orientation and predisposition to teach social studies in a particular way with new possibilities that may appear foreign or daunting. In some respects, this is because of our past socialization to the subject. Each of us comes to the role of "social studies teacher" having already experienced many hours of "teacher training" while attending social studies classes as a student in elementary and secondary school. During this time, ideas about the purpose of social studies and how it is supposed to be taught have been etched on our minds. These past experiences will likely profoundly shape our approach to teaching the subject. As the old adage goes, "We teach as we were taught."

> Take a moment to think back over your own experiences as a social studies student in elementary and secondary school. What were your best experiences? What were your worst experiences? What do you need to learn so that your own teaching will reflect more of your positive experiences and fewer of your negative experiences?

Reassured by our own social studies experiences, many of us may ask: "Surely these established patterns of teaching social studies are still adequate?" I believe they are not. Even if we personally enjoyed social studies in school, the subject as a whole has been largely unsuccessful both in achieving its aims and in motivating students. According to John Goodlad's seminal study of over a thousand North American classrooms, social studies is one of the least popular of all the commonly taught subjects. Upper elementary students liked it less than any other subject (1984, 210–212). At the secondary level, Goodlad observed that:

> The topics commonly included in the social sciences appear as though they would be of great human interest. But something strange seems to have happened to them on the way to the classroom. The topics of study become removed from their intrinsically human character, reduced to the dates and places readers will recall memorizing for tests (Goodlad 1984).

It is also disturbing that students generally perceive social studies to be one of the most difficult subjects, largely because of the volume of information they must remember and not because of the amount of thinking required. Studies of British Columbia social studies teachers, for example, found that the importance they attach to critical thinking is not adequately reflected in the teaching strategies they use in their classrooms (Bognar, Cassidy, and Clarke 1997; Case 1993).

The challenge—and it is a difficult one—is for each of us to recognize and understand both the strengths and the limitations of our inherited visions of social studies and then to build upon and beyond these experiences to enliven social studies for more of our students. I offer three typical vignettes of social studies teaching as a way to begin a critical conversation about the "what" and "how" of social studies. These snapshots of teaching practice invite us to recognize ourselves in them and then to look both for the positive elements and, even more importantly, for the areas where improvement is possible.

> Read the vignette on the following page, but before reading the author's comments, conduct your own analysis of the lesson: What are its positive aspects? What shortcomings do you notice? How might you improve upon the lesson? Repeat this process after you've read the other two vignettes.

VIGNETTE #1: FINDING THE FACTS

"Okay, let's turn to page 83 in the text, please." James quietly groans and slouches a little lower in his seat. Glancing to the front, he recognizes the predictable signals. Ms. Knowles is about to launch into today's discussion. James' slight anxiety about not having read the assigned chapter on Canadian pioneers for homework is balanced by his confidence that most of his friends are probably in the same boat.

He opens the textbook and begins to flip through the pages. With a quick glance up at Knowles, James is reminded that she is an okay teacher. In fact, most kids quite like her. She is sincere and always keen about the subject. But in spite of her own enthusiasm, she isn't able to excite most students about this stuff. For most of them, the definition of social studies is "a school way to talk about the dead."

Knowles' first question dislodges James from his musings. "What jobs did pioneers in Canada perform?" Her eyes scan the room. James hasn't a clue. He mentally replays his survival strategy. If Knowles looks in his direction for an answer, he will first avert his eyes; if she asks him for the answer directly, he will look up politely with a shy, vacant look on his face, fumble through the pages, and mutter that he doesn't remember that part of the chapter. Be polite and uninformed. That usually suffices. He will stay in Knowles' good books, and she probably won't bother him again for the rest of the lesson.

The teacher-directed questioning now begins in earnest. Page by page, the information emerges from the memories of the "regulars," those five students who always seem to appreciate the discussion and who recall the information well enough to offer intelligent comments. Slowly, relentlessly, Knowles extracts the desired facts and painfully constructs a picture from them, as if they were pieces of a jigsaw puzzle. Finally, she proclaims that the chapter has been "covered." James muses that this chapter, like the others before it, has been "buried"—but it will be resurrected very briefly at test time.

A writing assignment is next inscribed on the board: "Describe how early pioneers contributed to the development of Canada." James spends the next fifteen minutes summarizing a few key ideas he remembers from the discussion: that many pioneers became hard-working farmers, while others worked on the construction of the railroad. He receives some help from Alex, an "A" student sitting beside him. He then scans the text, finds one or two other ideas, and copies them verbatim into his assignment. Enough to hold up the A– average, he thinks to himself. After staring dreamily into the pages of the text for a few minutes, then taking a drink at the water fountain, James sighs deeply and heads off to the library, where he is expected to continue his research project on Canadian pioneers.

In reviewing the first vignette, it is important to acknowledge the lesson's positive attributes. The teacher was perceived by James to be both knowledgeable and enthusiastic in her approach to teaching social studies. She systematically exposed students to important background facts that might serve as a platform from which students could build a greater understanding of Canadian history. For a handful of students, the class discussion enabled them to make personal the information contained in their reading assignment.

The lesson, however, raises several basic questions. What organizing themes or concepts frame students' investigations? There is no evidence that the information presented amounts to anything more than a series of facts. It may be what Walter Parker (1989, 40) calls "teaching by mentioning" or the "parade of facts" approach: "the teacher tells students a few facts about a person or event and then moves on to telling a few facts about another person or event."

What insights or lessons are students asked to draw from the information? The larger picture—the general significance of the jobs performed by pioneers—is neither apparent to nor appreciated by most students.

What level of responsibility or accountability should individual students take for their own learning? The lesson relies heavily on the textbook, with the teacher engaging students in a "search and rescue" attempt to discover the facts contained within it. This methodology tacitly encourages compliance from most students, and does little to increase the number of students who actively participate in discussions or think critically about underlying issues. Although the lesson is presented clearly, and represents a solid effort to introduce new knowledge, students have little opportunity to connect this knowledge to previously learned facts and concepts, nor are they motivated to do so. Finally, the teacher does not develop a segue to subsequent investigations that may invoke fuller and more critical analysis by students.

We are left to conjecture how this lesson might be enlarged beyond the mere acquisition of facts to learning that would be both compelling and challenging for students. This challenge brings us to a second vignette, one that moves outside the textbook to the world beyond the classroom.

A number of positive features are apparent in this scenario. Students are actively engaged in the experiences, at least insofar as they all show genuine interest in how each organization they visit functions. Their teacher is committed to providing them with positive experiences that carry them beyond textbooks into the real workings of their community. He is well-organized and uses a broad variety of community resources. Students clearly expand their general knowledge of occupations in their community.

The levels of student enthusiasm in this scenario are

VIGNETTE #2: TREKKING THROUGH TOWN

Mr. Stevens is upbeat. He is continually drumming up enthusiasm among his young students for their community study, tirelessly opening up new avenues for exploring local organizations. Mr. Stevens quickly steps out of the line of children and parent helpers in front of the school and checks off each student's name. After a quick review of the field trip rules, the class walks single file for three blocks, soon reaching the local fire hall where the chief and four firefighters await them.

For the next hour, the class tours the facility. The hosts explain their jobs, telling students about some of the funny and sad things that they encounter in their work. They describe the various pieces of firefighting equipment. Children slide down the fire pole from half-ceiling height, try on rubber boots and coats, and clamber onto the fire truck. When asked by the fire chief whether they have any special questions, silence ensues among the students, broken only when one student asks whether all firefighters are permitted to drive the truck. Another asks whether the chief has ever seen anyone die, and then a third asks what the firefighters do all day and night when there are no emergency calls. At this point, the allotted time is up, and the class heads back to school, arriving just in time for gym class.

In the next social studies period, the class visits the local grocery store and spends time talking with the staff. They tour the back of the store, look at the butchers' work area, examine the throwaway vegetable section, and visit the offices. After a brief conversation with the manager, the students return to class and resume other activities. The community study proceeds in a similar fashion for three weeks, with field trips to two local businesses, the town hall, and a farm. Three parents also volunteer as guest speakers to explain their occupations. The students listen, and the teacher encourages them to ask the guests questions about their work. At the end of the unit, Mr. Stevens presents a summative assignment: "Pick your favourite job or organization and write five things about it."

---

higher than those described in the first vignette; many of the same questions must, however, be asked. To what extent are students motivated to learn from these experiences? Kieran Egan (1990, 1997) contends that children are typically underwhelmed with the study of everyday experiences, and that greater learning potential exists within the more distant worlds of fantasy and imagination. When social studies concepts are taught in the context of legends and mythology, for example, students are propelled by the power of story to consider important lessons about honour and shame, trust and betrayal, and other fundamental human notions. Egan believes these to be far more relevant and motivating than a trip to the fire hall could ever be. Involving students in direct experiences, as portrayed in this field trip vignette, should not be assumed to be educationally sound simply because students eagerly participate in them.

A related concern is student accountability. In field trip activities, what responsibility do students have for their own learning? Much as James did in the first vignette, these students are participating in a free ride (albeit with legs moving), and feel little obligation to inquire into their community. The field trips might have been enriched if students had identified and completed specific investigations during the trips. After collecting data in the field, students might then have reported their findings to the class. The field "trip" could thereby have been transformed into a field "study," and provided a rich source of fresh concepts and ideas emerging from well-constructed investigations. Such a scenario best comes as a result of a teacher working with students to decide upon the most interesting and challenging questions to guide their inquiries.

In this field trip lesson, what insights of importance have students gained? What new knowledge or concepts have these students acquired? Although they may pick up tidbits of information incidentally, it is unclear from the vignette that students entered or exited the field trips with a rich context for framing and extending their study. The experiences appear as serial pop-up activities with only a modest expectation that students will connect or apply this information to some larger question or problem. It is too large a stretch to expect that students will make these connections by themselves. Engaging children in direct experiences for the sake of active learning without helping them make the important connections may be interpreted as largely providing entertainment. John Dewey (1938), the twentieth-century advocate of experiential education, exhorted teachers to legitimate active learning by systematically linking it to reflective practice and helping students make meaning out of their experiences by drawing conclusions from them. The main message: direct experiences such as field trips must be linked closely to concepts and theories through reflective thought. But this brings us back to our primary question.

What will make the teaching of social studies a motivating and educationally significant experience for students? It is frequently suggested that schooling should do more to help students learn how to learn and to assess knowledge critically, solve problems, and make sound decisions. The third vignette seems to more directly address this vision of social studies teaching. But, as we review the lesson, we will see that it too provides some cause for concern.

Clearly, students in the third and last vignette are actively engaged in a series of diverse activities. Each student has in-

VIGNETTE #3: TACKLING THE BIG ISSUES

It seemed a bit funny. Grade 4 students reading fairy stories in social studies, especially the old version of "The Three Little Pigs." Then Mrs. Arnell—"Ms. A," the students call her—reads them a version of the tale told from the wolf's point of view. In *The True Story of the 3 Little Pigs* (Scieszka 1999), the wolf defends his badly tarnished reputation. Students begin to understand how selected events may be interpreted and reported in very different ways, depending on the point of view taken. Students compare the events of the classic version of the tale with the wolf's version and prepare to take on the different roles of the story characters in a simplified mock trial. The trial is going to determine whether the wolf is innocent or guilty of first-degree murder in the death of two pigs.

The wolf (the defendant), who pleads not guilty, works with his legal defence team to review the events reported in the story and to select information that supports his claim of innocence. Crown Counsel and her team of students are given one hour to study the case and develop arguments supporting their position that the wolf is guilty of premeditated murder. The judge and jury study the general background of the case and learn about their responsibilities in the trial proceedings. The next day, the wolf's trial is held. The teacher videotapes the proceedings, and, using jointly generated criteria, helps students assess their own and their peers' presentations. "Interesting," the students think, "a lot of work and even a bit of fun. So what does this have to do with what we are supposed to be studying about Canadian history?"

Ms. A starts the third day's class with a story and drawings showing Captain Cook's first encounters with the "Nootka" peoples of the west coast of Canada in the late eighteenth century. She summarizes the European views of the key events and, for homework, asks students to read Cook's account reprinted in the textbook. The next day she provides students with an entirely different perspective—this time from some of the recently published accounts of Maquinna and the Nuu-chah-nulth peoples who were the inhabitants of Friendly Cove on Vancouver Island. These accounts present an entirely different side of the story that has been passed on through oral tradition. They contain detailed descriptions of humiliation and assaults endured by the coastal peoples at the hands of European explorers. Ms. A. then asks the class to compare the two versions of "The Three Little Pigs" with the two versions of the encounters between Cook and the Nuu-chah-nulth people. She helps students use the proper language to compare the fictional with the historical events, and to refine their rough ideas so they are able to write in their journals about the similarities and differences between them.

Next, the students prepare for a second mock trial. This time, Captain Cook is charged with destroying the way of life of an indigenous people. Students employ the same model they used in the wolf's trial. Each student, first independently, then in a group, researches events related to the first contact in Friendly Cove. They write a summary of these events and with the help of a small group of peers construct arguments either defending or prosecuting Cook. As a culminating activity, they present their arguments in a mock trial.

dividual responsibilities within the learning tasks. Students such as James in the first vignette would have had difficulty evading this kind of assignment. To succeed in the mock trials, for example, each student is required to produce written arguments based on research and analysis, and then present them in a persuasive manner. It was intended that students would develop these skills first in relation to the fairy tale, and later by applying them to historical events related to European and aboriginal contact on the west coast of Canada. The objectives for the lesson extended well beyond the text of a classic piece of children's literature. Building on Egan's idea that story and literature can serve as a vehicle to teach important concepts, students learned about "points of view" by comparing the traditional version of the fairy tale with a modern counterpart. The teacher invited students to think critically—asking them to analyze information, decide what information would support their arguments, create and present arguments, and, ultimately, to make ethical judgments about an important historical figure. All is well thus far.

So what are the problems in this teaching scenario? The concerns with this vignette are found in the manner in which students are cast into an extremely complex historical context with insufficient background information, concepts, and skills for them to analyze the issues competently.

If students are to move beyond a superficial indictment or vindication of Captain Cook, they need a more thorough knowledge of both peoples involved: the Nuu-chah-nulth people—their history, economy, and social patterns, their previous and subsequent experiences with European and American traders, and their changing attitudes towards the white visitors; and, on the other side, the European explorers—their methods of pursuing trade, and the competition that drove their sponsors to expand their boundaries and increase the volume of trade. Without this understanding, students may be unable to judge responsibly whether or not Cook was guilty of destroying a nation of indigenous people.

A related concern stems from the skills and concepts presupposed by the very sophisticated challenges students were given. Expecting each student to successfully develop a cohesive argument is an immense stretch if students are not coached and supported in the requisite "tools." For example, will students recognize when a reason supports a conclusion and when it is largely irrelevant? Can they distinguish unfounded or exaggerated statements from grounded ones? Are students disposed to look at potential counter-arguments to their position or will they quickly reach a conclusion and be closed to all other options? Fundamental, too, is students' appreciation of the ethnocentrism that may colour each group's perceptions of events. Even the question posed—guilty or innocent—may fuel an unproductive "all or nothing" view of an issue that may better be cast in shades of gray. As exciting and challenging as they might appear, the trials and associated debating exercises are highly sophisticated and complex practices that may result in superficial outcomes unless preceded by deliberate and comprehensive preparation. The required abilities in critical thinking do not come naturally to most students, and many will need the support of a systematic progression of instruction and guided practice to prepare them for such complex challenges. Thus, although there is much that is educationally exciting about this third vignette, there are significant gaps that may undermine student learning.

As our discussion of these three vignettes suggests, effective social studies teaching is a complex and demanding enterprise. There are many choices to make concerning what to teach and a great deal of thought is involved in making these studies educationally rewarding for our students. In reviewing the three vignettes, we see how each offers a piece of the puzzle, yet each left on its own presents an incomplete picture. Students must acquire knowledge, yet our teaching must reach beyond transmitting factual information to developing thoughtful understanding. There is a need to involve students in mindful exploration of the world around them. This involves much more than providing active, hands-on experiences; it requires helping students frame, think about, and apply these experiences in meaningful and fruitful ways. As well, there is more to promoting thoughtfulness than posing provocative issues or dilemmas for discussion; we must identify and carefully develop the requisite skills and knowledge that will empower students to competently and responsibly tackle these challenges. Finally, the diverse curricular and pedagogical decisions regarding what and how to teach social studies must be influenced by one additional consideration—students have to be engaged in and by their social studies before they can be expected to learn what this subject has to offer.

REFERENCES

Bognar, C., W. Cassidy, and P. Clarke. 1997. *Social studies in British Columbia: Results of the 1996 provincial learning assessment.* Victoria, BC: Evaluation and Accountability Branch, Ministry of Education, Skills and Training, Province of British Columbia.

Case, R. 1993. *Summary of the 1992 social studies needs assessment.* Victoria, BC: Queen's Printer.

Dewey, J. 1938. *Experience and education.* New York: Free Press.

Egan, K. 1990. *Teaching as story telling.* London, ON: Althouse Press.

———. 1997. *The educated mind: How cognitive tools shape our understanding.* Chicago: University of Chicago Press.

Goodlad, J. 1984. *A place called school.* New York: McGraw-Hill.

Parker, W. 1989. How to help students learn history and geography. *Educational Leadership* 47 (3): 39–43.

Scieszka, J. 1999. *The true story of the 3 little pigs.* New York: Viking.

2 Purposeful Teaching in Elementary Social Studies

Roland Case and Mary Abbott

SOCIAL STUDIES IS... A POEM

What is social studies?
What a question to ask.
How will I answer?
What a difficult task.

Should the focus be religious?
Early settlers felt it was the key
The Revolutionary War
Brought a new philosophy.

Is social studies history
With a focus on the past?
Or sociology
Where the subject seems so vast!

Is social studies geography?
Where we look at population.
Or is it anthropology?
Where we look at culture's creation.

Is social studies political science?
And a view of government.
Or is it economics?
And a view of money spent.

When I am learning social studies
Should I start with me?
This is called the spiral curricula
And it could hold the key.

Should my lessons be directed
By the teacher or me?
Or can I learn about the subjects
By my own discovery?

While writing this poem
It seems I do digress.
Overall, I think the definition of social studies
Should include human development and progress.

—Donna Robinson

An Enduring Dilemma

Although social studies has been a part of the school curriculum for almost a century, there is little agreement on what constitutes a worthwhile social studies program. As the preceding poem suggests, there are likely as many answers to the question "What is social studies?" as there are social studies educators. Although lack of consensus is not necessarily undesirable—standardization, *per se*, is not a precondition for sound social studies teaching—the current diversity of conceptions is often characterized as a confused mess. As Marion Brady suggests, social studies is in "a chaotic state" little more than "an incredible heap of miscellany" comprised of:

> some odd pieces of the past held together by habit, a few bits of several social sciences (themselves in need of major rethinking), the remnants of a dozen ill-digested fads, an assortment of responses to demands of state legislators and special interest groups, and other odds and ends assigned to social studies because they do not seem to fit anywhere else (1989, 80).

The problem is captured in the cartoon "What Should be Included in the Social Studies Curriculum?", which shows bewildered educators peering at many jigsaw puzzle pieces. Each piece represents a different dimension of social studies (for example, citizenship education, generalizations, global education, skills, social action, history). The onlookers are unable to figure out how all the pieces fit together. Significantly, the caption reads: "It might help if we had a picture of what this is supposed to look like."

This lack of a clear picture is evident in the disconnected, irrelevant learning that many teachers report when asked what they remember of their own elementary studies classes. Isolated facts, endless colouring of maps, and tedious research reports figure strongly in their recollections. We recently asked a group of pre-service teachers to survey intermediate level students to determine their attitudes towards social studies. The majority of students cited social studies as their

WHAT SHOULD BE INCLUDED IN THE SOCIAL STUDIES CURRICULUM?

Cartoon by John Anfin. Courtesy of the artist.

least favourite subject. The very title of a popular professional book, *If This Is Social Studies, Why Isn't It Boring?* (Steffay and Hood 1994) is a further indictment of the subject. Clearly, social studies has the potential to be an exciting, dynamic, and thought-provoking subject, but all too often it fails to achieve this potential. So how do we decide what we should be doing and where would we begin to look?

Our goal here is to suggest how teachers might develop clearer pictures of what meaningful social studies looks like. The solution is not to be found in a definition of social studies, but in the answer to a fundamental question: "What am I really supposed to be teaching in social studies?" It is not imperative that everyone identifies exactly the same answer. Rather, it is important that individual teachers come to a coherent and defensible purpose that drives their social studies teaching. Developing this "picture" is a long-term aim that may take years to realize fully. But the alternative of not bothering to figure it out is much less satisfying—it results in what Brady referred to as "a chaotic state" and "an incredible heap of miscellany."

Finding Purpose in Curriculum Documents

Faced with the dilemma of what to teach, a teacher might reasonably turn to the prescribed curriculum for direction. Surely all we need to do is look at the provincial documents to learn what the government expects us to teach in social studies. As we will see, it is not as simple as that, but it is important to know what we will find in these documents and

to understand their role in developing a purposeful social studies program.

SPECIFIC CURRICULUM OUTCOMES

In provincial curriculum guidelines, the most specific and, one would think, most practical place to look is the lists of specific learning outcomes for a particular grade level—also called specific expectations or objectives. Let's see if these outcomes provide a clear sense of direction and purpose. In Table 2.1 are listed typical outcomes from three social studies curricula and sample activities that a teacher might use to address these outcomes.

In each of these examples, undertaking the suggested activity would satisfy the identified knowledge outcome and address (at least partly) the skill outcomes. The teacher could then confidently proceed to the next knowledge expectation in the curriculum and begin to address it.

The Ontario teacher might move from daily life in medieval times to castles and castle life (sports, entertainment, and justice). Students might draw pictures of a castle showing people undertaking typical activities. From here, the teacher could move to the next curricular outcome, which involves tracing the effects of various events including the Crusades, the opening of the Silk Road, and the Black Death.

The Alberta teacher might turn from uses of natural resources to an outcome dealing with competing demands on the land (for example, recreational use, food production, resource extraction). Students might brainstorm potential uses for a particular plot of land in their community or region.

The British Columbia teacher might move from the distribution of resources to explore the difference between renewable and non-renewable resources. Students might do this by sorting various resources into the two categories.

In each case, the teacher would continue in a similar vein until all outcomes had been covered. But it is worth asking what has been achieved. What is the reason for wanting students to learn about daily life a thousand years ago or to web different products developed from a natural resource? The effect of attempting to "cover" each outcome is to drag students through the curriculum for no apparent reason other than that the ministry curriculum guide states that topic X and skill Y must be taught. The problem is compounded when we realize that a given grade level may list many dozens of outcomes. For example, the Ontario grade 4 social studies curriculum lists 45 specific expectations, the Alberta grade 4 curriculum lists 102 specific outcomes, and the BC curriculum for grade 5 prescribes 24 learning outcomes.

"Covering" the specific outcomes in the curriculum doesn't lead to engaging, meaningful learning for at least four reasons.

- **Outcomes don't dictate teaching method**. Curriculum that is specified in terms of outcomes or expectations

TABLE 2.1 TYPICAL OUTCOMES AND ACTIVITIES

ONTARIO GRADE 4 (ONTARIO MINISTRY OF EDUCATION 2004)	ALBERTA GRADE 4 (ALBERTA LEARNING 2006)	BRITISH COLUMBIA GRADE 5 (BC MINISTRY OF EDUCATION 2006)
Knowledge outcome: describe aspects of daily life for men, women, and children in medieval societies (e.g., food, housing, clothing, health, religion, recreation, festivals, crafts, justice, roles) (27)	**Knowledge outcome:** analyze how Albertans interact with their environment by exploring and reflecting upon… How are natural resources used by Albertans (i.e., agriculture, oil and natural gas, forests, coal)? (14)	**Knowledge outcome:** describe the location of natural resources within BC and Canada (93)
Skill outcome: use graphic organizers to summarize information (e.g.,… timeline showing dates of innovations and events, T-chart showing comparison of peasants' and lords' lifestyles) (28)	**Skill outcome:** use graphic organizers, such as webbing or Venn diagrams, to make meaning of information (22)	**Skill outcome:** gather a body of information from a variety of primary and secondary sources (86)
Typical activity: Students might gather relevant information from the textbook about medieval societies and complete a three-column chart comparing aspects of daily life for men, women, and children.	**Typical activity:** Students might research an assigned resource using a government website. Groups could create a web diagram showing the uses that Albertans make of an assigned resource.	**Typical activity:** Students might research the distribution of resources in a particular province or territory using atlases, CD-ROMs, or online maps. Groups could present their research through models or maps that use grids (for example, longitude and latitude) and scales to show location.

describes what students should know or be able to do as a result of completing the lesson, but it doesn't indicate how teachers might involve students in learning the topic in the first place. For example, asking students to describe life in medieval times may be a way of assessing what they have learned, but we might teach them this information by reading a novel that transports students back to that time period. The tendency to teach the topic by asking students to perform the task mentioned in the outcome fuels this pattern of "covering the curriculum" that students find boring.

- **Outcomes aren't organized in teachable clusters.** Specific outcomes need not be taught in the order in which they are listed, nor for that matter need they be taught individually. The pattern when "covering" the curriculum is to proceed from one outcome to the next, often in a drawn-out manner. This is what Brady (1989, 80) is referring to as an "incredible heap of miscellany." This need not be the case. For example, all eighteen outcomes in the Medieval Times strand of the grade 4 Ontario curriculum (plus numerous language arts outcomes) could be addressed through one large project—namely, inviting students to research, write, and perform a play about medieval life.
- **Outcomes don't specify priority.** Not all outcomes are of equal importance nor will they have equal value for students in a given class. Consequently, each outcome

does not warrant the same amount of teaching time. In fact, a few outcomes may have great priority and deserve extended treatment, whereas others should be touched upon very quickly. The tendency when "covering" the curriculum is to teach a topic for as long as it takes to complete the selected activity—even if this means less important outcomes receive more attention than do vitally important ones.

- **Outcomes don't indicate purpose.** As previously mentioned, outcome statements don't indicate why we want students to achieve these results. If a teacher doesn't know why, it is almost certain that students won't know either. A likely result when "covering" the curriculum is to do things because the curriculum says so or because it's in the textbook.

Think back to your own experiences as a student in elementary social studies. Make a list of your clearest memories of these experiences—both positive and negative. Review these experiences in light of the four factors listed above: teaching method, meaningful organization, clear priorities, and a sense of purpose. To what extent can the nature of your experiences be attributed to choices your teachers made in light of these four considerations? What implications might this have for your own choices as a teacher of elementary social studies?

GOING BEYOND SPECIFIC OUTCOMES

Ken Osborne suggests that the danger of a preoccupation with specific outcomes is that "teachers come to see themselves, or be seen by others, not as teachers of history [or social studies] but as achievers of outcomes, and history becomes little more than a sequence of outcomes to be checked off in a teacher's day-book" (2004, 4).

The antidote to this problem is a return to the question "What is our purpose?" If we know why we are teaching something, we have a better idea of its priority relative to other outcomes and we can better decide how to structure learning effectively to achieve this end.

As the highlighted text suggests, educational writers use different terms to identify the important ideas that guide teachers' interpretation of curriculum outcomes. It does not matter whether one's reason for teaching a specific outcome is characterized as a "big idea," "linchpin," "essential understanding," or "enduring understanding." What does matter is that we know why we are teaching the outcome.

Let's return to the example of the grade 4 Alberta curriculum and consider possible reasons for studying how Albertans use their natural resources.

- **Economic purpose**: to decide which of Alberta's natural resources are the most promising to develop. If Alberta intended to reduce its dependence on oil and gas, which would be the best resources to develop?
- **Geographical purpose**: to investigate why some resources are more plentiful in some regions than in others.
- **Environmental purpose**: to explore how Albertans could better conserve and sustain their resources. Which resource uses are the most wasteful? Should we continue to use coal to generate electricity?
- **Personal purpose**: to appreciate the importance of these resources in the students' own lives. How do students and their families benefit from Alberta's natural wealth?
- **Historical purpose**: to learn about the directions that Alberta's resource use are taking by studying past and present patterns. Can we learn anything about our present challenges by studying how resources were used in the past?

Each of these purposes offers plausible reasons for teaching the identified outcome. Some may be more interesting or relevant to students, and may be more important in the bigger scheme. Developing a coherent purpose that excites and challenges students requires thoughtful consideration of what learning will contribute to their ability to interact in and contribute to the world. Perhaps any one of these reasons would work. Does it simply depend on the direction we personally want to take our students?

Asking "why" helps us uncover important aspects of

IDENTIFYING THE IMPORTANT IDEAS

Big ideas

Selma Wasserman describes the reason for learning as the "big idea" which answers the questions "What is worth teaching?" and "How does what I am required to teach fit with matters of importance or consequence?" Learning experiences grounded in big ideas illuminate content in relation to "important issues and concepts" as opposed to "content that deals with acquisition of facts." Wasserman suggests that "curriculum that reflects big ideas will enrich classroom life and promote deeper and more sophisticated understanding of the world we live in" (1990, 96). Big ideas emerge from the curriculum content in the form of substantive issues that are worth knowing. In other words, identifying an overarching reason is necessary when planning for teaching. Similarly, James Duplass (2004) refers to "big ideas" as powerful, long-lasting concepts or generalizations that invite students to consider new ideas and examine their beliefs. The teacher needs to identify a relevant big idea that will resonate with students and teach towards that goal in order to create a meaningful social studies program.

Essential understandings

Lynn Erickson's strategy for identifying matters of importance is to distinguish between topic-centred (for example, memorizing facts related to the American Revolution) and idea-centred curriculum (for example, developing and sharing ideas related to the concepts of freedom and independence as a result of studying the American Revolution) (1998, 50). The focus of idea-centred curriculum is conceptual ideas and the use of facts to support understandings. Identifying what is important requires teachers to think beyond the topic and facts to the important transferable ideas or essential understandings that transcend time and culture. For example, in studying immigration, an essential understanding might be "People migrate to meet a variety of needs. Migration may lead to new opportunities or greater freedom" (52).

Linchpin ideas

Grant Wiggins and Jay McTighe present a model of curriculum design that focusses on the "linchpin" idea. A linchpin idea identifies what is worth knowing and is essential for developing understanding—"to what extent does the idea, topic or process represent a 'big idea' having enduring value beyond the classroom?" (1998, 10). Curriculum designed around linchpin ideas promotes meaningful learning rather than the acquisition of easily forgotten fragments of knowledge.

content and to situate learning experiences in a more relevant context. But how will we know which learning experience is the best one or even the one intended by the government? The answers to these questions require us to look at various elements embedded in curriculum documents that typically provide the bigger picture.

The Bigger Curricular Picture

Teachers are expected to work within the guidelines provided by the provincial curriculum. This is the framework within which instructional decisions are made. It is teachers' responsibility to connect specific outcomes in meaningful ways and develop them in a context that furthers an overall vision for social studies. Identifying these connections and planning towards this purpose breathes life into the curriculum.

Three features of the curriculum are central in formulating this broader vision for social studies. These are the general goals that social studies promote, the strands around which subject matter is organized to promote the desired goals, and the ultimate rationale for the subject. We consider each of these elements and their role in giving purpose to social studies. As we will see, they leave much for the teacher to fill in.

GENERAL GOALS

The goals of a course or a unit are the general educational outcomes that are to be promoted by addressing the specific outcomes. Although the precise wording differs from jurisdiction to jurisdiction (for example, they are called "Overall Expectations" in Ontario and "General Outcomes" in Alberta), their common function is to provide a more general description of what we are trying to achieve. Perhaps these goals will help in giving purpose to our teaching.

Goals are typically categorized into types. The most widely used categories of goals are knowledge, skills, and attitudes. Despite its popularity, this categorization is confusing. Supposed "skills"—such as conducting research—require knowledge (of the strengths and key features of various information sources) and attitudes (attention to detail, curiosity). For this reason, we identify five categories of goals that are described in the adjacent highlighted text.

One obvious purpose in categorizing the kind of goal we are trying to achieve is that it orients us in a particular direction. For example, it is helpful to realize whether our primary goal is to promote content knowledge (understanding of certain ideas) or to foster individual action or to teach how to access information.

This direction is evident in the Ontario grade 4 curriculum, which identifies three "overall expectations" that students should achieve by the end of the Medieval Times section of the course.

- **Knowledge:** "identify and describe major features of daily life and social organization in medieval European societies from about 500 to 1500 C.E. (Common Era)" (27).
- **Skill:** "use a variety of resources and tools to investigate

the major events and influences of the era and determine how they shaped medieval society" (27).
- **Application:** "relate significant elements of medieval societies to comparable aspects of contemporary Canadian communities" (27).

As is typical of many curricula, these goals summarize in general terms what is stated in the specific outcomes. Unfortunately, they don't seem to suggest why we would teach these outcomes. What is the point of having students learn about medieval European societies and compare elements in these societies with contemporary elements in Canadian communities? We won't find the kind of clarity of purpose that we need from these goals.

The Alberta curriculum offers the following "General Outcome" for the cluster of specific outcomes we have discussed previously:

> Students will demonstrate an understanding and appreciation of how elements of physical geography, climate, geology, and paleontology are integral to the landscapes and environment of Alberta (2006, 13).

This broad outcome appears to include both content and attitudinal goals and suggests a geographical or environmental orientation, but it is not clear why we would want to further these goals. Are we to nurture environmentalism or perhaps to cultivate mini-geographers and geologists? It seems that the stated goal helps to some extent by eliminating some options, but we are still left with choices to make. These examples are instructive: general curriculum goals may sometimes suggest directions for our teaching, but they don't eliminate all the possibilities and often provide little help in understanding why we might want students to achieve this goal.

CURRICULUM STRANDS

Strands are another element commonly featured in social studies curriculum documents. The word "strand" refers to the parts that are bound or woven together to form the whole. There are two kinds of strands: "underlying themes," which are main threads or concepts that run throughout the curriculum, and "organizing themes," which are the categories used to structure or cluster segments of the curriculum (units within a single course or different courses within a kindergarten to grade 12 program). Both kinds of strands serve a similar purpose: they provide ways to identify the focus and organize the delivery of the curriculum.

UNDERLYING THEMES

The underlying themes highlight the continuing emphasis or the backbone of the curriculum. For example, Alberta (2006, 6–7) identifies six strands as the threads running throughout the entire K–12 curriculum:

- time, continuity, and change—essentially history;

- the land (places and people)—essentially physical and human geography;
- power, authority, and decision-making—essentially politics and law;
- economics and resources—essentially economics;
- global connections—essentially global education;
- culture and community—essentially anthropology and sociology.

The curriculum specifically links two of these strands—essentially geography and economics—to the outcomes that we have used as our example. These strands are described as follows:

> **The Land: Places and People.** Exploring the unique and dynamic relationship that humans have with the land, places, and environments affects decisions that students make and their understanding of perspectives, issues, citizenship, and identity. Students will examine the impacts of physical geography on the social, political, environmental, and economic organization of societies. The examination also affects students' understanding of perspectives and issues as they consider how connections to the land influence their sense of place (7).

> **Economics and Resources.** Exploring multiple perspectives on the use, distribution and management of resources and wealth contributes to students' understanding of the effects that economics and resources have on the quality of life around the world. Students will explore the basic economic systems, trade, and the effects of economic interdependence on individuals, communities, nations and the natural environment. Students will also critically consider the social and environmental implications of resource use and technological change (7).

The many ideas raised by these two strands suggest that several of the previously identified purposes—economic, geographical, environmental, and personal—may apply. It seems that here too the teacher must choose among the possibilities.

Running through the Ontario curriculum are six underlying themes or "fundamental concepts": systems and structure; interactions and interdependence; environment; change and continuity; culture; and power and governance (4). But the curriculum does specify which of these strands might apply to the medieval life outcome we have been discussing.

ORGANIZING THEMES

Organizing themes are the topics that subdivide a given grade level or distinguish one course focus from another. For example, in the Ontario curriculum, each social studies course (grades 1 to 6) is divided into two strands: "Heritage and Citizenship," which is very loosely a historical theme and "Canada and World Connections," which is loosely a geographical theme. The subject "social studies" disappears in grade 7 and beyond and is then organized in separate history and geography courses (and in later grades, into courses in economic, civics, and law). The elementary curricula in British Columbia (2006) is organized around five strands at each grade level:

- skills and processes of social studies
- identity, society, and culture
- governance
- economy and technology
- human and physical environment

Across grades the most common organizing theme for elementary social studies is the expanding horizons approach. In the early grades, the focus is on what is near and familiar to students and progresses to the distant and increasingly unfamiliar. Although there are variations, the organizing themes of the British Columbia, Alberta, and, to a lesser extent, Ontario curricula are the individual, family, school, community, province, nation, and the past.

On the next page are two diagrams that illustrate the structure of the Ontario social studies curriculum for grades 1 to 6 and the structure of the grade 4 curriculum for Alberta.

PROGRAM RATIONALE

While curriculum strands suggest how the outcomes are to be divided (in a discipline-based or a social dimensions arrangement), they don't tell us why we are teaching them. The rationale identifies the ultimate reasons for a program. In other words, a rationale for a social studies program explains the point of pursuing the goals discussed above. In this respect, the rationale is the "bottom line" of a program. In the face of uncertainty or conflicting directions, the rationale provides a basis for deciding which direction to pursue.

The tendency among some teachers is to regard discussion of the rationale for a subject as a rather abstract and irrelevant exercise. This attitude is unfortunate. Getting clear about our rationale—the reason for doing something—gives us a sense of purpose. The danger when we are unclear about the ultimate reason for doing what we do is that we will teach a topic merely for the sake of covering it. Thus, the rationale for a subject—whether it is clearly spelled out in the curriculum or one we develop and refine individually—should serve a practical function: it should give us some sense of direction when interpreting and implementing the curriculum. This direction is especially important since, as we have tried to illustrate, curricula leave teachers considerable latitude in deciding the specifics of what will be taught and how.

Consider the following official rationales for social studies:

- **Ontario:** prepare students "to function as informed citizens in a culturally diverse and interdependent world and to participate and compete in a global economy.... [and] to develop attitudes that will motivate them to use their knowledge and skills in a responsible manner" (2).
- **Alberta:** enable students "to become engaged, active, informed, and responsible citizens" with an emphasis on "recognition and respect for individual and collective identity" in a diverse, pluralistic, inclusive, and democratic society and awareness of "their capacity to effect change in their communities, society and world" (1).
- **British Columbia:** "develop thoughtful, responsible, and active citizens who are able to acquire the requisite information to consider multiple perspectives and to make reasoned judgments" (11).

All of these rationales refer to preparing citizens, but there is vagueness and variation in what this means. On first glance, the qualities of an ideal citizenship are so general and open-ended—"informed" and able to "function" in a "diverse" world—that almost any kind of citizen might be implied. On closer investigation, the tone of the visions suggests some differences. The Ontario curriculum stresses an economically viable citizenry, whereas Alberta has a more socially active vision of the ideal citizen. The British Columbia rationale emphasizes informed decision making as a quality of citizenship. Our challenge, then, is to use these rationales to inform and give purpose to our teaching of the specific outcomes listed in these respective curricula. A more extensive discussion of the visions of citizenship embedded in social studies curricula is the focus of the next chapter, "Four Defining Purposes of Citizenship Education."

For the time being, it will be useful to consider briefly how a rationale might shape our teaching. What, for example, are the implications of the Ontario rationale for the grade 4 curriculum? How does teaching about medieval life foster the development of an ideal citizen? Several possibilities come to mind:

- **Understanding of diversity**. The study of medieval life might be used to foster understanding of diversity as students learn that individuals within societies haven't always had the same rights, opportunities, values, and beliefs.

FIGURE 2.1 ONTARIO SOCIAL STUDIES CURRICULUM GRADES 1–6

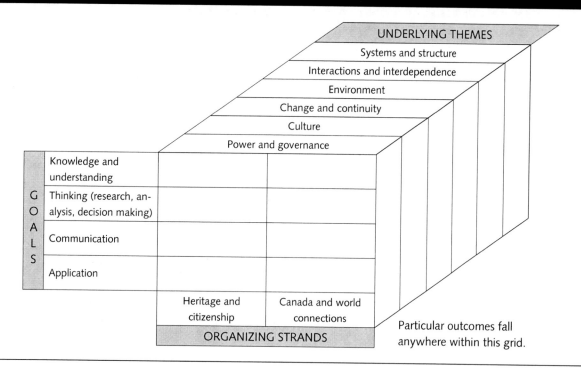

FIGURE 2.2 ALBERTA SOCIAL STUDIES CURRICULUM GRADE 4: THE LAND, HISTORIES, AND STORIES

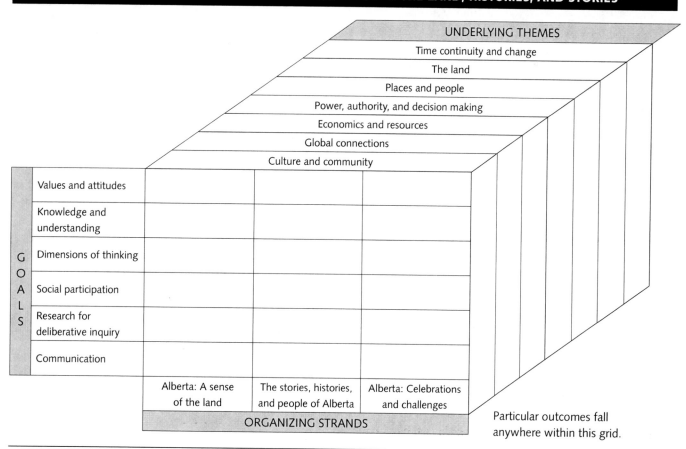

- **Understanding interdependence.** The study of medieval life might be used to foster understanding of interdependence as students learn how various aspects or sectors (for example, religion, innovations, architecture, social structures) of medieval life were dependent upon and influenced each other.
- **Respect for rights and peaceful problem solving.** The study of medieval life, especially the violence and abuses that were common, might be used to foster respect for others and encourage responsible behaviour.
- **Building teamwork.** The study of medieval life in and of itself may not be especially important to developing the ideal citizen, but it might provide an opportunity (for example, by mounting a play and getting an audience to attend) to nurture students' ability to work co-operatively in pursuit of a common goal.

The specific expectation for the grade 4 curriculum states: "describe aspects of daily life for men, women and children in medieval societies (e.g., food, housing, clothing, health, religion, recreation, festivals, crafts, justice, roles)" (Ontario 2004, 27). The teaching activity offered when we first introduced this outcome was to ask students to gather information from the textbook about life for men, women, and children in medieval societies. We can see how adopting any of the suggested rationales listed above would give meaning and relevance to the activity. Students are no longer collecting information for its own sake, but using this as an opportunity to understand interdependence or develop competence in working together. Having a purpose is not simply motivational for students, it influences what they learn from the activity. As Van Sledright notes, "How students view the purpose of engaging in topical or disciplinary study appears deeply connected to what they eventually learn and understand" (cited in Osborne 2004, 37).

Comparable examples could be developed for other curricula, but the conclusions would be the same. The stated rationales in curriculum documents indicate the kinds of purposes that we should set for our teaching, but even these leave open possibilities we must choose among.

This does not mean that we are free to do whatever we wish—we must work within the parameters set out by the curriculum even if the form and emphasis of that understanding may vary among us. As professionals, we have a responsibility to develop a program that is educationally sound and ethically defensible. In reaching decisions about the substance and shape of our social studies teaching—in refining the vision for our program—several factors are particularly relevant:

- the needs and expressed wishes of our students;
- the expectations embedded in the provincial curriculum in its stated outcomes, goals, strands, and rationale;
- the nature of social studies as a subject and the range of purposes that social studies is expected to serve;
- the expressed wishes of the local community;
- the priorities and needs of society generally;
- our own priorities and strengths as educators.

The Task Ahead

The word curriculum is derived from the word *curricle* which means "the path to follow"—hence, the notion of a course of study. Teachers must know where they are going if they are to lead students through the curriculum in a meaningful and productive way. One might think by covering each of the outcomes that a more complete picture would emerge—just as joining the dots by tracing lines between each point reveals a hidden image. It is not obvious that there is a single clear picture embedded in prescribed curriculum documents— joining the dots (covering the outcomes) may not reveal any image—it may simply mean a string of activities. As a British Columbia Ministry of Education document noted:

> Curriculum is no longer "ground to be covered." Instead, curriculum evolves from the teacher's mediation between the goals of the program and the curriculum and the individual learning styles, interests, and abilities of students (1990, 25).

An earlier British Columbia curriculum guide explained that "A curriculum is an organized statement of *intended* learning outcomes that serves as a framework for decisions about the instructional process [emphasis added]" (1988, 4). In other words, curricula are guidelines to assist teachers in developing a program of study for their own students.

It is incumbent on us as social studies educators to explore and assess the nature and implications of each of the elements of a curriculum—rationale, strands, goals, and specific outcomes (or expectations)—when developing our social studies programs. To some extent, choices will have been dictated by the provincially prescribed curriculum, but surprisingly, most curricula require considerable teacher discretion in deciding what specifically to include and emphasize, and how to organize these items for instructional purposes.

Engaging in purposeful social studies is not an easy task—it will no doubt evolve over years of teaching and reflection. However, we can begin by thinking about our vision for social studies. If we have only the vaguest idea of what social studies is supposed to look like, how will our students learn from us?

Identify one or more specific outcomes prescribed in social studies curriculum for a particular grade. Make a list of different activities you might undertake to help students meet this outcome. Review the rationale offered in the curriculum guide and formulate a particular purpose that would give meaning to the specific outcome(s) you identified and shape the activities you might ultimately select to meet the outcome. Justify your choice of rationale and teaching activity.

ENDNOTE

1 Ontario organizes its goals into four categories: (1) knowledge and understanding; (2) thinking, which includes research, analysis, and decision making; (3) communication; and (4) application, which is the use of knowledge and skills to make connections. Alberta has three categories of goals: (1) values and attitudes; (2) knowledge and understanding; and (3) skills and processes, which are subdivided into thinking, social participation, inquiry, and communication. British Columbia has no formal set of categories for its goals. Instead the curriculum guide simply describes a diffuse range of types of outcomes including developing understanding, making connections, applying knowledge, practising active citizenship, and demonstrating respect (2005, 11).

REFERENCES

Alberta Learning. 2006. *Social studies—Kindergarten to grade 12.* Edmonton, AB: Author. Available online at http://www.education.gov.ab.ca/k_12/curriculum/bySubject/social/default.asp.

Brady, M. 1989. *What's worth teaching? Selecting, organizing and integrating knowledge.* Albany, NY: State University of New York Press.

British Columbia Ministry of Education. 1988. *Social studies curriculum guide: Grades 8–11.* Victoria, BC: Author.

———. 1990. *The intermediate program: Learning in British Columbia.* Victoria, BC: Author.

———. 2006. *Social studies K to 7: Integrated resource package 2006.* Victoria, BC: Author. Available online at http://www.bced.gov.bc.ca/irp/irp.htm.

Chiodo, J. 1990. Social studies poems. *Social Education* 54 (7): 466–468.

Duplass, J.A. 2004. *Teaching elementary social studies: What every teacher should know.* New York: Houghton Mifflin.

Erickson, L. H. 1998. *Concept-based curriculum and instruction: Teaching beyond the facts.* Thousand Oaks, CA: Corwin Press.

Ontario Ministry of Education. 2004. *The Ontario curriculum—Social studies grades 1–6; History and geography grades 7 and 8* (Revised). Toronto: Author. Available online at http://www.edu.gov.on.ca/eng/curriculum/elementary/sstudies/html.

Osborne, K. 2004. Canadian history in the schools. Unpublished report by Historica Foundation, Toronto, January. Available online at http://www.histori.ca/prodev/default.do?page=.rp_index.

Steffay, S. and W.J. Hood. 1994. *If this is social studies, why isn't it boring?* York, ME: Stenhouse Publishers.

Wasserman, S. 1990. *Serious players in the primary classroom.* New York: Teachers College Press.

Wiggins, G. and J. McTighe. 1998. *Understanding by design.* Alexandria, VA: Association of Supervision and Curriculum Development.

3

Four Defining Purposes of Citizenship Education

Penney Clark and Roland Case

itizenship has been recognized as the rationale or defining aim of social studies since its inception as a school subject. In 1916, the report that marked the formal introduction of social studies in the United States argued that the "conscious and constant purpose" of social studies was "the cultivation of good citizenship" (cited in Dougan 1988, 14–15). Since then citizenship has been called "the primary, overriding purpose" and the "distinctive justification" of social studies.[1] As Fitzgerald aptly describes it, again and again social studies reformers have come "reeling back to the old lamppost of citizenship training" (1979, 187). In Canada, George Tomkins claims that "the goal of 'citizenship' probably comes closer than any other to identifying the purpose that Canadians have usually believed that the social studies should serve" (1985, 15). Echoing Benjamin Barber's sentiments, Larry Booi writes that "public education is the vital vehicle for developing citizens of a democratic society and that social studies teachers have the main role to play in this regard" (2001, 22).

Unfortunately, general acceptance of citizenship education as the *raison d'être* for social studies does not provide much guidance or direction since there is little agreement as to what constitutes the ideal citizen. Citizenship is such an amorphous concept that it may be used to legitimize virtually anything in social studies (Longstreet 1985). Apparent consensus about the centrality of citizenship education is almost meaningless because of widely disparate conceptions of citizenship (Marker and Mehlinger 1992; Sears 1996), which range from nationalistic loyalty to international solidarity (Cogan and Derricott 2000).

In this chapter, we outline four interrelated rationales underlying citizenship education; each at varying times in the history of social studies has served as the defining purpose of the subject. Before looking at each of these, it is useful to explain why as social studies teachers we should care about which purpose (or mix of purposes), if any, undergirds our teaching.

A Direction for Social Studies

For many of us, decisions about what to teach in social studies will likely be informed, consciously or not, by our image of the type of person and world we hope to promote. If our model citizen is someone who is well-informed about social matters, we will devote much of our time to helping students acquire a breadth of knowledge. If our focus is the ability to make ethically sound decisions about complex issues, then we will likely engage students in investigating and discussing social issues. Perhaps our ideal citizen is someone who is committed to acting on his or her beliefs. In this case, students might undertake community enhancement projects or explore ways of living and acting in personally responsible ways. Each of these choices should, and likely will, be influenced by an implicit view of what our subject is all about.

For some of us, our conception of the "good" citizen may be so completely established that further discussion will make no difference. For others, however, exploring options may help us become more focussed and resolute in our orientation or perhaps cause us to modify our outlook in light of an appreciation of alternative purposes that might be served. If we take seriously our role as educators charged with making complex judgments about our students' well-being, then we must articulate with some clarity our ultimate educational aims. As Ken Osborne writes in *Teaching for Democratic Citizenship*:

> Good teachers possess a clear vision of education and of what it will do for their students. They are not simply technicians who take prescribed curriculum, or the textbook, and work their students through it. They incorporate the curriculum into their philosophy of education and use what it has to offer in ways that make educational sense. This involves thinking carefully about goals and about how to achieve them, and such thinking inevitably takes a teacher beyond the confines of the classroom. Educational

18

goals do not exist in a vacuum. They emerge from thinking about what one wants for students and for the society in which they live (1991, 119).

During the ninety-year history of social studies in North America, the four ideals listed below have traditionally been offered as "competing" rationales for citizenship education.[2] Two of the rationales identify specific *social* purposes—that is, their focus is the type of society we hope to promote through social studies—and the other two rationales serve *individual* purposes—these focus on the type of individuals that we want social studies to foster.

- **Social initiation**. This rationale posits that the primary purpose of social studies is to initiate students into society by transmitting the knowledge, abilities, and values that students will require if they are to fit into and be productive members of society.

- **Social reform**. This rationale holds that the primary purpose of social studies is to empower students with the understandings, abilities, and values necessary to improve or transform their society.

- **Personal development**. According to this rationale, the primary purpose of social studies is to help students develop fully as individuals and as social beings. Its direct purpose is neither to reform society nor to maintain the status quo, but to develop each student's talents and character.

- **Intellectual development**. This rationale suggests that the primary purpose of social studies is to develop students' capacity for understanding the complex world

TABLE 3.1 FOUR "VISIONS" OF A CURRICULAR TOPIC: BUILDING THE CANADIAN PACIFIC RAILWAY			
UNDERLYING GOALS			
Social initiation: to promote knowledge of and pride in important events in Canadian history	**Social reform**: to encourage scepticism about the official versions of history and a concern for past injustices in Canada	**Personal development**: to nurture students' ability to work with each other and to plan and carry out self-directed studies	**Intellectual development**: to introduce students to the methods used by social scientists to inquire into the world
SAMPLE ACTIVITIES			
- learn about the "glorious" saga of the CPR's construction and the impressive engineering feats that occurred - learn about famous people who were instrumental in building the railroad, including John A. Macdonald, Donald Smith, William Van Horne, and Sanford Fleming - explore the historical significance of the railroad—opening the West to European immigration, defence against American Manifest Destiny, fulfilling the Confederation promise - explore the railroad as a symbol of Canadian nationhood—the iron ribbon that binds Canada and the Last Spike at Craigellachie, BC—the linchpin joining East and West	- learn about the alternative story of the railroad's construction, including the exploitation of immigrant workers and the corruption and greed that resulted in the "Pacific Scandal" - learn about the personal sacrifices of the Asian workers who actually constructed the railroad	- allow students to select any aspect of the topic that interests them personally and decide on a way to represent their learning - explore potential career choices—engineers, developers, politicians—by considering the contribution each made to the railway	- learn about historical inquiry by developing an account of an event using primary sources - learn about geographical inquiry by plotting the demographic effects of the railway on local terrain or by planning a route using contour maps - learn about archaeological inquiry by developing an account of camp life based on artifacts recovered from a simulated "dig"

[Handwritten annotations:
Maintain status quo — Reform — Indiv. talents — Understand Complexity
critical thinking going into world, think for self explore their world - collaboration Let's work together. Intellectual orientation - how to find/resear...
important too see great accomplishments inspires, teaches what humans can do]

they face by introducing them to the bodies of knowledge and forms of inquiry represented in history and the other social sciences.

Each of these camps themselves comprise variations. For example, the particulars of a social initiation rationale will vary depending on whether we are more liberal or conservative; similarly, social reformers may be radical or moderate in their outlook on social improvement. There is, as well, inevitable blurring of the lines between these camps—for example, at what point does a concern for social justice move from an accepted principle of mainstream Canadian society towards a commitment to social reform? Even pedagogical approaches overlap considerably. For example, although social initiation is typically associated with textbook-based programs, and intellectual development with engaging students in analysis of primary documents and social science research, the reverse is not inconceivable. The point of categorizing different rationales is not to pigeonhole each of us in one camp or another, but to invite reflection about the options facing us when deciding upon our purpose—*our* ultimate reason—for teaching social studies.

The choices we are forced to make each day of our teaching lives should reflect these priorities. Although the differences are more matters of emphasis than of mutual exclusivity, in important respects the different purposes require choices among competing objectives. As illustrated by the examples in the "four visions" of the building of the Canadian Pacific Railway in Table 3.1 and the study of families in Table 3.2, the underlying rationale will significantly affect the nature and outcomes of the study.

It is likely—even desirable—that many of us will endorse aspects of all four camps. We might, for example, think that promoting a sense of responsibility for others and a recognition of the need to pull one's own weight are part of a core set of values that all citizens ought to abide by. To this extent we have some affinity for the social initiation camp. Perhaps we are concerned that many students are overly accepting of mainstream attitudes that contribute to environmental destruction, exploitation, inequality, and other social ills. In this case, we are espousing elements of a social reform perspective. We must also decide how best to prepare students for these civic responsibilities. If our inclination is to emphasize students' feelings, needs, values, issues, and problems, we are

TABLE 3.2 FOUR "VISIONS" OF A CURRICULAR TOPIC: STUDYING FAMILIES

UNDERLYING THEMES

Social initiation: promote students' knowledge of the role of the family and a sense of responsibility towards their family	**Social reform**: encourage sensitivity towards and support of family structures and predicaments that may not be universally accepted by students	**Personal development**: nurture students' pride in their families	**Intellectual development**: teach students how to gather and represent information used by social scientists

(handwritten: role = diff for all) — *(handwritten: what if they don't have a good one?)* — *(handwritten: - Brochures - Aboriginal Tribe Pres.)*

SAMPLE ACTIVITIES

• learn about the important needs that families meet in society • learn about different family roles and the ways that family members work to support one another • learn about the responsibilities that each child has to contribute towards the harmonious operation of a family • learn about important celebrations that acknowledge parents' contributions (Father's Day, Mother's Day)	• explore and promote acceptance of less traditional family structures (including families with same-sex parents) and unfamiliar family practices from other cultures • learn about families who are less fortunate and what might be done to assist these families • carry out a project to help a family in need • learn how to recognize and respond when family members are acting improperly	• each child learns about his or her own family background • each child develops a treasure box representing the most powerful, positive family memories • each child plans a personal commemoration or personal act of kindness for a family member	• learn to interview family members and identify important information and ideas obtained • learn various ways of recording and presenting information and ideas (family tree, timelines, graphs, webbing) • learn how to formulate powerful questions to ask of a guest who is coming to talk about families

in effect adopting a personal development view of citizenship. This is certainly a widely held rationale for social studies, but we may nevertheless be concerned that helping students become "personally and socially fulfilled" may not do enough to prepare them to thoughtfully address the issues that they will encounter. The often quoted expression by George Santayana, "Those who do not remember the past are doomed to repeat it," suggests that students who have not studied much history will have little insight into or context for making sense of contemporary questions. Perhaps, then, preparation for civic life should focus on the knowledge and the principles of inquiry that drive history and the other social science disciplines. If this is the case, we have moved towards an intellectual development focus.

> Think of a social studies unit you have taught or have seen taught. Using the "four visions" chart as a guide, identify the dominant rationale or rationales underlying this unit. Select a rationale not significantly represented in the unit and think of activities that would reflect this new rationale.

In formulating our own more specific set of purposes for social studies education, it is useful to view the four traditional camps as positions on two intersecting continuums (as shown in Figure 3.1):

- **Social acceptance/social change spectrum**. Social initiation and social reform represent a range of positions on a social acceptance/social change spectrum. At one extreme, the point of citizenship education is to promote complete conformity with mainstream social norms and practices; at the other extreme, it is to promote total transformation of the social fabric. Seen in this light, the differences between the social initiation and social reform camps are matters of degree about the extent and depth that citizenship education should encourage social conformity/social transformation.

- **Subject-centred/student-centred spectrum**. Personal development and intellectual development represent a range of positions on a subject-centred/student-centred spectrum. At one extreme is a view that the best form of citizenship preparation is achieved by nurturing the whole child by focussing exclusively on his or her interests,

FIGURE 3.1   CITIZENSHIP EDUCATION MATRIX

Social studies rationales tend to be defined exclusively in terms of one of the continuums, either "social acceptance/change" or "child/subject-centred." Labelling a view as "social initiation" simply means that the dominant but by no means exclusive purpose is social acceptance. The closer the rationale is, for example, to the left of the social acceptance end of the continuum, the greater the emphasis placed on promoting the status quo. As a rationale moves towards the "social change" pole, the emphasis on the status quo diminishes until, at some point, the social reform purpose begins to dominate.

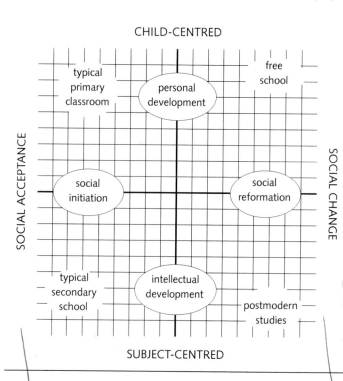

Plotting rationales within a matrix allows us to position camps in light of both sets of poles. For example, the "free school" movement in the 1960s was a radical child-centred approach to education with a strong social change mandate. Consequently, it belongs in the upper right-hand corner of the matrix. The typical secondary school program with a liberal arts emphasis is strongly subject-centred with a clear social acceptance mandate. Hence it belongs in the lower-left quadrant. Many primary classrooms would be located in the upper-left quadrant because of their child-centred, social acceptance mandate. Postmodern studies with their emphasis on making problematic the position from which scholarship is written would fall in the lower-right corner because of its critical discipline-based focus. A view of schooling in the very centre of the matrix would weight all four purposes equally: encouraging students to accept some aspects of society but to challenge others, and nurturing students' individual development in certain domains while seeking intellectual development through the disciplines.

2 ends of spectrum

concerns, problems, values, and so on; at the other extreme, the best form of citizenship preparation is thought to be achieved by disciplining the mind exclusively through exposure to the bodies of knowledge and forms of reasoning found in the social sciences.

Let us look at each of the traditional camps of citizenship education and consider how the differences between the camps can be explained in terms of where they fall within the matrix created by these two continuums.

The Social Acceptance/ Social Change Spectrum

[handwritten: false & dangerous →]

As indicated above, two of the traditional visions of citizenship education—social initiation and social reform—can be distinguished by the extent to which conformity with mainstream values, social practices, and world view are encouraged.

[handwritten: no in between]

[handwritten: textbook style?]

CITIZENSHIP EDUCATION AS SOCIAL INITIATION

The most common and long-standing view of the purpose of social studies, and, for that matter, of public schooling in general has been to promote a core body of beliefs and to instill the essential values and skills that are thought necessary to function in and contribute to society (Barr, Barth, and Shermis 1977, 59). The socializing role of schooling that prevailed in the 1800s was evident in the teaching of patriotism and character training, the primary components of social education at that time. Aspects of it were also evident in Canadian social studies curricula in the 1930s and 1940s, in which teachers were urged to use fables and stories about heroes (and occasionally heroines) as a means of inculcating values such as patriotism, loyalty, and courage. The "back to basics" movement of the 1970s reinvigorated, in a very conservative voice, the call to provide all students with core knowledge and values. This tradition continues with the recent emphasis on learning the essential facts of our culture and history. J.L. Granatstein's (1998) call to teach Canada's "common cultural capital" and E.D. Hirsch's (1988) "cultural literacy" and Charles Quigley's (1991) "civic liberty" in the United States are well-known examples of this vision. Headlines in Canadian newspapers on July 1 of each year reporting on the Dominion Institute's Canada Day History Quiz attest to continuing public interest in promoting knowledge of the basic facts of Canadian political and social history. Social initiators are likely to espouse the kinds of values (such as respect, responsibility, honesty, perseverance, optimism) advocated by the character edu-

[handwritten left margin: I agree but... I agree but...]

cation movement (Glaze, Hogarth, and McLean 2003) and the workplace skills of personal management, teamwork, and communication outlined in the *Employability Skills Profile* published by the Conference Board of Canada.

→ The social initiation rationale appears to be widely shared by social studies teachers. Jim Leming believes that in the United States, social studies teachers generally espouse a conservative version of social initiation involving "the transmission of mainstream interpretations of history and American values" (1992, 294). Linda McNeil (1986) found in an ethnographic study of teachers in six schools that a major goal was helping students maintain positive attitudes towards American institutions. In order to achieve this goal, teachers avoided content that would expose students to the injustices and inadequacies of economic and political institutions. In a survey of almost 1,800 elementary and secondary social studies teachers in British Columbia, approximately 70 per cent supported social initiation as a dominant purpose for social studies (Case 1993, 3). This compared with approximately 57 per cent who supported a social reformist role, and 38 per cent who supported intellectual development. (Respondents were not asked to comment on a personal development rationale.)

Social initiation does not necessarily require indoctrinating students into a narrow set of beliefs and values. Although nineteenth- and early twentieth-century versions of social initiation in Canada had a decidedly pro-British assimilationist bent, more recent versions embody a more multicultural, pluralistic aim (Sears 1994). An individual's perception of the prevailing, mainstream image of a good citizen may be broad-minded, including values such as an abiding respect for the rights of others and, in particular, tolerance of individual and cultural differences and freedoms. As Ken Osborne suggests, "While avoiding nationalistic chest-beating, history curricula are designed to instill in students a sense of Canadian identity, which all provinces describe as based upon respect for diversity, pluralism, and democracy" (2004, 6). Nor is social initiation inconsistent with critical thinking; but there are parameters within which this questioning is to occur—students would not be taught or encouraged to question the received interpretations of history and the foundations of the dominant world view. For example, advocates of a social initiation rationale would be less inclined to invite students to question seriously issues such as whether Confederation is something to celebrate, whether Canada is a token democracy, and under what conditions students should engage in civil disobedience. Social initiation is compatible with an active participatory citizenship; however, it would be more likely to emphasize community service projects rather than boycotts of consumer products, and voting in elections rather

[handwritten: +, proactive]

[handwritten: "Static"]

[handwritten bottom: involves: (all important) critical values thinking, respect, pride, resp.]

than political lobbying (see, for example, Alter 1997; Rappoport and Kletzien 1997).

[handwritten: Critical thinking   We need change!]

CITIZENSHIP EDUCATION AS SOCIAL REFORM

As its name implies, social studies as social reform focusses on encouraging a better society. It posits that there is much to be improved about society and that the role of social studies is to help students acquire the understandings, abilities, and values that will launch them on this path. Although both social initiation and social reform approaches would teach students about the history and workings of our nation and the world, their dominant purposes pull in opposing directions. In the case of social initiation, the overriding point is to get students to endorse the implied world view, whereas social reformers believe the emphasis should be to prepare students to critique the existing society. And unlike the social initiation approach, where the emphasis is on getting students to participate in and contribute to the established ways of operating, the social reform approach aims to empower students to work towards a "different" society. The reform position need not imply a radical anarchistic view of social change, but by definition social reform is more controversial than the social initiation position. Jim Leming (1992) and others believe it is for this reason that social reform is espoused more often by university professors than by classroom teachers. *[handwritten: due to controversy]*

Social studies' closest turn towards a social reform orientation occurred in the 1970s. Jerome Bruner, earlier a proponent of an intellectual development rationale, announced in a 1971 article entitled "The Process of Education Revisited" a "moratorium" or at least a "de-emphasis" on teaching the structure of history and instead argued for teaching history in the context of the problems facing American society (21). He identified social problems such as poverty, racism, the unpopular war in Vietnam, and the extent to which schools had become "instruments of the evil forces in our society" (20) as desired foci for social studies instruction. Osborne points out that Canada, too, had a "crisis of values" at this time, with the October Crisis of 1970, new societal concerns such as sexism, the stirring of discontent among Native peoples, and a breakdown in federal/provincial relations (1984, 95). Others point to Black studies, women's studies, and third world or development studies, which have been regularly offered in Ontario as examples of a social reform vision of social studies (van Manen and Parsons 1985, 6). More recently, some environmental education programs have raised critical consideration of local problems such as land use and conservation, as well as larger issues such as overpopulation, pollution, and resource depletion. The recent Alberta curriculum has elements of social reform in that it encourages debates around unresolved issues in Canadian identity such as the nature of federalism,

the meaning of democracy, and differing conceptions of social justice (Osborne 2004, 7). *[handwritten: Moving toward]*

An important thread of the social reform camp is teaching students to be what Walter Werner and Ken Nixon call "critically minded"—to be inclined as a general orientation to ask hard questions about much of what we encounter (1990, 2). Students need, for example, to be taught that public media do not simply convey information but, as Neil Postman suggests, they "conceptualize" reality: "They will classify the world for us, sequence it, frame it, enlarge it, reduce it, and argue a case for what it is like" (1979, 39). The very fact that public media pay attention to or ignore an event determines what we come to see as important or worth knowing. So too with what gets taught in schools. We shape students' perceptions of what is important in school and in life by celebrating the individual efforts of famous figures (for example, Van Horne built the CPR, Cheops built the Great Pyramid) and not the collective toil of ordinary, often exploited people, or by focussing on the military outcomes of battles and not on their environmental outcomes. A social reformer would want students to be critical (in an intellectually healthy way) of the very sources and selection of information they encounter—including their teacher and their textbooks. In contrast, a social initiator, even one close to the reform camp, would want students to be more generally accepting of these sources. *[handwritten: in curric   Be careful!]*

Within the last thirty years, a more radical version of social reform espoused by critical theorists has appeared in the social studies literature. This version presumes that knowledge is never impartial but always represents a value position because it is constructed by people with particular values and interests (Smits 1997; Stanley 1981). Representing any knowledge as a given or as objectively true obscures its social, economic, political, and historical contexts. Social science knowledge shapes our society in conformity with some values and in opposition to others since the dominant culture within society has a major influence on the development and maintenance of social institutions. This radical form of social reform calls for "root criticism" of all knowledge in the social sciences, including critical study of gender, race, nationalistic, or social class domination of social structures and knowledge (Nelson 1985, 370). Canadian proponents of this conception include van Manen, who espouses the "emancipatory" suggestion that "a socially conscious person" ought to engage in "social criticism of all forms of hegemony including the authority of the knowledge and value orientations taught in school" (1980, 114).

A second key element in many versions of social reform is the importance attached to social action. Since the overarching goal is to improve society, students should be assisted in acquiring the abilities and the inclinations to act on their beliefs. Fred Newmann's book *Education for Citizen Action*

[handwritten bottom: 2! ours has flaws, we change we might find better ways 3! Controversial yet called for today (points about society)]

[handwritten: "Moving Forward"]

has been influential in urging that students develop "environmental competence" (1975, 157) and engage in social action as the natural outcome of considering public issues. There has been a somewhat spotty and ambiguous inclusion of "social action" in Canadian social studies curricula. For example, the new Alberta curriculum identifies "social participation" as one of four core skills. Most of the examples refer to developing leadership skills in school and community groups, but the curriculum document does indicate that this goal "could include social action" (2006, 9). Similarly, the current social studies curriculum in British Columbia (2006, 1997) mandates action projects outside the classroom for students at several grades. However, it is ambiguous as to the rationale. It is consistent with a social initiation rationale to engage students in non-controversial forms of social participation such as cleaning up the litter around the school grounds and raising money for a local charity. A reform purpose for social action would involve students in projects that do more than perpetuate the way things are done by filling in the gaps in existing social services (Wade 2000). For example, elementary students have been involved in social reform by writing letters to the newspaper about the way baboons were caged at a Calgary zoo (Dueck, Horvath, and Zelinski 1977) and McDonald's use of styrofoam packaging (Roth 1991).

The Child-centred/ Subject-centred Spectrum

Unlike the two purposes of citizenship education already discussed, which have an implied stance towards the status quo—either that the existing state of affairs is basically sound or that it is not and should be changed—the next two camps that we discuss posit no such assumption. Perpetuating or altering the social order are not their preoccupation. Rather, their concern is where to focus in identifying and developing the desired knowledge, abilities, and values. Are they found with the individual by looking to and working with the range of personal needs and everyday predicaments of students, or do they reside in the subject area, in this case in the storehouse of intellectual insight offered though the social science disciplines? The tension between these two poles was expressed by the principal of a prestigious school in India that we visited. His school and many other élite schools in India have a strong intellectual development focus. This principal implicitly acknowledged the social development emphasis of a certain rival school when he commented with a hint of criticism, "Oh yes, you can tell students from that school, they are always so well-adjusted."

|1 better for younger
|2 important for learning, ex piano

CITIZENSHIP EDUCATION AS PERSONAL DEVELOPMENT

The whole child

The focus of personal development is on nurturing students who are fulfilled—personally and socially. It is believed that the "good" society will follow from creating well-adjusted individuals. Important elements of this tradition are traced to John Dewey's progressivist philosophy. Osborne suggests that "Canadian progressivism spoke in terms of the growth and development of students, of meeting students' needs, of teaching the whole child, and much less of social reform or reconstruction" (1996, 42). Instead of an imposed body of knowledge or predetermined direction for social studies education, the desired understandings, abilities, and attitudes are very much those that are required to cope with and make sense of students' own lives and experiences. As Shermis explains, in this tradition "a problem is not a problem unless an individual senses it as such" (1982, 49).

The personal development rationale has had a long history. It can be seen in the 1916 report of the National Education Association Committee on Social Studies in which it was suggested that instruction be organized "not on the basis of the formal social sciences, but on the basis of concrete problems of vital importance to society and of *immediate interest to the pupil* [emphasis added]" (cited in Jenness 1990, 77). This progressive-inspired tradition came into prominence in Canada in the 1930s, a decade during which every province initiated major curricular reform. Revised provincial curricula exemplified new "child-centred" approaches, which implied correlation of subject matter to the needs and interests of the child. The emphasis was on the "whole" child who would "grow physically, emotionally and spiritually, as well as mentally" (Newland 1941, 12). Curricula were activity-oriented, with a focus on group investigation of problems or issues of interest to students; the activities were intended to promote co-operation, communication, and decision making. Social studies formed the basis of these group investigations, called "enterprises" at the elementary level in many provinces (Alberta Department of Education 1936, 288). "The social studies classroom instead of being a place where children 'learn' history, geography, and civics, is to be a real laboratory, where co-operation, initiative, originality and responsibility are developed" (Alberta Department of Education 1935, 36). At the secondary level, this approach found expression in programs referred to in different provinces as core curriculum, life adjustment curriculum, or an integration of social studies with language arts and the humanities.

In the 1960s, the values clarification movement was an important addition to the personal development orientation. Values clarification is a model for teaching values developed by Louis Raths, Merrill Harmin, and Sidney Simon (1966). It encourages students to choose their own system of values.

The values clarification model has been described as "extraordinarily influential" in the development of the 1971 Alberta social studies curricula (Milburn 1976, 222).

The personal development rationale remains in evidence in contemporary social studies, especially in the elementary school. Key features of this vision include: (1) a belief that the content of what is learned is not as significant as students finding what they study personally relevant to their lives, (2) an emphasis on supporting students in pursuing their own directions and developing their own interests, (3) an emphasis on exposing students to a wide range of situations and experiences where they can work out their beliefs and develop their own positions on issues, and (4) a priority given to supporting students in feeling confident about themselves and their beliefs over challenging students to think differently or to question their values.

CITIZENSHIP EDUCATION AS INTELLECTUAL DEVELOPMENT

The definition of social studies which exemplifies the intellectual development rationale is Edgar Wesley's: "the social studies are the social sciences simplified for pedagogical purposes" (1937, 4). The defining feature of this tradition is not simply or even essentially a matter of acquiring a body of knowledge as it is mastery of the norms and methods used by scholars to gain new knowledge. It is believed that the various social science disciplines have generated the richest insights and investigative techniques for understanding our social world. Hence, developing the minds of students as social scientists and historians is thought to provide the best preparation for citizenship in a complex world. Unlike the personal development camp, intellectual development rationales see the disciplines, more than the students, providing the problems worth considering. Initiation into the academic traditions is more important than exposure to problems of immediate and personal concern, and coming to one's own conclusions is not as important as coming up with intellectually defensible conclusions.

This tradition came into its own with the publication of Jerome Bruner's slim book *The Process of Education* in 1960. Bruner referred to the "structure of the disciplines," by which he meant teaching the component parts or basic structures—the concepts, canons of reasoning, and techniques of inquiry—particular to each discipline. He believed that the basic ideas lying at the heart of the disciplines are simple enough for students at any level to grasp. Bruner argued that "intellectual activity anywhere is the same, whether at the frontier of knowledge or in a third-grade classroom" (14). Consequently, rather than simply presenting students with the findings of a discipline, students should take on the role of social scientist and use the inquiry techniques of the disciplines to make dis-

coveries themselves. Before social studies was itself a subject, proponents of history education were stressing the importance of analysis of source documents for the "mental training which may be obtained from their use" (Caldwell, 1899, reported in Osborne 2003, 482). This tradition has been evident in Canada in the texts and other curriculum materials used in the late 1960s and 1970s. It also appeared in texts used for university social studies curriculum and instruction courses, such as *Teaching the Subjects in the Social Studies,* where the authors identify helping school children begin to learn the thinking patterns, or structure, of the social sciences as a major purpose of elementary social studies (Moore and Owen 1966, v). These authors explain that "a better democratic citizen [is one] who can think historically or geographically, who can think as an economist or as a political scientist, whenever these approaches are relevant to the assessment of contemporary situations" (ibid.).

A similar philosophy underlies a 1960s approach to teaching geography in the elementary school:

> the child learns, at his own level, the structure of geography and the methods used by the professional geographer. He will learn of, through use at his own level, the various subjects which contribute to the subject of geography. He will also learn through practice in the field, and later with pictures, to observe details carefully, to record these details in many ways, to analyze the data, and then to synthesize selected data to answer a problem (Social Studies Advisory Committee 1962, 139).

While the structure of the disciplines approach has been somewhat discredited,[3] the calls to promote disciplined historical and geographical understandings are as strong as they ever were. In fact, there is considerable pressure, including calls from Canadian academics (Seixas 1994, 1997; Granatstein 1998), to replace social studies with the teaching of history and geography. As Peter Seixas (1997) argues, students should approach historical accounts critically. Yet this is unlikely to happen as long as students are taught only generic critical thinking or information processing approaches. The distinct challenges of thinking within the disciplines—notions in history such as what counts as a historically significant event, the difficulties of developing historical empathy, and the bases for accepting historical claims—require discipline-specific instruction. Without a developed capacity for historical thinking, teaching about the past is little more than the "simple accretion of increasing amounts of information" (Seixas 1994, 105). According to proponents of an intellectual development rationale, since the social science disciplines are the most rigorous and insightful forms of inquiry about our social world, they represent the best tools that social studies educators can offer students in preparation for citizenship. As Osborne wrote in the context of history, "The important tasks in teaching history are to arouse in students an interest in, and even love for, the past; to give them a sense of connectedness linking the present with both the past and the future; to help them think historically; and to show them the range of human behaviour" (2000, B3).

Having a Sense of Purpose

It is evident from the foregoing discussion that the factors that influence adoption of a particular conception include deep-rooted assumptions about the role of schooling, the perceived nature of challenges facing society and students, and the teacher's personal values and theories of knowledge and learning. Because of these ideological divisions, many have despaired of arriving at a common vision for citizenship education (Marker and Mehlinger 1992, 832). Attempts to reach consensus typically result in statements of purpose that are so vague they provide no helpful direction and are of dubious educational value. For example a 1982 survey of provincial curricula by the Canadian Council of Ministers of Education concluded that the common focus is on inquiry approaches towards a goal of providing "students with the knowledge, skills, values and thought processes which will enable them to participate effectively and responsibly in the ever-changing environment of their community, their country and their world" (4). This statement could include anything imaginable and can be interpreted to apply to any of the four camps. Not only is consensus on an identifiable set of desired attributes of citizenship not currently present, the prospects of it are remote. It is no wonder that it is frequently observed that "The content of social studies is a smorgasbord of this and that from everywhere; it is as confusing and vague as is the goal of citizenship" (Barr, Barth, and Shermis 1977, 2).

In order to fill this serious gap, each of us must of necessity develop our own guiding purpose for social studies. After reading the above discussion, we may be inclined to actively promote aspects of all four rationales for citizenship education. Perhaps the most appropriate way of framing the challenge is by asking "In what respects should each of these purposes be promoted?" However, we must be careful that this does not amount to unfocussed borrowing from all four camps. Vague and indiscriminate choices have produced the smorgasbord referred to above. Barr, Barth, and Shermis, later in the same book, characterize social studies in even less flattering terms, referring to complaints that the subject is "social sludge" and "social stew" and amounts to "a confusing hodge podge" (57). One reason for developing a focussed and discriminating sense of purpose is that few of the attributes of citizenship that are truly worthwhile can be nurtured quickly.

Those that we are most serious about will require considerable thought and effort to bring about. Students will not, for example, develop mastery of the social science disciplines without considerable exposure to the body of knowledge and standards of reasoning in these areas. Promoting all of the purposes in a half-hearted way may mean that nothing is done very well. Besides, there is never enough time. We must inevitably establish priorities, even if these priorities change over time and depend upon the particular class we are teaching.

Table 3.3 provides a sampling of the ways in which each of the main goals in social studies might be developed, depending on the rationale. This table suggests that the range of social studies goals will be present in any given vision, but that the particular emphasis of each will vary.

In addition to our conscious choices as teachers, the influences of the hidden curriculum subtly but pervasively impose a tacit vision of citizenship on us. For example, reliance on a *single* "authoritative" text is likely to suppress key attributes of social reform and intellectual development, as will an emphasis on recall of received "accepted" facts over student-initiated interpretations of events. One way or another, consciously or unconsciously, we will likely advance a particular rationale. For all of these reasons, we should be cautious about assuming that we can do it all, or that it does not much matter which vision or collection of attributes we judge to be most defensible. It should be stressed that the choice of a dominant purpose should not be a whimsical personal preference. Rather, it requires thoughtful and professional judgment based on a number of factors including the needs, best interests, and rights of our students, their parents, and of society, more broadly.

The vague generalities common in most social studies curriculum frameworks create considerable latitude for teachers to interpret and implement their own clear sense of purpose. Many teaching activities and materials—such as use of textbooks and primary documents, analysis of issues, field trips—are common to all four camps. These standard teaching approaches may be employed in different ways depending on the ultimate purpose for teaching social studies—for example, by varying the topics debated, the amount of deference to the authority of the textbook, and the importance attached to students' wishes. This possibility of massaging teaching objectives, activities, and resources to align with a particular purpose offers the most compelling reason for each of us to think clearly about the sort of citizen that ought to guide our social studies teaching. Every day in countless, often unconscious ways we shape students' development as members of society. If we are unclear about the direction, we will likely perpetuate the bland smorgasbord that has typified mission statements in social studies. If this is the case, we can hardly complain about a passive, unreflective, and apathetic citizenry,

TABLE 3.3 ILLUSTRATIVE GOALS FOR EACH RATIONALE

GOALS	SOCIAL INITIATION	SOCIAL REFORM	PERSONAL DEVELOPMENT	INTELLECTUAL DEVELOPMENT
Content knowledge	• mainstream view of history and the world • knowledge of core facts about Canada and the world • knowledge of rights and responsibilities	• alternative world views (post-colonial, feminist) • knowledge of "overlooked" facts about Canada and the world • knowledge of human rights	• self-knowledge • knowledge of personal events and background	• principal and core concepts of social sciences • broad general knowledge in each social science area • knowledge of historiography
Critical thinking	• framed social issues—thinking within "givens"—for example, how to better contribute to society, evaluate situations	• probing issues at the foundations of society • deconstructing media	• personal issue analysis • exploring personal viewpoints	• canons of histori-cal reasoning and evidence • discipline-based academic issues
Information gathering and reporting	• use of mainstream sources including electronic technology • established conven-tions for presenting information	• accessing "alterna-tive" sources of information and viewpoints • persuasive presentations	• mainstream sources of information to meet personal infor-mation needs • exploring personal forms of expression and representation	• use of academic resources including original sources and field research • research papers and other forms of academic presentations
Personal and social values	• national pride and trust in civic institutions • honesty, loyalty, and respect for others • work ethic and as-sume responsibility for self	• global affiliations • abiding social and environmental conscience • sceptical attitude	• personal and cultural pride • personal integrity • individual values clarification	• academic self-confidence • intellectual curios-ity and pursuit of knowledge • intellectual work ethic
Individual and collective action	• community service, school enhancement projects, and work placement • ability to work with others to solve problems	• direct political and social action (lobbying) • public advocacy and networking	• self-help and personal interest projects • personal advocacy	• field studies in academic areas • team research projects

Handwritten annotations:
- careful
- Assimilate
- info
- challenge
- ask questions = learn
- Slightly touch but allow movement
- "Cookie cutter" citizens
- creativity
- in BC curric gr.5
- learn from both points this way
- know history accept it
- finding info = imp.
- in an emergency = imp.
- careers get attn.

since we may have nurtured this "vision" by default—by failing to infuse our teaching with a coherent direction. Each of us needs a clear and reasonable rationale, even if it differs from the teacher's rationale that students encountered the year before and will encounter the year after. In fact, a diversity of well-conceived rationales may be healthy. Doing things well even if the goals differ is preferable to consistently doing things in a tepid and diluted manner. Far fewer students will be inspired or assisted by a social studies program that lacks clear focus and strong direction. To paraphrase a familiar proverb, "Where there is no vision, programs perish."

> Refer back to the "Citizenship Education Matrix" on page 21. Locate the most defensible position for you on this grid by thinking of the students you currently teach or anticipate teaching, and the problems facing them and their society. Which mix of rationales would best meet these needs? Justify your position by thinking of why you would not want to be farther along each of the continua that form this grid.

ENDNOTES

1   These comments are by Barr, Barth, and Shermis (1977) and Jenness (1990).

2   The conceptual framework for social studies developed by Robert Barr, James Barth, and Samuel Shermis (1977, 1978) has had the most impact and the greatest longevity. Their typology, which places citizenship as the ultimate goal of social studies, consists of three traditions: citizenship transmission, social studies as social science, and social studies taught as reflective inquiry. Our four-rationale framework differs from the three traditions of the Barr et al. model in three ways. Our "social initiation" is a narrower notion than their "citizenship transmission." They include any form of transmission of a world view—one which may be a mainstream view or a rather esoteric view held by a minority. For our part, we limit "social initiation" to mainstream world views and any vision of society that is different from the mainstream view as "social reform." Following Jean Fair (1977) and Brubaker, Simon, and Williams (1977), we believe that "reflective inquiry" neglects an important tradition in social studies—the child-centred, personal fulfillment vision. We offer "personal development" to reflect this strand. Finally, following Suzanne Helburn (1977), we collapse the Barr et al. account of "reflective inquiry" with "social science" into what we call "intellectual development." Other conceptual frameworks include the five-camp model (Brubaker, Simon, and Williams 1977), seven program types (van Manen and Parsons 1985), and "elitist and activists" conceptions (Sears 1996).

3   The structure of the disciplines approach has been criticized on numerous counts (Fenton 1991; Massialas 1992; Dow 1992). Criticisms include charges that it relies overly on knowledge objectives and inquiry procedures from the social science disciplines, while ignoring the needs and interests of students and

societal problems; that it uses materials that are too sophisticated for the students for whom they are intended; that it fails to involve typical teachers in material development; that it ignores the hidden curriculum of gender, social class, ethnic, and religious issues; that the logistical complexity of many of the projects is problematic; and that it fails to bridge the cultural gap between theory and the real world of teaching with its large classes, multiple preparations, and often resistant students.

REFERENCES

Alberta Department of Education. 1935. *Programme of studies for the elementary school.* Edmonton, AB: Author.

———. 1936. *Programme of studies for the elementary school.* Edmonton, AB: Author.

Alberta Learning. 2006. *Social studies—Kindergarten to grade 12.* Edmonton, AB: Author. Available online at http://www.education.gov.ab.ca/k_12/curriculum/bySubject/social/default.asp.

Alter, G. 1997. The emergence of a diverse, caring community. *Social Studies and the Young Learner* 10 (1): 6–9.

Barr, R., J.L. Barth, and S.S. Shermis. 1977. *Defining the social studies.* Arlington, VA: National Council for the Social Studies.

———. 1978. *The nature of the social studies.* Palm Springs, CA: ETC Publications.

Booi, L. 2001. Citizens or subjects? *Alberta Views* March/April: 28–33.

British Columbia Ministry of Education. 2006. *Social studies K to 7 integrated resource package.* Victoria, BC: Author.

British Columbia Ministry of Education, Skills and Training. 1997. *Social studies 8 to 10 integrated resource package.* Victoria, BC: Author.

Brubaker, D.L., L.H. Simon, and J.W. Williams. 1977. A conceptual framework for social studies curriculum and instruction. *Social Education* 41: 201–205.

Bruner, J. 1960. *The process of education.* Cambridge, MA: Harvard University Press.

———. 1971. The process of education revisited. *Phi Delta Kappan* 53: 18–21.

Case, R. 1993. *Summary of the 1992 social studies needs assessment.* Victoria, BC: Queen's Printer.

Cogan, J. and R. Derricott, eds. 2000. *Citizenship for the twenty-first century.* London: Kogan-Page.

Council of Ministers of Education, Canada. 1982. *Social studies: A survey of provincial curricula at the elementary and secondary levels.* Toronto: Author.

Dougan, A.M. 1988. The search for a definition of the social studies: A historical overview. *The International Journal of Social Education* 3 (3): 13–36.

Dow, P. 1992. Past as prologue: The legacy of Sputnik. *Social Studies* 83: 164–171.

Dueck, K., F. Horvath, and V. Zelinski. 1977. Bev Prifit's class takes on the Calgary zoo. *One World* 17: 7–8.

Fair, J. 1977. Comments of Jean Fair. In *Defining the social studies,* R. Barr, J.L. Barth, and S.S. Shermis, 106–109. Arlington, VA: National Council for the Social Studies.

Fenton, E. 1991. Reflections on the "new social studies." *Social Studies* 82: 84–90.

Fitzgerald, F. 1979. *America revised: History schoolbooks in the twentieth century.* Toronto: Little Brown.

Glaze, A.E., B. Hogarth, and B. McLean, eds. 2003. Can schools create citizens?: An exploration of character and citizenship education in Canadian, US, and UK schools. Special issue, *Orbit* 33 (2).

Granatstein, J.L. 1998. *Who killed Canadian history?* Toronto: Harper Collins.

Helburn, S.W. 1977. Comments of Suzanne W. Helburn. In *Defining the social studies*, R. Barr, J.L. Barth, and S.S. Shermis, 110–113. Arlington, VA: National Council for the Social Studies.

Hirsch, E.D. 1988. *Cultural literacy: What every American needs to know.* New York: Vintage.

Jenness, D. 1990. *Making sense of social studies.* Toronto: Collier Macmillan.

Leming, J.S. 1992. Ideological perspectives within the social studies profession: An empirical examination of the "two cultures" thesis. *Theory and Research in Social Education* 20 (3): 293–312.

Longstreet, W.S. 1985. Citizenship: The phantom core of social studies curriculum. *Theory and Research in Social Education* 13 (2): 21–29.

Marker, G. and H. Mehlinger. 1992. Social studies. In *Handbook of research on curriculum*, ed. P.W. Jackson, 830–851. Toronto: Maxwell Macmillan.

Massialas, B.G. 1992. The "new social studies": Retrospect and prospect. *Social Studies* 83: 120–124.

McNeil, L. 1986. *Contradictions of control: School structure and school knowledge.* New York: Routledge and Kegan Paul.

Milburn, G. 1976. The social studies curriculum in Canada: A survey of the published literature in the last decade. *Journal of Educational Thought* 10: 212–224.

Moore, E. and E.E. Owen. 1966. *Teaching the subjects in the social studies: A handbook for teachers.* Toronto: Macmillan.

Nelson, J.R. 1980. The uncomfortable relationship between moral education and citizenship instruction. In *Moral development and politics*, ed. R. Wilson and G. Schochet, 256–285. New York: Praeger.

———. 1985. New criticism and social education. *Social Education* 49: 368–371.

Newland, H.C. 1941. Report of the supervisor of schools. In *Thirty-sixth annual report of the Department of Education of the Province of Alberta.* Edmonton, AB: A. Schnitka, King's Printer.

Newmann, F.M. 1975. *Education for citizen action: Challenge for secondary curriculum.* Berkeley, CA: McCutchan.

Osborne, K. 1984. A consummation devoutly to be wished: Social studies and general curriculum theory. In *Curriculum Canada V: School subject research and curriculum/instruction theory. Proceedings of the Fifth Invitational Conference of Curriculum Research of the CSSE*, ed. D.A. Roberts and J.O. Fritz. Vancouver, BC: Centre for the Study of Curriculum and Instruction, University of British Columbia.

———. 1991. *Teaching for democratic citizenship.* Toronto: Our Schools/ Our Selves Education Foundation.

———. 1996. Education is the best national insurance: Citizenship education in Canadian schools—past and present. *Canadian and International Education* 25 (2): 31–58.

———. 2000. Who killed Granatstein's sense of history? Misguided criticisms. *National Post*, May 27.

———. 2003. Fred Morrow Fling and the source-method of teaching history. *Theory and Research in Social Education* 31 (4): 466–501.

———. 2004. *Canadian history in the schools.* A report prepared for Historica Foundation, Toronto. Available online at www.histori.ca.

Postman, N. 1979. *Teaching as a conserving activity.* New York: Delta Books.

Rappoport, A.L. and S.B. Kletzien. 1997. Kids around town: Civic education through democratic action. *Social Studies and the Young Learner* 10 (1): 14–16.

Quigley, C.N, 1991. *Civitas: A framework for civic education.* Calabasas, CA: Center for Civic Education.

Raths, L.E., M. Harmin, and S.B. Simon. 1966. *Values and teaching: Working with values in the classroom.* Columbus, OH: Charles E. Merrill.

Roth, A. 1991. Battle of the clamshell. *Report on Business Magazine*, April: 40–43, 45–47.

Sears, A. 1994. Social studies as citizenship education in English Canada: A review of research. *Theory and Research in Social Education* 22 (1): 6–43.

———. 1996. "Something different to everyone": Conceptions of citizenship and citizenship education. *Canadian and International Education* 25 (2): 1–15.

Seixas, P. 1994. A discipline adrift in an "integrated" curriculum: The problem of history in British Columbia schools. *Canadian Journal of Education* 19 (1): 99–107.

———. 1997. The place of history within social studies. In *Trends and issues in Canadian social studies*, ed. I. Wright and A. Sears, 116–129. Vancouver: Pacific Educational Press.

Shermis, S.S. 1982. A response to our critics: Reflective inquiry is not the same as social science. *Theory and Research in Social Education* 10 (1): 45–50.

Social Studies Advisory Committee, Faculty of Education, University of British Columbia. 1962. *History and geography teaching materials.* Vancouver, BC: University of British Columbia.

Smits, H. 1997. Citizenship education in postmodern times: Posing some questions for reflection. *Canadian Social Studies* 31 (3): 126–130.

Stanley, W.B. 1981. The radical reconstructionist rationale for social education. *Theory and Research in Social Education* 8: 55–79.

Tomkins, G. 1985. The social studies in Canada. In *A Canadian social studies*, rev. ed., ed. J. Parsons, G. Milburn, and M. van Manen, 12–30. Edmonton, AB: University of Alberta.

van Manen, M. 1980. A concept of social critique. *The History and Social Science Teacher* 15: 110–114.

van Manen, M. and J. Parsons. 1985. What are the social studies? In *A Canadian social studies*, rev. ed., ed. J. Parsons, G. Milburn, and M. van Manen, 2–11. Edmonton, AB: University of Alberta.

Wade, R.C. 2000. Beyond charity: Service learning for social justice. *Social Studies and the Young Learner* 12 (4): 6–9.

Werner, W. and K. Nixon. 1990. *The media and public issues: A guide for teaching critical mindedness.* London, ON: Althouse Press.

Wesley, E.B. 1937. *Teaching social studies in high schools.* Boston: D.C. Heath.

PART 2 Ends & Means

Content Knowledge

Critical Thinking

Information Gathering and Reporting

Social and Personal Values

Individual and Collective Action

4

Beyond Inert Facts
Teaching for Understanding in Elementary Social Studies

Roland Case

Only one in three Canadians knows who scored the winning goal that long-ago day in Moscow. Just half can place the significance of the Last Spike and almost no one knows the name of the judicial decision that gave women the right to be appointed to the Senate. These are the findings of a new poll that shows that Canadians continue to be dismally ignorant of their own history. (Campbell 2000, A1)

It cannot be too strongly impressed, that Education consists not in travelling over so much intellectual ground, or the committing to memory of so many books, but in the development and cultivation of all our mental, moral, and physical powers. The learned Erasmus has long since said: "At the first it is no great matter how much, but how well you learn it." (Ryerson 1847, 56–57)

The annual release of the Dominion Institute's Canada Day quiz fuels newspaper reports, such as the first quotation above, decrying students' ignorance of national historical facts and petitioning educators to teach more Canadian history. Similar reports are made about Canadians' geographic illiteracy based on students' inability to recall basic information (Canadian Council for Geographic Education 2005). Should we be alarmed about these consistently poor results?[1] Does this necessitate spending more time on content knowledge in history and geography?

Alternatively, the problem may not be that we don't teach enough history and geography but, as suggested by the second quotation, the ways in which these subjects are taught may contribute to the forgetting of these facts. Ironically, if we stress covering more facts, we may fuel a worse problem than lack of recall of details. Consider the following interview between Sam, a ten-year-old student, and Pauline, a student teacher at the University of Calgary:

Pauline: Out of the things you do in school, what would you say is the subject that you like least?

Sam: Probably language arts and social studies because they're boring. I don't like writing that much, so I don't like language arts too much, and social studies you've got to listen and learn words and stuff.

Pauline: So in social studies you're sitting there, listening to the teacher talk, are you?

Sam: Yeah, but it's still boring. We listen to her talk and we have to read these things. Last year we did about the war, Alberta, its history and stuff like that. And we had to read stuff and the teacher had to read stuff too. Just have to memorize these vocabulary and stuff and write them down.

Pauline: So if someone said, "What do you do in social studies?" what do you think you'd tell them?

Sam: Listening, memorizing, and writing. (Carswell 1990, 15) *critical thinking?*

Perhaps for similar reasons, a 1943 American survey by prominent social studies educator Edgar Wesley found very little difference in the scores on a general knowledge test of American history between high school students who had studied American history and those who had not. It is also revealing that the same test was administered to a sample of adults drawn from *Who's Who in America*. The study concluded that "many well-informed, useful, successful, and even distinguished persons cannot answer 75 per cent of the items" (Wesley, cited in Barr, Barth, and Shermis 1977, 40). This last finding underscores another key conclusion: there is an important difference between "remembering" historical or geographic information—factual recall—and "understanding" these events. For example, students may not remember that the term "Last Spike" refers to the final joining of the Canadian Pacific Railway in 1885, yet they may nevertheless have some understanding of the significance and key features of this event. As historian George Wrong noted in 1924, "Education is what is left when we have forgotten most of the facts we have learned" (cited in Osborne 2000, 36). Clearly, understanding the key ideas is more complicated and more important than simple recall of dates, place names, and terminology. Unfortunately, many public reports calling for the teaching of more "content" fail to make this distinction clear.

In this chapter, I explore how we might teach social studies content in ways that foster understanding rather than mere recall of information and that stimulate student interest, not irrelevance. My reference in the title of this chapter to "inert" facts comes from Alfred North Whitehead's famous book, *The Aims of Education*, in which he suggests that "the central problem of all education" is in preventing knowledge from becoming inert (1929/67, 5). By inert, Whitehead means "ideas that are merely received into the mind without being utilized, or tested, or thrown into fresh combination" (1). Harvard educational psychologist David Perkins defines inert knowledge as "knowledge that learners retrieve to answer the quiz question, but that does not contribute to their endeavours and insights in real complex situations" (1993, 90). His colleague at Harvard, Howard Gardner, notes that "Coverage is the enemy of understanding" (cited in Antonelli 2004, 42). The paradox of "less is more" may be especially true in this respect: less direct teaching of facts may result in greater understanding of and interest in the content which may produce increased long-term retention of information.

Calling attention to the need to see our task as engendering understanding, not transmitting information, has been a persistent theme in social studies. John Dewey wrote in his influential book, *How We Think,* that "the aim often seems to be—especially in such a subject as geography—to make the pupil what has been called a 'cyclopedia of useless information'" (cited in Hare 1994, 72). In 1960, Shirley Engle warned of a "ground-covering fetish" by which he meant the practice of "learning and holding in memory, enforced by drill, large amounts of more or less isolated descriptive material" (302). Walter Parker (1989, 41) urges that learning not be seen as "the warehousing of facts" but as the "progressive construction of understandings" and teaching not be the "telling of fact" but the leading of a construction project in which the teacher acts as a contractor—not actually building the house but contracting to students the sorts of labour that will culminate in their building of a house.

These admonitions to engage students in thinking about and with the content of the curriculum are easier said than done. Numerous challenges must be identified and overcome. This chapter focusses on teaching factual information in ways that promote understanding; in the next chapter, John Myers and I consider how to teach concepts in ways that promote conceptual understanding. By factual information, we mean beliefs about the way the world is and why it is this way. These include what in social studies are typically called "facts" and "generalizations." "Confederation occurred in 1867" and "John A. Macdonald was Canada's first prime minister" are examples of facts. "Early European exploration of North America was motivated by the desire for economic and political gain" and "Natural resources have dominated Canada's economic and social development" are examples of generalizations.[2]

Teaching for Understanding

Before examining how to teach factual knowledge in ways that increase students' understanding, it may be useful to clarify what it means to understand as opposed merely to possess (or recall) information about something. Three attributes seem especially significant:

- **Understanding implies basic comprehension of information**. Understanding a fact is not mere patter off the lips in response to a stock question. At the least, understanding implies that students can thoughtfully rephrase the answer in their own words. Richard Lederer has compiled an amusing "history" of the world gathered from students who apparently so poorly understood what was taught that they got their facts wrong. His report of students' account of ancient Rome is as follows:

  > Eventually the Romans conquered the Greeks. History calls people Romans because they never stayed in one place very long. At Roman banquets, the guest wore garlics in their hair. Julius Caesar extinguished himself on the battlefields of Gaul. The Ides of March murdered him because they thought he was going to be made king. Nero was a cruel tyranny who would torture his poor subjects by playing the fiddle to them. (1987)

- **Understanding implies appreciation of significance and interconnection**. Remembering that Confederation occurred in 1867 is not the same as understanding this fact. Understanding something about Confederation requires knowing the significance of this event and how it fits into the larger historical picture. Imagine asking students: "Which is the more important event in Canada's development as a nation—Confederation or the first basketball game?" We would have little confidence that students really understand Confederation if they chose the first basketball game. This is because we would doubt that they correctly appreciated the relative magnitude of the implications of these events. Imagine also asking: "What is the relation between Canadian self-rule and Confederation?" If students could not see any connection, we again might doubt that they understood Confederation, since they seem to have little appreciation of the constellation of ideas that interconnect with the specific event or phenomenon. For this reason, amassing discreet facts adds little to understanding since it is the interrelationships that are central. Ken Osborne (2004, 4) supports this view when be observes that "It is possible, for example, for a student to master a whole list of outcomes describing the First World War, but still have no real understanding of the War as a historical phenomenon."

- **Understanding implies some grasp of the warrants for belief**. A final aspect of understanding is the need to appreciate, to some extent at least, what kind of evidence is required in deciding whether one should accept or reject a proposed statement of fact. Imagine students are told that certain statements in their textbook are thought to be false, say, that Confederation was not in 1867 or that early European exploration of North America was not motivated by the desire for economic and political gain. If students had no idea whatsoever what might count as supporting or refuting evidence for these claims, then we might wonder how well they understood what these claims signify.

Our task, if we are concerned to promote understanding, is to help students comprehend, connect, and seek justification for the information they receive. Much can be said about teaching in ways that engage students and foster understanding. In the following sections, I explore various suggestions clustered around two general themes:

- Inviting students to think critically about the content
- Strategies for framing effective critical challenges

Thinking Critically about the Content

According to Whitehead, ideas remain inert if students do not use or test them. A similar sentiment was expressed in the very first assessment of "best practice" in Canadian schools by Egerton Ryerson in his *Report on a System of Public Education for Upper Canada* (1847, 58):

> If the mind of the child when learning, remains merely passive, merely receiving knowledge as a vessel receives water which is poured into it, little good can be expected to accrue. It is as if food were introduced into the stomach which there is no room to digest or assimilate, and which will therefore be rejected from the system, or like a useless and oppressive load upon its energies.

One hundred and sixty years ago, Ryerson concluded that students must, in some fashion, "digest" the ideas they

encounter—they must put the knowledge into use and assimilate or own the ideas. Answering comprehension questions after reading a text and/or taking notes while listening to the teacher are merely acts of receiving transmitted information. As Alfie Kohn reports, "Lecturing was defined by writer George Leonard as the 'best way to get information from teacher's notebook to student's notebook without touching the student's mind'" (2004, 189).

Students are digesting the content only when they think deeply about the material—that is, they begin to make reasoned judgments about or with it. As Parker notes, "Thinking is how people learn" (1988, 70). This certainly does not mean that it is inappropriate to transmit information—we must transmit information to our students. The point is that passing on information—including "covering" the pioneers and "doing" human migration—is not the heart of our task. This is merely a means to an end. Our real objective must be to support students' ability and inclination to think rigorously with and about these ideas.

The need for students to think continually about the content is crucial. It is not sufficient to "front-end load" considerable content and at a point near the end of a unit or term invite students to reflect on the ideas they have heard and read about. As Ryerson's metaphor suggests, information that has been passively acquired is not digested in a way that makes it available for future use. It ceases to be—because it never was—food for thought. For this reason we must find ongoing ways to involve students in thinking as they learn, so that they will, in fact, learn.

The most powerful way I know to help students digest what they are learning is to invite them to think critically about it using an approach I helped develop as part of The Critical Thinking Consortium.[3]

RECOGNIZING WHEN WE INVITE CRITICAL THINKING

The obvious place to begin to engage students in thinking critically is with the questions and tasks we invite them to consider. What does a question that invites critical thinking look like and how does this differ from other good questions we might ask students? We may often ask students to "think" about things, but only some of the time do we ask them to think "critically" about these things. To illustrate this difference, consider the questions in Table 4.1.

Although all three types are appropriate and valuable questions to ask of elementary students, only one type invites students to think critically.

- **Factual questions**. The questions in Column 1 ask students to recall or locate a correct answer from a source. Typically,

TABLE 4.1 THREE TYPES OF QUESTIONS

TOPIC	COLUMN 1 QUESTIONS OF FACTS	COLUMN 2 QUESTIONS OF PREFERENCE OR LIKING	COLUMN 3 QUESTIONS REQUIRING REASONED JUDGMENT
Communities	Where is Medicine Hat?	Would you prefer to live in Toronto or Medicine Hat?	Would moving to Toronto or Medicine Hat better meet your family's needs?
Community roles	How do police officers contribute to our community?	If you could be anyone you wished, would you want to be a police officer?	Which contribution made by police officers is the most important to our community?
Inuit	What did the Inuit traditionally use to make tools?	Which Arctic animal would you like to have as a pet?	Which animal—the seal or the caribou—contributed more to traditional Inuit life?
Explorers	What three Native peoples did Simon Fraser encounter on his descent down the river?	How would you have felt if you were with Simon Fraser on his journey?	Was Simon Fraser a rogue or a hero?

these questions have a single correct answer. The answer already exists and the student's job is to locate it. For this reason, I sometimes refer to these as "Where's Waldo?" questions after the children's picture book series with the same name. The books consist of sets of pictures each containing hundreds of figures including a funny-looking character named Waldo. Children are challenged to locate Waldo among the maze of other individuals in each picture. Although finding the correct answer can be difficult, it is not a "critical thinking" challenge because the essence of the task is to find a predetermined object as opposed to thinking through a problem. Often questions such as "Which factors led to the changes in traditional aboriginal lifestyle?" and "How does the harvesting of natural resources affect the environment?" are simply "Where's Waldo" questions because the correct answer can be found in students' notes, their textbooks, the library, or in their memory. The students' task is to locate the answers in the source. Despite this limitation, these questions are useful in raising ideas to the fore. However, if we asked only these questions, we should not presume that students have digested the information, rather they will have simply regurgitated it.

• **Preference questions**. The questions in Column 2 invite students to share their feelings—what they like and dislike. There are no wrong answers to these questions, in that they are matters of taste: some students like living in large cities, others prefer smaller communities; some students welcome adventure, other students do not. This type of question invites students to offer their "opinions" on matters where their answers are essentially personal

preferences. Almost no answer could be said to be unacceptable. Who is to say that all students should prefer to be a police officer or a teacher? Or that no one should prefer Toronto over Medicine Hat or vice versa? All answers are valid.

• **Reasoned judgment questions**. Both factual and preference questions are valuable questions to ask of students—they both have a place in any teacher's repertoire. But they do not invite students' "critical" reflection. Only the questions in Column 3 invite students to think critically because only they require students to make a judgment about which of the possible answers they might select makes the most sense or is the most reasonable. Although there may be several (in some cases many) reasonable answers to these questions, some answers are unreasonable. For example, although plausible arguments can be made for having either a hamster or a frog as a class pet, it is unlikely that a lion would be a good idea. Questions in Column 3 ask students to go beyond locating facts and merely espousing a personal preference. When thinking critically, students are not merely reporting what they know or like. They are, in effect, offering a judgment or an assessment among possible options, determining which would be the more reasonable or justifiable choice.

The significant feature of a reasoned judgment is that we must resort to criteria. We require some basis other than our own preferences and whims for selecting one option over another. For example, in deciding whether Toronto or Medicine Hat would better meet a family's needs, it would be useful to consider health factors, availability of suitable employment, quality of life, safety, and ease of travel. These factors form the criteria involved in making a reasoned judgment about Toronto or Medicine Hat as places to move the family.

The close relationship between the term "critical" and "criteria" is instructive. Mathew Lipman (1992) suggests that "critical" thinking is "criterial" thinking—to think critically is to think in light of or using criteria. A useful definition of critical thinking is as follows: *To think critically is essentially to assess the reasonableness of various options in light of appropriate criteria.* Notice that students may judge whether Simon Fraser, for example, was a hero on very narrow and dubious criteria, such as looks, fame, and wealth. Other criteria might include contribution to society, hardship endured, personal attributes, and respect for others. A central part of our job in helping students think critically includes inviting them to consider an appropriate set of criteria when deciding on the wisest conclusion to be derived from them.

THE "SUBURB OF HAPPY HOMES"

Illustration by Fraser Wilson.

JUDGING EFFECTIVE CRITICAL CHALLENGES

Developing effective questions or tasks that invite students to think critically is not a straightforward matter. We need to think critically about our questions. As mentioned above, if thinking critically involves thinking with criteria, we need to consider what criteria to use in judging whether a question or task is an effective critical thinking activity.

We believe an effective critical challenge will meet four criteria, which are listed in the left-hand side of Table 4.2. In the right-hand side, these criteria are applied to a question we might ask about the illustration "The 'Suburb of Happy Homes'" (Wilson, in Evenden 1995, 20), showing life in Burnaby, British Columbia in 1942.

We could, of course, ask any number of questions including Column 1, information or factual questions (e.g., "How many people do you see in this picture?"), and Column 2, preference or feelings questions (for example, "Would you like to live in this house?"). Instead, let us focus on a Column 3 question inviting reasoned judgment: "What is the season and the period of day (morning, afternoon, evening, or night) of the scene depicted in this illustration?" Older elementary students may be asked a more specific and challenging question: "What is the month, day of the week, and time of day (within an hour) of the scene depicted in the drawing?" Let's explore the merits of this question by considering four criteria for an effective critical challenge.

TABLE 4.2 THE BURNABY PICTURE ACTIVITY	
CRITERIA FOR EFFECTIVE CRITICAL CHALLENGES	**CRITERIA IN ACTION: WHAT IS THE SEASON (OR MONTH) AND TIME OF DAY?**
Clearly invite reasoned judgment among plausible alternatives It is essential that challenges pose questions or tasks that invite students to judge the reasonableness of plausible options or alternative conclusions. Since criteria give judgments rigour, the appropriate criteria should be implicit in the question. For example, when deciding which solution is the most reasonable, students might consider feasibility, effectiveness, and fairness.	Students must choose among the various seasons (or months) and time periods. Determining whether this requires "reasoned" judgment or mere expression of preference depends on whether we use criteria as the basis for our judgment. On what grounds might students judge whether summer or winter (June or January) is a more reasonable suggestion for the time of year? The implicit criterion for judging the more reasonable answer is consistency with the available evidence. Students are to judge which conclusion (spring or winter) is most consistent with the evidence in the picture (for example, the clothing worn, height of the vegetation), and with general knowledge about the world (for example, the look of plants at varying times of the year).

continued on next page

TABLE 4.2   THE BURNABY PICTURE ACTIVITY (CONT.)

CRITERIA FOR EFFECTIVE CRITICAL CHALLENGES	CRITERIA IN ACTION: WHAT IS THE SEASON (OR MONTH) AND TIME OF DAY?
Are perceived as meaningful by students If students view a challenge as irrelevant and unimportant, they are unlikely to engage seriously in the activity and, over time, are likely to regard critical thinking as a boring or trivial exercise.	The challenge to decipher the time period of the scene is likely to be more engaging than the suggested Column 1 question about the number of people in the picture and the Column 2 question asking whether the students would like to live in the house. If students had just studied about the seasons and about the times of the day, they might be especially intrigued by the invitation to apply their knowledge to solve the puzzle. Generally speaking, it is engaging to be asked a question that invites exploration, discovery, or reflection.
Advance students' understanding of the content of the curriculum Critical thinking should not be an add-on, nor should it interrupt the pursuit of other curricular goals. Rather, challenges should involve students in thinking critically about what we want them to learn from the curriculum. In this way, they are more likely to develop an understanding of the desired curriculum outcomes.	Meeting this requirement, of course, depends on what students are supposed to be studying. By examining the picture, students are likely to learn about life for a family living in a suburban community more than sixty years ago. This might be one of the outcomes in the curriculum. Alternatively, if the curricular outcome deals with the differences between past and present communities, then a more appropriate critical challenge might be to decide whether the quality of life was better for people living at the time of the drawing or in contemporary times.
Are focussed in order to limit the background knowledge required If students are without crucial background knowledge, then the value of posing challenges may be lost. Elementary students, particularly in the primary grades, are likely to flounder if they lack basic information presupposed by the challenge.	The proposed challenge is relatively focussed if we compare it to related questions we might ask, for example, "What is the month, day of the week, and hour of the day of the scene depicted?" Notice that the greater number of choices (twelve months as opposed to four seasons; four time periods as opposed to twenty-four hours) requires more sophisticated knowledge. The addition of the question about the day of the week adds further complexity, including requiring knowledge of the customs operating in Burnaby in 1942 (Would a family toil in their garden on a Sunday? Would the adults be at work on a Saturday morning? Would the children go to school?). Compare the knowledge required to determine the time of day for the scene depicted in the picture with that required to answer the following question: What is the average annual income of this family? Clearly, this later question would require considerably more background knowledge about the living conditions of wartime Canada.

Applying the criteria for an effective critical challenge is an important step in developing critical challenges. None of the following questions are effective invitations to think critically. For each question, decide how many of the four criteria discussed in Table 4.2 are missing to a significant extent:

- Which African animal is the fastest?
- What is your favourite part of the school playground?
- Name three things that you noticed about this website.
- After reading this passage, identify the reasons why ozone is being depleted.

Strategies for Creating Effective Challenges

Initially, at least, it is deceptively difficult to generate effective critical challenges. Many experienced teachers have observed that it is much like the early days of planning lessons. Our very first lesson plan took many of us days to create. Our second lesson plan was a little quicker and by the time we had planned our tenth lesson we could do several in an hour. A similar pattern applies with developing critical challenges: initially it takes time and persistence to develop effective critical thinking questions and tasks, but eventually it can become second nature to us. In this section, I offer strategies to help you learn to develop critical challenges that satisfy each of the criteria discussed in Table 4.2.

INVITING REASONED JUDGMENT

The crucial criterion for a critical challenge is that it invites students to offer a reasoned judgment—otherwise it won't require students to think critically. Over the years we have noted the various forms that critical challenges may take. There are at least six ways of inviting students to make reasoned judgments. Each of these ways is discussed in Table 4.3. It may help you to think of these different forms when creating your own critical challenges.

TABLE 4.3   SIX WAYS TO INVITE REASONED JUDGMENT

CRITIQUE THE PIECE One way of framing a critical challenge is to invite students to assess the merits or shortcomings of a designated entity, such as the following:

- a person (for example, a historical figure, a literary character, a contemporary leader)
- an action (for example, the proposed solution to a problem, a historical event)
- a product (for example, a passage in the textbook, a poster, an essay)
- a performance (for example, a speech, a presentation)

Primary level critical challenges	• Are our proposed questions about (topic) powerful? (Possible criteria: give lots of information, are not obvious, are relevant to the person)
	• Has the author provided a fair and full account of what actually happened?
	• Is the Wolf in *The True Story of the 3 Little Pigs* good or bad?
	• Is the person in the (picture, story) contributing a lot, some, or a little to the family (or community)?
	• Were the good old days that good? (Possible criteria: shelter, diet, health, wealth)
Upper elementary level critical challenges	• Is Simon Fraser a hero or a rogue? (Possible criteria: contribution to others, hardship endured, noble character traits, respectful of others)
	• Rate the quality of life of a slave in ancient Rome.
	• Is this poster an effective visual presentation for the intended audience? (Possible criteria: catchy, convincing for the audience, clearly and concisely presented)
	• Evaluate the effects of Confederation. Was it a positive or negative event for aboriginal peoples?
	• On a scale ranging from great to horrible, assess what it would it be like to live at this time considering the quality of the environment, comforts, and fun things to do.

JUDGE THE BETTER OR BEST Perhaps the easiest way to frame critical challenges is to invite students to judge which of two or more options (teacher-provided or student-generated) best meets the identified criteria. For example, you might ask students to determine the best solution to a problem.

Primary level critical challenges	• Which community (X or Y) would best meet the needs of all your family? (Possible criteria: safe, healthy, fun, jobs)
	• Of the three ways, which is the best contribution you can make to your (family/environment)? (Possible criteria: is safe, possible for you to do, would help someone)
	• Best thing about: What is the best thing about being in (school, a family, other groups)?
	• Most important contribution: Which of the four ways that (community, industry) helps the (community, family, school) is the most important? (Possible criteria: helps most people in important ways)
	• Greatest legacy: Which (tradition, celebration, story) from the past is the most impressive? (Possible criteria: applies today, means a lot)
	• What is the biggest (physical, daily life) difference between our present community and (past community, another community)?
	• Which of the two characters in the story would make the better friend? (Possible criteria: helps people, doesn't say mean things, forgives mistakes)

continued on next page

TABLE 4.3 SIX WAYS TO INVITE REASONED JUDGMENT (CONT.)

Upper elementary level critical challenges	• Who was the greater explorer—Vancouver or Cook? • Which is the more effective form of Arctic transportation: the dogsled or snowmobile? • Which of the five selected items is the most impressive legacy of ancient Egypt? • Fresh water is an endangered commodity. Identify all the threats to safe water supplies. Which threat is the greatest concern and why? Identify possible solutions to the threat and justify which one offers the most realistic chance of success. • You have been asked by the curator to select from a nominated list of paintings the one that best exemplifies the Group of Seven. Which painting do you choose? • Should this potential recreational site be developed or left untouched? • Would life be better sixty years ago or right now for a young person in our community?

REWORK THE PIECE In a third approach, students are invited to think critically as they transform a product or performance in light of new information or an assigned perspective or focus. For example, they might be asked to rewrite an account from the perspective or point of view of someone other than those in the original text—describing how a logger as opposed to an environmentalist, or a king as opposed to a peasant, would look upon relevant issues, for example. The criteria they would consider might include detailed and specific information that is consistent with the given facts and reveals the new perspective.

Primary level critical challenges	• Rewrite the story from another (person/character's) point of view. (Possible criteria: must include same details, be believable, show a difference) • After reading the traditional version of the Three Little Pigs (told from the pigs' point of view) and *The True Story of the 3 Little Pigs* (told from the wolf's point of view), write a fair-minded account of what happened at the third pig's house. • Picture the quality: Take a photograph that captures a community quality (for example, peaceful, safe, active). (Possible criteria: fits the quality, has sufficient detail)
Upper elementary level critical challenges	• Write two letters, one from the traditional perspective of First Nations peoples and one from a historical non-aboriginal perspective, about the practice of holding potlatches. • Create a picture book that shows changes in your community as seen though the eyes of many groups. • Predict what might have happened if any one of the historical events had turned out differently. • Redraw the picture showing the Burnaby family scene as it would appear in the present time (or in a different season of the year).

[handwritten margin note: works well with reform #2 - cindrella? Billy Goats gruff]

DECODE THE PUZZLE Another approach to framing critical challenges invites students to use clues to solve a mystery or to explain a confusing or enigmatic situation. For example, asking students to use evidence from the Burnaby picture to determine the season and time is an example of decoding the puzzle.

Primary level critical challenges	• Tell the story: Based on our simulated dig of (dinosaur remains, pioneer community), tell the story of what occurred on this site. (Possible criteria: uses all the facts, is believable, clearly tells the story) • Using the personal qualities and characteristics as clues, identify the mystery class member. • What am I? Offer an informed guess of the purpose and functioning of a mystery object. (Possible criteria: fits all the facts, makes sense) • Using clues in the pictures, explain who, what, where, when, and why. (Possible criteria: based on information in the picture, uses lots of clues) • Interpret the pictures and determine their proper sequence.

TABLE 4.3 SIX WAYS TO INVITE REASONED JUDGMENT (CONT.)

Upper elementary level critical challenges	• What is the cartoonist really saying in this drawing? Reformist
	• Using the clues in the various images, identify the four different communities represented.
	• Find out as much as you can about the region using the mapping technique you have been assigned (for example, scale, colour, contours).

DESIGN TO SPECS   Another effective means to frame a critical challenge is to ask students to develop a product that meets a given set of specifications or conditions. These specifications provide the criteria for judging which of the possible choices will be most effective. For example, if asked to design a rich habitat that meets the needs of an assigned animal, students would consider factors such as need for exercise, shelter, and safety to determine the specific objects to include in the habitat.

Primary level critical challenges	• Using the materials provided, build a structure that will achieve the specified results.
	• Design a plan for a website that meets class-developed qualities.
	• Design a symbol that best shows three of our community's qualities. (Possible criteria: fits the qualities, has sufficient detail)
	• Prepare a package of three helpful items for a homeless person. (Possible criteria: easy to carry, meets needs, shows we care)
	• A picture is worth a thousand words: Take a photograph that captures a community quality (for example, peaceful, safe, active). (Possible criteria: fits the caption, has sufficient detail)
	• Create a family shield that represents your family heritage and tells something about your identity.
	• Write a poem about the key features in a community that represent its land and people.
Upper elementary level critical challenges	• The premier has asked for concise notes on the day's front-page news. Your notes must be less than one-half page in length, focus on the important issues, and clearly summarize the main points.
	• Create a travelogue or itinerary to be used by an out-of-province family when planning their vacation to learn about the natural and human-made features in our province.
	• Prepare a persuasive letter (or an oral statement) directed to a specific group expressing your views on the preservation of national parks.
	• Create a poster-size advertisement to discourage fellow students from smoking, effectively employing the techniques of persuasion without distorting the evidence.
	• Generate three "powerful" questions to ask a classroom visitor. (Possible criteria: informative, relevant to the person, requires some thought in order to answer)
	• Create a plan to address a community or national concern. (Possible criteria: effective, efficient, sustainable, culturally responsible)
	• Write a story that is true to the time period, involves all the characters in a meaningful way, and captures the mood of the scene.

PERFORM TO SPECS   A final approach to critical challenges invites students to perform a task or undertake a course of action that meets a given set of specifications or conditions. Perform to specs is very similar to design to specs with one important difference: the focus on the latter is on the design of a product whereas perform to specs involves acting in real time. Role-playing can be an opportunity to perform to specs if students don't simply act as they wish, but instead think carefully about which actions would be consistent with their assumed character, plausible given the context or situation, and believable.

continued on next page

TABLE 4.3   SIX WAYS TO INVITE REASONED

Primary level critical challenges	• Personally ma[...]ity member, the school). • Charades: Po[...]ief, simple, no words, and informat[...] • Passing alon[...]er of the class. (Possible criteria[...]s simple to do)
Upper elementary level critical challenges	• Mount a sc[...]dents. • Undertake [...]lse's life. • Create a ta[...]nd tensions present during the ass[...] • Provide fe[...]ve, respectful, clear, and honest. • Dramatiz[...]e characters in a meaningful wa[...]

[Handwritten note overlaying table:] Drite what happened when the 3rd Goat crossed? — How is it S.S.? — PLO's — gr.2 units —SS?? —textbook —email teachers last —ask —web — $ instead —in curric

FRAMING MEANINGFUL QUESTIONS

Terrell Bell offers the following advice: "There are three things to remember about education. The first one is motivation. The second one is motivation. The third one is motivation" (source unknown). In addition to ensuring that our questions or tasks invite critical thinking, it is important they motivate students to want to learn.

One of the most compelling reasons for using critical challenges as a method of teaching subject matter is the inherent appeal of being invited to think about one's own beliefs and not simply to find answers that others have produced. "The Power of Critical Challenges" is typical of many testimonials I have received about the motivational effect of inviting students to think critically.

In developing critical challenges, the following kinds of qualities in a task have greater likelihood of appealing to students:

- real-life consequences (for example, sending a letter to an actual official instead of drafting a letter to a fictional person)
- connections to present-day, topical issues
- personalized to students' lives
- tied to compelling themes (for example, justice, mystery)
- sensational details or images
- fun or engaging activities (for example, simulations)
- activities that open with an engaging hook (for example, an anecdote, role play, or a powerful example)

Another way to promote student engagement is to reduce the impediments that are likely to confound or bore students. Following are a few suggestions:

- Strip away many of the trivial or extraneous details. For example, students need not study every major explorer or region, but perhaps only two or three representative examples.
- Minimize the kinds of tasks that student will regard as drudgery:
  - Provide manageable "inputs" (for example, avoid assigning long reading passages).
  - Limit the burden of the products that students will be required to produce without sacrificing the core understanding. For example, instead of requiring that students write an extended paragraphs, ask them to summarize their arguments in note form on a chart.
- Minimize the likelihood of student frustration:
  - Keep the task focussed so students are unlikely to get bogged down. For example, if the main purpose of an activity is to develop students' ability to analyze a current issue, supply them with a few relevant background pieces rather than expecting everyone to find their own sources.
  - Ensure that students have the "tools" they will need to successfully address the task.

PROMOTING UNDERSTANDING OF THE CURRICULUM

The underlying theme of this chapter is the importance of fostering student understanding of the content of the curriculum. To do this requires making the content problematic in some way so students think critically about it, and not merely regurgitate it. Thus, a key requirement of any critical challenge is that it addresses the content we want students to

THE POWER OF CRITICAL CHALLENGES

Recently I was selected to be a part of the team that would be writing the Online Teacher's Guide for the new Alberta grade 7 social studies curriculum. As a part of this process, the team was given the opportunity to learn how to develop critical thinking challenges. After spending a few intensive days in Edmonton learning about critical challenges and how to create them, I decided to create one for my current junior high social studies class. These lessons were some of my most successful classes of the year. One particular lesson with my grade 8 class stood out.

I created a critical challenge on the historical figures involved with the War of 1812. We focussed on three individuals: Tecumseh, Laura Secord, and Isaac Brock. The challenge asked students to decide which of the three historical figures was the "most heroic." After creating criteria as a class for what would constitute a "hero," students were given fact sheets for the three individuals. Once the students had decided which of the three was the most heroic according to their criteria and prepared their arguments, we were to debate the heroism of the three historical figures.

I was not prepared for the lively debate that ensued. Rarely have I seen my students so engaged as they debated the heroism of Brock, Tecumseh, and Secord. My role changed quickly from teacher to referee, as I almost needed to restrain some students physically. As the bell rang, the debate raged into the hallway and on into their next class. I felt very satisfied with the lesson, as this level of engagement is rarely seen at the junior high level. However, it was not until later that night that the impact of that critical challenge really hit home.

I am the school basketball coach and that night we were playing in the city championship. It was a thrilling back-and-forth game that ended with the other team hitting a last second three-point shot to beat us. After the excitement had died down, I was in the gym cleaning up when I heard some players arguing in the hallway. I thought that some of my players were upset about the game so I went to investigate. As I opened the door, the first thing I heard was one of my players yell:

"How can you seriously say Isaac Brock was not the most heroic of the three, when he risked his own life and *died* for what he believed in?"

A smile crept across my face as I realized that the players were not arguing about the championship game they had lost only moments before, but rather, they were arguing about the topic introduced that morning in social studies. This seemingly simple critical challenge had fostered curricular understanding in a way that was perceived as meaningful and important to my students. I left the school that night as a critical challenge convert anxious to engage my students by creating more.

This story was written by Chris Good, vice-principal, École St. Gerard School, Alberta.

---

understand. The examples in Table 4.4 illustrate the curricular understanding that is promoted through various critical challenges.

While developing critical challenges that help students "uncover" the curriculum takes practice, the bigger perceived obstacle is finding the time to address all of the subject matter that needs to be taught (Onosko 1989).

I want to explore this claim that inviting critical thinking means that teachers will be unable to "cover" as much of the curricular terrain as they would otherwise do if they dealt with everything in a more transmissive and less probing manner. One reason for this claim is a perception by some teachers that they are responsible for covering the entire textbook or for addressing all the main features of every era, region, or civilization mentioned in the curriculum. In a study of 1,800 social studies educators in British Columbia, one teacher wrote, "I don't have enough time to cover even 10 per cent of the textbook and other resources." Another recommended that steps be taken to "ensure that teachers do not feel that they have to 'cover' everything in the book (content) to pre-

---

TABLE 4.4 LINKS TO CURRICULAR UNDERSTANDING

CRITICAL CHALLENGE	CURRICULAR UNDERSTANDING PROMOTED
Decode the Burnaby picture	Learn about the customs and lifestyle within a suburban community in the 1940s.
Ask powerful questions of a World War II veteran who has come as a class visitor	Learn what the war meant to people who were involved in it and why society continues to commemorate this event.
If you were required to move either to Medicine Hat or Kingston, which community would best meet your family members' needs?	Learn how different communities meet people's basic needs in different ways.

pare their students for their next year" (Case 1993, 6). More recently, Osborne noted that the pressure of high-stakes testing forces teachers to "cover" their courses even when they know that they need to spend more time on certain topics if students are to properly understand them (2004, 25–26).

The perceived need to cover large quantities of material may arise to some extent from a belief that our crucial task as elementary social studies teachers is to transmit information about the world. One of my objectives in this chapter is to encourage teachers to see promoting understanding as our crucial task. This would mean that we need not "get through" the textbook or "cover" every explorer or region in a unit in order to meet our responsibilities to the curriculum.

Years ago, Hilda Taba offered useful advice about balancing the quantity of information with the quality of understanding. She believed that "coverage" of topics was impossible—there was always too much to cover. Instead teachers should sample rather than survey the content. Thus, the important question for Taba was not "how many facts, but which facts we want students to think about" (Fraenkel 1992, 174). John Dewey talked of "generative knowledge"— knowledge that had rich ramifications in the lives of learners (Perkins 1993, 90). The most generative knowledge is found in powerful conceptual and factual insights that apply across many circumstances. For example, is it important that students study all the major early Canadian explorers or is it sufficient that they consider one or two explorers and come to appreciate the extent to which personal, economic, and cultural motives drove early exploration? Is it imperative that students study all the major technological inventions and their effects or is it sufficient that students come away with a few broad understandings, grounded in specific instances, of the way technology has transformed (for better and worse) almost every aspect of Canadian society? These broader insights, which span cultures and time periods, are the sorts of generative understandings that are worth emphasizing.

It is sometimes thought that devoting considerable amounts of time to in-depth studies means that students are in danger of acquiring very narrowly circumscribed understandings. There are two ways in which this shortcoming can be mitigated using a sampling approach. The notion of a geological survey of the surface of an area followed by more probing exploration at carefully selected sites is an apt metaphor for the sampling of topics. Students may receive via minilectures, films, or fact sheets highly condensed overviews of a period or culture, which then sets a context for more focussed case studies of particularly promising issues.

It is also useful to consider that critical challenges need not be large-scale undertakings. Although in-depth challenges are valuable, there are many opportunities to pose "mini" challenges that take ten or so minutes to complete

(for example, which of the three differences between an Inuit and a southern community would have the biggest impact on daily life?). Even when critical challenges are extensive, the time spent can be justified provided many curriculum outcomes are addressed during the course of working through the challenge. "Bundling Curriculum Outcomes" illustrates the dozen or so outcomes in the grade 2 Alberta curriculum that would be addressed by bundling them within the critical task of deciding who would be most deserving of the honour if the school was to be renamed.

MANAGING THE ACQUISITION OF BACKGROUND KNOWLEDGE

Students need background knowledge in order to deal competently with critical challenges. If students lack this information, and if they do not acquire it as they address the challenge, the value of posing challenges may be lost. Students are less likely to develop their ability to think critically if they are fumbling in the dark. For this reason, it is important to anticipate and manage the information required by a challenge either by narrowing the challenge or by finding effective ways to help students acquire the information.

LIMIT THE INFORMATION REQUIREMENTS

One way to limit the amount of background knowledge required is by narrowing the challenge or, as my colleague Selma Wassermann would say, "make it compact." Critical challenges must be sufficiently delimited so students need not possess encyclopedic knowledge in order to realize success.

Answering the question "Who is the greatest hero in our community's history" is a task that could fill a book. A more focussed challenge is preferable, possibly, "Of the three people we have studied, who is the greatest hero?" Similarly, completing the task "Assess the legacy of the Industrial Revolution" could fill volumes. A more focussed challenge would ask, "Based on the following two reports and your own knowledge, is the steam engine the most significant invention originating from the Industrial Revolution?" or, perhaps, "In the first fifty years of the Industrial Revolution, which invention most altered industry and commerce?"

PROVIDE BACKGROUND INFORMATION EFFICIENTLY

Acquiring background knowledge is obviously necessary, but teaching it often gets in the way of critical thinking. It is useful to remember that "background knowledge" is the focussed information needed to address the task at hand; this is *not* the same as "general information" which might be described as the fuller

BUNDLING CURRICULUM OUTCOMES[4]

Critical Challenge

If we had to rename our school to honour a person in our community's past, who would you choose as the most deserving person?

Outcomes

The following grade 2 outcomes in the Alberta social studies curriculum could be addressed by this challenge.

Values

2.2.1 appreciate how stories of the past connect individuals and communities to the present

2.2.2 appreciate how aboriginal and Francophone peoples have influenced the development of the student's community

Knowledge and understanding

2.2.6 inquire into: What individuals or groups contributed to the developments of their community?

2.2.7 inquire into: How have the people who live in the community contributed to change in the community?

2.2.7 inquire into: How is the presence of aboriginal and/or Francophone origins reflected in the community today?

Dimensions of thinking

2.S.1 compare and contrast information from similar types of electronic sources

2.S.2 arrange events, facts, and/or ideas in sequence

Social participation

2.S.6 participate in activities that enhance their sense of belonging within their school and community

Research

2.S.7 access and retrieve appropriate information from electronic sources for a specific inquiry

2.S.7 organize information from more than one source

2.S.7 process information from more than one source to retell what has been discovered

2.S.7 draw conclusions from organized information

Communication

2.S.9 identify keywords from gathered information on a topic or issue

---

range of facts about a topic that is acquired for general interest or potential value. We often tell students more than they need to know and thereby reduce the amount of time available for them to think about what they really need to know. The following list includes several strategies to teach background knowledge:

- **Don't presume that background knowledge needs to be front-end loaded**. Students can acquire necessary information as they work through the challenge and even after they have answered the challenge provisionally (for example, after students offer their considered response invite them to undertake further study to confirm whether they are right or not).
- **Deliver it economically**. One way to communicate background knowledge is to embed critical challenges in picture books. In this way, students should acquire the information they need simply by listening to or reading a story. Other mechanisms for the efficient communication of information include the following:
  - Provide point-form notes
  - Deliver short mini-lectures on the key ideas
  - Distribute teacher- or student-prepared briefing sheets
  - Use visuals to communicate information
- **Make use of students as information sources**. It is often productive to tap into the collective wisdom of the class through class and group sharing. For example, in analyzing the Burnaby picture, each student might work

with a partner and then share their tentative conclusions with the entire class so that everyone has the benefit of each others' insights. Only after a common basis of background information has been developed, might students individually produce their own definitive response to the critical question. Another strategy is to divide topics among groups of students who pursue specific areas in some depth and then share their findings with the rest of the class, thereby broadening the scope of everyone's understanding.

- **Think carefully about student research**. Despite its popularity, independent library research is typically neither efficient nor reliable as a means of providing background knowledge: many students waste considerable time looking for material that does not give them all the information they need. Library research projects may be best directed to teaching students how to conduct research and not used as a means for acquiring background knowledge.
- **Where possible, frame the very acquisition of background knowledge as a critical challenge**. Find ways to chunk the acquisition of a body of knowledge into smaller bits and then frame a challenge for each segment. For example, if students were eventually to consider whether life was better now than it was sixty or more years ago, the Burnaby picture challenge could be used to teach them about life in the 1940s. In addition, students might be asked to think critically about questions they

Travel Brochures/Aboriginal Pres

I should have taught them + provided background info

would ask of people who were alive at the time as another information-gathering strategy requiring critical thinking. The following critical challenges can be used to invite students to think critically as they acquire background information:

- Select the five most important facts or events from the chapter.
- Decode the contents of the picture (answer the 5Ws, who, what, where, when, and why).
- Rank the causes or benefits in order of importance.
- Rate the effect of a particular event or policy from the perspective of various groups.
- Which of the provided sources offers the least reliable information?
- Think of a powerful question and a thoughtful answer on an assigned topic.

Conclusion

The focus of this chapter is on using critical thinking as a method for teaching content knowledge. I have argued that knowledge acquisition is not a matter of transmitting bits of information, but of developing student understanding of the ideas behind the facts. Superficial coverage of information or acquisition of facts for their own sake is of marginal value—if for no other reason than it appears that much of it is forgotten almost as soon as it is taught. Our primary task is not to present students with prepackaged information for mental storage but to help them internalize, question, and utilize relevant information. I have suggested that engaging students in thinking critically about and with the content of the curriculum is most effectively accomplished through meaningful, focussed challenges for students to address.

Using a curriculum guide or learning resource as a focus, create several critical challenge questions or tasks. Endeavour to meet all of the following criteria when framing each critical challenge:

- Does it invite students to make a *reasoned judgment*?
- Is it likely to be perceived as *meaningful* by students?
- Does it *promote understanding* of curriculum content?
- Is it *focussed* to limit the amount of background knowledge?

criteria ↑

ENDNOTES

1 Surveys throughout the twentieth century show repeatedly that students remember very little of the history learned in schools (Osborne 2004, 35–36).

2 The word "concept" is used ambiguously in social studies by some to refer to generalizations and by others to refer to the ideas or meanings captured by words such as "justice," "table," "sustainable," and "community." We use "concept" exclusively in this latter sense.

3 For further information about The Critical Thinking Consortium, which has worked with many thousands of social studies teachers and published numerous resources, go to www.tc2.ca.

4 This example was developed by The Critical Thinking Consortium for Alberta Education as part of its online guide to support implementation of the provincial social studies curriculum. Many other critical challenges can be found on the LearnAlberta website: http://onlineguide.learnalberta.ca/.

REFERENCES

Antonelli, F. 2004. *From applied to applause.* Toronto: Ontario Secondary School Teachers' Federation, November.

Barr, R.D., J.L. Barth, and S.S. Shermis. 1977. *Defining the social studies.* Arlington, VA: National Council for the Social Studies.

Campbell, M. 2000. Our young show dismal ignorance of history. *Globe and Mail,* July 1.

Canadian Council for Geographic Education. 2005. GeoForum: About geographic education online. Available online at http://www.geoforum.ca. Accessed November 26, 2005.

Carswell, R. 1990. Social studies through students' eyes. *One World* 27 (2): 14–16.

Case, R. 1993. *Summary of the 1992 social studies needs assessment.* Victoria, BC: Queen's Printer.

Engle, S.H. 1960. Decision making: The heart of social studies instruction. *Social Education* 34 (8): 301–306.

Evenden, L.J., ed. 1995. *The suburb of happy homes—Burnaby: Centennial themes.* Burnaby, BC: Community Economic Development Centre and the Centre for Canadian Studies, Simon Fraser University.

Fraenkel, J.R. 1992. Hilda Taba's contributions to social education. *Social Education* 56 (3): 172–178.

Hare, W. 1994. Content and criticism: The aims of schooling. In *Papers of the annual conference of the Philosophy of Education Society of Great Britain,* ed. J. Tooley, 72–89. Oxford: New College, University of Oxford.

Kohn, A. 2004. Challenging students—and how to have more of them. *Phi Delta Kappan* 86 (3), November: 184–194.

Lederer, R. 1987. The world according to student bloopers. *Verbatim: The Language Quarterly* 13 (4). Available online at http://www.verbatimmag.com/sampler.html.

Lipman, M. 1992. Criteria and judgment in critical thinking. *Inquiry* 9 (2), May: 3–4.

Onosko, J. 1989. Comparing teachers' thinking about promoting students' thinking. *Theory and Research in Social Education* 17 (3): 174–195.

Osborne, K. 2000. Who killed Granatstein's sense of history? Misguided criticisms. *National Post*, May 27.

———. 2004. Canadian history in the schools: A report prepared for Historica Foundation, Toronto. Available online at www.histori.ca.

Parker, W. 1988. Thinking to learn concepts. *Social Studies* 79 (2): 70–73.

———. 1989. How to help students learn history and geography. *Educational Leadership* 47 (3): 39–43.

Perkins, D. 1993. The connected curriculum. *Educational Leadership* 51(2): 90–91.

Ryerson, E. 1847. *Report on a system of public education for Upper Canada.* Montreal: Lovell and Gibson.

Whitehead, A.N. 1929/1967. *The aims of education and other essays.* New York: Free Press.

5 Beyond Mere Definition
Teaching for Conceptual Understanding in Elementary Social Studies

John Myers and Roland Case

A few years ago, my niece (Roland's) came home with the results of an end-of-unit quiz on thirty of the most difficult concepts in social studies. The concepts included capitalism, communism, totalitarianism, liberalism, and dozens of other complex political notions. She received 96% on the quiz—the highest mark in the class. Seeking to celebrate her success and engage her in political conversation, I asked what "capitalism" meant. She immediately recited in a rather hypnotic tone a dictionary-perfect definition. I responded, "Yes, but what does it actually mean?" and my niece said she wasn't exactly sure. So I agreed that it was a difficult concept to explain and asked if she knew whether or not Canada was a capitalist country. My niece responded, "How should I know?" She was the top student in the class and she didn't really understand anything of these concepts.

Concepts are the neglected content dimension in social studies. While generally speaking we may be in danger of having an obsession with teaching factual information, we are guilty of devoting very little attention to teaching concepts. Even when concepts are taught, we often do little more than provide a definition and an example. This is unfortunate because concepts are powerful tools for making sense of our world, and memorizing definitions doesn't go very far in helping students understand their meaning. The result, to use Hilda Taba's phrase, is "the rattle of empty wagons," where students learn to parrot the labels for concepts without grasping their meaning (Parker 1988). This chapter makes a case for the importance of teaching concepts, explains what this involves, and offers teaching and assessment strategies for conceptual understanding.

The Role of Concepts

A concept is "a mental construct or category represented by a word or phrase" (Wiggins and McTighe 2005, 340). Although concepts are abstractions—meaning they are ideas—examples representing concepts do exist. For example, the concept "mountain" is a mental construct, but individual mountains do exist. Concept groupings help us organize our experiences—we can distinguish mountains from hills, and both of these from plains and valleys. Our ability to make sense of the world would be greatly impaired if we did not use concepts as organizing constructs. For example, there may be as many as 7.5 million distinguishable colours, but we can manage this diversity by grouping them into a dozen or so basic categories (Bruner 1973). In short, concepts provide the intellectual categories or lenses through which we recognize and classify the world.

A simple way to illustrate this point is to draw attention to the drawing on the following page. When asked what they see, people will typically answer "a rabbit," "a duck," "a puppet," or some other creature. These answers arise only because we possess the concepts "rabbit," "duck," and "puppet." If we were not familiar with these concepts, we would not recognize them in the drawing. Hence, the difference when looking at the drawing between seeing undefined markings and seeing representations of objects is the possession of relevant concepts. Even animals recognize and classify objects as "food" or "non-edible" and distinguish fellow animals as "prey," "mate," "predator," or "other." Concepts actually shape what we see or, as a Chinese proverb puts it, "We see what is behind our eyes." If our students do not understand, for example, the concepts "justice" and "rights," they will not see injustice in a situation where a person's rights are being violated. Similarly, Roland's niece couldn't recognize Canada as a capitalist country because she did not truly understand the concept of "capitalism."

The metaphor of concepts as intellectual lenses is especially apt in that some individuals' glasses or eyesight are not

DUCK OR RABBIT?

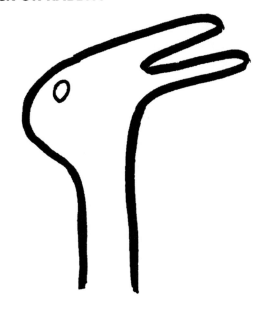

well focussed—they see the world in a blurred, sometimes incorrect form. The possession of rather crude concepts means that everything is reduced to vague dichotomous categories such as "awesome" and "gross" or "fun" and "boring." Our task, then, is not solely to introduce students to new concepts in social studies, but also to continually refine their conceptual understandings so that they learn to see the world in increasingly discriminating ways. In fact, the major focus of the primary social studies curriculum is on helping students grasp concepts that are central to understanding social life (such as teaching students to distinguish "needs" from "wants," to recognize when a group of people is a "community" and when it is not, and to understand the difference between a "right" and a "responsibility"). Because concepts organize or categorize our world, they often make most sense when paired with what they are not; we typically distinguish "need" from "want," "renewable" from "non-renewable," "capitalism" from "communism," and so on.

In addition to helping us classify and find meaning in our world, conceptual understandings are the essential building blocks for knowledge. Concepts are the basis upon which facts, theories, principles, and generalizations are constructed. Consider the following examples.

> **Fact**: Lake Superior is the largest of the Great Lakes.
> **Generalization**: Large bodies of water such as the Great Lakes have a moderating effect on climate.

> **Fact**: Sir John A. Macdonald was Canada's first prime minister.
> **Generalization**: Prime ministers are the most powerful members of their governments.

Students might memorize these statements, but they would not understand or be able to use them without knowledge of the concepts relied upon in these statements. The first pair of statements presupposes that the concepts "large," "lake," "moderating," "effect," and "climate" are understood; the second pair of statements presupposes that the concepts "prime minister," "power," "membership," and "government" are. Roland's niece might eventually learn that Canada is a capitalist country, but this fact still won't mean anything to her until she understands the concept of "capitalism." Studies going back almost a century in the area of history-learning show that emphasizing the facts at the expense of teaching the concepts impairs understanding and even retention of these facts (Wineburg 2001).

References to students' understanding or lack of understanding of a concept are potentially misleading since this may imply that concepts are either/or—either students grasp the concept or they do not. In many cases, students have an incomplete or distorted sense of a concept, which in some cases is worse than if they hadn't any conception whatsoever in the first place. For example, many students believe the opposite of "democracy" to be "communism." Since most North American students believe that democracy is a good thing, this implies that communism must be a bad thing. Communism may or may not be desirable, but it is not inherently undemocratic, as many students' misconception leads them to believe. But notice they will see communism in this light because of a conceptual confusion between economic systems (such as capitalism or communism) and political systems (democracy or dictatorship).

Challenges in Teaching Concepts

Despite their importance in helping us make sense of our world, concepts are not, generally speaking, taught effectively (Seiger-Ehrenberg 2001). Common impediments to effective conceptual teaching include:

- uncertainty over the very large number of concepts to teach, and which of those are most important to reinforce with students;
- lack of clarity about the precise distinctions between the various concepts we hope to teach (for example, How is "bias" different from "point of view"? Is the statement that "Black holes exist" or "God exists" a "fact" or an "opinion"?);
- conflation of concepts with other constructs such as facts and generalizations, and assuming that concepts can be taught the same way we teach facts;
- teaching concepts in a superficial manner by providing a definition and possibly an example or two.

Much of the rest of this chapter is devoted to suggestions on how to address these challenges.

One of the obvious difficulties is the sheer number of concepts we use in social studies. Every sentence contains concepts. Because of this, it is important to be selective. There is no point in teaching a concept merely because it is found in the curriculum or textbook. Students may already have a good grasp of the idea. For instance, most primary students will have some understanding of "family" before they begin to work with it in social studies. Most students will have lived in a family of one type or another for much of their life. Rather, they need experiences such as looking at pictures, reading stories, and talking with other children, which will help them see that some families are different from the ones they are familiar with (for example, they may have only one parent living in the home), but they are nevertheless families. Our efforts should be directed towards extending understanding and correcting misperceptions of familiar concepts.

As well, we should introduce students to unfamiliar concepts that have significant generative potential. By "generative," we mean concepts that represent significant ideas and can be linked with other important concepts. Consider the following pairs of concepts: "plateau" and "renewable resource" or "fashion" and "culture." The first concept in each pair identifies a rather narrow notion that does not have nearly the same breadth of use as does the second concept in each pairing. Clearly, we must prioritize our teaching towards developing those concepts that will have the biggest payoff in shaping and refining students' ability to make sense of their world.

Key Features of a Concept

It is helpful, when learning to teach concepts in ways that promote student understanding, to recognize four key features of any concept (Bennett and Rolheiser 2001).

- **Concepts have a label or a name.** Even before they can speak, infants struggle to classify things with names and labels, beginning with their own name. While they will invent their own names for these groups, they will also classify objects into categories: dogs, birds, hot, painful, and so on. In fact, young children understand many sophisticated concepts long before they learn the conventional terms or labels for them. For example, long before they learn the word "discrimination," many children will understand that some individuals are picked on unfairly simply because they happen to be different. Similarly, many young students can draw conclusions from a given fact without knowing that this is called an "inference" (for example, the fact that the person waves his hand in a

particular way suggests that he wants me to come towards him). As teachers, our role includes connecting students' existing conceptual understanding with the traditional words used to label these concepts. While it is helpful to know and use these labels, it is more important that students understand the meaning behind the vocabulary than for them to be able to use the words themselves.

- **Concepts are explained when examples are identified.** According to Gagné (1985, 95), concept learning refers to "putting things into a class" and being able to recognize members of that class. The American philosopher William James said: "A word is a summary of what to look for" (cited in Parker and Perez 1987, 164). Thus, recognizing the examples that fall within the concept and those that do not is at the core of understanding the concept. For instance, it would be difficult to claim that students understand the concept of "responsible citizenship" if they cannot identify picking up litter as responsible and throwing a candy wrapper on the sidewalk as irresponsible.

- **Many concepts are matters of degree.** Although some concepts are black or white—either a body of land is an island or it is not—many others are matters of degree. For example, at what point does a river become a stream? What is tall for the height of a child is not tall for a tree. If democracies take away rights of citizens during times of war or other disasters, at what point does a country cease to be a democracy and become a dictatorship instead? So-called "free market" economies are not completely without regulation, but under what conditions would an economy cease to be "free"?

- **Concepts are delineated by shared attributes.** The criteria that determine which examples belong within a conceptual category can be called attributes (also referred to as features, characteristics, or traits). For example, having three sides is an attribute of the concept "triangle"; an attribute of the concept "rule" is that it regulates actions. Some attributes are absolutely necessary for inclusion. These are essential attributes (for example, we cannot refer to an object as a triangle if it doesn't have three sides; the right to vote is an essential attribute of a democratic society). Some attributes may not be shared by all examples of a concept (for example, being able to vote for political parties, while a feature of most democratic societies, is not essential, since democracies such as ancient Athens operated without a party system as do some municipal governments today).

Helping students recognize non-essential attributes deepens their understanding of a concept. Non-essential attributes include "typical" features that are often associated with the concept and may be helpful in understanding it but are not necessarily present in all cases. For example, "mountains are (often) very high" and "mountains may have snow" are typical but non-essential attributes. Typical attributes of "rules" are that they often involve punishment or negative consequences if broken, and that they often prohibit or prevent action but may also protect or permit action. Another typical attribute of rules is that they are often written down. It may be the case that teaching students about typical features is as important as teaching them about essential features. But students must understand that a typical attribute need not always be present for the concept to apply (for example, heroes are often famous, but someone may not be famous yet may still be a hero).

The task of identifying attributes can be challenging, es-pecially in the case of abstract concepts. (Many social studies concepts are concrete in that they represent physical objects such as lake, mountain, ocean, valley, map, and globe; other concepts are abstract such as large, prime minister, power, time, culture, and discrimination.)

Clarity about the attributes is key when teaching for conceptual understanding. Table 5.1 suggests key attributes for a sampling of elementary social studies concepts. Once the key essential and non-essential attributes of a concept have been identified, it is important to select from this list those items about which students are most in need of instruction. It is generally unwise to attempt to teach all attributes of a concept at any one time. Instead, begin by teaching the particular at-tributes that students most need to understand.

TABLE 5.1   KEY ATTRIBUTES OF SELECTED SOCIAL STUDIES CONCEPTS

CONCEPT	ATTRIBUTES
bias	• an unfair preference or prejudice that colours observations or conclusions • a predisposition to praise or blame without sufficient evidence • comes in many forms: ethnocentrism, sexism, racism
change	• all things change over time • growth is change • change is necessary for survival • change may be negative or positive • change may be gradual or dramatic
co-operation	• co-operation does not always mean doing what you are told or that you have to "give in" • involves listening to each other in decision making • means working together for a common goal • not all "group work" is "co-operative" work
culture	• human response to the surrounding environment • changes over time • includes many different aspects of a society (for example, language, religion, customs, laws, art, music) • is more than costumes, clothing, and food • shapes our beliefs and values in powerful ways
needs	• refers to things that are basic for survival or a minimal level of functioning; are not simply wanted • different types of needs exist, both psychological and physical • some needs are common to everyone and some vary from person to person
perspective	• orients what we see and how we see things • can be physical (standing on top of or at the bottom of a hill) or mental (viewed from a teacher's, parent's, or student's perspective) • can't be avoided: everything must be viewed from some perspective • may be narrow or broad, empathetic or closed, biased or fair-minded • some perspectives are more defensible than others • we can and should be self-conscious about the perspectives we take on a given issue

TABLE 5.2   THE CONCEPT "PENCIL"

ATTRIBUTES	ESSENTIAL ATTRIBUTE	NON-ESSENTIAL ATTRIBUTE	EXAMPLES AND NON-EXAMPLES
contains lead	✓		if it did not contain lead, but ink, it would be a pen
needs to be sharpened		✓	mechanical pencils do not need to be sharpened
made of wood		✓	mechanical pencils can be made of metal or plastic
used for writing or drawing	✓		if it wasn't, it would be a stick or pointer
has an eraser		✓	erasers are a typical but not essential attribute

Promoting Conceptual Understanding

Learning a concept involves more than simple transmission of a label or a definition. It is centrally connected with recognizing the range of application or scope of the concept. For this reason, learning to recognize whether something is or is not an example of the concept lies at the heart of conceptual understanding.

In teaching concepts that refer to concrete objects such as "chair" or "tree," young students need to see numerous examples of the range of chairs and trees that exist. This is also the case with concepts that refer to non-physical notions such as "co-operation" or "needs." For these, students require examples that highlight the particular attributes you plan to teach. For example, in teaching that "needs can be both psychological and physical," we would include examples of psychological needs such as hope and emotional security along with examples of physical needs such as food and clean water.

Equally important in coming to understand a concept is knowing the limits or boundaries beyond which the concept does not apply. For this reason, non-examples are very useful in teaching. Non-examples are not simply any noninstance of the concept. Rather, they are closely related nonexamples—instances that are frequently confused with the concept or are very similar but different in important respects (for example, a much-wanted toy or a special privilege are non-examples of a "need").

In Table 5.2, we see examples and non-examples that might be offered to help students recognize the various attributes (essential and non-essential) of the concept "pencil." For example, students might be asked whether or not a pencil has to be made of wood and, if it is not, why not (it could be a mechanical pencil made of plastic or metal).

Strategies for Teaching Concepts

Considerable scholarly and professional attention has been devoted to methods for teaching concepts, most of which focus on the use of examples/non-examples. There are three general approaches offering different orientations to the use of examples and non-examples in fostering conceptual understanding:

- **concept recognition**, where the teacher identifies attributes and asks students to recognize which of the supplied items are examples and non-examples of the concept.
- **concept attainment**, where the teacher supplies items that are identified either as examples or non-examples and students must identify the attributes that distinguish the two categories.
- **concept formation**, where the teacher supplies neither identified examples and non-examples nor a list of attributes; instead, students create their own conceptual categories by sorting the items and explaining the attributes that distinguish their groupings.

Test how well you have understood some of the ideas related to the teaching of concepts. Table 5.3 contains a list of features that may or may not be necessary attributes of a mountain. For each feature, identify whether it is essential, typical, or not an attribute of a mountain. In each case, provide an example or a non-example to illustrate this feature. A sample answer for the first feature is provided.

TABLE 5.3 THE CONCEPT "MOUNTAIN"				
FEATURES	ESSENTIAL ATTRIBUTE	TYPICAL ATTRIBUTE	NON-ESSENTIAL ATTRIBUTE	EXAMPLES AND NON-EXAMPLES
has snow on top		✓		a mountain need not have snow
is found with other mountains				
is taller than a hill				
has trees on it				
rises above its surroundings				

CONCEPT RECOGNITION

Concept recognition is the most straightforward of these approaches. It begins with the selection of the concept(s) to teach, identification of a few key attributes, and creation of a list of relevant examples/non-examples for students to consider. Students are introduced to the concept and explicitly or implicitly to the attributes that define the concept. Students then sort the examples and non-examples according to the identified attributes and discuss the reasons for their choices. The teacher checks for understanding and then involves students in applying the concept in some meaningful context.

In the following example, adapted from Abbott, Case, and Nicol (2003, 83), the objective is to help students understand short-term and lasting differences. In particular, three attributes were identified:

- some differences don't last very long and others continue for a very long time.
- short-term and lasting differences can result from objects and from actions.
- short-term and lasting differences can be positive or negative.

The concepts are introduced by reading a story about a girl who tried to make a lasting difference in the lives of others. The teacher also discusses the different effects particular actions can have, such as doing someone's homework for them rather than helping the person learn how to do their own homework. Students are then given sets of cards with situations or actions similar to those reproduced in Figure 5.1

and asked to work with a partner to sort them into two labeled piles: "short-term differences" and "lasting differences." Finally, in applying the concept, students are asked to think of and carry out an action that would make a lasting difference in someone's life.

CONCEPT ATTAINMENT

The idea of concept attainment originates with cognitive psychologist Jerome Bruner (Bruner, Goodnow, and Austin

FIGURE 5.1 RECOGNIZING SHORT-TERM AND LASTING DIFFERENCES

Sort the following cards into short-term or lasting differences.

Give someone a photograph album as a gift	Give someone candy as a gift	Build a toy house with string and paper	Build a toy house with nail and wood
Talk over a problem with a person who made you angry	Try to hide from a person who made you angry	Drop garbage in the classroom	Cut down a tree

1967). It is a structured inquiry approach in which students are given examples and non-examples, but the particular concept is not indicated to them. In this approach, teachers select the concept they want students to attain, decide in advance on the attributes they want students to "discover," and then create or control a set of approximately ten paired examples/non-examples that will help students decipher these attributes. The examples/non-examples might be recorded as single words, phrases, actions, or images, and they may be introduced all at once to students or introduced one pair at a time as an unfolding mystery. The students' task is to ascertain which attributes explain why the examples fall into one category and the non-examples in another.

The scenario described in "Teaching About Natural Resources" illustrates a grade 3 teacher's efforts to use a concept attainment approach to teach about "natural resources." The teacher begins by introducing the task and a set of ten appropriately paired examples and non-examples. She presents the clearest contrasting pairs first and asks students to think about the difference between them. Gradually she presents pairs representing increasingly subtle distinctions. Meanwhile, students are generating and testing their hypotheses about the attributes that distinguish the examples from the non-examples. Students who catch onto the idea are able to identify the concept and are invited to suggest their own examples, while other students continue to try to formulate the concept. A "no call-out" rule allows everyone to stay involved. At an appropriate stage, the teacher offers test examples for students to classify. These serve as initial checks for understanding. To conclude, the teacher shares the conventional label or phrase for the concept and helps the class reach consensus on the concept and its defining attributes. Students discuss the changes in their thinking during the analysis of the paired examples.

The successful use of concept attainment as an unfolding mystery that students are to decipher depends on the

TEACHING ABOUT NATURAL RESOURCES

Serena Pierre has decided to use a concept attainment approach to teach her grade 3 class about natural resources. The night before class, she makes a list of the attributes of a natural resource that she believes are key to understanding the concept:

- natural resources are products that are considered valuable in their relatively unmodified (natural) form;
- natural resources are extracted from the earth or purified; they are not made or created by humans;
- mining, oil extraction, fishing, and forestry are generally considered natural-resource industries, while farming is not.

In a subsequent lesson, she will consider introducing a more complex attribute, the idea that natural resources can be classified into renewable and non-renewable resources.

For each attribute, she thinks of approximately three or four pairs of examples and non-examples. She makes a simple drawing and caption for each one on flash cards.

When it is time for social studies, she begins: "We are going to play a guessing game about some of the things we use in our world. I am placing pairs of things on the board under the headings YES and NO." Ms. Pierre puts a card with the word "trees" under the YES column and another card with the word "paper" under the NO column. Then she takes a second pair of cards. She puts "bears" under the YES column and "steak" under the NO column. Next she puts "wind" under the YES column and "plastic" under the NO column. She then asks the class to consider the three examples under the YES column and discuss how they are alike. "What do they have in common?

"No call-outs, please. If you have an idea, I want you to hang onto it and see whether your idea works with the next few sets of pairs." She proceeds to put "sunlight," "clay," and "crude oil" under the YES column and "electricity," "bread," and "gasoline" in the NO column.

Now there are six cards under each column. She asks, "What idea links all the items in the YES column? If you know, can you think of a new pair of items to go in the YES and the NO columns?"

Several students raise their hand. At the teacher's request, Maria offers "water" for the YES column and "ginger ale" for the NO column.

"That's correct," replies Ms. Pierre.

"I have another pair," says Gorinder, " 'wild berries' for the YES and 'wheat' for the NO column."

Other students nod their heads in agreement. Most raise their hands when asked whether they think they know the idea that links the items in the YES column. At this point, Ms. Pierre selects a card and holds it up. She asks: "Which column does 'plastic bag' go under?"

"NO."

"What about 'sand'?"

"YES."

"Where would 'cars' belong?"

"NO."

"How about 'gold'?"

"YES."

Ms. Pierre concludes by asking what the YES items have in common and offers the label "natural resources" to describe things that we use and that occur in nature. These two features are essential attributes of the concept. She invites students to describe their thinking during the analysis of the data as a way of reconfirming the critical attributes. The teacher and students discuss the purpose of distinguishing natural from human resources, and begin their study of Canada's natural wealth.

choice and sequencing of the paired examples. The initial set of paired examples shared with the class ought to suggest several hypotheses. Midway through the set, more clearly discriminated sets of pairs should be presented to help students eliminate various hypotheses. For example, in the scenario described above, the first two pairings might suggest that the YES examples are words ending in "s." The third set of pairings opposes this hypothesis. The teacher has to be clear about what to do if the ten or so pairs of examples and non-examples do not lead students to identify essential attributes and how to deal with incorrect or partially correct hypotheses. Practice in concept attainment can help students develop skills and habits of mind useful in inquiry lessons. With experience, children become skilled at identifying relationships in the cards or specimens.

CONCEPT FORMATION

The concept formation approach evolved out of the work of social studies educator Hilda Taba (1967). In this instructional method, students begin by examining data that may be generated by the teacher or by students. Students are encouraged to explore ways of classifying or sorting the data and attach descriptive labels to their groupings. Working individually, or better yet, in teams, students might use a mind map.[1] Students are helped to form their own understanding of a concept by linking the examples to the labels and by explaining their reasoning. Finally, students apply their understanding of the concept or concepts by predicting consequences, explaining unfamiliar phenomena, or hypothesizing and testing their hypotheses.

Consider the use of concept formation after a field trip in the local community. The teacher might engage students in discussing what they saw and heard. After listing the items on the chalkboard, the teacher invites students to look for ways of grouping the items (for example, "What things belong together?"). Students might arrange items by identifying common properties (such as clustering houses, apartments, and townhouses into one category, and grocery stores, clothes stores, and hardware stores into another). The teacher might prompt students with questions such as:

- How are these categories different from or similar to …?
- What does this tell us about …?
- Why do you think this would happen …?

Each group would be asked to explain its rationale for the classification system. Drawing attention to the different ways in which students classify is an important purpose of the activity. At some point the teacher should ask students to assign labels or names to grouped items (for example, "living places," "shopping places," "office places," "fun places").

In another class on communities, the teacher might provide students with sets of photographs of various types of communities (such as urban, suburban, and rural). Working in groups, students could sort the photographs into categories and distinguish among the categories. Students could then explore the differences and similarities, and perhaps also the advantages and disadvantages, of living in urban, suburban, or rural communities.

Concept formation provides students with an opportunity to explore ideas by making connections and seeing relationships between items. This method can help students develop and refine their ability to recall and discriminate among key ideas, to see commonalities and identify relationships, to formulate concepts and generalizations, to explain how they have organized data, and to present evidence to support the way in which they have organized the data.

In concept formation, students often develop the data set and even if the teacher provides the data, it is the class that establishes the classification system. This means that the concepts are identified by the students. These may or may not match the teacher's specific intentions. The strength of this approach is its open-ended opportunity for students to explore their own connections.

CHOOSING AMONG THE APPROACHES

A decision about which of the three approaches to use depends partly on the nature of the concept to be taught. Concept recognition and concept attainment are best used with concepts that have clearly defined attributes. Most concrete concepts such as "island" have one clear set of attributes that define examples (that is, either it is completely surrounded by water or it is not). Many concepts in social studies are of this type (for example, democracy, primary source, secondary industry, hypothesis, fact, assimilation), as are most concrete concepts found in geography and economics. Other concepts are "relational"—best defined when compared to other concepts (for example, an aluminum can might be considered as waste when thrown out as garbage but would not be if it were recycled). Examples of this class of concept include "strong," "deep," "opposite," and "pollution." Relational concepts can also be taught using concept recognition or concept attainment when the pairs represent examples at opposing ends of a continuum (such as comparing the size of a needle to that of an elephant). If a concept has an "or" in its definition, it likely has two or more sets of alternative attributes (for example, a citizen can be either a native-born or a naturalized member of a state). Such concepts as "symbolism," "equality," "justice," "controversial," and many abstract concepts in history are of this kind. Concept formation may work best with such concepts. Table 5.4 contains examples of concept teaching using a continuum of real to abstract sources and activities.

OTHER STRATEGIES

Although the use of example/non-example pairs is the most powerful means to help students understand concepts, other strategies are potentially useful complementary strategies. These strategies include the following.

- **Provide an opportunity to "experience" the concept.** Whether it is concrete or abstract, it is important for students to "experience" a concept. The need for tangible first-hand experience is especially acute with primary students (Seefeldt 2005, 197). With concrete concepts, these experiences may be provided by using actual physical objects or pictures, rather than merely referring to examples. In the case of abstract concepts, it is often more difficult, but even more necessary, to provide students with opportunities to "experience" key attributes of the concept. In teaching about "co-operation," for example, we might involve students in simulated situations where they work at odds with each other's goals, side by side in parallel, and in interdependent ways. It may be useful to examine Table 5.4, which represents a continuum from real to abstract. Where feasible, start as far as possible to the left of the chart in providing students with opportunities to experience a concept.
- **Provide or generate a definition.** Although on their own definitions do not capture all the attributes of a concept, providing or having students create a definition (especially if they have explored examples and non-examples) contributes to their conceptual understanding.
- **Explore the etymology of the word that represents the concept.** Etymology explores the linguistic origins of a word and its formation and development through time. Sometimes a word's origins provide a clue identifying an essential attribute of the concept. For example, the origin of the concept word "rule" is the Latin word that refers to a straight stick.
- **Compare derivative words.** Derivative words are words that come from the same stem as the concept under investigation. It is interesting, for example, to compare the notion of a ruler (that is, a straight edge) with the concept of a rule. A ruler is a physical device for guiding the making of lines, whereas a rule is a verbal device for guiding our actions.
- **Examine synonyms and antonyms.** Often synonyms and antonyms are helpful because students may be more familiar with these other words and their understanding of the concept under investigation can be reinforced.

Table 5.5 summarizes the strategies mentioned above and their specific applications to the teaching of the concept of "rules." All five strategies would rarely be used at any one time.

Assessing Conceptual Understanding

Numerous strategies can be used to assess how well students have understood a concept.

- **Recognize instances of the concept.** Provide students with original examples and non-examples and ask whether they are instances of the concept. Are the following examples of rules?

TABLE 5.4   A CONTINUUM OF LEARNING EXPERIENCES FROM REAL TO ABSTRACT

	REAL EVENTS AND ACTUAL OBJECTS	PHYSICAL REPRESENTATIONS AND ROLE PLAYS	VISUAL REPRESENTATIONS	VERBAL REPRESENTATIONS
Sources	On-location sites and actions; genuine artifacts	Toys or replicas; simulations	Photographs, drawings, and picture books	Stories and words
Samples of teaching the concepts "hill" and "co-operation"	• during a field trip, climb a hill • take part in classroom activities where students are allowed to work together and where they must work alone	• make a papier mâché model containing hills, mountains, and valleys • role-play situations where students are co-operative and where they are not	• examine photographs of hills and mountains • look at pictures depicting people both co-operating with each other and not co-operating	• read a story involving someone who lives atop a hill • read stories and discuss situations where students are co-operative and where they are not

TABLE 5.5 OTHER STRATEGIES

TEACHING IDEAS	"RULES"
Experiential introduction	Play a "rotten rules" game. Without any introduction, throw an inflated balloon into the class. Students will automatically react by batting the balloon back and forth. As students do this, assign points on the blackboard and draw students' attention to this by verbalizing the process: I am giving Suzy one point for hitting the balloon the highest. I am giving Joshua a point for hitting it quietly. Points can be given for highest, lowest, sex, colour of hair, or type of clothing of the hitter, and so on. Be inconsistent in scoring; take off a point for the same action or characteristic for which a student earlier received a point. Students will react with frustration and will try to figure out the basis for assigning points. End the game when the frustration level gets high. Discuss the following questions: • When the game began, what did you think you had to do? • Did you ever figure out the rules for the game? • How did you feel when you realized you didn't know what was going on? • Did anyone enjoy playing this game? Why or why not? • What were the rules? • How could we improve this game if we played it again? • How many would like to play the game again under the new conditions? • Are there times in real life when rules are needed or when rules that exist seem unfair?
Definition	• a principle or regulation governing conduct
Etymology	• "regula," meaning a straight stick, pattern
Derivative words	• to rule—to control, guide, direct, or govern • a ruler (straight edge)—a device for guiding the drawing of lines • unruly—uncontrolled • a (court) ruling—a decision as to what is to be done in a particular case
Synonyms or antonyms	• laws and regulations

- No one is allowed to use my radio without my permission.
- Every sentence must end with either a period, a question mark, or an exclamation point.
- Many people vote in federal elections.
- I don't like it when people run in the school hallway.

- **Generate examples.** Ask students to provide their own original examples of the concept:
  - Give two examples of a family rule or a school rule.
  - List two problems that you sometimes encounter at school.
- **Explain specific attributes.** Ask students to address questions about specific attributes:
  - Do all rules forbid action and are all rules written down?
  - Give an example of a rule that prohibits and a rule that enables.
- **Distinguish similar concepts.** Ask students to distinguish non-examples from examples:

- Explain in your own words the difference between a request and a rule. Give examples of each.
- Explain in your own words the difference between a problem and a question. Give an example of each.

- **Apply the concept.** Ask students to apply the concept in an assignment:
  - Create a set of class rules to guide how we should treat each other in class.
  - What problems were faced by the character in the story we have just read? Which of these was the most difficult?

The rubric in Figure 5.2 might be used to assess young students' ability to recognize examples of problems and solutions, match problems with solutions, and provide an example of a solution to a particular problem.

	SOPHISTICATED UNDERSTANDING	EXTENDED UNDERSTANDING	BASIC UNDERSTANDING	PARTIAL RECOGNITION	PRE-RECOGNITION
Distinguishes problem from solution	Correctly identifies problems and solutions, and correctly states in own words the difference	Correctly identifies problems and solutions and offers a simple explanation of their difference.	Correctly identifies simple examples of problems and solutions, but without any explanation.	Understands what is being asked, but has difficulty consistently identifying even very simple examples of problems and solutions.	Does not understand what it means to identify something as a problem or a solution.
Recognizes matching problems and solutions	Correctly recognizes the matching problem and solution when given less obvious examples.	Correctly recognizes the matching problem and solution when given various examples.	Correctly recognizes the matching problem and solution when given very simple examples.	Understands what is being asked, but has difficulty consistently recognizing the matching problem and solution when given very simple examples.	Does not understand what it means to match a problem with its solution.
Proposes possible solutions	Provides two or more reasonable solutions even with less obvious problems.	Proposes two or more obvious solutions that match a problem.	Proposes a single predictable solution that matches a simple problem.	Proposes a solution that seems unrelated to the problem or is otherwise inappropriate.	Cannot propose a solution when given a simple problem.

Identify an abstract concept that is not discussed in this chapter but that is central to social studies at a particular grade level. Identify at least three important attributes and develop a set of between six and eight paired examples/non-examples that you might use in a concept recognition or concept attainment lesson to teach these attributes.

Conclusion

The focus of this chapter is on teaching concepts in ways that foster understanding. We have argued that conceptual knowledge is not a matter of transmitting bits of vocabulary to students. Rote acquisition of definitions is not worthwhile—students can't use the concepts and they will have difficulty making sense of any factual information that relies on these concepts. In promoting conceptual understanding, we have emphasized the importance of identifying key attributes for selected concepts and teaching these largely through the use of examples and non-examples. Providing opportunities to "experience" concepts is also valuable, especially for younger students. Our goal should be to teach important concepts using strategies powerful enough to make them meaningful, memorable, and usable.

ENDNOTE

1   Mind maps and other visual tools such as Venn diagrams can be used to help students explore concepts and for teachers to assess student understanding. For ideas and resources on using visual tools such as mind maps, concept maps, and other graphic organizers, see Bennett and Rolheiser (2001) and McEwan and Myers (2002).

REFERENCES

Abbott, M., R. Case, and J. Nicol. 2003. *I can make a difference.* Richmond, BC: The Critical Thinking Consortium.

Bennett, B. and C. Rolheiser. 2001. *Beyond Monet: The artful science of instructional integration.* Toronto: Bookstation.

Bruner, J.S. 1973. *Going beyond the information given.* New York: Norton.

Bruner, J., J.J. Goodnow, and G.A. Austin. 1967. *A study of thinking.* New York: Science Editions.

Gagné, R.M. 1985. *The conditions of learning and theory of instruction,* 4th ed. New York: Holt, Rinehart & Winston.

McEwan, S. and J. Myers. 2002. Graphic organizers: Visual tools for learning. *Orbit* 32 (4). Available online at http://www.oise.utoronto.ca/orbit.

Parker, W. 1988. Thinking to learn concepts. *Social Studies* 79 (2), 70–73.

Parker, W. and S.A. Perez. 1987. Beyond the rattle of empty wagons. *Social Education* 51 (3), 164–166.

Seefeldt, C. 2005. *Social studies for the preschool/primary child,* 7th ed. Columbus, OH: Pearson.

Seiger-Ehrenberg, S. 2001. Concept development. In *Developing minds: A resource book for teaching thinking,* 3rd ed., ed. A.L. Costa, 437–441. Alexandria, VA: Association for Supervision and Curriculum Development.

Taba, H. 1967. *Teacher's handbook for elementary social studies.* Palo Alto, CA: Addison-Wesley.

Wiggins, G. and J. McTighe. 2005. *Understanding by design,* expanded 2nd ed. Alexandria, VA: Association for Supervision and Curriculum Development.

Wineburg, S. 2001. *Historical thinking and other unnatural acts: Charting the future of teaching the past.* Philadelphia: Temple University Press.

6 Children's Conceptions of Space and Time

Dennis Milburn

As children develop, they constantly receive information that they sort and classify so that they may come to know the world around them. This drawing together of information into a pattern of thought, speech, and action results in the formation of concepts. In this chapter, I will discuss two of these concepts: the concepts of space and time.

We all acquire spatial and temporal concepts in some measure, though they are more highly developed in some people than in others. From their very earliest years, children look at the world by organizing space and the objects within space. Children organize time not only in the conventional sense for the convenience of day-to-day living, but also more abstractly by projecting thoughts ahead and reflecting on what has passed. In concrete terms, the development of both concepts is a necessary feature of school life and, in the simplest form, we can see these concepts applied in the case of geographical space and historical time. Children do not come to school with these concepts firmly established and influences in the early years of schooling may help children move towards understanding time and space in their own conception of the world.

Space

Acquiring the concept of space involves more than learning to estimate distance, draw in perspective, or judge how far to throw a ball. The refining of spatial concepts is a more complex operation. At school, this process can be seen in holding a pencil, drawing a circle, writing one's name, painting a picture, tying shoelaces, climbing the monkey bars, or threading one's way through the classroom without falling over. All such activities demand both physical control of the objects and manipulation of "spatial data." This development may be supported by direct instruction from parents and teachers, but it also requires construction of internal sorting criteria that depend greatly on practical activity and experience.

The analysis of children's activities in the early grades re-veals how children acquire the frames of reference by which they can mentally organize space. The coordinates that make up this framework may appear to adults, at first glance, to be relatively simple. They may be such features as understanding what is vertical and horizontal, or knowing what is meant by right or left, in front or behind. These concepts must be learned (Russell 1956). All of us have had problems at some time with right and left and have seen children move slowly and painfully to understand them. We should not take such apparently simple things for granted. Children not only reason differently than adults do, they have quite different world views (Piaget 1950). At times, children seem to acquire philosophies as if by magic. For example, children at a very young age will act upon a hypothesis of "fairness" although they are not able to describe this moral precept.

In *Psychology and Perception*, Vernon (1962) states that each of us has a series of body axes by which we understand ourselves in space and that help us conceptualize space. As has been previously mentioned, an understanding of "vertical" and "horizontal" is a coordinate children gain early in life. An even more difficult coordinate is an understanding of right and left, and still more difficult is a perception of depth or distance. Children need these understandings to situate themselves in space. Space to a child is a kind of all-enveloping container made up of a network of sights and objects that need to be sorted using consistent criteria.

Often teachers tell children that vertical lines are lines that go up and down and horizontal lines are lines that go across. However, when the lines join to make angles or to construct the shape of an object, a further explanation of horizontal and vertical is necessary. Is a door a vertical line? Is a door two vertical lines and two horizontal lines? Many children will not be able to transfer the idea of vertical or horizontal from what they see to what they draw. For example in Figures 6.1 and 6.2 we see two first-grade drawings of a teacher standing at the chalkboard. The teacher is wearing clothing with a pattern of vertical stripes. One child has drawn the stripes correctly, the other has turned the stripes in space and made them hori-

FIGURE 6.1

FIGURE 6.2

zontal. As far as the second child is concerned the clothing is striped, and whether the stripes are vertical or horizontal is immaterial.

Since maps, and particularly local maps, show the space things take up on the ground, it is important for children to be able to draw objects from above. Piaget places the ability to do this around the age of eight, though other authorities disagree and place this ability even later. Normally, in their early years, children will "map" any object pictographically. That is, they will draw houses on their sides and they will place on maps things that are impermanent, such as cars or dogs. They will, in essence, draw a picture. If we wish to ask children to attempt to draw things from above it is necessary to use a phrase such as "Draw a bird's-eye view." However, this may lead to questions such as "How high is the bird flying?" (In one case, a child drew a lawn with a worm in the middle, this being considered as a suitable answer to the request "Draw a bird's-eye view.") To draw a "pilot's-eye view" may be a more useful approach. However, young children have difficulty drawing "from above" even in the simplest situation.

For example, first-grade children cannot usually draw a bottle from above. Almost all children draw bottles as seen from the side. This reinforces Piaget's claims that children draw objects from their own point of view. It is a comparatively late stage of development that allows them to draw all objects uniformly from a "pilot's-eye view."

The developmental nature of such cognitive processes, as stressed by Piaget, can be observed by analyzing drawings or maps on a topic such as "My route to school."

Figure 6.3 shows the work of a six-year-old Chilean boy. He orients himself spatially by recording the various turns he makes to go from home to school. The fact that he places his school near his house is subordinate to the mental path he has traced in his mind and recorded. Of further interest is that questioning revealed that the only road the child traversed was "Sevastian Elcano," which ran by his home. Other turns marked are within the school's gates and grounds. The reason for this is problematical. It may be that the turns in space within the grounds of the school are well known. In any case, these turns bring the child to the end of his journey, relatively close to his starting point. This is not an uncommon feature in children's drawings of their route to school and it could be said that they are conditioned by the size of the paper they are using. They may start in one corner, draw around the edge of

the paper and reach their destination at a point on the paper convenient to them.

Figure 6.4 is a map by a seven-year-old boy in which he has attempted to coordinate space, or perhaps more simply, to organize a journey in proportion. The first part of the journey is well drawn, since there is both a traffic "island" and a gas station to serve as points of reference. Then, near two pools and a river, the route becomes discontinuous and disjointed, returning to greater accuracy near the school in the bottom left-hand corner. Such discontinuity is a common feature in a child's developing ability to organize space. Space is organized in "sections." Those parts that have been well observed are drawn in detail. Other sections of the route are drawn less precisely (for example, a long straight road may be shortened). Sections of the journey are well drawn when the child has found a need to concentrate on detail. Recreating this type of journey in a representational form is complex and, as J. and S. Sauvy (1974) remark, "Dimensions are not respected."

We must also take into account, as has been mentioned, that the child is limited by the confines of the paper. Adults behave in the same way when drawing maps on subjects such as "How to find my house." They begin with panache, but as they begin to fill the paper, the relative scale alters. Their drawings become cramped and overly detailed.

In the classroom, this problem may be overcome by supplying an additional sheet (or sheets) of paper so that the journey may be continued. If this is done, the scale has some chance of remaining constant.

FIGURE 6.3

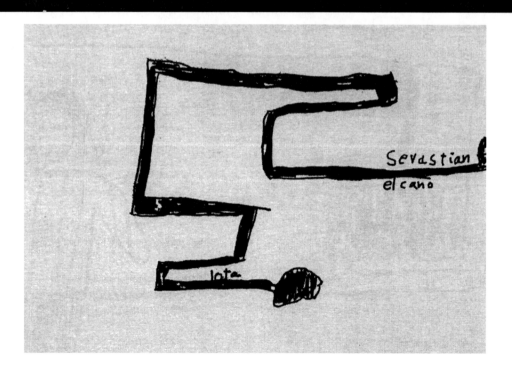

FIGURE 6.4

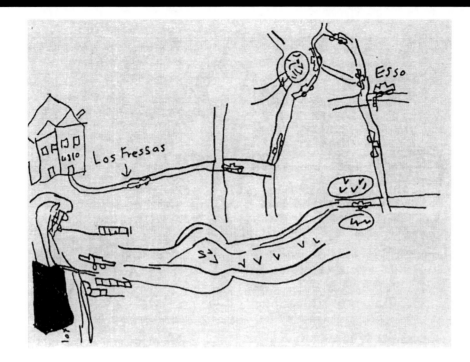

FIGURE 6.5

Figure 6.5 is a drawing by an eight-year-old Chilean girl. Her frame of reference is the street "block." Names are added as further pointers and a route is shown to assist the "reader." The journey has apparently been formalized in the child's mind. Houses and poplar trees are drawn in profile and, since the original drawing was brightly coloured, serve more for decoration than accuracy. However, this is an accurate representation of a journey.

Figure 6.6 shows a nine-year-old boy's reduction of his journey in a map of stark simplicity. In this case the boy's route to school represents a long cycle ride, and the mental map is therefore of greater complexity. At the age of nine, however, the child is also progressing to a stage where he is able to draw a map from a "pilot's-eye view." His map is consistent in technique and contains no extraneous or impermanent details.

Finally, Figure 6.7 shows a map drawn by an eight-year-old girl from Vancouver. Like her Chilean counterparts, she draws some objects pictographically, though the organization of data in space is fairly accurate. However, there is a further complication because this child wishes to show slopes. The apparent curves in the roads are in fact gradients, and, in the bottom left-hand corner, a flight of steps climbs a steep wooded incline.

Though such children's maps may appear to be a comparatively simple exercise, the children have been asked to do a number of concurrent tasks: to observe, to recall their observations, to plot the data, and to construct techniques for doing so. They have been asked to give points of reference with reasonable accuracy and, most difficult of all, to coordinate space in representational form.

The development of the concept of space in the three-year span from six to nine years is marked, as a comparison of the figures will indicate. There is, however, no strict adherence to chronological age in the development of spatial concepts, except perhaps in the ability to shift to a "pilot's-eye view" in the seven- to nine-year-old age range.

An exercise such as mapping "My route to school" probably calls for a more abstract level of thought than, for example, conducting the same exercise using toys as models. In toy play, the environment is more actively controlled and the process of trial and error allows for greater flexibility. Blaut and Stea (1974) indicate that children as young as the age of three can produce reasonable mental maps using toy play. They postulate that initial exercises carried out in preschool or kindergarten classes support formal map learning at the age of school entrance. However, the examples given in the previous figures reflect the infinite variety of ways in which children could draw their route to school. Children can, and do, invoke fantasy; they note objects that are impermanent; their eidetic imagery is extremely selective; and, in the end, they may become tired or frustrated and simply bring the exercise to a hurried close.

A number of conclusions may be drawn from such responses from children. Not only is a developmental pattern clearly in evidence, the child also draws considerably on his or her own perception of the environment. This internal ac-

FIGURE 6.6

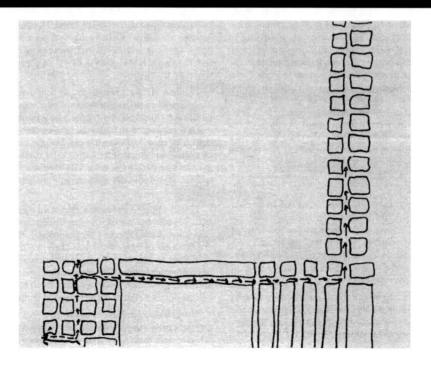

FIGURE 6.7

tivity, which can technically be called "spatial cognition," can only take place if the child has satisfactory frames of reference and can call upon them when solving spatial problems. When we ask students to "Draw a map to show X" we are asking them to represent ideas in a factual and visible manner.

The developmental understanding of maps is clearly seen to contradict any instructional pattern that requires a child to draw a map of a state or a province, complete with rivers and towns. Children may draw such maps accurately, but the maps may also be meaningless to the child. For this reason, many children's introduction to maps through world maps or national maps may be an unsatisfactory exercise for both children and teacher. Most children have simply not developed a conception of space adequate for them to understand this type of aerial distribution. There is no reason, for example, why young people should "know" that the blue on a map or the blue areas on a globe usually represent water. Nor can they be expected to know that the continents are the "shapes" we concentrate on. While adults who look at a world map may well have some conception of the shape of the major continents, young children have none. To many children under the age of seven, world maps appear merely as colourful patterns. This fact highlights the danger of glib references to "the basic skills of mapping."

The first steps in spatial cognition appear to be the building up of frames of reference. However, as experience and awareness grow, these frames of reference are complemented by the development of cognitive maps. A cognitive map is not necessarily a map in the traditional sense. It is a scheme within our mind which has the functions of the familiar map, but does not necessarily have the physical properties of such a graphic model.

Cognitive maps are in our mind when we respond to advertisements such as "Come to sunny Florida," or "Would you like to get away from it all?" Cognitive maps are, in a sense, an interpretation of the real world and are assembled in a highly individual manner from known data. For example, when a motorist gets stuck in a traffic jam, he may use his cognitive awareness of the route that he travels to attempt to bypass the obstruction. In this situation, the motorist is calling upon his experience and attempting to interpret what he knows.

Saarinen's (1969) work on students' views of the world shows that school children depend very much on "centrality." For example, African children in secondary school tend to place Africa in the centre of their world map, while their knowledge of the other continents remains fairly vague and the shapes they draw of them are indeterminate.

Some mental leap is needed in the classroom between the conjuring up of spatial information which, as it were, lies within our heads and transferring that information into a visible and representational form. There is a great difference between actual spatial perception and the ability to record it. The analogy is somewhat akin to the ability of a child to explain a concept verbally and the ability of the child to be accurate in his verbal explanation. An example of this can be seen in a 5-year-old child's definition of "sharing." Although this concept is difficult to verbalize, the child offered a reasonable definition—adequate to his stage of development—when he said "He can have it when I have finished with it." While this is not a dictionary definition of sharing, it is a definition that the child can operate and can represent by speech.

Research suggests that children pass through various stages of seeing and drawing objects from a highly egocentric point of view. Children move from the house drawn from the side, for example, to the more difficult task of organizing data in space. It is in this task that children encounter the projective element where they must assume an entirely different position and ultimately move from a two-dimensional viewpoint to a "pilot's-eye view." Such movement is not controlled by the cultural environment since it has been shown that children in different countries go through the same stages. There does appear to be some order or transformation from one stage to another. We know from working with children that their ideas, impressions, and mental structures do not atrophy but continue to change constantly just as concepts do not remain fixed, but are enlarged or altered as new information is assimilated. While children's conceptions of space may vary widely, they are valid referents for the children concerned. All children attempt to fashion an orderly model of the universe through various encounters with experience.

The author stresses the importance of practical activity and experiences as much or more so than instruction in developing a child's conception of space. Thinking about various dimensions of space (for example, left/right; front/back; high/low; altitude/depth; distance), make a list of tasks and experiences that you might design for children (primary or upper elementary) to help develop their understanding of these dimensions of space.

Time

"Time" may at first appear to be a more concrete and manageable notion than the concept of space. Time, as we know it, is measured in seconds, minutes, hours, days, weeks, months, years, and centuries. Yet the concept of time is projective even in a personal sense, since all of us interpret time in a highly individual manner. Measured time can become, in fact, a restraint on our actions.

Benjamin Franklin said "Do not squander time, for that's the stuff life is made of." Young children, however, find time in the adult sense to be supremely unimportant. Events are important, time is not. After five minutes of a car journey parents often hear the question "Are we nearly there?" Young children are concerned with the present and find it difficult

to categorize the past in a rational and orderly manner. An adult may say "When I was on my holidays last year," whereas a child will say "When I was on my holidays." To project into the future is difficult for us all. "Soon" is a relative term for young children and to project a verbal statement indicating that an event will occur "in a few weeks" or "next month" is most often meaningless.

Many children learn to tell the time in their early days of school. Exercises with, for example, play clocks are a common feature in kindergarten and grade 1. Nevertheless, time is still related to events. Consequently, in teaching children, time will be linked with known events, for example, "At three o'clock we go home," or "I go to bed at eight." Some authorities say that the first point in time that a child comes to understand is bedtime, and few would argue that children become reasonably prescient in anticipating events that affect them.

Once at school, children assimilate daily and weekly events very quickly. From this they learn to "name" time in hours or days. However, children have more difficulty understanding the concept of a year or any greater span of time. Many children must wonder why during most months we count to thirty or thirty-one and then start again, except for the fact that those numbers grade imperceptibly into the next month. Our own acceptance of days and months is a direct result of a socially imposed pattern. We rarely question the pattern and we may even see this pattern as immutable. Children can only begin to recognize the passage of time by identifying a number of discrete points which they then begin to put in some form of order. Passages of time between these points will remain unclear throughout life. In our early years we cannot envisage the future, and as adults we telescope what has passed into isolated and discontinuous incidents. Nevertheless, some points in time remain crucial for children.

A child's birthday is usually the most important event of the year for children in Western societies. Typically, children's knowledge and appreciation of time heightens as their birthday approaches. The word soon becomes next week, then two days from now and, ultimately, tomorrow. A year's chart showing "our birthdays" is one of the most useful ways to introduce children to the fact that there are twelve months in a year.

After their birthdays, Christmas is the next most important event in many children's lives. Using these events, children can begin to see the passage of time through events that are important to them. That is, they approach time through utilizing concepts that are adequate to their stage of development. They can, in essence, "perform" in a time frame which is credible to them.

A useful activity to get children thinking about the order of events and the meaning of "before" and "after" is to have them sort a series of cards with symbols on them illustrating events or festivals (for example, a card with a heart on it to denote Valentine's Day). Pick an event such as the child's birthday (write "My birthday" on the card) or a common cultural event as the centre point around which other events occur. Although the order of events can be learned fairly quickly, young children have little awareness of the passage of time.

Indeed, even adults find the passage of time difficult to display when faced with a practical exercise. These difficulties are illustrated by an experiment where a group of adults are asked to write down a historical event on a card. It is not necessary to know the date. They then take turns arranging the cards in chronological order because each new card may reorganize chronological time.

Two main features emerge from this experiment. First, in the construction of such a time scale it is noticeable that the scale becomes structured after the first person has laid down the first card. In general, people will use the first cards as a starting point in the same way as a child uses a card for "My birthday" as a point of reference and subsequently places all the cards relative to the first card, using the basic logic of "before" and "after." Second, the "spread" of cards (in physical space) on the time scale becomes relative to historical time only when cards have to be moved in order to place a new card between them. For example, if someone has laid down a card marked "Henry VIII, Dissolution of the Monasteries," and next to it a card is placed marked, "Death of Queen Elizabeth," a subsequent card which may have noted "The Spanish Armada" must then be placed between the two existing cards. This action usually prompts adults to attempt physically to spread the cards out "in time" though in the early part of the experiment they merely place the cards in some sort of historical order.

Thus we see that adults, themselves, have a concept of time and perhaps an idea of the spread of historical time. In general, however, adults' sense of the spread of historical time remains very sketchy. Adults will probably know that "The Greeks came before the Romans," though they will have little idea of the amount of space (or time) that these civilizations would take up on a time scale. Historical time must, of necessity, be selective. The facts, as points of reference known and understood by adults, will be a viable basis for understanding chronology.

Just as ideas of horizontal and vertical become reference points to assist in the organization of space, similarly, events become reference points in the organization of time for both children and adults. A knowledge of historical time, therefore, may occur through acquiring knowledge of disparate "events" that are then ordered chronologically. We see again in this activity the role of sorting and classifying as a fundamental part of concept formation. Historical events may be kaleidoscopic,

but in order to make some sense out of them we must attempt to order them in some way. Certainly the chronological method is not the only method of teaching history; there are a number of other methods of "order." What we are discussing here is the method or methods though which children can move towards their own conception of both personal time and historical time.

Research evidence suggests that children can manipulate and understand those broad sweeps of time such as geological time (Milburn 1966). Children between nine to fourteen years old seem to be able to assimilate a basic premise like "Mountains rise and fall, climates change," more easily than adults. They can use the names of geological eras correctly, and with understanding.

Thus, children who have been discussing the geological time scale can say with understanding that the deserts of the Permian and Triassic periods were eventually drowned by the Jurassic and Cretaceous seas. Children at this age are not inhibited by attempting to understand geological periods in years, as are adults. Adults will constantly ask "How many years ago were there swamps in existence that eventually turned into coal?" To say in response that the coal measure swamps of the Carboniferous period occurred approximately three hundred million years ago has really very little meaning. If, however, one has studied the broad sweep of geological periods from the Precambrian period to the present day, the point that coal measure swamps existed in the late Paleozoic era at least places this period in relation to other events.

This exercise in geological time illustrates an important stage in children's understanding of time. Here, children are ordering events in temporal sequence where successive events constitute a series: "x" comes before "y" and "x" and "y" before "z." Piaget and Inhelder (1956) suggest that the concept of seriations is grasped by the age of 7 or 8.

In addition to seriation, duration is another feature of the conception of time. Duration refers to attempts to classify time by setting one "piece" of time against another. To do this requires some form of classification that time span "A" is longer than "B," and that "A" is relative to "B," and that "A" and "B" are relative both to "C" and to each other.

The factors of succession and duration need to be coordinated so that time can be classified by both the event and the span of that event. Children are quick to point out that someone is younger than they are. However, if questioned they may say he is younger because "he is smaller." In other words, they have an idea of seriation but not of duration. Similarly, children may understand that events happened "before" the time span between the events. This attribute is built up slowly and it is not until the age of nine to ten years that phrases such as "still four days to wait," or "I was there last month" acquire significant meaning. We may all reflect that our sense of temporal duration becomes vague when we relate it to periods of sleep. Between falling asleep and waking, time apparently ceases to exist. In this respect, our understanding of time is a highly personal attribute. Time "words" are acquired with varying degrees of understanding. For example, "before" and "after" may present the same amount of difficulty to a six-year-old that "five centuries ago" may present to an adult.

Both time and space concepts are acquired by experience with the world around us and by the development of frames of reference. Children start establishing coordinates early in life that make up their frames of reference and these are not necessarily "taught" (Milburn 1980). The danger when attempting to introduce these coordinates is that we may start too far along the conceptual path. We often assume that facts must be self-evident; for example, that a child must surely know that the blue expanse on a map represents lakes, seas, or oceans (Milburn 1972). Not only may a child not understand this symbolic reference, they may not even know what lakes, seas, and oceans actually are. The internal system of coordinates is reinforced by the specific understanding implied through verbal definitions. Since most concepts are represented by verbal symbolism, an understanding of words is a visible sign that concepts are understood to some extent. Space and time are in themselves difficult concepts to explain and all people differ in the extent and manner in which these concepts are understood. Nevertheless, the input of experience transmitted through perception, memory, and even imagination ultimately lead to generalized conclusions by which we organize the world around us and attempt to understand both the past and the future.

Given the importance of practical activity and experience in developing a child's conception of time, identify various dimensions appropriate for the students you will teach (for example, quick/slow; sooner/later; ancient/modern; younger/older; day/week/month/year/decade/century/millennium). List tasks and experiences that you might design to help develop a child's understanding of time.

ACKNOWLEDGEMENT

This chapter is an abridged and edited version of "Children in Time and Space" in *A Canadian Social Studies*, 2nd ed., ed. J. Parsons, G. Milburn, and M. van Manen. (Edmonton: University of Alberta, 1985), 120–141.

REFERENCES

Blaut, J.M., and D. Stea. 1974. Mapping at the age of three. *Journal of Geography* 73 (7).

Milburn, D. 1966. *A first book of geology.* Oxford: Blackwell.

———. 1972. In *New movements in the study and teaching of geography,* ed. N.J. Graves. London: Temple Smith.

———. 1980. Mapping in the early years of schooling. In *Canadian geographical education,* ed. R. Choquette, J. Wolforth, and M. Villemure. Ottawa: University of Ottawa Press.

Piaget, J. 1950. *The psychology of intelligence.* London: Routledge & Paul.

Piaget, J., and B. Inhelder. 1956. *The child's conception of space.* London: Routledge.

Russell, D.H. 1956. *Children's thinking.* Boston: Ginn.

Saarinen, T. 1969. *Perception of environment.* Commission on College Geography, Resource Paper No. 5, Washington, DC: Association of American Geographers.

Sauvy, J., and S. Sauvy. 1974. *The child's discovery of space.* Harmondsworth, UK: Penguin.

Vernon, M.D. 1962. *Psychology and perception.* Harmondsworth, UK: Pelican.

7 Enriched by Teaching Aboriginal Content

Lynn Newbery, Cathy Morgan, and Christine Eadie

What We Learned

We are three West Coast educators whose combined teaching experience represents about eighty years in the classroom as elementary and secondary teachers and as faculty associates at Simon Fraser University working with student teachers. We are not aboriginal; however, we arrived at places in our teaching careers where we became passionately committed to seeking out aboriginal content and incorporating it into our curricula. We share some of our stories, called "Beginnings" here. We share the lessons we learned. We learned to handle racism and stereotyping, to infuse the provincial curriculum with aboriginal content, to become co-learners with our students, and to discover and appreciate the richness of local sites for learning, and the magic of traditional stories. We share the ways in which we have changed. Underlying our work is the belief that our students have achieved a fuller understanding of the Canadian story, a broader knowledge and understanding of aboriginal experiences and cultures, and a deeper connec-

BEGINNINGS #1: LYNN

I was fortunate. As a young teacher, I learned three valuable lessons: the importance of confronting racism and stereotyping, how to infuse the curriculum with aboriginal content, and that there were rewards to becoming a co-learner with my students. This is how it happened.

In the mid-sixties I moved to a British Columbia coastal community from Toronto, where I had taught social studies and English for four years. A teacher shortage in the community of Alert Bay led to my agreeing to teach half days. The assignment included grade 7 social studies—Canadian history, beginning with the explorers. A few days before school started, I was given a textbook that seemed ancient. I knew my class contained about 60 per cent aboriginal students. I was also aware of problems of racism that existed in this small but vibrant fishing community. As I examined the textbook, I was dismayed to find words like "savage" and "uncivilized" used to describe Native people. My impulse was to hide the book, because I was afraid that I could not protect my Native students if other students chose to use this language to make fun of them. My alternative plan for social studies was to focus the year's work on traditional ways of life on the coast. I was ignorant of First Nations culture or history (I realized how deficient my education, which included a degree in modern history from the University of Toronto, had been), any sense of what I could or should do, or how to go about it. This was probably a good thing. In my naive state, I saw no barriers.

And so began a year of exciting learning for us. We were all teachers and we were all learners. I plunged into reading each night from books I gathered; the students brought their learning and knowledge from home. Together, we shared a rich experience. The non-Native students joined in the project, working with their Native friends and researching in the library. We ended the year by travelling in a fishing boat to the mouth of a river where the students engaged in a "dig" in an old abandoned village midden. It was a year that changed me as a teacher.

I discovered that it was a positive experience to become a co-learner with my students and explore with them the tasks of seeking resources and organizing and sharing knowledge. I learned about First Nations culture on the coast, which was reviving after a hundred years of repression. I began to learn about the history of First Nations because this community had been subjected to the brutal application of the anti-potlatch laws enacted by the Canadian government. I learned that with my increased knowledge I could infuse provincial curriculum with aboriginal content. Since then I have learned that all subjects can be infused with aboriginal content. I also learned that I didn't need to hide biased textbooks but that I could use them to help students deal with racism and stereotyping.

tion to our land. We direct our stories and learning to non-Native teachers who have not travelled this road in the hope that our experiences will encourage you to discover and share with your students the richness of teaching aboriginal content.

Confront Racism, Bias, and Stereotyping

Students are exposed to bias against aboriginal people in print, music, and film, and in real day-to-day situations. We can help them identify, name, and combat this by introducing them to the concepts of racism, bias, and stereotyping; by building awareness and understanding of these problems; and by providing positive role models. I have outlined some ideas about how to accomplish these goals in the highlighted text below. Many more ideas can be found in a number of professional resources (see, for example, British Columbia

Ministry of Education 1998, 2000; Manitoba Education and Youth 2003; McCue and Associates 2000a, 2000b; Sawyer and Green 1990; Sawyer and Lundeberg 1993; Sawyer and Napoleon 1991).

Become a Co-learner with Students

The Canadian history we learned in high schools and universities often omitted aboriginal peoples. As noted by the Royal Commission on Aboriginal Peoples, "From the Commission's first days, we have been reminded repeatedly of the limited understanding of aboriginal issues among non-aboriginal Canadians and of the obstacles this presents to achieving reconciliation and a new relationship" (1996, volume 5, 92). Yet we live with this story today even if we do not know the story. A Gitxsan elder, Marie Wilson, talked about being surrounded by her ancestors whenever she spoke. The Gitxsan have a saying, "We walk on the breath of our grandfathers."

STARTING POINTS FOR CONFRONTING RACISM

Teach the concepts

- Work on the vocabulary: bias, opinion, viewpoint, prejudice, discrimination, stereotyping, racism. (See chapter 5 in this volume for suggestions on how to introduce these concepts.) Discuss prejudices students have encountered as young people ("you are too young"), as males or females, or as members of ethnic and religious groups.
- Expose older students to the use and inadequacy of the common stereotypical references to Native peoples— "noble savage," "silent hunter," "drunken Indian." For an exposé of Native stereotypes in Canadian culture, read *The Imaginary Indian* by Daniel Francis (1992).

Promote awareness of the problems

- Collect pictures that show people of various ages, gender, and ethnicity. Number each picture and post them around the classroom. Distribute a questionnaire containing questions about people in various contexts, for example, "If you were lost in a strange city, which person would you feel most comfortable approaching for help?" Ask students to respond to each question by selecting one of the numbered pictures. Use students' answers to explore stereotypical assumptions and to discuss the problems of systemic discrimination.
- Pose problems that touch upon discrimination. Ask students, for example, to imagine they live in a lovely three-bedroom house but the family is being transferred for a year and the house must be rented. Who will they rent it to? Create applications from a variety of people (for example, three nurses who work in the local hospital; two East Indian male university students; a First Nations family—the dad works for the hydro company and the mom looks after

three young children; a Caucasian bank executive whose wife is a social worker with no children). Distribute the applications to groups of students for review. Each group is to select the applicant to whom they would rent the house. Debrief by having a student from each group explain the reasons for their choice and for their reservations about the other applicants.
- Look at First Nations names used for cars and sports teams (for example, Braves, Pontiac, Chieftains, Cadillac) and the use of the "tomahawk chop" by sports fans.
- Examine your textbook for examples of bias or stereotyping.

Provide powerful role models

- Arrange for older students to watch movies that offer powerful portrayals of aboriginal perspectives. Notable examples include *Whale Rider* (New Zealand), *Rabbit-Proof Fence* (Australia), *Atanarjuat* (Canadian), *Powwow Highway* (American with Canadian actor Gary Farmer), and *Smoke Signals* (produced completely by aboriginal people and featuring two Canadian actors in the lead roles).
- Introduce students to aboriginal role models. Most aboriginal groups have produced excellent poster series featuring actors (Adam Beach, Gary Farmer), writers (Thomas King, Eden Robinson, Tomson Highway), doctors, judges, musicians, lawyers, prominent educators, and politicians who have achieved national prominence. Historical figures to introduce include Tom Longboat, Alwyn Morris, Lady Amelia Douglas, Pauline Johnson, and Joseph Brant.
- Watch the National Aboriginal Achievement Awards each spring on CBC television.

BEGINNINGS #2: CATHY

I arrived in a small northern community in 1971 to teach primary grades, without much background knowledge about the isolated rural area. As a member of the dominant culture, it never occurred to me while I attended public school in the 1950s and '60s that aboriginal people were not represented in the curriculum (except in stereotypical ways such as "Ii" for Indian and "Ee" for Eskimo on the alphabet chart).

I wanted to know more about the local Gitxsan culture in my area, but it was not a topic discussed by the parents of the children in my classroom. I sought books about the local community to familiarize myself with the stories and history of local First Nations groups. I began to make posters and big books that incorporated First Nations material in pattern books such as Bill Martin's *Brown Bear, Brown Bear, What Do You See?* which I adapted to *Eagle, Eagle, What Do You See?* I began to involve children in writing captions for their own stories rather than read from readers that depicted an urban circus story in which all the faces in the crowd were white.

In those early stages, I tried to adapt materials myself without consulting the Native community. Now I seek resources that have been locally developed or approved by Elders or by First Nations Education Committees. I try to find an aboriginal resource person to bring into the class. I recall a quote about the importance of sharing the community's history with my students: "Without history, a society shares no common memory of where it has been, of what its core values are, or of what decisions of the past account for present circumstances" (National Centre for History in the Schools, cited in Bredekamp and Rosegrant 1995, 116).

I understand that history began here long before Europeans arrived so I take my students to visit the First Nations historic sites in the community. I am learning to build lessons that connect students to these sites and to the traditional stories of their aboriginal ancestors. After visiting a local site, students simulated a midden dig in the classroom to think critically about how the various animal bones may have been used in the diet of the original inhabitants of the site. We learned about the prevalence of rabbit bones and understood why some aboriginal inhabitants were called "People of the Rabbit." Building my knowledge of First Nations history and cultures has taken some work, but I learned that I did not have to invent everything and that many resources were available.

I learned to handle my fear of being "politically incorrect." This concern can be simply illustrated by considering the confusion that arises over nomenclature. What terms should be used? What are the distinctions between "First Nations," "indigenous peoples," "aboriginal," "Native," and "Indian"? When considering a specific group of people should we speak of a house, a clan, a tribe, or a nation? And then there are the proper names of specific groups. Many of those names have changed in the last twenty years as First Nations have reclaimed their traditional names. The language groups can also cause confusion. For example, the Gitxsan (formerly spelled Gitksan) language is part of the Tsimshian language group but the Gitxsan cannot be called Tsimshian since that name applies to the First Nation that lives in another area of the West Coast.

It takes a bit of effort to learn the proper terms. I accepted that I was a learner and that I will make mistakes. As I learned, my knowledge deepened. As my knowledge increased, the danger of being trivial lessened. I learned to seek out the human resources living in nearby communities, to seek out the conferences that offered First Nations presenters and themes, and to have the confidence to ask questions. I am also learning to hear quieter voices, to listen before speaking, and to seek the wisdom of the Elders. My classroom was enriched with new learning, new resources, and new strategies, and my classroom became a better place to be.

The past is alive around us and even though people may not know the events of history, they live with the attitudes and emotions and consequences engendered by past events.

My appreciation for the experiences of aboriginal peoples in this country has grown as I learned about the Indian Act, the denial of the right to vote for aboriginals in the late nineteenth century, the return of the right to vote in the late 1950s and early 1960s, the fight for aboriginal fishing rights, the denial of language and culture (especially as acted out in residential schools), and the loss of the land. Blaming people for their difficulties is easy to do. Understanding the causes of the difficulties requires learning on our part. Many excellent resources on aboriginal history and culture are available for educators and students wishing to learn more (for example, Campbell et al. 2003; Carlson 1997; Kainai Board of Education et al. 2004, 2005a, 2005b; Manitoba Education and Youth 2003).

I invite all of us to leave behind any need to be "the classroom expert" for our students and, instead, acknowledge that we too are constantly learning about aboriginal peoples. The key is to participate in this shared inquiry with enthusiasm, respect, and commitment. The Nova Scotia teachers' guide for the Mi'kmaq history and culture course expresses this well:

> [T]he nature of instructional leadership provided by non-Native teachers will necessarily be different. They will actively share in the learning process with their students. In their attitudes and behaviours they will demonstrate their interest in the history of the

Mi'kmaq people, their respect for Mi'kmaq culture and spirituality, and their commitment to open-minded dialogue between the inheritors of different cultures (cited in Pohl, 2003).

Identify various outcomes or topics in the social studies curriculum for your grade level that provide opportunities to incorporate aboriginal history, culture, and issues. In each case, briefly describe how this might be done in a way that increases understanding both of the curricular topic and of aboriginal people.

Infuse Aboriginal Content

The goal of building understanding and admiration for the resilience of aboriginal peoples everywhere in Canada will not be advanced simply by creating a designated course or unit. We should look for opportunities to infuse aboriginal points of view and issues throughout the social studies curriculum and beyond. Suggestions for integrating aboriginal discussions into the study of traditional topics in social studies, current events, and other curricular subjects are found in the highlighted text below.

INTEGRATING ABORIGINAL CONTENT

Embed into traditional social studies topics

There are many opportunities to infuse aboriginal content into the topics normally addressed in social studies. Below are a few examples:

- **War of 1812.** The War of 1812 provides an opportunity to explore the concept of great leaders by studying the visions, activities, successes, and failures of three prominent aboriginal leaders of the time—Joseph Brant, Tecumseh, and Pontiac.
- **Confederation.** This classic event in Canadian history is often studied from French and English perspectives and from the colonial points of view. It would be interesting to explore Métis and First Nations reactions.
- **Human rights.** International instances of human rights abuse can be supplemented with examples of the Canadian government's treatment of aboriginal peoples (for example, the removal of the right to vote, and to meet to discuss land claims, to hire lawyers, or to raise monies to pursue land claims; and the setting up of residential schools for Native children and banning these children from speaking their own languages).
- **Forts and military.** Elementary students enjoy the study of forts, weapons, and knights. First Nations had forts, weapons, armour, rigorous warrior training, and systems of defence and battle tactics.

Infuse aboriginal concerns into current event discussions

Aboriginal perspectives can enrich the study of current events as suggested by the following examples:

- **Catastrophic diseases.** Germ warfare and smallpox epidemics were not new in the twentieth century. Aboriginal peoples suffered the ravages of disease after contact with Europeans. Smallpox epidemics in British Columbia in 1862 reduced the population of Haida Gwaii from about ten thousand to five hundred in a very short period of time. Germ warfare was first used in North America by General Amherst in 1763 when he distributed smallpox-infected blankets to the Mik'maq.

- **Repatriation of cultural treasures.** The plundering of cultural artifacts by the Nazis, the destruction of antiquities by the Taliban, and the looting of museums in Iraq can be connected to the experiences of First Nations peoples whose art and bones linger on in many museums and private collections around the world, or whose totems and masks were destroyed in huge bonfires in British Columbia. Recently the Field Museum in Chicago returned the bones of 150 Haida to Haida Gwaii.
- **Arranged marriages.** First Nations had marriages arranged for controlling property rights and status, and as a method of selecting and training chiefs.

Integrate with other subjects

Aboriginal content can be integrated with other subject areas. The following ideas are drawn from *Shared Learnings* (British Columbia Ministry of Education 1998):

- **Physical Education.** Invite elementary students to research and learn a traditional aboriginal game or dance to teach to the class.
- **Science.** Investigate traditional uses of plants by aboriginal peoples, traditional ceremonies for honouring the animals and conservation practices, and stories that teach children how to respect plants and animals. Instead of studying simple machines in the context of pyramid-building in ancient Egypt, focus on West Coast First Nations practices that allowed them to raise huge cedar beams for building their large communal houses.
- **Mathematics.** Graph aboriginal information. For example, bar graphs can be used to illustrate the population of aboriginal peoples in each province and territory.
- **Health.** Discuss with students the ideas of balance and symmetry, and their importance in aboriginal life (that is, for a healthy life, the mind, body, and spirit must be in balance). Explore the implications of these qualities for students' own well-being.

Access Resources: Materials and People

There are many excellent resources developed by aboriginal educators, writers, artists, and filmmakers. This list identifies some of them.

- The seven-video series *First Nations: The Circle Unbroken* (National Film Board) is an excellent resource covering a range of important topics. It is designed for high school students and contains lesson ideas. Historical footage of aboriginal people in traditional settings can be found on the National Film Board website at www.nfb.ca (go to "Educational Resources" and click on "Documentary Lens").
- Curriculum materials developed by school districts and government agencies. Lists of materials can be obtained by contacting almost any school district or provincial ministry of education.
- The Royal Commission on Aboriginal Peoples is available online at www.ainc-inac.gc.ca/ch/rcap/sg/sgmm _e.html.
- Contact Indian and Northern Affairs Canada to locate teaching resources. There is a separate listing for each province in the blue pages. Or call Info Canada, 1-888-O-Canada (622-6232) or go to www.ainc-inac.gc.ca.
- Contact your local friendship centre. Publications by the Ministry of Indian Affairs and Northern Development provide contact information for hundreds of aboriginal cultural centres and friendship centres across Canada (McCue and Associates 2000a, 54–67; 2000b, 60–73). Use the yellow pages in the phone book and check listings under "aboriginal."
- Use the internet to find resources. Some useful sites include:
  - Aboriginal Rights Coalition of BC at arcbc.tripod .com
  - Links to aboriginal resources at www.bloorstreet .com/300block/aborl.htm
  - BC Archives at www.bcarchives.gov.bc.ca/index .htm
  - Aboriginal Resources and Services of the Library and Archives of Canada at www.collectionscanada .ca/Aboriginal/index_e.html
- Visit your public library and your school library. You might be surprised at the collections there.
- Speak to someone at your local community college or university to locate human resources. First Nations courses are increasingly available across the country.
- Tune into the Aboriginal Peoples Television Network (APTN).

- Visit the reserve or friendship centre closest to your school on June 21, National Aboriginal Day.
- Make connections with educators, historians, traditional teachers, and chiefs on the nearest reserve. These people are valuable resources who can help secure guests for your classroom, suggest learning resources, and answer questions about protocols.

Explore Local Sites

No matter where you live in Canada, you are living on someone's traditional territory. The sites are beneath your feet and local aboriginal people can tell you about them. In many places the rocks themselves explicitly point to stories. Here are some points of interest, to name just a few:

- mysterious stone faces at the end of the Baie Verte Peninsula, Newfoundland;
- hundreds of petroglyphs at Bella Coola, British Columbia;
- petroglyphs outside Peterborough, Ontario;
- Dreamer's Rock, Manitoulin Island, Ontario, where visions were sought;
- Siwash Rock in Vancouver, British Columbia.

Sometimes these sites are in the news because of government decisions with regard to the land. Students can discuss the ethics of turning burial grounds into garbage dumps, paving them over for parking lots, or making golf courses over them (an issue in the Oka Crisis in 1990). Teachers have used government decisions to increase sensitivity in students to First Nations concerns and at the same time to practise critical thinking skills and debating techniques.

Teach Local Aboriginal History

The land where we live had ten thousand years of stories embedded in the rocks prior to the arrival of Europeans and a few hundred years of stories since. Until we appreciate what the land means to aboriginal peoples, we will not be able to comprehend the issues surrounding land claims. We should make an effort to seek out the stories of the land where we live. We can learn the stories that are told on the totem poles and in the traditional and the more recent stories. Even something as simple as learning the local aboriginal place names can enrich our knowledge of where we live. Even where the land is paved over, as it is in our major cities, the stories still exist. Finding them can build a sense of belonging and commitment to the land for all students. Imagine being in Wanuskewin Heritage Park in Saskatoon and thinking about the thousands of years that the nomadic tribes of the plains gathered there. Several pre-contact sites have been identified in this place whose Cree name is loosely translated as "living in harmony." People who are aware of the events and stories of the place they are in find their experiences are enriched by their knowledge.

As teachers, we can help our students experience this rich connection to the land. We can do this by seeking the local history of an area. I have learned to ask the following questions wherever I am:

- Who were the original people who lived here? Do their descendents still make it their home today?
- How can we learn about the culture of the local aboriginal people?
- What are the aboriginal names for places here and what do the names mean?
- What stories and oral histories are part of the local aboriginal people's culture?
- Where can we obtain information regarding the history and the stories of this place?
- Who might be able to share these with us and what is the protocol in using this information with our students?
- How can we have all of our students share in this local knowledge?
- What pictures can I find of this area in local, provincial, and national archives?

Teach Aboriginal Stories

Traditional stories are a fundamental part of aboriginal cultures. As Thomas King wrote, "The truth about stories is that that's all we are" (2003, 2). They are the truth on which cultures are built and land is claimed. The stories contain everything of importance—who the people are, how they came to be, how they obtained their crests and territories, what the events of their histories and everyday lives were, what the lessons are that they want to teach their young. Title to land is invested in the stories that are sung and told. Until we try to appreciate the stories, we will never understand land claims. This point is illustrated by the following incident:

> One of the Gitxsan elders asked government officials at a land claims meeting, "If this is your land where are your stories?" He spoke in English, but then he moved into Gitxsan and told a story. All of a sudden everyone understood … how stories give meaning and value to the places we call home; how they bring us close to the world we live in by taking us into a world of words; how they hold us together and at the same time keep us apart" (Chamberlin 2004, 1).

I have learned much from aboriginal teaching stories. One example in our area is the story "The Mountain Goats of Temlaham." In this story, young boys are mistreating a young goat. They pay no attention to the voices of their Elders warn-

BEGINNINGS #3: CHRISTINE

From my experiences, I learned the importance of teaching local aboriginal history and the importance of integrating aboriginal stories into my teaching. In the summer that I turned twelve, my family emigrated to northern British Columbia from Holland. We lived many miles out of town trying our hands at dairy farming so there was little time for meeting classmates. Many of my new classmates were of aboriginal ancestry and they had their own challenges to deal with since some of them had experienced being sent off to residential schools in the Lower Mainland and Alberta.

The summer I turned fifteen, I got a part-time job working in a Hudson's Bay trading post in Hazelton. This was when I learned about the power of story. I became very interested in the town's history and local characters. Many of the Gitxsan relatives of Simon Gunanoot and Alex McIntosh were customers at the store. From them, I heard the famous story of the shooting and the manhunt that lasted twenty years. (The story of the shooting of Alex—the manhunt for Simon, his survival in the wilderness, and his trial and subsequent acquittal—has been made well known by writer Pierre Berton and filmmaker Monty Bassett.) A kindly neighbour told me about the riverboat days when steamers came all the way up the Skeena River from Prince Rupert, disgorging people and supplies for the Omineca goldfields. I heard about the miners who, while camping near Gitsegukla, set the village on fire, and all the totems burned down. The chiefs blockaded the Skeena River and stopped all traffic until officials came from Victoria to pay compensation.

I went off to university to become a teacher and moved to a larger community but for me it has always been important that all my students learn about their local history—both before and after Europeans came. It is through better understanding that we can respect and appreciate each other. It has been wonderful to pass this understanding on to student teachers and to observe them using local stories and materials to enrich their content.

ing them that the whole community will suffer from their lack of respect to the kid. The kid is rescued by one boy who defies the rest. The mountain goat people then invite the boys' people to a feast up on the mountain. When everyone is there feasting, the mountain shakes and tumbles and the people are killed except for the one exceptional boy who had saved the kid that was being mistreated. The mountain that rumbled and fell is now called Roche des Boules: "mountain of the tumbling rocks"—and every once in a while, even today, we hear the rockfalls. It reminds us of the need to be respectful of nature. The equality of all life—human, animal, and plant—is clear and all life is to be respected and treated well.

There are a number of ways to help students appreciate and understand traditional aboriginal stories:

- Expose students to a large selection of the stories, including many local ones. A Ministry of Indian Affairs and Northern Development (2000) publication lists a wide selection of children's literature about aboriginal peoples. Collections of traditional stories can be found at www .hanksville.org/storytellers/alfa.html.
- Provide models for the class of the various types of stories: creation stories, humorous stories, everyday stories, teaching stories, trickster stories, transformation stories, and stories containing the oral histories.
- Form literature circles in which four to five students can share a story they have read and analyze it as to type, purpose, what it reveals about values and beliefs, and about aboriginal world view.
- Ask students to choose the story they like best as a group and present it using the oral traditions to the class.

Conclusions

The three of us were fortunate that our lives took us into areas where First Nations cultures were strong. Most teachers do not have this opportunity, but our experiences have led us to believe that important benefits are available to all Canadian teachers who make an effort to learn about and include aboriginal content wherever we teach to whomever we teach. However, as the cartoon implies, this is unlikely to happen if we remain on the narrow, mainstream culture road.

Some of us began our journey taking very small steps—a lesson here or there, perhaps a guest speaker, perhaps a craft or art approach. Eventually we graduated to integrated units in social studies and language arts. Others of us plunged in, planning an entire year with an aboriginal emphasis. Regardless of where we began, we have arrived at the same place—committed to incorporating aboriginal content into the mainstream

THE ROAD LESS TRAVELLED

Cartoon by Erica Ball. Courtesy of the artist.

of our teaching. It has been a wonderfully enriching journey. We invite the reader also to choose this less-travelled road and find the richness there.

Research the aboriginal history of your immediate area and locate notable sites nearby. Look for sources of information including people, publications, and educational facilities (museums, libraries, cultural centres) that might assist you in planning and delivering an engaging study of this history.

REFERENCES

Bredekamp, S., and T. Rosegrant, eds. 1995. *Reaching potentials: Transforming early childhood curriculum and assessment*, vol. 2. Washington, DC: National Association for the Education of Young Children.

British Columbia Ministry of Education. 1998. *Shared learnings: Integrating BC aboriginal content K–10*. Victoria: Author.

———. 2000. *BC First Nations studies 12: Integrated resource package 2000*. Victoria: Author. Available online at http://www.bced.gov.bc.ca/irp/irp_ss.htm.

Campbell, K., C. Menzies, and B. Peacock. 2003. *BC First Nations Studies*. Victoria: British Columbia Ministry of Education.

Carlson C.T., ed. 1997. *You are asked to witness: The Sto:lo in Canada's Pacific coast history*. Chilliwack, BC: The Sto:lo Heritage Trust.

Chamberlin, J.E. 2004. *If this is your land, where are your stories? Finding common ground*. Mississauga, ON: Knopf Canada.

Francis, D. 1992. *The imaginary Indian: The image of the Indian in Canadian culture*. Vancouver: Arsenal Pulp.

Kainai Board of Education et al. 2004. *Aboriginal perspectives (Aboriginal Studies 10)*. Edmonton: Duval House.

———. 2005a. *Aboriginal perspectives (Aboriginal Studies 20)*. Edmonton: Duval House.

———. 2005b. *Aboriginal perspectives (Aboriginal Studies 30)*. Edmonton: Duval House.

King, T. 2003. *The truth about stories*. Toronto: House of Anansi Press.

Manitoba Education and Youth. 2003. *Integrating aboriginal perspectives into curricula*. Winnipeg: Author. Available online at http://www.edu.gov.mb.ca?ks4/docs/policy/abpersp/index.htm.

McCue, H. and Associates. 2000a. *The learning circle: Classroom activities on First Nations in Canada (ages 8 to 11)*. Ottawa: Ministry of Indian Affairs and Northern Development.

———. 2000b. *The learning circle: Classroom activities on First Nations in Canada (ages 12 to 14)*. Ottawa: Ministry of Indian Affairs and Northern Development.

Ministry of Indian Affairs and Northern Development. 2000. *An aboriginal book list for children*. Ottawa: Author.

Pohl, A. 2003. Handling aboriginal curriculum studies appropriately. Coalition for the Advancement of Aboriginal Studies, Faculty of Education, York University, Toronto. Available online at http://www.edu.yorku.ca:8080/~caas/AbStudies.html.

Royal Commission on Aboriginal Peoples. 1996. *Final report of the Royal Commission on Aboriginal Peoples*. 5 vols. Ottawa: Queen's Printer. Available online at http://www.ainc-inac.gc.ca/ch/rcap/sg/sgmm_e.html.

Sawyer, D. and H. Green. 1990. *The NESA activities handbook for Native and multicultural classrooms*, vol. 1. Vancouver: Tillacum Library.

Sawyer, D. and W. Lundeberg. 1993. *The NESA activities handbook for Native and multicultural classrooms*, vol. 3. Vancouver: Tillacum Library.

Sawyer, D. and A. Napoleon. 1991. *The NESA activities handbook for Native and multicultural classrooms* vol. 2. Vancouver: Tillacum Library.

8

Teaching the Tools to Think Critically

Roland Case and LeRoi Daniels

Neither the hand nor the mind alone would amount to much without aids and tools to perfect them.
    —Francis Bacon, *Novum Organum* (1620)

The idea of critical thinking is not new. For decades—no, for centuries—it has been recognized as an important educational goal by practitioners and theorists alike. Curriculum documents and learning resources in all subjects and at every level of schooling recommend that students be taught to think critically. Despite this long-standing expectation, the extent of critical thinking and the manner in which it is taught are disheartening. Many studies document the preoccupation with transmission of information and rote application of "skills," and how little class time is devoted to thinking. The depressing irony is that critical thinking is much valued and yet inadequately addressed. Or, as Walter Parker (1991, 234) puts it, the teaching of thinking remains "more wish than practice."[1]

Numerous factors contribute to this situation. One enduring reason is the dilemma of how to get students to think for themselves and simultaneously teach the subject matter we want them to learn. This tension is captured in the so-called division between the teaching of "content" and "process." Confusion surrounding how to integrate these seemingly competing goals has led to opposing camps, with some educational theorists urging a focus on content, while others espouse an emphasis on general skills. The former are preoccupied with covering the subject matter of the curriculum, the latter with teaching mental operations. This division is educationally bankrupt since it is based on a false dichotomy: thinking without content is vacuous, and content acquired without thought is mindless and inert. As Richard Paul (1993, 277) notes, "one gains knowledge only through thinking."

The problem of transmitting information without getting students to think is that students frequently adopt ideas without understanding them. Research suggests, for example, that a large proportion of university students who have passed examinations in physics are unable to provide credible explanations for simple real-world problems, such as which of two balls, one heavier than the other, would hit the floor first when dropped (Mackenzie 1988). In explaining this anomaly, teacher-author Richard Feynman concludes: "After a lot of investigation, I finally figured out that the students had memorized everything, but that they didn't know what anything meant" (cited in Mackenzie 1988, 61).

Even educators who endeavour to engage their students in thinking critically about the content of the curriculum are often hampered by vagueness about what that would involve for the students they teach. Without a clear understanding of what is involved in critical thinking, we are likely to adopt a superficial approach, have significant gaps in our treatment, or proceed in an ineffectual if not counterproductive manner.

Profile of Exemplary Critical Thinkers

A useful general strategy to assist in unpacking vague or confusing notions is to consider actual examples of the concept—both positive examples (what it looks like when it is demonstrably present) and negative examples (what it looks like when it is demonstrably absent). We use this strategy in our professional development workshops to help educators refine their understanding of critical thinking. We invite workshop participants to think of individuals whom they deem exemplary critical thinkers and to identify the attributes or traits these individuals exhibit that distinguish them as such.

In the highlighted text is a list of attributes exhibited by exemplary critical thinkers. What can we learn from this list about the nature of critical thinking? You will notice that the

Before examining a representative sample of the responses we receive, take a moment to think of an exemplary critical thinker you know and list several qualities that make this person such a good thinker.

list is divided into five parts. We have created these divisions to better reveal the diverse attributes reflected in our collective ideas about what makes a good critical thinker.

ATTITUDES OR HABITS OF MIND

Part I of the list contains more items than any of the other parts. The inference is that the salient qualities of critical

TYPICAL ATTRIBUTES OF EXEMPLARY CRITICAL THINKERS

Part I Habits of mind (attitudes)

- are open to new ideas
- persist, have staying power, while thinking through a problem
- have empathy; can appreciate others' points of view
- have the courage of their convictions and aren't afraid to take an unpopular stand
- question ideas; don't accept everything at face value
- don't jump to conclusions
- are flexible and willing to change tactics
- don't take themselves too seriously—can laugh at themselves
- are willing to live with ambiguity; don't require black-or-white answers
- welcome challenges

Part II Thinking Strategies

- restate a problem in unambiguous language or in graphic form
- confirm understanding by restating in their own words
- ask questions to probe for more information
- examine issues from varying perspectives
- look for connections between what is already known and what is new
- test ideas using a "reality check"
- focus on one thing at a time, breaking complex challenges into manageable bits
- consider the assumptions presupposed by a position
- look for possible counter-arguments or negative consequences

Part III Background knowledge

- have extensive general knowledge; are experienced; are well-read
- are knowledgeable about the specific topic

Part IV Conceptual knowledge

- recognize common informal fallacies (for example, "straw person," "slippery slope," ad hominem arguments, hasty generalizations)

Part V Criteria

- recognize arguments that are well supported
- value clarity and specificity

thinkers are most frequently of this first type. But what is the common feature of this set of qualities? It may be somewhat surprising to realize that they are attitudes. This suggests that an individual's attitudes—or, to use the term that we prefer, habits of mind—are key constituents of good critical thinking. People who are, for example, closed to new ideas or inflexible in their thinking are seriously impaired in their ability to arrive at justifiable resolutions.

Recognizing the role of attitudes in critical thinking challenges a popular perception that critical thinking is a skill or set of skills. This perception is unfortunate since no amount of "skill" will overcome the limitations of closed-minded prejudicial thinking. The case of people who deny the Holocaust illustrates this point. Such individuals may be clever, have extensive knowledge of the events, be able to marshal persuasive arguments, and possess many other qualities on our list of attributes. Despite considerable critical thinking ability, however, these individuals are fundamentally mistaken in their belief that the Holocaust did not happen because, in many cases, their racial prejudices prevent them from impartially considering the evidence. Open-mindedness is but one habit of mind needed by critical thinkers. The tendency of some people to leap to conclusions underlies yet another crucial mental habit of a good thinker: the inclination to deliberate—to think before acting. As we will illustrate, successful critical thinking is significantly (but by no means exclusively) a matter of attitude.

THINKING STRATEGIES

The qualities listed in Part II are most closely aligned with what are loosely called skills, although for clarity we refer to them as thinking strategies. In addition to possessing certain attitudes, good critical thinkers use a variety of tactics or supports to work their way through the challenges they face. These strategies may be very elaborate, such as following a comprehensive decision-making model that begins with identifying the issue, then considering the consequences, researching each option, and so on. Alternatively, we may employ focussed strategies when addressing a specific task (for example, gaining clarity about a problem by restating it in one's own words, asking others for clarification, or representing the problem graphically). There are literally thousands of strategies—in the form of procedures, models, graphic organizers, and other types of heuristics—that guide individuals in working through challenges. Because critical thinking typically has been labelled a skill, such attributes have received considerable attention by teachers. But the strong association of critical thinking with skills has often meant that the other attributes of good thinking have been overlooked.

BACKGROUND KNOWLEDGE

Looking at Part III of the list of attributes of exemplary critical thinkers, we see that critical thinking involves more than strategies and attitudes; it also requires background knowledge. Many of us are incapable of thinking very critically about certain difficult topics, for example, nuclear physics or baroque art—not because we lack appropriate habits of mind or thinking strategies, but because we are largely ignorant of these subjects. Obviously, students cannot think critically about a topic they know little or nothing about. Yet this fact is overlooked if we treat critical thinking as a set of general skills that can be applied regardless of context.

Consider the example of teaching students the so-called operation of analysis. A generic strategies approach expects students to learn to analyze any object or event, without reference to the need for knowledge of the topic. Without adequate background knowledge, students must, of necessity, guess or speculate blindly. We cannot effectively teach students the process of analyzing, say, a poem for its metre, rhyme, and symbolism in the same way as they would analyze a historical document for its authenticity. Although both forms of analysis share a few strategies (such as isolating each discrete part and reading between the lines), successful completion of the task is determined, in large measure, by possession of the relevant background knowledge in poetry or history. Students won't be able to make sense of a historical document if they know little of the events mentioned in the document or of the general climate of the times.

In this respect, the "generic" approach to critical thinking is not only ineffective but potentially counterproductive since it may reinforce an undesirable habit of mind—that of being prone to making hasty or uninformed judgments. Our alternative conception—at least the picture emerging from the first three parts of our list of attributes—suggests that "analysis" requires a variable array of at least three types of attributes. Depending on the context, good thinkers will possess suitable habits of mind (such as an inclination to attend to detail and refrain from jumping to a conclusion), as well as relevant background knowledge in the field under investigation, and appropriate thinking strategies (such as isolating each discrete part and listing the features of each).

CONCEPTUAL KNOWLEDGE

There is another relevant type of knowledge—conceptual knowledge or knowledge of vocabulary. Although this is not frequently cited as a key attribute of critical thinkers, it is reflected in Part IV of our list of attributes: avoidance of fallacies.

Teachers of young students or students who are not native speakers of the language of instruction have long rec-

ognized the importance of concepts. For example, we teach students key vocabulary before reading a story in language arts and explain concepts in science or social studies before analyzing physical or social phenomena. What has not been so widely appreciated is the need to teach the vocabulary of thinking. Students cannot enter deeply into conversations about their thinking if they do not have the words to identify or recognize key distinctions. For example, if students cannot distinguish evidence from a conclusion or do not know what a reason is, they are less likely to provide sound justifications for their opinions.

Knowledge of a seemingly simple distinction between, for example, the concepts "what I like" and "what is worthwhile" is key to students' ability to think critically. When asked to determine the better dietary choice—hamburger or salad—many students, especially younger ones, will select what they like to eat. They do not think about the relative merits of each option but merely report their preference. Critical reflection occurs only when students have the conceptual lens to distinguish between considering what is worthwhile, such as what would be a good dietary choice (nutritious, environmentally sound, easy to prepare, tasty, widely available, inexpensive)—and what is likable, merely a pleasing personal choice. Conceptual distinctions such as "what I like" and "what is worthwhile," "evidence" and "conclusion," or "cause" and "effect" allow us to see important features of good thinking, without which we are left in a conceptual haze. Knowledge of the vocabulary of critical thinking is another of the underacknowledged attributes of good thinkers.

CRITERIA

The final, and possibly least acknowledged, set of attributes of exemplary critical thinkers is reflected in Part V of our list. Attributes such as concern for well-supported arguments and for clear, unambiguous statements refer to commitments to applying relevant criteria when thinking critically. As we suggested above, when thinking critically we are not merely espousing a personal opinion or belief. We are, in effect, offering a judgment or an assessment of the worth or reasonableness of some idea, product, or action. We can see why this is so by imagining a poor critical thinker.

A typical profile of the quintessential non-critical thinker is likely someone who simply accepts at face value everything he or she is told, or typically rushes to conclusions without deliberation. The missing ingredient is the individual's lack of any assessment or judgment as to whether or not the ideas or conclusions are sensible. Or, putting it positively, thinking critically requires that individuals assess the reasonableness of the alternatives before them. And assessments inevitably are done on the basis of criteria. For example, in deciding whether or not a particular movie is good, typically we will have reasons for our assessment. It may simply be that the movie made us laugh—in which case, our criterion for good movies is the amount of humour. Alternatively we may have a more elaborate set of criteria: we might feel that the movie had a poignant message, that the visual effects were breathtaking, and that the actors were engaging. These reasons reveal additional implicit criteria for our assessment of the movie (such as the significance of the message, the quality of the cinematography, and the believability of the acting). To think critically is essentially to engage in deliberations with the intention of making a judgment based on appropriate criteria. Notice that students may judge movies on quite narrow and dubious criteria, such as the amount of adventure and violence. Our job in helping students think more critically about movies includes encouraging them to care about a wider and, arguably, more adequate, set of criteria. For this reason, an important category of critical thinking tool is awareness of and concern for the relevant "criteria for judgment."

The close relationship between the term "critical" thinking and "criteria" is instructive. Matthew Lipman (1988) suggests that the word "critical" should be seen as a synonym for "criterial"—that to think critically is to think in light of, or using, criteria. To put it another way, the grounding on criteria is what gives our judgments rigour. When thinking critically about a movie, we are not asserting a personal preference ("It's good because I like it") or reaching a conclusion based on a dubious set of considerations ("It's good because it contains lots of bloodshed"). Rather, we are offering a reasoned assessment of the merits of the movie, a judgment based on an ample set of relevant criteria. An important critical thinking objective is to help students identify and appreciate relevant criteria for judging diverse endeavours across the curriculum, from what makes for an appropriate classroom pet, or a sound solution to a social problem, to the qualities of a good argumentative essay or an effective visual display.

The "Tools" Conception in a Nutshell

Summarizing the points made thus far, we believe that the basic building blocks of thinking are not usefully cast in terms of generic skills or mental operations. We do not learn to analyze, interpret, evaluate, predict, and so on and then simply apply these "processes" to a particular situation. Extrapolating from our discussion of the five types of attributes possessed by exemplary critical thinkers, we suggest that promoting critical thinking among our students is largely a matter of helping them to develop mastery of an increasingly broader repertoire of five types of intellectual resources.

We offer the notion of intellectual resources or "tools" to explain the development of good thinking. The ability to think critically develops over time as individuals acquire more of the tools of good thinking. The metaphor of intellectual tools is preferable to that of mental operations because we cannot teach students to be good analyzers or predictors per se; students can learn to analyze or predict in specific contexts only by acquiring the diverse tools required in that context. Students will not become better at predicting weather, earthquakes or story endings unless they acquire the relevant information, learn to attend to detail and develop other tools required for thoughtful completion of these tasks. Notice, too, that there is no "process" of predicting that is discrete from "content": we cannot (thoughtfully) predict weather without knowledge of meteorology.

It is also significant that our categories draw support from within the diverse body of literature on thinking. We have come across schools of thinking that focus separately on each of the five categories we identify. More specifically, in the critical thinking as background knowledge camp, we find advocates such as John McPeck (1981), E.D. Hirsch (1988), and Daniel Willingham (2007) arguing that sound thinking is best served by promoting student mastery of the discipline's subject matter. David Perkins and his associates (1993) believe that the central ingredients of good thinking are thinking dispositions—what we call habits of mind. Similarly, Harvey Siegel (1988) suggests that these are the most important features of a critical thinker, while Stephen Norris and Robert Ennis (1989) list dispositions as one of two categories of essential ingredients of critical thinking. Prominent among advocates of the centrality of criteria for judgment (also called intellectual standards) are Matthew Lipman (1988) and Richard Paul (1988). The informal logic school of thinking stresses two categories from among our tools: those criteria for judgment reflected in the formal and informal rules of logic (for example, the rules of class, conditional, probabilistic reasoning) and what we refer to as critical thinking vocabulary—concepts such as argument, validity, credibility, truth, soundness, induction, deduction, and various informal fallacies. The final category of tool—thinking strategies—is arguably the most widely espoused. Much of the literature on promoting thinking skills is a matter of teaching strategies for carrying out various operations (see, for example, Glaser 1984). The fact that collectively the different camps espouse all of our categories of tools is grounds for believing that our conception represents a more complete synthesis of the range of critical thinking attributes than is otherwise found.

It should be obvious that nurturing critical thinking is a long-term evolutionary goal. The ability to think critically develops gradually as students expand upon and enrich their pool of intellectual resources or tools. It requires incremental, collective effort; no one teacher can do it quickly or on her own. Clearly we must take the long view. The work of promoting critical thinking is a K–16 (kindergarten to university) challenge. But each of us is responsible for doing his or her part in promoting the tools that will help students to reason carefully and effectively in the range of endeavours addressed in the various subject areas.

Based on scholarly research and professional work with thousands of teachers, we are convinced that developing the tools for thought requires teacher effort at every level in the educational system in marshalling a four-pronged approach. The four prongs are represented graphically in Figure 8.1.

CREATE A CRITICAL COMMUNITY

Critical thinking cannot be learned independently of the broader forces operating within the classroom and the school. Consequently, it is essential to foster "critical" communities in which teachers and students interact in mutually supportive ways to nurture critical reflection. The point of forming a critical community is to create an environment, or climate, that embodies and reinforces the tools of thought. This is especially significant for acquisition of the desired habits of mind that are likely to develop only if they are modelled and continuously supported. Building a community of thinkers

is also instrumental in countering a tendency to view thinking as a solitary enterprise. Although we want students to be independent-minded and to make up their own minds, we should not expect them to do so entirely on their own. There is a key difference between thinking for oneself and thinking by oneself. Good critical thinkers regularly engage in dialogue with others to broaden their knowledge, test their ideas, and secure alternative perspectives. Learning to contribute to and make use of other people's wisdom can only be learned through participation in a critical community. Further discussion of this dimension of critical thinking is found in chapter 9, "Supporting a Community of Critical Thinkers."

PROVIDE CRITICAL CHALLENGES

The contextual nature of the tools means they are best learned within the context of a curriculum-embedded challenge that students may think through. Students need abundant occasions to employ the tools as they work through meaningful "problematic" situations. If a situation is not problematic (that is, there is only one plausible option or a correct answer is obvious), then it does not call for critical thinking—it is not a critical challenge. Further discussion of this dimension of critical thinking is found in chapter 4, "Beyond Inert Facts."

FIGURE 8.1 PROMOTING CRITICAL THINKING

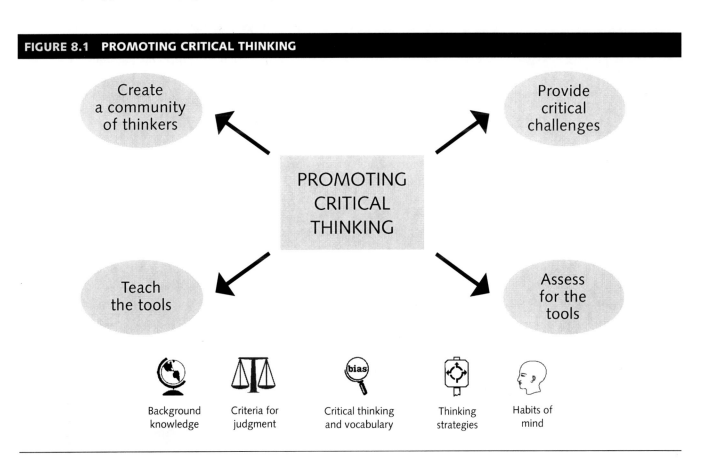

TEACH FOR THE TOOLS

Students require "enabling instruction" in the tools if they are to develop as critical thinkers. In relevant contexts, students should be introduced to the range of tools required for the tasks. The ability to think critically develops over a lifetime by acquiring and refining the vast repertoire of tools that an expert would draw on in responding to problematic situations. As we have seen, there are five kinds of tools:

- **Background knowledge.** Critical thinkers possess relevant information about a topic that is required for thoughtful reflection.
- **Criteria for judgment.** Critical thinkers understand the appropriate criteria or grounds for deciding which is the most sensible or defensible response to the challenge before them.
- **Critical thinking vocabulary.** Critical thinkers possess the concepts and distinctions that facilitate thinking critically. Although the other tools also refer to concepts, "critical thinking vocabulary" refers to concepts that are not included in any of the other tools and that address distinctions foundational to thinking critically about thinking—for example, the difference between "conclusion" and "premise," or "cause" and "effect."
- **Thinking strategies.** Critical thinkers are fluent in the repertoire of procedures, heuristics, organizing devices, and models that may be useful when thinking through a critical challenge.
- **Habits of mind.** Critical thinkers possess a wide range of the values and attitudes of a careful and conscientious thinker.

ASSESS FOR THE TOOLS

It is not sufficient merely to teach the tools. Because assessment influences what is learned, we must also assess for critical thinking. Teachers signal to students what is and is not important by assigning marks to some assignments and not to others and by "weighting" parts of assignments with different values. If student mastery of the tools is not assessed, not only are students (and teachers) left in the dark about their growth, but they are implicitly encouraged to believe that critical thinking is unimportant.

The "Tools" of the Trade

Growth as a critical thinker depends ultimately on developing understanding and competent use of five types of intellectual resources or tools. As we have stressed, students' ability to undertake any task thoughtfully depends on the range of tools they have for that particular task. The value of conceiv-

ing critical thinking as the competent use of contextually relevant tools is best seen in examples of individuals attempting to think through particular challenges.

THE TOOLS IN ACTION

Our first example, Table 8.1, is adapted from work by our colleague Jerrold Coombs. It illustrates the varied range of tools brought into play when thinking critically about an environmental issue. Specifically, it describes a hypothetical student's deliberations over what stance to take on a compromise proposal to develop and conserve various areas of a mature (or old-growth) forest. The tools she employs at each step of her deliberations are identified to reveal the adequacy of our model in accounting for the diverse elements of sound thinking.

In this example, the young woman's possession of an array of diverse tools empowers her to reach a critically thoughtful decision. It is important to note that critical thinking does not require reaching a single "correct" answer. An equally thoughtful person might reach a different position on this controversial issue. What would make both their conclusions critically thoughtful is the extent to which their deliberations reflect the use of the intellectual tools characteristic of a careful and conscientious thinker.

Also noteworthy is the observation that critical thinking is a matter of degree; an individual's sophistication and ability as a thinker is related to the range and level of mastery of the tools. All of us, including young children, think critically to some extent in some circumstances at least. That is to say, all of us possess and use some of the tools for thought. Equally true is the claim that all of us can improve our ability to think critically. We can do so both by deepening our grasp of the tools with which we currently have some familiarity and by acquiring additional tools.

TEACHING THE TOOLS

As illustrated by the young woman in our hypothetical scenario, any given intellectual task will require a range of tools for thinking critically. An important function of the tools approach is to help teachers identify what students need to be taught in order to undertake a given task in a critically thoughtful manner. To illustrate the instructional value of our model, we examine two cases in which students are taught the tools they need to ask thoughtful questions. We begin with a scenario in which primary students are taught to think critically about developing "powerful" questions.

In "Developing Powerful Questions," Tami systematically aided her primary students to construct questions thoughtfully by teaching four tools. Notice that teaching the tools

TABLE 8.1 THINKING CRITICALLY ABOUT LOGGING OLD-GROWTH FORESTS[2]

Outlined in the left-hand column below is a hypothetical response by a young woman to this issue: Should she endorse or reject the government's plan to permit logging in some areas of a forest and to designate other areas as a wilderness park? The tools embedded in her critically thoughtful response are indicated in the right-hand column.

SCENARIO	CRITICAL THINKING TOOL
The young woman has read a number of arguments for and against the government's plan that have appeared in the local newspaper. The arguments are presented roughly as follows:	
Anti-Development Side Environmentalists claim that the government has sold out to the forestry industry and unions. Some of them claim that they cannot afford to lose any more old-growth forest. They point out that forests are needed to prevent the buildup of carbon monoxide that causes global warming, that the forests are home to many species that are increasingly endangered by reductions to their habitat, and that old-growth forests enrich the aesthetic quality of life in the area. Some persons feel so strongly about the need to preserve old-growth forests that they have publicly announced that they have "spiked" (driven long nails into) many trees in the area and plan to recruit volunteers to spike many more.	**Background knowledge:** knowledge of the arguments made by the proponents of the anti-development side
Pro-Development Side Supporters of the government plan argue that the forestry industry needs to log at least part of the area and other old-growth forests if it is to continue to provide jobs for people, supply lumber to build houses, and contribute to government revenues. They claim that the land set aside for the park and for limited logging will be more than enough to maintain the aesthetic beauty of the area and to preserve the animal life there. They also argue that, since the logged areas will be replanted, there will not, in the long run, be any reduction in forested land in the area.	**Background knowledge:** knowledge of the arguments made by the proponents of the pro-development side
Several of the young woman's friends have joined demonstrations protesting against the government's decision to permit logging. The young woman checks her immediate impulse to rush out and join her friends because she wants to be sure that she is doing it for the right reasons, not simply for fear of disappointing her friends.	**Habits of mind:** open-mindedness and independent-mindedness
The young woman considers whether the consequences of stopping to deliberate about the best thing to do would likely be worse than acting without further deliberation. She decides that there is sufficient time for more careful deliberation before acting.	**Criteria for judgment:** extended deliberation is not always desirable
She attempts to understand clearly all the reasons for supporting the government's decision and those for protesting and trying to change that decision.	**Criteria for judgment:** possession of an adequate body of evidence
In doing this, she considers whether the claims of the government, the forestry industry, and environmentalists about the likely consequences of the government's policy should be believed.	**Habits of mind:** an inquiring or "critical" attitude
She knows that all of these groups have access to experts in economics and ecology, but also that they stand to gain by misrepresenting the facts about the likely consequences.	**Criteria for judgment:** concern for reliability of authorities
She also considers how adequate the newspaper accounts of reasons for and against the government's decision are likely to be.	**Criteria for judgment:** attention to the accuracy and unbiased nature of information sources
She is also aware that the emotionally charged language and other fallacious forms of persuasion used in the newspaper reports could influence her to adopt views not supported by good reasons. She makes a point of watching for and dismissing these fallacies.	**Critical thinking vocabulary:** can recognize informal fallacies

continued on next page

TABLE 8.1   THINKING CRITICALLY ABOUT LOGGING OLD GROWTH FORESTS (CONT.)

SCENARIO	CRITICAL THINKING TOOL
She considers whether she has any assumptions or preconceptions that would prevent her from making an unbiased assessment of reasons for this case.	**Habits of mind:** fair-mindedness
She decides her attachment to environmentalism and lack of contact with persons whose livelihood depends on logging may lead her to undervalue economic reasons for permitting logging.	**Habits of mind:** open-mindedness
Consequently, she decides to talk to forestry workers to get a more sympathetic understanding of their point of view.	**Criteria for judgment:** concern for a broadly grounded inquiry Thinking strategy: seeks counsel from a variety of parties in a dispute
She is aware that there may be other options open to her besides simply accepting the government's decision or joining protest marches. She tries to think of other plausible courses of action that would produce more desirable consequences.	**Thinking strategy:** looks for multiple possible options
Because she is aware that others may already have thought of plausible alternative courses of action, she seeks out knowledgeable people to discuss with them what they think ought to be done and why.	**Thinking strategy:** confers with recognized experts
In the course of the discussions, she often asks for clarification of the terms other people use and gives examples of what she means by various terms she uses to make them clear to others.	**Thinking strategy:** check for clarity and shared meanings of terms by asking for and providing examples
Having identified the likely consequences of each of the courses of action that seem plausible, she considers whether any of the courses of action involves treating others unjustly or otherwise acting immorally.	**Criteria for judgment:** concern that her decision does not unnecessarily harm others or treat them unfairly
She decides to rule out the option of joining the tree-spiking expeditions, because she has good reason to believe that this course of action could cause serious injury to persons working in the lumber industry and would subject her to criminal prosecution.	**Criteria for judgment:** seek to make an impartial judgment that would be acceptable even if the person were one of the other parties who may be adversely affected by the action
Accordingly she tries to imagine what it would be like to be a lumber mill worker facing the choice of not working or risking serious injury. She decides it would be morally wrong to subject them to such risk if there are other options available for adequately preserving forests.	**Thinking strategy:** test the fairness of moral judgments by sensitively imagining oneself in the predicament of others
Having ruled out those options that she has good reason to regard as immoral, she considers which of the remaining courses of action would produce the best consequences overall—which, that is, would most fully realize the things she values without producing unacceptable negative consequences.	**Habits of mind:** commitment to decide on rational grounds
Having made a tentative decision about which course of action is best, she decides to discuss it with others (including those who might have reached a different decision), explaining her reasoning and inviting counterarguments.	**Thinking strategy:** talk through one's thinking on an issue, inviting others to poke holes in the reasoning
She wants to be sure she hasn't overlooked any important considerations or failed to appreciate the significance of any of the likely consequences for other things she values.	**Habits of mind:** intellectual work ethic
Lacking any good reasons for changing her decision, she proceeds to act on it.	**Habits of mind:** commitment to act on the basis of reasoned judgment

is not the same as giving students the answers or doing the thinking for them. Tami did not give students questions they might ask; rather she helped them develop the intellectual resources to complete the task thoughtfully for themselves. Not only was the students' ability to pose powerful questions aided by the tools their teacher helped them acquire, but their understanding of the subject matter—in this case, the significance of Remembrance Day—was enhanced by the experience.

We can appreciate the contextual nature of teaching the tools—and by implication the limitations of generic thinking models—by contrasting the tools Tami developed with those developed by a junior high school teacher as she helped students think critically about questions for an end-of-unit test in social studies, described in "Developing Examination Questions."

We can see the contextual nature of the tools involved in posing effective questions by contrasting the two situations. The required background knowledge in one case was knowledge of World War II; in the other, it was knowledge of the Civil War period in seventeenth-century England. Karen's sample

"question frames" offered a thinking strategy—a strategy that complements brainstorming—to help students generate questions. Karen's articulation of the criteria (different from the criteria offered in the primary class) focussed students' thinking on the features of good examination questions.

Significantly, teaching students to think critically about the questions they posed contributed to their understanding of the subject matter. The criteria that Karen set, notably that students ask non-trivial questions, required them to think about what was important about the historical period. So too did her inclusion of student-generated test questions. Since these questions went beyond mere recall of information, studying for the test required that other students think about the issues raised. Karen insists that had she posed the very questions her students produced, she would have been bombarded with complaints: "How do expect us to know this? You never told us the answers to this!" Instead, not only did students take seriously the assignment to create the questions (in some cases reading the textbook for the first time), but they were more motivated to study for the test since the questions were posed by their peers.

DEVELOPING POWERFUL QUESTIONS[3]

As part of their social studies curriculum, Tami McDiarmid's kindergarten to grade 3 class was to learn about the significance of Remembrance Day (November 11). In fostering appreciation of this event, Tami invited her students to think of questions they might ask a classroom guest who was to speak about his World War II experiences. Left to their own devices, many students would likely have asked rather trivial or irrelevant questions. Tami sought to support her students in thinking critically about the questions they might ask by focussing their attention on four tools: some critical thinking vocabulary, criteria for judgment, a thinking strategy, and background knowledge.

A few days prior to the visit, Tami reintroduced key vocabulary by reminding her students that they had talked previously about two kinds of questions: "weak" questions and "powerful" ones. Armed with this distinction, the class discussed what powerful questions "look like or sound like"—or, to use our terminology, they discussed the criteria for judging powerful questions. Tami recorded on chart paper the following student-generated criteria:

Powerful questions …

- give you lots of information
- are specific to the person or situation
- are open-ended; can't be answered by yes or no
- may be unexpected
- are usually not easy to answer.

Next, Tami made use of a thinking strategy—that of brainstorming—that her students had already learned to use. Brain-

storming does not invoke critical thinking, but it is a useful strategy to help with the generation of ideas. While brainstorming, individuals are discouraged from making judgments about the proffered ideas; the point is simply to come up with as many ideas as possible. The critical thinking began in earnest when students, working in pairs, began to assess the brainstormed questions. Using the agreed-upon criteria as their guide, students discussed whether their proposed questions were likely to elicit lots of information, were obvious or predictable, and so on. Some "weak" questions were rejected; others were modified to make them more powerful.

Tami had developed a fourth tool—that of relevant background knowledge—during the three weeks preceding the guest's visit by reading and discussing various children's stories involving the war. Without the knowledge acquired from these stories, many students would have been incapable of asking a thoughtful question.

Here are a sampling of the student-generated questions asked the World War II veteran:

- Where did you live during the war?
- Were there any women in World War II? If so, what were their jobs?
- What started the fighting?
- Why was Canada involved?
- What was your safe place?
- Why did you fight in the war?
- Do you remember some of your friends from the war?
- Which countries did you fight over?

DEVELOPING EXAMINATION QUESTIONS[4]

Karen Barnett, a junior high humanities teacher, borrowed an idea from a fellow teacher, Bob Friend. Rather than simply assigning exam questions, she had her students create an end-of-unit quiz consisting of six questions and an answer key focussed on their study of seventeenth-century England. Students were informed that their test would be drawn exclusively from their questions. To support her students in completing this task, Karen provided them with three tools: background knowledge, criteria for judgment, and a thinking strategy.

The required background knowledge—knowledge of the focus of the questions—was acquired by reading the relevant chapter in their textbook and by undertaking a variety of related assignments. When framing their six questions, students were instructed to consider four criteria. Questions:

- must be clear so that fellow students will understand what is required;
- should address a non-trivial aspect of the contents of the chapter;
- can be answered within a half page (or twenty minutes); and
- must require more than mere recall of information.

Karen further supported her students' efforts by offering a thinking strategy—the use of "question frames"—to help generate questions that went beyond mere recall of information. More specifically, students were invited to frame questions using prompts such as the following:

- Compare ... with ...
- What conclusions can be drawn from ...
- Decide whether ... was correct when ...
- Predict what would have happen if ...
- What was the effect of ...
- Decide which choice you would make if ...

A list of the best student-generated questions was distributed to the class well before the test. The following questions were submitted by one of the students in Karen's class:

1. Compare the ideas of Thomas Hobbes and John Locke on government.
2. Do you think Cromwell was correct in chopping off the king's head, and what advantage did government gain over royalty because of this?
3. What were the effects of the civil war on the monarchy and the peasantry?
4. If you were the king, how would you handle the pressures of government and the people?
5. Compare the power of the government in the early 1600s to the power it has today.
6. What do you think would have happened if the people hadn't rebelled against the king?

This last point—the motivational value of critical thinking—is important. Although not all students will welcome opportunities to think critically, more often than not students prefer to think about matters than to regurgitate facts or apply undigested ideas. This is especially true when the issues or topics students are asked to think critically about are meaningful to them.

ASSESSING THE TOOLS

Thus far we have focussed on teaching the tools. Another useful feature of the tools approach is the parallel between instruction and assessment. Assessment is a major obstacle for many teachers in their efforts to promote critical thinking. If there is no single correct answer to look for in student responses, knowing what to assess is often difficult. As our last two examples illustrate, students might pose any of a nearly infinite number of effective questions. Does this mean that virtually any question is acceptable? If not, on what basis should we assess these questions?

The topic of assessing critical thinking is discussed more extensively in the final three chapters of this book. Let us say here simply that the key consideration is not whether we agree or disagree with the conclusions students reach but instead assess the quality of the thinking that supports their answers. In assessing critical thinking, we should look for evidence that shows that students' answers embody the relevant tools competently. Assessing students on the complete range of tools that a particular task requires may be unrealistic. A more appropriate approach is to assess only those tools that students were expressly expected to employ in the task before them. In other words, we should endeavour to assess the tools that the students were instructed to use. Returning to the two examples of teaching students to pose effective questions, let us see what this looks like in practice.

ASSESSING THINKING ABOUT POWERFUL QUESTIONS

In learning to pose powerful questions to the war veteran, the primary students were expressly taught four tools, all of them potentially forming the criteria for assessing students' thinking. Notice our use of criteria in two contexts: we talk about assessment criteria and criteria for judgment. Assessment criteria are the grounds for assessing students' work and, in the area of critical thinking, we recommend using all five tools as sources of assessment criteria. The tool we refer to as criteria for judgment is but one of the criteria that may be used to assess critical thinking.

The actual questions could be evaluated on two criteria: judgment and background knowledge about World War II.

We could assess the former by seeing how well the question each student posed met the agreed-on criteria. (Alternatively, students might be asked to explain how their question satisfies each criterion). Students' questions could be used to assess background knowledge by looking to see whether or not any question reveals factual errors. The teacher could circulate among the groups, assessing use of the brainstorming strategy by observing whether students readily volunteered questions and accepted all suggestions without criticism. Students' understanding of the conceptual distinction between weak and powerful questions could be assessed by providing sample questions and asking students to identify which are weak and which powerful.

ASSESSING THINKING ABOUT TEST QUESTIONS

In the second example, students were provided with three tools to support their thinking about examination questions: a range of criteria for determining effective test questions, the "question frame" strategy for generating questions, and background knowledge on the historical period. The student-generated questions could be assessed on all three grounds: how well they satisfied the stipulated criteria for judgment, the extent to which the questions represent a variety of question frames, and on the knowledge of the period implied by the questions asked. (A more appropriate source for assessing students' background knowledge would be the answer key that was to accompany each student's six questions.)

Since the focus of the second example was on posing test questions, we made no mention of the tools needed to help students think critically about their answer key (and, by implication, about their answers on the actual end-of-unit quiz). It would be instructive to briefly consider what these tools might be. Obviously, there is no definitive list of tools that teaches students to answer exam questions thoughtfully. Often the identified tools depend on the teacher's priorities for the assignment, the perceived needs of the students, and the demands of the curriculum. Consequently, our suggestions are just that. We do think, however, that there will be considerable agreement on the sorts of tools that we would recognize as being appropriate.

A useful place to begin thinking about which tools to assess is to imagine a weak student response to a sample question (poor responses are often more revealing). Using the question, "What do you think would have happened if the people hadn't rebelled against the king?", consider the following obviously flawed answer: "If the people hadn't rebelled they would have quickly forgotten their troubles and gone back to watching television."

What relevant tools appear to be absent in this answer? The historical error of assuming the existence of television in the seventeenth century comes immediately to mind. That is, the background knowledge is incomplete. The bald assertion that the citizenry would quickly forget their problems is vague, somewhat implausible, and is not supported with any evidence. These deficits suggest gaps in understanding the criteria for judging a thoughtful response.

The historical error about watching television might suggest stressing the need for students to read the chapter carefully. In addressing the gaps in criteria for judgment, we might explore with students the importance of a detailed (or specific) answer and whether it is plausible and amply supported by evidence (or reasons). The specification of these three criteria for judgment might raise the need to teach critical thinking vocabulary: all students would not know the difference between plausible and actual outcomes. (An outcome need not be actual, or even likely, for it to be plausible.) We might also try to nurture an empathetic habit of mind. Empathy, and in this particular case historical empathy, involves an appreciation of how others in different situations and contexts might feel. If students were inclined to put themselves, metaphorically speaking, into the heads and hearts of those living in the seventeenth century, their answers to the questions might be more detailed and plausible. In casting about for thinking strategies to help students construct a thoughtful answer we might recommend a "template" for their answers. Perhaps students might employ a three-point outline:

1. briefly summarize the position taken;
2. elaborate on what is meant or implied by the position; and
3. offer several pieces of evidence to justify the position.

We might imagine other hypothetical student answers, including ideal answers to help us elaborate on and refine our list of requisite tools. For example, our imagined exemplary answers might include refutation of possible objections to the stated position, or suggested alternative positions and evaluations of the relative merits of each. If we thought these were reasonable and appropriate expectations, we might introduce additional tools, including teaching the concepts of "argument" and "counter-argument" and revising the suggested three-point outline to add a new step:

4. anticipate possible objections to their position and provide a counter-argument for each.

Needless to say there are other possibilities for tools to teach and, in turn, to assess. The point to appreciate is how varied the tools, and how much better students' answers will likely be, if they have been taught to use some of these tools.

Think of an assignment involving critical thinking that you have recently given to students or, better yet, are about to assign. As a way of furthering your understanding of the ideas in this chapter, think of the tools you might teach your students to help them complete the assignment more thoughtfully. It is inevitable in any critical thinking task or question that background knowledge and criteria for judgment are needed. Tools of the other three types—critical thinking vocabulary, thinking strategies, and habits of mind—are often, but not always, applicable. As an aide, you might want to employ the strategy of anticipating student answers (both exemplary and poor) to help you develop a list of realistic and appropriate tools (these two qualities are your criteria for judging what to include and what to leave off).

ENDNOTES

1   The widely cited study of one thousand American classrooms by John Goodlad (2004) concluded that from the early grades school-based activities and environments condition students to reproduce what they are taught, not to use and evaluate information. Fred Newmann's (1991, 324) research on sixteen schools observed that most instruction "follows a pattern of teachers transmitting information to students who are expected to reproduce it." Sandra McKee (1988) found in her study of high school teachers that four per cent of classroom time was devoted to reasoning and an average of only 1.6 student-posed questions per class.

2   Developed by Jerrold Coombs, first published in Bailin, Case, Coombs, and Daniels (1999). Used with permission of the author.

3   This example is based on a lesson described in McDiarmid, Manzo, and Musselle (2007, 115–119).

4   Based on personal communication with Karen Barnett.

REFERENCES

Bailin, S., R. Case, J. Coombs, and L. Daniels. 1999. Conceptualizing critical thinking. *Journal of Curriculum Studies* 31 (3): 285–302.

Glaser, R. 1984. Education and thinking: The role of knowledge. *American Psychologist* 39 (2): 93–104.

Goodlad, J. 2004. *A place called school: Twentieth anniversary edition.* Whitby, ON: McGraw-Hill.

Hirsch, E.D. 1988. *Cultural literacy: What every American needs to know.* New York: Vintage Books.

Lipman, M. 1988. Critical thinking: What can it be? *Educational Leadership* 45: 38–43.

Mackenzie, J. 1988. Authority. *Journal of Philosophy of Education* 22 (1): 57–65.

McDiarmid, T., R. Manzo, and T. Musselle. 2007. *Critical challenges for primary students.* Rev. ed. Vancouver, BC: The Critical Thinking Consortium.

McKee, S.J. 1988. Impediments to implementing critical thinking. *Social Education* 52 (6): 444–446.

McPeck, J. 1981. *Critical thinking and education.* New York: St. Martins.

Newmann, F.M. 1991. Promoting higher order thinking in social studies: Overview of a study of 16 high school departments. *Theory and Research in Social Education* 19 (4): 324–340.

Norris, S.P. and R.H. Ennis. 1989. *Evaluating critical thinking.* Pacific Grove, CA: Midwest Publications.

Parker, W., Achieving thinking and decision making objectives in social studies. In *Handbook of research on social studies teaching and learning,* ed. J. Shaver, 345–356. Toronto: Collier Macmillan.

Paul, R.W. 1988. *What, then, is critical thinking?* Rohnert Park, CA: Center for Critical Thinking and Moral Critique.

———. 1993. The critical connection: Higher order thinking that unifies curriculum, instruction, and learning. In *Critical thinking: How to prepare students for a rapidly changing world,* R. Paul, 273–289. Santa Rosa, CA: Foundation for Critical Thinking.

Perkins, D.N., E. Jay, and S. Tishman. 1993. Beyond abilities: A dispositional theory of thinking. *Merrill–Palmer Quarterly* 39 (1): 1–21.

Siegel, H. 1988. *Educating reason: Rationality, critical thinking, and education.* New York: Routledge.

Willingham, D.T. 2007. Critical thinking: Why is it so hard to teach? *American Educator,* Summer: 8–19.

9

Supporting a Community of Critical Thinkers

Roland Case and Philip Balcaen

Critical thinking does not develop in a vacuum and lasting gains cannot be expected from isolated efforts. Nurturing critical thinking requires establishing on-going practices and structures that reinforce thoughtful reflection in our classrooms and schools. As Barbara Rogoff suggests, this requires more than "piecemeal incorporation of innovative techniques into an otherwise inconsistent fabric" of traditional teaching and learning (1994, 214). This chapter discusses what it means to support, and what is involved in supporting, a community of critical thinkers.

The Nature of Classroom as Community

Over the past two decades it has become popular to talk about a particular classroom atmosphere in terms of a community. This is an especially attractive metaphor for the kind of atmosphere that is conducive to critical thinking. Various writers identify four principles that define a group of individuals as a community (Lipman 1991; Newmann 1990):

- Participants are "committed to a common goal" that gives them unity.
- Participants do not work in isolation, but "interact in collaborative pursuit" of their goal (in other words, communication is key to a community).
- Participants "agree on the general procedures" to follow.
- Participants assume "individual responsibility"—each individual is responsible for contributing to the common goal.

Of course, there are many variations of classrooms as communities. These classrooms are variously referred to as caring communities, learning communities, communities of learners, and communities of inquiry. The underlying commonality is the commitment to creating a community atmosphere within the classroom; the qualifier indicates subtle differences in the particular common goal and some of the general procedures that are followed. A "caring" community,

for example, would give primacy to creating feelings of trust and emotional support, whereas a community of "inquiry" would emphasize the shared pursuit of knowledge. These differences in emphasis are relatively subtle—the conditions that support a community of inquiry overlap extensively with those to be found in a caring community—as students cannot learn from each other under conditions of distrust, lack of co-operation, and disrespect.

We must emphasize that our conception of a community of critical thinkers has more in common with the other variations of community than there are differences. For example, a critical community presupposes a deep and abiding concern for each other's feelings and ideas, and in this respect must be, to a significant extent, a caring community. The common feature—the notion of a classroom as a community—is central to understanding the kind of atmosphere recreated in a critical community or, for that matter, in other types of classroom communities.

Distinguishing "Traditional" and "Community" Classrooms

It may be helpful in getting further inside the notion of a classroom as community to distinguish it from other kinds of classroom atmospheres. In an illuminating article, Rogoff (1994) distinguishes a classroom community from teacher-run and student-run classrooms. She argues that teacher- and student-run classrooms exist at opposite ends of a spectrum, whereas classrooms as communities are in a different category altogether. Studies suggest that traditional teacher-directed classes may not create an atmosphere conducive to student thoughtfulness (Newmann 1991, 330). Goodlad's study of more than a thousand schools in the United States noted that despite the rhetoric of promoting creativity, individual flexibility, and independent thinking, the practice in many schools was quite different: "From the beginning, students experience school and classroom environments that condition them in precisely opposite behaviours—seeking 'right' answers, conforming, and reproducing the known" (2004, 291).

Many have thought that the alternative to a teacher-run classroom is a student-run classroom. Rogoff argues that this is not the case. Neither teacher-run nor student-run classrooms support thinking as well as a classroom as community does. This last comment is potentially confusing because a classroom community is often referred to as a student-centred classroom. Consequently, it will be useful to distinguish teacher- and student-run classrooms and then to contrast these with the notion of community-based classrooms. While doing this, we will explain the key advantages of the community approach. Key differences between teacher- and student-run classrooms are summarized in Table 9.1.

Rogoff suggests that on the spectrum of teacher- and student-run classrooms any diminution of teacher control directly increases student control. In the area of decision making in the extreme teacher-run class, the teacher makes all the rules, determines what is studied, sets the schedule for the class, and so on. The student's role is passive, merely to comply with the teacher's dictates. Conversely, in a student-run classroom, in order not to inhibit students' creativity and initiative, teachers assume a laissez-faire or "hands-off" approach. In the most extreme version, individual students are left to decide for themselves what to study, when, and how. Teaching and learning in a teacher-run classroom is largely through direct instruction in the accepted beliefs and ways of proceeding. In a student-run classroom, there is no direct instruction, no telling, no "right or wrong" answer, and no correct way of doing anything (Richardson 2003). Consequently, the teacher's role is largely to encourage students as they individually make their own sense of the material they engage with.

The dominant values of the teacher-run classroom are control and student replication of received beliefs and correct ways of acting. This point was vividly espoused by prominent nineteenth-century American educator William Torrey

Harris when he commented that "the first requisite of the school is order: each pupil must be taught to conform his behaviour to a general standard, just like the running of the trains" (cited in Barell 1991, 29). In a student-run classroom, the dominant values are a permissive atmosphere to nurture the free expression of ideas and actions. Apart from rare notable experiments such as the "free" schools movement in the 1960s and 1970s, student-run classrooms, in any pure form, have not operated extensively. However, some proponents of such movements as student-centred education, values clarification, discovery learning, whole language, and teaching for creativity seem to espouse a student-run philosophy within certain areas of the curriculum. For example, one elementary science teacher who had recently been introduced to "constructivist learning" but had developed a misconceived idea about it was reported to state, "Constructivism has taught me I do not need to know any science in order to teach it. I will simply allow my students to figure things out for themselves, for I know there is no right answer" (MacKinnon and Scarff-Seatter 1997, 53).

Clearly, choosing either a completely teacher-run class or a completely student-run class seems extreme. Teacher-run classes reinforce conformity and discourage individual thoughtfulness, whereas student-run classes abandon standards and preclude developing shared understandings. This seems to suggest the need to find a middle ground between these extremes. Herein lies the value of Rogoff's comparison of these two types of classroom structures. The middle ground between these poles—a classroom that is partly teacher-run and partly student-run—might be seen to imply that some of the time the teacher would initiate, direct, and control and at other times students would. When it was the teacher's turn to decide, students would be expected to comply, and conversely when it was the students' turn to decide, the teacher would stand back and permit—so, too, in the teaching and learning dimension. In those topics where a right way or a

TABLE 9.1 TEACHER- AND STUDENT-RUN CLASSROOMS

	TEACHER-RUN CLASSROOM	STUDENT-RUN CLASSROOM
Decision making	teacher initiates and dictates; students react and comply	students initiate and decide for themselves; teacher responds and permits
Principles of teaching and learning	teacher transmits received knowledge and practices; students absorb and adopt	students construct their own understandings and ways of doing things; teacher encourages but doesn't "interfere" in student learning
Teaching practices	teacher-directed instruction (for example, show and tell, repetition, drill and correction)	student-directed learning (for example, self-discovery, unaided exploration, hit and miss)
Dominant values	compliance and replication	permissiveness and individual expression

correct answer was required, the teacher would transmit the received knowledge and students would accept it; in other areas, where no received answer was expected, students would freely discover and individually conclude for themselves. Any compromise between these polar philosophies is a matter of determining when students are free to decide by themselves and when they must do as they are asked, and, by extension, when teachers are to assume a laissez-faire role and when they are to "call the shots."

THE THIRD WAY: CLASSROOM AS COMMUNITY

Rogoff invites us to see the classroom as community as a qualitatively different option to any position on the teacher/student–run continuum. It is not a matter of deciding whether the teacher or the student is "in charge." Rather it requires collaborative participation and decision making—a community effort—involving differentiated roles and responsibilities. Before looking at these elements, consider the description in the highlighted text of Roland's efforts at creating a community of learners in his own university teaching.

ROLAND'S ATTEMPT AT A COMMUNITY OF THINKERS

After years of talking about the classroom factors that promote student thoughtfulness, I decided to "walk the talk" and try to implement them in my methods course for pre-service social studies teachers. My typical routine would have been to open the first class with a talk about my expectations for the course supplemented with a detailed written syllabus outlining the topics and required readings for each week, and the precise nature of the assignments including their length, format, and due day (including, in some cases, the precise hour by which they were to be handed in). Instead, I said surprisingly little beyond welcoming students to the class and almost immediately invited them into a set of activities to help design the course contents.

We began by sharing in small groups and then as a class our most memorable (both positive and negative) experiences as students in elementary and secondary social studies. Students then examined two documents—the provincial curriculum and a recent Ministry of Education report on the state of social studies teaching. The students' task was to identify key elements of effective social studies teaching and the challenges these presented to prospective teachers. Finally, I offered my own critique of the "good, the bad, and the ugly" of social studies.

Working in groups, students identified the most important areas or topics they would need to master if they were to teach the prescribed curriculum in a manner that realized the successes and avoided the pitfalls they had identified in their personal experiences, the published documents, and my observations. As well, they were to suggest in general terms the kinds of activities, readings, assignments, and resources that might help them to achieve these ends. We compiled a collective list of these objectives and strategies and I indicated that I would return the following week with a proposed outline of our course of study that represented my best attempt to accommodate their recommendations. I warned that some of their suggestions may not be feasible given my limitations, realistic given the constraints we faced, or consistent with university policy (I did have to assign grades). I indicated that I might add a few topics of my own that past experience had taught me were valuable for beginning teachers, but that I would provide a rationale for these additions. Also, I announced that the next few classes would address topics that I had prepared in advance since I would need time to make the necessary preparations.

The "extra" preparations that I had to make were quite minimal since the kinds of topics and activities the students had identified were remarkably similar to those that I would have included anyway. The students and I were "on the same page" so to speak because, in the past, I had designed my course trying to answer the very questions I had put to them, and the documents and comments I presented to them informed (oriented) their thinking in directions that I thought desirable.

There were various other strategies that I implemented in my efforts to create a "critical" community. Three of these were especially significant:

- During the second class, we discussed and affirmed that my proposed course outline captured the spirit and many of the specifics of their recommendations. I then suggested that there were two kinds of questions that students could ask of teachers: "Tell me what to do and say" and "Help me advance my thinking and actions." I announced that for the first three weeks of class students were allowed to ask either kind of question, but that after that date, I would respond only to "Help me advance my thinking" questions. I offered examples of the first kind of question that students might pose if they wanted more information about the first assignment for the course (for example, How long does it have to be? Must it be typed? Should we offer our own opinion? What kind of answer are you looking for? Do we have to cite our sources?). I then inquired what these questions might look like if they were reframed as questions that wouldn't simply dictate what to do but would assist students in furthering their own thinking on these issues. Initially, several students offered what essentially were more specific restatements of the first kind of question (for example, Can it be less than five pages? Is it okay if I don't type it?). The class grew silent as they realized they were hard pressed to frame a question that satisfied the new requirements. I offered an example:

  "I see the first assignment is worth only 10 per cent of the final grade, that it has two parts, and you have not asked us to access outside sources. Given that the assignment is largely a personal reflection and I do

continued on next page

write in a rather concise manner, I think I could do a competent job in about three pages. Does this seem reasonable to you?"

We practised reframing other questions around the first assignment and almost immediately students began (with limited success) to attempt "Help me advance my thinking" questions. My typical response to their partial efforts was "Well, what do you think?" followed by, "Why do you think that?" This promoted students to think through the topic so they could eventually frame the second kind of question. But more often than not, by then students realized that they had actually worked out their own thoughtful answer and, with a few exceptions, didn't need me to affirm it.

- Every class (they were three-hour sessions), we arranged our chairs in a circle and spent approximately thirty minutes discussing emergent concerns, offering news and updates, and listening to students present on an assigned "mini-topic" that we had wanted to look at but didn't have time to devote a full class to. My role was to moderate the conversation and listen. Wherever possible, I returned the week following with an action that took up one or more of the ideas discussed in the previous week. In this way, I signalled to students by my actions that their opinions mattered.

- Students were expected to self- and peer-assess the major assignments using detailed rubrics that I had carefully developed and which the class had reviewed and, when necessary, modified. It was difficult initially to get students to use the descriptors as the basis for their assessments. Either the students hadn't really internalized these criteria or they ignored them, preferring to assign the rating they hoped to get. This was especially problematic when students were invited to assign marks. Things improved after much practice and with the addition of a rubric in which I evaluated stu-

dents on their ability to self- and-peer assess in a criterion-based, fair-minded manner. The result, as those who have been able to get their students to use a rubric effectively will attest, was a significant shift away from the teacher as the sole arbiter of standards to a shared responsibility with students.

The result of my various efforts was the most satisfying teaching experience of my career. Students acquired a much deeper understanding and competence than I had previously seen. Students reported they worked much harder in the course and found it very satisfying (this is not the same as enjoying the course, as many students agonized over tasks that pushed the boundaries of their teaching). Most felt that they had not simply acquired ideas and strategies from the course, but that it had changed them as teachers.

I can't close this story without noting that I tried to replicate these conditions in the next course I taught with much less satisfying results. Although many of these students reported similar results, one-third of the students did not. I was so dissatisfied with this group's performance in the course that I felt compelled to withhold their grades until they had redone the major assignment. I suspect the disappointing results with this group were because of things I had neglected or done differently and their modest level of commitment to the course and to teaching. They likely lacked a defining element of a community—namely a genuine commitment to a common goal: instead of caring about advancing their professional learning, they seemed more interested in getting through the course. The moral of this epilogue is not to undermine the power of creating a community of thinkers—in the first course and for the majority of students in the second course, the results were superior. However, I offer this cautionary note to remind us that, despite the value of this approach, there are no quick fixes or universal remedies in education.

The principles of a classroom as community, which to some extent are embodied in this example, can be summarized in Table 9.2.

Decision making in a community is not an "either/or" proposition; rather, it is a shared responsibility. Notice that Roland and the students negotiated the course contents.

Similarly, the regular implementation of ideas emerging from the weekly circles signalled to the students that their voices were being heard. According to some researchers, students' sense of being able to influence their learning, as opposed to relying exclusively on someone else—typically a teacher—to direct them, is a significant factor in encouraging students to

TABLE 9.2 CLASSROOM AS COMMUNITY	
Decision making	teacher and students negotiate mutually acceptable decisions within established parameters
Principles of teaching and learning	teacher orients, mentors, and monitors while students engage rigorously with the subject matter in concert with others
Teaching practices	teacher teaches the "tools" to enable students to reach thoughtful responses to structured but open-ended tasks
Dominant values	norm-guided participation and collaboration

think for themselves (Barell 1991, 71; Resnick 1989, 9). In a classroom as community, teaching and learning are collaborative—the teacher does not tell students what to think, and, conversely, students are not free to think whatever they happen to feel like. The teacher's role is to frame the tasks, actively mentor students, and support students in developing the "tools" they need in order to reach thoughtful conclusions. For their part, students must work within the negotiated structures and shared norms as they engage seriously with the subject matter. Norm-guided participation and collaboration among all community members are the dominant values.

The picture of a classroom as a community may sound idealistic. So how would one systematically undertake to nurture such an environment in an elementary or secondary classroom? Before looking at specific strategies to support a community of critical thinkers, we want to offer a few thoughts on the importance of carefully scrutinizing our existing practices to ensure their consistency with our overarching goal.

The Role of the Hidden Curriculum

The need to look closely at our practices arises not simply because we may miss out on opportunities to support critical thinking. The situation is more disturbing: many classroom practices actually undermine thinking. A particularly important dimension of classroom climate is what is loosely called the "hidden curriculum." The term "hidden" is thought by some to be misleading in that it suggests a conscious but covert attempt to teach contrary to the formal or official curriculum. Many believe that the so-called hidden curriculum is largely unintentional—that many of us do not deliberately send mixed messages to our students, but in large part we are unaware of the messages that our students draw from their classroom experiences. These unintended messages often have a more significant effect on student learning than do our deliberate efforts. This point was affirmed by studies of various educational programs to promote respect for others (Daniels and Case 1992). For the most part, specific programs and activities intended to increase respect for others had a marginal impact; the determining factor was the climate within the classroom. What mattered was whether or not teachers provided a safe forum for student dialogue, solicited and valued student opinions, and otherwise acted in ways that modelled respect for the feelings and ideas of others.

Even a commonplace activity such as teacher talk may have an unintended message for students. For example, studies of the factors that influence students' willingness to contribute to class discussions suggest that teachers commonly monopolize the talk. Not only does this reduce the opportunities for student to contribute, it creates the impression in students' minds that their opinions don't really matter (Hess 2004, 152).

One study suggested that 80 per cent of students would talk less in class if they felt their opinions weren't valued.

Consider the implications of the hidden curriculum in the context of the traditional classroom debate. The objective for each team in this activity is to prove that the other side is without merit by refuting, belittling, or ignoring opposing arguments. There is a tacit prohibition against changing one's mind partway through the debate. Crossing to the other side is akin to politicians switching party allegiance—both are seen as betrayals. Increasingly, teachers are replacing this adversarial format with more open-ended discussions in which students are encouraged to see the merits of all sides and to recast binary options as polar positions along a continuum. To facilitate this approach, class discussions may be configured in a U-shape. Students with polar views (either strongly agreeing or strongly disagreeing with the proposition) seat themselves at either tip of the "U"; students with mixed opinions sit at appropriate spots along the rounded part. At varying stages in the discussion students are encouraged to move along the spectrum as their intellectual positions on the issue change. In this way, less dogmatic attitudes are encouraged: the implicit messages of the traditional debate—black or white, fixed opinions with the objective of winning the argument—are supplanted by different messages of the U-shaped discussion, the value of provisionally held positions as one tries to figure out the most defensible personal stance from a continuum of options.

The lesson to be learned from these examples is that nurturing a classroom community of thinkers is an orientation that pervades all of our actions. Not only must we be proactive in introducing elements that will support thinking, we should be vigilant in identifying and altering habits that may undermine our efforts.

Take a moment to recall a class situation you have recently been part of, either as a student or as a teacher. Make a list of all the teaching and learning actions that in some way supported thinking and a parallel list of the actions that did not support thinking. Consider why each action had the effect that you believe it had. Identify ways you might strengthen the supportive actions and alter or diminish the non-supportive actions.

Strategies for Building Community

Each of us can build and sustain communities of thinkers in our classrooms by working on five fronts:

- setting appropriate classroom expectations;

- implementing appropriate classroom routines and activities;
- personally modelling the attributes of a good critical thinker;
- shaping the communicative interactions within the class to encourage thinking; and
- developing the tools students need to participate in a reflective community.

Before exploring specific strategies in each of these areas, we offer an account in highlighted text of Philip's efforts at creating a virtual community of learners among his students.

PHILIP'S ATTEMPT AT A VIRTUAL COMMUNITY OF THINKERS

For several years I have been using various online technologies with pre-and in-service teachers to support the teaching of thinking. Initially, my approach was to rely on electronic technologies as convenient tools to communicate with students between class periods. I began with e-mail exchanges to monitor concerns and address student questions. Later, I used a dialogue forum (First-Class) to post logistical information about the course and provide a forum for students to discuss the syllabus and other practical matters. Both these approaches afforded some benefit; notably all of us (including me) arrived to the face-to-face sessions better informed about each other's views and questions.

Recently, I have begun creating more authentic virtual learning communities that do more than act as peripheral technical support to the face-to-face sessions. I now use Knowledge Forum (KF) software (discussed in Scardamalia and Bereiter 1991) to support "knowledge building" where my students actively collaborate to develop the content of the discussions—the topics and resources we will consider—and how we will operate and be assessed. This software provides the architecture through which forum participants structure the discussion and collectively construct emergent understandings. It has played a significant role in nurturing communities of thinkers.

I have tried to support these virtual communities by acting on the five fronts discussed above:

- **Setting appropriate expectations**. At the outset, all of us agree on general expectations. These expectations include that participants take seriously the topic being discussed, attend to responses made by others, and contribute to the building of a positive virtual community. In one group, participants began to add their expectations as they identified a negative tone in some notes. As a consequence, the group developed a code of etiquette for our deliberations. These included expectations that we would always acknowledge contributions made within a note before offering contrary points of view, and that we would focus on the ideas while avoiding any personal criticism.
- **Implementing appropriate routines.** The most fundamental routines involve making frequent contributions to the forum: we post regular messages (usually one per week) intended to "advance understanding of the topic" and respond to several messages (usually two per week). Building on the KF framework we routinely provide structural clues to help everyone keep up with the discussions. These include the following:
  - creating informative and engaging titles for each

note (for example, Kohn trashes standardized testing: Does he make sense?);
  - mentioning the question we are addressing (for example, What assumptions is Alfie Kohn making? Or, Do cell phones have a constructive role to play in the classroom?);
  - identifying "keywords" in our notes (for example, inference, bias, conclusion, opinion) to help others search and organize the database;
  - making explicit references to other participants' notes (for example, X says "...," but I think ..., because ...);
  - embedding outside sources including internet links, graphics, and video clips.
- **Personal modelling of critical thinking attributes**. I try as best I can to model sound thinking and respectful discussion in my own notes. To encourage student use of the features of the software, I make a point of using various "scaffolding" labels ("An Alternative Point of View," "My Conclusion," or "Flaws in the Argument") to identify the kind of contribution I am making to the discussion. Such declarations help participants identify the thinking concepts in play.
- **Communicative interactions**. The structure and deliberative pace of online communication within a virtual community provide rich opportunities to ask probing questions and offer thoughtful responses. The KF software is particularly effective at helping participants move beyond merely offering observations and opinions to the weighing of multiple options and the seeking of informed consensus on topics. I have found these virtual interactions have transferred to more thoughtful face-to-face discussions in the classroom.
- **Tools for a reflective community**. Success is unlikely if a majority of participants lack the skills needed to contribute to a virtual community. I have found it imperative to teach participants both how to use the software to build community and the thinking tools needed to contribute.

While I am generally pleased with the results, every group has not been entirely successful in building a virtual critical community. One explanation for the less successful cases is participant unwillingness to use technology to support their work together. Another factor is the vulnerability felt by some participants over "publishing" their thoughts within the virtual environment. This sense of vulnerability requires careful attention during face-to-face encounters and assurances, supported with actions, that participants will be treated with the thoughtful consideration they deserve.

Classroom Expectations

The expectations we set for our students influence the tone of our classrooms. One of the significant factors in Roland's attempt to create a community was the kind of questions students were expected to ask. Typically, at the outset of each year we devote considerable time to establishing behavioural expectations (for example, students are expected to be punctual, keep the classroom clean, treat each other respectfully). It is worth considering the following kinds of classroom expectations that support thinking:

- Students are expected to make up their own minds—not simply take someone's word for things.
- Students and teacher are expected as a matter of course to provide reasons or examples in support of their observations, conclusions, and behaviour.
- Students and teacher are expected to seriously consider other perspectives on an issue and alternative approaches to a problem before reaching a firm conclusion.
- All persons are to be treated respectfully by everyone, even if their ideas seem wrong or silly.
- It is not simply permissible but expected that students will disagree with one another; however, differences of opinions must never be directed personally as attacks on the person.
- It is not acceptable merely to criticize and complain—the pros of a position should always be examined as should possible solutions to problems.
- The insincere use of critical techniques to show off or to be contrary is not tolerated (this does not mean that there is no place for well-intentioned devil's advocacy).

Classroom Routines and Activities

A community of thinkers is supported by building into the daily classroom operation various routines and activities that habituate students to particular frames of mind. The weekly discussion in Roland's class provided an ongoing mechanism by which students could air their concerns and influence the direction of the course. The following list includes some of the routines that support a critical community:

- Using the vocabulary of critical thinking as a matter of course in classroom discussion (for example, "What can you infer from this picture about the individual's mood or feelings?" "What assumptions are you making?").
- Consistently assigning tasks, including those that are for marks, that contain a non-trivial commitment to thinking critically.
- Involving students in scrutinizing accounts, textbooks, news articles and reports, and other "reputable" sources of information for bias, stereotyping, overgeneralization, and inaccuracy.
- Regularly soliciting student ideas and suggestions and (when appropriate) using them in setting assignments, establishing rules for the class, and establishing criteria for evaluation.
- Praising thoughtfully supported, insightful, or empathetic responses (even if flawed) over merely correctly recalled responses.
- Inviting students regularly to explore and defend positions from particular points of view, especially from perspectives that are not personally held by them.
- Involving students regularly in identifying and defending criteria to evaluate their classroom behaviour and work, and then applying these criteria to themselves and their peers.
- Providing students with adequate time to reflect on their learning and to think about their answers before being asked to respond.

Teacher Modelling

Albert Schweitzer is reported to have noted, "Example is not the main thing in influencing others, it's the only thing" (reported in Norman 1989, 27). This principle applies to critical thinking. If we want our students to be good critical thinkers we must model these attributes ourselves in the kinds of ways suggested below:

- Don't be dogmatic and don't always have an answer. Live with ambiguity—be satisfied with tentative conclusions until full review of complex issues can be carried out.
- Sincerely attempt to base all comments and decisions on careful and fair-minded consideration of all sides.
- Be willing (if asked) to provide "good" reasons for your decisions and actions (this does not mean that the lesson must be interrupted every time a student asks for a justification).
- Be careful to avoid making gross generalizations and stereotypical comments about individuals and groups, and seek to expose stereotypes in books, pictures, films, and other learning resources.
- Be willing to change your mind or alter your plans when good reasons are presented.
- Regularly acknowledge the existence of different positions on an issue (for example, looking at events from different cultural, gender, and class perspectives).
- Don't be cynical—adopt, instead, a realistic but questioning attitude towards the world.

Communicative Interactions

The "talk" that goes on within a classroom exerts a powerful influence on the atmosphere. Classroom communication can be divided into three categories:

- whole class discussions on a common topic;
- teacher interactions with individual students; and
- communication among students.

WHOLE CLASS DISCUSSIONS

Teachers can support a community of thinkers by attending to their communicative interactions with the class as a whole. Diane Hess (2004, 152) has identified four impediments to successful classroom discussions:

- a tendency for teachers to talk too much;
- "discussion" questions that don't invite discussion;
- lack of focus and depth in student contributions; and
- unequal participation by students (some students monopolize discussions and others are marginalized).

The obvious solution to teacher dominance of class discussions is to remind ourselves constantly that most of the talk should come from our students. It may also help to avoid signalling to students our own opinions on the issue under discussion. Instead, we might raise questions or offer statements that invite disagreement, not end it.

Another significant determinant of student participation in whole class discussion is the nature of the questions asked. If the questions are essentially matters of factual knowledge (for example, What was urban life like one hundred years ago?) or personal preference (for example, Would you have liked to have lived then?), there is little real opportunity for students to engage each other in genuine debate. In the case of factual questions, either students remember (or can guess) the answers or they don't know the answer and therefore have little to offer. Disagreements typically hinge on factual details (for example, Did they or did they not have cars?). There is relatively little to discuss other than to assert an answer. Preference questions are difficult to debate since they are largely matters of personal inclination (for example, You would to like live without electricity and I wouldn't). The most productive kind of questions for classroom discussions are ones that we have referred to in chapter 4 as critical challenges. These are questions that do not have a pre-specified right answer. To respond to them, students must render their own judgments based on relevant factors (for example, Considering social, physical, and mental health, was the quality of life for the average young person better now or a hundred years ago?). Such questions leave lots of room for debate, especially if students are well prepared for the discussion.

On the point of student preparedness for class discussions, the following strategies intended to support reluctant discussants contain useful advice to increase the likelihood that all students are ready for a discussion (Wilen 2004, 53):

- Base classroom discussions on a common text that students have read or an experience they have shared.
- Invite students to think about the topic beforehand and to write down a few questions they might have.
- Provide students with an opportunity to review information or to gather their thoughts prior to discussing the topic as a class.
- Divide students into pairs to develop questions and to prepare and rehearse a few points they might offer.

Teacher questioning is a key aspect of classroom discussion. Although there are no hard and fast rules for the kind and order of questions to ask, it does make sense to consider a general sequence when trying to engage students in group discussion. In the following questioning pattern, a discussion is initiated by asking one student to state and support a position and, if necessary, to clarify the position or the supporting reasons. Other students are invited to offer their positions and supporting reasons, and then to respond to those who disagree with them. Finally, the teacher might draw attention to unrecognized information or add provocative clues to stimulate further discussion. The objectives in asking these questions are to help students articulate their beliefs, extend their thinking, and engage with others. The questions listed below illustrate non-intimidating ways of framing each kind of prompt:

Invite a judgment and a reason or two
- What is your conclusion and what causes you to think this?
- Can you tell me what you think about the issue and a reason why?

Seek greater clarity (only if judgment or reason is unclear)
- That's interesting; can you give me an example?
- Can you help me understanding what you're saying? Is your point "this" or "this"?

Solicit other students' judgments and reasons
- Does anyone have a different opinion? Why or why not?
- Who has the same opinion, but for different reasons?

Invite students to respond to each other's comments
- What might you say to those who don't agree with your position?
- Some have mentioned [a reason]; does everyone agree that this is a convincing reason?

Add new information or provide clues to push students' thinking

- No one has mentioned [piece of information]. Would this make a difference to your thinking?
- Do you think it is important that [new piece of information]?

INTERACTIONS WITH INDIVIDUAL STUDENTS

In addition to whole group communications, a community of thinkers is also affected by teacher interactions with individual students. There is a delicate trade-off when responding to student questions. On one hand, answering their questions helps them learn; on the other hand, knowing that the teacher will provide the answer may discourage students from thinking for themselves. The difficulty that students in Roland's university methods class had in framing a question that advanced their own thinking illustrates the concern when students are freely given the answers. Although there are many occasions when student questions should be answered directly, it is worth considering ways of encouraging students to answer their own questions:

- Turn the question back on the student or onto others in the class (for example, Well, what do you think? What is your best guess as to the answer? How would you respond?).
- Prompt students with clues or hints or present an example or new situation that might help them see their response as problematic (for example, Have you considered…?).
- Suggest tentative answers, including those that many students would see as flawed (for example, Well I'm wondering if it could be…? I'm not sure, some people might think…).

INTERACTIONS AMONG STUDENTS

There is much that could be said about helping students learn to communicate respectfully and thoughtfully with each other. The area we will touch upon is peer feedback, which is one of the important occasions for inter-student communication involving critical thinking. When asked to offer peer feedback, students are in effect thinking critically about another's work—they are offering assessments based on identifiable criteria (for example, I think your work is interesting and well organized). The following suggestions may help to guide students during feedback sessions:

- Emphasize peer feedback as an invitation to see the positives, not just the negatives.
- Begin by critiquing the work of those not in the class, and

before asking students to put their work on the line, have the class critique something you have done (for example, an essay you wrote as a student, a class presentation you made). When it is time for peer critique, start with group assignments so the responsibility is shared among several students.

- In the early days of peer critique, do not allow negative comments—only allow remarks on positive features. A good indication of the time to make the transition to concerns/areas to consider is when students voluntarily ask each other to identify what is missing from or could be improved with their work.
- Model and set a few simple guidelines for peer critique: perhaps insist that each student start with two (or more) positive comments before offering a (single) concern, and that negative comments be phrased in the form of a query (for example, "I'm unclear why you did it this way. Could you explain what you had in mind?").
- Ensure that the early instances of peer feedback are low-risk, relatively easy to perform, and have an obvious benefit.

Tools for Community Participation

Just as students need instruction in how to function as citizens in society, so too do they need to be taught how to be effective contributors to a classroom community of thinkers. The classic image of the isolated thinker is a misleading one; we should not expect to be able to think through all of our "problems" by ourselves. Rather, we should actively develop, supplement, and test our ideas in conjunction with others—put our heads together. Many students may be unwilling or unable to contribute to and benefit from collaborative reflection. Perhaps they do not listen very well, or they cannot accept any form of criticism, or they do not know how to monitor what they say, or they have no confidence in their ability to contribute to the discussion. Students need these tools if they are to participate as effective members in a community of thinkers. Some of the key tools[1] are suggested below:

Background knowledge
- knowledge that individuals may see things in significantly different ways;
- knowledge of how individuals are likely to react in various situations.

Criteria for judgment
- consider whether their comments are relevant to the discussion (on topic);
- consider whether their comments will be clear to everyone.

Critical thinking vocabulary
- unanimous, consensus, minority positions.

Thinking strategies
- group-management strategies such as taking turns, assigning co-operative roles, active listening, and keeping a speaker's list;
- strategies for critiquing in a non-threatening manner including putting the comment in the form of a question, preceding a comment with a caveat, or preceding a comment with positive remarks;
- strategies for presenting information in group settings include limiting comments to a few points, speaking from notes, and connecting remarks to a previous speaker's comments.

Habits of mind
- independent-minded—willingness to make up one's own mind;
- sensitivity to others—attention to the feelings of others;
- self-monitoring—attention to how one's actions are affecting the group.

Review the list of strategies for each of the five fronts:

- Setting appropriate classroom expectations.
- Implementing appropriate classroom routines and activities.
- Personally modelling the attributes of a good critical thinker.
- Shaping the communicative interactions within the class to encourage reflection.
- Developing the tools for student participation in a reflective community.

Select one or two strategies from the list that you think would be realistic and most effective to implement in your teaching situation.

Conclusion

In this chapter we have argued how important it is to attend to the atmosphere that pervades a classroom, particularly as it relates to student thinking. Building on the metaphor of classroom as community, we distinguished classrooms in which students are partners in the decision-making process from those that are typically referred to as teacher- or student-run classrooms. The core features of a classroom community include a commitment to a shared purpose, agreed-on procedures, and joint responsibility. Using examples from our own university-based teaching, we illustrated various ways in which teachers might nurture a community of thinkers in their own classrooms.

ENDNOTE

1   The tools referred to in this list are explained in chapter 8, "Teaching the Tools to Think Critically" by Roland Case and LeRoi Daniels.

REFERENCES

Barell, J. 1991. *Teaching for thoughtfulness: Classroom strategies to enhance intellectual development.* New York: Longman.

Daniels, L. and R. Case. 1992. *Charter literacy and the administration of justice in Canada.* Ottawa: Department of Justice, June.

Goodlad, J. 2004. *A place called school: Twentieth anniversary edition.* Whitby, ON: McGraw-Hill.

Hess, D.E. 2004. Discussion in social studies: Is it worth the trouble? *Social Education* 68 (2): 151–155.

Lipman, M. 1991. *Thinking in education.* Cambridge: Cambridge University Press.

MacKinnon, A. and C. Scarff-Seatter. 1997. Constructivism: Contradictions and confusions in teacher education. In *Constructivist teacher education: Building new understandings,* ed. V. Richardson, 38–56. London: Falmer.

Newmann, F.W. 1990. Higher order thinking in teaching social studies: A rationale for the assessment of classroom thoughtfulness. *Journal of Curriculum Studies* 22 (1): 41–56.

———. 1991. Promoting higher order thinking in social studies: Overview of a study of 16 high school departments. *Theory and Research in Social Education* 19 (4): 324–340.

Norman, P. 1989. *The self-directed learning contract: A guide for learners and teachers.* Burnaby, BC: Faculty of Education, Simon Fraser University.

Resnick, L.B., ed. 1989. *Knowing, learning and instruction: Essays in honor of Robert Glaser.* Hillsdale, NJ: Lawrence Erlbaum.

Richardson, V. 2003. Constructivist pedagogy. *Teachers College Record* 105 (9): 1623–1640.

Rogoff, B. 1994. Developing understanding of the idea of communities of learners. *Mind, Culture, and Activity* 1 (4): 209–229.

Scardamalia, M. and C. Bereiter. 1991. Higher levels of agency for children in knowledge building: A challenge for the design of new knowledge media. *The Journal of the Learning Sciences* 1: 37–68.

Wilen, W.W. 2004. Encouraging reticent students' participation in classroom discussions. *Social Education* 68 (1): 51–56.

10 Historical Thinking in the Elementary Years

Amy von Heyking

Contrary to the prevailing opinion, history is not the story of the past. It is not a purely factual record of events that happened long ago. Rather, it is best seen as a form of inquiry that helps us construct an understanding of our individual and collective lives in time. It is an interpretive discipline, requiring students to determine the validity and credibility of evidence in order to analyze, construct, and reconstruct narratives about past people, events, and ideas. The Alberta social studies curriculum describes historical thinking as "a process whereby students are challenged to rethink assumptions about the past and re-imagine both the present and the future" (Alberta Learning 2006, 9). This approach is a significant departure from past practices. Traditionally, the history taught in many elementary schools has consisted of a single narrative—for example, the heroic contributions of settlers, or the wondrous achievements of ancient civilizations.

Understanding the interpretive nature of history is essential if students are to value the construction of valid alternative stories about the past and acknowledge the controversial nature of those constructions. For example, How different is the settlement of the West when seen through aboriginal eyes? Ancient Egypt is a "great" civilization from an architectural point of view, but what about from a human rights perspective? Creating this opening helps children explore their own and their families' connection to the past, empowers them to imagine possible futures and consider significant themes and questions in history, encourages them to be critical readers of historical narratives, and acknowledges the diversity of questions and topics of interest to historians beyond past politics and basic needs. History of this kind is powerful and exciting. It requires that children move beyond memorizing isolated facts or accepting a given story, and instead engages them in creating stories about the past. How can elementary school children do this?

Children's Historical Understanding

Early studies of children's cognitive development seemed to indicate that history was largely meaningless to students until the age of fourteen. Using Piaget's stages of cognitive development, researchers concluded that students under the age of sixteen could not be expected to cope with abstract concepts or tasks such as hypothesizing beyond what is readily apparent in source material or synthesizing ideas drawn from different sources. Clearly, if this assessment was valid, history as investigation, analysis, and interpretation would be beyond the ability of elementary school children.

Researchers now have largely rejected universal cognitive development theories. Instead, they define learning as a re-ordering of prior knowledge according to "scripts" that vary depending on the subject area (Levstik 1993). In other words, learners use their existing mental structures when confronted with something new. Accordingly, teachers should acknowledge that elementary children do indeed bring considerable prior beliefs to the learning of history. Seixas (1996) reminds us that from a very young age children encounter traces of the past in the natural and human landscape (weather-worn trees, deserted houses), in the relics of the past (old coins, antiques), in the language they use ("when I was little," "in Gramma's day"), and in the cultural institutions of which they are a part (school, church). Moreover, children experience many accounts of the past on television and film, in books, in family stories, and in commemorations. British researcher Hilary Cooper argues:

> [T]he past is a dimension of children's social and physical environment and they interact with it from birth. They hear and use the vocabulary of time and change: old, new, yesterday, tomorrow, last year, before you were born, when mummy was little, a long time ago, once upon a time. They ask questions about the sequence and causes of events: when did we move here? Why? What happened in the story

next? Children encounter different interpretations of past times in nursery rhymes and fairy stories, family anecdotes, theme parks, films, and pantomime. They encounter historical sources: old photographs, a baby book, an ornament, a statue, a church, maybe a closed-down factory or a derelict cinema being replaced by new roads and flats … before children start school there are many contexts in which they are implicitly aware of the past (1995, 1–2).

Research on children's prior understanding of time and history suggests that students have some conception of history as the study of significant events in the past and, as early as grade 2, may have some understanding of particular historical events (Levstik and Pappas 1987). Consequently, every elementary teacher would be well advised to provide opportunities within their history units for students to share prior beliefs.

Many studies indicate that elementary children can develop sophisticated historical thinking within an appropriate context of active engagement with source material, exposure to alternative accounts, and teaching that scaffolds their emerging understanding and skills (Barton 1997b; Foster and Yeager 1999; Levstik and Smith 1996; VanSledright 2002b). It is helpful, therefore, to examine the specific elements of historical thinking that define this domain, review current research in order to determine the extent and nature of children's work with these elements, and suggest ways in which teachers can nurture children's understanding of history.

Select a historical event that might be familiar to elementary school children. Identify two or three children who are willing to discuss this event with you. Individually, explore their understanding by asking the following questions:

- Who was involved?
- What were the main events?
- Where did it take place?
- When did it occur?
- Why is it an important event?
- How did it come about?

Compare the children's responses and identify areas of understanding and misunderstanding. Look beyond what may be simple factual errors for evidence of more foundational perceptions of the event in particular, and of history in general.

Historical Thinking

Although there are different explanations of historical thinking, Peter Seixas (1996) offers a coherent framework and a useful entry point for deepening students' historical thinking. He identifies six elements:

- historical significance;
- epistemology (grounds for historical knowledge) and evidence;
- continuity and change;
- progress and decline;
- empathy;
- historical agency.

These elements are interrelated. If students are investigating whether life is better now or in "the good old days," they would address concepts of change and continuity over time, of progress and decline, and would likely consider the validity of the evidence they collected (part of what Seixas includes in epistemology and evidence). A role-playing exercise in which students explore Chief Donnacona's perspective on his meeting with Jacques Cartier requires empathy with aboriginal people of the past and use of valid historical sources to create a plausible account. It may also challenge students to consider the significance of this historic meeting. In other words, the six elements are not typically addressed in isolation in separate learning activities. Without these concepts, students lack the tools needed to make sense of historical accounts and to construct their own interpretations.

HISTORICAL SIGNIFICANCE

History is not a chronicle of everything that happened in the past, but only a filtered representation of a very small part of what has occurred. Consequently historians must make decisions about what is significant and students need to be able to distinguish between what is historically trivial and what is important.

Instead of simply noting similarities and differences between historical periods, a table like the one illustrated in Figure 10.1 might be used to invite young students to reflect on the significance of the differences they notice. On their own or as a class, students might record or draw the features being compared in the left-hand column (for example diet, modes of travel, health conditions). Students would circle the rating that best represents their assessment of the amount of difference between the two time periods and explain their thinking.

In some cases, historical significance is determined by the long-term impact of an event, idea, or person. For example, we might study the use of cedar by First Nations peoples because

FIGURE 10.1   COMPARING THEN AND NOW

FEATURES WE ARE COMPARING	HOW BIG A DIFFERENCE?	WHY I THINK THIS
	nearly the same ◯ ◯	
	some difference ◯ ◯	
	a big difference ◯ ◯	
	nearly the same ◯ ◯	
	some difference ◯ ◯	
	a big difference ◯ ◯	

it had a great influence on their lives at the time, or we might learn about the battle on the Plains of Abraham because of its lingering effects on Canada's cultural and political landscape. But historical significance is also determined by our current interests and values. The priorities of the present shape the questions we ask about the past and the nature of the evidence we use. For example, comparing social studies textbooks from fifty years ago with modern ones, we would notice a greater focus on women and children in the latter. This is because earlier writers of these texts were preoccupied with political or economic concerns, for example, Why do we have this form of government? How did these particular patterns of trade develop? The everyday lives of people—particularly women, children, people of the working class, and people of ethnic minorities—were not thought of then as particularly significant from a historical point of view, whereas it is now thought important to encourage students to investigate the history of their local communities and of everyday life in the past.

Research suggests that even children as young as seven can distinguish between "history" and "the past" (Levstik and Pappas 1987). By the time they reach grade 6, students are able to explain and support their definitions with examples, suggesting that historical events are often rooted in conflict and result in social change. But teachers must be deliberate in their discussions with children about historical significance. Researchers stress the important opportunities available to teachers for engaging students in discussions about why some events, people, or ideas are included in school history curricula and texts while others are omitted. Historical events that are significant to students or are contentious because they occurred within the living memory of parents and grandparents provide particularly rich opportunities to consider what makes certain episodes and people of the past

important. CBC Television's *The Greatest Canadian* contest in 2004 sparked lively discussion and debate over just this question. The choice of Tommy Douglas, widely championed as the creator of Canada's public health care system, is a powerful illustration for children of the extent to which history embodies the viewpoint of the present.

Young children can address the element of historical significance by considering for whom their school or other places in the community are named. Why are these people important? Have students learned about other individuals in their community for whom something should be named? They could consider what will be significant in their own lives by creating time capsules to illustrate life in the beginning of the twenty-first century. Students should explain why they have included certain artifacts and omitted others. They might compare the choices they have made with those of students in a more senior grade or with those their own parents might make. Such exercises prepare children for later studies that further illustrate that historical significance depends largely on the purpose of the account (for example, to create a positive impression, to focus on a particular theme, to tell all sides of the story) and that this in turn depends on one's point of view.

EPISTEMOLOGY AND EVIDENCE

Another important element of historical thinking involves understanding the basis for claiming to know about the past. How do we determine what happened at a given time? For example, What was Champlain's role in the conflict between the Huron and the Iroquois? What evidence do we have? How reliable is this evidence? How can we explain historical accounts that offer different, even contradictory, interpretations of past events? We should not leave children with the impression that there is one true story of the past. Nor should they think that historians make things up. Children need to understand that historians draw inferences based on evidence, but that some inferences are better than others and some evidence more credible.

Researchers suggest that children have difficulty determining the credibility of evidence, weighing different kinds of evidence, and understanding how historians use evidence to weave different narratives of a single event or period. For example, the British researcher Peter Lee (1998) found age-related differences when elementary school children were presented with rival accounts of the same historical event. Primary-level children were more likely to take both accounts at face value, suggesting that the accounts differed more in the vocabulary used than in their content. When obvious contradictions in the claims contained in the accounts were pointed out to them, students assumed that one narrator had more information or dismissed the other as mistaken. Upper elementary children were more likely to see the accounts as written by people with particular biases. Some understood that accounts would vary according to the questions historians asked or the nature of their investigations. This observation seems to support Piaget's assertion that young children cannot hold more than one perspective at one time (and therefore critical analysis of historical evidence appears to be of little value for elementary school children). Contemporary researchers, however, reach different conclusions.

While young children may have difficulty with the nuanced and varied interpretations of historical evidence, they are quite comfortable recognizing and accepting multiple perspectives in literature. Young children can compare and contrast versions of fairy tales and nursery rhymes from different cultures, appreciating the differing perspectives. They can debate varying interpretations of stories they listen to or read. Hilary Cooper suggests that young children can begin to appreciate the interpretive nature of history and why there may be more than one version of a story about the past. But to do so, students "need opportunities to create their own interpretations, based on what they know, and to see how and why they may differ" (1995, 17). In other words, children must gain first-hand experience with the interpretation of evidence by engaging in historical inquiries within the context of their family history or other familiar surroundings. Children can examine photographs, analyze physical artifacts, and interview relatives in order to create accounts of their own past. They can compare and contrast these with those of their parents or siblings. They can draw inferences from a school backpack or an antique trunk full of objects. Who do you think this belongs to? What do you think this person is

ANCIENT EGYPT

Illustration by Danna deGroot. Courtesy of the publisher.

like? What does he or she like to do for fun? These activities require children to make tentative assumptions based on the evidence they have and generate questions to guide further inquiry. Peter Knight reminds us that even very young children can improve their historical reasoning by responding to three questions when presented with any traditional primary source: "What do you know for certain about it? What can you guess? What would you like to know?" (1993, 95).

Students might be invited to reach conclusions about life in an earlier period by interpreting images depicting past scenes. For example, in one resource (Case and Misfeldt 2002), students study various illustrations, including the one of political life in ancient Egypt included here, looking for clues and drawing conclusions to answer the 5W questions (who, what, where, when, and why). Their conclusions must be well supported by clues and provide a detailed portrayal of life (for example, Is the man sitting to the left of the stage an accountant? a scribe? a tax collector? What clues can we find? Is the figure sitting on the throne kind or nasty? poor or wealthy? What clues can we find?). Students are invited to reserve judgment and consult other sources if the clues are insufficient for them to reach a clear conclusion. Multiple interpretations, provided they are supported by plausible evidence, are accepted provisionally, subject to the discovery of additional sources of evidence that might support a more conclusive interpretation.

Many studies indicate that upper elementary children are capable of sophisticated reasoning when appropriately supported through analysis of historical evidence and accounts (Barton 1997b; Foster and Yeager 1999; Levstik and Smith 1996; VanSledright 2002a, 2002b, 2002c; VanSledright and

Kelly 1998). But researchers concede that several challenges remain. For example, although twelve-year-olds in one study were able to critique sources by detecting bias and identifying gaps in the evidence, they naively insisted that finding a kind of "middle ground" among their sources would yield a definitive account (Foster and Yeager 1999). They had difficulty assessing the validity of sources and using that assessment to weigh differing viewpoints. Other students, without sufficient content background or contextual information, assessed the validity of a source solely by the amount of information provided (VanSledright and Kelly 1998). Students' use of this criterion is not surprising given that this is often how multiple sources are used in elementary classrooms. Clearly, teachers need to help children analyze accounts and assess the quality of evidence upon which they are based.

Barton (1997b) was impressed with the ability of grade 4 and 5 students to identify historical sources, evaluate evidence, and reconcile contradictory accounts of a famous battle during the American Revolution. His study, however, revealed that when asked to construct their own accounts of the battle, students ignored the evidence they had spent so much time and effort analyzing. Instead, they largely invented their own stories. These students did not see the need to ground their historical narratives in the available evidence. This suggests that elementary teachers should exercise caution when using fictional narratives in their history teaching. Since students at this age are most familiar with narrative as a fictional (invented) form, they need explicit instruction as well as opportunities to examine the evidence on which such narratives are constructed. They should, for example, use source material to determine which episodes in a story or novel are likely to be true and which invented by the author. They need to compare and contrast historical fiction with non-fiction. They also need to engage in historical inquiries of immediate relevance to them that require using evidence to create original narratives.

CONTINUITY AND CHANGE

Understanding change over time is central to historical thinking. So, too, is the need to recognize the constants that continue through time. Obviously, age is an important factor in gaining this understanding: an older person simply has had more direct experience with historical change and continuity—in technology, social values, customs—and therefore has a better sense of what has and has not changed. But researchers suggest that age is not the only factor. Life experience can help even young children appreciate the nature of change. A young person who has lived through a war or a refugee experience, who immigrates to a new country, or who has had to move because a parent lost a job, may better understand

historical change than one who has always lived in a stable environment. But beyond experience, there are concepts that children must understand.

First, children must have a grasp of time-related concepts, such as "past" and "present," "yesterday," and "long ago." Primary children's understanding of time concepts is generally vague. They can read clock time; recite days, months, and seasons in order; and can use terms like "tonight" or "tomorrow" to describe a point in time. Units of time that require an understanding of decades and centuries must wait for the upper elementary grades. But researchers stress the importance of helping even very young children with time categories such as "past" and "present" or "then" and "now." Children should begin by examining objects and photographs from their own childhoods and learning about the lives of elders in their community (Seefeldt 1993). They can also examine archival and current photographs of familiar scenes—schools or local streetscapes—and categorize them as past and present (H. Cooper 1995). Illustrated picture books provide opportunities to identify elements of the story or illustration that provide clues as to its setting in time (for example, When did this story take place? How do you know? Are there clues in the illustrations?).

Sequence is another key concept in understanding temporal change. Researchers working with very young children stress the importance of developing students' understanding of a sequence of events by using familiar contexts (C. Cooper 2003). Early primary children can begin by sequencing photographs that show the activities and routines of their school day and gradually learn to sequence months and special events in the year for a classroom "memory line" or a personal timeline. Students can examine photographs of the school and its playground dating from ten years previously to compare and contrast their school "then" and "now."

Studies indicate that when faced with pictures and photographs from various eras, even young children can place them in the correct chronological sequence (Barton and Levstik 1996). Using clues from the material culture portrayed in the photographs, they could identify the sequence even if they lacked the appropriate time vocabulary to label the pictures. Upper elementary children are more likely to identify historical eras and include references to political history; they also rely less on evidence of technological change when sequencing pictures, but draw on their background knowledge of school history as well as information gleaned from the media, family history, and popular fiction and non-fiction.

Sequencing activities do not by themselves aid students' understanding of change and continuity. It is important to structure opportunities for young children to observe and record changes in themselves, their school, and their community, perhaps by following seasonal changes of a tree in the schoolyard, keeping records of children's own growth, or tracking a neighbourhood construction project. These activities help children understand that "(1) change is continuous and always present; (2) change affects people in different ways; and (3) change can be recorded and become a record of the past" (Seefeldt 1993, 147). While it is a useful starting point, we should not limit young children to exploring personal dimensions of change. With appropriate support, they can begin to think about changes over time in their families, schools, and communities.

Researcher Keith Barton believes that upper elementary students are adept at observing changes in material culture, technology, and social life, and are able to categorize events according to broad historical periods, especially if they explore when those things happened: "which came earlier or later (sequencing), what other things were going on at the same time (grouping), and how far apart they are from each other or the present (measuring)" (2002, 178). In other words, students need to see connections if they are to make sense of the broad sweep of time.

Children, however, are prone to constructing simplified narratives that distort history. They seemed to assume, for example, that historical change follows a uniform and linear pattern: immigrants came to North America, they lived in small cabins, they built cities. They are confused by evidence of "pioneer" life well after the establishment of cities in some parts of the country. Students tend to believe that once a "problem" has been solved, it is no longer an issue. For example, Barton reports that children believed that once women's suffrage was achieved, women were equal and no longer faced discrimination. Children should be exposed to a wide range of lifestyles and experiences in any given historical period:

> [W]hether studying ancient Egypt, colonial America, or the 1960s, for example, students should constantly be comparing the experience of men and women, urban and rural residents, and upper, middle, and lower socio-economic classes. Moreover, students should learn about the relationships among these groups, so that they see historical societies as consisting of many connected groups rather than as idealized stereotypes of explorers, settlers, and so on (Barton 1996, 74).

Children who can make connections with their own experiences are better able to appreciate the subtleties of historical change. Clearly, historical investigations of questions relevant to children are likely to lead to more sophisticated historical understanding.

PROGRESS AND DECLINE

The concepts of progress and decline address the crucial question of whether conditions have improved with the passage of time. Textbooks typically convey an underlying positive message of physical, intellectual, and social advancement. Many studies suggest that elementary students believe that history is the story of constant progress, that life—whether in terms of political participation, technological advantages, or amount of leisure time—has always improved over time. In fact, when American children were asked to identify the most important events in their country's history, they rejected any idea or event that challenged the dominant message that the nation has continuously progressed towards greater liberty and freedom for all. Challenging these dominant messages by provoking students with examples that encourage alternative readings might create the cognitive dissonance necessary for a more balanced understanding.

When studying a particular era in history, it may be helpful to ask students to consider in what ways life has improved and in which ways life has worsened since the period being examined. If children are interviewing parents or elders about their childhoods, they could be directed to ask these adults whether life had improved or declined and in what ways. The purpose of such considerations is not to produce cynics or sunny optimists, but rather to encourage a more complex understanding of change.

EMPATHY

According to historian Gerda Lerner, meaningful historical study "demands imagination and empathy, so that we can fathom worlds unlike our own, contexts far from those we know, ways of thinking and feeling that are alien to us. We must enter past worlds with curiosity and respect" (1997, 201). British researcher Christopher Portal explains that "empathy is a way of thinking imaginatively which needs to be used in conjunction with other cognitive skills in order to see significant human values in history" (1987, 89). Historians must make a creative leap from the documentary evidence available in order to create coherent narratives. Foster and Yeager define empathy as "a considered and active process," one that allows students to bridge the gap between what is known from evidence and what may be inferred given what we know about the context of the time and the individuals involved (1998, 1–2).

Hilary Cooper emphasizes the role of history in developing children's moral awareness, because it encourages children "to ask questions, to discuss and to speculate about the reasons for people's behaviour, attitudes and values in other times and other places" (1995, 3). Many teaching strategies—including using imaginative play stimulated by stories about previous times—can help very young children empathize with people in the past. Although play is largely driven by fantasy rather than any connection to historical evidence, Cooper believes that setting play in a historical context helps children find out about and try to understand and reconstruct past times (1995, 21). Activities such as role plays, simulations, and field trips to historic sites—if supported with appropriate structure, guidelines, and constructive intervention by the teacher—can help elementary children develop empathy with earlier times.

The paradox of empathy, and its value in developing historical understanding, is that it involves confronting difference at the same time that we recognize a common humanity that transcends time. It allows us to recognize something familiar, while at the same time acknowledging that times have changed in profound ways. Ultimately, it cultivates humility and prudence in our attempts to understand the past.

HISTORICAL AGENCY

The final element in Seixas's account of historical thinking refers to causation: historical agency is concerned with who makes things change and why. Research suggests that elementary children hold simplistic notions of the reasons for historical change. They tend to see history as a record of the accomplishments of a few important people: Sir John A. Macdonald was responsible for the confederation of the British North American colonies, or the five women involved in the "Famous Five" case convinced Canadians of the need for women's equality. This is hardly surprising given the traditional "great people" interpretations of history presented in many elementary textbooks.

Research suggests that children often misunderstand the scale or numbers of people involved in historic events. After studying the American Revolutionary War, for example, grade 5 students "did not understand that there were many thousands of soldiers, engaged in many different conflicts throughout the colonies; they thought there were simply two bodies of troops who kept meeting each other in battle" (Barton 1996, 66–67).

Elementary children have difficulty appreciating the social, economic, and political factors that lead to change; they do not understand the role of social and political institutions (Barton 1997a). Children would view the deportation of the

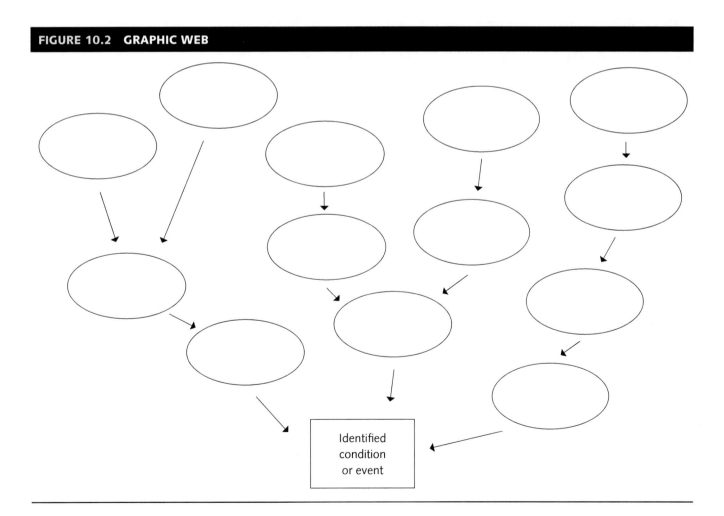

FIGURE 10.2   GRAPHIC WEB

Acadians between 1755 and 1763, for example, as the action of a bullying British governor in Acadia rather than the tragic consequence of a global conflict between two empires. Lengthy or detailed study of political, military, and economic history is inappropriate for elementary children. Yet the biographical approach to history should also be approached with caution. Because children appreciate so readily that history is about real people, history teaching at the elementary level may encourage an inflated sense of personal efficacy if students do not understand the institutional constraints on individual action. Teachers can help children analyze the complex questions of historical agency by distinguishing between direct and indirect influences on events.

A graphic web such as the one in Figure 10.2 is useful when students are analyzing the chain of factors or influences that contributed to a particular historical event. For instance, in considering why nineteenth-century immigrants moved to Canada, students might identify economic hardships, political conditions in their home country, the promise of free land, and so on. They would then investigate how these influences came to be (for example, economic hardships might be traced to unfair land practices). For young students, the activity may be more appropriately done using a simple wall-sized web while the class considers the reasons a particular historical figure acted as he or she did. Older students might complete the chart individually and then discuss their findings collectively.

Conversely, history's essential contribution to citizenship education lies in helping students understand that the actions of people in the past have an impact on us today and to appreciate that our own actions will have consequences for future generations. Thinking historically does not just mean thinking about the past; it involves seeing oneself in time, as an inheritor of past legacies and as a maker of the future. As the historian Gerda Lerner says,

> It gives us a sense of perspective about our own lives and encourages us to transcend the finite span of our lifetime by identifying with the generations that came before us and measuring our own actions against the generations that will follow.... We can expand our reach and with it our aspirations (1997, 201).

History teaching in elementary schools should offer opportunities for children to make a difference in the future of their communities. Projects such as the preservation of historic sites or the erection of historical monuments, or activities that involve them in environmental conservation would empower children and help them see the benefits of community service. This is why history is not only appropriate for elementary children, but essential.

Conclusion

It is possible for primary and upper elementary students to think historically, to understand the interpretative nature of history, and to engage in the creation of stories about the past. They need to see the relevance of their historical inquiries and to participate to the extent possible in hands-on activities that explore how people lived in the past. It is helpful to encourage children to share their thoughts at the beginning of historical inquiries, develop their own questions about the past, and examine evidence in order to reach their own conclusions. History teaching that focusses on developing children's understanding of these six elements of historical thinking will ultimately help create citizens who are critical thinkers, and who look to the future with imagination, empathy, and hope.

The author's fundamental point is that it is not enough to teach elementary students about the past; we should also help them think critically about any historical account. Select a topic from the curriculum that involves some historical thinking (whether about personal memories or earlier civilizations). Identify at least two of Seixas's elements of historical thinking (for example, significance, agency, empathy) and identify various activities that would help students think about this topic in a historically more meaningful way.

REFERENCES

Alberta Learning. 2006. *Program of studies: Social studies—Kindergarten to grade 12.* Edmonton: Author.

Barton, K.C. 1996. Narrative simplifications in elementary students' historical thinking. In *Advances in research on teaching, vol. 6: Teaching and learning in history,* ed. J. Brophy, 51–84. Greenwich, CN: JAI Press.

———. 1997a. "Bossed around by the queen": Elementary students' understanding of individuals and institutions in history. *Journal of Curriculum and Supervision* 12 (4): 290–315. Retrieved September 10, 2004 from Proquest database. Available from http://www.library.ualberta.ca/getit/.

———. 1997b. "I just kinda know": Elementary students' ideas about historical evidence. *Theory and Research in Social Education* 25 (4): 407–430.

———. 2002. "Oh, that's a tricky piece!": Children, mediated action, and the tools of historical time. *The Elementary School Journal* 103 (2): 161–183.

Barton, K.C. and L.S. Levstik. 1996. "Back when God was around and everything": Elementary children's understanding of historical time. *American Educational Research Journal* 33 (2): 419–454.

Case, R. and C. Misfeldt. 2002. *Legacies of ancient Egypt.* Richmond, BC: The Critical Thinking Consortium.

Cooper, C. 2003. History: finding out about the past and the language of time. In *Teaching across the early years 3–7* , ed. H. Cooper and C. Sixsmith, 153–167. London: Routledge Falmer.

Cooper, H. 1995. *History in the early years.* London: Routledge.

Foster S.J. and E.A. Yeager. 1998. The role of empathy in the development of historical understanding. *International Journal of Social Education* 13 (1): 1–7.

———. 1999. "You've got to put together the pieces": English 12-year-olds encounter and learn from historical evidence. *Journal of Curriculum and Supervision* 14 (4): 286–317.

Knight, P. 1993. *Primary geography, primary history.* London: David Fulton.

Lee, P. 1998. Making sense of historical accounts. *Canadian Social Studies* 32 (2): 52–54.

Lerner, G. 1997. *Why history matters.* New York: Oxford University Press.

Levstik, L.S. 1993. Building a sense of history in a first-grade classroom. In *Advances in research on teaching, vol. 4: Research in elementary social studies,* ed. J. Brophy, 1–31. Greenwich, CN: JAI Press.

Levstik, L.S. and C.C. Pappas. 1987. Exploring the development of historical understanding. *Journal of Research and Development in Education* 21: 1–15.

Levstik, L.S. and D.B. Smith. 1996. "I've never done this before": Building a community of historical inquiry in a third-grade classroom. In *Advances in research on teaching, vol. 6: Teaching and learning in history,* ed. J. Brophy, 85–114. Greenwich, CN: JAI Press.

Portal, C. 1987. Empathy as an objective for history teaching. In *The history curriculum for teachers,* ed. C. Portal, 89–99. London: Falmer Press.

Seefeldt, C. 1993. History for young children. *Theory and Research in Social Education* 21 (2): 143–155.

Seixas, P. 1996. Conceptualizing the growth of historical understanding. In *The handbook of education and human development,* ed. D.R. Olson and N. Torrance, 765–783. Cambridge, MA: Blackwell Publishers.

VanSledright, B. 2002a. Confronting history's interpretive paradox while teaching fifth graders to investigate the past. *American Educational Research Journal* 39 (4): 1089–1115.

———. 2002b. Fifth graders investigating history in the classroom: results from a researcher-practitioner design experiment. *The Elementary School Journal* 103 (2): 131–160.

———. 2002c. *In search of America's past: Learning to read history in elementary school.* New York: Teachers College Press.

VanSledright, B. and J. Brophy. 1992. Storytelling, imagination, and fanciful elaboration in children's historical reconstructions. *American Educational Research Journal* 29 (4): 837–859.

VanSledright, B. and C. Kelly. 1998. Reading American history: the influence of multiple sources on six fifth graders. *The Elementary School Journal* 98 (3): 239–265.

11

Escaping the Typical Report Trap
Teaching Elementary Students to Conduct Research

Penney Clark

Consider this scenario: We assign a research report on some topic—a famous person perhaps, or ancient Greece, or pioneers. Students head for the library and select from the shelf or the world wide web the first three sources they find. They copy or download the first paragraph from the first source, the second paragraph from the second source, and so on until their report meets the required word count. Come presentation time, students troop one by one to the front of the class to read their reports in low, monotonous voices. It seems that they understand little of the content since they can't answer questions based on the information they've just presented. And judging from the largely irrelevant questions from other students, the rest of the class wasn't listening either, or simply didn't understand the presentation.

What can we do to avoid this disappointing, yet all-too-common, scenario? Perhaps the place to begin our escape from this largely fruitless, time-consuming trap is to clarify why we engage students in conducting research and preparing reports in the first place. Is it primarily so students can learn about famous people, ancient Greece, or pioneers? No, because while acquiring information may be one of our objectives, there are faster, more efficient ways to achieve this end. Surely the more important purpose is to develop students' ability to conduct research independently, to synthesize that research in meaningful ways, and to clearly communicate their findings to others. As the above scenario suggests, many so-called research projects may do little to help students develop these abilities.

In this chapter, I present a seven-step model for teaching students at primary and upper elementary levels how to carry out and present research. The key to success is to devote as much, or more, attention to the process of conducting research as to the final product, a report. Teacher and teacher-librarian guidance along the way is crucial. We should not send students unaided to the library, assignment in hand,

and expect them to present a well-written, original, and thoroughly researched report on the due date. The complex task of conducting and reporting on research can be interesting and educationally useful if we implement strategies that actually teach students how to complete the various tasks involved in a research project:

- select and focus a topic;
- formulate guiding questions;
- identify relevant information sources;
- extract information from sources;
- record and organize information;
- synthesize information into an effective presentation format;
- assess and revise at each stage of the project.

Select and Focus a Topic

Any successful research project begins with thoughtful selection of a topic and the narrowing of that topic to manageable proportions.

SELECT A TOPIC

Three interrelated considerations are relevant when choosing a topic:

- **Curricular importance**. Student research provides an opportunity to develop a richer understanding of curriculum content than would be achieved by using a single resource or textbook, because it can involve a variety of resources and perspectives. But since research is time-consuming, topics should be selected carefully for their relevance to the broader goals of the curriculum. This may mean research questions set by the teacher that demand more than mere information summaries: they can encourage students to draw conclusions from their research and defend a position.

- **Availability of resources.** The choice of topic depends to some extent on the resources available. Teacher-librarians can be a great help in locating resources with diverse perspectives and rich detail. They will often place materials on reserve so they are available to students when needed. If school resources are limited, teacher-librarians can also assist by borrowing outside resources on a short-term basis.

- **Student interest.** Research projects provide opportunities for students to explore individual interests. They can have powerful motivational value if students care about the topic. The teacher can stimulate interest in topics by raising provocative questions that students might expect to encounter. Allowing students a say in selecting topics is another way to increase interest. This can be as simple as providing students with a list of curriculum-related topics from which they can choose.

FOCUS THE TOPIC

Research projects are unmanageable if the scope is too grand or vague. Since students often have trouble zeroing in on a topic, they may need assistance in articulating the scope of their research. Before directing students to choose their own topic, model with the entire class the focussing strategy illustrated by the following example.

Begin with a broad general theme, such as "European Exploration and Trade in North America" and, as a class, brainstorm a list of categories within this theme. The list might include:

- famous explorers and their contributions
- reasons for exploration
- inhabitants of North America
- the fur trade

Then select one of these categories and generate more specific topics that fall within its scope. For instance, narrower topics under the heading "Fur Trade" might include:

- fur forts
- fur trade routes
- methods of catching the animals
- daily life on the traplines
- role of women in the fur trade
- beaver hats and fur fashion
- aboriginal peoples and the fur trade
- the Hudson's Bay Company

These narrower topics then become the focus for individual research projects. After modelling this procedure with the entire class on a topic unconnected to the theme(s) of the actual research project, invite students, individually or in small groups, to undertake a similar process when selecting their own topics. Students may want to consult with friends and family and scan the textbook or other resources for help in generating a list of categories and topics. Before allowing students to proceed with their research, check that their topic choices are not too broad.

Formulate Guiding Questions

Inviting students to frame questions they will endeavour to answer through their research is often helpful in providing even greater focus and purpose. When generating guiding questions that will have meaning for the students, start with what they already know about their topic and then move to what is unknown.

START WITH WHAT STUDENTS KNOW

Students are often pleased to discover that they already know quite a bit about a topic. Getting them to record this information at the outset encourages them to connect it with the information they acquire during their research. One caution: some of the information that students already "know" may be incorrect. But it can be recorded anyway. Then, as they gather new information, students can check the accuracy of their original claims.

As demonstrated in Figure 11.1, "What We Already Know about Fur Forts," webbing is a way to generate and record what is already known. Ask students to think of everything they can that links to the keywords or ideas contained in their topic. Webbing encourages the free flow of ideas since students make any links that come to mind, rather than fitting information into predetermined slots.

MOVE TO THE UNKNOWN

Once students have reviewed what they already know about the topic, they can turn their attention to what more they would like to know. If students are interested in a topic, there will be many questions. Listing and then organizing these can help students target the most important and interesting aspects of the topic.

One strategy is to list student questions about a topic on chart paper, and then cut up the paper so that each question is on a separate piece. Either as a whole class or in smaller groups, students can sort the questions into categories and

FIGURE 11.1   WHAT WE ALREADY KNOW ABOUT FUR FORTS

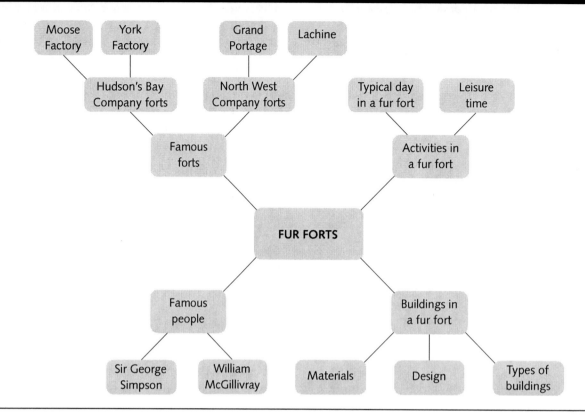

develop a single, more general question for each one. As Table 11.1 shows, the topic of fur forts might elicit specific questions that could be grouped under three general questions.

A variation of this approach for use with primary students is to ask every student to write (or have scribed) on an index card a question about the chosen topic. Arrange students in a circle and invite them individually to place their card on the floor in the centre. If others think they have a question that could be grouped with one already presented, they place their card in line just below the first card and explain why it belongs there. When all questions have been clustered in this manner, students choose a general question from those in each group, or formulate a new question which subsumes the specific questions on the index cards.

Armed with a few general questions (that summarize the many specific ones they have), students are better able to use information sources effectively. With a clear focus for reading, students have less difficulty separating relevant from

TABLE 11.1   STUDENT QUESTIONS ABOUT FUR FORTS

BRAINSTORMED QUESTIONS	GENERAL QUESTIONS
• Were there schools in the forts? • What did people do if they didn't take part in the fur trade? • Was life hard or easy for people living in the forts?	*What was it like to live in a fur fort?*
• Where were the forts built? • What materials were used to build the forts? • Who built them?	*How and where were fur forts builts?*
• When did fur forts stop being used? • Are there any fur forts still standing?	*What happened to the fur forts and what is the status of fur forts now?*

less relevant information. Otherwise, they will often assume that if the author considered it important enough to mention, it must be important enough to include in their notes. With questions in mind, students can scan for answers, rather than reading every word and constantly wondering what they should be looking for.

Identify Relevant Information Sources

A third step in conducting research is to help students learn how to identify possible sources of information and then select the most relevant and reliable sources. Identifying information sources is an area where the teacher-librarian can be of particular assistance, both in making appropriate resources available and in helping students locate the most useful ones.

IDENTIFY POSSIBLE SOURCES

The possibilities for information sources are infinite. It may be useful, before students begin their research, to brainstorm specific options as a group. If this is not feasible because individual projects are too varied, encourage students to brainstorm individual lists. Information sources can include print, people, and places, audiovisual materials, computer resources, and the internet.

- **Print texts**. These include encyclopedias and other reference books, magazines, almanacs, non-fiction trade books, literature, and newspaper clipping files, which can all be found in school and public libraries. Printed information can also be found in the kinds of materials that are not meant to be long-lasting. Many such items are not found in libraries because they are are frequently updated and therefore not saved, for example, pamphlets and bulletins published by advocacy groups such as environmental organizations, government departments, and agencies such as tourist bureaus and travel agencies. (See chapter 26, "Bringing the Outside In," for use of these kinds of print resources.)
- **People and places**. Parents, businesses, professional and lobby groups, and community organizations such as local historical societies and ethnic group associations can all be sources of guest speakers or interviewees. Places might include historic sites, museums, parks, zoos, and various kinds of resource centres. These can be particularly useful information sources for less capable readers. (See "Bringing the Outside In" for suggestions on interviewing people, hosting guest speakers, and conducting field trips.)
- **Visual and audiovisual sources**. These include pictures, drawings, graphs, slides, posters, videotapes, DVDs, and CD-ROMs. (See chapter 28, "Training the Eye of the Beholder," for use of visual and audiovisual materials as information sources.)
- **Electronic information sources**. The internet, electronic databases, and other computer-related materials have become increasingly useful for conducting research. It is crucial, however, that students learn how to use search engines and similar tools to manage these sources and assess their credibility. (See chapter 13, "Integrating Computer Technologies into Elementary Social Studies," for a discussion of locating and selecting appropriate electronic information sources.)

SELECT RELEVANT AND RELIABLE SOURCES

Once students have generated a list of possible information sources, encourage them to think about which sources seem the most promising. With young students, it might be best to simplify by presenting them with a pair of resources and asking them to explain which would be the better source for a given research purpose (for example, "If we want to know what 'voyageur' means, should we consult a newspaper or a dictionary?" and "If we want to know what voyageurs do, should we consult an encyclopedia or a dictionary?").

Older students require more complex challenges. Figure 11.2 presents the chart that teacher-librarian Elizabeth Smith and teacher Rachelle Beaulieu used to help grade 4 students at Shaughnessy Elementary School in Vancouver evaluate the suitability of various information sources on early Canadian explorers. In groups, students researched their assigned explorer using the eight sources listed on Figure 11.2. While doing this, they assessed the quality of the content in light of student-generated criteria. They were asked to offer reasons for each rating. After totalling the scores and rank-ordering the sources, each group reported its findings to the rest of the class.

Select a topic in the social studies curriculum and locate three relevant print or electronic information sources suitable for students at this grade level. Plan an activity with student-ready materials to teach students how to judge which of these sources is the most appropriate for the assigned topic.

FIGURE 11.2 EVALUATING RESOURCES ON CANADIAN EXPLORERS

3 = Effective   2 = So-so   1 = Ineffective

	Detailed (depth of info)	Up to date (currency)	Information from "around the world"	Includes the "whys" of history (determiners)	Includes the "consequences" of history	Not biased	TOTAL	RANK
Canadian Encyclopedia **CD-ROM**	3 2 1	3 2 1	3 2 1	3 2 1	3 2 1	3 2 1		
Encarta **CD-ROM**	3 2 1	3 2 1	3 2 1	3 2 1	3 2 1	3 2 1		
World Book **CD-ROM**	3 2 1	3 2 1	3 2 1	3 2 1	3 2 1	3 2 1		
Ebsco Magazine **Search Tool**	3 2 1	3 2 1	3 2 1	3 2 1	3 2 1	3 2 1		
Internet	3 2 1	3 2 1	3 2 1	3 2 1	3 2 1	3 2 1		
Non-fiction books	3 2 1	3 2 1	3 2 1	3 2 1	3 2 1	3 2 1		
Canadian Encyclopedia **Print Edition**	3 2 1	3 2 1	3 2 1	3 2 1	3 2 1	3 2 1		
World Book **Print Edition**	3 2 1	3 2 1	3 2 1	3 2 1	3 2 1	3 2 1		

Extract Information from Sources

The next step in conducting research is to extract the desired information from the source. To do so effectively and efficiently, students need to use such tools as tables of contents, indices, keywords, and site menus competently. It should not be assumed that all students are adept at using these information retrieval tools, especially electronic resources.

This is yet another step in which the teacher-librarian can be of assistance. Some teachers and teacher-librarians team-teach research skills. Preparation work is cut in half when the teacher and teacher-librarian each prepare a lesson on a specific skill (for example, using a table of contents or an index, or navigating a website) and teach that lesson to one-half the class and then to the other.

Record and Organize Information

The next step—learning to record and organize information in a form that will be helpful in completing a report—requires specific teaching. Four strategies for helping students record and organize information are described below: partner talk, guiding question folders, note-taking columns, and data charts.

PARTNER TALK

Partner talk is a strategy for organizing information that relies heavily on extended discussion prior to any written recording. Before beginning to write their reports, individual students explain to a partner what they already know or have found out. This approach can be used whether students in each pair have different topics or the same one.

Here is one way to organize a partner talk, developed by Ann McIntyre, who was a teacher-librarian in Edmonton public schools:

- Students work in pairs. Each partner tells the other what he or she already knows about the topic, and explains what they have found out about each of the guiding questions. The partners also ask each other questions.
- Individually, partners find a resource book and read relevant sections.
- Partners return and relate the new information they found.
- Partners question each other to find out what additional information is required.
- Partners turn to the resources used previously, or to new ones, to answer these additional questions.
- Partners share answers. Repeat previous steps until all needed information has been gathered.
- Students prepare their reports.

GUIDING QUESTION FOLDERS

Students can use a folder to store the results of their research. They begin by writing each of their general questions at the top of a separate sheet of paper. They create an additional final sheet with the title "Bibliography." All sheets are kept in a folder. As students conduct research, they record information on the appropriate sheet, always remembering to record the source on the bibliography page, indicating the title, author, date and place of publication, and the publisher's name. When students write their first draft, the needed information is organized for them.

The following list is an adaptation of this procedure for a group report with primary students:

- Brainstorm with students information already known about the topic. List these "facts" on strips of cardboard and place them in a pocket chart for easy reference.
- List the questions students have about the topic. Choose three or four key ones.
- Write each key question at the top of a sheet of chart paper. Ask students to print the questions at the tops of their own sheets of paper. Add a sheet called "Book List," where the books used as information sources are recorded.
- Read aloud all or parts of the books chosen as information sources. Encourage students to draw information from the pictures as well as from the words. Students are to raise their hands any time one of their questions is answered. Record answers in note form on the appropriate piece of chart paper. Students can print the answer on

their papers as well. As they listen, they can also check the validity of the information they already knew. They may find some of their information is incorrect. If a "fact" is incorrect, discard the card on which it is written. If correct, tape the card to the appropriate sheet of chart paper.

- Students generate and print on chart paper statements based on the information gathered. The information from each page will form one paragraph of the report.
- Choose a title for the report.
- Invite students to copy the report for themselves and illustrate it.

NOTE-TAKING COLUMNS

Note-taking columns are made by taking sheets of paper and drawing a line down the middle of each one. Write each guiding question on a separate sheet, as in the guiding question folder strategy. Students use the left-hand column to jot down information from the reference source. An alternative way to use the left-hand column is for students to paste a photocopy or printout of every text they are referencing. If necessary, they may use the back, or make their own form. Then they underline or highlight sentences directly in the photocopied or printed text. Stress that they are to focus only on information that pertains to their research question. In the right-hand column, students restate the information in their own words. This increases the likelihood that they will understand what the notes mean. Emphasize that their notes should be clear and understandable (so they can remember the important information) and expressed in point form (so that the notes are not too long). Student note-taking can be assessed using the rubric reproduced in Figure 11.3. Afterwards, students can cut the notes in the right-hand column into strips and use them to create an outline for their report. To reduce the likelihood of plagiarism, compare the ideas (underlined or recorded) in the left-hand column of the sheets with the student's final report in order to ascertain how closely these sources match the final product.

DATA CHARTS

Data charts are an effective format for recording information for three reasons: the limited space requires students to record information in point form; the framework encourages use of several information sources; and the listing of only a few questions or topics focusses students on the major issues. Until everyone is comfortable with the format, it is advisable to use data charts as a class rather than having students use them individually. Group practice runs should focus on topics unrelated to the topics students will explore for their individual projects.

FIGURE 11.3 ASSESSING STUDENTS' NOTES

	WELL-DEVELOPED 5	COMPETENT 3	UNDERDEVELOPED 1
Relevant ideas in left-hand column	Almost all relevant ideas and no irrelevant ideas are highlighted or listed.	Many relevant ideas and several irrelevant ideas are highlighted or listed.	Very few relevant ideas and many irrelevant ideas are highlighted or listed.
Clear and understandable notes	Almost all the relevant ideas and no irrelevant ideas are highlighted or listed.	Approximately half of the notes are expressed clearly and with enough detail to be understandable.	Very few of the notes would make sense to someone reading them.
Brief and in point form	All of the notes are written in very brief phrases.	Approximately half of the notes could be shortened without any loss of meaning.	Almost all of the notes are too long.
In student's own words	Everywhere appropriate, notes are in the student's own words.	Approximately half of the notes are copied exactly from the text.	Almost all of the notes are copied exactly from the text.

FIGURE 11.4 DATA CHART: PERU

OUR GENERAL QUESTIONS	WHAT WE ALREADY KNOW	SOURCE:	SOURCE:	SOURCE:
1. What are the most interesting physical features of the country? Summary statement:				
2. What are the major ethnic groups? Summary statement:				
3. Would it be fun to live here? Summary statement:				
4. Do women play important roles in this society? Summary statement:				

The steps involved in class use of data charts are illustrated in Figure 11.4, Data Chart: Peru and are listed as follows.

- Prepare a blank data chart on an overhead transparency and individual charts for every student. Ask students to record information on their individual sheets as the information is recorded on the overhead.
- Identify and record a title for the research topic.
- Generate numerous questions. Invite students to discuss which of these questions are the most important or interesting. List four or five major questions in the first column.
- In the second column, record what students already know in response to each question.
- Provide students with the titles of two or three brief sources which they will use as information sources. So that students do not become bogged down in any one source, choose brief ones. Pictures or poems are useful not only because they are brief but also because they illustrate the variety of possible information sources. Record the titles at the top of the remaining columns.
- Read or show the first source to students. Invite students to share information from this source that answers any of the questions in column one. Decide as a class on the best and briefest response to each question. Record each response in point form.
- Repeat this procedure with all other sources.
- Working together as a class, develop a summary response statement for each question.

Synthesize and Present Information

The most common methods of synthesizing and presenting research information are written reports and oral presentations.

STRATEGIES FOR WRITTEN REPORTS

- **Explain to a colleague**. Ask students to explain their topics to other students, using their notes as a guide, prior to drafting a written report. This lets them practise expanding their notes into sentences and to sequence their information logically. In addition, questions asked by other students may indicate information gaps that need to be addressed. (This approach is similar to partner talk except that students work from notes. Partner talk is oral until the final step.)
- **Draft without notes**. It can be useful to have students write the first draft of the report without reference to their notes. This encourages students to think carefully about what they are writing and helps them to make the

report their own. They can return to their notes for their second draft.

- **Selective efforts**. Polished written reports require several drafts, each of which must be edited. It may not be necessary, however, to take every report through to final polished product. One option is to allow each student to choose from among the reports assigned over the given year which one will receive the extra effort. These are the ones that will receive a professional-looking laminated cover and be displayed publicly.
- **Writing from a point of view**. Students can represent what they have learned from their research from a particular point of view. It is more interesting for students to write—and for the teacher to read—a letter from a settler on the Prairies to relatives in the Ukraine than a straightforward description of life on a prairie homestead. Similarly, a child's day-to-day journal of a hypothetical visit to contemporary China may be more engaging than a summary of historic sites, industries, and cultures.

  This type of writing is often referred to as RAFT writing—Role, Audience, Format, Topic. Students write in role (for example, from the point of view of a world leader, journalist, pioneer, inventor, or famous person in history) to a particular audience (to newspaper readers, a relative, prospective employers, or television viewers) using a particular format (newspaper editorial, poem, letter, journal entry, telephone conversation, or rap song) on a certain topic.

Offer students opportunities to display their reports in prominent locations. The teacher-librarian can help in this regard since the school library is an appropriate place for public displays of student work.

Elementary students should be expected to include a bibliography in a formal written research report, but they will need help. Upper-elementary students can be expected to write a simple reference list using an example as a model:

Braid, Kate. 2001. *Emily Carr: Rebel Artist.* Lantzville, BC: XYZ Publishing.

Primary students can be provided with a simple format such as the following and they can simply fill in the blanks.

SOURCES

Author	_____
Title	_____
Publisher	_____
Place	_____
Date	_____

STRATEGIES FOR ORAL REPORTS

- **Using visual aids.** Visual aids help make presentations more interesting to an audience. Students who are not aural learners may have difficulty listening for any length of time to an oral presentation. Visuals also provide memory cues to guide the oral delivery. Visual aids help presenters feel more at ease; they will know that the eyes of the audience will be directed elsewhere for at least part of the presentation. In addition, pointing to a picture or map gives presenters something to do with their hands, thus reducing nervousness.

- **Synthesizing another student's report.** To encourage students to listen carefully when others are presenting their reports, it is useful to ask students to take notes. One approach is to ask each student to use his or her notes to write a summary of another student's report. The example in the highlighted text, "Summary of Emily's Talk," was done by a student in a grade 3 class, where students made oral presentations on a topic of their choice.

There is no rule that says oral reports must be made by a student standing in front of a group of thirty others. There are alternatives to the whole class presentation:

- **Rotating presentations.** Locate speakers at different spots around the room and arrange for small groups of students to rotate from one speaker to the next. It is not essential that every student hears every other student's presentation. This approach has several advantages over the whole class/one-speaker-at-a-time method. First, it is far less intimidating for a student speaker to make a presentation to a small group than to the entire class. Second, the speaker has the opportunity to repeat the speech several times, gaining confidence and improving delivery with each presentation. Third, members of the audience may be more attentive in this format because they are not forced to sit in one place for long periods. Also, they have more opportunity to ask questions because there are fewer questioners.

- **Co-operative group presentations.** In this approach, a group of students works together to make the presentation, each focussing on a particular aspect of the topic. One student might serve as a moderator, introducing the topic and panellists, calling on questioners, and keeping things running smoothly. This approach is helpful to the speakers. They can assist one another with difficult questions and the burden of response does not fall on a single individual. In addition, students have an opportunity to develop group participation skills such as co-operating with and listening to others and taking responsibility for contributing to discussions. Students, however, should not simply be thrust into a co-operative project without being helped to develop the tools needed for effective co-operation. These include the willingness and ability to listen carefully to others in the group, await one's turn to speak, and share materials. (See chapter 21, "Co-operative Learning in Elementary Classrooms," for skill-building strategies.)

ALTERNATIVE REPORTING FORMATS

There are many alternatives to formal oral and written reports. "Alternative reporting ideas" lists a number of suggestions, any of which can be approached in various ways. For instance, a timeline may consist entirely of words, it may be illustrated, or it may be presented "live." Pat Shields (1996) suggests that in a "living timeline" format, students prepare role plays using costumes and props to suggest historical figures, either real or fictional, whom they have researched. The role plays are presented in chronological order so viewers can see how perspectives changed over time.

The depth of understanding of the subject need not be diminished when students use an unusual format. In fact, the level of understanding must often be greater in order to make the writing ring true. For instance, it would be more challenging for students to write entries in the diary of the gold miner Billy Barker during his exploits in the Cariboo than a straightforward account of the Cariboo gold rush. To write entries in Barker's journal, students must know about key events and also understand how Barker might have viewed

---

SUMMARY OF EMILY'S TALK
by Laura Brown

If you want to know anything about anaesthetics just ask Emily.

Anaesthetics are drugs that make it possible for operations and other medical treatment to be carried out painlessly. Anaesthetics are made from laughing gas. Horace Well invented anaesthetics.

A long time ago even the most minor operation was quite painful because back then they didn't have anaesthetics.

The main anaesthesias are local and general. A general anaesthetic is when you get a needle put through your vein.

A local anaesthetic is when they don't put you to sleep such as when the dentist puts a needle through your gum when you have a filling.

The other anaesthetic is when some ointment is swabbed on with a Q-tip or a cotton ball to numb the feeling in a certain area. The method called inhalation is when the doctor gives you gas through a mask.

This example of a summary was written by a grade 3 student at Caulfeild Elementary in West Vancouver.

---

them. Instead of writing a straightforward description of the building of the CPR, they could describe the events from the perspectives of various stakeholders by means of "interviews" with individuals such as the general manager William Van Horne, the financier Sir Donald Smith, an Irish or a Chinese navvy, Chief Crowfoot, or Agnes Macdonald (the wife of John A. Macdonald, who travelled through part of the Fraser Canyon sitting on the "cowcatcher" of the locomotive pulling the train). In trying to view events through the eyes of different participants, students will develop a richer understanding of circumstances, individual motivations, limitations, and causes and effects.

Alternative reporting ideas

role play	journal or diary
model	mobile
photo essay	advertisement
mural	game
cartoon	bulletin board display
panel discussion	collection
debate	chart
newspaper	play
film strip	letter
videotape	audiotape
story	poem
map	diorama
scrapbook	slides
collage	demonstration
illustrated timeline	song
position paper	field trip (student-planned)
TV or radio quiz show	computer program
banquet	poster
itinerary for imaginary trip	crossword puzzle
resumé	simulated interview
review	learning centre
annotated bibliography	skit
poster	

Assess Student Research

It is misleading to place assessment at the end of this model, since assessment should not be viewed as the last step in a research project, but rather as an ongoing part of the entire process. Three strategies for effective assessment of student research projects are:

- to generate and share assessment criteria prior to completion of any assignment;
- to assess research procedures in addition to products;
- to include self- and peer-assessment.

SET CRITERIA BEFOREHAND

Set out, or better yet, negotiate the assessment criteria at the very outset or at an early stage of the research project. This way, there are fewer surprises. Assessment is less menacing for students if they know how their work will be assessed and if they have had some say in establishing the basis for assessment. Encourage students to use the criteria to assess their own work before presenting it for teacher assessment. For example, the criteria listed below could be discussed with students when preparing an oral presentation or a written report.

Criteria for assessing an oral or written report

Content
- is accurate
- covers major points
- is sufficiently detailed
- is interesting

Organization
- begins with an effective introduction
- is arranged in logical sequence
- has an effective closure

Presentation (oral)
- is easily heard
- is delivered while looking at audience
- is delivered with an expressive speaking voice

Presentation (written)
- is clearly written
- uses correct spelling and punctuation
- uses descriptive language

Visual aids
- effectively illustrate key points
- are clear
- are visually appealing

ASSESS PROCEDURE AND PRODUCT

All aspects of the research process can and should be assessed, starting with students' ability to focus their topics and frame guiding questions, through the effective use of data charts, to the quality of the final written, oral, and visual products. Assessing along the way makes the task less onerous for the teacher and provides students with ongoing feedback, which reduces the likelihood that mistakes made early on in the process will scuttle the entire project. A form such as the "Research Project Feedback" illustrated in Figure 11.5 could be used for ongoing teacher notes on each student's progress through the research project.

FIGURE 11.5 RESEARCH PROJECT FEEDBACK

Topic:_____	Name:_____
SKILLS	**COMMENTS**
Topic ☐ is worth pursuing; ☐ is narrow enough to be manageable.	
Guiding Questions ☐ are relevant to topic; ☐ adequately summarize specific questions.	
Information Sources ☐ are relevant to topic; ☐ provide reliable information.	
Extracting Information ☐ uses appropriate locator aids (for example, index, table of contents, guide words, computerized directory to library resources).	
Recording and Organizing Information ☐ notes are brief; ☐ notes are well organized; ☐ notes cover important points related to topic; ☐ notes are drawn from several sources; ☐ notes are expressed in student's own words.	
Presenting Information ☐ written drafts have been carefully edited and corrected; ☐ presentations are appropriate for audience and topic; ☐ visuals are thoughtfully designed and constructed; ☐ written and oral reports are thoughtfully sequenced; ☐ reporting (in any form) clearly and accurately presents the collected information.	

INCLUDE SELF- AND PEER ASSESSMENT

Self-assessment and peer assessment should be part of every research project because they provide students with additional, more immediate feedback than a teacher alone can provide. Students must learn how to provide constructive feedback to others; this in itself is a valuable learning experience. Students need to think about and learn ways to make comments in a positive and sensitive manner (for instance, precede any concerns with several positive features, put forth concerns in the form of a query or issue to think about). Figure 11.6 is an example of a joint assessment sheet that can be used by students and teachers to assess a poster presentation.

Parting Comment

Throughout this chapter, I have pointed to the value of making maximum use of teacher-librarians. They can be helpful in many ways, including identifying appropriate resources in the school resource centre, obtaining other materials from outside sources, designing activities that require resource centre support, instructing students in skills needed to work

FIGURE 11.6   SELF- AND TEACHER ASSESSMENT OF A POSTER

	TEACHER RATING				SELF RATING			
	Definitely	Mostly	Partly	Not at all	Definitely	Mostly	Partly	Not at all
Important content/ message								
Clear content/ message								
Well laid-out/ designed								
Visually appealing								

through the research process, and providing a public venue for displaying finished reports.

The most dramatic example I have heard of co-operative planning and teaching between a classroom teacher and a teacher-librarian involved a grade 2 class researching dragons. Under the guidance of their teacher and the teacher-librarian, students examined portrayals of dragons in literature, determined the characteristics of dragons, and then formulated three questions they would ask a dragon if they happened to meet one. As students were discussing possible questions, a dragon (the grade 6 teacher) burst into the classroom and attempted to kidnap their teacher. Of course, she was eventually saved by St. George (the custodian). But, true to form, the librarian played a key role in keeping the dragon from being ripped apart by students until St. George could arrive. This life-saving gesture was necessary because St. George had been momentarily delayed by a custodial emergency, and these grade 2 students were determined to protect their beloved teacher. The now subdued dragon turned out to be meek and mild, and only too happy to be interviewed—and, of course, forever grateful for the services of the teacher-librarian.

Research projects are more time-consuming than simply supplying students with information. How should we decide when a topic is best addressed through student research? Examine the topics for a specific grade in the social studies curriculum. Decide which and how many of these topics over the course of the school year might best be addressed in a research project. Would you structure each research assignment in a similar manner? If not, how might you alter them to best achieve the information-gathering and reporting outcomes in the curriculum?

ACKNOWLEDGMENT

I wish to thank Marg Franklin, a retired elementary school principal and University of British Columbia sessional instructor in elementary social studies, for her helpful suggestions on the revision of this chapter.

REFERENCES

Harrison, J., N. Smith, and I. Wright, eds. 2004. *Selected critical challenges in social studies—Intermediate/middle school.* Richmond, BC: The Critical Thinking Consortium.

Nicol, J. and R. Case, eds. 2002. *The resourcefulness of the Inuit.* Richmond, BC: The Critical Thinking Consortium.

Shields, P. 1996. Experiencing and learning through simulations and projects. *Canadian Social Studies* 30 (3): 142–143.

12 Infusing a Spirit of Critical Inquiry

Garfield Gini-Newman and Laura Gini-Newman

From Piaget to the present, educational research suggests that students learn best when actively engaged: arithmetic is mastered through the use of manipulatives, science through experimentation, and physical education through participation in athletics. So how do we engage students in the study of far-off lands or long-ago events? The answer, we believe, lies in critical inquiry. Teachers can engage students in learning about social studies by involving them in shaping questions that guide their study, giving them ownership over the directions of these investigations, and requiring them to analyze critically rather than merely retrieve information. In these ways, we shift classrooms from places where teachers "cover" the curriculum to places where students "uncover" the curriculum.

This uncovering of the curriculum occurs only when students investigate questions that have a clear, worthwhile purpose and present problems or challenges that they perceive as meaningful. We use the term "critical" inquiry to mean inquiry that is not essentially the retrieval of information but rather a process of reaching conclusions, making decisions, and solving problems. Of course, some students may enjoy gathering information, but all students' depth of learning and sense of engagement are greatly enhanced when tasks require them to think critically at each step of the way. This point is illustrated by the typical research-project scenario described in the highlighted text, "Researching a Topic."

If we expect students to become critical thinkers and problem solvers, then we must challenge them to solve problems and embark on personally relevant journeys of inquiry. This outcome is unlikely if students are fed mounds of information with little opportunity to pose their own questions or to thoughtfully re-examine their emerging conclusions. Even well planned, interesting, and colourful lessons can fail to involve students in thinking meaningfully about the ideas. Active involvement requires that students digest and make personal sense of the ideas, not simply to listen and recite or to read and record.

Building motivation to learn is an important reason for encouraging critical inquiry (McGaugh 2003). Linking social studies to issues meaningful to students is crucial if we expect to engage them (McMahon and Portelli 2004; Armstrong and McMahon 2002). Where there is no engagement, students do not pay attention and consequently are unlikely to learn. Engagement is more likely when our curriculum is built around meaningful questions (including ones formulated by students

RESEARCHING A TOPIC

Students in grade 2 are asked to select any topic they wish, provided it deals with animals, and to prepare a short presentation supported by a display board summarizing their research. Samantha chooses cats. On the day of the presentation, she relays to her classmates the information she has found. Soon her classmates begin to ask questions. "Do you have a cat?" asks one student. "No," replies Samantha. "Do you want to have a cat?" asks another classmate. "No," replies Samantha. "Do you like cats?" asks another. "No!" Samantha exclaims, becoming somewhat frustrated by the questions. "Why is there a dog on your display?" comes a final question. "Let's move on to the next presentation," the teacher interjects.

What went wrong with this task? The absence of purposeful inquiry made Samantha select a topic and prepare a report without needing to think critically about the choices she was making or the significance of the information she was gathering. Had she been supported in asking a more purposeful question and processing the information critically, she might have selected a topic of genuine interest to her that would have led her to think more deeply about her findings. Samantha could have been asked, for example, to consider what kind of pet would make the best addition to her family. She then could have generated criteria for a suitable choice, including personal preference, cost to purchase and maintain, amount of care needed, habitat requirements, and diet. Using these criteria, she might then have researched several animals before making her choice. What's more, she would need to reach a conclusion and explain her thinking. Clearly, in this scenario Samantha would have been more involved, cognitively and emotionally, in her inquiry.

themselves), stimulating challenges, and relevant projects. In a classroom of critical inquiry, unsolved problems, intriguing mysteries, and purposeful questions are used to excite students to learn.

While recognizing the need to challenge students, teachers also must provide the necessary scaffolding for student success such as building on prior learning, providing concrete experiences, and arranging many opportunities for students to engage in focussed dialogue with their peers. This helps anchor students' learning and develop the knowledge and skills they need to direct their research, analyze their findings, and draw their own conclusions. Creating a safe environment where risk-taking is encouraged and students are not being marked down for their mistakes is also important. Students should be allowed to "fail forward" by having opportunities to practise, revise, edit, and polish their work before submitting it for marking.

In this chapter, we explore five dynamic elements of critical inquiry and suggest teaching strategies for creating a classroom built around it.

The Dynamics of Critical Inquiry

Critical inquiry is an attempt to infuse a spirit of exploration throughout the curriculum. At its heart is a provocative question or challenge which arises out of the interplay of asking, investigating, reflecting, creating, and sharing. With these multiple entry points, teachers are better able to tailor instruction to meet the varied needs of their learners. For example, students may respond to a challenge first by reflecting on what they know, sharing initial thoughts and ideas with peers, and then carrying out an investigation. Others may choose to investigate, share their preliminary findings, reflect on what they know and do not know, and then return to further investigation. Similarly, once students have completed their investigation, opportunities to share and reflect are integral parts of any creative process. Figure 12.1 outlines the dynamic nature of critical inquiry.

FIGURE 12.1 DYNAMIC ELEMENTS OF CRITICAL INQUIRY

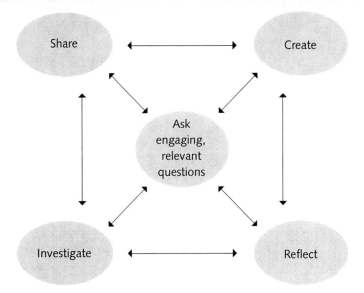

Ask: Inquiry begins with meaningful questions that are connected to the world around us, build on prior knowledge, and excite curiosity.

Create: The invitation to create a product or other representation of learning provides an opportunity to link new ideas with prior knowledge. This coalescence of ideas leads to the generation of additional thoughts and theories.

Reflect: Reflection on the path taken and the conclusions formed is an integral part of the dynamics of inquiry as it assists in the consolidation of learning. Reflection may lead to revisions in the investigation, affirm conclusions, or open new lines of inquiry.

Investigate: Investigation puts curiosity into action. As they gather information, students are likely to refine or redirect their questions, clarify ideas, and begin to make connections.

Share: Sharing with others the product of their journey of inquiry allows students to refine their ideas and reflect on how they arrived at this point.

Asking Questions

As suggested by the scenario described earlier in this chapter, students are too often detached from their research projects, a situation which usually guarantees that learning will be limited and of little lasting value. Framing effective inquiry questions is an important first step in any research.

Building on prior knowledge and asking questions of broad significance are vital to the success of social studies curricula. Students are more likely to become engaged if they are working from a question of more universal than particular importance. Also, the open-ended nature of the questions asked is crucial to the success of an inquiry-based classroom. Questions that send students to textbooks and other sources seeking the "correct answer" or which encourage them merely to prepare lists for their response do little to develop critical thinking or create genuine interest in social studies. Consider, for example, this question: "When and why did each province and territory join Confedera-

tion?" The question requires students to locate information and prepare a list of dates and reasons. When revised to read "Considering the interests and needs of your assigned province or territory, would you have supported entry into Confederation at the time each joined?", the question is more thought-provoking and exposes the historical reality that not everyone supported Confederation.

INQUIRY QUESTIONS AS UNIT ORGANIZERS

A powerful and engaging method of curriculum development is to build the entire year around provocative questions that challenge students to explore and apply their learning. When a course has a central inquiry question at its heart, it assists students in looking for the "big ideas" or the "enduring understandings," to use the term of Grant Wiggins and Jay McTighe (1998). Overarching questions reduce the likelihood of students bogging down in the details of history and geography. A provocative inquiry question provides them with a central reference point to reflect on as the year unfolds.

SAMPLE "BIG" INQUIRY QUESTIONS

Rules and Responsibilities
- What are the three most important rules you must follow each day, at home, at school, and in your community? How might your day change if there were no rules and no one had any responsibilities?
- What are the biggest differences between the rules and responsibilities in your life and those that your parents, grandparents, or teachers had to follow?

The Medieval World
- When people of the future study us, they will learn that tall office buildings and huge stadiums were built in most cities. When we study the medieval world we see that cathedrals and castles were often the most important buildings. What can we learn about a society by its buildings?
- Would you like the opportunity to live in medieval Europe if you could be taken back in time? Would you change your mind if you found out you would be a peasant? A member of the clergy? Nobility? Who had a better life in medieval Europe, men or women?

Early Civilizations
- In some areas such as Egypt, China, and India, early civilizations developed along river valleys. In other areas such as Mexico, Chile, and Japan, they did not. How important was the role of geography in shaping early civilizations?
- How should we measure the greatness of past civilizations? Which of the early civilizations did the best job at meeting the needs of the people who lived in them?

Twentieth-Century Canadian History
- At the beginning of the twentieth century, Prime Minister Sir Wilfrid Laurier commented that "as the nineteenth century belonged to Canada, so shall the twentieth century belong to Canada." If Laurier were alive today, would he believe that his words have come true or would he be disappointed?
- More elusive than the sasquatch is the search for Canadian identity. Have the events of the past century forged a unique Canadian identity and how have those events defined who we are as a country?

World History
- The historian E.H. Carr and others of the liberal tradition portray history as a steady march forward. In stark contrast, Felipe Fernández-Armesto claims that the very thought of history as progress is Eurocentric and repugnant, that history merely lurches chaotically from event to event. Do the trends of the past five hundred years offer more support for Carr's view of steady historical progress or for Fernández-Armesto's view of random chaos?
- What effect would it have on our textbooks if we changed how we measure the greatness of past civilizations (for example, lasting monuments they have built, size of the empire they established, degree to which they extended basic rights to all who lived in their society, respect for the environment)? What are the hallmarks of a truly great civilization? Which past civilization best embodies these attributes?

Such central questions serve as excellent summative assessment questions. For example, a central question such as "Is Canada a country we can be proud of?" provides a focus for learning about the history of the country. Around this central question, more specific critical inquiry ones addressing particular aspects of the curriculum might be framed:

- Was the deportation of the Acadians justifiable?
- Were French Canadians treated fairly and respectfully following the Conquest of New France?
- Have Canada's aboriginal people been treated with dignity and respect?
- Does Canada act more responsibly towards the environment today than it did in the past?
- Have science and technology improved the lives of all Canadians?

EFFECTIVE QUESTIONS FOR CRITICAL INQUIRY

Not all questions are created equal. As illustrated in Table 12.1, care must be taken to distinguish between questions of factual recall, questions of preference, and questions of critical inquiry. While each have value when used correctly, inappropriate use can become a barrier in meeting the intended learning objectives. If critical thinking is considered an integral part of a social studies program, then questions of critical inquiry are vital to the program's success.

Factual recall questions that have a single correct answer or a limited range of responses are useful as checks for understanding. When the purpose is to assess students' comprehension of key facts and processes, narrowly focussed questions are useful; but if the purpose of posing a question is to prompt student thinking, then open-ended questions of critical inquiry are necessary. Critical inquiry questions require thoughtful consideration of evidence gathered against a set of criteria. Although answers will often vary, a question such as "What is your favourite flavour of ice cream?" is not an inquiry question but rather one of preference. A question such

as this does not build on human curiosity; it does not require investigation, the convergence of new learning with prior understandings, or the application of criteria. (For more about framing questions that invite critical thinking, see chapter 4, "Beyond Inert Facts: Teaching for Understanding in Elementary Social Studies.")

SUPPORTING STUDENTS IN ASKING QUESTIONS

Equally important to the quality of questions posed by teachers is the students' own ability to ask powerful questions. In genuine critical inquiry, provocative questions, which form the basis of the inquiry, should emanate from students as well as the teacher. Yet all too often, students are unaccustomed to or ill-equipped for asking critical questions. Beginning in the primary grades, students are presented with research projects that often follow a similar process: students select a research topic, reflect on what they already know about the topic, consider what more they would like to know about it, and, following their research, summarize what they have learned. The intent of this type of exercise is commendable, though it often has a glaring flaw: rarely are students taught how to frame meaningful critical inquiry questions. As a result, their questions are typically limited to factual retrieval. Consequently, there is often little purpose to their research and no expectation that students will draw conclusions, merely that they will gather information.

If students are to become effective critical thinkers, they must learn to ask as well as respond to powerful questions. Throughout the school year, teachers should encourage students to ask critical inquiry questions on important issues, including events in the news and issues related to their school and community. Explicit teaching of the three types of questions, accompanied by opportunities to practise answering them, are vital if students are to move from questions of factual recall to critical inquiry questions. Teachers may wish to consider beginning a unit with factual recall questions and invite students to work in small groups to tweak the questions

TABLE 12.1   THREE TYPES OF QUESTIONS

FACTUAL RETRIEVAL	PERSONAL PREFERENCE	CRITICAL INQUIRY
Ask students to locate information.	Ask students to express a personal opinion or preference.	Ask students to reach a conclusion or solve a problem.
<ul><li>Answers are often "right there."</li><li>Answers have a single correct answer.</li><li>Useful in assessing comprehension of key facts.</li></ul>	<ul><li>Answers are not grounded in careful reasoning, but invite an emotional or "gut" response.</li><li>There are no wrong answers; it depends entirely on how each person feels towards the topic.</li></ul>	<ul><li>Answers require thoughtful consideration of evidence in light of a set of relevant factors or criteria.</li><li>Typically open-ended and there are often several reasonable answers.</li></ul>

into critical inquiry questions. For example, students might move from considering "What three challenges did aboriginal peoples encounter during this period?" (factual retrieval) to "What was the most significant challenge that aboriginal peoples encountered during this period?" (critical inquiry). Students could also review questions from a chapter in their textbook and group the questions into the three types, then suggest rewording of several of the factual recall questions so that they become questions of critical inquiry. Activities such as these support students in learning to frame effective questions while deepening their understanding of the subject matter and developing their capacity for critical thinking.

Throughout the process, encourage students to sustain their focus on critical inquiry by continuous self-monitoring and reflection on the quality and relevance of their questions. This helps to create self-directed, self-motivated students as their research empowers their thinking, leading to the creation of new knowledge rather than merely inviting regurgitation and organization of a body of information culled from other sources.

Assemble a list of five research questions or topics (either think of ones you have completed, look in a teacher resource, or ask students to suggest examples). Critique their effectiveness in light of the criteria discussed in this chapter (are open-ended, have broad significance, require thoughtful consideration). Keeping the same general topics, reframe each of these research projects into a more engaging critical inquiry.

Reflecting on Ideas and Strategies

Metacognition is a vital part of learning. Throughout an inquiry, students should be encouraged to take time to reflect on how the new information they uncover either challenges or affirms their beliefs, and to consider the validity of their conclusions in light of the evidence. Also important is self-reflection about the choices students make in conducting their research. Careful reflection occurs as students consider the nature of the questions they pose, assess the sources they are using, generate the criteria for guiding their decision making or judgments, weigh the evidence gathered in light of these criteria, consider the process by which they arrived at their conclusions and the validity of their conclusions, and finally, consider how purpose and audience will inform the presentation of their conclusions.

Instead of simply noting similarities and differences between people, places, or things (for example, in one community people make houses out of wood and in another, they make houses of ice), invite young students to reflect on the significance of the differences they notice. On their own or as a class, students might record or draw the features being compared (for example, types of houses, modes of travel, health conditions). Students would offer an assessment of the amount of difference between each of the compared features (for example, the houses are nearly the same, contain some differences, or are very different), and explain their thinking. After comparing individual features, students might offer an overall assessment of the degree of difference between the communities, then share their summary conclusions with the class.

Earlier we saw how provocative questions can be an effective means to frame a unit of study. These same questions can be used at the beginning of a unit to prompt student reflection on their prior knowledge and beliefs. Posing questions as an anticipation guide (see Figure 12.2 for an example) can be useful for raising important questions and garnering a sense of students' prior knowledge and attitudes before delving into a unit of study. Anticipation guides are generally used as a literacy strategy to prepare students to read a piece of text. Adapted, they become an excellent framework for a unit and a diagnostic activity. After responding to the anticipation guide questions, the teacher might debrief with students and explain that these are the essential questions for the unit. In fact, the questions can became focus questions for individual lessons and serve as the basis for an end-of-unit assessment.

Investigation

Being engaged by provocative questions primes the pump for learning, but providing support to meet the varying students' needs is vital if all students are to experience success. Before setting students free to conduct research, teachers need to lay some foundations. One such support are graphic organizers that can help students structure and make sense of the information they uncover in their investigations.

A teacher presentation road map can be a useful tool to help students learn from short lectures. Essentially, the road map "chunks" the teacher's presentation into meaningful pieces much like the outlines that are often put on the board before a talk begins. When using a road map, encourage students to record three or four key points in each box. Remembering that students can only pay attention for 10 to 15 minutes before needing to process what they have taken in, teachers should employ a think/pair/share strategy after addressing a couple of points on their presentation road map. This allows students to review what they have heard, share and support one another, and consolidate their learning by explaining their notes to their peers.

Another strategy to support students is collaborative note-taking (see Figure 12.3). Collaborative note-taking en-

FIGURE 12.2 ANTICIPATION GUIDE

Circle the answer that best describes your opinion.

1. Considering the causes of the War of 1812, it is difficult to assign blame to one country.

    Strongly agree   Agree   Don't know   Disagree   Strongly disagree

My explanation:

2. There were several heroic figures in the War of 1812.

    Strongly agree   Agree   Don't know   Disagree   Strongly disagree

My explanation:

3. The outcome of the war was determined by several key battles.

    Strongly agree   Agree   Don't know   Disagree   Strongly disagree

My explanation:

4. Considering the causes and outcome of the War of 1812, Canada was the winner of the war.

    Strongly agree   Agree   Don't know   Disagree   Strongly disagree

My explanation:

courages students to make point-form notes from a reading or during a presentation and then exchange notes with a peer. Each student reviews a fellow student's notes, adds information that was missed, and asks reflective questions. Afterwards, students jointly discuss and make notes on how the noted information connects with their world or with the central question(s) of the unit.

Students most often encounter Venn diagrams in mathematics classes. But consider their power when they are used to invite students to draw conclusions about the relationships between people, places, and things. For example, students might be asked to determine which of the Venn diagrams in Figure 12.4 best represents the relationship between the role of women in ancient Egypt and in contemporary Canadian society. In responding to this question, students would search a variety of sources including textbooks and websites, in order to locate words, phrases, or visuals that they can place within each circle to support their conclusion. It would be helpful for students to explain their conclusions in small groups and to adjust their findings based on the discussion.

Students need to search broadly for evidence and to consider multiple perspectives. To do this, they should consult a variety of sources to gather as many views as possible. They should be encouraged to gather information from various textual and non-textual sources (books and magazines, electronic sources, field visits to museums and other sites, visuals, interviews). They need to be taught how to read various text forms including a wide range of primary source material. Teachers should explicitly teach students how to read and decode visual text forms such as cartoons, artworks, and maps. (See other chapters in this volume for strategies on promoting these forms of information literacy.)

FIGURE 12.3 COLLABORATIVE NOTE-TAKING

Reflective questions:	My point-form notes on key facts, terms, ideas, and concepts:	Fellow students' additional notes:
Reflective questions:	• • • • • • • • •	• • • • • • • •
Reflective questions:		

Connections with other topics or the contemporary world:

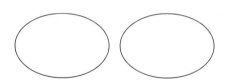

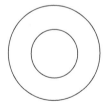

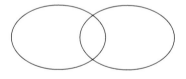

This graphic suggests that the role women played in the two societies was completely different and that there was no overlap or continuity.

This graphic suggests that the role of women expanded from ancient times (centre) so that by the present day in Canada, women were continuing to fulfill all the roles they had in ancient Egypt and had added several more roles.

This graphic suggests that while there were some roles they played in both societies, there were also roles unique to each society.

Sharing of Ideas

The opportunity to seek assistance, receive feedback, and hear responses from peers, parents, and teachers is a vital part of critical inquiry. As the previous examples suggest, graphic representations of ideas and conclusions are excel-lent vehicles enabling students to share their thoughts and conclusions prior to completing a summative task. Similarly, various forms of in-class debate and discussion, such as the "Academic Controversy" strategy described in the high-lighted text, provide a forum for the exchange of ideas that, when combined with reflection, extend student learning and challenge students' thinking. Infusing opportunities to share through inquiry provides students with feedback that will enrich their understanding of the curriculum.

Creating

Students' opportunities to create new knowledge through the fusion of prior knowledge and current learning are largely dependent on the nature of the tasks assigned by teachers. Tasks that are narrowly focussed on recall of pre-determined information preclude critical inquiry and present fewer opportunities for students to take ownership over their learning. Conversely, assessment tasks that invite students to engage in critical inquiry tend to encourage students to apply their learning in ways meaningful and relevant to the learner.

In effective classrooms, assessment drives instruction. Knowing what students are to achieve and how they will demonstrate it should be the basis on which daily instruction is planned. Differentiated assessment ensures that students with varying learning styles, interests, and aptitudes are given opportunities to demonstrate their learning. The key to differentiated assessment is establishing clear targets and not confusing methods with targets. For example, assessment targets might include student understanding of the "big ideas and concepts" being studied and the abilities to conduct research, think critically, and communicate their findings and conclusions effectively, considering purpose and audience. If these were the assessment targets (or objectives), then a variety of methods might be used to assess student learning. Students could write a report, prepare a visual essay, create a bulletin board display with relevant images and captions, or deliver an oral presentation. Encouraging students to select the best method to demonstrate their learning is yet another way to shift the focus of learning from teacher- to student-directed learning.

Assessment tasks can further student learning and not simply measure it; when clear targets are provided from the outset and when students receive frequent feedback, they then have opportunities to improve their work through revision, editing, and polishing. Throughout these tasks, students need appropriate scaffolding to ensure success and to encourage them to reflect on what they are learning (Earl 2003). At some time this may require allowing students to "fail forward." Learning from their mistakes can often provide powerful and lasting learning. But to have the confidence to fail forward, students need to know that their teacher is available to support them as needed and that failed attempts will not affect their final grade negatively. This requires that teachers embrace the concept of "assessment as learning" and provide feedback and guidance without grading students on the process of learning. Of course, at some point, students

ACADEMIC CONTROVERSY

Academic controversy is a strategy created by David and Roger Johnson (described in Bennett and Rolheiser 2001) that establishes small co-operative groups of four to six students to explore both sides of a designated issue. Each group is divided into A and B teams. The controversy is then identified in the positive (for example, "Canada should work with the United States to provide direct and indirect military aid to eradicate terrorism"). The A students prepare the "pro" side and the B students prepare the "con." Once students have prepared their opening arguments, each team shares its ideas with the opposing students. To encourage students to present ideas concisely, each team is allowed no more than ninety seconds. While each team presents its points, the opposing team practises active listening and takes notes. There should be no interruptions. Once both sides have presented their views, the A and B teams each gather to plan a rebuttal. In planning their rebuttal, they should consider the flaws in the opposing team's arguments. Each team has approximately sixty to ninety seconds to present its response. Once both sides have presented their rebuttal, the teams switch sides and repeat the process. The final step in the academic controversy, after students have presented opening points and rebuttals from both sides of the issue, is to hold a round robin. During the round robin, students explain where they stand on the issue individually.

will need to demonstrate their learning through some kind of performance; and teachers do need to grade students on performances.

The authentic assessment task described in the highlighted text "The Great Sandcastles/Snow Sculptures Competition," which is built around critical inquiry, challenges students to create and explain a replica of an ancient landmark.

> Think back to a research project you were asked to undertake in social studies. Using ideas discussed in the five elements of critical inquiry (ask, create, reflect, investigate, and share) suggest revisions to your original research project that would make it more personally engaging and educationally worthwhile.

Concluding Comments

Organizing the social studies curriculum around critical inquiry ensures a focus on key curricular ideas and concepts while allowing students to explore topics and issues of personal interest and relevance. In addition to engaging students,

THE GREAT SAND CASTLES/SNOW SCULPTURES COMPETITION[1]

The Challenge

Throughout the ages, people have created lasting landmarks. From the Great Pyramids of Egypt to the Great Wall of China, from the soaring cathedrals of medieval Europe to the grace and perfection of the Parthenon, architecture tells us much about the people who created the buildings.

The Great Sand Castle/Snow Sculpture Competition invites you to build an accurate scale model of an ancient site at a local beach or in the snow. To prepare for the challenge, you will need to find books with pictures and information about the site and the society that constructed the architecture. You will need to look carefully at the pictures and take research notes. Once you are familiar with the structure, its purpose, and the sponsoring society, you should prepare a detailed plan including a sketch, required tools, and any extra materials needed to construct the model out of sand or snow. You are also to prepare an informative viewers' guide in the form of a brochure that provides details of the original structure and explains why this structure best represents the early civilization from which it came. Information you might include in the brochure:

- Who built it?
- What was its purpose?
- Where was it built?
- When was it built?
- How was it built?
- Why is it an important site?

In meeting this challenge, you will work in groups of three to complete the steps outlined below.

Each Student's Responsibilities

- Prepare a bibliography of between four and seven sources.

- Prepare two to three pages of research notes and gather four or five visuals related to the society and the structure.
- Prepare a sketch of the structure.
- Write a 250- to 300-word summary explaining the purpose of the structure, its method of construction, and how the structure was reflective of various aspects of the society that built it, including:
    - the influence of religion on the social and/or political structure of the society;
    - social divisions within the society; and
    - the relationship between those in positions of authority and the general population.
- Actively participate in the construction of the scale model.
- Be able to explain the structure, its purpose and its relationship to the civilization which built it to observers.

Each Group's Responsibilities

- Establish deadlines for each of the steps relative to the date established by the teacher for the building of the structure.
- Assign responsibility to individuals for preparing the final sketch and gathering the tools and materials needed (one student), and preparing a viewer's guide (two students) and produce a group agreement which clearly lists the agreed due dates and individual responsibilities.
- Collaboratively scan sources to select a suitable structure.
- Prepare a detailed plan for the construction of the scale model drawing on the sketches and notes of group members.
- Gather necessary tools and resources in preparation for the construction of the model.
- Construct the scale model in sand or snow.

---

critical inquiry contributes to their cognitive development by challenging them to make decisions, solve problems, and draw connections. The ability to conduct focussed research and to analyze critically are crucial life skills.

There is no question that the most efficient means to "cover" an over-built curriculum is to teach from a teacher-focussed, lectured-based approach. Teaching students the skills they need to be successful takes time. Putting the proper scaffolding in place to assist them in meeting the expectations of the curriculum requires time spent on teaching critical thinking skills. And so the age-old debate rages on. Should teachers take the time to teach effectively or make sure they cover the entire curriculum? On closer inspection, however, it is evident that this debate exists only when curriculum is viewed through the eyes of the teacher. When viewed through the eyes of the learner, can there really be any debate? Should

we quickly cover curriculum knowing that little of what is taught is retained beyond the final exam, or should we develop students' ability to learn independently and to think critically about the world around them, thus preparing them for the challenges they will face for a lifetime? Perhaps we need to consider the success of our classes based on what students retain in the years to come rather than on ephemeral results of tests.

ENDNOTE

1   Details of the Great Sand Castles/Snow Sculptures Competition can be found in Newman (2001).

REFERENCES

Armstrong, D. and B. McMahon. 2002. Engaged pedagogy: Valuing the strengths of students on the margins. *Journal of Thought*, Spring.

Bennett, B. and C. Rolheiser. 2001. *Beyond Monet: The artful science of instructional integration.* Toronto: Bookation.

Earl, L. 2003. *Assessment as learning: Using classroom assessment to maximize student learning.* Los Angeles: Corwin Press.

McGaugh, J.L. 2003. *Memory and emotion.* London: Weidenfield and Nicolson.

McMahon, B. and J. Portelli. 2004. Engagement for what? Beyond popular discourses of student engagement. *Leadership and Policy in Schools* 3 (1): 59–76.

Newman, G. 2001. *Echoes from the past: Teacher's resource.* Toronto: McGraw-Hill Ryerson.

Wiggins, G. and J. McTighe. 1998. *Understanding by design.* Alexandria, VA: Association for Supervision and Curriculum Development.

13 Integrating Computer Technologies into Elementary Social Studies

Susan Gibson

Electronic information has assumed a new importance in schools. Teachers are under increasing pressure to ensure student mastery of the technological skills required in an information-based society. According to Leu, "The internet is entering classrooms at a rate faster than books, newspapers, magazines, movies, overhead projectors, television or even telephones" (2000, 425). This move to computerize has significant implications for social studies educators. Although computers are commonplace in most Canadian schools, many questions remain regarding their use in supporting and enhancing student learning. This chapter explores ideas and resources for making effective use of computers as a tool to support students in constructing knowledge in elementary social studies. More specifically, I address five areas:

- using the internet to access information;
- using the internet to organize and synthesize information;
- using computers to represent constructed knowledge;
- using computers as problem-solving tools; and
- using computers to facilitate communication and collaboration.

Before doing this, I want to briefly discuss what we know about the most effective uses of computers and the benefits they provide.

Educational Uses and Benefits

Over a decade of research indicates that the most effective uses of computers are in information processing and to enhance productivity in student completion of tasks. Software that allows students to apply new learnings as they work on projects—including databases, spreadsheets, multimedia, e-mail, and network search engines—show the most potential (Jonassen 1996). This is especially true when computer resources are used to support authentic tasks; when they facilitate visualization, analysis, and problem solving; and when they offer opportunities for feedback and revision (Means 2001). Computer resources used in these ways have the potential to develop intellectual skills of inquiry, reasoning, problem solving, decision making, and critical and creative thinking (Adams and Burns 1999; Boethel and Dimock 1999). An inquiry approach to learning with computers places less emphasis on acquiring and presenting information and more on constructing knowledge, making meaning, drawing on personal life experiences, and taking responsibility for one's learning. The most meaningful learning experiences with technology are those that are active, co-operative, constructive, intentional, and authentic (Jonassen, Howland, Moore, and Marra 2003).

The benefits of using computer tools such as the internet in these ways include the following:

- providing quicker and easier access to more extensive and current information in a variety of forms (graphs, pictures, text) and through a variety of modalities (auditory, visual), all of which increase students' motivation to further explore ideas;
- providing opportunities to research independently and explore more varied, real-world topics in greater depth at the learner's own pace, which puts more control over the learning into the hands of students, increases active engagement in their learning, and creates greater feelings of empowerment;
- enabling students to represent their learning in a variety of ways through the creation of original and innovative work that can be shared with a global audience;
- allowing students from different cultural or linguistic backgrounds with limited English proficiency to learn through the visual aspect of the information available and providing opportunities to use computers to improve their written and spoken abilities;
- providing assistive technologies for students with disabilities, including voice recognition systems, speech synthesizers, talking books, Braille display, image mag-

nifiers and specially designed keyboards that give visual, aural and tactile support and allow students to be more in control of their own learning experiences.

There is a wide variety of computer-related tools to facilitate students' inquiry and knowledge construction. Internet websites are useful resources for various stages of inquiry, including accessing information, organizing information, and representing results. The remainder of this chapter looks at specific examples of how to design meaningful computer-based learning experiences around inquiry, problem solving, communication, and collaboration. All of these uses treat students as active creators and shapers of their own knowledge who are able and willing to think for themselves (Boyer and Semrau 1995).

Using the Internet to Access Information

The internet is a valuable resource for supporting students in search of information related to an inquiry. The greatest advantage of the internet is that students have access to an abundance of up-to-date information from a variety of perspectives. Locating useful and accurate information can be a struggle, however. The profusion of things to access via the internet can easily sidetrack students, leading to a great deal of time off task. Information gathering can easily become a mindless exercise in which quantity overrides quality. This sort of information-gathering exercise does little to promote deeper thinking and understanding. There is also a danger that students will stumble on inappropriate sites, despite the use of Net Nanny and other protective software. Consequently, students need to become critical thinkers who can determine for themselves what makes a website inaccurate or inappropriate.

The teacher in the highlighted text "Ms. Stukowki's Internet Research Project" developed a strategy for helping her elementary students who were engaged in an inquiry project to identify useful information sources and decide what to do if an inappropriate site is accidentally accessed.

Ms. Stukowski recognizes that the "information glut" requires that students become information managers by developing the ability to use information purposefully and effectively (Todd, Lamb, and McNicholas 1992). Students must be taught to define the tasks for which information is needed, locate appropriate sources of information, select and record relevant information from sources, interpret and organize information for best application, present the information in an appropriate way, and evaluate the outcomes in terms of task requirements and knowledge acquired.

MS. STUKOWSKI'S INTERNET RESEARCH PROJECT[1]

Ms. Stukowski teaches a split grade 4/5 class this year. She wants her students to learn to be good problem solvers, users of multimedia software, and producers of their own multimedia presentations. In social studies, as a part of their study of Canada and the world, her students undertake a project that requires them to conduct research and create a computer presentation. The class has been divided into groups representing different regions of Canada and countries of the world. The challenge for each group is to prepare a multimedia production designed to "sell" their particular area to an audience of their peers. The grade 4 students are investigating provinces of Canada and the grade 5 students are looking at various countries. The class begins by brainstorming a list of topics to investigate including climate, resources, industries, occupations, population, cities, landscape, and interesting facts. Students begin data retrieval by accessing information from a number of sources to support each of the topics. The internet is the primary research resource. Ms. Stukowski teaches the children how to use search engines and how to judge the usefulness of a website using a strategy called "The Four As"—Accessible, Appealing, Appropriate, and Accurate. To ensure that they visit appropriate sites only, the children are also taught "If the picture isn't nice, hit the back button twice." This directive is posted in the computer lab as a reminder. The students use Google as their search engine. As well, students have access to electronic encyclopedias including Microsoft Encarta (IBM), The New Grolier Multimedia Encyclopedia (Mac), PC Globe (IBM/Mac) and The New Canadian Encyclopedia Plus (IBM/Mac) to provide images, video, text, and narration. Data collected from these various sources are recorded, organized, and stored initially in ClarisWorks (IBM), a word-processing program. The spreadsheet program found in ClarisWorks is used to organize and tally comparative information on Canada's regions and the selected countries of the world. Once the data are collected, organized, and synthesized, students create a multimedia presentation using HyperStudio (for Mac). Each group presents its slide show on their region/country to the whole class using a Smartboard device attached to a classroom computer.

Critical literacy skills must be carefully taught and monitored to ensure students are developing proficiency in their use. Children need to be instructed and have opportunities to practise examining critically and making appropriate informed, ethical choices. They must be taught to recognize that each website represents a particular viewpoint and that it is important to examine several points of view on any issue.

It is also important to address concerns about plagiarism and copyright involving the internet. The website of the Media Awareness Network (www.media-awareness.ca) is an excellent Canadian source for ideas about developing critical literacy and for information on plagiarism and copyright.

There are countless controlled educational sites that deal with social studies topics. The highlighted text "Controlled Educational Sites" describes three kinds of these sites: scavenger and treasure hunts, virtual field trips, and virtual museums.

> Select a topic from the curriculum or from a student textbook. Search the internet to locate possible sources that students might access, or consult resources prepared in an abridged form. Develop an activity in which students are not simply finding information at these sites but also using the information to reach a conclusion on some issue.

Using the Internet to Organize and Synthesize Information

In addition to learning to locate and evaluate information on the world wide web, students' inquiry and knowledge construction can be supported with web-based tools for synthesizing and organizing. Databases, such as the Statistics Canada database featured on the next page, are useful for integrating information from a variety of sources, stimulating critical thinking, visualizing complex historical relationships, and developing conceptual understanding (Ehman and Glenn 1991). Databases can be structured by the teacher or left open-ended so students can select the information they wish to represent and then design the database to represent that information. The spreadsheet is another tool that can be used to store, organize, and analyze data. Most word-processing programs

CONTROLLED EDUCATIONAL SITES

Scavenger Hunts and Treasure Hunts

Scavenger-hunt and treasure-hunt websites are good places to introduce searches to students by getting them used to accessing information, navigating around different types of websites, and reading to locate specific information. Scavenger hunts and treasure hunts provide topic-related searching challenges for students using pre-selected websites. One example, the Ancient Olympic Cyberhunt (found at www2.lhric.org/pocantico/olympics/ancienthunt.htm), provides a series of questions about the first Olympics and then provides links to specific websites where children search for appropriate responses. This is also a good way to begin a resource list for further research support throughout a unit of study on ancient Greece. Another site, the Cyberhunt Kids' Library (found at www.teacher.scholastic.com/products/instructor/cyberhunt_kids.htm), offers similar activities on the Aztecs, ancient Chinese, Vikings, and Columbus.

Virtual Field Trips

Virtual field trips can be used to support student inquiry and knowledge construction as they allow students to travel through time and space to places that would otherwise be out of reach. Often these tours provide images and text describing the particular site being toured. For example using the topic of China, students can access interactive sites (such as www.cobb.k12.ga.us) and then type "China" in the search space. This site features the Great Wall of China, the Forbidden City, the terracotta soldiers, Tiananmen Square, views of the cities and the countryside, and other geographical features of the country. These visuals give children important contextual information to help them personalize their study of a country from afar. The VirtualTourist website (www.virtualtourist.com) allows children to take virtual trips through any country in the world simply by highlighting their choice on a world map. The study of the history of Canada's peoples can be enhanced through

the Underground Railroad site (www.nationalgeographic.com/features/99/railroad) which is a virtual field trip following the footsteps of Harriet Tubman, who led hundreds of runaway slaves to freedom.

Virtual Museums

Students can access the collections of a number of virtual museums. Through these sites, they can analyze primary documents and engage in the processes that historians use (Bass and Rosenzweig 1999). One site, assembled by the Canadian Broadcasting Corporation (archives.cbc.ca) contains clips from radio and television stories about people, conflict and war, disasters and tragedies, arts and entertainment, politics and economy, life and society, science and technology, and sports. The site has a teacher section that includes educational materials and activity ideas for using the resources provided at the website. Other web-based news services can also be used to help students develop critical awareness of current events. (See, for example, www.newsworld.cbc.ca and www.mycanadiannews.com).

Canada's Digital Collections (collections.ic.gc.ca) provides artifacts addressing Canadian history, culture, aboriginal communities, and Canadian landscapes. Students can submit proposals to create their own web pages about some aspect of Canadian history. From this website, students can also access the Canadian Aboriginal Digital Collections by clicking on "First Peoples." The Memory Project (www.thememoryproject.com) involves students in sharing the oral history of Canadians in three areas: Passage to Canada, Peace and War, and Heroes and Heroism. Two other web-based Canadian museum collections that social studies teachers should find useful are the Canadian Museum of Civilization (www.civilization.ca) and the Virtual Museum of New France (www.civilization.ca/vmnf/vmnfe.asp).

have built-in spreadsheet and database applications that make these tools easily accessible for teachers and students.

Visual organizers are another set of tools that can be used for organizing information. Inspiration (www.inspiration.com) and the more child-friendly version, Kidspiration (linked from the Inspiration Software home page), are concept-mapping tools that can be used in the early stages of research to brainstorm ideas and check on children's understanding of a topic or concept. "By uncovering students' individual understandings, teachers can determine the influence of students' prior knowledge and further their education through new experience" (Adams and Burns 1999, 25). Graphic organizers can also be accessed at the Graphic Organizer website (www.graphic.org).

Using Computers to Represent Constructed Knowledge

The internet can be useful for representing the results of the inquiry. Children can create and post their own work on web pages. Not only does this add authenticity and relevance to the learning, but it also allows students to become designers and publishers rather then simply users of information (Staley 2000). For example, Our Roots: Canada's Local Histories Online (www.ourroots.ca) contains web pages featuring the results of student inquiry. In one project entitled "The Artistry of the Land: Ancient Stories of our First Nations Peoples," grade 2 and 3 students have posted journal entries about their explorations into the culture of the First Nations people in their area. In the highlighted text, "Madame Garnier's Constructed Research Project," a grade 3 teacher tells why she chose to use a webpage to represent what her students had learned during their study of ancient civilizations.

HyperCard programs are another kind of a computer-based presentation tool. Earlier, I discussed Ms. Stukowski's use of this tool with her grade 4 and 5 students. HyperStudio (www.hyperstudio.com) is a multimedia student-authoring program that provides students with the opportunity to experience a multi-sensory learning environment. With this tool, students can create their own interactive multimedia presentations, including graphics, video, animation, and sound to meet their differing learning needs. Slide shows can also be created in ClarisWorks, KidPix, Microsoft PowerPoint, Adobe Persuasion, or Corel Presentations. Using computers for product-oriented projects such as designing multimedia presentations can be highly motivating for students. Students learn not only how to organize information for their presentation using these tools, but also how to create their own representations of their knowledge about a topic, which increases their ability to express their individuality and their unique perspectives (Boethel and Dimock 1999).

Using Computers as Problem-Solving Tools

Although the majority of school-related work on the world wide web is directed to searching for information on a topic, it has great potential as a motivating force in social studies by engaging students in simulations and WebQuests. Simulations can be powerful tools for making abstract content and complex ideas more accessible to learners (Goldman, Cole, and Syer 1999; Schacter and Fagnano 1999). "Utilizing computer modelling as a visualization (can be) a powerful bridge between experience and abstraction" (Dede 2000, 172). Participatory simulation software can also help students "develop a sense of empathy for the subject and jettison contemporary assumptions and values to understand an event as it really was" (Staley 2000, 9). Providing students with such alternative ways to learn, including both verbal and non-verbal ways, can be of help to those with mild learning disorders (Shields and Behrmann 2000).

Careful selection is important to an effective social studies program if simulation software is being used. Before deciding on a software program, familiarize yourself with its contents, as you would with any other resource. Consider the level of interactivity the software promotes. Software that has a drill-and-practise format tends to have the purpose of transmitting information and then ascertaining student recall of that information through lower-level questioning and built-in right-answer tests. Some software programs cover only a very narrow slice of a topic and at times deal with content that is outside the curriculum. For example, game-like simulations like The Yukon Trail and The Oregon Trail provide opportunities to engage students in decision making, but their content is limited. While students are asked to role-play and make decisions about such things as the best route to take

and the necessary supplies to buy, they remain largely passive in these activities. Others like Where in the World is Carmen Sandiego? and Carmen Sandiego's Great Chase Through Time teach some knowledge about world geography and history respectively, but they are highly game-like and may perhaps be best used during "free time" or in an interest centre. However, software like the Tom Snyder series Decisions, Decisions 5.0 engages students in collaboratively and interactively investigating issues such as prejudice, violence in the media, lying and cheating, and saving the environment. (See "Geography-Related Simulations" for additional resource ideas.)

You will want to consider how much of a particular unit the software covers and where it would best be used. Some software is excellent as a unit opener because it can act as a motivator and pique students' interest in a topic. For example, as part of a social studies unit on the study of the geography of Canada, a game like Cross Country Canada could be used to begin the investigation of the topic since children are actively engaged in facing many problem-solving situations as they "drive" an eighteen-wheel truck across Canada to pick up and deliver various commodities. Other software programs may best be included as part of the development phase of the unit to assist in the teaching and learning of specific content and skills. A software selection such as Adventure Canada would help students learn about Canada by actively involving them in explorations of Canadian culture, people, and history. Other pieces of software may be selected because they would be useful as a closure to the unit. A good fit as a closure to the study of Canadian geography, for example, might be The Great Canadian Adventure because students could use it to review their learning about the geographical features of Canada. (See "Web-Based Historical Artifacts" for additional online opportunities to engage students in solving problems using primary documents.)

Another web-based activity for developing problem-solving skills is WebQuest. WebQuest is a specially designed website that engages students in a task or inquiry to solve a problem using web-based resources (Dodge 1996). Most of the resources used for the inquiry are other websites that have been vetted and linked directly to the WebQuest site. Through WebQuest, students can actively explore issues from a number of different viewpoints, find answers, and reach moral and ethical decisions about real contemporary world problems. A WebQuest can help to develop critical and creative thinking, problem-solving, and decision-making skills. WebQuests can easily be tailored for diverse needs in the classroom.

A WebQuest is typically divided into five sections (see the samples on the next page). The first part of the WebQuest lays out the task or the problem to be investigated. Students are then assigned roles or provided with differing perspectives on the issue or problem being investigated. Working either in-

GEOGRAPHY-RELATED SIMULATIONS

Tom Snyder Productions has several pieces of software that could be used to teach children geography skills. A program like Geography Search engages students in learning about latitude, longitude, the earth's rotation, weather, and wind patterns by simulating an ocean voyage. The Inspirer Geography Series has students investigate issues related to world geography collaboratively. The Neighbourhood Map Machine involves younger learners in constructing maps to learn about directional terms. Another program, The National Geographic Atlas of the World, allows young learners who are unfamiliar with a term to interact with the text through voice replication and pictures. Such use not only develops mapping skills but provides reading instruction as well (Wood 2000). Further opportunities for authentic learning can be built into a unit on geographic skills through a site like the ESRI corporation's website (www.esri.com), which allows students to create and manipulate layers of maps to collect detailed information about a place. Two other internet resources that provide opportunities for map creation are the Map Maker pages at the Canadian Geographic website (www.canadiangeographic.ca/mapping/mapmaker/default.asp) and Natural Resources Canada's Atlas of Canada website (www.atlas.gc.ca/site/english/index.html).

WEB-BASED HISTORICAL ARTIFACTS

Websites can also provide problem situations for students to solve. The UK National Archives Learning Curve website (www.learningcurve.gov.uk) is an excellent example of a web-based museum collection that presents a number of issues for students to investigate using primary documents. For example, there is a section on the evacuation of British children to Canada during World War II. Using this website, students can engage in a problem-solving activity that requires them to examine primary source evidence, including official Canadian and British government documents and records, to investigate the issue of child evacuation during wartime. The Children of World War II site (www.bbc.co.uk/history/ww2children/index.shtml) addresses a similar issue. Here students use photos, posters, letters, documents, radio clips, and sounds to investigate topics including a wartime home, rationing, and being an evacuee.

The McCord Museum offers a free online "history laboratory" in which images and objects from 1840–1945 are given a central role (www.mccord-museum.qc.ca). This laboratory draws upon the Keys to History resource, a database of 110,000 images of artifacts, developed in collaboration with seven other Canadian museums. This fully bilingual world wide web resource provides tools that allow students to access information, organize and synthesize facts, and share knowledge. They are invited to analyze primary documents and engage in the process that historians or museologists use. Thematic tours (through video, images, and text) provide insights into major events in Canadian history and aspects of daily life that shaped the Canadian experience.

Observation, quizzes, and role-playing games include: placing objects in their proper context; recreating period dress; discovering the identity of unusual objects; locating the odd man out in period settings; finding the link between two historical figures; and Mind Your Manners! (a game that explores the Victorian period and the Roaring Twenties). Although these resources and tools were developed for the general public and for secondary schools, they would also be of interest to upper elementary classes.

Another creative tool at the McCord Museum site is the Web Folder that allows users to create their own visual presentation based on images from the collections, adding comments, personal images, and hyperlinks. Using this tool, students carry out their inquiry and can integrate resources from elsewhere. The Web Folder presentations are saved on the server, where they can be printed, downloaded to the user's computer, or presented in front of the class.

dependently or in groups, they explore the issue or problem under guidance and in a manner that is meaningful to them. Students access the information provided, analyze it, synthesize and evaluate it, then transform it in some way to demonstrate their understanding of the particular view which they are to take in response to the problem being investigated. They then share their findings with the whole class. The teacher acts as a facilitator, checking to see that students understand the role they are to take, and that they are on task.

Using Computers to Facilitate Communication and Collaboration

Computer technologies can be helpful in developing communication and collaborative skills. Students are fascinated by the possibilities of electronic communication for exchanging ideas about topics of mutual interest with other students and adults in different parts of the world. Collaboration among learners within and beyond the classroom walls can be enhanced through the use of computers. Information gathered

SAMPLE WEBQUESTS

In a WebQuest entitled "Does the Tiger Eat Its Cubs?" (www.kn.pacbell.com/wired/China/childquest.html) students explore the way children in orphanages in China are treated. The question that students investigate is "What's the truth about how children are treated in China?" Students are directed to investigate the information from various perspectives. They are divided into three teams. One team reads international news reports, another reads responses from the Chinese people, and a third examines the government of China's position using China's One Child Policy. The class then collectively discusses their findings with the challenge of reaching a consensus decision on the issue. The culminating task is to write a letter to the government expressing their opinion on what can be done about the situation.

In the Ancient Egypt WebQuest (www.iwebquest.com/egypt/ancientegypt.htm), students are sent on a mission to locate the burial mask of the ancient Egyptian Pharaoh Tutankhamun which contains a coded message that if decoded could help solve the earth's environmental crisis.

WebQuest databases can be searched both for specific grade levels and subject areas (see, for example, webquest.sdsu.edu).

in this fashion is viewed by students as being more connected to "real" local, national, and global issues. Interactive web-based collaborative projects are an excellent way to engage students in projects with other students and experts from around the world. Some research contends that gender bias pervades computer technologies and makes computers less friendly for girls; however, electronic participation has been found to be more gender-equitable and can counteract male dominance (Linn 1999). As well, providing opportunities for collaborative activity through the use of technology has been shown to heighten girls' interest in computing (Butler 2000).

Communication tools such as e-mail, listservs, bulletin boards, newsgroups, and chat groups build on students' desire to communicate and share their understandings. Computer networking also allows students to communicate and collaborate with content experts and fellow students around the globe. Online conversations through e-mail can prompt reflection and help students to think about their ideas and how best to articulate those ideas so that they are clear to others. Such conversations also encourage self-checking for understanding and identification of inaccuracies in one's own expressed ideas, which can lead to rethinking and reframing of former ideas.

According to a report from SchoolNet (Industry Canada 2002, 1–2) the benefits of a telecollaborative approach to learning include:

- placing students in a position where they can discover the world and share the results of their experiences;
- involving learners in new roles as active participants, creative interpreters of the world, and experienced collaborators; and
- providing for a greater range of learning by doing and constructing content.

Through the use of electronic communication, children are able to speak for themselves. Online chat allows more than one student to "talk" at the same time. As well, a world wide web opportunity like e-mates gives students an opportunity to interact with a real audience without the inhibiting factor of peer pressure (Richards 2000). It "frees the child with special needs from fear of being stigmatized as well as enabling them to network with other children to share feelings about having a disability" (Shields and Behrmann 2000, 13). E-mail and threaded discussions can "act as a conduit rather than an impediment to conversation" (Richards 2000, 4).

There is great potential for computer technologies to help develop effective citizens, since students gain first-hand knowledge of other cultures through online learning communities. Such increased exposure to first-hand information could potentially overcome students' insular views of the world. Some scholars suggest that broader exposure to other cultures through increased internet access can spread democratic ideals internationally and help stem the growth of potentially incendiary nationalism (Githiora-Updike 2000, 63). Staley (2000, 9) calls online discussions "a type of democratic performance."

The highlighted text "Mrs. Brown's Telecollaboration Project" is the story of one teacher who used daily electronic updates to enhance her students' learning about life in the Far North. Other examples can be found on the next page.

Making Do With Limited Computers

Before closing I would like to discuss the possibilities for making maximum use of computing if a computer lab is not avail-

MRS. BROWN'S TELECOLLABORATION PROJECT

Mrs. Brown's grade 6 students are working on an Iditarod project, a study of the dogsled race held annually in the Arctic. The Iditarod project is part of a unit on survival that integrates science (focussing on weather, snow studies, and animals of the North) with social studies (through map work and a study of life in the North on the tundra). Activities include reading novels; writing; construction of models, puppets and dioramas; drawing; weather and newspaper reporting; and winter survival experiences such as quinzhee building, outdoor cooking, and snow studies. Students interact via e-mail with outside experts, including a former racer. A major aspect of this project requires students to choose a particular dogsled team and musher to follow through the course of the race, updating their information and standings each day. For this project, students have to access the internet because the information required for daily updating

and following the race is not available elsewhere. Working in groups, students use the internet to read online stories, investigate weather conditions along the route, track and report on the mushers, and check for survival conditions associated with the race. On one particular day, they are surprised to discover that one of the teams in the lead the previous day is now in thirteenth place. Another team is running with one less dog and two teams have been scratched from the race. The teacher challenges the students to find out why through further internet investigations. They locate information about care of dogs, care of the runners, and surviving outdoors in winter weather conditions, including dressing for warmth and attention to dehydration, all of which is then used by students to plan an outdoor excursion as a culmination to the unit of study.

CONNECTED LEARNING PROJECTS

The Global Schoolhouse (www.globalschoolnet.org/GSH/index.html) provides opportunities for students to engage in over nine hundred telecollaborative projects, many of them relevant to social studies. One project, Friends and Flags, is designed for K–12 classrooms to promote multicultural awareness by assigning children to international learning teams. Students interact through discussion boards and chat rooms as well as view each other's work. Some examples of their work include peace poetry, art galleries, quilt patches, and a holiday corner. At this website, children can engage in online expeditions with adventurers as they travel around the world. Through daily updates on the world wide web and through conversational discussion boards, students can ask questions of the adventurers and keep in touch with the latest discoveries as the journeys unfold. There are also opportunities to plan an individualized online expedition and to find worldwide partners who may wish to partner up with other classes for an adventure.

Global Learn Day (www.gsn.org/GLD/index.cfm) is another website that offers online expeditions twice a year where a team of explorers is sent to different parts of the world to document local environments and ways of life. These explorers post journals, research logs, and photos to the website each day. Classes can send messages to the explorers, and teachers can customize their study of the expedition to meet students' needs and interests by choosing materials and activities suited to their students' needs.

able and you have only one computer in your classroom. One idea is to set the computer up as a learning station where students work in groups on certain aspects of research projects that require access to the internet. Rotate each group through the computer station so that everyone has access to internet resources at some point in the inquiry. Only one computer is needed if you have a projection device to allow you to share simulations and WebQuests with the entire class. In the case of a WebQuest, the home page of the site can be projected onto a screen at the front of the class and the teacher can walk the class through each step. When students are divided into task groups, the materials can be printed off for each group and the remainder of the WebQuest can be completed without accessing the computer, or with rotating access to the one classroom computer by each group. You can also use educational software or internet sites from the front of the classroom to anchor learning or guide a discussion. (See www.teachnet.com/how-to/organization/onecompclass040799.html for other ideas about using one or a few computers in the classroom).

> Select a topic from the curriculum or from a student textbook. Using electronic resources mentioned in this chapter or located elsewhere, develop an activity in which students use computers not to gather information but to solve problems or organize and synthesize ideas. Plan how you will help students undertake this knowledge-construction task using the computer.

Concluding Remarks

The main focus of this chapter is the efficient and effective integration of computers into the curriculum and specifically the use of the internet to help students construct knowledge. I believe that the most effective uses of computer technologies are those that foster meaningful learning by engaging learners in authentic, inquiry-oriented learning experiences that recognize the active role of the learner in constructing meaning about the world. A number of internet-based tools provide support for students throughout their inquiry. These tools—including virtual museums and field trips, spreadsheets and databases, concept-mapping tools, and simulations—have the potential, if used in meaningful ways, to develop students' ability to think critically and creatively, solve problems, make sound decisions, and collaborate with one another.

ENDNOTES

1   The teacher stories provided in this chapter are based on actual classroom examples collected as part of a three-year study supported by the Social Sciences and Humanities Research Council on internet use in Canadian schools. The teachers and their schools have been given pseudonyms to guarantee anonymity.

REFERENCES

Adams, S. and M. Burns. 1999. *Connecting student learning and technology.* Southwest Austin, TX: Educational Development Laboratory.

Bass, R. and R. Rosenzweig, R. 1999. Rewriting the history and social studies classroom: Needs, frameworks, dangers, and proposals. *Journal of Education* 181 (3): 41–61.

Boethel, M. and V. Dimock. 1999. *Constructing knowledge with technology: A review of the literature.* Southwest Austin, TX: Educational Development Laboratory.

Boyer, B. and P. Semrau. 1995. A constructivist approach to social studies: Integrating technology. *Social Studies and the Young Learner* 7 (3): 14–16.

Butler, D. 2000. Gender, girls, and computer technology: What's the status now? *Clearing House* 73 (4), March–April: 225–229.

Dede, C. 2000. A new century demands new ways of learning. In *Digital classroom: How technology is changing the way we teach and learn,* ed., D. T. Gordon, 171-174. Cambridge: MA: Harvard Education Letter.

Diem, R. 1997. Paradigms for pre-service teachers: emphasis on technological integration. *Technology and Teacher Education Annual.*

Dodge, B. 1996. Active learning on the web. Available online at http://edweb.sdsu.edu/people/bdodge/active/ActiveLearningk-12.html.

Ehman, L., and A. Glenn. 1991. Interactive technology in the social studies. In *Handbook of research in social studies teaching and learning,* ed. J. P. Shaver, 513–522. New York: Macmillan.

Githiora-Updike, W. 2000. The global schoolhouse. In *Digital classroom: How technology is changing the way we teach and learn,* ed. D.T. Gordon, 60–66. Cambridge, MA: Harvard Education Letter.

Goldman, S., K. Cole, and C. Syer. 1999, July 12–13. *The technology/content dilemma. Evaluating the effectiveness of technology proceedings.* Washington, DC: Eric Document No. ED452821.

Industry Canada. 2002. A study of grassroots projects: Online project-based collaborative learning. Available online at http://www.schoolnet.ca/alasource/e/resources/toolkit/tele/index.asp.

Jonassen, D. 1996. *Computers in the classroom: Mindtools for critical thinking.* Englewood Cliffs, NJ: Prentice-Hall.

Jonassen, D., J. Howland, J. Moore, and M. Marra. 2003. *Learning to solve problems with technology.* Upper Saddle River, NJ: Merrill Prentice Hall.

Leu, D. 2000. Exploring literacy on the internet. *The Reading Teacher* 53 (5), February: 424–429.

Linn, E. 1999. Gender equity and computer technology. *Equity Coalition* V, Fall.

Means, B. 2001. Technology use in tomorrow's schools. *Educational Leadership* 58 (4): 57–61.

Richards, G.A. 2000. Why use computer technology? *English Journal* 90 (2), November: 38–41.

Schacter, J. and C. Fagnano. 1999. Does computer technology improve student learning and achievement? How, when, and under what conditions? *Journal of Educational Computing Research* 20 (4): 329–343.

Shields, M.K. and R.E. Behrman. 2000. Children and computer technology: analysis and recommendations. *Future of Children* 10 (2), Fall–Winter: 4–30.

Staley, D.J. 2000. Technology, authentic performance, and history education. *International Journal of Social Education* 15 (1): 1–12.

Todd, R., L. Lamb, and C. McNicholas. 1992. The power of information literacy: Unity of education and resources for the 21st century. Paper presented at the annual meeting of the International Association of School Librarianship, Belfast, North Ireland.

Wood, J. 2000. Literacy: *Charlotte's Web* meets the world wide web. In *Digital classroom: How technology is changing the way we teach and learn,* ed. D.T. Gordon, 117–125. Cambridge, MA: Harvard Education Letter.

14 Reading Comprehension Strategies in Social Studies

Paul Neufeld

Historical Neglect

The importance of teaching reading comprehension strategies in social studies should be obvious. Since social studies is, after all, a text-laden subject, being able to read and comprehend texts effectively is crucial for success. Despite research confirming that students can effectively be taught strategies for improving their reading comprehension (National Reading Panel 2000), such instruction rarely occurs (Durkin 1978/79, Pressley 2002a).

Before World War I, little thought was directed towards teaching students how better to comprehend what they were reading. Reading instruction consisted of oral reading practice, the hallmarks of which were accurate and fluent recognition and pronunciation of words. In the decade after the war, the emphasis shifted from improving oral reading towards gaining meaning from text. For the next forty years, reading comprehension instruction consisted largely of students answering teacher-presented questions about specific selections (Pearson and Dole 1987). Dolores Durkin, after observing more than ten thousand minutes of instruction in her landmark study of reading and social studies instruction, concluded that giving, completing, and checking assignments consumed a large part of the teaching periods and that no actual instruction in how to comprehend was taking place (1978/79, 481). Despite the importance of reading in social studies and other subjects, and a growing body of research suggesting the efficacy of teaching students how to comprehend, more than two decades after Durkin's famous study, researchers continue to document the limited extent to which such instruction actually occurs (Pressley 2002b).

In this chapter, I present the basic principles and introductory tools required to teach reading comprehension in social studies. In the process, I hope to communicate why reading comprehension instruction should not be viewed as the exclusive domain of English/language arts but instead has an important place in social studies. I begin by defining reading comprehension and outlining the role of thinking in reading comprehension. The bulk of the chapter looks at specific reading comprehension strategies and offers a framework for developing self-regulated student use of a repertoire of these strategies.

Reading Comprehension as Thinking

Comprehension is defined here as constructing a reasonable understanding of a text. Three principles underlie this deceptively simple definition: 1) comprehending a text requires active, intentional thinking through which a reader constructs meaning (Alexander and Jetton 2000); 2) varying interpretations of texts are to be expected because of differences in people's background knowledge and experiences; and 3) not all interpretations of a given text can be considered valid (Pressley 2002b). Clearly, comprehension is a function both of what the reader brings to the text (for example, his or her background knowledge of the topic) and the ideas conveyed through the words themselves. Thus, two students reading the same historical account may reach differing impressions about some aspects of the text. If both readers have comprehended the text, however, the essence they extract from the story should be similar (Pressley 2002b).

Comprehending a written text is a multifaceted undertaking, requiring both automatic and intentional thinking. Readers must engage in thinking at the word level (for example, decoding of words, accessing one's memory of word meanings) and at what has been called the above-word level. Thinking at the above-word level consists of the purposeful use of procedural or "how-to" strategies when attempting to comprehend a text (Alexander and Judy 1988). Although my focus in this chapter is solely on developing above-word-level strategies, other challenges to reading comprehension must not be overlooked. These include attending to the reader's general knowledge of the world and specific knowledge of the particular topic; knowledge of relevant vocabulary; the ability to activate such knowledge; and competence in word-level processes such as decoding and fluency (that is, the ability to read at an appropriate rate and with expression). Difficulties in any of these areas may render above-word-level strategies unavailable to the reader. Consequently, comprehension-strategy instruction should complement, not replace, various long-standing practices such as providing vocabulary instruction and building students' background knowledge prior to having them read.

A substantial body of research supports the value of teaching students to use question asking and answering to support their efforts to comprehend what they read (Rosenshine, Meister, and Chapman 1996). Question asking and answering can be viewed as the foundation for all the other strategies. In other words, the process of asking and then answering questions of oneself and of the text activates the other strategies. What differs from one to the next is the type of questions one asks. Developing the ability to ask and answer questions of oneself and the text before, during, and after reading is an essential part of becoming a strategic reader. The ultimate goal is for question asking and answering to become a habit—a natural and pervasive part of a student's reading routine.

Without guidance, many students will not spontaneously generate and use effective question asking and answering strategies. These students will benefit from explicit instruction in a few well-researched strategies, and ongoing guidance in learning to select, activate, and use the strategies without direct prompting from others (Pressley 1998). The strategies described below can be applied regardless of the kind and length of the text—whether one is reading whole books, research articles, chapters within books, or passages within chapters.

Reading Comprehension Strategies

Researchers have identified many individual reading comprehension strategies that are both teachable and useful. These strategies can be clustered into two groups: pre-reading strategies, and during- and after-reading strategies (Schuder 1993).

PRE-READING STRATEGIES

As the name suggests, these strategies help students comprehend texts by involving them in thinking about the text before they actually start to read it. Four of these strategies are discussed below.

- **Clarify a purpose for reading.** A simple but important first step is to encourage students to think consciously about the crucial question: why they are about to read a particular text. Some common reasons for reading social studies texts are to prepare for a class discussion, study for a test, or gather important information for completing a task such as writing a paper. Questions for students to ask include:
  - Why am I reading this text?
  - How should my purpose affect the way I read the text?
- **Overview the text.** Overviewing involves quickly surveying the text before reading it. The intent is to develop an overall sense of the text, determine its relevance to the purpose for reading, and identify sections that are particularly relevant to the purpose. Implementing this strategy involves considering the title and major headings, reading the introduction and conclusion, and examining text support features such as tables and graphs, with the purpose of answering questions such as the following:
  - What does this text appear to be about?
  - What major topics are covered in the text?
  - What text structure(s) does the author use to present the information? (for example, enumeration, time order, compare and contrast, cause and effect, problem/solution)
- **Activate prior knowledge.** Having developed a general sense of the content and organization during the overviewing process, readers can invoke knowledge they already possess that may be relevant to the text. Prior knowledge provides a mental connection linking ideas in the text with the reader's existing knowledge of the topic and the world. This practice has been shown to improve both recall and comprehension (Anderson and Pearson 1984). At this point, typical questions for students to ask and answer include:
  - What do I already know or think I know about this topic?
  - How does what I already know about this topic relate to this particular text?
- **Make predictions about the text.** Students can learn to make predictions about a text by drawing on answers produced using the overview strategy and by drawing on prior knowledge of the topic (Pressley 2002b). For instance, after scanning an article on the history of the Olympics, a student might forecast that the text will provide information about sports such as wrestling that were popular in ancient Greece. Such predictions can then be used as hypotheses to test as the student is reading. A typical prediction question for students to ask and answer is:
  - I think this text is going to be about …

Before reading any further, review the questions to ask and answer when overviewing a text. Apply this strategy to the rest of the chapter and then read the chapter to test how well you were able to develop an overall sense of this part and to identify particularly relevant sections.

DURING- AND AFTER-READING STRATEGIES

According to Pressley and Wharton-McDonald (1997), students should learn to use strategies while reading a given text and after they finish reading it, as well as use strategic thinking before beginning. Strategies applied during these phases are intended to help students: 1) understand and remember what they have read; and 2) monitor their comprehension and remedy misunderstandings when breakdowns in comprehension occur. As was the case with pre-reading strategies, readers' ability and inclination to ask and answer questions of the text, and of themselves, drives the use of any particular strategy. Three types of strategies are addressed.

- **Analyze text structure.** The term "text structure" refers to the organizational logic of a text. It identifies the form in which information is organized for presentation. Most texts are written using relatively few organizational structures—enumeration, time order, compare and contrast, cause and effect, problem/solution, and description (see Table 14.1, "Common Text Structures"). As shown in Table 14.2, adapted from categories proposed by Vacca and Vacca (1999), each of these text structures, with the exception of description, is typically associated with a set of keywords that readers can use to identify the particular structure or structures.

Helping students identify organizational structure facilitates their comprehension (Taylor and Beach 1984). For instance, recognizing that a particular text compares and contrasts the leadership styles of former prime ministers provides a framework for understanding the information presented. Not surprisingly, once students learn to identify organizational structures, they can apply this strategy when overviewing texts before reading them.

TABLE 14.1	COMMON TEXT STRUCTURES	
TEXT STRUCTURE	**EXPLANATION**	**VISUAL REPRESENTATION**
Enumeration	Lists items or ideas that follow in order (for example, stages in the passage of legislation, instructions for building an igloo).	
Time order	Lists a sequence of events in time (for example, the daily schedule of a pioneer, major events in the history of a civilization).	
Compare and contrast	Highlights similarities and differences between two or more things or events (for example, comparing life in nineteenth and twenty-first century Canada, differences between capitalism and communism).	
Cause and effect	Shows how events (causes) lead to other events (effects) (for example, causes of poverty, escalation of violence in a dispute).	
Problem/solution	Shows the development of a problem and one or more solutions (for example, dealing with pollution or traffic congestion).	
Description	Presents the main features of a person, event, object, or scene (for example, conditions for new immigrants, daily life in a community).	

TABLE 14.2 USEFUL WORD CLUES

	ENUMERATION	TIME ORDER	COMPARE AND CONTRAST	CAUSE AND EFFECT	PROBLEM/ SOLUTION
Keywords	to begin with first secondly next then finally most important also in fact for instance for example	on (date) not long after now as before after when following	however but as well as on the other hand not only … but also either … or while although unless similarly yet	because since therefore consequently as a result this led to so that nevertheless accordingly if … then thus	

Key questions for students to ask are:

* Do I see any keywords associated with specific text structures?
* What text structures are used to present the information? (for example, enumeration, time order, compare and contrast, cause and effect, problem/solution)

* **Summarize the text.** Another strategy is to teach students to summarize coherently and briefly what they have read. Creating well-developed summaries is difficult. To support this task, students are advised to ask and answer questions such as "What organizational structure(s) does the author use to present the information?", "What is the gist of the text?", and "What are the author's main points?".

  * *Oral summaries.* Duke and Pearson (2002) recommend the use of oral summaries for "on-the-fly" comprehension checking that involve pausing momentarily after reading a section and checking comprehension by constructing a brief oral summary of what has just been read.
  * *Visual summaries.* Visual summaries include visual organizers such as semantic webs and Venn diagrams, strategies that are not typically regarded as summarizing tools. Vacca and Vacca (1999) point out that visual organizers provide graphic representations of both important information and the structure of knowledge contained in the text. Visual organizers also depict how these ideas relate to one another. Keep in mind that constructing appropriate organizers requires that readers be able to identify the organizational structure of a text. For instance, as suggested in Table 14.1, a Venn diagram or matrix can be used to summarize and compare and contrast text structure, but neither can be used to summa-

rize a cause and effect or problem/solution organizational structure. There are many commercially produced instructional packages to teach about visual organizers. Such products, however, may not be necessary and may in fact get in the way of students' learning to use visual summaries effectively on their own. The power of visual organizers is realized only when students learn to construct them to accurately represent the particular texts they are reading—something mass-produced visual organizers can seldom accomplish. Most importantly, students find it liberating to create their own tools.

  * *Written summaries.* Teaching students to write summaries in complete or partial sentences is another useful strategy. A common approach, as suggested below, is to teach students rules to apply when constructing written summaries (McNeil and Donant 1982):
    1. Delete unnecessary material (for example, delete interesting details that are not germane to the topic at hand).
    2. Delete redundant material (for example, delete repetitious statements made in the text).
    3. Select a word to replace a list of items (for example, replace "beans, flour, sugar, and dried fish" with "food").
    4. Select a word to replace the individual parts of an action (for example, replace a long description of explorers crossing a mountain pass with "the explorers crossed the mountain pass").
    5. Select a topic sentence (that is, one that captures the main idea or gist of a paragraph or passage).
    6. Create a topic sentence if one is not available.

FIGURE 14.1   DOCUMENTING THE DETAILS

One way to introduce students to the 5W questions is to use a chart in which the reader provides evidence from the text to support a response to each question.

	READER'S RESPONSE	EVIDENCE FROM THE TEXT
WHO are the main actors in the text?		
WHAT have they been doing?		
WHERE did the actions take place?		
WHEN did the actions take place?		
WHY have they done these actions?		
Questions I have:		

- **Monitor comprehension.** As with previous comprehension strategies, the ability to ask and answer questions is essential for clarifying, comprehending, and correcting misunderstandings. Baker (1985) points out that many readers, particularly younger ones or poor ones, are unable to monitor their understanding while reading. Examples from the seemingly endless number and type of questions that students could ask to assist in monitoring are:
  - Is what I just read clear to me? Do I "get it?"
  - Can I answer who, what, when, where, why questions about the text?
  - What about the text is still fuzzy or unclear?
- **Use fix-up strategies.** Following the identification of a breakdown in comprehension, students must know to clarify the failure and apply "fix-up" strategies to remedy the situation. Two questions to help remediate a breakdown in comprehension are:

  - Given my purpose for reading, how important is it that I clearly understand this portion of the text?
  - What strategies could I use to help me better understand what I'm reading?
    - Re-read part or all of the text.
    - Look ahead in the text.
    - Relate the information in the text to what the reader already knows about the topic.
    - Examine other resources on this topic (for example, books, web pages, videotapes).
    - Consult someone who might resolve my confusion (for example, student, teacher, parent).

Review each of the text structures outlined in Table 14.1 and decide which one (or ones) are evident in this chapter.

Instruction in the Strategies

Thus far I have discussed strategies that will help students become better at comprehending what they read. Next I focus on how to teach these strategies. Two phases for teaching reading comprehension strategies are described below: explicit instruction in individual strategies (Roehler and Duffy 1984) and teaching for self-regulated use (Collins-Block and Pressley 2002). The move from explicit instruction to teaching for self-regulated strategy use is not entirely sequential. Instead, there is considerable movement back and forth between the two phases. Students are more likely to master independent self-regulated use of a given strategy if it is taught and learned in a meaningful context that directly applies to the course material they are expected to read (Gambrell, Kapinus, and Wilson 1987). This is accomplished by using actual content area materials during both phases of the process.

EXPLICIT INSTRUCTION OF INDIVIDUAL STRATEGIES

This initial phase of instruction focusses on helping students become competent users of the specific comprehension strategies discussed above. I recommend a four-step framework in which the teacher explicitly teaches the strategy to be learned, rather than simply presenting it, hoping that students "catch on."

- **Introduction.** A first step is to introduce the strategy by explaining what it is and why it is useful. This can be done by offering a simple description and/or definition of the strategy (Baumann and Schmitt 1986). Next, ask students what, if anything, they already know about the strategy, provide a rationale for learning the strategy, and offer evidence of how it can improve their reading comprehension.
- **Modelling.** An effective way to teach students how to use a strategy is to show how it works (Dansereau 1987). Generally speaking, reading and learning processes are covert thinking activities that students seldom get to view in others. As students look on, teachers are advised to demonstrate while thinking aloud and explain their thought processes while using the strategy.
- **Guided practice.** Guided practice involves providing students with numerous opportunities to use a strategy in an environment where support and feedback are readily available. In this step, the teacher and students together share responsibility for implementing a comprehension strategy. For example, after modelling several examples of identifying organizational structure(s), highlight several relevant words in a new passage and ask students to identify the text structure. Gradually release to students the responsibility for executing the strategy through a progression, starting with the whole class then proceeding towards small-group and individual guided practice. The transition from teacher-directed to student-directed execution with extensive practice in a supportive environment is essential for developing independent use of a strategy (Pearson and Dole 1987). Perhaps the biggest and most crippling deficiency in prevailing approaches to teaching reading comprehension strategies is the failure to provide numerous opportunities for supported practice.
- **Independent practice.** In the final stage, independent practice, students assume full responsibility for using the strategy (Baumann and Ballard 1987). Teacher monitoring and feedback are important, however, to ensure correct use of the strategy and to build student confidence. To reduce the likelihood of a pattern of failure, it is wise after the first few instances of independent practice to discuss students' responses along with their methods of reasoning (Pearson and Dole 1987).

The highlighted text "Teaching a Comprehension Strategy in Action" provides an example of explicit instruction in a reading comprehension strategy using this framework.

TEACH FOR SELF-REGULATED USE

The goal of teaching reading comprehension is to foster student mastery of a growing repertoire of individual strategies in a self-regulated fashion The challenge in becoming an independent strategic reader is not simply a matter of acquiring knowledge of various strategies, but also of knowing exactly when, given the specific purpose and text, to employ particular strategies (Malone and Mastropieri 1992, 278). When assisting students in learning when and where to use each strategy, it is helpful to review why such strategies are useful and to provide multiple opportunities to practise them using actual course content (Gersten and Carnine 1986).

Teaching for self-regulated use should begin as soon as students understand what the particular strategy is and how it works. In practice, then, the two phases are more nearly parallel than sequential, with the teacher providing instruction in when and where to use different strategies as the opportunity arises. For instance, a teacher might model a previously taught strategy while introducing students to text structures. Nonetheless, as students acquire increasingly larger repertoires of strategies, there is a natural progression from explicit instruction of individual strategies towards instruction on the coordinated and self-regulated use of multiple strategies.

If students are to become competent strategic readers,

TEACHING A COMPREHENSION STRATEGY IN ACTION

The scene is Mr. Carling's Canadian history class. Mr. Carling has a well-deserved reputation as an excellent teacher who works tirelessly to instill a passion for history and learning. To this end, in addition to having a strong focus on content, his classes are directed towards helping students become more effective learners. It is late September and Mr. Carling is eager to start helping his students learn how to better comprehend the history texts they will be reading through the year. He has chosen to begin with teaching them to overview a text before reading it.

Introduction

Sitting on the table at the front of the class, Mr. Carling addresses the students: "Okay, today I'm going to introduce a strategy, a thinking tool if you like, that will help you become a better reader of your social studies textbooks, and other information books, for that matter. With time and practice, this tool will, if you choose to use it, help you better comprehend what you read in this course and in other courses. The strategy is called overviewing.

"Does anyone have an idea what I mean by overviewing?" A few students raise their hands and take a stab at answering his question. Mr. Carling points to Kevin who says, "This is just a guess but I'm thinking it might be when you skim over what you're supposed to read before you actually read it." Marcy jumps in and adds, "Yeah, I think it means looking over the chapter and trying to figure out what it's about before you actually read it." Nodding in agreement, Mr. Carling says, "You're certainly on the right track." He then adds clarity to the informal definitions provided by the students. "Overviewing," he says, "involves reading through the title, introduction, major headings, and conclusion of a chapter or book prior to reading it in an effort to get a rough idea of what the text is about. Often people will also have a look at things like pictures and graphs as they overview a chapter.

"Now, I hope you're thinking to yourself, 'Why would I want or need to do that? Why wouldn't I just start reading?' Well, the answer to those excellent questions is that because doing so will help you better understand and remember the information in the chapter. In a minute, I'm going to show you how and why this is the case."

Modelling

Mr. Carling jumps down from his perch on the table and says, "Okay, now I'm going to show you how this strategy works. I'm going to demonstrate it for you. As I'm doing this, I want you to pay very close attention to what I am saying. I'm going to share the way I'm thinking with you so that you can think in the same way when it's your turn to do an overview." He then asks students to take out their textbooks and open to page 84, the chapter on the War of 1812. Once the students are settled, he models overviewing for them.

"The title of the chapter is 'The War of 1812.' All right, I'm thinking things are looking pretty straightforward then. It seems obvious that I'm going to be learning about the War of 1812 when I read this chapter, now doesn't it?" Next, Mr. Carling reads the introduction to the chapter, pausing to reflect on what he has read after he finishes. "Hmm, that refreshes my memory a bit, I'm remembering now hearing somewhere that the War of 1812 was between Canadians and Americans. I'm now going to read through the headings and see if I can get a big picture of where the author is going with this chapter. I want to identify the major topics."

He then flips through the chapter pausing to read each of the major headings aloud and then to "think out loud" about how they relate to one another and what he knows or thinks he knows already. In addition, he looks over various illustrations and text boxes that provide interesting tidbits about the war. After reading aloud the first few lines of one text box, he pauses and says as if to himself, "That's kind of interesting. I didn't know Laura Secord was a real person. Okay, but I need to be careful here; as interesting as that blurb is I don't think it's crucial at the moment. Remember, I'm trying to get a broad sense of what the chapter is about." When Mr. Carling reaches the end of the chapter he reads the chapter summary and then says, "All right, I think I've got a pretty good idea of what this chapter is about. Based on my overview, I'm quite sure, pretty much certain in fact, that I'm going to be learning about the War of 1812, which was a war between Canada and the States, and it looks to me as if we won."

Once he has completed his overview, he discusses the processes he went through. He asks the students if they agree with his assessment and asks them to provide him with reasons for their positions. For instance, when Isabella jumps in and says, "Yes, I totally agree with you," he asks her to explain why she agrees. Isabella says, "Oh that's easy, because the title is 'The War of 1812.'"

After they've spent some time discussing the content of the overview, Mr. Carling says, "Now I want you to think about the thinking I did and the questions I asked and answered as I conducted my overview of the chapter. Can you help me generate a list of things I did?" With guidance from Mr. Carling, the students generate the following to-do list and list of questions to ask and answer for conducting an overview, which he writes on the chalkboard:

Overviewing to-do list:
- Read the title.
- Read the introduction.
- Read the major headings.
- Look at the pictures and other extras (be careful not to get sidetracked).
- Read the conclusion.

Questions to ask and answer when overviewing:
- What does the chapter appear to be about?
- What are some of the major topics?
- Do I know anything about this already?

continued on next page

- How can I use this to help me get ready to read?
- After reading: Was I right?

Finally, after going over a few key vocabulary terms and engaging in an informal discussion with the students centred around what they think they know about the War of 1812, Mr. Carling assigns the chapter for students to read.

Guided practice

After a day working through a series of activities associated with the introductory chapter on the War of 1812, Mr. Carling revisits the overviewing strategy with students. He begins by reminding them about the strategy and his modelling of it. Through discussion, he elicits from the students the goal of the strategy and the major steps involved. Then he tells them that today they will have an opportunity to implement the strategy of overviewing as a class as they prepare for another reading on the War of 1812. After handing out the reading, Mr. Carling asks if anyone can suggest how they might start. Anton answers, "Yeah, we could read the title and talk to ourselves about it like you did the other day." Mr. Carling laughs and says, "Okay, so what would you say to yourself, Anton?" Anton replies, "I'd read the title, 'The War in Upper Canada,' and then I'd say to myself, 'It looks like this is going to be about the part of the war that took place in Upper Canada, wherever that is." Mr. Carling says, "Anton has got us off to a good start. Can someone suggest what we might do next?" Carlos suggests they should be able to get an even better idea about the chapter by reading the introduction. After reading the introduction

aloud and eliciting student thoughts on what it tells them about the chapter, Mr. Carling and the students read the headings and the conclusion, working through the overviewing process together as they go. An important aspect of the guidance provided by Mr. Carling is his continual requests of students to provide the reasoning behind their statements. He wants to be sure that students are not simply randomly guessing about the content, but offering informed guesses based on the text and their background knowledge. When they have completed their overview, students read the text.

The process described above occurs repeatedly over the next few weeks. Each time Mr. Carling assigns a new chapter, he and the students overview it before reading. As the class grows more proficient at this strategy he withdraws from the process, allowing students to take increasing responsibility for its implementation. Moreover, there is a corresponding shift in grouping structures used for the practice sessions, from whole class modelling and practice to small group and ultimately individual practice.

Independent practice

As students develop fluency with overviewing, Mr. Carling provides opportunities to practice this strategy independently as they seek to learn from texts they are reading for assignment purposes. He has already introduced them to making predictions about what they are about to read, and students are adding this technique to their repertoire of reading comprehension strategies.

they require many opportunities to discuss the texts they read (Pressley et al. 1992). While discussing the content of the texts is important, such discussions should also extend to the process students engaged in while trying to comprehend the text. These discussions should take place in small groups where the students discuss both their understandings of the text and the strategies they used to construct those understandings. In the beginning, students will need considerable teacher input, but as they become more capable, the teacher should gradually withdraw his or her support. Teacher support should focus on prompting students to be active readers by asking them to think about the kinds of strategies they should use (Pressley 2002b). For instance, following reading, a teacher might ask students what kinds of strategies would help them retain the important information from the text and why they would use these strategies. After students implement such strategies, the teacher might ask them to share the information and critique the strategies they used to help retain it. Without making these discussions teacher-centred, the teacher should participate by sharing the understandings he or she constructs and by modelling the strategies used to construct them.

Conclusion

Achieving success in social studies requires that students be able to comprehend the texts of the discipline. Unfortunately, many students struggle to read such texts and learn from them if they are not provided with instruction in how to do so. Moreover, despite research supporting its effectiveness, instruction in how to comprehend is not a feature of many social studies classes. It is my hope that this discussion will help social studies teachers make comprehension instruction a meaningful component of the instruction they provide.

I offer five principles to keep in mind while planning and providing this instruction:

- Remember, the purpose of comprehension instruction is to help students better comprehend challenging texts. Comprehension strategies are a means to this end, not an end in themselves.
- Teach a few comprehension strategies well rather than teaching many strategies poorly.
- Provide many opportunities for students to practise the strategies they are learning for real purposes.
- Help students learn to adapt comprehension strategies to

their needs, individual preferences, and the text at hand, instead of using them in a lockstep fashion.

- Be patient. It may take several years to become an effective teacher of reading comprehension.

REFERENCES

Alexander, P.A. and T.L. Jetton. 2000. Learning from text: A multidimensional and developmental perspective. In *Handbook of reading research*, vol. III, ed. M.L. Kamil, P.B. Mosenthal, P.D. Pearson, and R. Barr, 285–310. Mahwah, NJ: Lawrence Erlbaum.

Alexander, P.A. and J.E. Judy. 1988. The interaction of domain-specific and strategic knowledge in academic performance. *Review of Educational Research* 58: 375–404.

Anderson, R.C. and P.D. Pearson. 1984. A schema-theoretic view of basic processes in reading. In *Handbook of reading research*, ed. P.D. Pearson, 255–291. New York: Longman.

Baker, L. 1985. How do we know when we don't understand? Standards for evaluating text comprehension. In *Metacognition, cognition, and human performance*, ed. D.L. Forrest-Pressley, G.E. MacKinnon, and T.G. Waller, 155–206. New York: Academic Press.

Baumann, J.F. and P.Q. Ballard. 1987. A two-step model for promoting independence in comprehension. *Journal of Reading* 30: 608–612.

Baumann, J.F. and M.C. Schmitt. 1986. The what, why, how, and when of comprehension instruction. *The Reading Teacher* 39: 640–646.

Collins-Block, C. and M. Pressley, eds. 2002. *Comprehension instruction: Research-based best practices*. New York: Guilford Press.

Dansereau, D.F. 1987. Transfer from cooperative to individual studying. *Journal of Reading* 30: 614–619.

Duke, N. and P.D. Pearson. 2002. Effective practices for developing reading comprehension. In *What research has to say about reading instruction*, 3rd ed., ed. A. Farstrup and J. Samuels, 205–242. Newark, DE: International Reading Association.

Durkin, D. 1978/79. What classroom observations reveal about reading comprehension. *Reading Research Quarterly* 14: 481–533.

Gambrell, L.B., B.A. Kapinus, and R.M. Wilson. 1987. Using mental imagery and summarization to achieve independence in comprehension. *The Journal of Reading* 30: 638–642.

Gersten, R. and D. Carnine. 1986. Direct instruction in reading comprehension. *Educational Leadership* 43: 70–78.

Malone, L.D. and M.A. Mastropieri. 1992. Reading comprehension instruction: Summarization and self-monitoring training for students with learning disabilities. *Exceptional Children* 58: 270–279.

McNeil, J. and L. Donant. 1982. Summarization strategy for improving reading comprehension. In *New inquiries in reading research and instruction*, ed. J.A. Niles and L.A. Harris, 215–219. Rochester, NY: National Reading Conference.

National Reading Panel. 2000. *Teaching children to read: An evidence-based assessment of the scientific research literature on reading and its implications for reading instruction: Reports of the subgroups*. Washington, DC: National Institute of Child Health and Development.

Pearson, P.D. and J.A. Dole. 1987. Explicit comprehension instruction: A review of research and a new conceptualization of instruction. *Elementary School Journal* 88: 151–165.

Pressley, M. 1998. *Reading instruction that works: The case for balanced teaching*. New York: Guilford Press.

———. 2002a. Comprehension strategies instruction: A turn-of-the-century status report. In *Comprehension instruction: Research-based best practices*, ed. C.C. Block and M. Pressley, 11–27. New York: Guilford Press.

———. 2002b. *Reading instruction that works: The case for balanced teaching* (2nd ed.). New York: Guilford Press.

Pressley, M., P. El-Dinary, I. Gaskins, T. Schuder, J.L. Bergman, J. Almasi, and R. Brown. 1992. Beyond direct explanation: Transactional strategies instruction of reading comprehension strategies. *Elementary School Journal* 92: 513–555.

Pressley, M. and R. Wharton-McDonald. 1997. Skilled comprehension instruction and its development through instruction. *School Psychology Review* 26: 448–466.

Roehler, L.R. and G.G. Duffy. 1984. Direct explanation of comprehension processes. In *Comprehension instruction: Perspectives and suggestions*, ed. G.G. Duffy, L.R. Roehler, and J. Mason, 265–280. New York: Longman.

Rosenshine, B., C. Meister, and S. Chapman. 1996. Teaching students to generate questions: A review of the intervention studies. *Review of Educational Research* 66: 181–221.

Schuder, T. 1993. The genesis of transactional strategies instruction in a reading program for at-risk students. *Elementary School Journal* 94: 183–200.

Scott, D., C. Falk, and J. Kierstead. 2002. *Legacies of ancient Egypt*. Richmond, BC: The Critical Thinking Consortium.

Taylor, B.M. and R.W. Beach. 1984. The effect of text structure instruction on middle-grade students' comprehension and production of expository text. *Reading Research Quarterly* 19: 134–146.

Vacca, R.T. and J.L. Vacca. 1999. *Content area reading: Literacy and learning across the curriculum*, 6th ed. New York: Longman.

15 Nurturing Personal and Social Values

Roland Case

The teaching of values is one of the most important yet deeply controversial goals in social studies. Many believe that becoming educated is not simply, or even essentially, a matter of acquiring a body of knowledge, but that the nurturing of personal and social values that will guide our decisions and actions in just and productive ways is equally important. By personal values I mean those that individuals hold about themselves, such as self-esteem, integrity, personal responsibility for one's actions, and pride in one's work. Social values refer to the values that we hold about others and about society generally, including national pride, commitment to justice, respect for law, respect for the environment, and a co-operative and empathetic attitude. Many people see social studies in particular as providing an important opportunity to promote the fundamental values that society requires of its citizens. But despite the central role of values education, which is often referred to as character education (Burrett and Rusnak 1993; Glaze, Hogarth, and McLean 2003), in citizenship, there is considerable controversy about it.[1] The dominant historical objections to the teaching of values in schools revolve around three issues:

- **Should we nurture values?** Should values be taught in school, or should schools be value-free?
- **Which values to nurture and who decides?** Which values are to be promoted in schools? Who selects and defines these values, and on what basis?
- **How should values be nurtured?** What methods can and should teachers use to promote values in a manner that respects the rights of students and parents?

In this chapter, I deal mainly with the last question by exploring three overlapping approaches to promoting personal and social values. But before doing so, I offer a few remarks about the other two questions.

Should We Nurture Values?

In some respects, the question whether teachers should teach values in school is moot. Schools cannot be value-free and teachers cannot avoid promoting values. The fact that we praise children for being honest, thoughtful, and punctual signals the embedded values in our schools. Every time we permit or prohibit certain behaviour, we implicitly promote certain values over others: school rules against fighting or throwing rocks, for example, attest to how we value individual well-being and the protection of property. Such rules inevitably affect the values that students develop.

Whether educators want to or not, inevitably, through either the explicit curriculum or the "hidden curriculum"—the implicit norms and values that are promoted, often unintentionally, through the way we run our schools and conduct our classes—we influence student values and attitudes. For example, if we mark students' work for neatness or praise them for asking probing questions, we are encouraging them to act in particular ways; if we do not reinforce neatness or an inquiring attitude, we implicitly tell students that these behaviours are not valued. Such is the case with everything we do (or do not do) in school. The only real choice teachers have about promoting values is whether their influence will be largely hidden and inadvertent or explicit and systematic.

In an interesting article, Daniel Duke (1978) illustrates how schools may affect students' attitudes in unintended and undesirable ways. He suggests that many students may develop a cynical attitude towards our legal system because of common school practices. We can appreciate the hidden lessons schools teach students about the fairness of our system of laws by contrasting the espoused civic ideals with the regulatory practices that actually operate in many schools. Duke concludes that it is difficult for students to develop respect for law and principled behaviour if their experiences in school, which is the first and most extensive public institution young citizens encounter, consistently reinforce the opposite. Table 15.1 contrasts the rhetoric about the rule of law with the practices that Duke saw actually operating in many schools.

Ultimately, decisions about values issues—including whether schools should intentionally teach values—should be subjected to rational scrutiny. Teachers must thoughtfully assess the pros and cons before making their decision. Table 15.2 lists competing reasons for and against the intentional teaching of values in schools. It is interesting to note that, at least according to this list, the majority of objections to teaching values intentionally are not against the idea *per se*, but are concerns about which values to promote and how to do so responsibly. These are the issues to which I now turn.

Which Values to Nurture?

There are no simple answers for determining which values to promote intentionally in schools. Nevertheless, it is useful to consider the degree of consensus about the value (although this is by no means the only criterion, it is a promising starting point). On one end of the spectrum are values (especially very general values) that are widely acknowledged as acceptable or even highly desirable attributes of citizens. Honesty, pride in

TABLE 15.1 WHAT SCHOOLS "TEACH" ABOUT OUR LEGAL SYSTEM

WE TELL STUDENTS...	YET, OFTEN IN SCHOOLS...
• that we live in a society based on democratic principles	• school rules tend to be determined by those least subject to their application
• that all people are to be treated equally before the law	• many teachers fail to enforce school rules consistently
• that the punishment should be reasonable and that it should fit the crime	• the consequences for disobeying school rules frequently lack logical relationships to the offences; for example, the punishment for skipping classes is often suspension from school
• that society is committed to safeguarding the rights of individuals against abuse by the state	• students have few options if they disagree with a claim brought against them by school authorities
• that no one is above the law	• teachers frequently fail to model the rule-governed behaviour they expect of their students

TABLE 15.2 SHOULD SCHOOLS INTENTIONALLY PROMOTE VALUES?

REASONS FOR	REASONS AGAINST
• Teaching about values is part of the school's mandate. Official rationales for public education typically refer to the need to develop the values of productive citizenship. For example, the Ontario Ministry of Education (2004, 2) identifies the need to "develop attitudes that will motivate them [students] to use their knowledge and skills in a responsible manner." Alberta Learning (2003, 2) lists a number of values and attitudes that are necessary for active and responsible citizens, including respecting the dignity and equality of all human beings, social compassion, fairness, justice, honouring and valuing the traditions and symbols that are the expressions of Canadian identity, and valuing lifelong learning.	• Values promoted in schools may conflict with those shared by individual parents, local communities, or society more generally.
	• Students may be indoctrinated into accepting values that are essentially individual in nature (that is, teachers may fail to respect individual students' freedom of conscience or right to their personal inclinations).
• Teaching values is a precondition for many other objectives in the curriculum: knowledge and skills cannot be developed without accompanying value components. For example, students will learn little if they do not have self-esteem, curiosity, and open-mindedness. Students will be unable to work co-operatively unless they have some respect for the feelings of others, are willing to play by the rules, and so on.	• Despite their best intentions, it is feared that schools will do a poor job of promoting values (for example, instead of teaching about equality, schools may unintentionally promote condescending attitudes towards various cultural or racial groups).
	• Values often raise extremely sensitive issues that may profoundly upset students.
• Many important values need attention, and schools have a significant, perhaps unique, opportunity to make a difference. If racism and discrimination are promoted within some families, how will these undesirable—and in some cases illegal —values be countered if not by the educational system?	• Because values may be controversial, actively promoting them may, in certain circumstances, present a professional risk for the teacher (for example, the teacher may become embroiled in a controversy).

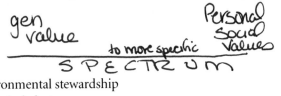

one's work, concern for the well-being of others, and respect for the property of others are examples of values that would likely have broad public support. A justification for including these values in the public education curriculum derives from the notion of *in loco parentis*—the notion that schools must, to some extent, take up the role and act on behalf of parents. Promoting certain values can be seen as an extension of the type of upbringing that reasonable parents would wish for their children. As was suggested in the 1931 Hadow report: "What a wise and good parent would desire for his [or her] children, a national educational system must desire for all children" (cited in Cassidy, 1994).

The kinds of personal and social values listed below seem indispensable for healthy human existence and would likely be broadly supported. No doubt some may object to these suggestions or insist on adding other essential values. This list is drawn largely from the values advocated fifty years ago by a social studies curriculum committee, cited by Ralph Tyler in his classic book on curriculum design (1969, 92–93). Promoting these values, at least in general terms, is unlikely to conflict with broadly held parental or community values, although from time to time individual parents and community members may not share them. This "consensus" list may serve as the starting point for identifying the values to be nurtured in schools.

Personal values

- acceptance of self; realization of one's own worth
- integrity, honesty, and frankness with self
- sense of hopefulness about the future
- willingness to seek adventure; sense of mission
- desire to make a productive contribution to society
- love of truth, however disconcerting
- respect for work well done
- appreciation of beauty in art and the environment
- pride in family and ethnic background
- personal hygiene and health
- self-discipline and self-direction
- independent-mindedness (the courage of one's convictions).

Social values

- respect for the dignity and worth of every human being
- commitment to equal opportunity for all
- tolerance and kindness
- desire for justice for all
- acceptance of social responsibility
- commitment to free thought, expression, and worship
- commitment to peaceful resolution of problems
- respect for privacy
- national pride

- environmental stewardship
- fair-mindedness
- concern for well-being of animals
- respect for the rule of law.

At the other end of the spectrum are personal and social values that are profoundly controversial, particularly positions or attitudes on specific issues such as abortion, same-sex parenting, affirmative action, and capital punishment. In these cases, since society generally is sharply divided, teachers should assume that there may not be a single most acceptable position; well-informed, thoughtful people may not share the same values. In such cases, if the issue is to be raised (and it may be that in many communities some value questions are too controversial to be raised in school), the objective should not be to promote a specific position, but rather to encourage students to the extent feasible to make up their own minds after thoughtful consideration. The teachers' responsibility would be to act in a respectful and fair manner, seeking to instill appreciation of the need for sensitivity when dealing with divisive issues and to facilitate students' gathering and assessing information pro and con before deciding for themselves. A fair manner may not mean that teachers devote identical attention to all sides. If students are already well aware of one side, it may be necessary to spend more effort helping them to see other sides. However, it should be clear that teachers are not favouring a side because it reflects their own position, but rather to ensure that students see all important viewpoints. Because students may be unduly influenced by their teachers, it is important to consider under what conditions teachers should withhold their own personal positions from students.

Many values are largely matters of personal inclination, such as the dictates of religious conscience, life choices, political affiliations, and personal aspiration. In schools that are committed to cultural and political pluralism, it is inappropriate to espouse or favour the values of one religious or political ideology over those of others. Consequently, it would be inappropriate, for example, to act as former US vice-president George H.W. Bush advised when he encouraged schools to teach about the law so as to "combat criticism of our representative government" (reported in American Bar Association 1982, 1). As Ken Osborne notes, "a well-informed, democratic and interested citizen need not be supportive of government policies" (1982, 59). Since in these matters there is no agreed-upon "correct" set of values (nor should there be), the teacher's role is to encourage students to explore and clarify these values for themselves. Although teachers should not presume which conclusions students will reach about these values, there may be considerable merit in providing them with opportunities to examine their own belief systems.

Teachers' concerns about indoctrinating or imposing personal beliefs may be reduced by resolving to encourage students to make up their own minds about values on which there is little agreement, and by communicating this commitment to parents, which may help alleviate suspicion and opposition. Yet some issues divide communities deeply, and taking the open-minded view may not satisfy everyone. Our dilemma is, on the one hand, a responsibility to develop students' ability to engage with and resolve value issues in non-violent, thoughtful ways, and on the other, a responsibility to respect, within limits, the parents' right to raise their children as they see fit. Ultimately, these decisions are matters of professional judgment—of deciding what is most defensible in light of the needs and rights of the individuals and groups whom educators have a responsibility to serve. The more contested or individualistic the value, the more sensitive and vigilant teachers must be about empowering students to make up their own minds thoughtfully, and about parents' right to be informed about and direct their children's education.

Merely because some values may be inappropriate in schools and others, if addressed at all, must be handled with extreme sensitivity, does not mean that there are values about which consensus among reasonable people cannot be reached. I believe there are many such personal and social values that are essential components of any social studies curriculum. And there may be many others that, if taught appropriately, have a legitimate place in public education.

> Take a moment to think of the five most important values—social or personal—that you would want to nurture in your classroom. Consider why you think these are so important. What might you do to reinforce and model these values in your teaching?

What Methods Should Be Used?

So much has been written on teaching about values that it is difficult to get a handle on this field. For our purposes, I believe it useful to focus on three broad approaches:

- creating classroom and school environments that reinforce desired values;
- facilitating direct "emotive" experiences that evoke desired sensitivities;
- engaging students in thoughtful deliberation about their values.

Although they will be discussed separately, these approaches overlap and should be mutually supportive.

CREATING REINFORCING ENVIRONMENTS

Values do not develop in a vacuum. In fact, they are more likely to be nurtured by the subtle yet pervasive influences operating within a social environment than they are by short-lived instructional techniques. The literature on the hidden curriculum attests to the power of environmental conditions in supporting or inhibiting the acquisition of attitudes. For example, the tone or atmosphere in a classroom is overwhelmingly cited as a primary factor in developing social attitudes (Leming 1991, Patrick and Hoge 1991). Studies reported by Judith Torney-Purta (1983) indicate that the particular content of the curriculum is less influential in developing students' political attitudes than is establishing a classroom climate where students feel free and have opportunities to express their opinions. Teacher behaviour is especially important in signalling to students what really counts. Teachers who are open-minded are more likely to foster these attributes in their students. Similarly, teachers who sincerely demonstrate their empathy for others are more likely to nurture empathetic tendencies in their students. There may be no more effective way of promoting values than by sincerely and consistently communicating to students through our actions that certain values matter. Examples of teacher behaviour, expectations, and activities that reinforce concern for others are suggested below:

Student expectations and activities

- A code of rules or principles of behaviour towards fellow students is clearly articulated and closely enforced.
- Verbal or physical abuse of students by students is as unacceptable as verbal or physical abuse of teachers by students.
- Good deeds by students are acknowledged.
- Students are frequently engaged in role reversals where they are asked to think of how others might feel in various situations.
- Students are frequently asked to express why they care or do not care about events or people that may seem remote from their lives.
- Students are invited to participate in projects in which they do something positive for others.

Teacher modelling

- The teacher refrains from put-downs and sarcasm, and is always conscious of treating students (and colleagues) with the utmost respect and deference.
- The teacher is willing to admit error, either publicly or privately, and attempts to redress the action if he or she treats a student unfairly.
- The teacher will often undertake random acts of kindness.

- The teacher is seen by students as a caring person with compassion for their concerns and difficulties.

FACILITATING DIRECT EXPERIENCES

A second approach to nurturing personal and social values is to provide opportunities for students to "feel" the effect of caring for such values. Unlike a reinforcing environment, whose goal is to habituate students gradually to particular frames of mind, direct experiences provide students with opportunities to encounter for themselves, vividly and emphatically, the power and merit of certain ways of being. Often these experiences will open students' minds and hearts to perspectives they would otherwise miss or downplay. There are at least three types of direct experiences that nurture values: vicarious, simulated, and first-hand.

- **Vicarious experiences.** To live vicariously is to encounter life through the experiences of another. Film and literature—both fiction and non-fiction—are especially effective in this regard. Vicarious experiences allow students to live the lives of others and in doing so to experience the power of feeling and caring about matters that may otherwise be foreign or remote. Susan Inman, a teacher at Windermere Secondary School in Vancouver, uses a National Film Board video, *Where the Spirit Lives*, to enhance student sensitivity to the feelings and concerns of First Nations individuals. Prior to viewing this moving film about the plight and courage of First Nations students in residential schools, several of her students had shown indifference, perhaps even callousness, to First Nations people. The video personalized—put a profoundly human face to—what were previously stereotypical images. I remember as an elementary student being moved profoundly by a historical novel about the Jesuit martyr, Isaac Jogues. Although I have since tempered my feelings towards these missionaries, I have never lost my sense of admiration for individuals who are so committed to a principle that they are willing to endure great hardship and sacrifice. At the primary level, children's stories provide powerful vehicles to invite the young to consider important values. The highlighted text below illustrates a few of the many thousands of stories that can serve this purpose. (See chapter 29 in this volume for more ideas on the use of literature in social studies.)

- **Simulated and role-play experiences.** Drama, role play, and other simulations allow students to adopt and act out the predicaments of others. One of the most famous examples of a simulated experience was described in the award-winning documentary *The Eye of the Storm* (Peters 1987). In an effort to help her grade 3 students appreciate the consequences of bigotry, Jane Elliott began, without announcing she was going to do so, to discriminate against the blue-eyed children in her class, and the next day discriminated against the brown-eyed children. Students were moved by the unfairness of this contact with prejudice. In a follow-up documentary, *A Class Divided*, filmed almost fifteen years after the simulation, the students in Elliot's class described the profound influence the earlier experience had in shaping their values.

- **First-hand experiences.** Powerful, evocative experiences need not be second-hand. Students can encounter value-nurturing situations in real-life contexts through guest speakers, field trips, exchanges, pen pals, and social-action projects. A skilled guest speaker can do much to change student attitudes. Certainly many of my own stereotypical attitudes towards ethnic and racial groups

---

VALUES-BASED STORIES FOR PRIMARY CHILDREN

Students are introduced to the unfairness of inequitable sharing of jobs through *Piggybook* by Anthony Browne (1986). It describes a mother who does all the household chores until she leaves home for a short time and the rest of the family learns to recognize their selfish behaviour. After discussing the unfairness of this situation, students list jobs done at home and develop criteria for assigning responsibility for them in their own family or in an imaginary family. Students are invited to decide on a new job they will undertake at home or at school. A week or so after assuming their new tasks, students report on their experiences and receive a note of appreciation for their efforts.

Students explore the idea of doing more than they are expected to do through *The Gardener* by Sarah Stewart (1997). In this story, a young girl undertakes a project to cheer up her sombre uncle. Using events from the story, students learn to distinguish acts of kindness from jobs that people have a responsibility to carry out. Students then discuss and apply the criteria for an act of kindness before choosing and implementing an appropriate action for a family or community member. When the kind actions are completed, students discuss their contributions to the happiness of others.

The story *Fly Away Home* by Eve Bunting (1991) tells how a homeless boy is given hope after seeing a trapped bird find its freedom. It is the anchor for a lesson on developing empathy for homeless people, exploring ways in which students might help them. Students listen to the story, then compare their own lives to that of the main character. After discussing the difficulties that homeless people experience, students select three helpful items that they personally would recommend giving to a shelter.[2]

were exploded when I first encountered articulate and impassioned individuals from these groups. Social-action projects can also be important value-nurturing experiences. As Mary-Wynne Ashford reports in her article "Youth Actions for the Planet" (1995), involvement in environmental and humanitarian projects can counter the global hopelessness prevalent among many students.

To illustrate the power of role-play experiences, imagine the effects of the activity "The Eporuvians Come to Call," described in the highlighted text, in helping students empathize with what others may feel about perceived inequities. A 1986 Australian Broadcasting Corporation film entitled *Babakiueria*—a phonetic spelling of "barbecue area"—offers a similar reversal of perspective with aboriginal explorers discovering a group of white inhabitants in a campground.

Experiences such as these—whether brought about vicariously, through simulation, or in first-hand encounters—help to evoke students' sensitivities to important values. The point is not to manipulate students into a particular perspective, but to ensure that students who may be self-absorbed will experience other predicaments and feelings.

PROMOTING THOUGHTFUL DELIBERATION

The third approach to values education encourages students to think about their attitudes. On its own, it will rarely be sufficient in itself, and perhaps may not be the best first step in promoting such change. But we are in danger of manipulating and indoctrinating students if at some point we do not encourage them to reflect on the implications and significance of their values. Eventually, students must thoughtfully make up their own minds. Generally speaking, the deliberative approach to attitude development has two strands:

- **values clarification**, wherein the objective is to help students clarify the values they hold and the implications of these values for other aspects of their lives; and

THE EPORUVIANS COME TO CALL[3]

The following three scenarios are intended to evoke empathy for the historical treatment of First Nations people. The teacher reads an imaginary scene and allows students time to reflect (and write) about their thoughts before proceeding to the next scene.

Scene 1: You're playing in your backyard when a group of odd-looking men dressed in strange clothes walks into your yard. They look dirty and hungry, and are shouting and gesturing in a strange language. They try hard to communicate with you, but you can't understand them. You can tell, though, that what they are saying is important.

Not knowing what else to do, and because they look hungry, you invite them into your house and give them some cake and tea. Soon you are able to communicate with them using hand signals and gestures. You still don't know what they want, but you begin to understand that they are from a far away land called Eporue. They really like your town and they want to stay.

- How would you feel? Scared? Flattered? Angry? Friendly? Annoyed? Curious? Excited?
- What would you do? Would you help them out? Ask them to leave?

Scene 2: Imagine that you welcome the Eporuvians. After all, you want to be helpful, and they seem so lost. You let them stay in your house, and you keep feeding them. You show them around the town and introduce them to your friends. You begin to notice, however, that they have a disagreeable habit of taking your things. All in all, they don't seem too considerate. You begin to wonder whether making friends with them was such a good idea after all. You also start to wonder if these house guests will ever leave.

After a while, you begin to realize that they want to keep living in your house and taking your things. In fact, they think that they own the place—and the land it's on, too. They stick the Eporuvian flag in the ground, and claim your yard for their leader.

- What would you do? Organize your friends to drive them out? Try to reason with them? Trick them into leaving? Give up and be friends?
- How would you feel? Scared? Angry? Puzzled? Disappointed?

Scene 3: By now, they don't bother talking to you much anymore, except when they want something from you. They bring their relatives, and lots of other Eporuvians, to live in your town. Eventually, they tell you and your family to leave, and give you a broken-down shack to live in, with no yard, no running water, and lots of other people crowded into it (who have all been forced off their land as well).

You never get your land back. For two hundred years, the story of how the Eporuvians forced you off your land is handed down. You tell your children, who tell their children, and so on, for ten generations.

- How will your descendants feel about the Eporuvians? Would you call them heroes or villains?
- If you were a descendant of the Eporuvians, how would you feel about what happened? Would you feel any responsibility to extend friendship to these people?

- **values analysis**, which proposes a more critical examination of student values and in which students assess the adequacy of the reasoning behind their value stances.

VALUES CLARIFICATION

Louis Raths, Merrill Harmin, and Sidney Simon (1966) are the best-known proponents of the values clarification approach, although many others have espoused it and it is widely evident in current educational practice. Its underlying premise is that individuals experience dissonance as a result of their being unclear, confused, or uncommitted to their values. Since values are seen to be an intensely personal and emotional matter, the teacher's role is to help students overcome this dissonance by inviting them to clarify and affirm their own values. This approach identifies three features of a sincerely held value:

- **choosing:** individuals must choose their values by considering the implications of a range of alternatives, without pressure or influence from others;
- **prizing:** once chosen, individuals should be happy with the choice and be willing to publicly affirm the value;
- **acting:** individuals should act consistently to reaffirm and strengthen their commitment to the value.

The teacher's primary responsibility is to encourage students to clarify their own values for themselves. Teachers facilitate this process by organizing activities that stimulate students to think about their values, and by providing occasions for students to publicly affirm, celebrate, and act on them. This was very much the approach followed in the previously mentioned use of literature to invite young students to consider what action, if any, they would like to adopt in response to a situation described in the story (for example, unfair allocation of tasks, people in need). In helping students clarify, teachers might ask questions that invite students to identify their values, to think about the personal meaning and implications, and to consider the consistency of their words and deeds through the use of clarifying questions such as the following:

- Is this something you value?
- How did you feel when it happened?
- What are some good things about it?
- Have you thought much about it?
- Where does this idea lead? What are its consequences?
- Do you do anything about it?
- Is what you have just said consistent with … [a previous action or comment]?

Other clarifying activities include inviting students to rank-order alternatives or locate values on a continuum and to reflect on and discuss provocative statements, problems, or issues posed by the teacher. Concurrent with activities to clarify values would be opportunities to publicly affirm and act on them. A classic values clarification activity, described in "A Personal Coat of Arms," is to create a personal coat of arms in which students symbolically represent and share their most cherished values.

VALUES ANALYSIS

Unlike the values clarification approach where the focus is on students personally clarifying their choices through reflection and action, the focus of values analysis is on students critically examining their value assumptions and reasoning. This latter approach holds that on their own students may not always see the gaps or inadequacies in their thinking and that students actually may hold discriminatory or prejudicial attitudes. As long as students are consistent and willing to act on them, the values clarification approach would find these values acceptable. Values analysis holds that some values may be unreasonable and that even if students sincerely hold them, they should be helped to seeing the position's limitations. This is especially important with social or ethical values: those we hold towards others. The similarities between the values analysis and values clarification approaches should not be overlooked. Both respect the importance of students making up their own minds after thoughtful consideration. The main difference is that the values analysis approach wants to teach students to think critically about their values, especially their ethical values. These values are seen to be far less private a matter than is presumed by the values clarification approach.

The Association for Values Education and Research (AVER) that used to operate at the University of British Columbia was a prominent advocate of the values analysis approach. AVER's work provides a structure to help teachers and students reflect on their values more critically. The AVER approach (1978, 1991) is based on a reconstruction of the logic of value reasoning into three elements:

- **the value judgment:** a statement about what the person judges to be desirable or undesirable or what ought, or ought not, to be (for example, "School is horrible" or "School should be illegal");
- **the factual evidence to support the judgment:** a descriptive or factual statement of what actually is, was, or is likely to be, which is seen to be relevant to the judgment taken ("I have to work very hard in school");
- **the implied or underlying value principle:** the more general value position that the person has accepted implicitly by virtue of the factual reason offered ("Situations that force people to work very hard are horrible—or ought to be made illegal").

A PERSONAL COAT OF ARMS

A popular values clarification project is to have students create a personal coat of arms that symbolically represents the values that each holds dear. The project integrates well with social studies units on knights and chivalry, First Nations peoples, patriotism and nationalism, cultural heritage, personal growth, and self-esteem. The undertaking can be more or less ambitious, but since the purpose is to help students identify and celebrate their own values, there is merit in taking the time to ensure that the project fosters self-discovery and personal pride.

- **Creating context.** Introduce the project by drawing attention to the historical and contemporary uses of coats of arms and heraldry (for example, First Nations, medieval and contemporary nobility, national flags, university and family crests). Explain that many citizens treat their national flag with great reverence because it is a symbol of their homeland. They may be outraged when people burn or trample on the flag. Soldiers carry the flag into battle as a symbol of what they are fighting to protect. Desecrating a flag or other personal crest shows disrespect or scorn for that person or group's cherished values. Ask students to consider for a moment the values they would fight to promote or protect.
- **Identifying the values.** Depending on the time available and student level, the crest may contain one or two panels only, although a crest will usually contain between four and six panels, each representing a different value. An outline of a coat of arms such as the sample represented here may be provided to students, either as a working copy (that is, as a prototype for a poster-size design that they will eventually create) or as the final copy. Typically, the teacher establishes the number of panels and the themes. The following are common themes for panels:

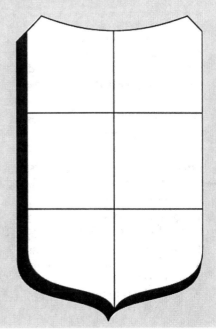

- most cherished family characteristic or event
- most cherished ethnic/cultural characteristic or event
- most cherished national characteristic or event
- most cherished personal character trait(s)
- most cherished character trait(s) sought in one's friends
- most significant personal accomplishment(s) to date
- personal motto or guiding principle
- most significant personal aspiration(s)
- most significant contribution(s) one could make to one's friends or family
- most significant contribution(s) one could make to the world at large
- what one would hoped to be remembered by—one's epitaph.

Selection of the themes should be guided by the specific goals of the project. For example, if increased cross-cultural awareness is an objective, then the first and second values on the above list would be especially relevant.

- **Exploring the values.** Once the themes have been established, students should then be assisted to explore thoughtfully what this means for them personally. Again, depending on the specific themes, students might be assigned one or more of the following tasks:
  - interview a relative about his or her family or ethnic background;
  - read about individuals who exhibit character traits that they admire;
  - as a class, brainstorm a list of character traits or life goals, and rank-order their priorities;
  - think about what they would do if they had one year to live and were guaranteed success in whatever they attempted;
  - discuss with others who know them well what is seen to be their strengths and ambitions.
- **Representing one's values.** Although words may be appropriate in some panels (for example, a personal motto or epitaph), a coat of arms' impact lies in its symbolic representation. Depending on student level, simple drawings, photographs, or magazine illustrations on regular-sized paper may suffice. Alternatively, students might be asked to create a shield-sized poster.

  Regardless of size, the effect is more powerful if students spend time exploring different types of symbols, including corporate logos (for example, the Nike "swish" represents the wing of the goddess Victory, and victory in Italian is *nike*) and national flags and crests (the dramatic rising sun in the Imperial Japanese flag, the olive branches of peace caressing the globe in the United Nations flag). It is especially valuable to point out the symbolism in each design (a dove symbolizes peace, lions symbolize courage).

continued on next page

The significance of particular colours may also be explored (white symbolizes purity, red symbolizes life). Encourage students to create original or adapted representations and not to rely exclusively on well-established symbols. Some students may be embarrassed about their inability to draw. This can be mitigated by downplaying the artistic element (by not assigning marks for technical merit) and by allowing pictures, computer graphics, and even "commission renderings" by fellow artists in the class.

- **Celebrating the values.** Since a primary purpose of the project is to publicly affirm students' values, it is important that there be an opportunity to share and celebrate the coats of arms. (Student should not be required to participate if they do not wish to.) There are several ways in which this might be done:

- Each person explains his or her coat of arms to other students in a small group, to the whole class, or in a gallery walk.
- The class might interpret the symbolism in each coat of arms and guess what it means before having the creator explain it to them.
- The coats of arms may be displayed around the classroom or in the school hallway or library for others to admire.

However the coats of arms are displayed, it is important that the atmosphere should be one where students feel safe about sharing their deeply held values and are helped to feel pride in their representations and in the values they symbolize.

When students offer and defend a position on a value issue (for example, whether it is wrong to tell a white lie, or whether Canada should accept more immigrants), their reasoning can be reconstructed using these elements into deductive arguments, consisting of a major premise (the implied value principle), a minor premise (the factual evidence), and a conclusion (the value judgment). For example, a student might offer the following judgment on the desirability of increased immigration quotas: "It's stupid for the Canadian government to increase immigration levels." When asked to provide factual evidence to support this conclusion, the student might respond: "The more new immigrants we accept, the more current residents are out of work." The implied value principle that the student must accept if the reasoning is to be valid is that "The Canadian government should not adopt policies that cause unemployment among Canadian residents." This reasoning can be roughly translated into the following syllogism:

Major premise (implied value principle)	The government should not adopt polices that cause unemployment among Canadian residents.
Minor premise (factual evidence)	Increasing immigration quotas causes unemployment among Canadian residents.
Conclusion (value judgment)	Therefore, the government should not increase immigration quotas.

The point of reconstructing value reasoning in this way is to provide teachers with three points at which to help students think critically about their views. Students can be taught to query whether or not: (1) the major premise (implied value principle) is acceptable, (2) the minor premise (factual evidence) is factually true, and (3) the conclusion (value judgment) follows from the premises, especially when all of the reasons are considered.

The unique contribution of the AVER approach is the tests or challenges that students and teachers can apply in assessing the acceptability of the implied value principle. University of British Columbia professor Jerrold Coombs (1980) has identified four ways to challenge our principles:

- **Consistency with other basic values.** An obvious test of the acceptability of an implied principle is whether or not it is consistent with other more basic tenets in one's own value system. It would not be justifiable to accept a principle that is inconsistent with one's fundamental values. For example, if I believe it wrong to discriminate against people on the basis of race, then I would be inconsistent in accepting a principle that suggested that white immigrants be given priority. Similarly, if I believe that the lives of people ought to be placed above money, then I would not be consistent if I rejected refugees whose lives were in danger merely in order to save tax dollars.

- **Consequences for everyone involved.** A second way to evaluate the acceptability of implied principle is to assess the consequences of adopting it for all of the people likely to be affected, especially those likely to be the most significantly affected. Students should take on these others' perspectives and ask: "How would I feel if I were in someone else's shoes? Would I judge the principle to be fair from that perspective?" If I would find it unfair to accept the implied principle if I were in someone else's position, then that is a reason for not finding the principle acceptable. Even young children use this test when they ask, "How would you like it if I did that to you?"

- **Consequences in other relevant situations.** A third way to test an implied principle is to consider the consequences in other similar situations. If using the implied principle in these situations would be undesirable, then this is a reason for rejecting or at least modifying it. Consider, for example, the implied principle that it is always wrong to tell a lie. It would be appropriate to imagine situations where telling a lie might be justified. Suppose I were living in Nazi Germany during World War II. Would I consider it wrong to lie to soldiers who asked if there were any Jewish people living in my house? If I think I am justified in lying in this situation then I should modify my implied principle to something like "It is wrong to lie unless it is to protect someone's life." It would then be useful to imagine situations that were not a matter of saving a life but in which I would still consider lying acceptable. The point of the test is to explore other situations where the same principle might apply to determine if I can accept the consequences of adopting the principle in these situations. If not, then the principle needs to be modified or rejected.

- **Consequences for repeated instances.** A final way to test the acceptability of an implied principle is by supposing that repeated instances of a situation were to occur. If the consequences of repeated applications are unacceptable, with no rational way to justify allowing only some instances of the act, then fairness requires preventing everyone from acting in that way. For example, although it may not be particularly undesirable for one person to walk across grass in a park or to throw a cigarette butt on the ground, the effect of everyone doing it is ruined grass or horrible litter. The philosopher Marcus Singer (1958, 162) refers to this as the generalization argument: "If the consequences of everyone's acting in a certain way would be undesirable, then no one has the right to act in that way without a reason or justification."

Each test would need to be explained to students, perhaps introduced one at a time. Students need to learn when a test is likely to be relevant, perhaps by having students apply a particular test to a list of principles that has been supplied to them.[4]

To illustrate how the AVER approach can help students think more critically about their value positions, the highlighted text, "Reasoning About Canada's Immigration Quotas," outlines a six-step model for values analysis applied to the issue of Canada's immigration quotas.

As I hope this discussion of the AVER approach indicates, there is need to teach students how to think critically about their values. Although there are multiple approaches to values education—classroom environment, direct experiences, and values clarification—teachers ultimately must encourage students to reflect critically on their values, especially on their social or ethical values: those pertaining to how others are to be treated.

Concluding Remarks

I want to close this chapter on values education with a plea for two virtues: sensitivity and perseverance. Although we should be sensitive to our students in all that we do, there is particular need for caution when dealing with values. Not only are values rife with controversy, they are deeply tied to students' feelings. We have a special responsibility to enter into this domain with the greatest of sensitivity for our students.

The consequences of a failure in this regard were demonstrated to me while visiting a high school in New York City several years ago. I had been invited to observe a lesson where an abbreviated version of the personal coat of arms activity described earlier was introduced. The teacher opened the lesson by sharing a personal coat of arms he had made. It was sketched in pencil on a regular sheet of paper and, consequently, was not readily visible to students. He explained to the class the four panels on his coat of arms, and assigned students to develop their own. The values they were to represent were an aspect from their cultural background, their favourite food, their favourite activity, and the epitaph they would like for their headstone. Their coats of arms were to be photocopied so that he could hand them out. Students were given

---

REASONING ABOUT CANADA'S IMMIGRATION QUOTAS

- **Identify and clarify the issue under discussion.** Before getting too far into a topic, students need to be precise about the issue. For example, is the dispute over the criteria for selecting new immigrants or the size of annual quotas of immigrants allowed into Canada? Students need to understand that Canada sets quotas for three classes of immigrants: (1) refugees who are fleeing political oppression or desperate conditions; (2) family immigrants who are applying to be reunited with their relatives; and (3) independent immigrants who have no political or family claims (many of whom are wealthy applicants willing to invest in Canadian businesses).

- **Generate possible factual reasons, pro and con.** Once an issue is clarified, students should consider the reasons, pro and con. It is important that the reasons be framed as factual or description statements (that is, what actually is, was, or is likely to happen). Individually or as a class, students may list pro reasons down one column and con reasons down the other column, as illustrated below.
  Issue: Should Canada increase its immigrant quotas for:
  - refugees?
  - family class immigrants?
  - independent immigrants?

continued on next page

PRO	CON
• many immigrants may be in desperate economic need	• many Canadians may feel invaded by more immigrants
• many immigrants may need protection from war and political persecution	• many immigrants take advantage of the system
• increased immigration adds to the population size of Canada;	• immigrants drain money away from other Canadians through increased need for social programs
• increased immigration results in enriched lives and lifestyle for many new immigrants	• increased immigration leads to overcrowding in some areas
• many immigrants bring talents and human resources that benefit Canada	• increased immigration drives down the minimum wage
• immigrants provide a pool of workers to fill low paid jobs that may otherwise go unfilled	• increased immigration discourages integration of ethnic groups into mainstream society
• increased immigration helps to unite separated families	• increased immigration fuels racial/ethnic tensions
• increased immigration adds to Canada's cultural diversity.	• increased immigration leads to higher housing prices
	• increased immigration will lead to the European culture becoming a minority in Canada
	• increased immigration will lead to the white race becoming a minority in Canada.

- **Investigate the accuracy of the factual claims offered.** Students should be discouraged from accepting at face value the factual reasons they offer. Often, students will have little evidence for their beliefs and, in some cases, their beliefs may be inaccurate or only partly true. For example, it is not obvious that increasing immigration drains money away from current residents. One of the government's motives for increased immigration is providing a larger consumer base of support for domestic industries and businesses. As well, Canada saves money if it accepts immigrants who have already been trained as, say, medical doctors or computer analysts, rather than educate candidates domestically. After seeking evidence students should, where appropriate, modify or reject suggested reasons. For example, the claim that immigrants drain money may be found to be clearly false in the case of independent immigrants, or the suggestion that increased immigration leads to higher house prices may be false in the case of refugees.
- **Test the acceptability of each implied principle.** With each factual reason that is thought to be true, students should be helped to identify the implied value principle by reconstructing the logic of their reasoning into a deductive argument. For example, the principle implied by the argument that many Canadians may feel invaded by increased immigration goes something like this: "The government should not adopt policies that cause Canadian residents to feel a sense of invasion." Students would then apply to each of the implied values one or more of the principle tests discussed earlier. Principles found to be unacceptable should be modified or rejected. Three of the tests are useful in assessing the acceptability of the above-mentioned principle:
    - *Consequences for everyone involved.* Students should endeavour to put themselves in the position of someone whose parents live in another country but who cannot immigrate because other Canadian

residents feel somewhat invaded. Or put themselves in the position of someone who is in danger of being tortured in their home country if their application for refugee status is rejected simply because some Canadian residents may feel invaded. Would students still think it fair to accept this principle if they were in these peoples' predicaments? If not, then the principle should be modified or rejected.

- *Consequences in other relevant situations.* Students should endeavour to think of a different government policy they support, but that many people might find invasive. Perhaps the issue is mandatory seat belts. Would students be willing to give up on the policy merely because many Canadians resent having to wear seat belts? If not, then they do not accept the principle that merely because people feel invaded, policies should be scrapped.
- *Consequences for repeated instances.* Students should consider the consequences if every government policy were to be scrapped because many people feel invaded. Would governments be able to act at all if this principle was accepted? There are few, if any, policies, including limits on gun control, smoke-free areas, and anti-discrimination laws, that would not threaten some group. The consequence of the implied principle, if accepted, might be that governments could never implement any policy.
- **Weigh all remaining (valid) reasons, pro and con.** After eliminating the reasons that are unwarranted because of unacceptable implied principles, the next step is to assess the collective weight of the remaining reasons. This involves deciding the importance of the values underlying each one (the implied principles) and the extent to which each position affects these values. For example, students must consider whether a relatively modest loss of economic

benefit to current residents should be given priority over the life-and-death protection afforded political refugees whose lives may be in danger.

- **Present and defend a judgment on the issue.** Finally, students should determine their own stand on the issue. This may be a simple for-or-against position, but more often it will be a qualified stance. For example, students might decide that immigration quotas should be increased in some areas and decreased in other areas, or that quotas should be increased across the board, provided immigration fraud is reduced. Students would be expected to demonstrate how their position is the stronger alternative and how it accommodates the valid concerns of the opposing perspective.

only a few minutes to think about and sketch a symbol to represent each value. A male student asked if he could complete the activity at home, but he was told to finish it before the end of class. He then volunteered to come back after school to complete the assignment, whereupon the teacher suggested that if he just got down to work immediately he would be finished in no time. With fifteen minutes remaining in the period, the teacher randomly divided the class into groups of four. Students were to explain their coat of arms to the other three members of their group. In one group, I noticed the sole female student being ignored by the three male students in her group. She sat the entire time with her coat of arms in her slightly outstretched arms, waiting to be invited by the others to explain her cherished values.

This values lesson was not sensitively handled. The young woman's self-esteem was damaged that day. The male student who wanted to take his coat of arms home to do a proper job learned that "getting it done" was the main thing. And the personal pride of everyone in the class was diminished by having their values treated in such a slapdash fashion and trivialized by such banal questions.

And now a point about perseverance. In talking about the slow pace of significant educational change, Ralph Tyler likens teachers' efforts to the effect of dripping water upon a stone: "In a day or week or a month there is no appreciable change in the stone, but over a period of years definite erosion is noted. Correspondingly, by the cumulation of educational experiences profound changes are brought about in the learner" (1969, 83). Clearly we must take the long view on nurturing personal and social values. It requires incremental, collective effort—no one teacher can do it quickly or on his or her own. Each of us is responsible for doing our small part to promote the values that will guide students in thinking and acting as responsible human beings and citizens. Arguably, there is no goal more important than this for social studies educators.

Think back to one of the five most important values that you identified earlier. Make a list of possible activities or resources that you might use to nurture each value. Be sure to think of ideas for each of the three kinds of approaches described in this chapter: creating reinforcing environments, facilitating direct experiences, and promoting thoughtful deliberation.

ENDNOTES

1 Alfie Kohn (1997) draws attention to the fundamental ambiguity in the term "character education." In its broad interpretation, character-building refers to any attempt to help children develop desired traits. In its narrow sense, it refers to an approach to inculcating a work ethic and other socially conservative values using exhortations to behave, extrinsic rewards, and other forms of moral training.

2 Lessons can be found in Abbott, Case, and Nicol (2003).

3 The Eporuvian role play was developed by Anne Hill, an elementary teacher in Terrace, British Columbia.

4 Teaching activities for introducing principle-testing are described more fully in the AVER teaching materials (1978, 1991).

REFERENCES

Abbott, M., R. Case, and J. Nicol. 2003. *I can make a difference*. Richmond, BC: The Critical Thinking Consortium.

Alberta Learning. 2003. *Social studies—Kindergarten to grade 12* (validation draft). Edmonton, AB: Author. Available online at http://www.education.gov.ab.ca/k_12/curriculum/bySubject/.

American Bar Association. 1982. What's happening in law-related education? *LRE Report* 3 (3): 1–6.

Ashford, M-W. 1995. Youth actions for the planet. In *Thinking globally about social studies education*, ed. R. Fowler and I. Wright, 75–90. Vancouver: Research and Development in Global Studies, University of British Columbia.

Association for Values Education and Research. 1978. *Prejudice*. Toronto: OISE Press.

———. 1991. *Peace: In pursuit of security, prosperity, and social justice*. Toronto: OISE Press.

Browne, A. 1986. *Piggybook*. New York: Alfred A. Knopf.

Bunting, E. 1991. *Fly Away Home*. New York: Clarion Books.

Burrett, K. and T. Rusnak. 1993. *Integrated character education.* (Fastback #351). Bloomington, IN: Phi Delta Kappa Educational Foundation.

Cassidy, W. 1994. An examination of caring and compassion in social studies education. Unpublished paper, Simon Fraser University, Burnaby, British Columbia, May.

Coombs, J.R. 1980. Validating moral judgments by principle testing. In *Practical dimensions of moral education,* ed. D. Cochrane and M. Manley-Casimir, 30–55. New York: Praeger.

Duke, D.L. 1978. Looking at the school as a rule-governed organization. *Journal of Research and Development in Education* 11 (4): 116–126.

Glaze, A.E., B. Hogarth, and B. McLean, eds. 2003. Can schools create citizens?: An exploration of character and citizenship education in Canadian, US and UK schools (special theme issue). *Orbit* 33 (2).

Kohn, A. 1997. How not to teach values: A critical look at character education. *Phi Delta Kappan.* Available online at http://www.alfiekohn.org/articles.htm#education.

Leming, J.S. 1991. Teacher characteristics and social education. In *Handbook on research on social studies teaching and learning,* ed. J. Shaver, 222–236. New York: Macmillan.

Ontario Ministry of Education. 2004. *The Ontario curriculum—Social studies grades 1–6—History and geography grades 7 and 8 (revised).* Toronto: Queen's Printer. Available online at http://www.edu.gov.on.ca.

Osborne, K. 1982. Civics, citizenship and politics: Political education in the schools. *Teacher Education* 20, 58–72.

Patrick, J.J. and J.D. Hoge. 1991. Teaching government, civics and law. In *Handbook on research on social studies teaching and learning*, ed. J. Shaver, 427–436. New York: Macmillan.

Peters, W. 1987. *A class divided: Then and now.* New Haven, CT: Yale University Press.

Raths, L.E., M. Harmin, and S.B. Simon. 1966. *Values and teaching: Working with values in the classroom.* Columbus, OH: Merrill.

Singer, M.G. 1958. Moral rules and principles. In *Essays in moral philosophy,* ed. A.I. Meldon, 160–197. Seattle: University of Washington Press.

Stewart, S. 1997. *The Gardener.* Vancouver: Douglas and McIntyre.

Torney-Purta, J. 1983. Psychological perspectives on enhancing civic education through the education of teachers. *Journal of Teacher Education* 34: 3–34.

Tyler, R. 1969. *Basic principles of curriculum and instruction.* Chicago: University of Chicago Press.

16 Embedding Global and Multicultural Perspectives

Roland Case, Özlem Sensoy, and Michael Ling

Much has been written about the importance of helping students understand the multicultural, globally connected world in which they live. Responding to this challenge should not, we believe, focus on teaching facts about various cultures and countries. Rather, our goal is better directed towards helping students view the world—and the events and people within it—in a different light. As Louis Perinbaum (1989, 25) observes, global education is a way of looking at the world more than it is the accumulation of information. The same can be said for multicultural education. This characterization is often discussed in terms of developing multicultural and global perspectives.

Before explaining what we mean by multicultural and global perspectives, we would like to clarify the difference between global education and multicultural education. These terms overlap to a great extent. Perhaps it is most helpful to view multicultural education as a subset of global education because the cultural dimensions of our global reality are one aspect—albeit a very significant part—of a wider set of political, economic, and social dimensions. It might be suggested that this characterization is potentially misleading since multiculturalism, especially in a country like Canada, is not simply a matter of international interests. Rather, multiculturalism is very much a part of our national reality and identity. However, even in this respect, Canadian multiculturalism cannot be separated from its global connections. Events such as the "war on terror," trade relations with China or the United States, and outsourcing of jobs to India, all have impact on cultural relations within Canada. The difference then is largely a matter of emphasis: the "content" of multicultural education is the national and international contexts of culture and cultural relations, whereas global education attends to a broader set of topics that include global development and trade, human rights, the environment, and culture.

What is a Global/Multicultural Perspective?

A perspective implies a "point of view"—a vantage point from which, or a lens through which, observations occur, and an "object" of attention—an event, thing, person, place, or state of affairs that is the focus of the observations. Thus an economic perspective (the point of view) would consider the financial costs and benefits of a proposed action (the object). Similarly, an ethical perspective would look at the morality of an action. A global/multicultural perspective refers to a point of view or set of lenses for viewing people, places, and things around the world. These perspectives consist of two elements—a substantive and a perceptual dimension.

- The **substantive dimension** refers to the "object" of focus within a global/multicultural perspective. These are the world events, states of affairs, places, and things that global and multicultural educators want students to understand. The substantive dimension is concerned with fostering knowledge about the people, beliefs, and customs beyond students' own cultural group and country, and knowledge of events, places, and issues beyond the local and immediate.

- The **perceptual dimension** refers to the "point of view" or lens of a global/ multicultural perspective. These are the habits of mind, values, or attitudes from which we want students to perceive the world and the plurality of cultures within it. The perceptual dimension, reflected in spatial metaphors such as narrow or broad, ethnocentric or cosmopolitan, and parochial or far-reaching, describes a mindset or outlook—a capacity to see the "whole picture" with its complexity and diversity. Nurturing the perceptual dimension of a global/multicultural perspective requires developing the mental lenses through which the local and international world is to be understood in more holistic, interrelated, and complex ways.

An attempt to explain global and multicultural education requires articulating both the range of phenomena to be explored (the substantive dimension) and the desired lenses through which this examination is to occur (the perceptual dimension). Before elaborating on this two-dimensional account, let us consider why we should care about nurturing global/multicultural perspectives.

Why a Global/Multicultural Perspective?

The aim in prompting global/multicultural perspectives is to expand and enrich students' views of the world so they are not ethnocentric, stereotypical, or otherwise limited by a narrow or distorted point of view. Unless students recognize that their particular lenses are not universally shared and see the need to adopt multiple and far-reaching perspectives, many students are likely to view the world predominantly through their own cultural lenses, lenses shaped narrowly by their own interests, location, and experiences.

Research on freehand maps drawn by students from different nations illustrates the importance of helping students perceive the world in diverse and encompassing ways. In a classic study, Thomas Saarinen (1973) compared sketch maps of the world created by high school students from four cities: Calgary (Canada), Helsinki (Finland), Makeni (Sierra Leone), and Tucson (USA). These sketches, which provide metaphorical pictures of students' images of their world, suggest how students' understandings are mediated by the lenses through which they view things. As might be expected, most students depicted their home country and home continent with a high degree of accuracy and detail, often locating them in the centre of their map. This positioning of themselves at the centre of the world is symbolic of their socialization and outlook. Typically, more distant continents were relegated to the "outer reaches" of the page and often reduced to vague blotches far smaller than their actual land masses warranted. These depictions symbolize the reduced levels of awareness of and significance attached to "foreign" regions.

Curiously, some international features such as Hawaii, the British Isles, and the "boot" of Italy were exaggerated or rendered with unusual precision. For varying reasons, these "distant" features had particular significance for the map-makers—perhaps the students had visited the place, had relatives living there, or had read about some event or place associated with that country.

Instruction in school may unintentionally reinforce students' parochial or distorted world views by focussing on quaint and superficial aspects and further estrange cultural groups by fostering a "we/they" dualism. For example,

many curriculum materials promote what might be called a "food–costumes–customs" approach to the study of cultures. However, learning about ethnic dishes and "strange" holiday practices is unlikely to promote an enlightened perspective on the lives and concerns of people in these "foreign" cultures (Zachariah 1989). Well-intentioned attempts to interest elementary students in other cultures by featuring the exotic and exceptional elements of these cultures may make these people more "alien" to some students. By attending to the bizarre, and to some extent trivial, cultural dimensions, we may actually reinforce stereotypical perceptions (Schuncke 1984, 249).

Other distortions are also commonplace. For example, students may regard Africa and South America as primitive frontiers if their exposure to these continents is entirely in the context of subsistence living, genocide, drug runners, and deforestation. Many students are often surprised to learn of the existence of well-educated, affluent people living in modern African cities because the media-based representations they often see are restricted to jungles and rural villages. Similarly, when poverty is discussed, students are likely to regard people in these situations with condescending paternalism unless students are also shown instances of initiative and self-sufficiency. Unfortunately, until quite recently, treatment of Africa, South America, and the Middle East in Canadian social studies curricula focussed predominantly on ancient (and now fallen) civilizations (Case 1989, 6) and the curriculum in at least one province referred to the study of "primitive" cultures (British Columbia Ministry of Education 1983, 40).

These types of lingering ethnocentric and stereotypical perceptions will not be resolved simply by teaching more about the world—merely having more information may not advance students' understanding—because much of what we notice and the interpretations we make depend upon the lenses through which we filter this raw data. Approaching a study with a parochial attitude is likely to confirm, not dispel, stereotypes and prejudices. We must attend directly to the perceptual lenses that colour students' sense-making.

What Comprises the Substantive Dimension?

As indicated earlier, the substantive dimension refers to the range of global/multicultural topics—world events, states of affairs, places, and things—about which students should be informed. Many writers have offered accounts of what we refer to as the substantive dimension of global/multicultural education. Kniep (1986), Hanvey (1976), and Banks (2004) are among the most widely cited. Kniep and Hanvey, for example, identify five topics that form the main objects of global study. Interestingly, the focus of the first topic is multiculturalism.

- **Universal and cultural values and practices.** Hanvey uses the term "cross-culture awareness" to refer to knowledge and respect for the diversity of ideas and practices to be found in human societies around the world. Kniep emphasizes the importance of teaching about both commonality and diversity: teaching about universal human values that transcend group identity (for example, equality, justice, liberty) and about diverse cultural values that define group membership and contribute to differing world views (for example, values related to aesthetics, lifestyle, or the environment).

- **Global interconnections.** Kniep talks of "global systems" and Hanvey speaks of "global dynamics" to describe knowledge of the workings—the key features and mechanisms—of the interactive economic, political, ecological, social, and technological systems operating worldwide.

- **Present worldwide concerns and conditions.** Both writers identify the need to know about current and emerging global issues and problems—Hanvey calls it "state of the planet awareness." These persistent, transnational issues, which span peace and security, economic development, environmental, and human rights concerns, include population growth, migration, poverty, natural resource use, science and technology, health, and international and intranational conflict.

- **Origins and past patterns of worldwide affairs.** Kniep stresses the importance of "global history"—seeing the historical evolution and roots of universal and diverse human values, of contemporary global systems, and of prevailing global issues and problems.

- **Alternative future directions in worldwide affairs.** Hanvey stresses the importance of "knowledge of alternatives"—also called "awareness of human choices"—learning of alternatives to the ways in which the world is currently run, including alternatives to unrestrained economic growth, current foreign aid and technical assistance policies, and consumption patterns.

Although the substantive and perceptual dimensions intertwine, this list of topics identifies the content that these prominent global educators see as the main focus for global education. In essence, they believe that students need to know that people across the world share some values and differ in others, that events and forces in the world interconnect in powerful ways, that the world is facing a number of serious issues with deep historical roots, and that humankind has the potential and, indeed, the obligation to alter the existing ways of "doing business."

An important concern in global, and, obviously in multicultural education, is the teaching about cultures. As was discussed earlier, there are many pitfalls, in part because of a stereotypical view of the notion of a "culture."

Contrary to the way in which it is often taught, culture is not a unified, fixed entity. In fact, culture is not a "thing" at all, but rather the name we give to the set of beliefs, values, behaviour, and ways of living that any community of people expresses. Culture is created by people collectively as a way of adapting to social and environmental circumstances. Therefore, as circumstances change, so does culture. One indication of the malleability of culture is the way that many peoples of the world have very quickly responded to and have made use of new technological innovations. The Inuit, for example, were incorrectly thought by many in the 1930s and '40s to live a static, unchanging existence. The snowmobile, however, was very quickly incorporated into Inuit culture and some would now suggest it has become essential to the Inuit way of life. We have to look no farther than the introduction into contemporary Western culture of cars or telephones during our grandparents' lives, television during our parents' lives, and computers into many of our own lives, to see how new inventions become so much a part of the cultural landscape that one often wonders how people ever did without them. They become so integral to our day-to-day existence that they seem almost invisible—a "natural" feature of our existence. We don't notice them as unique or novel in any way; they are just "there" in our lives.

It is important to appreciate that a culture should always be made sense of relative to the circumstances in which it was created and now exists. Material technologies (for example, costumes, food, housing) are not in and of themselves culture; they are simply physical objects that may reveal much about a group when we look closely at how they are used by a particular people. What is important to recognize is that "artifacts," and other material or cultural expressions, including words, manners, and gestures, are not just arbitrary "things" in our worlds. Rather, they embody sets of ideas about how members belonging to a particular cultural group perceive, relate to, and act in the world.

Ironically, we are often unable to see our own cultural responses and yet we are often excessively conscious of the practices of others. The case of able-bodiedness illustrates this "blindness" (left-handedness is another example). Those of us who are able-bodied may go about the entire day, perhaps even weeks and months, without thinking about our ability to access public space. This blindness is called *privilege*. Such privilege (able-bodied) causes us to "not see" that public space is not universally accessible. We overlook how our environment (for example, restaurants, schools, parks, and transportation systems) accommodates "our" bodies as the norm.

Only when we encounter those whose bodies are socially defined as outside the norm of the able-bodied do we notice "their" differences. This blindness is also illustrated in many aspects of social life. For example, many English-speaking Canadians would say that American and British English speakers *have* accents but that Canadians do not. Similarly, other groups are said to *have* cultural practices but "we don't."

These examples illustrate the importance of attending to the role of cultural traditions in shaping our behaviour, identities, environments, and assumptions, and to the fact that when we are part of the dominant group, our culture is the invisible norm against which other cultures are measured. Put another way, a culture provides an invisible screen or a lens through which participants interpret and respond to the world, a so-called world view. Why do I feel it is inappropriate for me to burp loudly after a meal in a restaurant, yet this may be entirely appropriate in another context? Such are the ways society, by way of culture, orients our views so that we may respond to "other views" with resistance or even hostility. Put this way, it becomes easier to see that any cultural expression should be seen as a particular response to social and environmental circumstances.

It is also important to recognize that often there is a *dominant* cultural tradition that has greater access to opportunity and power. For example, the dominant religious tradition in Canada is the Christian tradition. This historical fact has resulted in the dominance in "our" nation of Christian practices (such as Easter and Christmas) and institutionalization of these celebrations through state-sanctioned holidays. Although many other faith communities are celebrated for the diversity they bring to Canadian culture, these groups are not afforded comparable institutional recognition of their cultural practices. Of course, institutional holidays in Japan, India, Iran, and other countries will reflect the traditions of the dominant groups in these nations.

Examine the text and pictures dealing with cultural groups found in various textbooks and other teaching resources. What portrait of these cultures is depicted? To what extent are superficial or unusual aspects profiled? Is there greater emphasis on differences or similarities between these groups and students' cultural roots?

What Comprises the Perceptual Dimension?

A major—possibly the key—challenge in developing a global/multicultural perspective is to transform a parochial perspective (that is, making sense of the world from a superficial, narrow, or ethnocentric point of view) to a broad-minded multi-perspective (that is, making sense of the world from varied and "enlightened" points of view). There is little value in promoting knowledge of alternative future directions, for example, if students are going to immediately dismiss these ideas because they don't suit students' immediate and possibly narrow interests—hence the need to help students see things from a more "global" and "culturally diverse" perspective. To better appreciate both what this involves and how to promote it, we characterize the perceptual dimension in terms of three lenses, or habits of mind: open-mindedness, full-mindedness, and fair-mindedness.[1]

OPEN-MINDEDNESS

Open-mindedness refers to a willingness to consider new ideas and alternative ways of looking at people, places, and events. Its opposite is closed-mindedness—the unwillingness to explore other ways of looking at things or the inability to see things as others might. Nurturing open-mindedness involves encouraging two traits:

- **Recognizing differences in points of view.** Students must realize that individuals and groups do not always see the world, or explain events that occur in it, in the same way, thus it is necessary to develop the ability to see things from differing viewpoints.
- **Entertaining various points of view.** Students need to accept the right of others to hold points of view that differ from their own and to be willing to and able to consider varying perspectives—including diverse cultural points of view.

Open-mindedness is *the* crucial feature of the perceptual dimension. It identifies an openness to things that are unfamiliar or even strange to us. It involves more than understanding that people have different opinions on an issue—for example, some people are in favour of mandatory use of seat belts and others oppose mandatory use. It involves what Hanvey (1976, 4–5) refers to as "perspective consciousness"—an awareness that individuals and groups have world views or "cognitive maps" that are not universally shared by others and may be shaped by factors that we are unaware of and unable to control. Young students may need particular help in appreciating that there may be more ways to see an event than their own. Multiple points of view involves looking at issues from different disciplinary perspectives (for example, seeing the economic, environmental, and political implications of a position) and also from different personal and cultural perspectives.

In introducing point of view, it may be useful to encourage students to view and describe concrete objects from different physical locations (for example, the look of a pencil or a classroom from the front, back, and sides). Stories also provide opportunities for students to take on a role and describe events and feelings from different characters' perspectives. It is also useful to invite students to attend to shifts in their own perspectives when new information is added to a circumstance. Discuss, for example, how a person might feel if they saw another student sitting alone eating lunch in the cafeteria. Suppose the person moved further into the cafeteria and noticed that the solitary student was his or her younger sibling. How might this information affect the person's perception of the scene? Or what if the person him- or herself is the one sitting alone eating lunch? Each piece of information may create an internal shift affecting both feelings and the description of the event.

Encourage students to approach the study of other cultures from the point of view of an insider in that culture. Another strategy—a twist on the mental maps activity discussed earlier—is to invite students to draw mental maps from designated perspectives—say, from the point of view of someone living in their hometown, and then from the perspective of a group that students have been studying in class (Johnson 1997). Students would be encouraged to depict on their maps the characteristics of the world that would be most relevant to the people from whom the perspective is being taken—for example, Europe might be prominent on a map if many local immigrants had come from Europe, or Japan might be prominent if imported cars were popular.

When comparing cultural points of view, it is important to remind students of the heterogeneity within any group. Although "Europeans" or "Japanese" as a group might share some traits, not all members within the group necessarily share points of view on all (or even most) things. A useful analogy can be drawn with being a student in twelfth grade. As a group, twelfth-graders share experiences such as writing provincial examinations; however, it is simultaneously true that within this group there are very distinct points of view.

Students may be open-minded with regard to some issues and not others, often depending on the degree of personal investment or familiarity with the points of view. For example, we are less likely to be open-minded when self-interest or deeply held values are at stake. The difficulty in seeing the other side was confirmed during a workshop one of us offered for teachers in India. We asked participants to entertain possible reasons why a political group that had killed fourteen innocent people the day before may have acted in a principled manner. Many of the teachers were able to undertake this exercise in perspective-taking; others seem unwilling and incapable of doing so. Although we personally might believe that killing fourteen bystanders was not justified, unless we seriously consider the reasons for this group's actions, we should worry that we have reached an ethnocentric, closed-minded conclusion.

Teacher modelling is also an important way to encourage student open-mindedness (Torney-Purta 1983, 33). Modelling open-mindedness requires that teachers consistently and sincerely attempt to base their classroom comments and decisions on careful consideration of all sides, and to show a willingness to change their mind or alter their plans whenever good reasons are presented.

FULL-MINDEDNESS

Full-mindedness refers to the inclination to make up one's mind on the basis of adequate understanding of the whole story. Its opposite is simple-mindedness—a penchant for leaping to conclusions or settling for simplistic or incomplete explanations. Promoting full-mindedness includes helping students develop the following traits:

- **Anticipating complexity.** The inclination to look beyond simplistic accounts of complex issues, and to look for ramifications and interconnections and to see phenomena as part of a constellation of interrelated factors.
- **Recognizing stereotyping.** The ability to identify and dismiss portrayals of people or cultures that are superficial generalizations or objectifications that portray cultures or countries as quaint, eccentric, or objects of curiosity.
- **Suspending judgment when warranted.** A willingness when dealing with complex matters to withhold coming to a firm conclusion until varying viewpoints, and the evidence for them, have been considered.

Anticipation of complexity involves fostering student scepticism of explanations that fail to consider with sufficient imagination the range of interacting factors and consequences of most global events; it is a call to resist seeing events in the world as isolated and localized. Although it is inevitable, and often desirable, that global/cultural issues be simplified somewhat, it is important to discourage superficial or naive views (that is, black-and-white accounts and definitive lists of the causes of events). If students are not alerted to, or if they refuse to accept, the messy reality of many of our enduring global predicaments, they will be satisfied with crude and simplistic responses to problems. Simplified solutions, however, are unlikely to succeed—world famine will not be resolved by producing more food (we already produce enough food to feed everyone) and we will not eliminate poverty merely by creating more jobs (many people considered to be below the poverty line are fully employed or are not capable of working). Unless students anticipate the ramifications of a course of action, they are less likely to advocate proposals that adequately accommodate the interconnected nature of many global situations. A case in point is the Green Revolution, which failed to accommodate the social, psychological, financial, and agricultural implications of abandoning supposedly unsophisticated farming practices.

One of the most important implications of anticipating complexity is that any cultural practice should always be considered in the context in which it is expressed. In other words, we need to be sensitive to the situation in which cultural values and beliefs are expressed instead of simply leaping to conclusions. Historical, political, and social factors influence the expression of "culture." For example, Madonna's version of pop-culture dance may have been controversial in the mid-1980s, early in the development of music-video culture. In today's context, a similar dance style may well be viewed as "normal" in this genre.

Cultural stereotyping is the tendency to see individuals and societies in simple, superficial, and often negative ways. To avoid this requires an awareness of the breadth and depth of cultural practices. The activity in the highlighted text may help elementary students appreciate the sophisticated wisdom behind seemingly "silly" practices.

BELIEVE IT OR NOT

Students are introduced to and invited to react to the "unusual" practices of an unidentified group (the Inuit). It is anticipated that some students may initially find these actions "odd" or "unusual." The objective is to encourage students to respond more respectfully to situations that initially seem "foreign" by helping them see the rashness of their initial impressions.

WHAT DO YOU THINK OF A GROUP THAT ...	
Their behaviour	Your initial reaction
• once lived in snow houses in winter	
• plays soccer at midnight	
• used moss diapers for their babies	
• softened animal skin by chewing it	
• made sleds out of frozen fish	
• made sails for their boats from animal intestines	

After recording their initial reactions, students learn about the reasons for each practice (below are suggested advantages of two of these practices) and are invited to reconsider their initial impressions. In this way, students are helped to appreciate the resourcefulness of the Inuit and that the lifestyle of other cultures may seem unusual at first glance, but once they understand why people live a certain way, the actions are generally perceived to be thoughtful.

RATIONALE/ADVANTAGES FOR SELECTED INUIT PRACTICES	
Behaviour	Rationale
moss diapers	• moss is widely available • moss can be stored in the winter • moss diapers are free, absorbent, and soft • moss diapers are environmentally friendly (moss is biodegradable) • moss can be packaged tightly and is lightweight for travel
sails made of intestines	• intestines are strong (they won't rip easily) • intestines are lightweight (they will not slow down the boat and can be transported easily) • intestines are easy to sew together • intestines are available any time animals are killed • the sails are environmentally efficient (parts of animals that may not be eaten or otherwise be used are used)

Educators can discourage simple-mindedness by stressing the rationale for practices but also by attending to the interrelated factors involved in most events and the inevitability of ramifications for most actions. For example, solutions to global population problems should be discussed in the context of competing social and religious pressures, such as parents' reliance on their children to supplement family incomes and to provide for old-age security, deep-rooted religious beliefs and cultural values, and state-mandated rules regarding family size (such as China's one-child policy). Young students can be introduced to the complexity of events by having them trace the myriad consequences of a single action (for example, the effects of an environmental change) or the range of factors that have influenced an event (for example, all the people and countries that contributed to the breakfast eaten that morning). Fostering student appreciation of complexity may require replacing superficial exploration of many topics with fewer, but more in-depth, case studies. In general, teachers who model an appreciation of the complexity of most issues are likely to promote student acquisition of this attribute (Newmann 1991, 330).

Recognition of stereotyping refers to developing students' ability to identify the inadequacy of accounts of people, cultures, or nations that are limited to a narrow range of characteristics (that is, important features of the group are ignored) or that depict little or no diversity within them (that is, differences within the group are ignored). Unlike the previously discussed element of complexity, which focusses on explaining events with appropriate intricacy, resisting stereotyping involves describing groups of people with sufficient diversity. For example, during the Cold War period especially, the tendency in the West was to talk about Eastern Europe as if it were a single entity. Similarly, the crude treatment of African culture in many social studies textbooks fails to do justice to the fundamental differences among African cultures and to their richness (Beckett and Darling 1988, 2–3). As was mentioned earlier, stereotyping occurs when educators, however well-intentioned, focus on the quaint or exotic features of a culture. For example, curriculum resources regularly stereotype Egypt as a museum or curiosity piece—as the land of pyramids and sphinxes.

In addition to cultural stereotyping, a particularly relevant form of stereotyping is the inclination to focus on "we/they" dualisms. Casting issues as "our" cultural group against "other" cultures is stereotyping whenever it disguises the shared values that underlie supposedly competing interests. This tendency, sometimes called "essentializing" group characteristics, attributes to all members of a group a limited set of qualities. Similarly, dualisms among international sectors (for example, north-south, east-west, developed-developing countries) involve stereotyping whenever the interests of all countries in a bloc are reduced to the interests of the bloc and set in opposition to the interests of other blocs. The problem with these dualisms are their tendencies to ignore the cross-boundary similarities and shared interests in many issues and problems (for example, Eastern Europeans are likely as concerned about cancer as are North Americans) and to polarize camps on issues when divisions are not warranted (for example, ending the nuclear arms race was a goal shared by people on both sides of the Iron Curtain). Of course, we can go to the opposite extreme by exaggerating the extent to which one group's interests are shared by all nations and peoples.

Recognizing stereotypes is important because unflattering stereotypes of people, cultures, or nations are often deliberately encouraged. For example, creating hostile stereotypical images of people from an opposing country is sometimes used to fuel distrust or hatred against them (Silverstein 1989). Even in situations where the motives are benign, the effects of stereotyping are often undesirable. The eugenics movement in Western Canada and in many American states is an example of the disastrous effects of well-intended stereotyping. The so-called science of eugenics called into question the "fitness" of certain groups to have and raise children. Based primarily on unflattering stereotypes about people with mild disabilities, aboriginal peoples, and those of Eastern European origin, members of these groups, considered to be "feeble-minded" or to have loose morals, were evaluated by boards that had the power to sterilize those deemed to be socially undesirable. This occurred in North America during the same time in which similar claims about the superiority of certain races were the popular ideology in Western Europe.

As this example illustrates, condescending and paternalistic attitudes towards people from various cultures may be a function partly of our stereotypical images of these people (Werner, Connors, Aoki, and Dahlie 1977, 33). Building students' resistance to stereotypical accounts decreases their inclination to dehumanize or marginalize groups, because students see these groups as having a full range of human attributes. In other words, we should try to inoculate students against accepting portrayals of members of other cultural groups "as cardboard characters in a stilted puppet play" (Zachariah 1989, 51). On a positive note, we can develop students' resistance to stereotyping by increasing their appreciation of the similarities and shared interests among cultures, and by combatting tendencies to paint issues in black-and-white terms.

The previously mentioned strategies for promoting an appreciation of complexity are appropriate for encouraging appreciation of global/cultural diversity: gross generalizations about people and nations should be discouraged, and examples of differences within cultural and national groups should be provided. Although more extensive study of fewer cultures or nations may be preferred to the relatively superficial study of many peoples, we must guard against stereotypical impressions encouraged when a heterogeneous entity, say Africa or aboriginal peoples, is considered exclusively in the context of one sample, say Nigeria or Haiti. As a general rule, we should avoid presenting only the dominant images of a country or people—that is, avoid dealing exclusively with the poverty in Africa and with the civility in Japan.

Being open-minded also implies having a tendency to suspend making firm judgments when evidence is inconclusive or when a thorough examination of the issue has not been carried out. As the Scottish philosopher David Hume observed, a wise person proportions his or her belief to the evidence. Teachers can encourage full-mindedness in their students by not always having the answer and by being comfortable with uncertainty—that is, being satisfied with tentative conclusions until a full review of complex issues can be carried out.

FAIR-MINDEDNESS

Fair-mindedness refers to the inclination to give a fair hearing to alternative points of view—to judge matters on the basis of their own merits, and not simply in terms of our own interests and preferences. Its opposites are bias and self-absorption. Promoting fair-mindedness includes encouraging a willingness and ability to:

- **empathize with others:** to place oneself in the role or predicament of others or at least to imagine issues from the perspectives of other persons or groups;
- **overcome bias:** to resist imposing the interests or perspective of one's own group over those of other countries or peoples.

The ability to empathize does not imply that we must agree with the positions taken by others or be supportive in all cases—it requires solely that we try to understand in a vivid way what others think and how they feel. Empathy is not the same as open-mindedness, although the two are related. Empathy presupposes an openness to ways different from our own, but it goes further than openness, in that empathy requires that we "feel" the other person's predicament. The need to promote empathy arises because merely learning more about other people or countries may not increase students' appreciation of what other people's lives are really like. However, the inclination to empathize with others is not identical with promoting unqualified acceptance of others—a sensitive exposure to certain practices may legitimately redouble students' sense of another's oddness or unreasonableness. Thus, promoting empathy is not tantamount to encouraging moral relativism—students may still judge that certain practices are undesirable or unappealing. However, as the common expression suggests, we shouldn't criticize another until we have walked in that person's shoes.

Bias refers to an unwarranted or unfair preference for one's own interests or affiliations. It was reflected in contrasting descriptions of British and Iraqi actions provided by the British press at the height of the Persian Gulf War in 1991. More specifically, British forces were described as "cautious" and "loyal," and Iraqi troops as "cowardly" and "blindly obedient"; British sorties were "first strikes" and "pre-emptive" while Iraqi initiatives were "sneak missile attacks" and "without provocation" (*The Guardian* 1991). And more recently, in the reporting in the aftermath of Hurricane Katrina in New Orleans, black residents were said to be "looting," while white residents were merely "finding" provisions (Yahoo!News 2005). These accounts are prejudiced even if we all agree that Iraq deserved condemnation for provoking the war and that the residents were looting, because otherwise identical actions were judged differently merely because of which side performed them.

There are three forms of bias that are particularly relevant for multicultural and global education:

- **Ethnocentrism.** This refers to the view that one's own cultural group is superior to all others. It is not necessarily ethnocentric to prefer most features of North American life to customs and practices in other cultures; rather, it is ethnocentric to judge them better simply because they are our ways. Unless students are able to see the merits of other cultures, the study of other cultures will simply fuel the belief that "our ways are the best and the others are inferior." As Jenness (1990, 412) remarked in his extensive review of social studies, some educators are concerned that "the world studies program may well turn out to be a fatter photo album, ethnocentrically selected and arranged." In North America, for example, people typically bathe once a day, which is considered sufficient to maintain a socially acceptable measure of cleanliness. From a Japanese perspective, however, bathing merely once a day may be regarded as very unclean. Either perspective, seen from an ethnocentric point of view, would regard the other as inappropriate—either deficient or excessive cleanliness—missing the point that these behaviours are socially defined responses (or adaptations) to particular conditions.
- **National fanaticism.** This refers to a refusal to assess policies and events involving our own country impartially or to recognize that, on some occasions, national best interests, as opposed to the interests of other countries or people, should not be paramount.
- **Presentism.** This refers to a preoccupation with the in-

terests and well-being of current generations to the exclusion of the interests of persons yet to be born into the world. In other words, the felt urgency of our immediate needs and desires may preclude our fair-minded consideration of others' future needs. Concern with this form of bias underlies much criticism about our inadequate sensitivity to the long-term environmental consequences of national policies and consumer decisions.

To encourage fair-mindedness, students should regularly be expected to explore and defend positions from different points of view, especially from perspectives that are not personally held by them. For students who have difficulty in being fair-minded, teachers may try "challenging" their thinking in non-threatening ways by presenting opposing reasons and by looking for inconsistencies in their attitudes. More likely, however, reasoning with students will not be sufficient. Students may benefit from exposure to evocative situations where they can "feel" for themselves the power and merit of other perspectives. There are at least three sources of these sorts of visceral experiences:

- **Vicarious experiences** where students come to live the lives of others through films and stories. There are many collections of films and stories about various countries and cultures; many of these have been written or produced by people from other cultures.
- **Simulated experiences** where students act out through role play or another type of simulation activity the predicament of others.

- **First-hand experiences** where students encounter in "real-life" meaningful contexts—through field trips, classroom guests, exchanges, pen pals, social action projects—the points of view of others.

The highlighted simulation, "What's Fair," is intended to help students develop empathy for those who may be living in poverty. Experiences such as these—whether brought about by reading a story, participating in a simulation, or experiencing things first-hand—help to evoke students' sensitivities to points of view that they might otherwise downplay or ignore.

Conclusion

Our four objectives in writing this chapter have been to:

- illustrate the importance of helping students approach the study of their world from a more "global" and "diverse" perspective;
- explain five main areas of the substantive—or content—dimension of this perspective;
- explain three key traits of the perceptual—or attitudinal—dimension;
- suggest ways in which the perceptual dimension may be nurtured—through direct instruction, teacher modelling, and "experiential" activities.

Although our focus is social studies, it is apparent that promoting a global/multicultural perspective should not be limited exclusively to this subject, nor should it be an

---

WHAT'S FAIR?

At the start of the day, randomly distribute a coloured card to each student upon entering the class—in a class of thirty students have three gold cards (or ten per cent of the class), nine silver cards (thirty per cent), twelve green cards (forty per cent), and six white cards (twenty per cent). Offer no comment about the card, but at the break and/or at lunch time, distribute food according to the following schedule:

	SNACK	LUNCH
Gold card	21 Smarties (or raisins)	sandwich, milk, apple, and a cookie
Silver card	9 Smarties (or raisins)	sandwich
Green card	4 Smarties (or raisins)	plain slice of bread
White card	1 Smartie (or raisins)	crust of bread

It will take little time for students to erupt into complaints about unfairness. Debrief the activity by noting the parallel between, on the one hand, the unfairness of students getting more goodies than others merely because they happened to get a particular card when they came into the room and, on the other hand, the unfairness of people having greater wealth than others merely because they happened to be born in a particular country or social class. To avoid anxiety and resentment, it is wise to end the activity by equalizing the distribution of goods among students. If students who have more resist, this too is significant and worth exploring in class: why might those with wealth or power resist policies that may potentially take away their advantage?

occasional add-on that occurs within a designated unit. Rather, efforts to promote a global perspective can and should be embedded in much of what we do each day.

Locate the teaching instructions in a resource dealing with a specific cultural group. Look for evidence suggesting how the suggested activities support or undermine the following elements of a multicultural/global perspective:

- **Open-mindedness:** a willingness to entertain new ideas and alternative ways of looking at people, places, and events. It requires:
  - recognizing differences in points of view, and
  - entertaining various points of view.
- **Full-mindedness**: the inclination to make up one's mind on the basis of adequate understanding of the whole story. It requires:
  - anticipating complexity,
  - recognizing stereotyping, and
  - suspending judgment when warranted.
- **Fair-mindedness:** the inclination to give a fair hearing to alternative points of view—to judge matters on the basis of their own merits, and not simply in terms of our own interests and preferences. It requires:
  - empathizing with others, and
  - overcoming bias.

Design one or more activities to enhance a multicultural/global perspective on the featured cultural group.

ENDNOTE

1   In an earlier article, Case (1993) identified five interrelated elements of the perceptual dimension (open-mindedness, anticipation of complexity, resistance to stereotyping, inclination to empathize, and non-chauvinism). In a 1995 article intended for elementary students, these traits were collapsed into three more general categories: open-mindedness, full-mindedness, and fair-mindedness.

REFERENCES

Banks, J.A., ed. 2004. *Diversity and citizenship education: Global perspectives.* San Francisco: Jossey-Bass.

Beckett, K. and L. Darling. 1988. The view of the world portrayed in social studies textbooks. Occasional paper #13. *Explorations in Development/Global Education.* Vancouver: Research and Development in Global Studies, University of British Columbia.

British Columbia Ministry of Education. 1983. *Social studies curriculum guide: Grade 1–grade 7.* Victoria, BC: Author.

Case, R. 1989. Global perspective or tunnel vision? The mandated view of the world in Canadian social studies curricula. Occasional paper #23. *Explorations in Development/Global Education.* Vancouver: Research and Development in Global Studies, University of British Columbia.

———. 1993. Key elements of a global perspective. *Social Education* 57 (6): 318–325.

———. 1995. Nurturing a global perspective in elementary students. In *Thinking Globally about Social Studies Education,* ed. R. Fowler and I. Wright, 19–34. Vancouver: Research and Development in Global Studies, University of British Columbia.

The Guardian. 1991. Mad dogs and englishmen. February 22.

Hanvey, R.G. 1976. *An attainable global perspective.* New York: Global Perspectives in Education.

Jenness, D. 1990. *Making sense of social studies.* New York: Macmillan.

Johnson, C. 1997. Expressing a global perspective: Experiences in a Mexican classroom. Unpublished paper.

Kniep, W.M. 1986. Defining a global education by its content. *Social Education* 50: 437–446.

Newmann, F.M. 1991. Promoting higher order thinking in social studies: Overview of a study of 16 high school departments. *Theory and Research in Social Education* 19: 324–340.

Perinbaum, L. 1989. A new frontier for teachers. *Alberta Teachers' Association Magazine* 69: 23–25.

Saarinen, T.F. 1973. Student views of the world. In *Images and environment: Cognitive mapping and spatial behavior,* ed. R.M. Downs and D. Stea, 148–161. Chicago: Aldine Publishing.

Schuncke, G.M. 1984. Global awareness and younger children: Beginning the process. *Social Studies* 75: 248–251.

Silverstein, B. 1989. Enemy images: The psychology of US attitudes and cognitions regarding the Soviet Union. *American Psychologist* 44 (6): 903–913.

Social Studies and the Young Learner. 1994. Special theme: Global perspective in a new world, March/April.

Stewig, J.W. 1992. Using children's books as a bridge to other cultures. *The Social Studies* 83 (1): 36–40.

Torney-Purta, J.V. 1983. Psychological perspectives on enhancing civic education through education of teachers. *Journal of Teacher Education* 34: 30–34.

Werner, W., B. Connors, T. Aoki, and J. Dahlie. 1977. *Whose culture? Whose heritage? Ethnicity within Canadian social studies curricula.* Vancouver: Centre for the Study of Curriculum and Instruction, University of British Columbia.

Willms, J. 1992. The children next door: Bringing the global neighbourhood into the classroom. *Orbit* 23 (1): 14–16.

Yahoo!News. 2005. As discussed at http://www.media-awareness.ca/english/resources/educational/teachable_moments/katrina_2_photo.cfm.

Zachariah, M. 1989. Linking global education with multicultural education. *Alberta Teachers' Association Magazine* 69: 48–51.

17

Teaching for Hope

Walt Werner

One cannot live in this media-rich culture without feeling some unease about the future. Weekly we encounter disturbing images of urgent proportions. A litany of enormous challenges—including poverty and famine, human rights abuses and repression, desertification and ecological stress, social chaos, and international debts—confronts our increasingly interdependent world. After Lebanon, Cambodia, and Ireland came Ethiopia, Sudan, Bosnia, and Rwanda [then Iraq, Afghanistan, and Darfur—Ed.], and we have come to expect that a list of similar place names will continue. Systemic interactions among diverse problems are overwhelming in their complexity and ambiguity, and this leads to uncertainties. According to the Club of Rome,

> Never in the course of history has humankind been faced with so many threats and dangers ... the causes and consequences of which form an inextricable maze.... Individuals feel helpless, caught, as it were, between the rise of previously unknown perils on the one hand, and an incapacity to answer the complex problems in time and to attack the roots of evil, not just its consequences, on the other hand (King and Schneider 1991, 127–128).

Even though this barrage of bad news leaves us psychologically fatigued, we still need to rationalize the realities of what we see and hear, because no matter what our politics, we want a better future (Kennedy 1993; Roche 1993).

For children, though, pictures of a broken world speak directly to their own future. Implied is their tomorrow. Whether this realization occurs in a dramatic moment of insight or slowly awakens as a vague awareness, the consequence can be uncertainty about the future or, even worse, some loss of hope.

Classrooms are unwitting partners in this loss. It begins when youth encounter texts and images that imply a deeply problematic future. Through classroom projects, video and print resources, and discussions of current events, students glean bits of information from which they construct their personal views, often of a crisis-ridden and confusing world created by adults who seem unwilling or unable to change it. "Youngsters piece together these fragments in a jumbled patchwork of mixed perceptions that make them anxious," observed Van Ornum (1984, 16). "The world is not safe. If adults are scared and helpless, what chance do kids have?" When unchecked, these feelings lead over time to insecurity or cynicism about the prospects for individual and collective futures.

Such outcomes, however, are educationally unacceptable because schools are in the business of strengthening realistic hope in the future. Let me illustrate with an event from a grade 10 social studies class. Groups were organized around research projects related to a number of global issues. I thought they were learning well to sort through controversial problems when a young woman quietly informed me that she would rather drop out of her study group and do an individual project on cowry shells. When asked what social or economic issues were represented by these natural artifacts, she replied that she was not aware of any issues nor was she interested. She simply wanted to study the shells, as she said, "because they're beautiful." I suddenly realized that here was a sixteen-year-old whose sense of future was threatened. The cumulative effect of my "ambulance chasing" pedagogy was a sense of helplessness, a feeling that the range and complexity of issues were too difficult to understand, let alone solve. My focus on problems left her with a deepening uncertainty.

Anyone who is a teacher is necessarily an optimist. Our working with young people represents a commitment to the future. We are teaching for hope. But what does it mean to have hope? Many years ago, Philip Phenix reminded educators that "Hope is the mainspring of human existence." This is no idle slogan, for, as he explained, "conscious life is a continual projection into the future.... Without hope, there is no incentive for learning, for the impulse to learn presupposed confidence in the possibility of improving one's existence" (1974, 123). Essential to hope is a knowledgeable and reflective confidence in the future and a willingness to engage it.

The future, whether one's own or that of a larger group, is seen as open, having possibilities, rather than foreclosed or predetermined. This belief entails confidence that current problems and worrisome trends can be addressed in response to care and effort, that good planning and strategic action taken today can have significant consequences. In short, hope expresses itself as a "Yes" to tomorrow.

How can youth's sense of hope for the future be strengthened through classrooms? Part of the answer lies in the important roles that emotion, information, vision, and efficacy have in young people's coming to understand the problems and complexities of their larger world. Through a teacher's sensitive use of these four avenues, hope can be encouraged during discussions about global issues.

Select two current crises that are widely reported in the news. Arrange to discuss these crises with three or four students. Ask them what they feel about each crisis, what they know about them, whether they see the possibility of positive resolutions, and whether there is anything the students can do to help bring about a solution. Summarize their responses and draw several conclusions about the levels of hopefulness these students express.

Emotion

Honest treatment of subject matter, whether in the humanities or sciences, will at times give rise to emotionally loaded concerns and questions about the future. For decades, educators have known that harm to learning does not necessarily come from material that evokes emotion (Jones 1970, 69–86). Any learning that is memorable and important is also emotion-full. Expressions of feeling—such as surprise, anger, wonder, uncertainty, awe, consternation, commitment—engage the interest and imagination of students, extend their involvement with the subject matter, and imbue the curriculum with the kind of personal significance that impels rather than hinders learning.

There is an emotion, however, that is not a friend of learning: anxious students do not perform well. Anxiety about the future rests on feelings of helplessness and isolation in the face of threatening prospects (Jones 1970). And when children are unwilling to talk freely about topics that engender this sense of aloneness and hopelessness, their uninformed imaginations give rise to misperceptions of issues that can further reinforce anxiety (Stackhouse 1991).

How can the study of global problems and issues help youth feel less anxious about the future, less helpless about the prospects for change, and less alone in their imaginations?

That students feel threatened by questions about the future needs to be dealt with rather than avoided. Classroom discussions, when sensitively directed by the teacher, can counter anxiety. For example:

- Watch for *signs of anxiety*, and seek ways to ameliorate this feeling and to promote a sense of community and efficacy. Indicators of a loss of hope can be varied. For example, off-hand comments or jokes during conversations about world problems may indicate fear, confusion, resignation, or anger; these refusals to discuss issues seriously may be masking deeper ambivalences. Expressions of apathy or lack of interest—such as protesting the topic, disengagement from discussion, or incomplete or poorly done projects—may also be attempts to protect oneself.

- Take seriously *the sentiments* about anxiety or hopelessness that children express during discussions of current events and issues. Help them articulate the reasons for these attitudes, and where appropriate, provide counter-examples and new information that challenges narrow or unsubstantiated beliefs.

- Focus discussions not only on the informational content of issues, but also on their *emotional content*. How do students feel about the issue? Emotions have to be shared—listened to and discussed—in order to be understood and harnessed for learning. As concerns are expressed, children realize that they are not alone in their imaginations about the future; there are broader communities of concern embracing people around the earth.

Information

Shielding children from global problems cannot be a solution to preserving their sense of hope. Purging the curriculum of topics that raise concerns for young people, or focussing discussion only on "safe" areas, are not options except for making classrooms more sterile places. As Van Ornum suggests, "Today's young people, for better or worse, are savvy and cynical. Old before their time, they know a dodge when they see one" (1984, 3). They already know from television that many people lead wretched lives because of environmental degradation, armed conflicts, and poverty, and that some adults are not hopeful about change (Kaplan 1994). But if children hear little acknowledgement of these realities, they conclude that educators either do not care or are not being honest; neither case instills confidence in learning about global issues. The perceived dark side of the world calls for information rather than silence.

Thoughtful discussion of information is essential, though, because a source of hopelessness can be misinformation, misunderstood information, or a lack of information about the nature and extent of a problem. Any defensible belief in the future has to include, among other things, an adequate knowledge—a realistic understanding and honest appraisal—of what the situation is. Herein lies a responsibility of educators to ensure that students have accurate and balanced input when discussing global issues, and to check whether the inferences drawn from classroom conversations and other texts are reasonable. Sketchy or inaccurate "facts," as well as hearsay, casual comments, and a neglect of context, can lead to unwarranted conclusions, overgeneralizations, or false impressions of what the future might be like (Jickling 1994).

If we want students to develop a reasoned hope in the future, then during classroom discussions:

- probe for *inferences* that children hold about the future. Are these inferences warranted by the best information at hand? Could their conclusions lead to unfounded fears or unrealistic expectations? Uninformed or misinformed fears and confidences both constitute naiveté.
- provide greater awareness of the broad range of *institutions* dedicated to gathering and disseminating reliable information about issues, and of the many groups that use this information to lobby governments for new policies or changed laws. This research and development work is premised on a strong confidence in the future.

Emphasis in the classroom upon inert information—often packaged as worksheets and end-of-chapter questions—only provides youth with disconnected "facts" about the state of their world. Unless meaningful connections among these isolated bits and pieces are forged, the picture of the larger world may make little sense beyond a bewildering array of problems. Hope falters when the content learned by students does not lead to better understanding.

Vision

Hope cannot rest only upon an understanding of what is or will be the case (information), but also upon imagined alternatives and how these may be achieved (vision). "Where there is no vision," says an ancient proverb, "people perish." It is not enough to want a "better world" without articulating what this might mean: What are one's priorities for an improved world, and how could they be achieved? Alternative futures are defined as we "name" them through goals, plans, and policies. Problem solving calls for a willingness to project outcomes and to choose from among competing scenarios. Rich imagination is the stuff of hope. But imagination withers whenever young people are treated as less than mindful agents through unimaginative pedagogy.

Children's hope is strengthened as their imaginations are engaged in understanding and "making" their world:

- Introduce *visionary concepts* that define alternatives for the future. Some examples are "sustainable environment," "respect for the rule of international law," "the commons," and "human rights." That these concepts may be controversial does not disqualify them from classrooms, but highlights the fact that they represent important values for envisioning the future.
- Discuss why the world community has forged institutions that embody and implement *collective visions* for the future. Examples include the world court and international law, as well as the many other agencies and covenants of the United Nations (Department of Foreign Affairs and International Trade, 1994).
- Give students opportunities to define and share *personal visions* for the future. Imagination is clarified and enlarged as it is challenged in a context of alternatives (Boulding 1995; Korten 1995). Not only do the visual and performing arts offer multiple modes for expressing doubts and hopes about the future, but also through "writing and sharing stories, creating images, and participating in role plays, we can simulate events as though we are already in the future. Our objective in such visualizations is not to predict the future, but to perceive potential futures in the here-and-now and to conceptualize what it will take to get there from here" (Bryant 1995, 40). Visions can be created and shared through various avenues, including poetry, music, drama, dance, story, drawing, and painting.

Hope is never fostered when students' own creative envisioning of desirable futures is disallowed, when information about the world is treated as a given to be received rather than re-imagined. Youth need to theorize about possibilities.

Efficacy

A concern that youth express when they begin to recognize the extent of world problems is why adults are not solving them. This query is not about more information on specific government policies and projects, but more deeply about how the world of adults works. It is an attempt to understand the kind of world in which they live: Is it a world in which adults do not care about problems that occur elsewhere? where adults do not know what to do? or where adults care more about present interests than consequences for the future? Some of children's deepest fears about abandonment are here tapped (Hevesi 1990). They seek assurances that adults can be trusted to protect the new generation's future. No wonder they become apprehensive.

Our goal is to encourage the development of those abilities and dispositions that allow young people to engage in appropriate personal, social, and political action. Hope is indistinguishable from a belief that individuals and groups influence and shape their futures through action. A strong sense of personal efficacy is a driving force behind any achievement. Without it, there is little open-mindedness to new ideas, willingness to reflect on one's own plans, or motivation and confidence in becoming proactive. To paraphrase Saul Alinsky, "There can be no darker or more devastating tragedy than the death of people's faith in themselves and in their power to direct their future. Denial of the opportunity for participation is the denial of human dignity...." Students need to understand why they are not powerless to make a contribution at some level.

Fostering efficacy is not an add-on to studies of global issues, but should be part and parcel of the ongoing discussions:

- Focus on the worldwide extent of *agencies, partnerships,* and *networks* engaged in problem solving. Young people are not aware of the range of groups—whether governments, international institutions, non-governmental organizations, grassroots community initiatives, or the private sector—committed to action and what they are doing. The important understanding here is that the difficulties facing our interdependent globe are being worked on by many people in various ways.

- Infuse *good news stories* about the successes that individuals, groups, and institutions are having in their actions. Elicit examples of actions that have been and are being taken to solve problems. Valuable experience and skills have been gained over the past decades, and considerable progress was achieved in areas such as health, agriculture, and social justice (Canadian International Development Agency 1987). The purpose for introducing positive examples is to provide a balanced and honest, not utopian, view of the gains that are made locally and internationally.

- Encourage discussion of *personal actions* that could be taken at home and in the school or community. The complexity of issues and problems does not preclude consideration of meaningful action: What can I personally do? Is there collective action that we should plan? Depending upon the age and circumstances of students, activities may involve letter-writing, changing one's consumer habits, attending a seminar for further information, joining the work of a community organization, or forming a school club. Appropriate action is not only a way to apply what is learned, but also a means for understanding issues better and strengthening efficacy.

Curricula and classrooms are largely organized around and for passivity. Often students are taught political incapac-ity rather than efficacy through the large amounts of inert knowledge they are given. They learn inadvertently that "doing school work" is not meant to be "real work" that has any direct impact on (or even relevance for) larger issues. This is why discussions about efficacy are so important for undercutting learned helplessness.

Conclusion

Classroom discussions of global issues may increase student anxieties about the future. This is why educators need to reflect on the roles that emotion, information, vision, and efficacy may have in shaping young people's beliefs about their tomorrow. I am not advocating that we put a light and happy face on the world. Youth already have a sense of dark crises on the horizon, but these realities need not imply despair. Hope requires a careful understanding of issues, and the development of reasoned visions and a realistic sense of efficacy. It is then that the sobering images on TV screens and the problems they imply can be seen with possibility.

Let me conclude with a personal anecdote. Late one night I heard my son, who was in grade 1 at the time, call from his room. I turned on the light and noticed that he had been crying. "When I grow up," he announced, "there will be no more wilderness." Whatever he meant by "wilderness" was not as important at this point as his expression of a threatened personal future. This loss of hope had started earlier in the day during a classroom discussion about stresses on ecosystems around the world, followed that evening by a television documentary on the loss of wilderness in western Canada. Because he lacked adequate information and the necessary conceptual tools to appraise the issues, what little understanding he gained from these two events led to a confused and anxious inference about his own future. I assured him that, although wilderness was indeed under serious threat in places, many groups of concerned people just like him were working to protect ecosystems through new policies and laws, and that there were things that he and I could do as well. Over the next few days, we sought new information, shared our visions, and explored ways to enhance efficacy.

Think of a contemporary local, national, or international issue or problem that you would want to explore with students. Use the author's four key ideas of emotion, information, vision, and efficacy to develop a list of a dozen activities or discussion points that you could use to build hope in students as they explore the issue.

ACKNOWLEDGMENT

This chapter appeared originally in 1995 in *Thinking globally about social studies*, ed. R. Fowler and I. Wright, 57–60. Vancouver: Research and Development in Global Studies, University of British Columbia.

REFERENCES

Boulding, E. 1995. Why imagine the future? *Context: A Journal of Hope, Sustainability, and Change* 40: 50.

Bryant, B. 1995. Rehearsing the future. *Context: A Journal of Hope, Sustainability, and Change* 40: 39–50.

Canadian International Development Agency. 1987. *Sharing our future: Canadian international development assistance.* Hull: Minister of Supply and Services Canada.

Department of Foreign Affairs and International Trade. 1994. *Canadian reference guide to the United Nations.* Hull: Minister of Supply and Services Canada.

Hevesi, D. 1990. NY children feel both fearful, guilty about the homeless. *Globe and Mail*, , May 22.

Jickling, B. 1994. Studying sustainable development: Problems and possibilities. *Canadian Journal of Education* 19 (3): 231–240.

Jones, R. 1970. *Fantasy and feeling in education.* New York: Harper Colophon Books. Kaplan, R. 1994. The coming anarchy. *Atlantic Monthly*, February, 44–76.

Kennedy, P. 1993. *Preparing for the twenty-first century.* New York: Random House.

King, A. and B. Schneider. 1991. *The first global revolution: A report by the Council of the Club of Rome.* New York: Pantheon.

Korten, D. 1995. A new day's coming in. *Context: A Journal of Hope, Sustainability, and Change* 40: 14–18.

Phenix, P. 1974. Transcendence and the curriculum. In E. Eisner and E. Vallence, eds., *Conflicting conceptions of curriculum* (117–132). Berkeley, CA: McCutchan.

Roche, D. 1993. The new world order: Justice in international relations. *Global Education* 1 (1): 31–38.

Stackhouse, J. 1991. There's method in the misery. *Globe and Mail*, October 18.

Van Ornum, W. 1984. *Talking to children about nuclear war.* New York: Continuum.

18 Cultivating Legally Aware and Empowered Citizens

Wanda Cassidy and Margaret Ferguson

"That's not fair!"

"She hit me!"

"Stop peeking at my answers!"

"He called me a bad name!"

"She owes me five dollars!"

"Hey, do you want to hear the new CD I burned from the net?"

"Teacher, Ronnie isn't following the rules!"

"Someone rifled through my desk!"

"You're a bully!"

"I feel left out and picked on!"

When asked whether they teach law, elementary teachers usually are surprised by the question, and respond in the negative. Yet, as suggested by the sample student comments listed above, every day in elementary classrooms and hallways and on school playgrounds, teachers and students grapple with law-related issues. They may not immediately identify them as legal, but the law has much to say about getting along with others, respecting people's property and their right to privacy, making fair decisions, keeping promises, and ensuring that rules are applied fairly. Inevitably, students learn about law through the policies and practices at school.

In addition, the social studies curriculum provides many opportunities for elementary students to learn about law. Topics in each grade are directly or indirectly related to law, for example, rights and responsibilities of family and community members, government and the Charter of Rights and Freedoms, the founding of Canada, First Nations issues, immigration and our multicultural mosaic, the environment, and Canada and its place in the world.

Law is foundational to social studies education and to cultivating informed and empowered citizens. In this chapter, we explain the purpose of law-related education and its importance to elementary social studies. We explore three approaches—conceptual, practical, and participatory—to addressing the law component in the formal and informal curriculum, and suggest instructional strategies for each.

What Is Law-Related Education?

The term "law-related education" or LRE was coined over thirty years ago to describe the kind of education about law that is appropriate for students in public school. There is a tendency to think that studying law means learning the body of rules and procedures that lawyers acquire in law school or that adults learn in a piecemeal fashion as they proceed through life. This is not the recommended approach for elementary schools: most classroom teachers are ill-equipped to disseminate such information and the technical aspects of law are not the most appropriate law-related content to teach in public schools. For this reason, the term "law-related education" was coined to distinguish the teaching about law in the schools from the teaching of laws to lawyers and other legal professionals.

Rather than transmitting technical information about laws, LRE is more centrally concerned with promoting student understanding of the role that law plays in society and in their personal lives. Certainly, specific laws are studied from time to time, but the emphasis is on understanding why we have laws, the sources of law, legal institutions and structures, and other aspects of the foundations of law. The content of LRE is the ideas or concepts underlying the legal system—notions such as rights, responsibilities, authority, justice, and equality. LRE examines the values or beliefs embodied in our law, such as respect for property and human life. LRE involves developing basic citizenship attributes—such as critical thinking and conflict resolution—to help students participate effectively in a legally regulated world, and to effect change when the rules no longer reflect the kind of community we want, LRE encourages active learning and the use of community resources to gain a realistic look at the legal system in operation. Important LRE objectives include reducing cynicism, understanding the limitations of law, and assuming some responsibility for making the system responsive to people's needs.

LRE seeks to develop critically aware and socially responsible citizens who are willing and able to make a positive difference in their neighbourhood, community, and nation. These aims are intertwined with the goals of social studies education more broadly: preparing young people for citizenship, developing student's abilities to think critically about issues, and encouraging students to take action to make the world a better place (Marker and Mehlinger 1992, Newmann 1989). Law professor Hugh Kindred captures the value of law-related education in furthering social studies goals:

> In a participatory democracy, it is vital that students learn about their rights and duties as citizens. Knowledge of the institutions that control the society is a prerequisite to intelligent democratic action.... In addition, it is important that students know not only their civic responsibilities, but also their freedoms of action within the Canadian system of government. The measure of good citizenship is not inculcated conformity, but a healthy respect for the rights of others as well as one's own, and an allegiance to orderly processes, even in diversity. The character of law encourages such critical, yet constructive attitudes. Consequently its study will develop them in students, the next generation of Canadian citizen (1979, 534).

As well, there is a profoundly practical reason for learning about the law. LRE is basic to survival in a world where law is pervasive. We marry, have families, travel, conduct business, worship, and even die according to law. Our written laws proliferate at a staggering rate. The federal government has enacted hundreds, if not thousands, of statutes and every province has approximately five hundred statutes in place. Thousands of regulations appended to these statutes contain the procedural "nuts and bolts" that affect how we act. Add municipal bylaws to this list and it is easy to appreciate that the long arm of the law reaches into almost every aspect of our lives. Without some appreciation of the nature and scope of this influence, students' ability to function in society is impaired. Furthermore, ignorance of the law is not considered a justifiable excuse when a law is not followed.

Efforts to infuse LRE into elementary schools are typically organized around three approaches (Starr 1989):

- **conceptual:** focussing on the core concepts and principle in law;
- **practical:** stressing the day-to-day implications of law;
- **participatory:** involving students in the application of law-related procedures.

Most programs in Canadian social studies classes combine elements of all three approaches, depending on curriculum expectations, grade level, and teacher and student needs and interests.

THE CONCEPTUAL APPROACH

The conceptual approach examines central legal ideas such as liberty, justice, and equality—concepts that form the bedrock of a democratic society and which are lauded in school. Even primary students have strong notions about what is right or fair, and are intrigued by dilemmas that present opportunities to examine issues of power, authority, privacy, responsibility, and property. This approach to LRE focusses on broad principles and concepts, and emphasizes critical thinking.

One way to address concepts is through a case study. Cases can either be real (for example, historical events, actual court cases, or current events), based on stories from children's literature, or imagined dilemmas. In an article entitled "A Tale of Two Gates," James Lengel (1984) suggests how the story *Peter Rabbit* can involve students in analysis of abstract concepts such as punishment, justice (fairness), authority, and responsibility. In this classic tale, Peter Rabbit lived with Flopsy, Mopsy, Cotton-Tail, and his mother underneath the root of a very big fir tree. One morning old Mrs. Rabbit tells her children that they may go into the fields and down the lane, but they are not go into Mr. McGregor's garden because their father had an "accident" there—he was put in a pie by Mrs. McGregor. Like most children's stories, *Peter Rabbit* sets out a problem of obedience and disobedience, of adventure and misadventure, of making and breaking rules. This realistic, close-to-home conflict raises the following important legal issues:

- Was the father's fate really an accident?
- Was it fair for Mr. McGregor to punish the father so harshly?
- What could have been a fairer punishment?
- Did Mrs. Rabbit have the authority to make the rule she did?
- Was it a good rule?

In case studies, students wrestle with the facts, issues, and arguments, and come to a reasoned decision that can be justified according to the evidence. There are no "pat" or "right" answers in a case study. Rather, the purpose is to teach students to distinguish relevant facts from irrelevant ones, synthesize issues into a key problem or question needing resolution, articulate perspectives from more than one side, reach a reasoned decision, and justify their conclusion with sound reasons (Bognar, Cassidy, and Clarke 1997). The highlighted text "Case Study Method" suggests a five-step structure for a case study.

Many topics in the elementary social studies curriculum have a legal angle. When examining the roles and responsibilities in a community, for example, teachers can invite students to consider why we need laws, how a law might be changed, whether we need police officers to keep the peace, what role each citizen has in improving the neighbourhood, whether children should have rights, and what penalties are appropriate when someone damages the environment. Similarly, immigration may be studied through the notions of diversity, inclusion, and multiculturalism. Topics such as government and politics invite examination of the rule of law, the role of the judiciary, and the importance of the Charter of Rights and Freedoms to articulating the values we espouse as Canadians.

Figure 18.1, "Who Has a Responsibility?" (adapted from McDermid, Abbott, and Case 2003), describes an activity to help primary students understand when someone has a responsibility to do something. In assessing responsibility in the two hypothetical scenarios, students would consider two factors: whether the persons are able to help, and whether it is fair to expect them to help. Building on this understand-

CASE STUDY METHOD

- **Find the facts:** Who is involved? What happened? What is the complaint or charge? What facts are important? Which facts are irrelevant?
- **Frame the issues:** Identify the key issue and pose it as a question (for example, Should logging be restricted in the area of the Spirit Bear? Was an assault committed when Sally hit Sammy?).
- **Discuss the arguments:** An issue always gives rise to two or more points of view. What are the arguments for and against? Which arguments are most persuasive? Why?
- **Reach a decision:** After students wrestle with the case and reach a decision, the court decision may be discussed, a historical event replayed, or the story's ending communicated.
- **Examine the reasoning:** Students should back up their decision with reasons. In a real case, judges often disagree with each other. In appeal cases involving more than one judge, one judge writes the majority decision, and other judges may write minority opinions. Students may be invited to do the same.

FIGURE 18.1   WHO HAS A RESPONSIBILITY?

Imagine you have been asked by your teacher to bring back to your classroom a big box of books that is too heavy for you to carry. You think of three people who might have a responsibility to help you.

	Is _____ able to help you?	Is it fair to expect that _____ should help you?
A teacher who is standing beside the box	yes no	yes no
Your friend who is sick at home	yes no	yes no
A big boy who is very strong who has been sent with you by your teacher to help carry the box	yes no	yes no

Imagine you are in class working on an arithmetic problem that is too hard for you to do, but you must solve the problem before you go to recess. You think of three people who might have a responsibility to help you.

	Is _____ able to help you?	Is it fair to expect that _____ should help you?
Your teacher who is standing beside you	yes no	yes no
Your friend who is really good at arithmetic and sits next to you	yes no	yes no
The person who lives next door to you, who is very good at arithmetic, but who has left town for a long trip	yes no	yes no

ing, students would then examine responsibilities that other people in the community have and eventually responsibilities that students themselves have.

THE PRACTICAL APPROACH

The focus of the practical approach is law's impact on the daily lives and decisions of Canadians, including children. At the elementary level, students need to understand that law affects them each day in many ways, whether they are aware of it or not. A simple activity to sensitize students to the diverse ways in which laws touch their lives is to ask them to write a story describing who they are, where they live, and what they did from the time they got up in the morning to their arrival in the classroom. (Younger students can draw pictures representing the things they do each day.) After discussing the stories, help students see that law regulates everything from the kinds of homes they live in, to the beds they sleep on, what is written on their breakfast cereal boxes, the type of fabric in their clothes, how parents treat them, bicycle safety, school hours, the type of playground equipment at school, what can be said in school textbooks, what they can or cannot say or do to a fellow student, and the air they breathe.

A related activity to increase upper elementary students' awareness of the scope of the law is to circulate sections of the local newspaper. Ask groups of students to identify any article, advertisement, or section that relates to law. Initially, students may find a few obvious examples (such as a crime committed, a lawsuit, or a police matter). However, with guidance, students can see that almost every part of the paper is connected to law—including the sports pages, advertisements, classified section, comics, entertainment section, and most headline articles. As the highlighted text "Law in Our Everyday Lives" suggests, law regulates and shapes almost everything we do on a daily basis.

Appreciating the practical implications of rights contained in documents such as the United Nations Convention on the Rights of the Child or the Canadian Charter of Rights and Freedoms requires that students understand that human rights exist to protect the most basic of human needs. Students learn the importance of these entitlements by examining the consequences that follow when these rights are not respected. Using Figure 18.2, "Drawing the Line on Our Right to Food" (adapted from Nicol and Kirk 2004), students might consider the point along a continuum from total absence to complete luxury at which meeting this basic need becomes a right. Students would decide this by considering the implications, on the one hand, of not meeting the need for a person's well-being and, on the other hand, of placing an unfair burden on the rest of society who would have a responsibility to see that this right is respected. The articulation of this point can be used to generate a statement of rights (for example, every child has a right to enough food so that…), which can be posted to a class charter, and eventually compared with the UN Convention on the Rights of the Child or Canadian Charter of Rights and Freedoms.

LAW IN OUR EVERYDAY LIVES

- **Name.** Laws specify the surname a child can take. Everyone's name is registered on a legal document, the birth certificate. There is a legal procedure to follow for changing one's name.
- **Address.** Do students live in a village, city, or town? This designation is determined by law. Zoning laws specify the type of dwellings that can be built in an area. The procedures for numbering homes and naming streets in municipalities are regulated by law.
- **School.** Laws require children to attend school and these laws set the number of hours of instruction per day and per year. The law requires adults to pay taxes to support schools and sets out the rights and responsibilities of teachers and principals.
- **Pets.** Municipalities have laws that affect the type of pet one can have, and whether or not a pet requires a licence and a leash on public property. Cruelty to animals can be a criminal offence.
- **Family.** Laws specify how marriage must take place, how

people come to assume the rights and responsibilities as a mother or father, under what conditions divorce can occur, how adoptions occur, who is entitled to inherit property when a family member dies, and so on.
- **Food.** Laws regulate the handling and packaging of food, what foods can be imported and exported, and what businesses must do before they can sell food.
- **Transportation.** Drivers and owners of vehicles have many laws to obey—licensing, insurance, and traffic laws. Bicycles, scooters, and skateboards are also regulated by laws.
- **Contracts.** Any time goods are bought or sold, we are entering into a contract. Consumer protection laws ensure that contracts are fair.
- **Money.** Laws establish what currency is legal tender in a country.
- **Businesses.** The formation and operation of businesses are governed by law, including the rights and responsibilities of employers and employees.

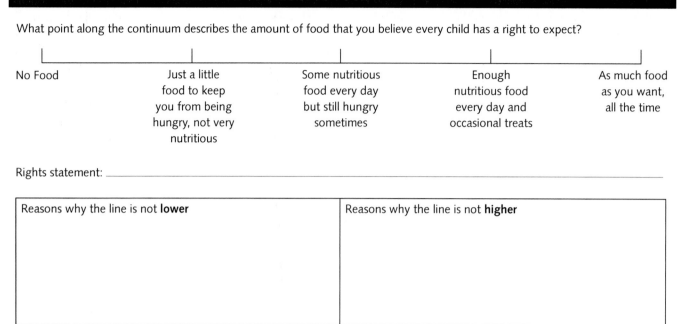

FIGURE 18.2 DRAWING THE LINE ON OUR RIGHT TO FOOD

What point along the continuum describes the amount of food that you believe every child has a right to expect?

| No Food | Just a little food to keep you from being hungry, not very nutritious | Some nutritious food every day but still hungry sometimes | Enough nutritious food every day and occasional treats | As much food as you want, all the time |

Rights statement: _____

Reasons why the line is not **lower**	Reasons why the line is not **higher**

Select an important legal principle (such as equality, justice, personal responsibility, or the rule of law) and develop one or more activities to help students better understand the concept and to nurture their appreciation of its importance as a personal and social value.

THE PARTICIPATORY APPROACH

Many LRE advocates stress a participatory approach to learning, where students engage directly with legal resources in the community and with real or realistic law-related problems. Judges, lawyers, legislators, human rights advocates, environmentalists, and others are invited into the classroom, and students interact with local law-related agencies. Courthouses are open to the public, and many courts (with prior permission) will allow classes to view a trial in session or conduct their own mock trial in a spare courtroom. Many law-related agencies are willing to share their knowledge with students (for example, immigrant services societies, Native friendship centres, human rights groups, mediation services, media watch, internet regulators, consumer protection agencies, animal rights groups, or multicultural groups). Exploring the roles that these agencies play in our society gives breadth to students' understanding of the richness of community resources, and complements their knowledge of more typical services like the police, firefighters, postal service, and recreational facilities. (See the Additional Resources section at the end of this chapter for contact information on public legal education agencies that have a mandate to support teachers in various provinces and territories.)

The participatory approach stresses that students learn about law by experiencing legal processes and decision making in ways that simulate real life. This means that mock trials and role plays based on legal procedures are central to LRE pedagogy. Simple simulations or role plays may be developed based on neighbourhood or school issues, historical events, or stories from literature. For example, as described in the highlighted text, "Resolving a Neighbourhood Conflict," students can experience the procedures of a small claims court by participating in a three-way role play involving two disputing parties and a judge.[1]

Mock trials, which involve more formal enactment of legal procedures than do role plays, have been used in elementary social studies classes to address historical and current events (Cassidy and Yates 1998, 2005; Norton 1992). In a mock trial, students put a character on trial and then enact the trial playing the roles of the accused, the witnesses, court personnel, and the media. Classes have examined a gold rush murder case tried by the infamous hanging judge, Matthew Bailey Begbie, charged a student in the case of a missing social studies exam, run a school Litter Court to try classmates accused of littering the school playground, and put such fairytale characters on trial as Goldilocks, Hansel and Gretel, Peter Pan, and Alice in Wonderland. Current events also provide engaging scenarios that can be used as the basis for mock trials.

Children's literature provides a rich source of material for mock trials or role plays involving law-related issues such as good and bad leadership, responsible and irresponsible behaviour, and freedom, equality, justice, and privacy. The case of Peter Rabbit, described earlier, illustrates this potential. Peter Rabbit could be put on trial for trespassing on Mr. McGregor's garden and for stealing Mr. McGregor's vegetables. The witnesses for the prosecution might include Mr. McGregor, Mrs. Mouse, the Scarecrow, and Constable Meadows. The witnesses for the defence might include Peter, Benjamin Bunny, Cotton-Tail, and old Mrs. Rabbit. Lawyers present the case with the help of a court clerk, court recorder, sheriff, and jury. Some students could assume media roles by preparing newspaper articles on the case or running a video camera. Unlike a scripted trial, students develop their roles based on the story, and the lawyers for the prosecution and defense prepare questions for their witnesses and to cross-examine the other side's witnesses. The prosecution presents the story and tries to prove that Peter is guilty of both charges beyond a reasonable doubt. The defence challenges the story, presents Peter's side, and calls witnesses to introduce doubt that Peter did the things as charged or that he intended to do them. The jury—classmates or another class in the school— determines the verdict.

In the additional resources listed at the end of this chapter, we provide annotations of other promising stories. Following is a list of stories for primary children organized by law-related themes (Doge 2004):

Rules
The Signmaker's Assistant, by Tedd Arnold
Aunt Chip and the Great Triple Creek Dam Affair, by Patricia Polacco

Honesty
Franklin Fibs, by Paulette Bourgeois and Brenda Clark

RESOLVING A NEIGHBOURHOOD CONFLICT

Scenario

Between the Sámi yard and the Finn yard next door stood a beautiful, massive tree. The Finn ancestors planted the tree a century ago, and over the years the trunk of the tree expanded so that half the trunk and many of the branches extended over the property line into the Sámi yard. The four Sámi children loved to climb the tree and played in it for hours. The Finns didn't seem to mind when Jo Sámi, the oldest child, built a tree house in the branches and slept there with a friend on hot summer evenings. The Finns' children had left home long ago, so they liked to see children playing outside.

The Finns, however, were getting older and hated to rake up the leaves and prune the branches. They also wished for more daylight because the tree blocked out most of the sunshine on that side of their house where they had two picture windows. The Sámis, on the other hand, were grateful for the shade the tree provided.

One day, while the Sámis were away, Mr. and Mrs. Finn arranged for the tree to be chopped down. When the Sámi family arrived home, they were devastated. The younger children cried for days. When the Sámis tried to talk to the Finns about it, Mrs. Finn just said, "Well, it was our tree and we had a right to do with it what we wanted." Mr. Sámi said: "Well, I'm not so sure; it was also on our property too; you had no right! Besides, we've used it for years, and you didn't seem to mind!"

The Sámis want to plant another tree in the empty spot, but can't afford to buy a large one unless they are given money for over their loss of the old tree. The Samis decide to take the Finns to court for loss of enjoyment of the tree, and to seek damages of one-thousand dollars to pay for a new large tree.

Role play

Divide the class into small groups of three students each. One student assumes the role of the plaintiff, the Sámis. The second student plays the defendant in the lawsuit, the Finns. The third student plays the role of judge who hears both sides of the issue, asks questions of each party, determines whether the Sámis have a legitimate case against the Finns and, if so, whether damages and court costs should be awarded.

Before the role play, each side should prepare its case and decide how best to present it to the judge. During the preparation time, the judge reads through the case and records questions to ask. The judge's options in deciding the issue include the following:

- rule in favour of the Sámis and make the Finns pay them one-thousand dollars plus court costs;
- dismiss the claim against the Finns, which would require the Sámis to pay the court costs of both parties; or
- decide on a middle ground where both parties pay their own court costs, and the Finns pay a lesser amount to the Sámis, or to require that both parties come to a mutually agreeable size and type of tree and plant it in a spot on which agree.

Once the judge in each trial has heard the case and made a decision, the judicial decisions and reasons for the decisions should be shared with the rest of the class. Discuss the following broader issues:

- Why were there different decisions?
- What were the most convincing arguments?
- What aspects of law would you have liked to know more about before you reached your decision?
- Is court the best place to resolve a problem like this one?

The Three Little Wolves and the Big Bad Pig, by Eugene Trivizas and Helen Oxenbury

John's Choice: A Story about Honesty, by Jane Belk Moncure

Pollution
The Tower, by Michael Twinn and Arlette Lavie
One World, by Michael Foreman
The World that Jack Built, by Ruth Brown

Vandalism
The Giants' Child, by Marcia K. Vaughan
Purple, Green and Yellow, by Robert Munsch and Hélène Desputeaux

Play Lady: La Señora Juguetona, by Eric Hoffman and Suzanne Tornquist

Street Safety
Traffic Safety, by Nancy Loewen and Penny Dann
Tin Lizzie, by Peter Spier
Curious George Rides a Bike, by H.A. Rey

Trespassing
Somebody and the Three Blairs, by Marilyn Tolhurst and Simone Abel
Deep in the Forest, by Brinton Turkle
Goldilocks Returns, by Lisa Campbell Ernst

ORGANIZING A MOCK TRIAL

Mock trials can be conducted informally inclass or conducted with costumes and props in a local courthouse or other public place with actual members of the judiciary or legal profession presiding. There are three phases to a trial: the preparatory phase, the trial itself, and the post-trial discussion. The phases for a criminal mock trial suitable for primary and intermediate level students are outlined below.

Preparatory phase
- Decide on the story or event for the trial, or choose one of the scripted or packaged mock trials available.[2]
- Help students understand the criminal charge, the facts of the case, and the key issues.
- Review basic information with students about the justice system (adversarial model, need for impartial decision, role of court personnel, innocent until proven guilty, concept of intent, reasonable doubt).
- Assign (or allow students to choose) their roles: the accused, witnesses, Crown prosecutors, defence lawyers, court clerk, court reporter, sheriffs, and media (court artist, newspaper reporters, television journalists). A lawyer or school principal should be asked to play the role of judge.
- Divide students into four small groups that will each prepare their case:
    - Crown prosecution and their witnesses;
    - defence lawyers, the accused, and their witnesses;
    - court personnel; and
    - the media.
    If following a script, emphasize that the case should be presented without notes as much as possible. For more complex trials involving role cards instead of a script, emphasize the development of arguments, writing good questions to be asked in court, and presenting one's evidence as convincingly as possible.
- Invite students to prepare costumes that represent their role.

Enacting the trial
- If the trial is conducted in the school gymnasium, library, or classroom, design the room to model a real courtroom, as illustrated in figure 18.3 (adapted from Cassidy and Yates 2005).
- Once the trial begins, it should continue without interruption until the jury reaches a decision and the sentence is rendered (if guilty), or the accused is set free (if not guilty). The teacher's role is to take notes and comment following the trial, not to guide or interrupt the trial.

Post-trial discussion
- Immediately after the trial, debrief with students, allowing them to share their feelings and thoughts about the trial, and to come out of role.
- With the full class listening/contributing, address each group:
    Jury: What evidence was most convincing? Which characters were most believable? Why did they decide the case as they did?
    Lawyers: Which arguments were most persuasive? Would you have changed your presentation in any way?
    Witnesses: What did you experience being in the witness box? Did any aspects of the trial surprise you?
    Court personnel: Why is the role of court clerk and court reporter important? Did the sheriff feel any differently about the role after donning a costume?
    Media: What parts of this trial are you going to write about or present to classmates? What role does the media play in real court cases?
    Whole class: What did you learn about the law and court system as a result of participating in this trial?
- The days following the trial provide other opportunities for reflection, or more in-depth investigation of aspects of the justice system and conceptual issues such as the advantages and disadvantages of the adversarial model, whether judgement by peers in a jury system is the best method of determining guilt, whether there are better ways to resolve disputes than through the courts, and so on.

FIGURE 18.3   COURTROOM LAYOUT

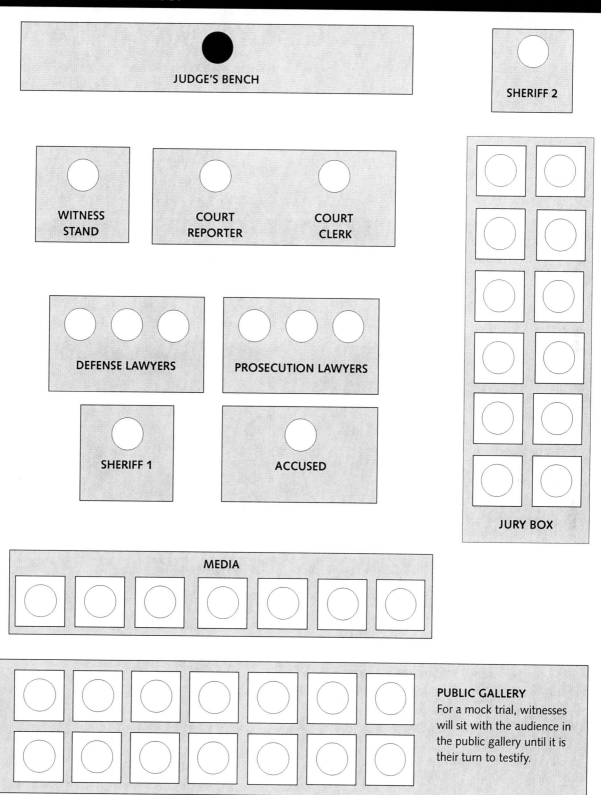

JUDGE'S BENCH

SHERIFF 2

WITNESS STAND

COURT REPORTER

COURT CLERK

DEFENSE LAWYERS

PROSECUTION LAWYERS

SHERIFF 1

ACCUSED

JURY BOX

MEDIA

PUBLIC GALLERY
For a mock trial, witnesses will sit with the audience in the public gallery until it is their turn to testify.

Law

A Small Lot, by Eros Keith

Old Henry, by Joan W. Blos and Stephen Gammell

Jonathan Cleaned Up—Then He Heard a Sound: or Blackberry Subway Jam, by Robert Munsch and Michael Martchenko

Annie Bananie and the People's Court, by Leah Komaiko

Carla Goes to Court, by Jo Beaudry and Lynne Ketchum

Parliament: Canada's Democracy and How It Works, by Maureen McTeer

Monkey Tales, by Laurel Dee Gugler and Vlasta van Kampen

Adjudicating actual classroom and school disagreements afford wonderful LRE opportunities. One such dispute resolution mechanism is mediation. In this method, parties work together with the help of a third party to come to a mutually agreeable decision. This involves give and take, with each side letting go of certain demands or moderating others in order to agree on a solution. This procedure may be simulated in class, with students learning listening and negotiating skills in the process. Students are presented with an issue, either from history or the current day, and then work in one of the disputant groups or in a mediator group to come to a solution.

Many schools have peer mediation programs where students involved in conflict learn to solve their differences with the assistance of trained student mediators and without the intervention of teachers. Student mediators might be coached to use the steps outlined in the highlighted text when assisting other students to resolve a dispute.

The growing interest in social responsibility and in restorative justice is also compatible with law-related education, particularly if the programs developed are respectful of individuals, give credence to due process, allow for diversity and reasonable dissent, seek to be just and fair, and work towards the good of all (Whitley 2002). It is important, too, that the whole school community be involved in these initiatives, working together to model and practise the values of responsibility or restoration, rather than expecting only the students to comply (Epstein 1999). Approaches that engage all stakeholders and become embedded in school culture have a far greater impact on learning than programs that merely formalize the goals and do not implement them into all levels of practice.

Teachers would be remiss if they focussed exclusively on the formal curriculum of social studies education, yet failed to consider the law-related implications of the informal or "hidden" curriculum. What we do in the classroom—what is modelled and prastised—has a powerful effect on children's learning (Jackson 1990; Jackson, Boostrom, and Hansen 1993). Establishing working principles for the classroom

GUIDELINES FOR PEER MEDIATORS

- **Who is involved?** Make sure every person involved in the conflict is present. List their names, grades, and teachers.
- **What happened?** Each student should be given a chance to say what happened without being interrupted or corrected by the others who are involved. You decide the order of speaking. Use active listening skills and ask open-ended questions to make sure you get as many facts as possible. After everyone has spoken, summarize the facts as you understand them. Does everyone agree this is what happened?
- **What is the real problem?** Help the students identify the issue that is causing the problem. Identifying feelings is often a first step (for example, "I feel angry because...."). Each person has to listen very carefully to what the others are saying. The real issues are often hidden.
- **How can we fix the problem?** Encourage students to think of as many solutions as possible. Do not let them discard any solution until all the options are understood. What solution is acceptable to everyone? When an agreement is reached, make sure everyone understands it. Write down what was decided. The problem may happen again and the agreement may have to be changed.

and a few rules to support these principles helps to model for students the ideals of thoughtful law-making and citizen involvement. These conditions for a "democratic" classroom can be nurtured at the beginning of the school year by considering and, if appropriate, inviting students to consider the following kinds of questions:

- What are the shared values and beliefs that will form the basis of the classroom community?
- Will these values be reflected in classroom rules or procedures?
- Will students' views be solicited?
- How many rules are needed and how will these rules be established?
- To what extent will students be able to have input into the rule-making, and how will this be done?
- How will rules be enforced and who will judge whether a rule has been broken?
- Will the consequences for the breach of a rule be fair and flexible so that the context of the offence is considered?
- Is there a need to clarify or modify the rules as situations develop? How will this be done?
- How does one measure the fairness or appropriateness of a rule? (Should all students find the rules acceptable, or is it sufficient that the majority agree?)

Conclusion

The law dimension is an essential part of an adequate social studies education. The kind of education in law we advocate is not that of mini lawyers-in-training, but rather sensitizing children to the role that law plays in their lives and in a democratic society. We have illustrated a range of opportunities and strategies for incorporating law-related topics into the formal and informal curriculum. No single approach to LRE is required—you are encouraged to start small with an approach that best suits your purposes and resources. By doing this, you will join elementary teachers across North America who are advancing children's awareness of legal concepts and procedures and empowering them as effective and responsible members of their classroom, school, and neighbourhood communities.

ENDNOTES

1   This story is taken from Cassidy and Yates (2005). Additional examples are provided in this book, as well as a discussion on how to use contemporary children's stories and multicultural stories to address law-related issues. Other references are Ferguson (1998) and Gascoigne (1998).

2   For a list of trials, see the Law Courts Education Society of British Columbia website or consult www.acjnet.org/teacher/ and www.lawconnection.ca.

REFERENCES

Bognar, C., W. Cassidy, and P. Clarke. 1997. *Social studies in British Columbia: Results of the 1996 Provincial Learning Assessment.* Victoria, BC: Province of British Columbia.

Cassidy, Wanda. 2000. Law-related education: Promoting awareness, participation and action. In *Weaving connections: Education for peace, social and environmental justice,* ed. T. Goldstein and D. Selby. Toronto: Sumach Press.

Cassidy, W. and R. Yates, eds. 1998. *Let's talk about law in elementary school.* Calgary: Detselig.

———. 2005. *Once upon a crime: Using stories, simulations and mock trials to explore justice and citizenship in elementary school.* Calgary: Detselig.

Doge, K. 2004. Books with law-related themes for primary students. In *Law in the Curriculum,* Education 448 Course Reader, W. Cassidy and R. Yates, Reading 5.4. Burnaby: Faculty of Education, Distance Education, Continuing Studies, Simon Fraser University.

Epstein, J. 1999. Creating school, family, and community partnerships. In *Contemporary issues in curriculum,* 2nd ed., ed. A. Ornstein and L.S. Behar-Horenstein, 422–441. Boston: Allyn & Bacon.

Ferguson, M. 1998. Learning law-related concepts through literature. In *Let's talk about law in elementary school,* ed. W. Cassidy and R. Yates, 89–116. Calgary: Detselig.

Gascoigne, H. 1998. Looking at law through story drama. In *Let's talk about law in elementary school,* ed. W. Cassidy and R. Yates, 71–88). Calgary: Detselig.

Jackson, P.W. 1990. *Life in classrooms.* New York: Teachers College Press.

Jackson, P.W., R. Boostrom, and D. Hansen. 1993. *The moral life of schools.* San Francisco: Jossey-Bass.

Kindred, H. 1979. Legal education in Canadian schools? *Dalhousie Law Journal* 5 (2): 534–542.

Lengel, J. 1984. A tale of two gates. *Update on Law-Related Education* (Fall): 27–28.

Marker, G. and H. Mehlinger. 1992. Social studies. In *Handbook of research on curriculum,* ed. P. W. Jackson. New York: Macmillan.

McDermid, M., M. Abbott, and R. Case, eds. 2003. *Rights, roles and responsibilities at school.* Richmond, BC: The Critical Thinking Consortium.

Newmann, F. M. 1989. *Education for citizen action: Challenge for secondary curriculum.* Berkeley, CA: McCutchan.

Nicol, J., and D. Kirk. 2004. *Caring for young people's rights.* Richmond, BC: The Critical Thinking Consortium.

Norton, J. 1992. The State v. the Big Bad Wolf: A study of the justice system in the elementary school. *Social Studies and the Young Learner* 5 (1): 5–9.

Starr, I. 1989. The law studies movement: A brief look at the past, the present and the future. In *Law vs. learning: Examination for discovery,* ed. W. Crawford, 11–15. Toronto: Canadian Law Information Council.

Whitley, C. 2002. Building citizenship, democracy and a community of learners within a context of a restorative justice model. Unpublished master's project. Burnaby, BC: Simon Fraser University.

ADDITIONAL RESOURCES

Websites suitable for elementary grades

Access to Justice Network. Classroom resources and Access to Justice Materials: http://www.acjnet.org/naresources/classroom.aspx.

BC Civil Liberties Association. Citizenship teaching module http://www.bccla.org/citizenship.

Canada's SchoolNet. Lesson plans and online mock trials for elementary students: http://www.acjnet.org/teacher.

Law Courts Education Society of BC. Resources and programs for teachers: http://www.lawcourtsed.ca.

The Centre for Education, Law and Society (CELS). Articles and lesson plans for classroom use: http://www.lawconnection.ca.

Public Legal Education Association of Saskatchewan. Elementary school resources related to the law: http://www.plea.org.

United Nations Cyber School Bus. Global legal issues from children's perspectives: http://www.un.org/pubs/cyberschoolbus.

Stories with law-related dimensions

Ering, Timothy Basil. 2003. *The Story of Frog Belly Rat Bone*. Cambridge, MA: Candlewick Press. Cementland is gray and ugly. One day, a boy finds a special and mysterious treasure that promises to change Cementland into an enjoyable place. When thieves steal the treasure, he must come up with a creative plan to thwart them and save the treasure.

Issues: Who does the treasure legally belong to? What punishment should the thieves face? What are the legal issues involved in the boy's plan to save the treasure? If the thieves have a change of heart, should the charges be dropped? What are the rights and responsibilities of the citizens of Cementland?

Levine, Arthur A. 1993. *Pearl Moscowitz's Last Stand*. Illustrated by Robert Roth. New York: Tambourine Books. The neighbourhood on Gingko Street has experienced many changes throughout the years. Friendships flourish as new families arrive from new cultures, but one by one, the cherished gingko trees have disappeared. When City Hall decides to remove the last tree, in the name of progress, Pearl Moscowitz gathers the community together to take a stand.

Issues: How can a community exercise democratic involvement and have a meaningful effect on civic decisions? Are there times when civil disobedience is the only option? Explore the issue of protection of the environment versus "progress."

Miller, William. 1998. *The Bus Ride*. Illustrated by John Ward. New York: Lee & Low Books. The story of an African American girl and her mom who challenge an unjust law. Though they must sit at the back of the bus, one day the little girl moves up to the front—causing a huge discussion across the city. This story is loosely based on Rosa Parks' historic decision not to give up her seat to a white passenger on a bus in Montgomery, Alabama in 1955.

Issues: This story examines discrimination, racism, individual rights, and changing laws.

Patron, Susan. 1991. *Burgoo Stew*. Illustrated by Mike Shenon. New York: Orchard Books. Five mean and hungry boys from a poor area go to their neighbour's house and demand that he make them some food, or else they will steal it. In the end, the neighbour teaches the boys to share and help.

Issues: This story looks at bullying, intimidation, theft, and sharing.

Wildsmith, Brian. 1993. *The Owl and the Woodpecker*. Oxford University Press. The animals in the forest hold a meeting to try to resolve a problem between two members of their community who are fighting. Woodpecker is creating a noise during the day when Owl is trying to sleep. Neither of them will move. The peaceful life of the forest is being destroyed.

Issues: How does a community resolve a problem between two members who both think they are right? Who has a legal right to stay? What legal obligations do the woodpecker and the owl have to do to preserve the peace? Explore the actions of each animal

in relation to social responsibility, diversity, democratic rights and responsibilities, and solving problems.

Public legal education agencies in Canada

There are a number of organizations and resources available to teachers who wish to enhance the program they offer in law-related education.

Alberta

Legal Resources Centre
201–10350 124 Street
Edmonton, AB T5N 3V9
Fax: 780 451-2341
http://www.legalresourcecentre.ca/index.html

British Columbia

Centre for Education, Law and Society
Simon Fraser University
3230–515 West Hastings Street
Vancouver, BC V6B 5K3
Tel: 604 268-7840
http://cels.sfu.ca
http://www.lawconnection.ca

Law Courts Education Society of BC
260–800 Hornby Street
Vancouver, BC V6Z 2C5
Tel: 604 660-9870
http://www.lces.ca

Legal Services Society
400–510 Burrard Street
Vancouver, BC V6C 3A8
Tel: 604 601-6000
http://www.lss.bc.ca

People's Law School
150–900 Howe Street
Vancouver, BC V6Z 2M4
Tel: 604 331-5400
http://www.publiclegaled.bc.ca

Manitoba

Community Legal Education Association
205–414 Graham Avenue
Winnipeg, MB R3C 0L8
Tel: 204 943-2382
http://www.communitylegal.mb.ca

New Brunswick

Public Legal Education and Information Service of New Brunswick
P.O. Box 6000
Fredericton, NB E3B 5H1
Tel: 506 453-5369
http://www.legal-info-legale.nb.ca

Newfoundland
Public Legal Information of Newfoundland
31 Peet Street, Suite 227
St. John's, NL   A1B 3W8
Tel: 709 722-2643
http://www.publiclegalinfo.com

Northwest Territories
Law Society of the Northwest Territories
Main Floor, 5004–50 Avenue
P.O. Box 1298
Yellowknife, NT   X1A 2N9
Tel: 867 873-3828
http://www.lawsociety.nt.ca

Nova Scotia
The Legal Information Society of Nova Scotia
5523 B Young Street
Halifax, NS   B3K 1Z7
Tel: 902 454-2198
http://www.legalinfo.org

Ontario
Community Legal Education Ontario
119 Spadina Avenue, Suite 600
Toronto, ON   M5V 2L1
Tel: 416 408-4420
http://www.cleo.on.ca

Justice for Children and Youth
Canadian Foundation for Children, Youth and the Law
415 Yonge Street, Suite 1203
Toronto, ON   M5B 2E7
Tel: 416 920-1633
http://www.jfcy.org

Prince Edward Island
Community Legal Information Association of Prince Edward Island
P.O. Box 1207
1st Floor Sullivan Building
Charlottetown, PEI   C1A 7M8
Tel: 902 892-0853
http://www.isn.net/cliapei

Quebec
Barreau du Québec
445 boulevard Saint Laurent, S215
Montréal, PQ   H2Y 2Y7
Tel: 514 954-3459
http://www.barreau.qc.ca/?Langue=en

Commission des Services Juridiques
2, Complexe Desjardins
Tour de l'Est, Bureau, # 1404
Montréal, PQ   H5B 1B3
Tel: 514 873-3562
http://www.csj.qc.ca

Gouvernement du Québec
Ministere de la Justice
1200 route de l'Eglise, 6th Floor
Sainte-Foy, PQ   G1V 4M1
http://www.justice.gouv.qc.ca/English/accueil.asp

Saskatchewan
Public Legal Education Association of Saskatchewan
300–201 21 Street East
Saskatoon, SK   S7K 0B8
Tel: 306 653-1868
http://www.plea.org

Yukon
Yukon Public Legal Education Association
c/o Yukon College Library
P.O. Box 2799
Whitehorse, YK   Y1A 5K4
Tel: 867 668-5297
http://www.yplea.com

19 Activism in Elementary Social Studies
The Chamberlin–Glassford Exchange

Chuck Chamberlin and Larry Glassford

This chapter contains three articles: an initial essay by Chamberlin, a response by Glassford, and a rebuttal by Chamberlin.

Citizenship as the Goal of Social Studies: Passive Knower or Active Doer?

Chuck Chamberlin

An Edmonton grade 4 class had been studying Alberta's forestry industry for over two months when their teacher asked her students whether they thought the new pulp mill proposals being announced were a good idea. To help them make an informed decision, Monique [the teacher] helped set up a chart listing the consequences of building the mills or not. Finally, students wrote letters to Premier Getty, Forestry Minister Fjordbotten, and news media telling about their decisions and reasons. The class received a reply from Getty, and CBC-TV came out to the school and interviewed students, then showed a clip on their six o'clock news.

This was particularly interesting because Alberta's social studies curriculum states that "Responsible citizenship is the ultimate goal of social studies." This is defined as follows.

Responsible citizenship includes:

- understanding the role, rights, and responsibility of a citizen in a democratic society and a citizen in a global community;
- participating constructively in the democratic process by making rational decisions;
- respecting the dignity and worth of self and others (Alberta Education 1989, 1).

The responsible citizen needs to participate constructively, then, and the curriculum underscores this by including a model for decision making that ends with:

- Take action (if feasible and desirable).
- What can we do? Do it.
- Was that a good thing to do? Why or why not?
- Was this a good way to answer our problem? Why or why not? (8)

This good citizen presented to us in the Alberta social studies curriculum is very much like these grade 4 students. They had done months of research; they knew a great deal about the environmental, economic, health, aesthetic, and recreational consequences of starting up more pulp mills and *used* their knowledge to make an informed decision on the issue. Most teachers would stop there, feeling that social studies time should be used for learning about the world, not helping students take action to make the world a better place. That raises the question of whether the traditional knowledge-building role of social studies is adequate to develop responsible citizens who not only understand the role, rights, and responsibilities of citizens in a democratic society, but also participate constructively in the democratic process.

If schools are to prepare actively participating citizens, they need to be concerned about the development of a strong sense of political efficacy, or a belief that it can make a difference if you all get together and writes letters to the premier, the minister of forestry, and the media. Unless students believe their efforts will be effective, all the knowledge in the world is unlikely to lead them to be responsible citizens who participate constructively. Monique began providing experience for her students in taking action, and in getting used to the role of exerting influence on public issues and decisions. Perhaps she made some progress, as half of her students answered "yes" when asked, "If a school rule was unfair, do you think you could do anything to get it changed?" Perhaps the effect of working together as a class had some influence on their answers, as nine of those eleven students who answered "yes" then explained they could get other kids to help work for change. Typical was the student who wrote, "I think I could because I would get a group together and go talk to [the principal] about it." Other students said they would "go for a petition" or more forcefully, "get a lot of kids and all tell the teachers and force them to change the rules," or "if all the students got together they could just stay home until the principal will forget the rule." Perhaps the sense of community solidarity and strong sense of political efficacy indicated in these statements reflects the experience of a whole class writing letters and appearing on TV to attempt to exert influence on a social issue, an experience planned and provided by their teacher.

It is instructive also to examine the reasons given by the eleven students who said "no," they didn't think they could do anything to change an unfair school rule. Three said the school rules were good ones, in the best interests of the safety and security of all, and shouldn't be changed. These students were so strongly convinced that the school authorities were completely virtuous that they couldn't even conceive of there being unfair school rules. One wonders how much encouragement they have been given over their five years of schooling to think critically, examine alternatives, or take responsibility for making independent judgments. It seems more likely that obedience, passivity, compliance, and respect for authority have been a heavy emphasis at home and in school.

Five other students who answered "no" said, "They won't listen," or "You can't fight rules." One wonders what experiences have led to this cynicism about attempts to influence people in authority.

These students were also asked four questions about their likely success in influencing other levels of government; the results are shown in Table 19.1.[1]

Such low levels of expected success in exerting influence are discouraging in a country that prides itself on being a democratic society where political participation is essential. How did these students come to hold such pessimistic views? Perhaps they have been subjected to such a heavy emphasis on obedience, politeness, respect for authority, and hard work that it seems wrong to expect to stand up and speak out. Some evidence for that conclusion is found in students' answers to the items in Table 19.2.

Vastly higher percentages of these nine- to ten-year-olds agreed with the importance of obedience, good manners, loyalty, hard work, and respect for Canada's institutions than agreed with likely success in influencing government. These attitudes and self-concepts are not innate, but are learned, and schools must be part of that learning process. However, these students are not nearly so likely to learn that part of their responsibility as a citizen is to stand up for what they believe in, and speak out to try and make our society a better place for all of us to live. Note the much lower percentages of agreement with these items as shown in Table 19.3.

It may well be that most of these children have had nine to ten years of home life emphasizing obedience not assertiveness, conformity not creative thought, respect not equality, acceptance not critical reflection. It may well be that their five years of schooling has mostly reinforced those home attitudes. Indeed, it seems likely that for most of these students' school lives they've been encouraged to *know* about the world, but not to *act* on it. Embedded in this role of only knowing but not acting is a hidden curriculum of passivity, not active citizenship.

Newmann has argued that teaching students to be passive knowers rather than active doers defeats the key principle of democratic government, consent of the governed. Central to Newmann's argument is the ethical importance of equality, based on the moral premise that every human being is entitled to respect and dignity. Dignity, Newmann asserts, is possible only if the claims and interests of each person are treated impartially, which in turn requires that society be organized so that power is distributed as equally as possible through rights to participate in periodic selection of leaders and direct participation to affect the outcome of specific issues. This emphasis on equal access to power minimizes the chance that equal rights can be violated. Newmann concludes, however, that the consent ideal is not being realized, and that "education is, in part, responsible for its failure" (1975, 46). He cites Verba and Nie's study, indicating that eleven per cent of citizens are extremely politically active and forty-seven per cent are relatively inactive, and that "high participators are overwhelmingly upper-status, wealthy, white, middle-aged citizens taking a 'conservative' stand on such issues as welfare" (50). Further, Newmann reports, government leaders in the Verba and Nie study:

> were more responsive to active than to inactive citizens. That is, they were more aware of the activists' views, tended to share those views, and spent more of their efforts trying to implement them. Views of the inactive citizens were not as consistently known, shared, or pursued by government leaders (53–54).

Newmann's solution is to develop skills, predispositions, and self-concepts needed for active participation in public affairs by all citizens, not just those who have developed a strong sense of political efficacy from seeing their upper socio-economic status parents exert power and influence. Programs that stop short at reflectively inquiring into issues and making decisions on them offer a version of citizenship that models knowing and deciding, but not acting: passivity. Hence education for knowledge rather than for action would seem to still bear responsibility for the failure of the consent principle and the continued inequality revealed in élite domination of political affairs.

Wood also has argued the case for a conception of active

TABLE 19.1 INFLUENCING GOVERNMENTS

	% AGREE	% DISAGREE	% DON'T KNOW
If I wanted to, I could get someone in the city government to listen to what I want.	36	36	23
When I grow up I believe I will have a fair chance of influencing people in government.	45	9	45
If I joined together with others, we could cause some rules and laws to be changed.	32	55	14
If people would quit complaining and get active, they could change what the government does.	55	18	27
Mean:	42		

TABLE 19.2 CHARACTERISTICS OF A GOOD CITIZEN

	% AGREE	% DISAGREE	% DON'T KNOW
A good citizen obeys the law.	86	0	14
A good citizen is always polite.	55	23	27
A good citizen is loyal to his or her family.	86	4	14
A good citizen works hard.	77	4	18
A good citizen has good table manners.	68	14	18
A good citizen studies hard in school.	86	4	9
A good citizen pays his taxes regularly.	82	4	14
A good citizen keeps up with what is happening in the world.	77	9	14
A good citizen stands up when "O Canada" is played.	73	9	18
A good citizen shows respect for a funeral.	86	0	14
Mean:	78		

TABLE 19.3 ACTIONS OF A GOOD CITIZEN

	% AGREE	% DISAGREE	% DON'T KNOW
A good citizen joins a political party.	27	27	45
A good citizen tells others what he or she thinks about political problems.	55	9	32
A good citizen tries to change things in the government.	32	45	23
A good citizen gets other people to vote in elections.	55	23	27
A good citizen works to get politicians to do what he or she wants them to do.	9	50	41
Mean:	36		

citizenship rather than the "passive knower-decider." Wood advocates participatory democracy, where citizens take "direct action on social issues—picketing, protesting, democratic takeovers" (1984, 226) as necessary if the hidden curriculum of the school is to change from one that promotes working-class passivity to one that nurtures a sense of political efficacy among all classes. Wood suggests we learn from theorists such as [Michael] Apple the school's social role, namely

> that schools teach a limited, very limited vision of democracy.... Removing from the curriculum any mention of citizen action or resistance, schools seem to limit our vision of democracy to an occasional trip to the ballot box. Gone is the active participant, enter the passive consumer (224–225).

AN ALTERNATIVE MODEL OF CITIZENSHIP EDUCATION

Wood's activist conception of citizenship was built into the provincial curriculum in Alberta during the decade 1978–88. It added the step of "acting on your decision" to the reflective decision-making model Engle and Ochoa (1988) advocate. Consequently, some Alberta teachers have had their students inquiring into a wide range of social issues, culminating their inquiry with varied forms of direct and indirect action. Some examples will provide a contrast to the passive knower method and to its implicit vision of good citizens and good society.

SPRAYING MOSQUITOES

Taylor and Moore (1983) described a four-and-a-half-month study by their grade 5 and 6 students of the use in Red Deer of chemical sprays for mosquitoes that culminated in some students preferring increased use of chemicals, some wanting to replace chemical use with spraying insect predators of mosquito larvae on ponds and ditches, and a third group advocating no control programs at all. The two classes requested time to present their findings and recommendations during a city council meeting, and, using effective forms of persuasion, put predators into an aquarium full of mosquito larvae to show how voraciously predation followed. The students read passionate poetry concluding "please spray not, we'd rather swat," and showed a slide-tape presentation on the effects of chemicals on the food chain and ecosystem. These teachers were influenced by the Hungerford and Peyton (1976) conception of a citizen who is both competent to take action on issues and willing to take that action. After the project, many of these students had a stronger sense of political efficacy than they'd had four and a half months before. When asked

how likely it was that they would really do something about changing an unfair school rule, they made statements such as the following:

> I think it would be likely because after the mosquito project I learned that even grade 5 kids can change council's minds.

> Very likely, because I have had experience with my school.

> We learned that you have to stick up for your rights, so I would go out and do it.

> Well, now that I know how to go about trying to get something done right that I think is wrong, I would probably try and change it (Chamberlin, Connors, and Massey 1983, 34–35).

Further, parents who were interviewed at the city council meeting were very positive about the depth of knowledge students had acquired and their confidence in making their cases before the august authorities on city council. The hidden curriculum in this program had involved learning roles and self-concepts, but not that of the passive knower.

BAN THE BARS

Bev Priftis had gotten to the section of [Jerome] Bruner's *Man: A Course of Study* where they learn about the behaviour of baboons when she decided to take her Calgary grade 7 class to the zoo to observe the nature and behaviour of a baboon troop. When her students found the primates kept in individual cages, they were upset by how this contradicted what had been learned about the social organization and territoriality of these animals. They wrote letters of protest to the Zoological Society, the mayor, the Queen, and the editors of the *Calgary Herald* and the *Albertan*. At first, the head of the Zoological Society charged that the students were uninformed, childish, and irresponsible. The "Ban the Bars" movement grew in the city, however, and eventually the baboons were removed from the zoo because a suitable environment could not be provided. Students' sense of political efficacy was reinforced by seeing that their actions could be effective in making their community a better place for all to live in (Dueck, Horvath, and Zelinski 1977).

CLEAN UP THE DUMP

Three grade 6 and 7 classes in rural Rimbey [Alberta] spent two months learning about provincial law on solid waste disposal, surveying other towns to learn about their dumps, observing the dripping pesticide cans and lamb carcasses in their dump, reading newspapers and magazines, surveying residents for their opinions, interviewing the district agriculturist, home economist, and mayor, and reading government studies on disposal. Finally, they were ready to propose a set of solutions. They wrote letters to the *Rimbey Record*, entered a float in the rodeo parade, wrote several letters to the town and country councils, put out more garbage cans on the rodeo grounds, made posters to advertise the issue, and presented their proposals at a town council meeting (Johncox 1983).

SAVE OUR PARK

When city planners proposed putting a freeway through a ravine in an Edmonton community, the whole school set out to prepare a submission to the Transportation Task Force hearings. Teachers from grade 1 to grade 6 worked with their students to write letters, draw posters, and speak to the hearings. Eight student representatives carried the school messages to the hearings, gave brief speeches on why they didn't want the ravine destroyed, and submitted picture books bearing their submissions. Later, the Task Force recommended the ravine be developed as a community park and that no freeway be routed there. City council later incorporated these recommendations into their transportation and parks plan, and today the ravine is preserved as a park (Chamberlin 1979).

Many more examples could be added to this list to illustrate how Alberta students have learned that the desired role of a citizen is to know what's going on, be part of it, and do something about it. The passive knowing model of citizenship seems to ignore the importance of a sense of political efficacy and its class-based distribution. In failing to include it, many teachers also fail to adequately strive for the moral principle of equality Newmann argued is essential to human dignity. The passive knower model of citizenship leaves the school and social studies open to the charge that they do too little to end the role of the school in reproducing a society in which a rich, well-educated élite dominates a passive working class. They seem to have ignored the work of such critics of the school as Apple, Bernstein, Bowles and Gintis, Giroux, and Freire who point out how the school transmits passivity and acceptance of the status quo to working-class students. The omission of an action component also seems to ignore the work on developing a sense of political efficacy and an internal locus of control done by Ehman, Verba and Nie, Massialas, Peyton and Miller, and others.

If students learn that it is enough to make an informed decision on an issue without acting on it, how can we expect them to say, "Well, now that I know how to go about getting something done right that I think is wrong, I would probably try to change it"?

Before reading the response to Chamberlin's position, consider how persuasive his arguments are. What are his strongest arguments? Which are his weakest arguments? Anticipate what objections might be raised. Overall, how convinced are you of his position?

Ten Reasons for Questioning the Activist Citizen Model of Elementary Social Studies

Larry Glassford

In the inaugural edition of *Canadian Social Studies,* Chuck Chamberlin (1991) argues for a vigorous emphasis on political action as an indispensable part of the elementary social studies curriculum. Pre-teen students, he asserts, should be encouraged to move far beyond the acquisition of passive knowledge of their world. In Chamberlin's view, they ought to be trained as active doers, not just in the classroom, but also in the political arena. As examples to be emulated, he reviews several instances in Alberta where "teachers have had their students inquiring into a wide range of social issues, culminating their inquiry with varied forms of direct and indirect action." In one case, a grade 4 class wrote letters to the provincial premier concerning a proposed pulp mill, and then was interviewed before TV news cameras. In another case, grade 5 and 6 students presented findings about the chemical spraying of mosquitoes to a city council meeting. Chamberlin is delighted that the teachers of these elementary classes utilized a decision-making model that culminated in taking public action. "Alberta students," he concludes, "have learned that the desired role of a citizen is to know what's going on, be part of it, and do something about it."

What could be wrong with that? Actually, there are a number of reasons to question this activist citizen model. First, though, let us be clear on one matter. As writer of this rejoinder, I do not hold up the traditional passive learner model as the ideal instructional situation. Active learning is, generally, more effective learning. And what about elementary students taking direct or indirect political action? Certainly, as Chamberlin describes the Alberta social studies curriculum, "if feasible and desirable." It's a big "IF"!

I now move to some objections to the activist model, listed here in descending numerical order.

10. Our kids are not always on the side of the angels.
Any conscientious parent knows this. Children are much the same blend of selflessness and selfishness as the adults

they eventually become. But oh, how the news media love children, especially in the assumed role of "informed innocence," questioning some established authority. Not even the advertising might and savvy of McDonald's could withstand the battering of Toronto-area elementary schoolchildren.... Brought by their teacher to stand in the shadow of the golden arches, they politely protested the use of Styrofoam containers before the eager news cameras. Never mind that the hastily summoned replacement packaging is deemed by some experts to pose just as daunting an environmental challenge. The kids are back at their favourite restaurant, munching fries and burgers much as before. A triumph of the active citizenship model? I don't think so!

9. Do real teachers picket City Hall?

Are there really an infinite number of absolutely clear-cut, white-hat vs. black-hat causes around, so that every elementary social studies teacher in every community can in clear conscience guide succeeding classes, year after year, to take meaningful action in the political arena? And what of the teacher who believes simulating the real world of politics in the classroom is a valid active learning approach? According to Chamberlin, the absence of direct or indirect political action at the end of the research and decision-making process is an alarming omission. Teachers who failed to lead their students all the way to community action would not be doing their job. They would be guilty of encouraging their pre-teen students "to know about the world, but not to act on it."

8. To everything there is a season.

The activist model as presented by Chamberlin is built on two questionable assumptions. First, in order to have a participatory citizenry, people must be trained for activism by the schools. Second, this activist training must be fully implemented by grade 6. Otherwise, he writes, "teaching students to be passive knowers rather than active doers defeats the key principle of democratic government, consent of the governed." To choose an historical example, would Chamberlin mean to imply that Thomas Jefferson and company waged resistance to British rule largely because their schools two or three decades earlier had specifically trained them in confrontational tactics? In fact, one assumes the American patriots took direct action because they decided it was both "feasible and desirable." With regard to the second assumption, why the insistence that the political action model be fully implemented by grade 6? Does all effective learning end then? Or is it simply the case that pre-adolescent children are less apt to think critically for themselves, and therefore more likely to reach the conclusions indicated for them by their well-meaning activist teachers?

7. What happens when political action fails?

Chamberlin writes "unless students believe their efforts will be effective, all the knowledge in the world is unlikely to lead them to be responsible citizens who participate constructively." It is vital, he maintains, that elementary students acquire a strong sense of political efficacy. And yet, many of these classroom-initiated campaigns are bound to fail. Even if every protest, every petition, every letter-writing project were totally valid (a most unlikely possibility), some of them would encounter opposing political forces of greater strength, and consequently would fail to achieve the children's objectives. Moreover, most public issues cannot be reduced to such stark good-vs.-evil terms. Political choices generally involve a complex assessment of possible outcomes, with no ironclad guarantees of right or wrong. Students who celebrated an apparent victory in grade 4 might come to see, with the passage of time, that the outcome they advocated and helped produce was turning out to be the wrong one. In either case—on the side of right but unsuccessful; or, successful but ultimately on the side of wrong—the students' sense of political efficacy would be diminished, not augmented.

6. Do real citizens picket City Hall?

Imagine a society where everyone is extremely active politically. This may be a vision of the perfect polity for Professor Chamberlin and the authorities he cites (chiefly F. Newmann and G.E. Wood), but others might see it as a recipe for chaos. In fact, one might argue that high rates of political activity by the citizenry are a sign not of a thriving political system, but of precisely the opposite: a political system that is not functioning well at all in the interests of its citizens. Most people in functional societies find other legitimate pursuits to occupy the bulk of their time: family, recreation, culture, religion, and community service. What happened to the "Big Chill" generation of 1960s-style activists? They grew up, got jobs, started families, took on mortgages, and assumed responsibility for running the institutions they once confronted. Direct democracy, with every citizen participating actively and continuously in the political process, does not seem to offer a viable long-term alternative. It must be remembered that ancient Athens, often seen as a role model for democratic citizen participation, disenfranchised both women and slaves, who together formed the great majority of the adult population (Kitto 1957).

5. Balance efficacy with trust and support.

Professor Chamberlin stresses the great importance of nurturing in students a sense of political efficacy, which he rightly associates with "active citizenship," but nowhere does he mention trust or support, also vital elements in a successful political system (Almond and Verba 1965). In fact, he is all but contemptuous of "these nine- to ten-year-olds [who] agreed with the importance of obedience, good manners, loyalty, hard work, and respect for Canada's institutions." Such apparently unworthy values are dismissed as mere evidence of "passive citizenship." Furthermore, he takes the schools to task for their success, along with the children's own parents, in developing these attributes. And yet, can we imagine a livable society without such qualities as loyalty, respect, and trust?

4. Power culture or counterculture?

"Picketing, protesting, democratic takeovers" were the core of 1960s-style radical campus politics. Are these really the most effective ways to achieve meaningful political change? In point of fact, these are marginal strategies, often the last resort of interest groups who have failed in more conventional attempts to influence the political process (Van Loon and Whittington 1987). Certainly students need to know that picketing and protesting are options one may select. It is not clear that every elementary student needs a direct experience in placard-carrying by the age of twelve. Furthermore, teachers owe it to their students to acquaint them with the deeper realities of political power. Most of it is wielded out of sight, not in the streets or on TV. No amount of instructional manipulation at the elementary level is likely to change that fact. Equating political efficacy with letter writing and public demonstrations may actually do students a disservice if it misleads them about who really gets what, when, how in this country.

3. Don't forget organized interest groups.

Professor Chamberlin argues that Canadian politics are typified by "working-class passivity," a state of affairs he finds intolerable. Evidence to sustain this conclusion is apparently based, at least in part, on an American study conducted some two decades ago. One wonders if this view takes proper account of the growth in profile and influence of such broad-based interest groups as the Canadian Auto Workers, the National Action Committee for the Status of Women, and the Assembly of First Nations. Surely factory workers, women, and Native people qualify as valid representatives of the working class in its broader sense. "Passive" does not come to mind as an accurate description of these groups in recent years (Sheppard and Valpy 1982).

2. English-speaking Canada is a distinct society.

The political culture of English-speaking Canada differs from that of the United States. Basic assumptions developed about American society do not necessarily apply in this country. The activist citizenship model is an apt illustration. The political sociologist S.M. Lipset, for instance, has written convincingly of the significantly higher levels of deference to constituted authority evident north of the Canadian-American border, as compared with south of it (1970). One may applaud or deplore this essential difference, but not ignore

it. When Chamberlin states that this is "a country that prides itself on being a democratic society where political participation is essential," he may be describing the United States more than Canada. This land of the maple leaf is, after all, the country that placed "peace, order, and good government" prominently in its founding constitution, rather than "life, liberty, and the pursuit of happiness." The difference is significant and persistent.

1. Let us not confuse ideology with pedagogy.

"Responsible citizenship" is the announced goal of the activist education model, but achieving fundamental changes to a perceived "class-based" society appears to be the real agenda. "The passive knower model of citizenship," Chamberlin writes, "leaves the school and social studies open to the charge that they do too little to end the role of the school in reproducing a society in which a rich, well-educated élite dominates a passive working class." The egalitarian ideal is appealing in theory, but one searches in vain for working models in countries the size of Canada. In recent years, several self-described parties of the working class have been driven from power in Eastern Europe and the former Soviet Union, after spectacularly failing to deliver the goods, either politically or economically. Marxian analysis of the failings of bourgeois capitalism and bourgeois democracy was, and is, perceptive (Marx and Engels 1959). Marxist prescriptions for a better society have been thoroughly discredited. As an alternative to the creation of a classless society of extremely active political participators, perhaps one might substitute the development of effective co-operation and leadership qualities in our students as a more realistic goal of citizenship education.

To know and then to act is insufficient. To know, and then to act wisely: there's the problem.

Has reading Glassford's concerns changed your original estimation of Chamberlin's position? What are Glassford's strongest arguments? Which are Glassford's weakest arguments?

What Vision of Democracy Should Guide Citizenship Education? A Response to Larry Glassford

Chuck Chamberlin

In spite of Professor Glassford's list of ten objections to the activist conception of citizenship education, it is clear that the root of our disagreement lies in our conceptions of the good society and the role of the school in preparing Canada's youth for citizenship in that society. Professor Glassford correctly recognizes that my vision of a good society is a democracy in which all citizens feel competent, confident, and responsible to participate in shaping the direction of change. To be competent, they must be knowledgeable about why the world is as it is and how it could be changed to make it better. To be confident they must have had life experiences in being accepted as legitimate participants in governance of classroom, school, community, or broader areas. To be responsible they need to see some of the positive and negative consequences of their decisions and feel the effects.

Contrasted to this conception of participatory democracy is one implied in Professor Glassford's article. He refers to participation as chaotic, points to the importance of loyalty, obedience, and respect for institutions, and suggests that simulating action is as good as real participation in social issues.

Two of the principles of democracy that mandate a social action model of citizenship education are consent of the governed and equal opportunity for all to actively participate in governance. Consent is not the same as passive acceptance of others' proposals, but rather informal and positive espousal. Newmann (1975) has developed this rationale, as have Oliver and Shaver (1966), Barber (1984), Wood (1984), and others. Freire (1972) uses the Spanish term *autogestion* in a similar way, meaning that a community takes responsibility collectively for the planning and action needed to shape their future together. At the school level, autogestion and consent of the governed means that students take an active role in openly debating what goals, rules, and projects will constitute their future, as Kohlberg (1981) described in his concept a "Just School," and as currently required by law in Denmark. At the community level, it means that current issues such as using chemical sprays for mosquitoes in Red Deer, or solid waste disposal in Rimbey be seen as public issues that all citizens feel responsible for helping resolve.

It must be noted that contrary to Professor Glassford's conclusion that black vs. white or good vs. evil issues would be used, these are complex issues involving competing values and long-term consequences, and are part of global as well as local dilemmas. [After spending] time with Danish primary school children who had just returned from two weeks in Minsk, Belorussia, and who spoke knowledgeably about how Denmark could help, I am convinced Canadian children are equally capable of learning to accept responsibility for understanding the social issues facing their communities and taking informal action. This is reinforced by having listened to Red Deer students show city council that they were much better informed about the economic, environmental, health, recreational, and social consequences of using chemical sprays than their elders were.

Central to the argument for a social action model of citizenship education is the importance of a sense of political efficacy. This feeling that our efforts to affect decisions about the future of our communities will be fruitful is not inborn, but is socially learned, and as Newmann (1975) shows, is primarily learned by children from wealthier families whose parents are used to effectively exerting influence. Children from poorer families are more likely to learn from their parents that "you can't fight City Hall," so why waste your time trying? Schools that provide no opportunity for all children, rich and poor, to develop a sense of political efficacy are contributing to the maintenance of a society where the wealthy confidently pick up the phone and invite the mayor to lunch at their country club to discuss changing the zoning of residential land to commercial use, while the poor despair of being heard. By providing children with an opportunity to see themselves as responsible for and capable of participating in social decisions, the school is taking a role in contributing to the kind of democracy in which active consent of the governed is more equally distributed among children of the rich and poor. Otherwise, schools by default contribute to inegalitarian participation in making social decisions where the children with a strong sense of political efficacy who are from wealthier families will be the movers and shakers.

I was pleased that Professor Glassford spoke up for the status quo and for passive citizenship education goals as it may provoke further critical reflection among Canada's citizenship educators about the kind of society they value and the role of the school in preparing students for their future in that society. To the extent that teachers more clearly think through the alternatives, they can accept conscious responsibility for their decision and teaching acts, thus being good citizens as well as good teachers.

> Where do you now stand on the issue of involving elementary students in responsible social action? What additional information, if you could obtain it, would make you even more certain of your position?

ACKNOWLEDGMENT

These articles, which are reprinted with permission of The Althouse Press, appeared originally in *Canadian Social Studies*, volumes 26 (1): 23–26 (1991) and 27(1): 28–29 and 30 (1992). Minor alterations to the original articles have been made for stylistic and format purposes.

ENDNOTE

1   These, and the items in Tables 19.2 and 19.3, come from an instrument developed by Dr. John Seymour, University of Manitoba.

REFERENCES

Alberta Education. 1989. *Social studies teachers' resource manual*. Edmonton: Alberta Education.

Almond, G.A. and S. Verba. 1965. *The civic culture: Political attitudes and democracy in five nations*. Boston: Little, Brown.

Barber, B. 1984. *Strong democracy: Participatory politics for a new age*. Berkeley, CA: University of California Press.

Chamberlin, C. 1979. A whole elementary school takes social action. *One World* 17 (4): 13–14.

———. 1991. Citizenship as the goal of social studies: Passive knower or active doer. *Canadian Social Studies* 26 (1): 23–26.

Chamberlin, C., B. Connors, and D. Massey. 1983. Project Athens: Can schools teach active citizenship? *One World* 22 (2): 33–39.

Dueck, K., E. Horvath, and V. Zelinski. 1977. Bev Priftis' class takes on the Calgary Zoo *One World*, 17 (4): 7–9.

Engle, S. and A. Ochoa. 1988. *Education for democratic citizenship*. New York: Teachers College Press.

Freire, P. 1972. *Pedagogy of the oppressed*. New York: Herder and Herder.

Hungerford, H. and R. Peyton. 1976. *Teaching environmental education*. Portland, ME: J. Weston Walsh.

Johncox, B. 1983. Rimbey environmental action project. *One World* 22 (2): 25–29.

Kitto, H.D.F. 1957. *The Greeks*. Harmondsworth, UK: Penguin.

Kohlberg, L., M. Lieberman, C. Power, A Higgins, and J. Codding. 1981. Evaluating Scarsdale's 'just community school' and its curriculum: implications for the future. *Moral Education Forum* 6: 31–42.

Lipset, S.M. 1970. *Revolution and counter-revolution: Change and persistence in social structures*. New York: Anchor.

Marx, K. and F. Engels. 1959. *Basic writings on politics and philosophy*. Ed. Lewis S. Feuer. New York: Anchor.

Newmann, F. 1975. *Education for citizen action*. Berkeley, CA: McCutcheon.

Oliver, D. and J. Shaver. 1966. *Teaching public issues in the high school*. Boston, MA: Houghton Mifflin.

Sheppard, R. and M. Valpy. 1982. *The national deal*. Toronto: Fleet.

Taylor, D. and R. Moore. 1983. Red Deer environmental action project. *One World* 22 (2): 8–13.

Van Loon, R. J. and M.S. Whittington. 1987. *The Canadian political system: Environment, structure and process*. 4th ed. Toronto: McGraw-Hill Ryerson.

Wood, G.E. 1984. Schooling in democracy: Transformation or reproduction? *Educational Theory* 34 (3): 219–239.

20 All Talk and No Action?
The Place of Social Action in Elementary Social Studies

Penney Clark

It is generally agreed that the preparation of citizens is the raison d'être of social studies. However, establishing that citizenship education is the ultimate purpose of social studies doesn't tell us very much. The crucial question to address is to determine exactly what the qualities of a good citizen are. Is it sufficient that students are capable of informed debate on social issues? Or does effective citizenship also require developing the will and the ability to "act" to address local, national, and global problems?

Prominent Canadian (Osborne 1982) and American educators (Newmann 1975, Goodlad 2004) have long argued that students should be taught not solely to discuss social issues but also to act on them. This attention to social action is apparent in recent provincial curricula. For example, the Alberta curriculum states that the role of social studies is to help students "become active and responsible citizens, engaged in the democratic process and aware of their capacity to effect change in their community, society and world" (Alberta Education 2003, 1). Starting with grade 3, the "Social Participation" outcomes in this curriculum include expectations that students will contribute to the well-being of their school or the broader community (Alberta Education 2005). Similarly, the British Columbia social studies curriculum expects elementary students to "practise active citizenship" (British Columbia Ministry of Education 2005, 7). In grade 6, for example, they are asked to "implement a plan of action to address a selected local or global problem or issue" (98). The curriculum suggests that this might involve a fundraising or letter-writing campaign, a clothing drive, writing an editorial for a school or community newspaper, or circulating a petition.

Of course, it is not enough simply to ask students to undertake a project. If they are to succeed in this endeavour and learn about active citizenship, they need to be taught how to plan and implement action projects responsibly. This chapter focusses on developing these abilities by discussing various examples of social action undertaken by elementary students and by presenting a framework to guide teachers in selecting and conducting social action projects.[1]

Types of Social Action

A useful starting point is to identify the different categories of social action that students might undertake. One classification views social action projects along a continuum extending from, at one end, "direct action" (directly addressing a problem oneself) to, at the other end, "indirect action" (influencing, or using as intermediaries, those who hold power and who are in a position to effect change). Both direct and indirect action can occur at local, provincial, national, or global levels.

INDIRECT ACTION

Elementary students in two North Vancouver schools engaged in indirect local action as a result of problems they examined in their social studies program.[2] They sought indirectly to bring about action by lobbying officials in political and government positions who had the authority and influence to take action if they could be convinced to do so. More specifically, the grade 4 and grade 5 French immersion classes at Ross Road Elementary made a presentation to North Vancouver District officials advocating the suspension of a proposed residential development in a wilderness area. Prior to the presentation, students toured the district hall and discussed forest management with the mayor and with a forest industry representative. They also performed a play involving a developer who wanted to cut down trees in a small town.

Kindergarten and grade 4 students from Maplewood Community School in the same school district engaged in indirect social action against the planned development of land owned by the Vancouver Port Corporation. These students sent letters to the port corporation, the North Vancouver District mayor, the federal transport minister, the prime minister, the provincial premier, and environment critics for the opposition parties. One grade 4 student wrote in his letter, "Without the mud flats no one will see the animals again. The only time you will see birds is when they pass by. How would you like it if animals took away your buildings? I do not think you would like that."

An example of indirect global action is fundraising to support relief organizations such as UNICEF (United Nations International Children's Emergency Fund). Students know they are helping in a general sense, but there is no direct contact with the people affected, they have no control over how the funds are administered, nor can they observe specific results of their actions, unless they are able to convince a relief worker to send them a video.

DIRECT ACTION

An example of direct action at the global level is "Project Love" (nd). This project is sponsored by CODE (Canadian Organization for Development through Education), an organization supporting literacy in the developing world. Students assemble Project Love kits containing basic school supplies—a pencil, eraser, notebook, and ruler—packed in a reusable plastic bag, and send them to developing countries such as Belize, Guyana, Ethiopia, and Tanzania. Students raise funds to help cover the cost of the supplies and shipping.

Other examples of direct local action include cleaning up the school grounds or a local park, raising money to purchase playground equipment, operating a "buddy" system for new students, visiting the elderly at a senior citizen's home, or caring for animals at a local wildlife habitat.

Framework for Social Action Projects

There are many things to consider when guiding students through a social action project. Below is a framework identifying six tasks. Depending on the project, not all will be required and with younger students especially it will be necessary to address the relevant steps in a more simplified manner:

Laying the groundwork

1. *Preplan for the project*
   What factors might a teacher consider before formally deciding to undertake a social action project? At this preliminary phase, a teacher should select a suitable focus for the project and secure advice and approval from key parties.
2. *Introduce the idea to students*
   How might undertaking a social action project be presented to students? The teacher might consider how to connect this project to students' interests and to topics in the curriculum.

Guiding students through the project

3. *Clarify the problem*
   What is the problem in need of attention? Students gather information and articulate a clear statement of the problem.
4. *Agree on a sound solution*
   What are the different ways in which the problem could be solved and which is the most promising solution? Students assess the relative merits of alternative solutions, and decide upon the best option.
5. *Plan an effective course of action*
   How will the proposed solution be put into effect? Students consider specific challenges, resources, and strategies in developing an action plan.
6. *Implement and evaluate the action*
   Is the planned action working? Students manage progress of the project and debrief the experience.

The rest of this chapter is devoted to unpacking the specific considerations involved in each of these tasks.

Task 1: Preplan for the Project

The preliminary planning for a project has two parts: selecting a suitable focus and securing the advice and approval of key participants.

SELECT A SUITABLE PROJECT FOCUS

Five questions are useful to consider when selecting and shaping the focus for a project:

- Is it relevant for my students?
- Is it appropriate for my school and community?
- Does it grow out of and support the curriculum?
- Are there adequate resources?
- Is it worth the effort?

STUDENT RELEVANCE

There is little point in attempting a project if students do not support it. Rahima Wade (1995) found, when working with a grade 4 class in a suburban American school over the course of a school year, that unless students saw a meaningful or enjoyable connection between a social action project and their own lives, they had little interest in further involvement. For example, Wade tried to interest students in fundraising to purchase a goat for a poor family in Haiti. Although most students voted in favour of participating in the project, only three students came to an out-of-school meeting to plan a course of action. Wade abandoned the project, concluding that it was too far removed from the students' own interests and life experiences.

Lewis describes how her upper elementary students from a low-income area became excited about school because of a social action project. As she says, "it was not an imaginary situation or a case study in a textbook—it existed in their neighborhood" (1991, 47). She describes how engagement in social action made the curriculum relevant for these students:

> Children anxiously await answers to letters, and track legislation. No one knows for sure what will happen next. When the Jackson children sat in the Utah Legislature watching the votes for their hazardous waste fund flash on the wall, they exhibited as much enthusiasm as if they had been counting points on the scoreboard at a basketball game (49).

We should not presume that students will always be enthusiastic about the same projects that would interest adults (Wade, 1995). For example, in the context of creating a class Bill of Rights, students in a grade 4 class decided to write letters to their principal requesting permission to chew gum and wear hats in class. Most adults would not consider these issues of great importance, but the grade 4 students felt differently and decided to act on their concerns. Students' sense of empowerment can result only when they take ownership of, and feel enthusiasm about, a project. Of course, all students need not participate in a particular project. Nor should those who do not wish to become involved prevent others from having the opportunity to do so. To the extent possible, we should allow for alternative routes for students who are not committed to the selected project or who want to pursue an alternative course of action.

APPROPRIATENESS FOR THE COMMUNITY

It would be inappropriate for a teacher to encourage students to engage in a project that violates the values of the community. The uproar caused by such an action may negate students' feeling of efficacy and make them unwilling to engage in future projects. When assessing a project's suitability in light of the cultural, religious, political, and economic characteristics of the school and community, we might ask ourselves the following questions:

- Does it respect the belief systems and cultural values of students and parents, as well as local histories and sensitivities?
- Would it lead to unproductive conflict or stress? A project that is appropriate in one school may create unproductive controversy in another. Although controversy will be part of any project related to sensitive issues, it may be

wise to modify a project's focus if there is potential for unproductive conflict.

CURRICULUM MATCH

Social action projects have the potential to promote many curricular outcomes, including the skills needed to organize information, write proposals and reports, deliver public presentations, co-operate with others to achieve a shared goal, listen thoughtfully to the ideas and opinions of others, construct a compelling argument, and interact effectively with adults. Teacher Syma Solovitch-Haynes (1996) details her grade 2 students' success in achieving many such curricular goals. These students in Central Harlem set out to rename a street Mary McLeod Bethune Place after they noticed there were no streets in their area named after African-American women. In the course of working to achieve this goal, students learned how to research needed information, access the legislative process, organize and get signatures on a petition, and prepare and present a compelling argument in public forums.

Content knowledge is also promoted through social action projects. For instance, academic peer-tutoring projects in reading and math have been shown to positively affect achievement scores for both tutors and their pupils (Hedin 1987). Lewis (1991) describes the academic benefits as her elementary students sought to eliminate hazardous waste sites in Utah. Not only did students hone their speaking and writing skills as they learned to communicate effectively by means of telephone calls, letters, and proposals, they also learned the process of passing a bill, and used mathematics to compile survey data and calculate the anticipated profits from their fundraising efforts.

ADEQUATE RESOURCES

Facilities, materials, time, knowledge, and abilities are needed to complete a project successfully. The following questions are worth considering in this regard:

- Do students have the background experience, prior knowledge, and developmental maturity for grappling with the concepts, complexities, and implications of this action? Can they be expected to acquire what they are missing or can "outside experts"—parents and community members—make up for any shortfalls in expertise?
- Can parents be counted on to provide assistance and materials that may be needed? If outside activities are involved, will adequate supervision and transportation be available?
- Is the project doable within the available time? Success

often depends upon having sufficient time. Would holidays interupt the project? How will it fit with the time demands of other school events?

WORTHWHILE

Social action projects may require students and teachers to spend considerable in-class and out-of-school time on the project. Thus, it is important that the benefits warrant the effort. In addition to achieving curriculum outcomes, an important measure of the success of a social action project is its impact on student empowerment. Involvement in social action projects contributes to student assertiveness and self-esteem (Kohn 1990). Students who work in projects where they see that they have made a difference feel valued and involved (Yaeger and Patterson 1996). Wade (1995) believes that student ownership of a project is central to developing a sense of empowerment. Students must see a connection between the activity and their own interests. Other critical factors are the teacher's willingness to relinquish some control over decision making, and the teacher's actions in fostering empowerment, such as providing choices and including time in the school day for student-initiated projects.

"You know, I didn't think something I did could really matter. Now I know that I can make a difference" (reported in Reindl 1993, 44). This was the message given by many students in grade 4 and grade 5 classes to their teacher following an extensive local action project. These students conducted food drives to help the needy in their community, persevering despite heckling from older students because the project was important to them. They also "adopted" a battered women's shelter and raised funds to purchase a swing set for children staying at the shelter. In the teacher's words:

I found myself trusting them more and more as the year went on and seeing that they could handle it, that it wasn't going to be devastating for them because they were having the opportunity to do something about it. With children you just can't let them feel hopeless. I think they can deal with almost anything as long as they know it doesn't have to be that way (44).

These students saw situations that disturbed them and, with the encouragement of their teacher, did something about them. As a result of their actions, they developed a sense that they could indeed change the world around them for the better. A second interesting point in this regard, as illustrated by the following comment, is that the teacher, too, felt a sense of empowerment: "If I never do anything else with kids for the rest of my life, I will feel that, in letting these kids do this, I made a contribution" (46).

If students feel they lack the abilities and resources to ef-

fect change, they are unlikely to wish to participate. For this reason, particularly for young children, it may be worthwhile to focus their social action on the classroom or school environments. These are places where they should feel comfortable and where they can actually see the changes that their actions have wrought. Such a project might involve forming a "Green Team" to promote recycling, sponsoring a bicycle safety program, forming a team of crosswalk guards, or tutoring other students who are experiencing difficulty.

SECURE SUPPORT FROM KEY PARTIES

It is always a good idea to secure community and administrative support for any proposed project. Social action projects are more public and may be more controversial than other school activities and some people may consider it inappropriate for students to be involved in social action projects during the school day. More often than not, potential criticisms can be avoided by keeping parents and the school administration informed about the project.

Clearing the project beforehand with the school administration by pointing out the congruence of project objectives with the curriculum will help if there is any negative parental or public reactions (Kreisberg 1993). Informing parents by letter of the proposed activities allows them to air concerns and helps to garner their support. This is preferable to explaining after the fact if some controversy emerges. It can also be helpful to have parents and others participate in planning discussions or as panel members when different perspectives on the issues are presented.

In the example described in the highlighted text, a grade 7 teacher and her class were criticized in the press for questioning the ethics of keeping animals in cages. Support for their actions came by pointing to the congruence between project objectives and curriculum objectives, and by securing approval ahead of time for the project from the school administration, curriculum specialists, and parents.

The author recommends five factors to consider when selecting a social action project:

- relevance for students
- appropriateness for the school and community
- curriculum match
- available resources
- whether it is worthwhile

Identify four or five possible projects for students to undertake at your grade level and use these criteria to assess each option. Identify and justify your selection of the one or two most promising options.

MONKEY BUSINESS

Bev Priftis took her grade 7 students to the Calgary Zoo in order to extend inquiry into the nature and behaviour of baboons and other animals as part of a study of the unique characteristics of humans.[3] The purpose of the unit, which was called "Man: A Course of Study," was to promote student inquiry into the question, "What is human about human beings?"

As a result of their field trip experience, many students became concerned with the contradiction between what they had learned in class about social organization and territoriality, and the practice of caging baboons and other animals. The students decided to write letters of protest to the Zoological Society, the mayor of Calgary, the Queen, and the editors of two daily papers.

The newspapers printed stories on the students' actions. One paper, in particular, emphasized the conflict between the attitudes of the Zoological Society and those of the students. The teacher was portrayed as incompetent, the students uncontrolled, and the zookeeper inflexible. The head of the Zoological Society wrote a three-page letter charging that the students' criticisms were childish and irresponsible and that they had not been properly prepared for their field trip.

The response to her students' actions could have had negative repercussions on the career of this teacher. It was only her second year of teaching and permanent certificates were not granted until the end of two years' teaching experience. Fortunately, Ms. Prifits had laid the groundwork. She had become acquainted with the resources for the unit she was teaching by means of a professional workshop. This program was clearly consistent with the provincial curriculum and the supervisor of social studies had promised to purchase the material in order to pilot the program in the Calgary school system. Parents had been given an opportunity to become familiar with the program through informational meetings. Many were pleased at the enthusiasm it generated in their children, particularly those children who had not previously been interested in social studies. This teacher also received a great deal of support from colleagues, including her principal and the professor who had originally introduced her to the program.

The teacher made use of the controversy that surrounded her students' social action to advance student learning. For instance, students compared the story as it appeared in the newspaper with the notes the teacher kept when the newspaper reporter interviewed her for the article. They examined the story for contradictions and evaluated it for bias and personal motives.

Largely because of the prior groundwork that was done, this story has a happy ending. The Zoological Society and the community as a whole eventually endorsed the "Ban the Bars" movement. The baboons were removed from the zoo because it was not a suitable environment for them. The program continued to be taught in Calgary schools. Bev Priftis was recognized for her expertise in social studies methodology and became a social studies consultant with the Calgary Board of Education.

Task 2: Introduce the Idea to Students

Many social action projects arise from students' interests and concerns. For example, in teacher Solovitch-Haynes' case, on the way to school one morning, her grade 2 students noticed the absence of street signs honouring female African-Americans and wanted to do something about it.

Other projects arise from curriculum units already taking place in the classroom. For example, while learning about community services, primary students might decide that there is a need for a swimming pool in their own community and then embark on a plan to see what they can do to help bring this about. Upper elementary students studying transportation networks might decide that sections of the Trans-Canada Highway require upgrading and begin lobbying efforts to that end. Even historical units can lead to social action projects. For instance, upper elementary students who are learning about Canada's aboriginal peoples in the past may wish to investigate current land claims issues and make their opinions known.

If a project does not naturally arise from student concerns or from the curriculum, it would be important to stimulate student interest through a guest speaker who has personal experience with the issue, a newspaper article, a news clip or documentary film, or a field trip to the site of the controversy. In the example that follows, teacher Steve Oldenberger directed his grade 6/7 students' attention to the pollution of the Fraser River by means of several field trips.

Task 3: Clarify the Problem

An important part of learning to participate in social action is developing the ability to clearly identify the problem to be solved. Two useful strategies are to involve students in researching the problem and then in exploring its complexities.

GATHER INFORMATION

Students need to collect information about a problem just as they would with any other research project, and they may need assistance with this research. This can involve helping students to frame clear questions, determine their information needs, and develop strategies for gathering the necessary

LEAVING A LEGACY

Steve Oldenberger's grade 6/7 classroom in Queen Elizabeth Elementary is just a stone's throw from the Fraser River, which winds through the community of New Westminster, British Columbia. Steve asked his students to see what they could discover about the river. They began by taking class field trips there in order to observe seasonal water levels, turbidity, and temperature, as well as water quality, what was floating on it, and what was on its banks. They recorded information by taking photographs and writing their observations in logbooks. They also collected samples of river water in different spots to test with the help of lab equipment lent by the Marine Science Centre at the Vancouver Aquarium. With the Science Centre's help, they dredged samples of the muddy bottom of streams that feed the Fraser. They used nets to gather insects from the water surface. They carried out systematic samplings of the invertebrate population that inhabited the tributaries leading to the river, and carefully examined the health of minnows in the local streams. They enlisted the help of marine life experts, environmentalists, and others to make sense of their data.

The students' findings were disturbing. There was litter on the riverbanks. Wood debris from upriver was stifling wetland growth. Pollutants such as oil and agricultural run-offs were threatening the more delicate inhabitants of the river. Large fish were rare and bird habitat was decreasing.

The students decided that they wanted to do something about the problems they had discovered. They considered a variety of alternative solutions, such as:

- writing articles for publication in the local newspaper;
- raising money for a particular campaign, such as building bird nesting boxes;
- producing a video about the river that could be shown at the school and perhaps other schools in the district; and
- creating a website to publicize the problems.

In the end, the students voted to launch a River Day in May for the entire school and the community. Students organized guest speakers, study stations, observation sites, publicity booths, and food tables. They prepared posters, brochures, and displays of their photographs, log entries, and drawings. They organized a shoreline cleanup to involve their visitors in a hands-on restoration activity.

The first River Day was an enormous success. The entire school, and many neighbours, participated. Reporters and photographers from the local media also attended, as well as a representative from City Hall. River Day has been held now for several years. Six students presented at the 2002 International Children's Conference on the Environment held in Victoria, British Columbia. The result of this ongoing social action project has been a great deal of effort directed at clean-up of the Fraser River environs. The students in Mr. Oldenberger's grade 6/7 classes have encouraged community members as well as students in other nearby schools to become involved. "And instead of tin cans and broken bottles, the riverbanks near Queen Elizabeth School are sprouting wildflowers and native grasses."[4]

information. See chapter 11, "Escaping the Typical Report Trap," for specific teaching suggestions.

RECOGNIZE COMPLEXITY

Successful projects depend on students recognizing the complexity of the problem under investigation, and appreciating the various perspectives that are held, as well as multiple contributing causes. The difficulties that emerge when this is not done are illustrated by an incident involving a grade 1 girl who came home from school and accused her logger father of being a murderer because his tree-cutting was eventually going to kill everyone. The little girl had been read a story at school about British Columbia's Carmanah Valley and environmentalists' efforts to save the old-growth trees there. Officials in the IWA-Canada (International Woodworkers of America) local were concerned about what they saw as an unbalanced treatment of logging and took the issue up with the local school board (Rees and Fraser 1992). This child should have been reminded that she used wood, in various ways, every day of her life. She needed to understand that loggers do not simply "murder" trees, but chop them down in order to meet very real human needs. Even at six years old, a child can begin to appreciate the complexity of environmental issues, and that their solutions are more often a matter of balance than of taking an either-or position. Teachers have a responsibility to see that students are well-informed about opposing views.

In another situation, after observing volunteer students at community food programs for three years, one researcher concluded that understanding of the underlying problems was not promoted through these experiences (Willison 1994). When asked why they thought people went to the programs to obtain meals, students responded that clients were "hungry, homeless, excessive users of drugs and alcohol, unemployed, sick, uneducated, and do not want to work. On some occasions, students responded that the clients 'did not have any self-respect'" (89). These exclusively negative stereotypes were reinforced by a teacher who made comments such as, "See how much sugar these people take, they need sugar because of drug addictions" (88). Willison points out that these stereotypical notions were true for only a portion of the food program clients. Many were actually employed, but their income was insufficient to meet their needs. Student preparation for this project should have included examination of the underlying conditions of poverty, and of the history of local food provision programs.

Advocates for total banishment of child labour in Third World countries have been cautioned by UNICEF about the complexity of the issues involved. Child factory workers in developing countries are often the sole support of their families. If all child labour were banned, the families might starve and these children might be forced to turn to more oppressive sources of income such as prostitution. Many aid workers advocate working instead to improve children's working conditions, and provide health care and educational programs, rather than outright banning of child labour (Vincent 1996). A recent UNICEF report recommends that governments focus on increasing educational opportunities, enforcing labour laws, and addressing social problems such as caste and ethnic divisions that exacerbate the problem (Stackhouse 1996). Clearly social action is complex, and unintended consequences must be considered carefully.

Task 4: Agree on a Sound Solution

The next stage after defining a problem is to agree on a solution. While it is impossible for students to anticipate all the consequences of their proposed action, they should carefully examine possibilities and likely courses of action under various circumstances. Careful consideration of an action project was evident when a grade 8 class considered "adopting" a child in Africa (Ashford 1995). After carefully considering this plan, class members realized that the project was not as desirable as it had initially seemed. It was a long-term project that could not be continued when students left grade 8, and there was no guarantee that the incoming grade 8 class would be willing to carry on with the commitment.

Students need to be well informed about the potential impact of various action options. Students in Toronto were highly successful in their efforts to have fast-food giant McDonald's change from its Styrofoam clamshell packaging to paper (Roth 1991). However, scientific experts, as well as environmentalists, have since argued that McDonald's has caused more harm than good by this move. For example, James Guillet (1990), professor of chemistry at the University of Toronto, states that his own twenty-five years of research, as well as other scientific studies, simply did not support students' claim that when the foam disintegrates, it produces a chemical that has been associated with a breakdown of the Earth's ozone layer. As well, the volume of trees that are needed to provide the new paper packaging, and the magnitude of pollution produced through paper production may be worse environmentally than the plastics previously used.

Guillet concludes with the following caution:

> Environmental problems are extraordinarily complex. There is no magic solution to pollution. What we must do to minimize environmental damage is to make informed and intelligent choices. Media-supported campaigns such as this make great television, but they also exploit the natural altruism of young children and do little to inform the public. Children's crusades should have no place in the formulation of public policy (1990, D7).

Grade 5 students in Surrey, British Columbia, sent letters to the *Vancouver Sun* (June 25, 1996) expressing concern about the exploitation of Indonesian factory workers who make Nike products. These students were justifiably angry at Nike for paying their workers wages of $2.20 a day, while at the same time paying basketball superstar Michael Jordan $20 million a year to represent the company. Many of the students called for a boycott of Nike products. These students thought it worthwhile to take the time to write letters in order to publicly air their concerns. They may well have chosen the best action under the circumstances. However, they would have confidence in their decision only if they had carefully investigated the situation before reaching their conclusion. For instance, did they consider the possibility that driving up wages in Indonesia might result in Nike moving its factories to another country where labour costs are lower? Did they anticipate that other large corporations considering options for locating their factories might also avoid Indonesia? What alternatives to a boycott of Nike did they consider? Perhaps it would be more desirable to encourage all companies or countries in the region to establish minimum-wage laws. Perhaps as more large corporations build factories in Indonesia they will compete for the labour that is available and wages will rise. Canadian businessman Subhash Khanna, who imports clothing from South Asia, argues, "If you don't do business with Third World countries you will increase their poverty and have more kids dying of hunger" (cited in Vincent 1996, 50). It is important that students consider potential consequences before reaching a decision.

Figure 20.1, "Consequences for Stakeholders," is intended to help students explore the implications of each proposed solution for one or more groups who may be affected by the actions.

Task 5: Plan an Effective Course of Action

After deciding on a solution, the next task is to develop a plan to put the solution into effect. The purpose of an action plan

FIGURE 20.1 **CONSEQUENCES FOR STAKEHOLDERS**

Stakeholder group: _____

Identify the anticipated consequences for each proposed solution and indicate whether they will be negative (-), positive (+), or mixed (?) for an assigned stakeholder group or for various stakeholders.

OPTIONS	ANTICIPATED CONSEQUENCES	
		+ - ?
		+ - ?
		+ - ?

is to guide students in implementing the project. The quality of the plan depends largely on the thoroughness of students' deliberations. Use of a simple task analysis chart such as Figure 20.2, "Action Plan," can support students in identifying the many steps to be taken, the resources required to complete each step, and the people responsible.

While planning a course of action invite students to reflect on the soundness of their proposals by considering the following criteria:

- **Clear.** Are the goals and tasks of the plan clear to us?
- **Effective.** Are the proposed strategies likely to lead to the desired solution? What might some other effects of these strategies be (i.e., unintended consequences)?
- **Respectful.** Does the proposed strategy respect the feelings of all sides? Have we judged how the strategies will affect people? Does it respect the rights and legitimate interests of those who might be affected?
- **Realistic.** Is the plan doable given our time and available resources? How much class time is realistically available to devote to the project? How much outside help will be necessary?
- **Comprehensive.** What did we have to leave out of the plan? Does it contain and sequence the important tasks necessary for successful implementation?

Task 6: Implement and Evaluate the Action

By this stage, students should have a good sense of their project and what needs to be done next. Now the teacher's task is to help students bring the project to a successful conclusion. Wade (1995) found that students responded enthusiastically to projects where they were closely supervised and assisted by their teacher or other adult. Students did not carry through on projects where they were left to their own devices. For instance, a group of students planned to write letters to American soldiers in Saudi Arabia after one student suggested the plan, but no one followed through. However, most students were enthusiastic about and participated in a project initiated, organized, and supervised by Wade in which students made puppets to send to India to teach villagers to make a simple solution for curing diarrhea, a common killer of children.

As students work through their project, and after its completion, encourage them to assess their decisions and actions in light of their own opinions, the opinions of other students, the responses of those who were affected by the action project, and both short- and long-term consequences. Figure 20.3, "Reflecting on Our Project," suggests questions to ask students as they debrief their experiences.

There is a risk that students will feel that, in spite of all their efforts, they were ultimately unsuccessful in achieving

FIGURE 20.2   ACTION PLAN

ACTIONS TO BE TAKEN	RESOURCES REQUIRED	WHO WILL BE RESPONSIBLE

their goals. Lewis (1991) gives a description of the discouragement one boy might feel early on in his project:

> Successful phone calling is a simple place to begin. Students often fail at this initial step. For example, Joe may get access to use the school phones (which might require a notarized letter from his parent). He dials the main number for the Department of Transportation seeking information on the placement of a street light near the school. It takes four transfers before he reaches the correct party who can help him. Ms. So-and-So says she will mail some information to Joe and asks for the school address.
>
> Joe panics. Although he can instantly recall all the states in the NFL, he doesn't know the school address. He asks Ms. So-and-So to wait, then runs into the secretary's office to find out the address. Seven people are lined up at the secretary's desk. By the time Joe gets the address and returns to the phone, Ms. So-and-So has hung up. Joe can't remember how to get through to her again and gives up. His first attempt to become involved in citizenship, and he stubs his toe and loses interest (48).

Two ways to reduce the likelihood of perceived failure are to prepare students to carry out the steps necessary to complete the project and to encourage students to define "success" very broadly. Suggestions for developing the necessary competencies have been discussed throughout this chapter. In terms of students' definition of success, this need not mean that the intended change is achieved. It can simply mean that students develop a sense of efficacy by actively participating in the process to affect change, even if, ultimately, that change does not occur. If students feel proud that they acted on their convictions, they are likely to want to engage in more such projects. Students should also be reminded that even though no immediate positive consequences stemmed from their social action, desirable changes may yet occur over the long term. (See "Teaching for Hope" in this volume for a discussion of the importance of nurturing student hopefulness and for factors that affect this goal.)

Conclusion

There is no doubt that engaging in social action involves uncertainties. It can place both teachers and students in situations where they are unfamiliar with the circumstances and

FIGURE 20.3   REFLECTING ON OUR PROJECT

Identify two ways in which you think this action project was successful.

List three factors that helped and three factors that hindered the success of the project.

HELPING FACTORS	HINDERING FACTORS
•	•
•	•
•	•

What might you and your fellow students have done differently to make the project more successful?

Identify the most important thing you have learned from this project about planning and conducting social action.

---

unsure how to proceed. Social action can be much more visible, and also more controversial, than other social studies activities and may invite criticism from outside sources. Nevertheless, there are significant benefits. Prominent among these is a sense of empowerment, possession of which increases the likelihood that students will become active citizens in their adult lives. In the final analysis, it is difficult to conceive of social studies as citizenship education without the possibility of social action. The "cost" of a social studies program that is all talk and no action is the preparation of citizens who are unqualified and unwilling to work to improve their community, their nation, or their world.

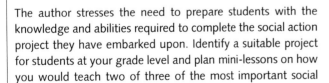

The author stresses the need to prepare students with the knowledge and abilities required to complete the social action project they have embarked upon. Identify a suitable project for students at your grade level and plan mini-lessons on how you would teach two of three of the most important social action competencies required by this task.

ACKNOWLEDGMENT

The author is grateful to Marg Franklin, retired elementary school principal and sessional instructor in elementary social studies curriculum and instruction at the University of British Columbia, for her helpful comments on the manuscript of this chapter.

ENDNOTES

1   This chapter draws heavily on the framework and ideas in *Active Citizenship: Student Action Projects* (Case et al. 2004), a teaching resource designed to develop student's ability to think through each step of a social action project.

2   These examples were described in "Students wake up to environmental concerns," by Michael Becker in the *North Shore News*.

3   This example of social action is based on an article by Dueck, Horvath and Zelinski (1977).

4   This example of social action was adapted from "Leaving a legacy" in (Case et al. 2004, 83–84). Thanks to Steve Oldenberger and his students at Queen Elizabeth School, New Westminster, BC and the Marine Science Centre at the Vancouver Aquarium. See www.riverworks.org for further information on school-based projects supported and aided by the Marine Science Centre.

REFERENCES

Alberta Education. 2003. *Social studies—Grade 4 to grade 9.* Validation draft. Edmonton, AB: Author. Available online at http://www.education.gov.ab.ca/k_12/curriculum/bySubject/social/default.asp.

———. 2005. *Social studies—Kindergarten to grade 3.* Edmonton, AB: Author. Available online at http://www.education.gov.ab.ca/k_12/curriculum/bySubject/social/default.asp.

Ashford, M-W. 1995. Youth actions for the planet. In *Thinking globally about social studies education,* ed. R. Fowler and I. Wright, 75–90. Vancouver: Research and Development in Global Studies, University of British Columbia.

British Columbia Ministry of Education. 2005. *Social studies K to 7: Integrated resource package 2005.* Response draft. Victoria, BC: Author. Available online at http://www.bced.gov.bc.ca/irp/irp.htm.

Case, R., C. Falk, N. Smith, and W. Werner. 2004. *Active citizenship: Student action projects.* Richmond, BC: The Critical Thinking Consortium.

Dueck, K., F. Horvath, and V. Zelinski. 1977. Bev Priftis' class takes on the Calgary zoo. *One World* 17 (4): 7–8.

Goodlad, J. 2004. *A place called school: Twentieth anniversary edition.* Whitby, ON: McGraw-Hill.

Guillet, J. 1990. Kids' crusades bad idea. Letter to the editor, *Globe and Mail,* December 1.

Hedin, D. 1987. Students as teachers: A tool for improving school climate and productivity. *Social Policy* 17: 42–47.

Kohn, A. 1990. *The brighter side of human nature: Altruism and empathy in everyday life.* New York: Basic Books.

Kreisberg, S. 1993. Educating for democracy and community: Toward the transformation of power in our schools. In *Promising practices in teaching social responsibility,* ed. S. Berman and P. La Farge, 218–235. Albany, NY: State University of New York Press.

Lewis, B.A. 1991. Today's kids care about social action. *Educational Leadership* 49 (1): 47–49.

Newmann, F. 1975. *Education for citizen action.* Berkeley, CA: McCutcheon.

Osborne, K. 1982. *The teaching of politics: Some suggestions for teachers.* Toronto: Canada Studies Foundation.

Project Love. Nd. Pamphlet. Canadian Organization for Development through Education.

Rees, A. and K. Fraser. 1992. Book turns 6-year-old against her father. *The Province,* February 20.

Reindl, S. 1993. Bringing global awareness into elementary school classrooms. In *Promising practices in teaching social responsibility,* ed. S. Berman, and P. La Farge, 27–49. Albany, NY: State University of New York Press.

Roth, A. 1991. Battle of the clamshell. *Report on Business Magazine* April.

Solovitch-Haynes, S. 1996. Street-smart second-graders navigate the political process. *Social Studies & the Young Learner* 8 (4): 4–5.

Stackhouse, J. 1996. Hazardous child labour increasing. *Globe and Mail,* December 12.

Vancouver Sun. 1996. Air Jordan comes in for a crash landing with Surrey students. Letters to the Editor, June 25.

Vincent, I. 1996. The most powerful 13-year-old in the world. *Saturday Night,* November.

Wade, R.C. 1995. Encouraging student initiative in a fourth-grade classroom. *Elementary School Journal* 95 (1): 339–354.

Willison, S. 1994. When students volunteer to feed the hungry: Some considerations for educators. *Social Education* 85 (2): 88–90.

Yaeger, E.A. and Patterson, M.J. 1996. Teacher-directed social action in a middle school classroom. *Social Studies & the Young Learner* 8 (4): 29–31.

SUPPLEMENTARY READINGS

Alter, G. 1995. Transforming elementary social studies: The emergence of curriculum focused on diverse, caring communities. *Theory and Research in Social Education* 23 (4): 355–374.

Association for Supervision and Curriculum Development. 1990. *Educational Leadership* 48. This issue is devoted to the theme of social responsibility.

Baydock, E., P. Francis, K. Osborne, and B. Semotok. 1984. *Politics is simply a public affair.* Toronto: The Canada Studies Foundation.

Berman, S. 1990. Educating for social responsibility. *Educational Leadership* 48 (2): 75–80.

Berman, S. and P. La Farge, eds. 1993. *Promising practices in teaching social responsibility.* Albany, NY: State University of New York Press.

Botting, D., K. Botting, K. Osborne, J. Seymour, and R. Swyston. 1986. *Politics and you.* Scarborough, ON: Nelson.

Chamberlin, C. 1979. A whole elementary school takes social action. *One World* 17 (4): 13–14.

——— 1985. Knowlege + commitment = action. In *A Canadian social studies,* rev. ed., ed. J. Parsons, G. Milburn, and M. Van Manen, 231–248. Edmonton, AB: Faculty of Education, University of Alberta.

Chamberlin, C., B. Connors, and B. Massey. 1983. Project Athens: Can schools teach active citizenship? *One World* 22 (2): 33–39.

Clarke, P. 1999. Smoking salmon for social justice. *Teacher: Newsmagazine of the BC Teachers' Federation* 11 (5).

Conrad, D. 1991. School-community participation for social studies. In *Handbook of research on social studies teaching and learning,* ed. J.P. Shaver, 540–548. New York: MacMillan.

Conrad, D. and D. Hedin. 1991. School-based community service: What we know from research and theory. *Phi Delta Kappan* 72 (10): 743–749.

Engle, S. and A. Ochoa. 1988. *Education for democratic citizenship.* New York: Teachers College Press.

Hartmann, T. 2000. Peace cranes. *Teacher: Newsmagazine of the BC Teachers' Federation* 12 (7).

Kielburger, M. and C. Kielburger. 2002. *Take action! A guide to active citizenship.* Toronto: Gage Learning.

Lyman, K. 1995. "AIDS—You can die from it." Teaching young children about a difficult subject. *Rethinking Schools* 10 (2); 14–15.

Nickell, P. 1997. Big lessons for little learners. *The Social Studies Professional: Newsletter of the National Council for the Social Studies* 127: 3–4.

Shaheen, J.C. 1989. Participatory citizenship in the elementary grades. *Social Education* 53 (6): 361–363.

Van Scotter, R. 1994. What young people think about school and society. *Educational Leadership* 52 (3): 72–78.

Wade, R.C. 1994. Community service-learning: Commitment through active citizenship. *Social Studies and the Young Learner* 6 (3): 1–4.

———. 1996. Prosocial studies. *Social Studies and the Young Learner* 8 (4): 18–20.

Wade, R.C. and D.W. Saxe. 1996. Community service-learning in the social studies: Historical roots, empirical evidence, critical issues. *Theory and Research in Social Education* 24 (4): 331–359.

Werner, W. 1999. Selecting "hot" topics for classrooms. *Canadian Social Studies* 33 (4): 110–113.

21 Co-operative Learning in Elementary Classrooms

Tom Morton

In the 1980s, co-operative learning marched—sometimes with considerable fanfare—to the centre stage of accepted educational practice. Researchers and practitioners alike applauded co-operative learning for its power to improve academic achievement, especially among students who had traditionally not done well in school, and for its potential to enhance interpersonal relations, especially among ethnic groups and between handicapped and able students.

Since then, many teachers have embraced co-operative learning. Many others, however, have run up against the common barriers to implementing a new practice, and abandoned the approach in favour of more traditional group work or whole-class instruction. In speaking of the United States, Seymour Sarason (1995, 84) suggests rather bluntly that what passes frequently for co-operative learning is a charade and often a misnomer for traditional group work. Although research on the current situation in Canada is sparse, the reality of co-operative learning, especially in secondary schools, may be less like a mainstage performance than a fringe festival play—creative, exciting, but marginal. This situation arises partly because of a failure to appreciate that co-operation is not merely a teaching technique, but a fundamental commitment to a set of core values.

Morton Deutsch (1949) coined the term "co-operative learning" sixty years ago, but the idea of group learning has been around for a longer time. At the beginning of the twentieth century, John Dewey recommended that students work together on problems that had relevance to their lives. However, the barriers to effective group work are long-standing and deeply rooted, often extending to the very core of teaching beliefs. Dewey wrote of his attempt to buy work tables for his elementary school. He could not find anything other than individual desks. Finally, a salesperson identified the problem: "I am afraid we have not what you want. You want something at which the children may work. These are all for listening!" (1916). Similar practical and philosophical barriers impede effective implementation of co-operative learning.

This chapter seeks to clarify key elements of effective co-operative learning and to suggest ways to implement co-operative approaches in social studies. I begin by offering three reasons why co-operative learning should play an important role in our subject and then explore three challenges to its implementation. I then introduce two of the best known approaches to co-operative learning—the Learning Together model, developed by brothers David and Roger Johnson with help from their sister Edythe Holubec, and the Structural Approach, first developed by Spencer Kagan and recently revised with help from his wife, Laurie, his son, Miguel, and many associates. I explore the principles behind each approach, offer sample lessons, and distinguish these models from each other and from traditional group work and direct instruction.

Why Co-operative Learning in Social Studies?

Co-operative learning is an approach to teaching in which students work together in small groups that are carefully designed to be cohesive or positively interdependent. At the same time, group members are individually accountable for their own learning and for contributing to the group's learning. This approach to learning can contribute to the goals of social studies in at least three ways:

- **Academic achievement.** Considerable research suggests that co-operative learning, properly implemented, promotes academic achievement—in the case of social studies, the acquisition of a body of knowledge in the social science disciplines and the ability to investigate and communicate these ideas. Two notable reviews, a meta-analysis of 475 research studies (Johnson and Johnson 1989) and a similar review with stricter selection criteria of 60 studies (Slavin 1989), concluded that co-operative learning produced moderately large gains in achievement when compared to control conditions.

- **Constructivist learning.** There is considerable cognitive research suggesting that learners must "construct" knowledge if it is to be internalized and integrated with other background beliefs. Co-operative learning facilitates the transaction or construction of ideas. One of the more effective ways of making personal sense of ideas is to explain them to others. Perhaps this contemporary approach was expressed earliest by the Roman philosopher Seneca when he said, "Qui docet, discit," meaning whoever teaches, learns (also translated: when you teach, you learn twice).

- **Citizenship values and attitudes.** Co-operative learning promotes the values and dispositions of a responsible citizen. Well-planned co-operative lessons offer students opportunities to express themselves and reflect on their civic competence—the abilities and values of citizenship (Myers 2003a, 2003b). Since its early years, co-operative learning has been closely linked with promoting mutual respect and liking regardless of differences of intellectual ability, ethnicity, race, gender, handicapping conditions, social class, or gender. It does this by encouraging students to appreciate their own background and those of others, and by fostering commitment to a set of foundational values including respect for civic responsibilities, freedom of expression, fairness, and equality.

Challenges to Co-operative Learning

A prominent researcher, Robert Slavin, warned educators during the rise to popularity of co-operative learning in the 1980s that it was being "oversold and under-trained." At the time, many teachers were encouraged to implement an approach to teaching that they may have inadequately understood and possibly were at odds with their beliefs and practices. If co-operative learning is to be more than the charade that Sarasan describes, we must recognize and commit ourselves to several basic principles.

NEED FOR TEACHER COMMITMENT AND STUDY

One of the preconditions for co-operative learning is recognition of the commitment and study required to implement it competently. Co-operative learning is not a mere technique to vary the usual instructional bill of fare. An occasional group task or a lesson or two on co-operation in the midst of business as usual will not create a learning community and improve interpersonal relations. As David and Roger Johnson (1992, 45) note: "Simply placing students in groups and telling them to work together does not in and of itself result in co-operative efforts—or positive effects on students."

Teachers must anticipate that implementing co-operative learning will create problems and raise questions: What do I do about students who resist being in the same group? What about the quiet students? What about the group that doesn't get down to work, finishes early, or talks too loudly? Most of us will need help in resolving these problems and, over time, forging a learning community from what may be very diverse and reluctant learners. Help may come from a co-operative support group formed by teachers themselves—much like the ones in which we expect students to participate—or through independent self-study or outside help from a school board consultant or support teacher. (Contact information for co-operative learning groups is listed at the end of this chapter.)

ALIGN CLASSROOM PRACTICES AND VALUES

The basic values of co-operative learning, such as collaboration, equality, and inclusion, may conflict with teaching philosophies, curriculum content, and classroom organization. Because of these conflicts, some teachers may be reluctant to extend co-operative learning beyond a few token lessons. One source of value conflict is the importance in co-operative learning given to social or interpersonal goals. Most co-operative models teach interpersonal skills and encourage group self-reflection, both to help students for academic purposes and for their own sake. In contrast, the norms in some classrooms, more in secondary schools than elementary, affirm that learning means academic learning only. Social goals may not merely be downplayed, they may be actively suppressed by factors such as the way seating is arranged into rows so as to minimize student interaction and maximize teacher control.

As well, co-operative learning may conflict with deeply held beliefs about individualism and competition. In a co-operative classroom, common watchwords are "Two heads are better than one" and "You have a right to ask any group member for help and you have a duty to help anyone who asks." Students sit facing each other, they know the names of their classmates, and they may ask for a chance to study together before a test or have a partner for a project. Teachers who believe strongly in individual learning and competition may be uncomfortable with this kind of a classroom.

Even if students are not separated from each other in the classroom, they are often pitted against each other. We send enduring messages that fellow students are potential barriers to success whenever we grade by the curve, display only the best papers on the wall, sort children into winners and losers in spelling bees, and encourage students during a teacher-led discussion to compete to get the answer quickly. In his book *No Contest: The Case Against Competition*, Alfie Kohn (1992) summarizes the research on the effects of these sorts of classroom practices when compared with co-operation. He found that competition is associated with less generosity, less inclination to trust, less willingness to see other viewpoints, and poorer communication.

Co-operative learning will never be more than a fringe methodology or a charade unless the practices and embedded values operating within our classrooms support co-operation. We must recognize that almost everything we do or say in our classes may influence co-operation (Sapon-Shevin and Schniedewind 1992).

BUILD STUDENT SKILLS AND HABITS OF CO-OPERATION

If co-operative learning is to be effective, we need to include considerable instruction and student reflection on interpersonal skills and attitudes. When problems occur, such as a conflict or a reluctant participant, students and the teacher should discuss them. One motto of the Johnsons' has been "Turn problems back to the group to solve," and they insist that co-operative groups put their academic tasks to one side and address personal problems first. By teaching social skills and establishing the habit of reflection on group dynamics, students can recognize that they have the power to make co-operation work.

Two Approaches to Co-operative Learning

Describing the essence of co-operative learning can be like "The Six Blind Men of Hindustan," the old poem about the blind men who touch various parts of the elephant—the leg, the trunk, the tusk—and declare the animal to be just like a tree, a snake, a spear, and so on. By one account, there are more than twenty co-operative learning models (Myers 1991). In this chapter, I explore two of the more popular models: the Johnsons' Learning Together model and the Kagans' Structural Approach. My purpose is to show the key ingredients involved in co-operative learning, identify the ways in which it differs from traditional group work, and give some useful ideas for implementing either of these models.

ELEMENTS OF THE LEARNING TOGETHER MODEL

The Johnsons' model offers one of the best-known explanations of the principles of co-operative pedagogy (Johnson, Johnson, and Holubec 1998). According to their model, five elements are essential for effective co-operation:

- **Establish positive interdependence.** Group work will be co-operative only if there is positive interdependence:

group members must believe that their success depends on the success of others or, as the Johnsons say, "We sink or swim together." Positive interdependence can be seen as both an element of lesson design and as a spirit of mutual helpfulness. Teachers might create positive interdependence by asking small groups to come up with a single product or to share a limited number of resources such as one instruction sheet, paper, felt pen, glue stick, or pair of scissors. Planning for positive interdependence is especially important in the early months of the school year, when students may not have developed the skills or motivation to co-operate.

- **Require individual accountability.** Individual accountability can be seen both as an element of lesson planning and, over time, a spirit that everyone contributes to the group effort and is valued for that contribution. On the one hand, when students know that they are accountable for their own learning and for helping the group learn, both group productivity and individual achievement are enhanced. On the other hand, resentment is likely if some members are not pulling their own weight. When some students hitchhike on the efforts of others, hardworking group members may lessen their effort to avoid being "suckers." To encourage individual accountability, we might require each student to be ready to explain the contents of a common product or assign each student a specific section of a shared product.

- **Encourage face-to-face interaction.** Co-operative learning requires face-to-face interaction where the conversation helps students advance their own thinking on the matter before them. This element is often referred to as "purposeful talk" and it emphasizes the role of talk in thinking. To achieve a high level of academic achievement, students must meet in groups to discuss and refine their thinking. To achieve a feeling of caring and commitment, students must encourage and help each other. Sitting together, but working independently and occasionally copying each other's notes, is not interaction.

- **Teach interpersonal or social skills.** Social skills refer to behaviours such as sharing, listening, and encouraging that enable a group to work together. Students do not necessarily know how to behave co-operatively. In the first few weeks of co-operative work, we may have to teach what might simply be called "good classroom manners," for example, students move quickly and quietly to groups, use a person's name, talk in quiet voices, stay with the group, avoid wandering around, and sit so that they face each other. In the primary grades or in classes with many impetuous students, it may be several months before we can introduce more advanced social skills such as encouraging participation or active listening. The timing and particulars may differ, but the need to teach rather than assume social skills is crucial.

- **Allow for processing.** Students require the time and procedures to analyze if their group is functioning and their individual mastery of the requisite social skills. Research suggests that academic achievement is greater when co-operative groups reflect on their process. It is advisable to devote regularly between five and fifteen minutes of group time for students to write about or discuss group interactions. The participation pie activity described in Figure 21.1 is one strategy for facilitating reflection about group interactions.

Planning an effective Learning Together lesson may take considerable time to master. The suggested sequence of steps outlined in the highlighted text, "Planning a Learning Together Lesson," is one way we can attend to key considerations in implementing co-operative learning.

As one can see by examining the list above, there are a number of operational details besides the five elements; group composition, especially, needs prior consideration. Group size should be small, ranging from two to five students, and the groups should be mixed according to academic level, ethnicity, gender, and socio-economic status. Compatibility is another ingredient in the mix. Considerable research and teacher experience suggest that heterogeneous groups enhance class cohesiveness, inter-group relations, and academic achievement for all students.

However, when unaccustomed to co-operative learning, students typically want to choose their own group members, mainly friends who are often similar to themselves. Consequently, there may be tension when teachers choose groups.

PLANNING A LEARNING TOGETHER LESSON

Specify lesson objectives
- academic content
- social skills

Decide about operational details
- group size
- assignment to groups
- room arrangement
- materials
- student roles

Introduce the lesson
- explain the academic task
- structure positive interdependence
- create individual accountability
- explain expected use of social skills
- set criteria for success

Monitor students
- look for evidence of the expected social skills (by student or teacher observation)
- provide opportunities for processing

Evaluate
- academic achievement
- group functioning

To lessen this tension spend some time explaining the reasons for mixed groups along the lines of the following:

- Social studies class is where we learn how to be good citizens and part of that is learning to work with others who may be different from us but with whom we share this classroom and this planet.

FIGURE 21.1 PARTICIPATION PIE

Divide the pie to illustrate how much each member of your group participated in the task. Write down their names in the appropriate section. Below give reasons why you divided up the pie as you did and suggest things you might do to improve the co-operative sharing of the group.

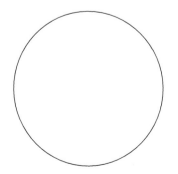

Reasons:
Ideas for improvement:

- Often we work better with those who are not our friends, there's less social talk about sports or movies and the like.
- Each student will probably work with everyone in the class at some point during the year.
- You don't have to like your teammates; you only have to work with them.
- When we play sports, go to church, temple, or synagogue, join a trade union, or are born into a family, we are in a team, so why not in the classroom?
- Especially for a highly diverse class: There are lots of different people in this classroom and in our neighbourhoods, but in this country we say that this is a good thing, and that we should respect each other and learn to work together.
- Especially for older students: Learning to work with others is key for a successful career; when hired for a job, we do not choose our fellow employees and we certainly do not choose the customers. Business research suggests that people who get fired from their first jobs do so because they can't get along with their boss and their co-workers.

Some students may still disagree with you, but they will know that you have a clear plan and purpose for your groupings.

Although most experienced practitioners argue strongly in favour of teacher-selected teams, during the early part of the year when we are unfamiliar with our students or for a break at any time of the year, random choice is recommended. There are several enjoyable, creative ways to do this such as counting off the names of famous figures, counting off in a foreign language, distributing playing cards with the common cards sitting together, or lining up according to birth date without talking—a challenge—and then grouping students next to each other. As a class develops into a learning community, one that is inclusive by habit, students may be able to choose their own heterogeneous groups.

MAKEOVER LESSON BASED ON LEARNING TOGETHER

The significance of the Johnsons' Learning Together model can be seen by contrasting its five elements and key decisions with traditional group work. In a lesson described in *Critical Challenges for Primary Students* (McDiarmid, Manzo, and Musselle 2007), students are asked to develop criteria for powerful questions in preparation for a visit by a classroom guest. The criteria might include "questions that will give you answers with a lot of information" or "questions that require some thought." Students then use the criteria to assess questions that they might ask the guest and each student selects

one question. Let us explore a Learning Together approach to this lesson and how it differs from traditional group work.

PREPARATION

If this were traditional group work, as stated above, students might select their own groups. Most students would choose their friends, meaning that most of the groups would be of the same gender, ethnicity, class, and status level. The group size might vary from two to twenty. With such homogeneous groups, few of the social goals of co-operation would be realized and probably neither would the academic goals in some groups. In contrast, the Learning Together teacher will carefully select groups to include a high achiever with a low achiever and one or two middle-level achievers for a group of three or four. In addition, the teacher would consider gender, ethnicity, and general compatibility. In the primary grades most co-operative work is done in pairs. (It's hard to get left out of a pair.)

Students also need to be comfortable with a number of routines such as seating arrangement—what the Johnsons call "eye to eye and knee to knee"—and some kind of quiet signal to indicate the time to stop group work and pay attention to the teacher. Often, the success of a lesson depends on these and other small lesson details.

POSITIVE INTERDEPENDENCE AND INDIVIDUAL ACCOUNTABILITY

The Learning Together teacher would next explain the academic task and set the interdependence and individual accountability criteria. For the first step of this critical thinking lesson, each group could have goal interdependence (namely, the common task of establishing criteria for a powerful question). There could also be resource interdependence if each group was given a single poster on which to write the criteria for powerful questions and role interdependence if there were different but complementary roles, such as the following:

- **Checker:** confirms that everyone in the group agrees with each decision and can explain the reasons for it.
- **Recorder:** writes down the group's questions and reads them back to the group to confirm the wording.
- **Encourager:** invites individual members who may be silent to share their ideas and encourages the group if it gets bogged down.
- **Gatekeeper:** ensures a balanced discussion by politely asking students who might be talking too much to give others a turn.

Individual accountability could be established by asking each student to be ready to explain the criteria and why their criteria are key to recognizing questions that are powerful. Circulating among groups or with the whole class, the teacher might randomly ask students to respond. If the student's answer is reasonable, the teacher compliments the whole group for the work, and not just the individual student, as is traditionally the case. If the answer is unreasonable, the group needs to go back to work and the teacher returns to ask the question again to the same student.

On the one hand, students might also be individually responsible if they are asked to take turns offering a criterion. As suggested above, assigning roles gives special responsibilities to each student. On the other hand, in traditional group work there would be little positive interdependence or individual accountability. All students would use their own notebooks and the groups would be instructed to create criteria and share their answers. Students who are co-operative by nature might do this and produce a common list but there would be no clear impetus to do so; and if they did do so, there would be little motivation to refine and develop the list. In addition, without individual accountability, some students would say and do little and would merely copy the work of others.

For the next step in the lesson, in which each student has a written question, a Learning Together approach would also ask student teams to have a common goal (for example, each student is to have a powerful question written down to ask the guest) and individual accountability (for example, individual students are able to explain how their question meets the agreed-upon criteria).

SOCIAL SKILLS

In traditional group work, social skills are often omitted entirely or are superficially addressed by general admonitions such as "I want you to listen." In the Learning Together model, the teacher discusses why listening is a good idea and teaches specific strategies, for example, by asking "What kinds of things would you be likely to say if you were listening carefully to someone? What would you look like as you were listening carefully?" The teacher might record responses on a poster or ask three or four students to role-play positive and negative examples. To understand the importance of social skills and to be able to use them well are major learning objectives for the Johnsons.

PROCESSING

At some point, co-operative groups will be asked to reflect on how well they worked together so they might improve their social skills, resolve any group problems, or simply celebrate their success. This reflection might be done in various ways: students may keep a journal, the teacher could make observa-

tions and report on them to the class, the group can discuss what they did well and identify areas for improvement, or individuals may complete a self-reflection form such as the Pair Reflections described in Figure 21.2. Typically, in traditional group work, student reflection at the end would be solely about the content of the lesson.

EXTENSIONS

Powerful questions could be added to a social studies unit where students interview community or family members or other students who are role-playing historical or literary characters.

Select a lesson, preferably one you have planned. Using the example of the remake of the "powerful questions" lesson into a co-operative lesson as a guide, modify the activities of your selected lesson so that it has the five elements of effective co-operative learning suggested by Johnson and Johnson.

The Structural Approach

Another popular co-operative learning model, the Structural Approach, includes similar elements to the Johnsons' but with a few key differences. The Johnsons' approach focusses on the elements of co-operative learning so that teachers can develop lessons embodying these principles. The Kagans and associates instead provide planned lesson structures that have the co-operative elements built into them. At first look, their repertoire of co-operative structures or lesson formats may appear to be a "cookbook," but each structure has a solid co-operative foundation and is suitable to different teaching situations.

The Kagans define structures as content-free ways to organize social interaction within the classroom. The structures are the "how" of instruction while the lesson content is the "what." The more than 150 structures in the Kagan model may seem daunting. However, there is no need to use all or even most of the structures. In fact, the Kagans advocate teaching students one structure a month. The large repertoire provides flexibility in choosing co-operative procedures for a specific topic or learning objective.

Structures can be as simple and brief as Think-Pair-Share, which can take mere minutes to complete. In the Think-Pair-Share structure, the teacher poses a problem or a question and individually the students think, write, or draw an answer, then one person shares ideas with his or her partner for a measured time—between twenty to sixty seconds depending on the activity—while the partner listens and offers feedback. The two students then switch roles: the next person shares his

FIGURE 21.2   PAIR REFLECTIONS

Name: _____

Name of partner: _____

	Never				Always
I made certain my partner and I both understood the material we were studying.	1	2	3	4	5
I listened to the contributions of my partner.	1	2	3	4	5
I felt that my partner listened to me.	1	2	3	4	5
We stayed on task.	1	2	3	4	5

List two adjectives that describe how you feel about your work together:

1. _____

2. _____

---

or her ideas while the other person listens. The teacher then asks students to share their ideas with the entire class.

A structure can also be as involved as Co-op Co-op, which is a structure for group research projects that has ten steps and involves considerable student autonomy. With this structure, students form groups with others who share an interest in a topic, research an aspect of that topic, then pool their knowledge to prepare a class presentation. Co-op Co-op may take a full semester to complete. Additional Kagan structures suitable for elementary grades are described in the highlighted text, "Co-operative Structures Appropriate for Elementary Students."

From grade 4 up, almost any structure can be used. The simplest structures are best for the younger grades and any class that is new to co-operative learning. For example, for groups of two, use RallyRobin or Timed-Pair-Share, and for students that are ready for a bigger group of three or four, use Placemat. These are most appropriate for primary students. More complex structures would be Numbered Heads Together and Academic Controversy (described in chapter 12, "Infusing a Spirit of Critical Inquiry").

Each Kagan structure incorporates the same positive interaction and individual accountability as the Johnsons, but the Kagans suggest two alternative principles: "equal participation" (the use of strategies such as taking turns that promote broad involvement of all students) and "simultaneous interaction" (as many students as possible contributing at the same time). The acronym for Kagans' principles is PIES:

positive interdependence, individual accountability, equal participation, and simultaneous interaction. Equal participation would be reflected, for example, in the timed aspect of Timed-Pair-Share or the turn-taking step in RoundRobin and RoundTable. Simultaneity is reflected in the importance given to pairs in most of the structures.

There is also a different emphasis from the Learning Together approach on social skills. In an article contrasting the two approaches, Kagan (2001) agrees with the value of social skills but argues that there is no need to take extra time to teach them and process their use when they are embedded in the structure. For example, a social skill such as active listening is integral in Corners and encouraging participation is important in RoundTable.

MAKEOVER LESSON USING THE STRUCTURAL APPROACH

To better understand the structural approach and its four principles let us consider how the structures described in the highlighted text might be used to compliment a direct, whole-class instruction. I will use as an example a critical thinking lesson called "What Is Canada Like?" (Harrison, Smith, and Wright 2002). In this lesson, students learn about metaphors and what makes a powerful metaphor. They then view the video *Kids' View of Canada* to identify the metaphors offered in the video about Canada. Finally, they analyze the metaphors in the video and create their own metaphor

CO-OPERATIVE STRUCTURES APPROPRIATE FOR ELEMENTARY STUDENTS

- **Numbered Heads Together.** Students number off within their teams. The teacher asks a question that has multiple answers or a complex answer and the teams discuss possible responses. The teacher calls a number and the student with that number from each group explains his or her group's answer.
- **Corners.** The teacher poses a question, statement, or issue and offers four or so possible responses each assigned to a corner of the room. Students move to the corner that best represents their choice and pair up to explain the reasons for their choice. The teacher then begins a whole-class instruction and calls on students to explain their choices. This is most effective if students have learned to paraphrase. In this case, the teacher would ask students to paraphrase the reasoning of students from other corners.
- **RoundRobin and RoundTable.** The teacher poses a question that has multiple answers. In RoundRobin, students take turns giving an answer or idea orally. In RoundTable, students write down or construct answers in turn or simultaneously on a single sheet of paper. For social studies, this might include listing jobs in the community, cities, details from a picture, or recollections from a field trip or video.
- **RallyRobin, RallyTable, or RallyRead.** These structures use the same steps as RoundTable and RoundRobin but are done in pairs. RallyRobin is organized turn-taking. Primary students might take turns saying the letters of the alphabet or counting numbers. Students could also take turns drawing part of the forest or impressions of a story passing the paper from partner to partner. In RallyRead, students take turns reading sentences or paragraphs to each other.
- **Timed-Pair-Share.** This is a very versatile approach that is a more carefully structured form of Think-Pair-Share, where students turn to a partner and talk about something. With younger students it helps to structure the think time and the share time or one person may do all the talking. In Timed-Pair-Share, the teacher poses a question to the students who are in pairs. The students then think by themselves or write or draw an answer to the question. Then one of the students shares his or her thoughts for a measured time—twenty seconds to two minutes—while the other student listens. The students then switch roles. Almost any thought-provoking question a teacher would normally ask of a whole class could become Timed-Think-Pair-Share: after looking at a picture or listening to a story the teacher could ask, "What does this tell us about...?"
- **Review.** Students could write down everything they remember and then share, or they could do an oral review, answering the question: what have we learned from reading this story or newspaper article? Other possible questions could include:
  - A question asking for a reason why something happened.
  - A question asking for a prediction.
  - A question that asks students to reflect on how they think, for example, what steps do we need to follow when we interview someone about their work? What should we be thinking about when we try to help someone?
  - Kindergarten and grade 1 students could draw their thoughts, for example, after looking at a picture or hearing a story, midway in a story to predict what happens next, or for reflecting on feelings using a sad face, happy face, silly face, and mean face.
- **Placemat.** This begins with a similar approach to Round-Table. Teams of two to four students are given a large sheet of paper divided into sections according to the number of students in the group with a square or circle in the middle. Students are given a question and they write or draw their answer in one of the sections. The steps include:
  - Assign students a topic or question that requires reflection, for example, what students know about the city, Canada, the government, or some controversial issue.
  - Each student writes down or draws what he or she knows or thinks in his or her own space, leaving the centre blank.
  - Students take turns sharing their thoughts with the group or rotate the paper to view each other's responses. Optionally, they may place a star beside the most important idea each of the other students has written.
  - As a group, students combine their ideas to write their best answer or a consensus answer in the central section of the placemat.
- **Team Web.** Each team is given a large sheet of paper and each student a different coloured pen. Students are asked to construct a web about a topic of study. Optionally, the teacher may provide all or some of the sub-topics and ask students to provide a detailed explanation and identify connecting links. The key to this exercise is the coloured pens: each student must contribute to the web and write in a different colour, thus making individual accountability easy to monitor.
- **Carousel Sharing.** One person from each team stays at the team's workplace to be a spokesperson for their topic. The other team members rotate from spokesperson to spokesperson learning as much as they can about a topic, which they must understand in order to complete a task. After the carousel, each rotating group of students provides feedback to their own spokesperson about what they learned from the other teams' spokespeople.

according to the agreed-upon criteria and then, using an image illustrating the metaphor, create a group poster.

The following description of the lesson activities will assume that the teacher has used the Learning Together model to form groups and arrange seating. In addition, it will assume that the class is familiar with the structures. Students will begin in a team of four, then separate into pairs and then reassemble in groups of four. Note that the description below uses more structures than most teachers would want in a single lesson, for the purpose of illustrating the variety of applicable structures.

As a team builder, anticipatory set, and just for fun, the lesson could begin by asking students to describe themselves metaphorically by choosing one of the following word pairs. Ask students to write an individual response to "How would you describe yourself? Are you more of a cat or a dog? … solid or liquid? … Monday or Saturday? … eagle or dolphin? … a radish or a strawberry?" After each of these questions, students use the RoundRobin structure to share their answers.

Next, students are asked to consider the meaning of these and other, more typical, social studies metaphors such as describing the United States as a cultural "melting pot" and Canada as a multicultural "mosaic." This could be done in pairs with a Timed-Think-Pair-Share followed by a whole-class instruction on the definition of a metaphor.

The teacher continues in the mode of whole-class instruction to explain the features that make a metaphor powerful: broad application (an accurate comparison usually on many points), original, revealing (gives insights), and surprising (intriguing or lively). Students are asked to use these criteria to consider which is the more powerful metaphor: "television is a fountain of information" or "television is bubble gum for the mind."

Returning to Think-Pair-Share, students now suggest metaphors to represent common things or events in their lives such as playing, eating, school, or family. They list these and ask which are powerful and why.

So far, the steps illustrate one aspect of the Kagan approach: a mix of short co-operative activities with teacher-directed instruction. According to the Kagans, a teacher will seldom give a fully co-operative lesson, but almost every lesson should have some co-operative activity.

The next activity, watching the National Film Board video *Kids' View of Canada*, contrasts clearly with direct instruction, or what John Myers calls "full frontal instruction." A typical form of direct instruction using a video might appropriately be labelled the "Whole Class View-Question-Answer" approach. It has three parts:

• The teacher shows the video.

PAIRS VIEW

• The teacher pairs students A and B and explains to the pairs that they have a common goal: to generate a list for each partner that contains the metaphors in the video used to describe Canada.
• The teacher shows the video and stops it every five to ten minutes or after a noteworthy metaphor.
• When the video is stopped for the first time, A tells B what he or she identified as a metaphor and what it means. B listens and then helps as needed.
• Both A and B take notes.
• After the explanation and notes are completed, the video is turned on again.
• After a suitable period, the pause is repeated but with B identifying the metaphors.
• The cycle repeats and the roles reverse with every pause until the video is finished.
• With the whole class, the teacher randomly calls on different As and Bs to explain the main ideas or answers.

• Students individually complete worksheets or answer questions during or after the showing.
• When the assignments are completed, the teacher calls on students one by one for their answers to the questions.

In this approach, during the showing of the video, there is little interaction among students nor with the teacher. If a section of the video is confusing or complex, students get little or no help until the end. The question and answer session is intended to help all students learn, but in many classes it may be competitive if students are vying for the teacher's attention with cries of "Me! Me!" and have their hands jabbing the air. Student-to-student interaction is competitive when strong students triumph, while those who are not quick with the answer or not aggressive enough to win the teacher's attention lose. This approach is quite different from Pairs View (Morton 1996), described in the highlighted text.

The next step in the lesson is for students to analyze interesting metaphors from the video and at least one metaphor of their own creation using the criteria for a powerful metaphor. This could be done co-operatively using Numbered Heads Together.

Following this, students choose the most powerful metaphor and create a group poster indicating the points of application between Canada and the powerful metaphor. This too could be done with Numbered Heads Together or perhaps a modification of the Team Web, in which each student uses a different coloured felt pen to draw the poster.

Finally, each group shares its posters. A Carousel structure might be appropriate so that students can listen to each group's explanation of the power of its metaphor.

Although I have suggested possible co-operative structure, these last few activities would be inconsistent with the Kagans' approach because they lead to giving a group grade. The Kagans oppose group grades over concerns about fairness and because they fuel negative reactions against co-operative learning on the part of high-achieving students. However, the Johnsons recognize the risks, but nevertheless believe that group grades may sometimes be acceptable if teams are well prepared and individual accountability is well planned. The Kagans would recommend that the Structural Approach be used for the introduction, the input of information, and guided practice aspects of the lesson, after which students would demonstrate their learning with an individual project or test. According to the Kagans, co-operative learning is a method of teaching, not an approach to the evaluation of learning.

The final few steps of analysis and a group poster could be preparatory work followed by individual team members writing a paragraph or illustrating one of the metaphors that the group has analyzed. Individual students might also be given a new metaphor, perhaps from a political cartoon about Canada, and asked to decide whether it is a powerful metaphor and why.

DICK TRACY'S CRIME STOPPERS, A.K.A. THE FOUR FATAL FLAWS

Growing up in the 1950s and 1960s, I often read the comic strip "Dick Tracy." At the end of Saturday's funny pages, there was a section called "Dick Tracy's Crime Stoppers Textbook" that contained hints for the amateur detective. For instance, when trying to memorize the face of a criminal to identify him later, make sure to note the size and shape of the ears and earlobes. What follows is a more serious educational version of my comic strip memories.

Paul Vermette of Niagara University probably did it best in identifying tips for stopping "crimes of co-operative learning" in his article "Four Fatal Flaws: Avoiding the Common Mistakes of Novice Users of Co-operative Learning" (1994). He considers the first fatal flaw to occur in the construction of student groups, that is, many novice users leave the choice to students with disastrous results. He argues, as I do, that teachers should build the teams.

The second fatal flaw is to launch students into a major group project before completing smaller activities to build teams and establish social skills and habits of co-operation.

The third common fatal flaw involves the issue of working in class. "To help monitor the effectiveness of co-operative learning, the teacher *needs to see it!*" writes Vermette. (The italics are his, but could have been mine.) He lists many advantages of doing co-operative work in class, for example,

teachers can offer suggestions and praise to students, boost the efforts of reluctant learners or shy students, and help groups reflect on their behaviour. When teachers give students group projects to complete outside class, none of this happens. Moreover, having seen many of these group projects assigned to my daughter, I have a visceral reaction against the almost inevitable unequal participation. There is almost always someone who does not participate fully.

The fourth fatal flaw is found with group grades: "Nothing offends an industrious student more than having someone else (Paul or Paula Parasite?) do nothing and share an A!" If group grades are to be assigned, it is imperative that all students get what, and only what, they deserve.

Co-operative learning is a valuable approach to teaching and learning, worthy of attention and thoughtful implementation by elementary school teachers. Although it does demand a commitment on our part, an alignment of our values with the approach, and a willingness to address the social side of learning, there is research, practical guides, and experienced teachers, some of which are listed in the following references, to help us.

Select a lesson, preferably one you have planned. Using the example of the remake of a traditional lesson into a co-operative lesson as a guide, modify the activities and structure of the selected lesson so that it embodies Kagan's four principles of effective co-operative learning.

REFERENCES

Deutsch, M. 1949. A theory of cooperation and competition. *Human Relations* 2: 129–152.

Dewey, J. 1916. *Democracy in education.* New York: Macmillan.

Harrison, J., N. Smith, and I. Wright. 2002. *Critical challenges in social studies for upper elementary students.* Richmond, BC: The Critical Thinking Consortium.

Johnson, D. and R. Johnson. 1989. *Cooperation and competition: Theory and research.* Edina, MN: Interaction Books.

———. 1992. Approaches to implementing cooperative learning in the social studies classroom. In *Cooperative learning in the social studies classroom,* ed. R. Stahl and R. VanSickle, 45–51. Washington, DC: National Council for the Social Studies.

Johnson, D., R. Johnson, and E. Holubec. 1998. *Cooperation in the classroom,* 7th ed. Edina, MN: Interaction Book Co.

Kagan, S. 2001. Kagan structures and learning together—what is the difference? *KaganOnLine Magazine.* Available online at http://www.KaganOnline.com/KaganClub/index.html.

Kohn, A. 1992. *No contest: The case against competition.* Boston: Houghton Mifflin.

McDiarmid, T., R. Manzo, and T. Musselle. 2007. *Critical challenges for primary students.* Rev. ed. Richmond, BC: The Critical Thinking Consortium.

Morton, T. 1996. *Cooperative learning and social studies: Towards excellence and equity.* San Juan Capistrano, CA: Kagan.

Myers, J. 1991. Cooperative learning in history and social sciences: An idea whose time has come. *Canadian Social Studies* 26 (2): 60–64.

———. 2003a. Assessing citizenship and character using co-operative learning. *Orbit* 33 (2): 47–9.

———. 2003b. Co-operative learning: Steps toward an anti-racist education. *Orbit* 33 (3): 29–32.

Sapon-Shevin, M. and N. Schniedewind. 1992. If cooperative learning's the answer, what are the questions? *Journal of Education* 174 (2): 11–37.

Sarason, S. 1995. Some reactions to what we have learned. *Phi Delta Kappan* 7 (1): 84.

Slavin, R.E. 1989. *Cooperative learning: Theory, research, and practice.* Englewood Cliffs, NJ: Prentice-Hall.

Vermette, Paul. 1994. Four fatal flaws: avoiding the common mistakes of novice users of cooperative learning. *The High School Journal,* February/March: 255–260.

ADDITIONAL RESOURCES

Bellanca, J. and R. Fogarty. 2001. *Blueprints for achievement in the cooperative classroom,* 3rd ed. Thousand Oaks, CA: Sage.

Bower, B. and J. Lobdell. 2003. *Social studies alive! Engaging diverse learners in the elementary classroom.* Palo Alto, CA: Teachers' Curriculum Institute.

Coelho, E. 1994. *Learning together in the multicultural classroom.* Markham, ON: Pippin.

DeBolt, V. 1998. *Write! Social studies.* San Juan Capistrano, CA: Kagan Publishing.

Johnson, D. and R. Johnson. 1992. *Creative controversy.* Edina, MN: Interaction Book Co.

Johnson, D., R. Johnson, J. Bartlett, and L. Johnson. 1988. *Our cooperative classroom.* Edina, MN: Interaction Book Co.

Kagan, S., L. Kagan, and M. Kagan. 2000. *Reaching the social studies standards through cooperative learning* (video and teachers' guide). San Juan Capistrano, CA: Kagan Publishing.

Stahl, R., ed. 1994. *Cooperative learning in social studies: A handbook for teachers.* Reading, MA: Addison-Wesley.

Vermette, P.J. 1998. *Making cooperative learning work: Student teams in K-12 classrooms.* Upper Saddle River, NJ: Merrill.

GROUPS

BC Cooperative Learning Association is the professional specialist association of the BC Teachers' Federation: http://psas.bctf.ca/BCCLA.

Cooperative Learning Center at the University of Minnesota: http://www.co-operation.org.

Great Lakes Association for Cooperation in Education (GLACIE) is based in Toronto: http://www.glacie.ca.

International Association for the Study of Cooperation in Education is a group of teachers and researchers from around the world who produce a magazine called *Co-operative Learning*: http://www.iasce.net.

Kagan Publishing and Professional Development: http://www.KaganOnline.com.

PART 3 Implementation

Instructional Planning

Learning Resources

Student Assessment

22 Course, Unit, and Lesson Planning

Roland Case

In this chapter I offer a framework that tracks teacher planning in social studies from the most abstract and general aims for an entire course to the most specific decisions about which method and resource to employ in a particular lesson. The framework consists of four levels:

- the vision for the year
- a course plan
- unit plans
- individual lesson plans

Before examining each level in detail I offer four overall principles to guide your deliberations. I introduce these principles by drawing parallels between successful planning and the practices of experienced hikers on a long-distance wilderness trek. The image of a journey through boundless, often unfamiliar territory is a particularly apt metaphor for the challenges of course, unit, and lesson planning.

Guiding Principles of Planning

Those with orienteering experience will know that hikers must be clear about where they are starting from and where they want to get to ultimately. Otherwise they are likely to lose their bearings in what may well be dense and confusing terrain. Without a clear sense of direction, even if they do not become completely lost, hikers may waste considerable time and energy and may fail to reach their intended destination. Although the ultimate destination may not be in view until near the end of their trip, which may be many days or weeks in length, hikers will always know the general direction to head towards in order to reach their long-term objective. Typically, they plot their route in outline form. They anticipate that their plans will change, but they recognize the value of having a clear plan, even if it is provisional. To keep themselves on track, hikers identify prominent features or landmarks within intermediate reach that will keep them working towards their final destination. These landmarks may be off in the distance,

several or even many kilometres ahead, but they nevertheless serve as a beacon—as the clear visible focus of their travel. If a landmark is vaguely defined, for example, if they select a feature as vast and undefined as a mountain range or an ocean, it will not keep them on a consistent path. From time to time, especially if conditions change or the going becomes very rough, hikers may reconsider whether or not heading towards the designated beacon is the best course to follow. Of course, the bulk of hikers' time is spent attending to their most immediate objectives—getting up the ravine, finding a suitable place to stop, checking their resources, making sure morale among the hikers is positive, and so on. They look for easy routes or pre-established paths that can expedite their travel, and they take detours if a route seems easier or if there is a site that offers an enticing diversion. They supplement the supplies they carry with resources found on the way, and they improvise should the need arise.

Although much of the trip consists of these moment-to-moment choices about which way to turn or where to step next, there is no point in staying on a path or turning towards a hill if it does not lead in the desired direction. Consequently hikers continually double-check—often in an intuitive or reflexive manner—that the specific choices they make are aligned with the more distant beacon they have set. Accordingly, they will follow a pre-established path only so long as it leads in the desired direction, and they may rejoin the path sometime later if it turns back towards their destination. Consistently, the direction hikers take is informed by the beacon they have set because, if clearly and properly determined, heading for it means they are on the track towards their ultimate destination.

There are many insights about effective planning to draw from this analogy with trekking though wilderness terrain. These insights can be consolidated into four general principles of planning: be purposeful, build thoughtfully, draw widely and wisely, and plan loosely.

BE PURPOSEFUL

The principle that planning should be purposeful is perhaps the most significant recommendation I offer. It emphasizes the need to decide where we want to take our students and to use that destination to orient everything we do. Without a clear and conscious direction, our teaching is aimless—likely amounting to little more than a string of activities leading nowhere in particular and serving no important purposes. Just as with trekkers, so too as teachers we need to set and be guided by long-, intermediate-, and immediate-term destinations:

- Our ultimate destinations are our rationale—our ideals or ultimate vision—for society and for our students.
- Our intermediate destinations are our goals for an individual unit and course.
- Our immediate destinations are our objectives for specific lessons.

The principle of being purposeful does not presuppose a "teacher-driven" approach to planning and teaching. The need to have a clear purpose is compatible with extensive student involvement in setting destinations by consensus or, to the extent feasible, in encouraging individuals to strike out in different directions. Given students' different preferences and abilities it often makes sense, even for those heading towards the same general ultimate destination, for individuals to pursue common goals by following different paths.

Effective implementation of purposeful planning implies four conditions:

- **Clear, focussed destinations.** Both in the long- and short-term, we should know what we hope to achieve with our students. Vaguely understood goals and objectives do not provide the sense of purpose that effective teaching requires.
- **Manageable destinations.** We should not expect to do it all and if we try to do too much—for an entire course or for an individual lesson—we may end up doing a superficial job that makes no lasting difference.
- **Justifiable destinations.** We cannot simply decide to pursue our own preferred direction without seriously considering students' best interests, parents' rights, and other curricular and professional responsibilities.
- **Aligned destinations.** Our long- and short-term destinations must be in alignment, so that we are continually working towards our ultimate destination. This requires that:
  - our rationale inform our goals;
  - our goals orient our objectives; and
  - our objectives determine our day-to-day decisions about teaching methods, resources, and assessment.

BUILD THOUGHTFULLY

The principle of building thoughtfully emphasizes the importance of anticipating the intermediate steps to be taken and developing the resources and tools needed to achieve our ultimate educational goals. The expression by the Chinese philosopher Lao Tzu that a journey of a thousand miles starts with a single step is especially relevant. It is not enough that we have a grand plan; we must also attend to how we will get there. Just as the trekker must decide what equipment is needed to cross a river or what supplies to sustain the team, as teachers we must also consider what our students will need to reach the desired goals and what we must do to support this growth.

Effective implementation of the principle of building thoughtfully includes at least three considerations:

- **Nurture an environment conducive to learning.** We must work to develop the type of classroom and school environment that supports the desired learning. If we want to develop student autonomy, we must nurture it by establishing a climate that encourages students to take risks and to make up their own minds. The mere planning of thoughtful lessons will not lead very far if the conditions in the classroom undermine these efforts. For example, inviting students to debate a very controversial issue before classroom trust and civility have been adequately established may lead to bitter and counter-productive results.
- **Provide meaningful contexts for learning.** A concern expressed by many social studies teachers that students do not perceive social studies to be relevant. We can help students better appreciate social studies by carefully planning activities that are motivating, and by framing our units and lessons in contexts that will resonate with students.
- **Teach the prerequisites.** Just as it is unfair to expect someone to construct an elaborate house without having the basic tools to do the job, so is it unfair to expect significant educational achievement without providing students with the intellectual tools they need for success. We must think through what students require for success at each step—for example, what knowledge, abilities, and attitudes are needed for students to become good researchers. Then we must plan how to assist students in acquiring each of these prerequisites.

DRAW WIDELY AND WISELY

The principle of drawing widely and wisely from many sources draws attention to the value of an eclectic approach to planning for content, teaching methods, and learning resources. Preoccupation with a narrow theme and over-reliance on a single method, such as lectures, or on a single resource, such as a textbook, are analogous to staying on pre-established paths long after they cease to lead in the direction that we want to head towards. We must draw imaginatively from varied sources in our quest for better ways to help our students get where we want them to go.

Effective implementation of the principle of drawing widely and wisely involves the following considerations:

- **Integrate the content of different disciplines and subjects.** We should help students make meaningful links among the disciplines within social studies, draw insights from other subjects to inform social studies, and connect what they study in school with their own experiences and concerns.
- **Use diverse learning resources.** We should plan to make effective use of diverse resources from computers to cartoons, from textbooks to picture books, and from feature films to guest speakers.
- **Use varied teaching methods.** We should plan for a rich array of activities from teacher-directed to student-directed, from written work to small-group conversation, and from seat-work to fieldwork.

PLAN LOOSELY

The principle of planning loosely arises because there is no guaranteed path for all students for all times. Planning is too messy and uncertain an affair to be reduced to a fixed plan. Not only will one path not work for all students, but conditions change, our students change, and we change. We should be prepared to reformulate our plans to accommodate these eventualities and the countless unanticipated turns that arise halfway though the year or in the middle of a lesson. However, this lack of predictability does not imply that planning is fanciful or useless. Planning is a deeply practical matter. The point of planning is to identify what is most worthwhile to teach and then to design a course, a unit, or a lesson that increases the likelihood that our teaching will be successful.

Effective implementation of the principle of planning loosely involves the following considerations:

- **Expect diversity.** Always expect and, to the extent possible, accommodate diversity in student interests and abilities.
- **Allow for student choice.** Entrench opportunities for student choice and self-direction as a feature of our teaching.
- **Stay flexible.** As teachers, we will be more effective if we remain open to change. Instead of viewing a lesson or unit plan as the fixed menu for the day or the month, we should look upon planning as the ongoing vehicle for

scrutinizing where we are going with our teaching and deciding what a good way is to get there.

I believe these four principles should permeate all of our planning, from decisions about the ultimate goals to our most immediate objectives. To assist in planning that embodies these principles, I offer a four-level framework:

- the vision for the year;
- a course plan;
- unit plans; and
- individual lesson plans.

These levels are akin to progressive snapshots of the earth beginning with the broadest global view and zeroing in on a particular site. Each provides increasing detail of a progressively smaller area of instruction. I begin by describing the most general level and proceed to the most specific level. Despite sequencing my discussion of the model in this order, planning should not necessarily proceed in a "general to specific" manner. Those who like to begin with the concrete will find it more productive to start with particular lessons and resources, and work from there to the more general vision. Regardless of where we start, all of us will likely move back and forth between levels as our ideas become clearer and more specific. Thus the four levels imply no particular planning sequence; but regardless of how we proceed, by the end of our planning deliberations, the issues raised at each level of the model should have been thought through in a coherent way.

Realistically, a fully completed set of plans as outlined in this framework would involve years of thinking about and trying out ideas. Nevertheless, all of us, and especially new teachers, can benefit from a deeper understanding of the considerations involved in the kind of comprehensive planning suggested by this framework. In this respect the framework is an ultimate destination. It is an invitation to strive for an ideal—even if never fully reached; only by attempting it will we come closer to where we want be.

Creating a Vision for the Year

The most general level of planning involves creating a vision for the entire year. In effect, it involves asking ourselves the following question: "In a hundred words or less, what am I really attempting to achieve in social studies this year?" The point of planning at this level is to give focus and direction to a course. Figure 22.1 illustrates a form that might be used to articulate the most general level of planning. A vision for the year may consist of three main components:

- **Rationale.** Our rationale should be a clear and defensible

FIGURE 22.1 VISION FOR THE YEAR

Theme for the year			Grade
Rationale			
PRIORITY GOALS		Classroom climate	
Content knowledge	Personal and social values		
Critical thinking	Individual and collective action		
Information gathering and reporting	Other		

account of our educational ideals—the underlying reasons or ultimate purposes for our efforts as educators.

- **Priority goals.** Our priority goals are the handful of educational goals that will be the major focus of attention for the year. These goals represent our priorities for the year—mindful that we cannot do everything well. If our goals are met, we will have gone some way towards moving students closer to the ideals set out in our rationale.
- **Classroom climate.** The classroom climate refers to the defining qualities and procedures of the learning environment within which we hope to promote the priority goals and, ultimately, our rationale.

FORMULATING A RATIONALE

Educational rationales are descriptions of the ideal individual or society we hope to promote through education. An earlier chapter in this collection, "Four Defining Purposes of Citizenship Education," identified four broad categories of rationales for social studies, positioned along two continua:

Social acceptance/social change spectrum

- **Social initiation.** Transmitting the understandings, abilities, and values that students will require if they are to fit into and be contributing members of society.
- **Social reform.** Promoting the understandings, abilities, and values necessary to critique and improve society.

Student-centred/subject-centred spectrum

- **Personal development.** Fostering the personal talents

and character of each student so that they develop fully as individuals and as social beings.

- **Intellectual development.** Developing understanding of and appreciation for the bodies of knowledge and forms of inquiry represented in the social science disciplines.

These rationales, in effect, are ways of categorizing the types of ideals that are typically offered for social studies. In the sample vision for the year, Figure 22.2, you will find elements from each of these four categories.

In thinking about our own rationale, we should be guided by two considerations: Am I clear about the ideals I am striving for? Are these justifiable ideals?

CLARITY OF FOCUS

Many of the ideals found in rationales for social studies—such as personal autonomy, critical thinking, productive citizen, or tolerant society—are potentially vague. Unless we are clear in our own minds what we mean by notions such as these, they will not serve as useful guides to our planning. Does a tolerant society mean that we will begrudgingly accept differences? And what sort of differences will we tolerate? Religious views? Alternative lifestyles? Political and economic ideologies? Perhaps we want to focus largely on racial, ethnic, and cultural differences. We may also want to pursue a more embracing vision, not merely putting up with differences but actually welcoming and accepting people because of the cultural contributions that they bring to mainstream society. These are different emphases, and clar-

FIGURE 22.2 SAMPLE VISION FOR THE YEAR

Theme for the year Canada before and after Confederation	Grade middle school

Rationale

My ideal citizen:

- is able to cope with a complex, uncertain world
- is willing and trained to think things through rigorously
- is knowledgeable about a wide range of issues
- is committed and willing to work to make the world better for all
- is emotionally mature and socially adept

PRIORITY GOALS		Classroom climate
Content knowledge • understands the complexities and interrelations of many of the historical and contemporary problems in Canada • has knowledge of both the ennobling and the regrettable events in Canada's past	**Personal and social values** • has empathy and respect for others • is committed to social justice • is respectful of different viewpoints • has tolerance for ambiguity • is independent-minded	• respectful, safe environment • challenge students in non-threatening ways • emphasis on self-directed learning —independent projects, peer and self-assessment • abundant opportunities for student choice • students expected to form personal opinions and support with reasons
Critical thinking • can competently analyze controversial issues • sees issues from varying perspectives • possesses the tools of a good critical thinker	**Individual and collective action** • is able and willing to work co-operatively with others, even in difficult situations • can plan thoughtfully to solve demanding problems	
Information gathering and reporting • can plan and conduct independent research • can effectively use media and other local sources of information	**Other**	

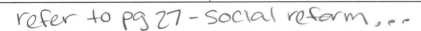

refer to pg 27 - social reform,..

ity about the particulars of our rationale are useful when planning.

JUSTIFIED IDEALS

In deciding whether or not our rationale is justifiable we should be guided by the following considerations:

- the broad needs of our students;
- the broad needs of the local community;
- the broad needs of society generally;
- our own values as educators.

The value of a clear, justifiable rationale is that it helps us to recognize and keep to what really matters. I remember teaching an especially troubled group of grade 6/7 students.

Whenever I got bogged down in the minutiae of the curriculum or was frustrated by the day's events, I would remind myself of why I was there. Long before I knew to call it my "rationale," I knew that my reason for persisting was to help these students learn to take personal responsibility for their lives. I had seen too many of their peers fall by the wayside, driven by a lack of trust of others and a lack of respect for themselves, into a world of glue sniffing and other forms of self-destructive escapism. I hoped I could teach them about literature and science along the way, but not if pursuing these goals interrupted my more pressing mission of helping them take control of their lives. My justification for this "personal development" rationale was obvious. When I thought about what these students most needed in their lives and what their parents most hoped for them, of paramount importance were notions such as functional literacy, personal responsibility, and self-respect.

ESTABLISHING PRIORITY GOALS

The priority goals identify our key educational emphases for the year. If we could make a real difference in several areas, what would we hope to achieve over the year? With the students described above, my priorities included teaching them to read at a level required to understand the newspaper, to commit themselves to a task and complete it, to treat each other with respect, and to develop pride in themselves.

In deciding what to emphasize in a given year, it is useful to consider how our rationale could be advanced through the general goals for social studies. Throughout this book, the following have been identified as representative of the range of goals social studies typically seeks to promote:

- **content knowledge:** the breadth and depth of factual and conceptual knowledge students should possess about their world;
- **critical thinking:** the ability and inclination to assess what to believe and how to act competently;
- **information gathering and reporting:** the ability to identify information needs, extract information from varied sources, and represent this information in appropriate forms;
- **personal and social values:** the desired values that individuals are to hold about themselves and towards others; and
- **individual and collective action:** the ability to analyze problems in students' lives and in society, plan appropriate courses of action individually and in collaboration with others, put into action their plans, and evaluate the efficacy of their efforts.

We need not be bound by these categories of goals, and may prefer to use the terminology provided in the provincial curriculum or some other document. If teaching an integrated course, we would include goals not exclusively from social studies but from other subjects as well. The important consideration is not the terminology, but to identify a manageable number of priority goals that will form our emphasis for the year. We will, of course, pursue many other goals; these merely represent the handful of goals that we have set as the most productive and pressing avenues to promote our ideals. Often our rationale overlaps with our priority goals because some of the ideals in our rationale are aims that are directly promoted in social studies. Typically, however, ideals are broader aspirations, and we will emphasize only some aspect of these. For example, a "social reform" rationale might include the ideals of promoting a world without poverty, hunger, and war. In a given year, we might emphasize only a few goals that promote these ideals, for example, teaching students to treat one another respectfully and to use peer-mediation and other non-violent forms of interpersonal conflict resolution.

The criteria for justifying a rationale are relevant to justifying our priority goals, although the focus in justifying priority goals is more on examining how social studies and we, as teachers of social studies, can best further ideals embedded in our rationale. In deciding upon this we should consider the following factors:

- the needs and expressed wishes of our students;
- the expectations embedded in the provincial curriculum;
- the nature of social studies as a subject and the range of purposes that social studies is expected to serve;
- the expressed wishes of parents and the local community;
- the needs of society generally; and
- our own priorities and strengths as educators.

SHAPING THE CLASSROOM CLIMATE

Although classroom climate has not traditionally been seen as part of the defining vision of a course, it is becoming increasingly obvious that this factor plays a significant role in supporting or impeding the achievement of social studies goals. Many of us will have been frustrated by our inability to get students, say, to think critically about issues or to take responsibility for their learning because the prevailing mood in the class undermined our efforts. The point of including classroom climate is to identify the basic principles that ought to guide the conduct of our class if we are serious about our rationale. For example, in the sample vision for the year, one of the elements of the rationale is to promote students' willingness and ability to think things through with rigour. Students are likely to take the risks involved in thinking for themselves only if the classroom is a safe and respectful place, and only if the inevitable "challenging" required to help students probe their thinking more deeply is done in a non-threatening manner. These features must, therefore, be important operating principles for the classroom. Identifying operating principles is a matter of thinking through the sorts of routines and norms that must be part of the daily business of our classrooms if we are to have any likelihood of advancing our rationale. See chapter 9, "Supporting a Community of Critical Thinkers," for more about nurturing classroom climate.

Developing a Course Plan

Although the vision for the year is our ultimate destination and should always be in the back of our minds, like trekkers, we will not have that vision constantly in our sights. Our conscious focus will likely be more immediate: deciding what we would have to teach in September, or in November, in order to get where we want to be in June. The purpose of the second level of the planning model—the course plan—is to set out the general sequence and structure of the pursuit of our goals by plotting the more specific objectives or outcomes that will be promoted in each unit. Just as a long trip may be broken into phases, so too the journey through the curriculum is typically divided up into units of study—usually between three and five units over the course of a year. Figure 22.3 contains a form that might be used to lay out a course plan. The tasks in developing a course plan include:

- deciding on an appropriate focus for each unit;
- identifying specific objectives for all unit goals; and
- sequencing objectives across units.

DECIDING ON A FOCUS FOR THE UNIT

Typically, planning a course begins by identifying the unit topics or unifying ideas for each phase of the course. The topic provides the context or vehicle for promoting the goals and specific objectives that will eventually be set for each unit. Selecting a topic is a common beginning step in deciding on an appropriate focus for a unit. Surprisingly, however,

---

FIGURE 22.3   COURSE PLAN

UNIT DESCRIPTION	Content knowledge	Critical thinking *P82,83 78-81*	UNIT OBJECTIVES Information gathering and reporting *Concept sets?*	Personal and social values	Individual and collective action
Unit 1 Synopsis Main goals					
Unit 2 Synopsis Main goals					
Unit 3 Synopsis Main goals					
Unit 4 Synopsis Main goals					
Unit 5 Synopsis Main goals					

identifying a topic need not determine in any definitive way what will be taught in a unit. For example, a unit on the topic "ancient Egypt" might focus on any number of studies, for instance:

- the environment's significant role in shaping human activity (for example, impact of the Nile);
- the thinking behind religious and cultural practices of other groups that may at first glance seem foreign to us (for example, studying the rationale for embalming, beliefs about reincarnation);
- the wondrous mathematical and engineering accomplishments of this civilization (for example, building of pyramids);
- the work of archaeologists in adding to our knowledge of ancient Egypt (for example, carry out a simulated dig, read about famous discoveries).

These underlying ideas within the topic are often framed as generalizations that we want students to come to understand. Various educators have stressed the power of unpacking the underlying idea through "essential" questions (Erickson 1998, Wiggins and McTighe 1998) that guide students in "uncovering" the curriculum. The examples in Table 22.1

TABLE 22.1   UNPACKING THE UNDERLYING IDEA

UNIFYING IDEA/BROAD UNDERSTANDING	CURRICULAR OUTCOMES ADDRESSED (BC CURRICULUM)	QUESTIONS TO BE EXPLORED
Families care for each other and work together to meet each other's needs.	• Describe some of the purposes of families. • Describe how families can be similar and different. • Identify and clarify a problem. • Identify strategies to address a problem.	• How does my family help me? • How can I best contribute to my family? • What are the benefits of a small/big family? • What are my most powerful family memories? • How might we help this family?
A community is more than buildings and places; it is a network of interdependent people who work together.	• Describe ways members of a community meet one another's needs. • Describe functions of local government. • Identify contributions of various occupations to BC communities. • Describe [students'] rights, roles, and responsibilities within the community. • Draw simple interpretations from personal experiences, oral sources, and visual and written representations. • Identify an issue and provide a reason to support a position.	• What people and places in my community are important to me? • Who contributes to my quality of life? • How can I contribute to my community? • What are the different experiences of people in my community? • What is community "spirit"? • What makes a good community?
Managing our natural resources in order to sustain our planet is a responsibility of global citizenship.	• Analyze the relationship between development of communities and the available natural resources. • Explain how supply and demand are affected by population and the availability of natural resources. • Describe the various ways of distributing natural resources within Canada. • Demonstrate understanding of sustainability, stewardship, and renewable versus non-renewable resources. • Assess the effects of lifestyles and industries on local and global environments. • Defend a position on a regional issue in light of alternative perspectives.	• How do we benefit from the natural resources of our country? • What is the connection between the environmental and economic impact of resource development? • How has resource development changed over time? • How do we balance the challenges of environment, economy, and sustainability?

illustrate how underlying ideas, curricular outcomes, and guiding questions help to create a focus around which learning activities can be developed.

In an important respect, a unit topic (for example, families, communities, our natural resources) is the shell within which the contents of a unit will develop. Although the most common type of topic is what is typically referred to as a theme, there are other types of unifying or central ideas of a unit. The highlighted text identifies six types of unit organizers, each of which could be unpacked into more specific essential or guiding questions.

The choice of the type of topic influences the shape or direction of a unit. For example, a unit organized around the theme of explorer Simon Fraser provides a different orientation than a project-based unit on researching, writing, and mounting a play about Simon Fraser's travels or an issue-based unit on deciding whether Simon Fraser was a hero or a rogue. Although there will be overlap in what is learned from these three units, there will likely be important differences in the outcomes. Accordingly, we should select unit topics that will best advance the goals we want to foster in each unit.

An important step in getting clear about a unit is to decide upon three or four goals that will be the main emphasis of the unit (other goals will be promoted but not stressed in the way the main goals will be) and, using these goals as a guide, to think through how the topic might best be handled.

TYPES OF TOPICS OR UNIT ORGANIZERS

Theme
A theme is an idea or feature that is shared by, or recurs in, a number of separate elements. The connection among elements in the unit is that they are in some way associated with a common theme. Some types of themes are:

- **Places.** For example, Egypt, our neighbourhood, deserts, the moon.
- **Events.** For example, building the pyramids, making the atomic bomb.
- **Eras.** For example, the Depression, pre-Copernican Europe.
- **Concepts.** For example, friendship, harmony, time, creativity.
- **Generalizations.** For example, man is a social animal, history repeats itself.
- **Phenomena.** For example, biological change, war, growing up.
- **Entities.** For example, bears, atoms, multinational companies.

Narrative
A narrative (Kieran Egan calls it a storyform) is a series of episodes that uses a familiar structure for building upon and connecting elements in a unit. The elements are united in that each must fit the story being told. Some sample narratives are:

- developing story of a country, province, or city
- tale of a people, family, or person
- evolutionary steps in a discovery or invention
- account of a quest or adventure

Issue
An issue identifies a specific question whose answer is a value judgment about what ought to be the case. The elements are united in that each is necessary to competently address the issue. Entire units might focus on issues such as:

- Should students have a right to select their textbook?
- Are large families better than small families?

- Should further technological innovation be encouraged?
- Which innovation arising from ancient Greece has had the most significant influence on our lives?

Inquiry
An inquiry identifies a specific question whose answer is a description of how things actually were, are, or are likely to become. The elements are united in that each is necessary to competently undertake the inquiry. Entire units might focus on inquiries such as:

- What motivated/drove famous people to greatness?
- How does the natural environment deal with its "waste"?
- What will my life be like thirty years from now?
- Is the United States more like ancient Sparta or Athens?

Problem
A problem identifies a specific question whose answer is a course of action. The elements are united in that each is necessary to competently solve the problem. Instead of merely talking about what should or might occur, entire units could lead students to act on problems such as:

- Can we reduce the amount of paper wasted in school?
- How can our school be made more personal/safe?
- What can we do to protect our parks and wildlife?
- What can we do to improve working conditions in developing countries?

Project
A project involves creation of a "product" of some kind. The elements are united in that each is necessary to competently complete the project. Entire units might focus on producing objects or events such as:

- models or replicas
- a play or performance
- a diorama or mural
- a written or audiovisual piece

(As a theme or an issue? And what theme or issue in particular?) The partial course plan in Figure 22.4 contains a synopsis, the main goals, and the objectives for the first unit in a year-long study of nineteenth-century Canada. The main focusses of this unit are to help students learn to work effectively together in groups, to teach them about conducting independent research, and to develop a broad understanding of key events leading up to Confederation. The unit organizer—a project to create a giant timeline of events during this period—was chosen because it is a good vehicle to serve these three goals.

IDENTIFYING SPECIFIC OBJECTIVES

As we think about our unit topic and main goals, we will inevitably begin to identify specific content. At some point it becomes necessary to outline more systematically and specifically the objectives or learning outcomes for the unit. At this stage we are not concerned about teaching methods—what we will have students do during the unit—but rather on what we hope students will learn. (Research suggests that many teachers prefer to begin with the activities then decide what the objectives might be. This simply means that once deciding on a unit focus some teachers may want to jump to the next, more specific level and think about the activities that students will be involved in before identifying the specific objectives that the unit will address.)

The key challenge in identifying the specific objectives is to unpack what is involved in promoting the goals we have set for the year, and especially the main goals that we have identified for the unit. Objectives are simply more specific elements of a goal; objectives often take a lesson or two to cover, whereas goals typically refer to general aims that may take an entire unit or longer to achieve. In developing the sample unit plan, we would want to think through what is involved in promoting independent library research. What are the crucial sub-skills or tools that students will need to develop this ability and which of these are best taught in this unit? Should my students learn to use library reference aids (for example, card catalogue, reference index), or should I introduce them to the internet and the various tools available for electronic research? Perhaps my students already know how to locate information sources. In that case, I might be better advised to help them improve at extracting information from these sources.

Although it is difficult to do, the best place to begin this articulation process is by developing lists of the more specific objectives that are implied by the goals for each unit—especially the main goals for the unit. Often the curriculum guide or other professional materials are helpful in providing details about the objectives for specific goals. Of course, we will not be able to do it all in any one unit; we must set priorities about the most important objectives to pursue. As a general rule, we are well advised to do a smaller number of things very well, rather than attempt to do too many things in one unit. This is why a few goals (perhaps three or four) should be designated as the main goals for the unit. If we run out of time, we will make sure that the key objectives associated with our main goals are not sacrificed.

The following factors are particularly relevant considerations when deciding the specific objectives for a unit:

- the overall rationale for the course and the main goals for the unit;
- our students' interests and prior learning;
- the requirements of the provincial curriculum;
- our own interests and competencies as teachers;
- the resources available in the school and district; and
- the possibilities of integration with other areas of study.

SEQUENCING OBJECTIVES ACROSS UNITS

The final task in developing a one-year overview is to develop a scope and sequence of objectives from unit to unit. The scope of objectives should be comprehensive so that over the course of a year the entire set of curricular objectives are adequately addressed. The sequence should be reasonable; for example, we should not teach objectives in an early unit that presuppose mastery of outcomes that we have planned to teach later in the year. In many cases, there may be no obvious prerequisites; for example, in teaching students to interpret visual documents it may make no difference whether we start with photographs or maps. The sequence may depend entirely on the availability of resources for the unit topics we have selected. In other cases, the sequence may be crucial. For example, we should teach simple procedures for using the internet, such as finding sites where the address is provided, prior to introducing more sophisticated variants involving student-designed searches. Although there are no hard and fast rules, the following are different ways to think about the scope and sequence of objectives over the course of a year:

- proceed from simple to more difficult;
- proceed from concrete to abstract;
- proceed from general to specific;
- proceed in chronological order (especially relevant with content objectives);
- process in reverse chronological order from present working back;
- proceed from near to far; and
- proceed from far to near.

FIGURE 22.4   SAMPLE COURSE PLAN

"Some activities might include:" *(handwritten)*

UNIT DESCRIPTION	UNIT OBJECTIVES				
	Content knowledge *(+ PLO's)*	Critical thinking *(p.78)*	Information gathering and reporting	Personal and social values *(+ PLO's)*	Individual and collective action *(unit w/ action)*
Unit #1 Timeline: The lead-up to Confederation **Synopsis** The class is divided into five teams that are to research and prepare a giant illustrated timeline that will be posted around the entire classroom depicting the major social, political, cultural, and economic events and people in Canada from 1815 to Confederation. Each team is responsible for researching, documenting, and illustrating major landmarks and key figures for a ten-year period. Groups must decide by consensus on the basis of agreed-upon criteria the most significant events and persons of their time period. Students are expected to share their findings orally and prepare a background sheet that all students receive. The unit will conclude with a student-created exam on events and people depicted in the timeline. **Main goals** • Learn to work effectively and co-operatively in groups. • Learn to conduct independent library research. • Develop a broad overview of events leading to Confederation.	• Understands the political, eco-nomic, social, and geographical factors leading to Confederation. • Has knowledge of key events and persons in the development of Canada from 1815 to 1867.	• Is able to assess appropriateness of information sources for a purpose. • Is able to use criteria to reach a reasoned decision.	• Uses library reference aids to locate sources (for example, biblio-graphy, catalogue, electronic search engines). • Uses textual aids to locate informa-tion (for example, index, glossary, keywords, head-ings, legend). • Summarizes ideas in his or her own words. • Uses graphics (for example, timelines, charts, graphs) to present information. • Oral and visual communica-tion is clear and accurate.	• Takes pride in preparing quality work. • Respects opinions and is supportive of others. • Respects the rights of everyone in the group. • Engages respect-fully in group discussion.	• Understands collaboration, co-operation, compromise, consensus. • Plans how to or-ganize the group, divide up the tasks, and sched-ule and monitor the work plan. • Fulfills roles and responsibilities effectively and fairly.

Handwritten annotations:
- *4-5 include (concept sets back knowl)*
- *4-5- bulk of lesson*
- *4-5 - how conclude unit (assessment)*
- *+ Critical thinking questions*
- *2*
- *27*
- *2*
- *★ use criteria to make reasoned judgement*
- *★ Can repeat alot*
- *- Able to read source & understand*
- *main idea*
- *p.12*

Using the social studies curriculum for a grade level of your choosing, develop a vision for the entire year and briefly outline the focus and main objectives for three or four units. You may want to use the templates outlined in this chapter ("Vision for the Year" and "Course Plan") or others of your choosing. Plan carefully so that the various aspects of your priority goals for the year are developed systematically throughout the units.

Outlining Unit Plans

A more specific level of planning occurs when we take each of the units described in the course plan and begin to develop their details. As illustrated in Figure 22.5, unit plans typically consist of summary notes outlining the objectives, the proposed methods or activities, the anticipated resources that will be needed, and the suggested assessment strategy for each lesson. A unit might contain anywhere from ten to twenty lessons. The following sequence is one way to proceed when developing a unit plan.

- Brainstorm possible teaching strategies and resources that would promote the identified goals and objectives.

Supplement your own ideas by looking for teaching resources in a local school library, in a teacher's resource centre, or in catalogues of print and multimedia resources. Talk to others who have taught this topic and may be in a position to suggest ideas or resources. Assemble as many ideas and resources as you can find.

- Identify an introductory activity or activities. We all know that first impressions are important. This same principle applies to the way new units of study are introduced. The introductory lesson(s) to a unit can serve several important purposes:

  ◆ Arouse student interest in the topic and provoke student questions.

  ◆ Provide students with background information and set the context for what is to follow.

  ◆ Provide the teacher with diagnostic information about the extent of students' present knowledge about the topic and attitudes towards it, as well as related skill levels.

  ◆ Help the teacher and students formulate a plan of action for studying the topic of the unit; the highlighted text, "Ways to Introduce a Unit," offers various suggestions for beginning new units of instruction in an engaging and effective manner.

- Identify a culminating activity or activities that summa-

FIGURE 22.5   UNIT PLAN

Unit topic			Grade	Unit #
Unit goals	1. 2. 3. 4.			

LESSON TITLE	SPECIFIC OBJECTIVES	METHODS/ ACTIVITIES	RESOURCES	ASSESSMENT STRATEGIES AND CRITERIA

rize or draw attention to the main goals and provide an occasion to demonstrate and celebrate students' learning. Often the culminating activity may refer back to the introduction or be previewed at the outset of the unit so that the unit is "framed" in a coherent manner.

- Begin to flesh out the rest of the unit plan by indicating the specific lessons and order in which the unit will unfold. Specify objectives for each lesson. Check to see that all relevant objectives listed on the course plan for that unit are addressed. From the list generated above, select the teaching strategies, student activities, and learning resources that will best serve the objective(s) for each lesson. Also, specify the assessment techniques (for example, a one-page report, an oral presentation, a poster) that will reveal how well students have met the objectives for that lesson. It is also very useful to specify

WAYS TO INTRODUCE A UNIT

- **Audiovisuals.** Viewing an audiovisual resource is motivating and provides students with information on which to build. Students may not attain a strong grasp of its contents on the first viewing. It can be viewed again later in the unit. When choosing audiovisual material to introduce a unit, the priority should be to stimulate interest rather than to provide a great deal of information immediately.

- **Brainstorming.** Brainstorming is a useful way to ascertain the depth of students' knowledge about a topic before beginning instruction and to help them organize the information they already have into a framework. The teacher's role is to record all responses without criticism, help students expand on others' ideas, and set a time limit and stick to it. Following the brainstorming sessions the teacher helps students sort the ideas into categories using approaches such as webbing or data retrieval charts. Retain the final organization so that students can examine it at the end of the unit to see how much they have learned.

- **Discrepant Event.** A discrepant event identifies unusual aspects of a situation in order to provoke student thought. For example, tell students that as the people in a sleepy town of five hundred inhabitants left church one Sunday, they heard much shouting and general hilarity issuing from the direction of the harbour. As they raced down for a look, they saw a steamship containing four hundred men entering their harbour. Many of the men wore bright red shirts and carried backpacks with supplies. Some had picks and shovels. Ask students why they think these men descended on this town. After students have advanced a number of possible explanations, tell them that the sleepy town was called Fort Victoria and it was the future capital of the province of British Columbia. The men who arrived on the ship had just come from San Francisco because they had heard that gold had been found on the Fraser River. They intended to purchase supplies in Fort Victoria and then continue on to seek their fortunes. The first step towards British Columbia becoming a colony and then a province was because of the influx of new people due to the gold rush.

  Here is another example. Tell students that a civilization began on the banks of a river that flooded regularly. A desert surrounded the civilization, which made the climate dry and hot. Ask them for their predictions as to the likelihood of this civilization surviving and ask for their guesses as to what civilization this might have been. If students are not able to guess correctly, tell them that the civilization was that of ancient Egypt and that it flourished on the banks of the Nile River in Africa for thousands of years. Ask students to hypothesize why the civilization of ancient Egypt established itself in this particular location. They can then begin data-gathering activities to verify or refute their hypotheses.

- **Displays.** A teacher-created display can arouse interest and provide initial information about a topic. The display should be set up a week or more prior to beginning the unit so that students will have plenty of time to browse among the items in the display and to talk about them informally with other class members. Alternatively, students can create their own displays by bringing pertinent items, newspaper articles, and magazine illustrations to school, or the teacher and students can contribute jointly to the display.

- **Field Experience.** A field experience is often considered to be most effective at the end of a unit because students have a greater understanding to bring to it at that point. However, such an experience can also be useful at the beginning of a unit because of its value in piquing interest and in the information it can provide, which can serve as a springboard to the acquisition of further information.

- **Guest Speaker.** Invite a guest who has special knowledge about the unit to speak to the students. The students' parents may be willing to speak about their occupations, countries of origin, or other areas of expertise. A way of finding out whether there are parents willing to make themselves available for this purpose is to send a questionnaire home at the beginning of the school year. Other sources of speakers include retired people's organizations, consulates, government departments and agencies, and public relations departments of large companies.

- **Music.** Play a tape that is representative of the time, place, or topic. For instance, if studying a particular country, music commonly enjoyed by people there could be played. Songs from Canadian children's singers such as Raffi; Sharon, Lois, and Bram; Fred Penner; or Charlotte Diamond could be chosen to illustrate topics such as friendship, family relationships, and roles and responsibilities of family members. "The Wreck of the Edmund Fitzgerald" by

continued on next page

- **Mystery Box.** Show students a gift-wrapped box containing several objects related to the unit. Let each student handle the box. Have students use a "twenty questions" approach to ascertaining which objects you have selected to include in the box; that is, they will be limited to twenty questions, and therefore must begin with very general questions in order to eliminate as many possibilities as they can as quickly as possible. Record the guesses on the blackboard. When twenty questions have been asked, open the box and explain each object.
- **Simulation.** A simulation can provide an extremely motivating introduction to a unit. Examples are beginning a unit on the growth of industrialization by having students simulate an assembly line or a unit on local government with a simulation in which they become members of a city council making a decision related to commercial versus recreational uses of land. Follow up with a discussion in which the simulation experience is related to understandings that will arise from the unit.
- **Story.** Stories can engage student interest in a unit of study and bring unit understandings to life. Examples are the use of the book *Maxine's Tree* by Diane Leger-Haskell to begin a unit on the environment or perhaps reading a Greek myth to begin a unit on ancient Greece.

what qualities will be looked for when assessing students' work—in other words, indicate the criteria that will be used to assess students' work (for example, the report is well organized, shows evidence of empathy for the people described, is historically accurate).

- Finally, review the draft unit plan with another person to ensure the following:
  - *Adequate emphasis on each goal.* Verify that the activities and objectives described in the unit plan match the main goals identified in the course plan. Has the unit shifted in a direction that does not do justice to the proposed emphasis? If so, either bring the unit back into line so that it promotes the main goals adequately, or change the proposed focus for the unit.
  - *Appropriate sequence.* Check to see that the lessons are ordered in such a way that the prerequisite objectives are taught in a reasonable sequence and that the unit builds towards a culminating activity, with a sense of completion for students.
  - *Reasonable flow.* Look to see if the transitions are connected or disjointed between lessons and over the whole unit. Although every lesson will not follow directly from the prior one nor lead smoothly to the next, the greater the flow of lessons, the less likely that students will be confused by the progress of the unit.
  - *Rich variety.* Review the proposed activities, resources, and assessment strategies to ascertain whether they contain sufficient variety and range. Without realizing it, the unit may rely excessively on one or two activities (for example, answering questions from a textbook) or assessment strategy (for example, journal reflections).

A sample of a partial unit plan is found in Figure 22.6.

Creating Lesson Plans

The most specific level of planning occurs at the individual lesson level. This is where we think through in considerable detail exactly what, when, and how things will be done for each lesson. The more experienced we become, the less detailed our lesson plans need to be. Although lesson planning may take different forms, I recommend dividing the planning of a lesson into the seven tasks described below and outlined in Figure 22.7.

- **Formulate lesson objectives.** Objectives specify the outcomes we hope to produce (that is, what we expect students to learn from the activities that we plan for them). These objectives will already be identified if a unit plan has been developed. Although there is no hard and fast rule, it may be unwise to have more than three objectives for any given lesson, especially if they are not closely connected to one another. Generally speaking, promoting one or two outcomes well is preferred over doing many things superficially. It is important not to confuse objectives with methods: an objective specifies the hoped-for outcome of having students complete the learning activity. Statements of method would include statements such as "Students will debate an issue" and "Students will experience what it is like to be discriminated against." A statement of the objectives is generated by asking what the students will learn by engaging in the debate (for example, learn to express their ideas clearly or to develop persuasive arguments to support their position) or what they will learn by experiencing discrimination (for example, acquire greater sensitivity to the feelings of others).
- **Introduce the lesson.** The introduction should provide an engaging and illuminating launch into the lesson. Its purpose is to create a "mindset" that will motivate students and focus their attention in ways that will increase

FIGURE 22.6 SAMPLE UNIT PLAN

Unit Topic: Our school community				Grade: 1	Unit # 1

Unit Goals	1. Develop students' ability to read simple maps. 2. Increase students' familiarity and comfort with the school setting and staff.		3. Develop students' appreciation of the contributions that others make to the school. 4. Develop students' ability to use criteria in thinking critically.		

LESSON TITLE	SPECIFIC OBJECTIVES	METHODS/ACTIVITIES	RESOURCES	ASSESSMENT STRATEGIES AND CRITERIA
Making school our home	• learn the layout of the school • learn the meaning of the concept "criteria" • learn to use criteria in making a decision	Read *Welcome Back to Pokeweed Public School*. Introduce map of your school and, just as in the story, lead students on a tour of their school. Make a list of people and places encountered. Brainstorm what might be done to make the school more "homey" (for example, get to know everyone, learn where everything is). Introduce the concept of "criteria"— what something "looks like" or "sounds like" when it is done right. Assist students in generating criteria for sound actions (that is, realistic, safe, serves desired purpose). Discuss which options for making school more "homey" meet the criteria for sound action. Plan how the class might carry out some of these options.	• *Welcome Back to Pokeweed Public School* by John Bianchi	• assess whether students recognize when a possible option clearly meets or clearly does not meet the criteria
Learning to read maps	• learn to read symbols and locate sites on simple maps	Read *Mandy and the Flying Map* to introduce the idea of maps. Discuss the concept of a "bird's-eye" view. Walk students through a classroom map pointing out things on the map and in the classroom. Play a game where students think of things in the classroom and give clues on the map to help others guess the object.	• *Mandy and the Flying Map* by Ann Powell • overhead or poster-sized map of the classroom	• using a game format, assess whether students correctly move to places identified on the classroom map • assess whether students can correctly point on the map to classroom objects
Touring our school	• learn to follow simple maps and locate objects on the map	Working in small groups and accompanied by a parent or helper, students go on another tour of the school. They are to trace the route followed and add features to their maps as they come to key spots in the school.	• copies of a simple school map	• assess students' ability to correctly locate their location on the map and draw objects in the school on their maps

continued on next page

FIGURE 22.6 SAMPLE UNIT PLAN (CONT.)

LESSON TITLE	SPECIFIC OBJECTIVES	METHODS/ACTIVITIES	RESOURCES	ASSESSMENT STRATEGIES AND CRITERIA
Who are the people in our school?	• learn who works in the school	Read *Who's Behind the Door at Our School?* Students list the people in their school and the position they have (that is, Ms. Smith is the principal; Mrs. Jones, the custodian; Mr. Chan, learning assistance teacher). Paste photographs of each person on a poster next to their name and position.	• *Who's Behind the Door at Our School?* by Michael Salmon • staff photographs	• using a game format, assess that students can correctly match the name, picture, and position of each staff member
What do the people in our school do?	• learn the duties performed by each staff member	Brainstorm questions students might ask to learn more about each person and what they do. Discuss the criteria for a good question (clear, gives lots of information—not "yes" or "no," may be unexpected). As a class, decide upon a common set of questions to use to interview each staff member. Pairs of students interview a designated person. Students trace the route to the interview on their map.	• interview question and recording sheets for each pair of students	• assess whether students recognize when a possible option clearly meets or clearly does not meet the criteria • assess whether students correctly trace their route on the school map
Who's contributing the most?	• appreciate staff contributions to school • learn to support their positions with a reason	Record information gathered from interviews on posters next to each person's picture. Discuss criteria for deciding who contributes most (that is, protects safety, affects largest number of students). Students vote for the three people who are doing the most to make the school a positive place, providing a reason for each choice.	• "ballot" to vote for three most significant contributors	• using the "ballot," assess whether students offer a relevant reason for each choice • observe informally during class discussions to see if students show appreciation for staff contributions

the likelihood of their benefitting from the lesson. Suggestions for creating a mindset include:

- Establish a connection with a previous lesson.
- Explain the purpose and value of what is to be learned.
- Provide an overview of what will take place.
- Invite students to share what they know about the topic for the day's lesson.
- Involve students in an enjoyable activity or pose a question or dilemma that will arouse curiosity and set a context for what students are about to learn.

• **Develop and sequence the body of the lesson.** The body of the lesson refers to the teacher instructions and student activities that will occur during the lesson. Suggestions for planning the body of the lesson include:

- Break down the component parts of each objective into teachable elements and think of how each can be taught.
- Vary the types of activities so there is a change of pace.
- Think about dividing the tasks/sessions into tightly orchestrated segments (between ten and twenty minutes' duration) to reduce the likelihood of students tiring of activities that go on for a long time.

FIGURE 22.7 LESSON PLAN

Lesson title	
Objectives	By the end of this lesson, students will: 1. 2. 3. 4.
Introduction	
Body of lesson	
Closure	
Assessment	
Extension	

- Although this sequence is not always appropriate, as a rough rule it is useful to think of six stages in the body of a lesson:
  - *Instructional input:* students are given new information or are introduced to a new notion (by the teacher or students, through reading or viewing).
  - *Modelling:* a demonstration (by the teacher or by the students) of what is to be done with this new knowledge.
  - *Trial run:* on their own or in small groups, students try one or two examples (or the first steps) to see if they have grasped the task.
  - *Group feedback:* issues and difficulties encountered during the trial run are discussed as a class.
  - *Application of knowledge:* students proceed with the main assignment for the lesson.
  - *Coaching:* as students work on their assignment, the teacher or students (in pairs or in cooperative groups) provide individual advice as problems and questions arise.
- **Prepare resources.** Resources refer to the instructional materials, activity sheets, readings, and questions that will be used to support the lesson.
- **Draw closure.** Closure refers to the proposed means for

debriefing the students and helping them consolidate what they have learned. Closure often involves the following tasks:
- Students summarize what they have learned.
- Students apply learning to a new situation.
- The teacher synthesizes key ideas and draws connections.
- **Assess student learning.** Assessment tells us how well the objective(s) have been met. Students should be provided, prior to completing an assignment, with a clear indication of the assessment, including:
  - the criteria that will be used as the basis for assessment of student learning; and
  - the standards or levels of performance for each criteria (that is, what does "very good" on the assignment look like, and how does it differ from "good"?).
- **Extend or follow up on the lesson.** The extension part of a lesson is a way to provide for those students who invariably finish early. Unless we plan educationally enriching activities for this eventuality, some students will often waste considerable class time. Extension activities are useful when the proposed lesson goes more quickly than anticipated. Extension is also useful to encourage students who may want to pursue ideas raised by the lesson further.

FIGURE 22.8 SAMPLE LESSON PLAN

Lesson title	Simon Fraser: Hero or Rogue?
Objectives	By the end of this lesson, students will: • understand the concepts of "directly observed fact" and "inference" and be able to identify inferences drawn by an author; • understand that different inferences may be drawn from the same event (and the most defensible inference is the one that is most plausible given the facts); • be able to generate and defend an interpretation of a historical event; and • know about Simon Fraser's experiences with the First Nations people.
Introduction	Mention to students that Simon Fraser was a famous Canadian explorer—among other forms of recognition, a major river and a university have been named after him. Suggest that there is some reason to suspect that history has been too kind to Simon Fraser—that possibly he really doesn't deserve his fame. The point of the lesson will be to find out exactly what sort of person he was. Before doing that, students must learn how to interpret facts.
Body of lesson	1. **Teaching about inferences** (that is, the difference between directly observable/audible fact and an inference). With little or no prior explanation perform the following gestures and ask students to explain what you are doing: • Point your finger at a student and motion for him or her to come. • Put your finger to your mouth to indicate silence. • Pretend to be thinking. After students have answered, suggest that they have interpreted or drawn an inference from what you were doing. Ask them to tell you exactly what they saw you doing. Use a chart such as the following to record student answers.

DIRECTLY OBSERVABLE FACTS	INFERENCES
Directing index finger at student and curling it inward.	Teacher wants student to come to her.
Putting index finger to your lip.	Teacher is trying to quiet class.
Looking upward pensively and saying "Well, I wonder…"	Teacher is thinking about something.

2. **Reinforcing understanding.** Ask the class to come up with a definition of: (a) a directly observable (or audible) fact, and (b) an inference. Ask students for examples of a directly observable fact and possible inferences to be drawn. Provide several examples and discuss the inferences implied in the statements (include some that are contentious inferences).

3. **Modelling the assignment.** Direct students' attention to the first paragraph of the reading for this lesson "The Descent of the Fraser River." Invite students to identify either directly observed facts or inferences in this paragraph. Ask students to speculate about other inferences that might be drawn from these events. For example, it is stated that "The route was so rough that a pair of moccasins was worn to shreds in one day of portaging." The wearing out of a pair of moccasins in one day is the directly observable fact. The author's inference seems to be that Fraser and his men were determined, persevering, and willing to endure great sacrifice.

4. **Application of learning.** Direct student attention to the Student Instructions sheet (for younger students present them orally) and the Data Recording Chart. Explain the tasks (which may be done individually or in small groups). Ask one-half of the class to focus on Simon Fraser and the other half of the class to focus on the First Nations people. Confirm that students understand what is expected before setting them to work.

Body of lesson (Cont.)	5. **Sharing of insights.** After students have had sufficient time to complete the assignment, invite them to share their findings. Begin by asking about the more interesting facts and inferences that students encountered in the text. Then ask individuals to share their assessments of the character of Simon Fraser and the First Nations people they encountered. Encourage debate and ask students to defend and qualify their answers on the basis of consistency with the evidence found in the text. Be careful to note that all First Nations people may not have the same character—some may be friendlier than others, and so on. 6. **Application of knowledge.** Based on their own deliberations and on the class discussion, ask students to list five or six words or phrases that they believe describes Simon Fraser's character fairly and five or six words or phrases describing the First Nations character(s). Students must support their character descriptions by referring to their interpretations of the events. Remind students that events may have several plausible interpretations, and their task is to decide which is the most defensible interpretation. For older students expect them to defend their interpretations of specific events in light of other evidence in the text.
Closure	• Discuss how differences of opinion about what sort of person Simon Fraser was could be resolved by finding out more about Simon Fraser from other sources (for example, Simon Fraser's diary; the diaries of some of his companions; what is known about Simon Fraser from his friends, employers, and competitors). • What do these differing stories tell us about the study of the past? Consider the following question: What is the true nature of history: fact or inference? In your own words, explain what the question is asking and support your position by referring to examples drawn from the report about Simon Fraser's trip and an account of the trip from a First Nations perspective.

Assessment	• Evaluate each student's character profile in light of the following criteria: adequacy of support for overall conclusion, sensitivity to alternative inferences, ability to support particular inferences in light of other textual evidence.
	
	• Present students with the drawing of Simon Fraser and his crew. Pose the following questions:
	    ◆ Which one of the men in the drawing is Simon Fraser? Explain the reasons for your choice.
	    ◆ What impressions does this drawing suggest about these explorers and about the region that they are travelling through?
	    ◆ Draw your own picture of Simon Fraser and his men as seen from a First Nations perspective. On the back of your picture explain the key differences in perspective on the explorers and the region between your picture and the drawing provided.
	
	• Use these criteria to assess students' picture study:
	    ◆ Correctly identify the middle person (in the front canoe) and suggest that clothing, physical appearance, and lack of a paddle are key reasons why this person stands out from the rest.
	    ◆ The number of plausible inferences that the students suggest (for example, the region is dangerous, uncivilized, and largely uninhabited, and the explorers are daring, afraid, and determined).
	    ◆ Assess students' pictures (and explanations) in terms of the number and plausibility of inferences drawn as seen from the First Nations perspective. An additional criterion might be imaginativeness of inferences drawn.

Extension	• Ask students to write a two-page detailed account of Simon Fraser's trip from the perspective of one of the First Nations people that Simon Fraser would likely have encountered. Their account should be consistent with the directly observable facts in the attached historical report. (It is expected that they will draw different inferences from these facts.) Criteria for assessment: the major criteria are the plausibility of inferences drawn and sensitivity to alternative inferences when facts are seen from different perspectives. Other criteria might include accuracy of chronological sequence, imaginativeness of inferences drawn, and completeness of account of all the major events. • Discuss factors that affect the credibility of reports, such as: Were the witnesses physically present? Do they have an obvious self-interest? Are they trustworthy sources?. Why might Simon Fraser's diary not be completely credible? Why might he be motivated to distort the truth, consciously or unconsciously? Perhaps you could introduce the concepts of primary and secondary sources.

SIMON FRASER: HERO OR ROGUE?

Simon Fraser is a famous Canadian explorer—among other forms of recognition, a major river and a university have been named after him. Has history been too kind to Simon Fraser? Does he really deserve this fame? What sort of person was he? What sort of people were the First Nations people that Simon Fraser encountered on his travels? Read the attached historical report, "The Descent of the Fraser River," and complete the following task(s).

Step 1

Circle all the statements in the attached report that provide any obvious insights about the character (personality traits, and personal strengths and weaknesses) of Simon Fraser and/or the First Nations people he encountered.

Step 2

Use the data recording chart to summarize what the report tells us about Simon Fraser and the First Nations people. The entries in the left-hand column should be descriptions of what occurred, the entries in the middle and right-hand column are character traits that the author and you attribute to the character of the person(s). In many cases, the author does not present directly observed facts, but simply provides his inferences. In these situations, indicate what you imagine are the facts that would have been observed. Examples have been provided on the data recording chart.

1) Simon Fraser's character: In the left-hand column, list any directly observable facts about the events and actions involving Simon Fraser. For each directly observable fact, indicate in the middle column what the author infers from the facts about his character, and in the right-hand column indicate what you infer from these facts about his character.

2) Characteristics of First Nations people: In the left-hand column, list any directly observable facts about the events and actions involving First Nations people. For each directly observable fact, indicate in the middle column what the author infers from the facts about their character, and in the right-hand column indicate what you infer from these facts about their character traits.

Step 3

1) List approximately five words or phrases that portray your assessment of Simon Fraser's character. Be prepared to defend your assessment.

2) List approximately five words or phrases that portray your assessment of First Nations people's character. Be prepared to defend your assessment.

SIMON FRASER'S CHARACTERISTICS		
Directly observable facts	**Author's inferences**	**Your inferences**
Example: The places where they had to carry their canoes were so rough that a pair of moccasins was worn out in one day.	Simon Fraser is a very determined individual— nothing will stop him.	Fraser may be determined, but perhaps he just doesn't know how to walk in this kind of countryside.
FIRST NATIONS CHARACTERISTICS		
Directly observable facts	**Author's inferences**	**Your inferences**
Example: The First Nations people said the river could not be canoed and Fraser believed them.	The First Nations people were truthful.	Perhaps the First Nations people were trying to scare Fraser.

THE DESCENT OF THE FRASER RIVER[1]

On May 28, 1808, Simon Fraser led twenty-three men on an expedition to find a route from the interior of British Columbia to the Pacific Ocean along the river that Fraser imagined to be the Columbia River. Day after day they encountered obstacles as they paddled down the river. The river was a continual series of rapids and the carrying places were extremely dangerous or very long. The places where they had to carry their canoes to get around the rapids were so rough that a pair of moccasins was worn to shreds in one day. Fraser decided the First Nations people he had met were correct in saying that the river was not passable for canoes. So Fraser and his men set out on foot, carrying packs weighing eighty pounds each. In his diary, Fraser wrote that they experienced "a good deal of fatigue and disagreeable walking" but he and his men continued on their journey.

Soon they met First Nations people who told them ten more days would bring them to the sea. One villager said that he had been to the sea and had seen "great canoes" and white men. When Fraser and his party proceeded, many of the locals walked with them. Two days later, at a large village near present-day Lillooet, First Nations people told them that the river was navigable from their village to the sea, whereupon Fraser bargained for two canoes. At another village (now Lytton), the people were so friendly that Fraser was called upon to shake hands with twelve hundred of them. In return, he and his men were well fed and were able to get two wooden canoes.

Despite what the First Nations people had said about the river being navigable, the explorers soon found their way blocked by numerous rapids. Two canoes were lost. More canoes were obtained from the Native people. During this time, the explorers toiled over the roughest country they had ever seen:

> We had to pass over huge rocks assisted by the Indians.... As for the road by land, we could scarcely make our way with even only our guns. I have been for a long period among the Rocky Mountains, but have never seen anything like this country. It is so wild that I cannot find words to describe our situation at times. We had to pass where no human being should venture; yet in those places there is a regular footpath impressed, or rather indented upon the very rocks by frequent travelling. Besides this, steps which are formed like a ladder ... furnish a safe and convenient passage to the Natives; but we, who had not the advantage of their education and experience, were often in imminent danger when obliged to follow their example. [extract from Fraser's journal]

At Spuzzum, Fraser was much impressed by a number of totem poles, each fifteen feet high and "carved in a curious but rude manner, yet pretty well proportioned." Friendly First Nations living in large frame houses presented them with roast salmon. Near where the town of Hope now stands, they were entertained at a large village where there was a huge com-

Illustration by Charles W. Jefferys.

munity house built of cedar planks. The First Nations people warned that the Natives of the coast were "wicked" and would attack them, but Fraser would not alter his plan. When these First Nations people refused to lend him a canoe, Fraser took one by force. For a short while canoes from the village followed them, their occupants waving weapons and shouting war songs, but Fraser and his men ignored them. Soon after, another group came at them "howling like wolves" and swinging war clubs, but they did not attack Fraser's group. Fraser ordered his men to paddle farther along to a second village, but the behaviour of the First Nations people forced them to turn back. On July 2, near what is now New Westminster, Fraser decided to return up the river in order to secure provisions before attempting to resume his descent to the ocean. This was the farthest point reached by the explorers. Fraser's reception by First Nations people on his return up the river was far from friendly—one group seized a canoe and began to pillage the baggage. Fraser forced a canoe from them and left a blanket in return. For several days hostile First Nations people followed them. They finally reached friendly villages and were guided over rough bridges and swaying ladders by Natives who "went up and down these wild places with the same agility as sailors do on board a ship."

Fraser finally arrived back at Fort George on August 6. Although Fraser had not accomplished his purpose of exploring the Columbia River, he really was the discoverer of the river that bears his name. Because of his voyage the confusion between the Fraser River and Columbia River was cleared up.

Select two of three outcomes from the social studies curriculum and develop a detailed lesson plan using the template outlined in this chapter or another of your choosing. Take care to ensure that the lesson teaches and assesses the identified learning outcomes.

The sample lesson plan in Figure 22.8 illustrates many of the suggestions just described. The focus of the lesson is the concept of inference—that is, interpreting or drawing conclusions from accepted facts. In this lesson, students consider whether or not Simon Fraser is a bona fide hero by reading a historical account of his explorations and dealings with the First Nations people he encountered.

Closing Remarks

As suggested by the analogy offered at the outset of this chapter, the challenges to thoughtful planning are a lot like trying to negotiate a wilderness. Just as it is easy to lose one's way in the forest, so too is it easy to become disoriented when planning for instruction at any level. We are especially likely to stumble if we fail to articulate or lose sight of our important educational destinations. The danger, if you will pardon the forced metaphor, is that we may lose sight of the forest through the trees. The immense volume of choices about what and how to do it, and our desire to do it all, may result in plans that are scattered and rather superficial. Setting a modest number of challenging goals and doing them well may be the best course to follow.

Having just emphasized the importance of a strong guiding direction to one's teaching, let me also caution that we should not feel bound to follow a preordained set of steps and activities when circumstances change. We need to monitor student reactions as we go, changing plans in midstream when appropriate. In addition, as we learn more about teaching, we should revisit our plans from year to year.

ACKNOWLEDGMENTS

Thanks to Mary Abbott for developing the examples found in "Unpacking the Underlying Idea."

Thanks to Penney Clark for the list found in "Ways of Introducing a Unit."

ENDNOTES

1   This is a shortened version of "The descent of the Fraser River" by Malcolm G. Parks in *Discoverers and Explorers in Canada—1763-1911* (Portfolio II #4), illustrated by Charles W. Jefferys and published by Imperial Oil Ltd. Used with permission.

REFERENCES

Erickson, L. H. 1998. *Concept-based curriculum and instruction: Teaching beyond the facts.* Thousand Oaks, CA: Corwin Press.

Wiggins, G. and J. McTighe. 1998. *Understanding by design.* Alexandria, VA: Association of Supervision and Curriculum Development.

23 Engaging Students in Learning History

John Fielding

It is easier to comment on how not to teach history, than it is to explain how to teach it successfully. I have only to recall the countless negative reactions I heard throughout my career from adults when I informed them that I was a history teacher. Some of their responses included: "Oh! That was my worst subject." "I hated history." "History was boring." "Names and dates, that's all it was, and I can't remember any of them!" Their responses to my question, "Why didn't you like history?" made reference to a typical list of complaints: memory work, recall, lists of names and dates, not relevant, uninteresting, the teacher talked all the time, and we didn't do anything.

I believe we can learn how to teach history effectively by considering the positive memories that people who enjoyed the subject have about history in school. Typically, positive responses come from people who had teachers who took them to historic sites, involved them in recreating history through drama, told great stories, and encouraged provocative discussions. In short, history learning was, to use the word these people often used, engaging.

What I have also learned by talking with people who enjoyed history in school is that they have continued to study and learn history throughout their lives. In most cases they continue their study not through formal academic study, but by reading history for pleasure, researching their family's history or genealogy, collecting stamps or antiques, telling stories of the past, or travelling to museums and historic sites. Their lives are richer and more interesting as a result of their enjoyment of history. The challenge for history teachers is to stimulate students' curiosity, interest, and engagement similarly.

Speaking personally, I trace the reason I studied history in university and eventually became a history teacher back to my grade 4 teacher. She was an austere woman who would slap any unsuspecting child with a ruler simply for looking sideways. But one day she did an unusual thing. She told us to get out of our seats and go to the huge windows at the side of the classroom. There we were instructed to observe the river outside. The school sat on a hill overlooking the Grand River, which flowed through the little town of Paris, Ontario. She said, "Try to imagine Father Marquette and his partner in exploration, Louis Joliet, in their birchbark canoes paddling down our river through the forested wilderness past our school. Of course, our school would not have been here!"

After a few minutes of scene-setting—dreamy gazing for some, but intense imaging for me—we were whisked back to our desks. Here the rest of the story with dates and details continued, but from that moment on I was fascinated with these explorers. I had imagined that I actually saw them. History came alive for me that day. Years later, in grade 12 and grade 13, when trying to decide what to do with my life, I couldn't get that moment with history out of my head. I now realize that my experience in that class was momentous because my teacher had engaged my historical imagination. She did this in various ways. She made history "active" because she got us to move out of our desks. She used historical facts to "create a story" of Marquette and Joliet's travel and explorations. And she made it "immediate and relevant" by encouraging us to look at locations and events in our own community.

Our first priority in teaching history is to develop strategies that arouse and engage our students' historical imaginations. It will not occur by lecturing students with lists of names, dates, and definitions for recall and test purposes. Certainly students need to learn historical facts, including names and dates, but students are more likely to understand and remember them if they are engaged by the study of history. The ineffectiveness of the traditional textbook and lecture methods were documented in a famous memory study conducted by Danielle Lapp of Stanford University. Her research concluded that we remember only 10 per cent of what we read, 20 per cent of what we hear, 30 per cent of what we see, 50 per cent of what we see and hear, and 90 per cent of what we do and say. The challenge then is to make the study of history something that students can see, do, and talk about.

Traditional Strategies for Increasing Student Interest

Like most history teachers, I have searched for years to find ways to interest my students and to make history fun. I tried many strategies before I understood the difference between lessons that are just interesting and those that are engaging and effective. Students may enjoy some activities, but they may not learn much of real substance from them. The following activities are examples of interesting but not necessarily effective strategies.

CROSSWORD PUZZLES, WORD SEARCHES, AND FILL-IN-THE-BLANKS

These activities can keep students busy and, for some students, may reinforce dates or vocabulary. However, students don't learn about historical context, and the activities don't invite imaginative re-creation of an era or event, and don't involve any of the skills of a historian. In fact, I wonder if they do much at all for learning history.

TRIVIA GAMES

With the popularity of various forms of trivia games and the annual Dominion Institute survey report about how little Canadians know about their history, there has been a push to teach young people more historical facts. History-related trivia games can be used for review or to conclude a lesson. However, for many students trivia games simply reveal how poor they are at memory work. Even those who remember the details may have little real understanding of their historical significance or context.

Traditional Engaging and Potentially Effective Strategies

There is a second category of activity that does have wonderful potential to interest students and to help them develop skills, including critical thinking and decision making. However, these activities are often deficient in another respect: they fail to engage students' historical imagination. The following activities can make history come alive for students, but typically they fall far short of this potential.

FILMS, VIDEOS, OR DVDS

Films, videos, and DVDs are more popular with students than word games. These resources can help students visualize an era or an event. However, too often students passively watch presentations without analyzing what is presented, why it is presented, and how it is being presented. While these presentations may stimulate students' interest, unless students raise questions about the experience we have to wonder what students are actually learning and if this is really an effective way of coming to understand history.

FIELD TRIPS

How can anyone be critical of a field trip? Students enjoy field trips because they include a change of scenery, involve free time, and introduce interesting places to see. Without ruining all the fun involved in a site visit (because we know our task is partly to interest students in studying history), we need to engage students in learning about the place they are visiting. We need to challenge students to think about what they are experiencing, why a site is important, and what we can learn from it. Pre- and post-field trip research and activities can make the difference between a merely entertaining outing and a significant history-learning experience.

DEBATES

Debates are a favourite activity for some teachers who like controversy and competition. The danger with debates is that students are often more interested in winning their argument than thoroughly examining an issue. I have steered clear of the "either/or" mentality encouraged by debates since I learned about Edward DeBono's PMI approach—P stands for plus or positive, M for minus or negative, and I for interesting or I wonder if. Using a PMI strategy, students would gather in groups to brainstorm an issue and then record the plus, minus, and interesting ideas. The PMI approach can lead to great discussions and thoughtful reflection.

Another alternative to the debate is the "U-shape" forum.

To facilitate discussion, classes may be configured in a "U-shape." Students with polar views (either strongly agreeing or strongly disagreeing with the proposition) seat themselves at either tip of the "U"; students with mixed opinions sit at appropriate spots along the rounded part. At varying stages in the discussion, students are encouraged to move along the spectrum as their intellectual positions on the issue change. In this way, less dogmatic attitudes are encouraged. The implicit messages of the traditional debate (fixed opinions with the objective of winning the argument) are supplanted by varying messages in the "U-shaped" discussion (provisionally held positions as one tries to figure out the most defensible personal stance from a continuum of options).

POSTERS

It has become increasingly popular to ask students to create posters, especially posters encouraging immigration to Canada at the beginning of the twentieth century or recruiting soldiers for World War I. Students who like to draw or paint enjoy making posters in history class, but too often this involves little or no research. Creating posters turns into a copying exercise, and involves no critical thinking about the use of propaganda and why certain images appealed to people at that time in history. Without these latter dimensions, creating posters may have limited value in a history class.

There are always exceptions, and one approach to posters that I recently encountered involves critical examination of an issue combined with an imaginative activity. It is called "Moving to New France" (Sandwell, Misfeldt, and Case 2002, 75). In this two-part critical thinking activity, students explore the "push/pull" and "retain/repulse" factors connected with immigrating to New France in the seventeenth century. In the first task, students examine and prioritize reasons for staying and leaving a community. Students then read about four fictional persons who contemplate immigrating to New France and assess the factors affecting each person's decision to immigrate. They then determine whether their assigned French citizen would stay at home or immigrate to the New World. In the second critical thinking task, students learn to recognize a poster's implicit message, target audience, and persuasive techniques by analyzing several Canadian immigration posters. They then create a poster encouraging or discouraging immigration to New France using appropriate techniques and appealing to the interests and fears of the target audience. In the final step, students analyze each other's posters.

MIND MAPS

The sounds of moaning can be painful when we ask students to write an essay or a report. For many students, extended written work is their worst nightmare. Yet when showing a video in class or assigning material for students to read we want to see what they have understood from the activity. In place of extensive writing tasks, I have found mind map assignments to be more satisfying and effective for many students. A mind map is a visual representation of students' thoughts and thought processes. It can show how they connect ideas and reveal their understanding of cause and effect relationships. Instead of asking students to share a report by reading it to the class, I have noticed that it is more effective to ask students to explain what they have learned by referring to a mind map that they can display for the class.

TIMELINES

I used to dread starting a new topic such as the French Revolution or World War II. I wondered how students would understand what happened without having some knowledge of the sequence of events. I certainly didn't want to lecture them for forty minutes. Instead of simply giving students a timeline of key events to introduce a topic, I started asking them to evaluate the significance of these events according to a set of criteria established by the class. For example, how many people were affected by the event? Did it cause subsequent changes? Did it cost lives or save lives? Was the impact of the event short- or long-term? In order to answer these questions, students had to read and do some independent research. I assigned this as a group activity so students could divide up the research, pool their knowledge, and discuss why they assigned the rankings they did. Students made a bar graph ranking each event's significance on a scale from zero to ten. Finally, students presented their findings using their graphs. The presentations led to many a lively discussion, for the students' interpretations of events were never the same.

Less Traditional Engaging, Imaginative, and Effective Strategies

In my opinion, the most important element of an effective strategy is its ability to activate students' historical imagination. It should involve students in using and talking about their learning. Some strategies that are not merely interesting but actively engage students in an effective and creative manner include role-playing, creating tableaux, stepping into history, and writing postcards and obituaries. One word of caution, however; there are no guarantees that these activities will work for everyone. Many elements must be in place for successful results. Good research habits are needed to avoid blatantly inaccurate, false history. And students need to know that inviting different interpretations is not permission to make errors in historical fact or to impose present-day thinking and values on the past.

ROLE PLAYS

I made sure my students participated in at least one role play or tableau exercise each semester. Why? Because year after year, for more than twenty years, when I asked my students to rate their favourite lesson, most said it was role-playing an event. Keep in mind that role-playing should involve historical accuracy, not remaking history.

The challenge with role-playing is that it can take longer to prepare. The good news is, once you find a good ready-made role-playing activity, you can use it for many years. There are many suitable role plays on the internet or you can create your own exercise. You can, with a little reflection, update it every year and it will just get better every time you use it.

Role-playing puts students into decision-making situations when they are asked to re-enact events such as famous meetings (for example, the Quebec City Conference of 1865) or encounters between historic individuals (for example, an immigration simulation in the *We Are Canadians* learning package [CRB Heritage Foundation 1995] provides the resources to support elementary students in playing the parts of immigrants and immigration officials during four different time periods of the twentieth century). Role-playing helps students learn not only about the event, rules, dates, and people, it makes the event come alive. In the case of the Quebec City Conference, students learn to negotiate, compromise, and even make good impressions. While re-enacting immigration scenarios, students learn about the process and may come to feel the emotions accompanying historical debates about immigrants, immigration, and immigration restrictions.

The following list outlines various strengths of role-playing as a learning activity.

- It can help students recreate the dramatic quality of a situation or historical setting.
- Open-ended role-playing situations provide students with an opportunity to analyze a problem or controversial situation.
- It provides an opportunity for students to develop a social conscience by putting them in the shoes of another person.
- It can help students learn to view issues from the perspective of other people.
- It can sensitize students to the idea that maintaining a win-lose posture in which "I am right and they are wrong" often serves to perpetuate a problem.

- Role-playing often leads students to decision-making activities. Decision making in itself can be motivating. It empowers students: they feel they have some control over their learning when they are encouraged to make decisions.
- It allows students to combine the cognitive and the affective domains of learning. Students are encouraged to feel as well as think.

Some cautions to address when using a role-play activity are listed below.

- It is very difficult to understand how people thought in the past. Too often, we impose our thinking on the past and do not dig deep enough to begin to enter the minds of our ancestors. Students need help in building a historical setting or context for their role play.
- The real complexities and subtleties of a situation may be overlooked or simplified to an unacceptable level. Some groups may be presented in a stereotypical way (for example, women, visible minorities, people in certain jobs, and religious groups).
- People's feelings, opinions, and attitudes might not be portrayed accurately. Try as we might, we can never really feel the pain, anxiety, fear, or even the joy of the original experience. We must encourage students to thoroughly and critically research the time period they are about to dramatize.

TABLEAUX

A tableau is a striking scene or picture created by organizing students in a staged pose, often in costume. A series of tableaux can be used effectively to recreate an event, especially when a narrator describes the various scenes and the progression of events. Tableau is a variation of role-playing and can be less intimidating because, while everybody can participate, not everyone needs to speak. I have used the following guidelines to recreate events in a tableau.

- Divide the class into teams of four to six students. Each team should do the research to create their series of tableaux.
- Include three to five tableaux or frozen snapshots in a series, each representing a dramatic moment.
- Explain to the students that everyone should be in the picture and visible from the same camera angle. Students should avoid clumping together to give the picture depth.
- Each person needs to decide on an interesting pose. Some exaggeration may be required in order to convey a point. Every feature is important, for example, wide-open eyes, reaching hands, or a tilted head.

- Costumes and props can be difficult to find, but you may be able to find one prop for each student. Props can add to the scene and also help shy students who need something as a distraction.

- When the picture freezes, the narrator steps out of the tableau and describes the scene and its significance with a prepared statement. The narration should be concise and dramatic, and include no more than two or three sentences. In order to get more students involved, encourage the group to have a different narrator for each scene. Perhaps the key person in each tableau could be the narrator.

- During the rehearsal, the actors should take turns stepping out of the tableau to take on the role of director. They should look for variation in the tableau scenes, visual impact, timing, and clarity for the narrators. If a digital camera is available, pictures can be taken so that the group can see themselves to analyze and assess their visual impact.

- Remind the students that in a tableau, each actor is aware of not only his or her role but also of the relationship to each other.

The crucial aspect of this activity is the debriefing. At the end of the activity, invite students to discuss the following questions:

- What was portrayed?
- Why was it important?
- Was it a plausible recreation of the event?
- What aspects do we need to learn more about?
- Are there other interpretations of what happened?
- What have we learned from this activity?

STEPPING INTO HISTORY

Role-playing and tableau can be combined into an activity called "Stepping into History." This is a concept I developed after participating in a History Alive! workshop presented by Bert Bower from the California Teachers' Institute. This activity involves students in role-playing people in a painting or photograph. Some of my favourite photographs for this strategy are famous ones, such as "The Last Spike"[1] or "Fathers of Confederation at the Charlottetown Conference." The idea is to assign roles based on the people in the picture. Students research their characters, and then they create a conversation about the issue that is the subject or reason for the picture. For example, in the two photographs I mentioned, the issues are obviously the building of the transcontinental railway and Confederation. This activity is excellent for stirring up the students' historical imaginations and encourages them to

research, discuss, and identify people and places in history. It can also, with thoughtful help from the teacher, involve critical thinking. By asking penetrating questions, we can encourage students to recreate a realistic historical context. Otherwise, students are likely to impose the present on the past. There are opportunities for some imaginative dialogue but avoid inauthentic dialogue—that is neither good history nor good history teaching.

POSTCARDS FROM THE PAST

Creating postcards from the past is an interesting alternative to essay- and report-writing. When studying a time period or an event, whether it is the Loyalists, Confederation, or settling the West, ask students to create postcards from the perspective of individuals living in that time period. The postcard should be historically accurate—we may have to suspend some historical accuracy for the Loyalists since they were far too busy and disoriented to be writing postcards even if they had had them back in the 1780s. The postcards are to be written in the first person and should have proper postcard format, including a representative picture on the front.

This is a more useful activity than simply writing a letter or drawing a picture. It involves student research, which often does not occur if you ask them simply to draw a picture or create a poster. The purpose of the research is to ensure accurate information and realistic portrayals of the character's opinions about the matters of the day. The 5W questions (what, where, who, when, and why) can provide a template for developing the postcard narrative.

I developed "Postcards from the Past" with the help of colleagues for the Historica Fair program. For more information about this lesson, including an assessment rubric and template, consult the Historica website (www.histori.ca). The Loyalists unit developed for the Library and Archives of Canada has an excellent Postcards from the Past activity (www.archives.ca). This activity satisfies all my criteria for an effective lesson: it invites imagination, requires research, and appeals to different learning styles.

HERITAGE OR HISTORY MINUTES

History minutes is a strategy that developed out of the popular television advertisements called "Heritage Minutes." These were produced originally by the CRB Foundation Heritage Project and more recently by Historica. In preparation for their own history minute, help students choose and research a person, event, or even a popular product of the time. Divide the class into small production teams and ask them to write a storyboard for their history minute. You may want to show an actual Heritage Minute and critically analyze it as a model. Information about the actual Heritage Minutes and about this type of lesson is easily found on the Historica website. It is not necessary that students actually produce a video, although students usually want to and it teaches them other skills in a real, worthwhile way.

OBITUARY OR EULOGY

I have lots of friends who read the obituaries every day—of course, I am older than elementary students, and so are my friends. An obituary can offer a wonderful summary and interpretation of a person's life. There are excellent models in most newspapers, especially the "Lives Lived" column in *The Globe and Mail*. I like the idea of finding primary documents about famous people such as Winston Churchill, Sir John A. Macdonald, or Billy Bishop and asking students to write an obituary based on them rather than on secondary sources that have already done most of the work. Of course, this suggestion will depend on the students' age and ability level. Even writing an obituary or eulogy from secondary sources requires research, creativity, storytelling ability, and writing skills. Encourage students to present their eulogy orally.

Conclusion

My purpose in writing this chapter has been to try to encourage teachers to see the value—even the necessity—of engaging students in the study of history. I have tried to explain how this is not the same as making history fun or amusing. Rather, it involves trying to excite students' curiosity about the past. They want to be challenged, but not overwhelmed. They want to be able to think, talk, and do history. They need to be given opportunities to make decisions, walk in other people's shoes for a while, and, most of all, to be engaged imaginatively.

Select one of the kinds of activities discussed in this chapter and develop a lesson plan on some past event included in the curriculum. For young children this may be an important family or community incident. Focus on trying to draw students into the time period and to engage their imagination.

ENDNOTE

1   A complete, ready-to-use "Stepping into History" lesson with the "Last Spike" photograph is available on the Historica website at http://www.histori.ca/prodev/lp.do?id=10086.

REFERENCES

CRB Heritage Foundation. 1995. *We are Canadians* (Kit #10: Changing Patterns). Toronto: Prentice Hall.

de Bono, E. 2000. *Edward de Bono's CoRT Thinking Lessons.* Oxford, UK: Cavendish Information Products.

Sandwell, R., C. Misfeldt, and R. Case. eds. 2002. *Early contact and settlement in New France.* Richmond, BC: The Critical Thinking Consortium.

24 Sample Primary Lesson
Passing Along Kindness
The Critical Thinking Consortium

This chapter provides a detailed lesson plan[1] that illustrates how primary students can be engaged and systematically supported in thinking critically about the effects of their actions. The main focus of the lesson is a critical challenge where students must choose and perform an act of kindness towards someone in the classroom so the person feels good enough to "pass it on."

The lesson is intended to help students experience the power of setting in motion a series of positive actions by being kind to someone who, in turn, is motivated to pass along a kind gesture to another person. The concept of a chain reaction of human kindness is introduced through the story *Because Brian Hugged his Mother,* by David L. Rice (1999). This story tells of a young boy who impulsively hugs his mom one morning and sparks a series of unselfish acts that extends to dozens of people. Students create a "chain of kindness" by role-playing and diagramming the kind acts described in the story. After developing criteria, students brainstorm a list of acts of kindness towards class members. Students individually select one act of kindness that they agree to carry out towards an assigned member of the class. Afterwards, students discuss how they have benefitted from giving and receiving their kind act and acknowledge each other's thoughtfulness in a letter of appreciation. As an extension, students undertake an act of kindness in their family or community and look for indications that it may have had an effect on the recipient's behaviour.

In the course of working through this task it is hoped that students will come to understand that treating others kindly creates positive feelings that may be passed on to others. In so doing, students will learn that both the doer and the receiver benefit from acts of kindness.

The premise of The Critical Thinking Consortium approach is that student success in any critical thinking task depends on their possession of the relevant "tools."[2] Following are the key tools that students are taught in this lesson:

Background knowledge
- understanding of a chain of events
- knowledge of the effects of actions on people

Criteria for judgment
- criteria for act an of kindness (for example, makes someone feel good about themselves, is thoughtful, shows appreciation for the other person)

Thinking strategies
- web

Habits of mind
- empathy

Preplanning

ASSEMBLE OBJECTS FOR CHAIN REACTION

In Session One, we suggest introducing the concept of a chain reaction by creating a configuration of dominoes or other objects that will visually demonstrate the string of events that one action can put in motion. Gather a sufficient number of objects so that after your demonstration, pairs of students might each receive a handful of objects with which to create their own mini chain reaction. You may want to tie in this activity with a science lesson on cause and effect.

PREVIEW STORY

As a follow-up to the demonstration, we suggest introducing the idea of a human chain of events using the picture book *Because Brian Hugged his Mother,* by David L. Rice. Since the lesson is structured around this resource, you will need to adapt the activities if you use a different book to introduce this theme.

Session One

DEMONSTRATE CHAIN OF EVENTS

Arrange the collected dominoes or other objects in a series so that one action will cause all of them to topple or move in some way. Hold aside three or four objects and place these in a separate configuration so that they do not create a chain reaction. Begin by drawing students' attention to the display of the three or four "non-connected" objects. Invite students to speculate on the number of objects that you would have to tap in order to get every object to move. After everyone has offered a guess, tap the first object and then the next until all of the "non-connected" objects have fallen. Now draw students' attention to the display of "connected" objects and invite students to guess how many objects you would have to tap to get every one of these objects to move. After students have offered their opinions, tap the lead object and watch the chain reaction. Discuss the difference between the non-connected and connected configurations, drawing out that in the first demonstration one action had an effect on one object only, whereas in the second demonstration one action had twenty or thirty times that effect. Explain that "chain of events" is the term used to describe a situation in which one action causes a string or set of events.

DEVELOP OWN CHAIN REACTIONS

Divide students into pairs and distribute five or more objects to each pair. Direct students to arrange their objects so that one action will cause all of the objects to move. Subsequently, ask students to create a second configuration in which no action will cause more than one object to move. Circulate among the pairs to confirm that students can create both types of configurations.

INTRODUCE STORY

After allowing time for students to explore chain reactions using the physical objects, ask students to describe how they feel when someone does something nice for them (for example, feels like someone cares about them). Discuss how making someone feel good might affect the way that person behaves (for example, the person may be more likely to smile or to share with others). Explain that the class is about to learn of the effects that a young boy had by doing something nice for his mother. Display the cover of the book, *Because Brian Hugged his Mother*. Ask students to suggest how Brian's mother might have felt when Brian hugged her. Invite students to imagine what she might have done differently because of Brian's action.

READ THE STORY

Start reading the story and pause to allow students to check their predictions about the mother's feelings and reactions. Invite students to listen as you read the rest of the story to learn of the events arising from Brian's hugging of his mother. As the story is completed, ask students to suggest why everyone did something for someone else (for example, kindness was passed on, people felt as if someone cared and they wanted to do the same for someone else). Inquire whether students notice any similarity between the events in the story and the effects on the objects they have just played with (one action causes another action, which causes yet another action, and so on).

ROLE-PLAY THE CHAIN OF EVENTS

Enlarge to ledger size (11 x 17) copies of Blackline Master 24.1, "Brian's Chain of Events." Cut out the individual strips indicating one of the twenty-three characters in the story and the kind act each performed. Arrange students in a large circle. Distribute the numbered strips in the order in which the characters appear in the story (Brian appears at the end and the beginning of the story). If your class has fewer than twenty-three students, assign students at the beginning of the circle to assume an additional role near the end of the chain. If your class has more than twenty-three students, either assign two students to play individual characters and share the task or expand the circle of kindness by inventing new characters and acts of kindness. Additional blank cards are provided for these additional characters and events at the bottom of the blackline master. For example, after receiving a hug from Brian, Mom made pancakes for Joanna and Brian. Students can imagine what might have happened to Mom after she sent the children off to school. Perhaps Mom came across a neighbour who was having trouble with his car and gave him a lift to work; as a result the neighbour may have helped a co-worker finish some urgent work. She may have handed in her work on time and made their boss so happy that the boss took the office staff to lunch, and so on. When everyone has been assigned a role(s), begin to reread the story. As the events are described in the story, students role-play their assigned character's action towards the next character in the chain. The class should end up full circle with Brian again hugging his mother.

DEBRIEF THE ROLE PLAY

Help students appreciate that as each person in the story did something kind for someone else, it was as if a chain of kindness was formed—each person was joined to someone else by an act of kindness. Explain that this chain of kindness shows how many people can be affected in some way by one gesture.

	PERSON	ACT OF KINDNESS
1	Brian	hugged his mother
2	Mother	made pancakes for the children
3	Joanna	complimented and helped the teacher get ready for school
4	Mr. Emerson	had the class make a banner for the principal's birthday
5	Ms. Sanchez	was patient with Lorreta
6	Lorreta	didn't embarrass Richard
7	Richard	praised Eddie
8	Eddie	gave his picture to the bus driver
9	Ms. Wong	let the truck driver get in front
10	Truck driver	helped the stock clerk
11	Stock clerk	gave Mrs. Johnson free dog food
12	Mrs. Johnson	let Jumbo watch his favourite video
13	Jumbo	didn't tease Tiffany
14	Tiffany	was friendly to Mrs. Gunderson

continued on next page

15	Mrs. Gunderson	praised the mechanic
16	Mechanic	thanked the mail carrier
17	Mail carrier	complimented the baker
18	Baker	made muffins for the dentist
19	Dentist	complimented the chef
20	Chef	made the police officer's favourite dish
21	Police officer	didn't give Brian's father a ticket
22	Brian's father	spent extra time with Brian and told him how much he was loved
23	Brian	hugged his mother again
24		
25		
26		
27		

Session Two

WEB CHAIN OF EVENTS

As a review of the previous day's lesson, invite the class to create a giant web of the chain of events in the story. In preparation, write the title "Chain of Kindness" on chart paper and attach it to the bulletin board along with one piece of coloured paper (the approximate size of an index card) for each student in the class. Arrange the pieces of coloured paper in a circle or other shape that eventually loops back onto itself, leaving space between the pieces of paper to indicate the actions between the characters. Direct students to locate the strip of paper (Blackline Master 24.1) they received in preparation for the role play. Instruct them to cut apart their assigned character from the action performed. In turn, invite students to attach their "character" card to the coloured paper and their "kind action" card in the space between the adjacent pieces of coloured paper. While doing this, each student is to explain to the class his or her part in the chain of events. Suggest that students use the following format:

I'm ___their assigned character___. Because ___the previous character who was kind to them and the action performed to them___, I decided to ___the kind act their character performed on the next character in the chain___.

CONNECT THE FEELINGS

Explain to the class that you are going to reread the story so students can focus on the characters' feelings when others acted kindly towards them. Make sufficient copies of the feeling bubbles (see example in Blackline Master 24.2) so that each student receives one bubble. Pause while rereading the story whenever a character's reactions are identified. Call on students to name or describe the feelings (for example, happy, positive, grateful). For each character, ask one student to write the feeling words inside the feeling bubble. After the story is completed, direct students to attach the bubbles just above the character's name on the Chain of Kindness board. As they post their bubbles, invite students to reconstruct the link, this time in terms of the feelings not the events. Suggest that students use the following format:

I'm ___their assigned character___. Because ___the previous character was feeling that character's feelings___, he/she was kind to me, which made me feel ___the feelings their character experienced___.

DEBRIEF CHAIN OF FEELINGS

Ask students to explain how the chain of positive feelings started (someone did an act of kindness for someone else). Point out to students that an act of kindness creates positive feelings and when people feel positive about themselves they are more likely to act positively towards others. Emphasize that even a very modest action, such as a hug, can turn out to make a big contribution because of all the people who "pass it on" by performing their own acts of kindness to others.

BLACKLINE MASTER 24.2   FEELING BUBBLES

BRAINSTORM POSSIBLE ACTIONS

Ask students if they would like to create their own chain of kindness in the classroom just as Brian did in his neighbourhood. If they agree, invite students to suggest ways that they might make students in the class feel good about themselves so they will want to "pass it on" to others in the class. Record all suggestions (for example, say something nice about the person, ask the person to play at recess, smile at others, say please and thank you with a smile, offer willingly to help if needed). Encourage students to keep their ideas simple. Title the list "Kind actions we might do."

Session Three

DEVELOP CRITERIA

Ask students to consider how they might decide which of the many kind acts on the list would be the best choice. Remind students that when making decisions it is helpful to have guidelines for good choices. Ask students to suggest factors for deciding whether something would be a suitable act of kindness. Alternatively, suggest possible actions that would be obviously "inappropriate," such as those mentioned below, and invite students to explain why these actions would be unsuitable:

- Offering candy to someone who does not like sweets (the action won't make the person happy or feel good).
- Giving someone a big hug in a way that shows you don't really mean it (the action is not sincere or honest).
- Agreeing to do everything the person wants for a year (the action is not easy to do; it is too difficult).

Record their explanations for rejecting these possibilities and other factors suggested by students as criteria for an act of kindness:

An act of kindness should...

- make someone else feel good;
- be honest, be something the person feels good about doing; and
- be simple to do; not be too difficult.

APPLY CRITERIA

Help students understand how to apply the criteria to possible acts of kindness by reviewing one or two incidents from Brian's chain of events. Create a chart such as the one suggested in Figure 24.1 and list a few actions from the Chain of Kindness display. Record the identified criteria along the top row. Ask students to indicate whether the identified acts of kindness meet each criterion. Place a "✓" or "✗" in the relevant column. Repeat the process with a few other possible acts of kindness that would not satisfy all the criteria.

ASSIGN RECIPIENTS

You will need to prepare beforehand the specific pairings of students who will give and receive each act of kindness so that an unbroken chain is produced. One method is simply to proceed down the class list, assigning students to carrying out their action on the next person on the class list. If you want to match particular students, be sure to pair each "recipient" with a person who has not already been designated as a "donor" (the final recipient in the chain must be the student who was the first donor). Make a copy of Acts of Kindness (Blackline Master 24.3) for each student. In preparation for distribution to students, record each donor's name in the top corner of Blackline Master 24.3 where it says "Name:" and record the name of the assigned recipient on the line "Planning an act of kindness for." Before distributing the sheets,

FIGURE 24.1   KIND ACTIONS WE MIGHT DO

POSSIBLE ACTIONS	MAKES SOMEONE ELSE HAPPY	IS SOMETHING THE PERSON FEELS GOOD ABOUT DOING	IS SIMPLE TO DO
help the teacher get ready for school	✓	✓	✓
hug a parent or grandparent	✓	✓	✓
give someone your age all of your toys	✓	✗	✗
give an adult all of your toys	✗	✗	✗

encourage students not to reveal whose name they have been assigned since it will be more effective if the acts of kindness are a surprise.

SHORTLIST POSSIBLE ACTIONS

When every student has a classmate for whom they are to plan an act of kindness, invite the class to refer to the previously developed list of "Kind actions we might do" and to think of other actions. Ask students to select three actions that would be suitable choices for their assigned person. Students are to draw or describe these actions in the boxes on the left-hand side of Blackline Master 24.3 and to place a "✓" or "✗" in the small box next to each identified criterion in the right-hand column. If a criterion is not met, students should explain why in the space below the small boxes.

PRESENT THE CRITICAL CHALLENGE

When everyone has identified three possible actions, introduce the critical task:

Choose and perform an act of kindness towards someone in the classroom so the person feels good enough to "pass it on."

Invite students to consider which of their three choices would make the best act of kindness for their assigned person. Ask students to indicate the action they intend to carry out and to explain the reasons for this choice on the bottom of Blackline Master 24.3. Collect the completed sheets to ensure that none of the selected actions are inappropriate. Explain to students that the chain of events will take place on the next day.

Session Four

IMPLEMENT THE CHAIN OF EVENTS

On the assigned day, return to students their copy of Blackline Master 24.3. You will need to decide whether to organize the class in a large circle and conduct the chain of kindness acts in a single public session, or to ask students to carry out

BLACKLINE MASTER 24.3   ACTS OF KINDNESS

Planning an act of kindness for _____	
POSSIBLE ACTIONS	**CRITERIA**
Choice #1 I could	☐ will make the person happy ☐ is something I feel good about doing ☐ is simple to do ☐ _____
Choice #2 I could	☐ will make the person happy ☐ is something I feel good about doing ☐ is simple to do ☐ _____
Choice #3 I could	☐ will make the person happy ☐ is something I feel good about doing ☐ is simple to do ☐ _____
I choose _____ because _____	

their actions covertly over the course of the day. If the latter option is chosen, ask students to bring their copy of Blackline Master 24.3 back to you very soon after they have carried out their action. This will enable you to monitor the chain in case some students do not realize that it is their turn to implement their kind act. Start the chain of events by quietly asking one student to carry out the planned action. The student receiving this kind act will then carry out the kind act that he or she has planned for someone else. The chain continues until all students have performed and received an act of kindness.

WEB THE CHAIN OF EVENTS

Duplicate several copies of Class Chain of Events (Blackline Master 24.4) and cut apart the individual strips so that every student has one strip upon which to record the name of the recipient and the kind act they performed for that person. Remove the slips of paper and feeling bubbles that students previously attached to the Chain of Kindness display when creating Brian's chain of events. Alter the number and configuration of pieces of coloured paper on the display so that there is one piece for each student in the class. Following the pattern used to recreate Brian's chain of events, invite stu-

BLACKLINE MASTER 24.4   CLASS CHAIN OF EVENTS

1		
2		
3		
4		
5		
6		
7		
8		
9		
10		
. . .		

dents in the order in which the kind acts were performed to attach their slips to the display, explaining their action using the following format:

Because _the student who was kind to them and the action performed to them_, I decided to _the kind act they performed on the next student in the chain_.

Session Five

CONNECT THE FEELINGS (OPTIONAL)

Revisit the Chain of Kindness board one final time so students can explore how they felt when others acted kindly towards them. Invite students to recall the kinds of positive feelings that characters in the story felt as a result of being treated kindly. Read to the class the feelings recorded on the characters' feeling bubbles. Now invite students to think of how they felt when their fellow students acted kindly towards them. Duplicate sufficient copies of the feeling bubbles found on Blackline Master 24.2 so that each student receives one bubble. Invite students to write the feeling words inside the bubble and to attach the bubble just above their name on the Chain of Kindness board. As they post their bubbles, students are to reconstruct the chain of feelings experienced. Suggest that students use the following format:

Because _the previous student_ was feeling _that student's feelings_, he/she was kind to me, which made me feel _the feelings the student experienced_.

CREATE NOTES OF APPRECIATION

Suggest to students that giving a note of appreciation is an act of kindness that makes people feel positive about themselves. Using Note of Appreciation (Blackline Master 24.5) to record their response, invite students to express their appreciation to the student who acted kindly towards them.

REFLECT ON INFLUENCE

Arrange for students to hand their notes of appreciation to the appropriate person. You may want students to read their notes aloud. Discuss how students feel when someone shows appreciation for their kindness. Also discuss students' feelings while performing their acts of kindness and seeing the recipient's pleasure. Invite students to comment on how the satisfaction of giving and of being acknowledged for acts of kindness may affect their future behaviour (for example, more acts of kindness, more consistent in thanking others, more signs of appreciation).

BLACKLINE MASTER 24.5   NOTE OF APPRECIATION

To _____

You are a very kind person because _____
_____
_____

It makes me feel _____
_____
_____

I am glad to pass it on by _____
_____
_____

Thank you from _____

DISCUSS "PASS IT ON"

Congratulate students on the difference they are making to their classroom community. Encourage them to continue to "pass it on." Remind students of the ripple effect that individuals can have on their class and community.

Evaluation

Assess each student's ability to identify and carry out an act of kindness using the rubric Assessing Acts of Kindness (Blackline Master 24.6). The sources of evidence and the two criteria for assessment are listed below:

- Use the responses to the checklist of criteria found on Acts of Kindness (Blackline Master 24.3) to assess each student's ability to judge possible actions in light of the identified criteria for an act of kindness.
- Use the choice and the accompanying explanation recorded on Acts of Kindness (Blackline Master 24.3) to assess student's ability to select a suitable action.
Reaching the "basic understanding" level on the rubric may be appropriate for many primary students.

Extension

CREATE AN "APPRECIATION" BOARD

Invite students to contribute to a class or school "appreciation" board. Include pictures that show students and adults being kind to each other. Attach notes of appreciation for actions such as the following:

- Thanks to the parents who made hot dogs for a fun day.
- Thanks to the custodian for keeping the school so clean and safe.
- Thanks to older buddies who helped in the class.

Invite other classes to contribute to the display.

CREATE A CLASS MAILBOX

Create a mailbox to collect student and teacher notes of appreciation for other members of the class. The mail might be delivered at the end of each day. Invite students to decide whether they prefer that the notes of appreciation be shared with the entire class or delivered to the person whose name is on the note. You may wish to model the procedure by placing a note in the mailbox each day. Monitor the notes of appreciation to ensure that no students are left out of the chain.

PASS IT ALONG AT HOME

Encourage students to extend the acts of kindness to people at home or in the neighbourhood. Invite students to look for evidence that people might be "passing it on" (for example, being nice to others, smiles more frequently, starts to say hello).

BLACKLINE MASTER 24.6	ASSESSING ACTS OF KINDNESS				
	SOPHISTICATED UNDERSTANDING	**EXTENDED UNDERSTANDING**	**BASIC UNDERSTANDING**	**PARTIAL RECOGNITION**	**PRE-RECOGNITION**
Assesses possible actions in light of criteria	Correctly assesses even less obvious actions in light of identified criteria.	Correctly assesses a range of possible actions in light of identified criteria.	Correctly assesses very obvious actions in light of identified criteria.	Understands what is asked, but does not always correctly assess even very obvious actions in light of identified criteria.	Does not understand what it means to assess possible actions in light of identified criteria.
Selects a reasonable kind action	Selects a reasonable choice and explains in own words why it meets each of the criteria for an act of kindness.	Selects a reasonable choice and explains in very simple terms why it meets the criteria for an act of kindness.	Selects a reasonable choice without any explanation why it meets the criteria for an act of kindness.	Selects an action that does not meet the criteria for an act of kindness.	Unable to select one choice as the best act of kindness.

Thinking of the intended student audience and the curriculum, critique this lesson. Be sure to identify its positive traits and shortcomings. Discuss what you could do to improve, adapt, or extend this lesson.

ENDNOTES

1 This lesson is taken from *I Can Make a Difference*, ed. by M. Abbott, R. Case, and J. Nicol. 2003. Vancouver, BC: The Critical Thinking Consortium.

2 Chapter 8 in this volume, "Teaching the Tools to Think Critically," explains each of these tools.

REFERENCES

Rice, D.L. 1999. *Because Brian Hugged his Mother*. Illus. K.D. Thompson. Nevada City, CA: Dawn Publications.

25

Sample Upper Elementary Lesson
Arctic Survival

The Critical Thinking Consortium

This chapter provides a detailed lesson plan[1] that illustrates how elementary students can be engaged and systematically supported in thinking critically about the conditions in the Arctic. The main focus of the lesson is a critical challenge where students must buy supplies for a four-day trip to the Arctic during the winter season.

The lesson is intended to help students learn about the necessities for survival as they decide what supplies are needed to outfit a four-day trip to the Arctic. Students begin by reviewing arctic winter conditions and the differences between needs and wants. They are given a budget of $3,000 to purchase the needed supplies from a catalogue or, if possible, from a sample "general store" set up in the classroom or from an online catalogue of outdoor equipment. Students categorize the supplies into needs and wants as they decide what supplies are necessary and which luxuries can be afforded within the limited budget. Finally, students are asked to provide specific, factually supported reasons for their choices.

In the course of working through this task it is hoped that students will better appreciate the resourcefulness of the Inuit as they learn that survival in arctic conditions requires careful selection of the important necessities.

The premise of The Critical Thinking Consortium approach is that student success in any critical thinking task depends on their possession of the relevant "tools."[2] Below are the key tools that students are taught in this lesson:

Background knowledge
- knowledge of arctic landscape and climate
- knowledge of the properties of various supplies

Criteria for judgment
- criteria for effective purchases (for example, meets all needs to survive in the Arctic, stays within budget, provides a pleasurable trip)
- criteria for a good explanation (for example, specific, supported with facts, more than one reason)

Critical thinking vocabulary
- needs (necessities) and wants (luxuries)

Thinking strategies
- data chart

Preplanning

ASSEMBLE SAMPLE SUPPLIES (OPTIONAL)

In this challenge, students select from a list of approximately fifty items—without exceeding the $3,000 limit—the supplies they will take on a four-day trip to the Arctic. An illustrated list and order form is provided in Arctic Supplies (Blackline Master 25.1). You may prefer to direct students to use an actual catalogue from an outdoor equipment store such as Mountain Equipment Co-op (www.mec.ca). It is even more engaging if students see the actual items. Consequently, you may want to create a "general store" in a corner of the classroom (or in a spare classroom, the gym, or the library). Assemble as many of the items as possible listed in Blackline Master 25.1. Substitute pictures for items that cannot be located. Mark the price on each item and arrange the goods in departments matching the categories of basic needs (for example, food, clothing, shelter, tools, transportation).

Session One

DISCUSS ARCTIC ENVIRONMENT

Invite students to imagine that they are in the Arctic during the winter. Ask them to identify the climatic and landscape conditions they would expect. If helpful, arrange to have several pictures to show to the class. Record students' ideas on the board. If needed, prompt students with questions such as the following:
- Would it be sunny? rainy? windy?
- Would the ground be slippery? covered in snow? wet or dry?
- Would the surface be flat or hilly? smooth or rough?

CLOTHING

Winter Boots
Waterproof winter boots with a heavy-duty rubber sole for great traction and support.
$100.00/pr

PRICE   QUANTITY   TOTAL

$100.00   _____   _____

ARE THEY NEEDED?   ☐ NO   ☐ YES

REASON FOR DECISION:

Winter Boots
Mid-calf length, lined, waterproof winter boots with rubber toes and soles.
$120.00/pr

PRICE   QUANTITY   TOTAL

$120.00   _____   _____

ARE THEY NEEDED?   ☐ NO   ☐ YES

REASON FOR DECISION:

Winter Socks
Pair of quick-drying socks for cold weather.
$9.00/pr

PRICE   QUANTITY   TOTAL

$9.00   _____   _____

ARE THEY NEEDED?   ☐ NO   ☐ YES

REASON FOR DECISION:

Winter Underwear
Pair of thermal underwear that helps trap body heat and keep it close to the body.
$45.00/pr

PRICE   QUANTITY   TOTAL

$45.00   _____   _____

ARE THEY NEEDED?   ☐ NO   ☐ YES

REASON FOR DECISION:

Winter Pants
Waterproof winter pants.
$70.00/pr

PRICE   QUANTITY   TOTAL

$70.00   _____   _____

ARE THEY NEEDED?   ☐ NO   ☐ YES

REASON FOR DECISION:

Winter Pants
Waterproof snow pants with suspenders.
$180.00/pr

PRICE   QUANTITY   TOTAL

$180.00   _____   _____

ARE THEY NEEDED?   ☐ NO   ☐ YES

REASON FOR DECISION:

Waterproof Suit
Waterproof hooded winter jacket with pockets that zip up and waterproof snow pants.
$310.00/ea

PRICE   QUANTITY   TOTAL

$310.00   _____   _____

IS IT NEEDED?   ☐ NO   ☐ YES

REASON FOR DECISION:

Waterproof Jacket

Waterproof winter jacket with hood.
$130.00/ea

PRICE   QUANTITY   TOTAL

$130.00   _____   _____

IS IT NEEDED?   ☐ NO   ☐ YES

REASON FOR DECISION:

Waterproof Jacket
Hooded waterproof winter jacket with elastic around the bottom.
$160.00/ea

PRICE   QUANTITY   TOTAL

$160.00   _____   _____

IS IT NEEDED?   ☐ NO   ☐ YES

REASON FOR DECISION:

Winter Jacket
Fake-fur-lined winter jacket with hood.
$200.00/ea

PRICE   QUANTITY   TOTAL

$200.00   _____   _____

IS IT NEEDED?   ☐ NO   ☐ YES

REASON FOR DECISION:

Winter Vest
Waterproof winter vest.
$100.00/ea

PRICE   QUANTITY   TOTAL

$100.00   _____   _____

IS IT NEEDED?   ☐ NO   ☐ YES

REASON FOR DECISION:

continued on next page

CLOTHING	FOOD

CLOTHING

Sweater
Wool turtleneck sweater.
$80.00/ea

PRICE   QUANTITY   TOTAL

$80.00   _____   _____

IS IT NEEDED?   ☐ NO   ☐ YES

REASON FOR DECISION:

Gloves
Warm pair
of gloves.
$40.00/pr

PRICE   QUANTITY   TOTAL

$40.00   _____   _____

ARE THEY NEEDED?   ☐ NO   ☐ YES

REASON FOR DECISION:

Sweatshirt
Thick hooded sweatshirt.
$60.00/ea

PRICE   QUANTITY   TOTAL

$60.00   _____   _____

IS IT NEEDED?   ☐ NO   ☐ YES

REASON FOR DECISION:

Winter Hat
$12.00/ea

PRICE   QUANTITY   TOTAL

$12.00   _____   _____

IS IT NEEDED?   ☐ NO   ☐ YES

REASON FOR DECISION:

Mittens
Warm pair
of mittens.
$30.00/pr

PRICE   QUANTITY   TOTAL

$30.00   _____   _____

ARE THEY NEEDED?   ☐ NO   ☐ YES

REASON FOR DECISION:

Winter Hat
Waterproof
baseball hat.
$15.00/ea

PRICE   QUANTITY   TOTAL

$15.00   _____   _____

IS IT NEEDED?   ☐ NO   ☐ YES

REASON FOR DECISION:

FOOD

Camp Food
One-day supply of nutritious
food for breakfast, lunch,
dinner and two snacks
(suitable for camping).
$30.00/ea

PRICE   QUANTITY   TOTAL

$30.00   _____   _____

IS IT NEEDED?   ☐ NO   ☐ YES

REASON FOR DECISION:

Water Filter
$90.00/ea

PRICE   QUANTITY   TOTAL

$90.00   _____   _____

IS IT NEEDED?   ☐ NO   ☐ YES

REASON FOR DECISION:

Stove
Portable cooking stove (fuel
included).
$80.00/ea

PRICE   QUANTITY   TOTAL

$80.00   _____   _____

IS IT NEEDED?   ☐ NO   ☐ YES

REASON FOR DECISION:

Cookware
Five-piece non-
stick cooking set.
$50.00/ea

PRICE   QUANTITY   TOTAL

$50.00   _____   _____

IS IT NEEDED?   ☐ NO   ☐ YES

REASON FOR DECISION:

Garbage Bags
Package of 10.
$3.00/ea

PRICE   QUANTITY   TOTAL

$3.00   _____   _____

ARE THEY NEEDED?   ☐ NO   ☐ YES

REASON FOR DECISION:

| SHELTER | | | TOOLS |

SHELTER

Tent
Waterproof free-standing tent that is easy to set up.
$250.00/ea

PRICE   QUANTITY   TOTAL

$250.00   _____   _____

IS IT NEEDED?   ❑ NO   ❑ YES

REASON FOR DECISION:

Heated Room
Shared bedroom in a cabin with electricity and indoor plumbing (includes bed sheets).
$60.00/night

PRICE   NIGHTS   TOTAL

$60.00   _____   _____

IS IT NEEDED?   ❑ NO   ❑ YES

REASON FOR DECISION:

Sleeping Bag
Waterproof sleeping bag that is good for temperatures as low as -20 C.
$200.00/ea

PRICE   QUANTITY   TOTAL

$200.00   _____   _____

IS IT NEEDED?   ❑ NO   ❑ YES

REASON FOR DECISION:

Sleeping Bag
Waterproof mummy sleeping bag that is good for temperatures as low as -50 C.
$1000.00/ea

PRICE   QUANTITY   TOTAL

$1000.00   _____   _____

IS IT NEEDED?   ❑ NO   ❑ YES

REASON FOR DECISION:

Blanket
Heavy-duty blanket.
$30.00/ea

PRICE   QUANTITY   TOTAL

$30.00   _____   _____

IS IT NEEDED?   ❑ NO   ❑ YES

REASON FOR DECISION:

Pillow
Waterproof lightweight camping pillow.
$20.00/ea

PRICE   QUANTITY   TOTAL

$20.00   _____   _____

IS IT NEEDED?   ❑ NO   ❑ YES

REASON FOR DECISION:

Sleeping Pad
Waterproof, lightweight.
$60.00/ea

PRICE   QUANTITY   TOTAL

$60.00   _____   _____

IS IT NEEDED?   ❑ NO   ❑ YES

REASON FOR DECISION:

TRANSPORTATION

Backpack
Waterproof, internal-framed backpack for carrying heavy loads.
$300.00/ea

PRICE   QUANTITY   TOTAL

$300.00   _____   _____

IS IT NEEDED?   ❑ NO   ❑ YES

REASON FOR DECISION:

Backpack
Waterproof backpack with several different-sized compartments.
$100.00/ea

PRICE   QUANTITY   TOTAL

$100.00   _____   _____

IS IT NEEDED?   ❑ NO   ❑ YES

REASON FOR DECISION:

TOOLS

Flashlight
Heavy duty flashlight (batteries not included).
$30.00/ea

PRICE   QUANTITY   TOTAL

$30.00   _____   _____

IS IT NEEDED?   ❑ NO   ❑ YES

REASON FOR DECISION:

Lantern
Lightweight butane lantern (fuel included).
$50.00/ea

PRICE   QUANTITY   TOTAL

$50.00   _____   _____

IS IT NEEDED?   ❑ NO   ❑ YES

REASON FOR DECISION:

Bear Repellent
Guaranteed to chase away all kinds of bears.
$8.00/ea

PRICE   QUANTITY   TOTAL

$8.00   _____   _____

IS IT NEEDED?   ❑ NO   ❑ YES

REASON FOR DECISION:

continued on next page

TOOLS

Knife
Swiss Army knife with 20 different attachments.
$80.00/ea

PRICE   QUANTITY   TOTAL

$80.00   _____   _____

IS IT NEEDED?   ☐ NO   ☐ YES

REASON FOR DECISION:

First Aid Kit
$20.00/ea

PRICE   QUANTITY   TOTAL

$20.00   _____   _____

IS IT NEEDED?   ☐ NO   ☐ YES

REASON FOR DECISION:

Toothpaste and Toothbrush
Small size; ideal for tavel.
$4.00/set

PRICE   QUANTITY   TOTAL

$4.00   _____   _____

IS IT NEEDED?   ☐ NO   ☐ YES

REASON FOR DECISION:

Batteries
Package of 4 "AA" batteries.
$4.00/ea

PRICE   QUANTITY   TOTAL

$4.00   _____   _____

IS IT NEEDED?   ☐ NO   ☐ YES

REASON FOR DECISION:

Camera
Disposable camera and film (batteries not included).
$15.00/ea

PRICE   QUANTITY   TOTAL

$15.00   _____   _____

IS IT NEEDED?   ☐ NO   ☐ YES

REASON FOR DECISION:

Sunglasses
Glare reduction.
$30.00/pr

PRICE   QUANTITY   TOTAL

$30.00   _____   _____

IS IT NEEDED?   ☐ NO   ☐ YES

REASON FOR DECISION:

Hairbrush
$4.00/ea

PRICE   QUANTITY   TOTAL

$4.00   _____   _____

IS IT NEEDED?   ☐ NO   ☐ YES

REASON FOR DECISION:

Binoculars
High-powered.
$300.00/pr

PRICE   QUANTITY   TOTAL

$300.00   _____   _____

ARE THEY NEEDED?   ☐ NO   ☐ YES

REASON FOR DECISION:

Two-Way Radio
Water resistant (batteries not included).
$100.00/ea

PRICE   QUANTITY   TOTAL

$100.00   _____   _____

IS IT NEEDED?   ☐ NO   ☐ YES

REASON FOR DECISION:

Heavy-duty rope
50' coil.
$50.00/ea

PRICE   QUANTITY   TOTAL

$50.00   _____   _____

IS IT NEEDED?   ☐ NO   ☐ YES

REASON FOR DECISION:

Watch
Waterproof with built-in compass.
$40.00/ea

PRICE   QUANTITY   TOTAL

$40.00   _____   _____

IS IT NEEDED?   ☐ NO   ☐ YES

REASON FOR DECISION:

TOTAL OF ALL ITEMS

$ _____

REVIEW NEED VS. WANT

Ask students what things they might "need" if they are to cope with these arctic conditions. In the course of this discussion remind students about the difference between "needing" and "wanting" something (for example, "need" means you cannot function without; "want" means you can get by without it, but you would like to have it). Suggest synonyms for the terms: necessities and luxuries. Ask students to offer pairs of related needs and wants as illustrated by the following examples:

- "I would 'need' clothing to keep me warm. I might 'want' Calvin Klein jeans and a Club Monaco sweatshirt."
- "I would 'need' shelter to protect me from the cold. I might 'want' to stay in a fancy hotel."

INTRODUCE THE CRITICAL CHALLENGE

When students understand the difference between needing and wanting something, present the critical task:

Buy supplies for a four-day trip to the Arctic during the winter season.

Explain to students that everything they bring on the trip must be purchased (students cannot bring anything of their own from home). Students will have a maximum budget of $3,000 to buy all the supplies they will need. Because of the limited funds, encourage students, first, to carefully choose the supplies they need; and second, to choose the supplies they might want to make the trip as pleasable as possible.

DECIDE ON NEEDED SUPPLIES

Distribute copies of Arctic Supplies (Blackline Master 25.1), from which all supplies must be bought. Alternatively, direct students to the online catalogue of an outdoor equipment store. Suggest that students use a pencil to record their purchases on the charts so they can make changes. Explain the procedure that students should follow. You may want to summarize the following steps on the board or walk the class though one step at a time, waiting for everyone to complete one step before proceeding to the next:

- **Identify needs.** Go through the list (and, if available, the actual items) looking only for those things students absolutely need, checking the "Yes" box (under the "Is it needed?" column).
- **Record individual cost of needs.** Determine how many of each of the needed items they will require and record the cost of these necessities in the "Cost" column. Remind students they will be gone for four full days and nights.
- **Calculate total spent on needs.** On a separate piece of

paper, direct students to copy down the amount spent thus far on necessities. Encourage students to ignore the cents and round off each cost to the nearest dollar. Determine how much is left to spend (or how much they have overspent).

- **Share decisions about needs.** When students have completed their initial selection of needs, invite three students to list their choices about clothing needs. If there are any discrepancies in their choices, ask them to explain the reasons for their choices. Proceed with other needs if this seems warranted. If students need considerable support in thinking through the implications of the choices about needs, organize students into groups of three or four and ask them to share their decisions for each category of basic needs.

Session Two

DECIDE ON REMAINING SUPPLIES

Explain the procedure that students should follow for the next step:

- **Add/delete supplies.** Go over the list again, adding (or deleting) necessities (for example, three pairs of underwear instead of one, or vice versa) and, if appropriate, adding luxuries that will make their trip more pleasurable. Students should keep track of the additional/reduced cost of purchases to make sure they do not exceed the $3,000 limit.
- **Calculate exact total cost.** When students have made their purchases, on a separate sheet of paper they should copy the exact amount (dollars and cents) of all purchases and calculate the total. Depending on the sum they may want to make final adjustments to their order.

PROVIDE RATIONALE FOR THEIR CHOICES

When students have completed their deliberations, ask them (possibly as a homework assignment) to provide written explanations for all of their purchases. Draw their attention to the space for recording their decision in each box on Blackline Master 25.1. Explain that they are to write their reasons for buying or not buying each item. In cases where students have a choice among similar items (for example, two different types of boots) they should indicate why they choose the particular option that they did. For each decision, ask students to provide more than one reason that includes details and evidence (for example, students should say more than "I needed it" or "I didn't need it," but explain in light of the conditions they will face in the Arctic how each item would be useful or not). As a class, model the rationale that students might offer in explaining their choice of which boots to purchase. Possible reasons include the following:

- Heavy soles are less slippery on ice.
- Thicker soles may be warmer than thin rubber soles.
- Taller boots may keep deep snow out.
- Waterproof boots are necessary in the snow and ice.

Encourage students to refer to what they have already learned about life in the Arctic to support their answers.

DEBRIEF THE DECISIONS

When students have completed their rationales, discuss issues that arose in deciding what to purchase for the trip and why:

- What questions do students have about what they would "need" to buy?
- Was there anything they "wanted" to buy, but did not have enough money?
- What was their best purchase (that is, the most interesting or resourceful choice)?
- What have they learned from this activity about the Inuit and their ability to live in the difficult arctic conditions?

You may want to raise specific issues that students may miss (for example, why sunglasses may not be needed because of the limited winter light or why bear repellent may be necessary since polar bears don't generally hibernate).

Evaluation

Assess students' selection and justification of their list of supplies recorded on Arctic Supplies (Blackline Master 25.1) using the rubric found in Assessing the Purchases (Blackline Master 25.2). According to this rubric, the assignment is worth fifteen marks and is assessed on three criteria:

- identification of needs and wants;
- reasonable selection of supplies; and
- sound reasons for each decision.

Extension

Compare modern survival supplies with what the Inuit traditionally used for their survival. For each of the basic needs, decide how they differ and how they are similar.

BLACKLINE MASTER 25.2   ASSESSING THE PURCHASES

	SOPHISTICATED	VERY GOOD	COMPETENT	SATISFACTORY	IN PROGRESS
Identification of needs and wants	The identification of needs and wants for all items seems very reasonable.	The identification of needs and wants seems reasonable in almost all cases.	The identification of needs and wants seems reasonable in most cases.	The identification of needs and wants seems reasonable in many cases, but major misidentifications are made.	Many items are obviously incorrectly identified as needs or wants.
Selection of supplies	The selected supplies will clearly meet all the necessities of arctic survival.	The selected supplies are generally adequate to meet the necessities of arctic survival.	The selected supplies will meet almost all the necessities of arctic survival, with only one or two major gaps.	The selection of supplies will probably meet many of the necessities of arctic survival, but there are several major gaps.	The selection of supplies is obviously inadequate to meet many of the necessities of arctic survival.
Reasons for choices	Sound reasons supported with relevant facts are provided for every item.	Sound reasons supported with relevant facts are provided for almost all items.	Reasons are provided for most items, with only a few questionable or unsupported reasons.	Reasons are provided for many items, but a number of reasons are questionable or without factual support.	Very few reasons are provided and supported with facts.

Thinking of the intended student audience and the curriculum, critique this lesson. Be sure to identify its positive traits and shortcomings. Discuss what you could do to improve, adapt, or extend this lesson.

ENDNOTES

1   This lesson is taken from *The resourcefulness of the Inuit*, edited by J. Nichol and R. Case. 2003. Vancouver, BC: The Critical Thinking Consortium.

2   Chapter 8 in this volume, "Teaching the Tools to Think Critically," explains each of these tools.

26 Bringing the Outside In
Using Community Resources in Elementary Social Studies

Penney Clark

Garnet McDiarmid (1970) tells the story of a teacher who wrote that he did not have science in his elementary school because the school had neither textbooks nor laboratory equipment. McDiarmid points out that the school was located in an area of uranium mines, moraines and other post-glacial deposits, running water, ponds, and abundant flora and fauna—all of which could have been exploited as fascinating sources for scientific investigation.

A similar point might be made about the availability of outside resources for social studies. Every school has many historic and geographically interesting sites to explore nearby or further afield. Every teacher has access to local people who are willing to be interviewed or come to school to share their expertise. Many organizations will send print and video materials free-of-charge. Students in urban areas can step outside their school to investigate traffic patterns, community development, museums, and recreational facilities. Students in rural areas can visit metropolitan areas, regional industries, local historic sites, and countless other places in the surrounding area. The value and accessibility of the community as a learning resource in social studies is richly illustrated by the examples described in "Globe-trotting Teddies." Unfortunately, many of us overlook the educational potential of what is outside our classroom walls.

Learning to making effective educational use of the community requires that these encounters become more than "isolated experiences," unrelated to curriculum learning outcomes. As one writer warns, field trips may involve little more than "wandering in a long line (rather like a snake that has just shed its skin and is doubtful about its boundaries) through museum corridors with half-minute halts to gape at an exhibit or collect stragglers"(quoted in Oliver 1970, 22). The lost educational potential of field experiences is reflected in an episode of the television show *The Wonder Years* in which the junior high school protagonist Kevin Arnold and his classmates visit a museum. In the episode, teacher and students have very different agendas. The teacher, of course, views the trip as an opportunity to expose students to the richness of the past. For Kevin and his friends, the exhibits become a mere backdrop to more important personal concerns—who likes whom, who is going to which party on the weekend, and so on.[1]

If students lack clear curricular purposes and educational context in which to place it, embarking on a community experience can become a mere diversion from classroom routine—a welcome relief perhaps, but ultimately not an experience that furthers the goals of social studies. In this chapter, I explore the value of and strategies for effectively bringing the outside into the curriculum in the context of three types of community resources: field experiences, local experts, and materials developed by non-educational agencies.

Field Experiences

Involving students directly in the community through field experiences can foster rich understandings not available from textbook study. For example, art galleries and museums can enliven the study of ancient civilizations or pioneer times. Field experiences, particularly those involving overnight stays, are ideal for outdoor studies and environmental investigations.

During a unit on pioneer life, a combined grade 3/4 class in Alberta visited a typical pioneer home, a wealthier pioneer home, a historical costume collection, and the first schoolhouse built in their school district more than one hundred years earlier. In the typical pioneer home, the students chopped wood, carded wool, and made butter, ice cream, scones, and candles. In the home of the wealthier family, they did needlework, baked cookies, and acted as guests in the drawing room. When viewing the historical costume collection, students imagined what it would be like to wear corsets and stiff collars. During the morning spent in the schoolhouse, they enacted a typical 1881 school day with a teacher "in role." Through these simulated experiences, students gained a feel-

GLOBE-TROTTING TEDDIES

Wendy Newport and Jenny Murdie, two primary teachers at Irwin Park Elementary School in West Vancouver, found an interesting way to help their grade 2 students learn about the wider world. Early in the year, each student brings a teddy bear to school. Each teddy is given an identification card, travel journal, instructions, and a tote bag. The first entry in the journal describes the student's/owner's interests and geographical location. Each teddy is then given to someone who will be travelling to other parts of the province, country, or world. This individual might be a family member, friend, parent's work colleague, or acquaintance. The traveller is asked to pass the teddy on to someone else, but only after that person agrees to one condition: an entry must be made in the travel journal and a postcard mailed to the student.

Each year the class receives several hundred postcards, as the teddies are passed from one person to another. One year, postcards arrived from more than fifty countries. When a postcard arrives, its content are read to the class and discussed, and its origin is located on a world map. Whoever has the teddy on April 30 is asked to mail it back to the school. By the end of the school year, at least 80 per cent of the teddies, with their travel journals and often souvenirs, make their way back to their owners. What a wonderful way for young children to begin to learn about the world! They read first-person accounts of places and events, living vicariously through their teddies.

The "Flat Stanley" project is a variation on this strategy.

More than one thousand schools around the world have sent paper dolls to classes in other countries. Flat Stanley's daily experiences are recorded in a journal, which is sent along when he is returned by mail. The idea originated with a book called *Flat Stanley* by Jeff Brown. The story is about a boy who is squashed flat by a bulletin board. He makes the best of his situation by embarking on adventures such as mailing himself to a friend in California. Flat Stanley has posed with US President George W. Bush, and spent a day at the White House after receiving security clearance. He has also been on an episode of *The West Wing*.

In a similar vein, Karlo Cabrera's grade 4 class at Fenside Public School in North Toronto mailed "Flat Mark" to Paul Martin shortly after he became prime minister. Martin welcomed the idea and invited Flat Mark to the swearing-in ceremony at Rideau Hall. Martin told the students that "Flat Mark got into some trouble, and there are stories I don't think I should tell you, but he did a terrific job.... He was extremely helpful when the transition team was devising policy." Flat Mark was returned to the students accompanied by a binder of photographs and captions and a journal describing his experiences. In exchange, students sent three books describing their "hopes and dreams and wishes for Canada," including wishes that there would be no more SARS, and that people would be kinder to animals, stop robbing banks, and cease waging war (Taber 2003; Galloway 2004).

ing for life during pioneer times in their community. This is evident from three students' unedited journals following the field experience in the schoolhouse (McKay 1990, 153–154):

> **Penney:** Today at the 1881 School I learned how things were back in the 18S mostly. Such as reading, games, aned a spelleing B. the teacher called us lassies and ladies. I also learned that there wre severeal additions to the school because the amount of children was growing alot the games were called Anti-I-over, marbles jacks, count the rabbits and fox and geese. I also learned that the old school was once a House and the people that lived in it loved walpaper and I learned that the school house was down by saskatchewan river and it flooded so they tied it down by a hool on the back of it so it wouldn't float away. I also learned that the first legestlatetive building was in the gym of Macy avenue school.

> **Adam:** I lrnd that 1881 school is srikt with the kids. The kids play anty anty I over and the boys playd kech and rabits

> **Timothy:** it was scarry when adam was talking to Jason and the teacher turned around and smacked the stick on the desk and said put your hands on the desk and I thought she was going to smack adams nuckles but she didn't. then she turned to me and said stand up and put your hands on your desk and then I thought she was going to smack me on the bum but she didn't.

> I also was intereted and thought that was neet was the little kinds of porjectors, one you would put a candel in it and that would be the light and you would put a little sort of film and it would show up on the wall.

Timothy's relief that both he and Adam were spared the teacher's wrath is palpable. Because they actually were pioneer children for a time, all three students gained a more powerful understanding than they might have attained through reading about or viewing such a scene. The students also acquired historical information on topics such as children's games of the time, the first legislative building in the province, audiovisual techniques used by nineteenth-century teachers, and disciplinary methods. This information enabled students to build their impressions of what life was like during the period—impressions that would expand as they engaged in follow-up activities upon their return from the trip.

When conducted in the context of an ongoing unit or theme, a field trip becomes much more than a pleasant break from daily routines. It can provide accurate information and direct experience that enrich social studies topics, such as:

- roles of community members
- community services
- community rules and laws
- cultural makeup of the community
- local government
- transportation networks
- industry and commerce
- architecture
- zoning
- recreation

Field experiences must be carefully planned. Activities that take place prior to and following the field experience may be of equal importance to those activities that take place during it. Prior activities set the context for the experience and help students participate with inquiring attitudes. Follow-up activities allow students to clarify impressions, share ideas, and apply what they have learned. The highlighted text contains a checklist of logistical and educational factors to consider when organizing a field trip. I will elaborate on three sets of considerations:

- choosing a field experience;
- deciding on a site;
- developing preparatory, on-site, and follow-up activities.

CHOOSING TO GO ON A FIELD TRIP

Two factors should govern the decision to include a field experience in a social studies program: feasibility and educational

FIELD TRIP CHECKLIST

Early preparation
☐ Review school and district policies regarding field trips.
☐ Obtain information about the field trip, including talking to other teachers who have organized similar outings.
☐ Clarify educational objectives. Make them as concrete as possible.
☐ Obtain permissions from principal and on-site authorities.
☐ Book trip and arrange transportation.
☐ Make students aware of objectives and solicit student input.
☐ Visit site. Could take along a student committee.
☐ Arrange for helpers.
☐ Inform parents of the purpose of the trip, departure and arrival times, eating arrangements, costs, supervision arrangements, and any special clothing or equipment requirements.
☐ Obtain permission from parents or guardians.

Just prior to trip
☐ Provide checklist for students:
  ♦ money
  ♦ equipment
  ♦ clothing
  ♦ food
☐ Collect money, if required.
☐ Prepare students logistically:
  ♦ discuss safety issues
  ♦ could role-play expected behaviour
  ♦ review rules of conduct
  ♦ establish work groups and buddy system

☐ Brief adult helpers:
  ♦ discuss purposes of trip
  ♦ discuss duties
  ♦ discuss safety issues
☐ Prepare students educationally:
  ♦ review objectives
  ♦ share students' prior knowledge about the place
  ♦ assign individual and group tasks

On the trip
☐ Use the travel time to the site as part of the experience (for example, have students take note of types of buildings, industries, and transportation observed en route).
☐ Once on site, point out boundaries and key spots (for example, washrooms, meeting area, lost and found space).
☐ Elicit student questions and discussion.
☐ Remind students about gathering and recording data:
  ♦ go over charts to be filled in or questions to be answered
  ♦ assign one or more students to take photographs as a record of the trip
  ♦ create field sketches
  ♦ interview people on-site
☐ Plan for return trip (for example, take a different route back to the school to capitalize on the commuting and what can be observed while travelling).

Follow-up
☐ Organize, synthesize, and present collected data.
☐ Formally thank hosts and helpers.
☐ Evaluate trip.

efficacy. Feasibility refers to the reasonableness of undertaking the proposed activity given the typical constraints—transportation logistics, insufficient adult supervisors, expensive admission fees, safety considerations, and parental resistance due to lack of understanding of the connection between the experience and curriculum objectives. Many of these difficulties can be overcome with careful planning.

A second consideration is educational efficacy—whether the benefits outweigh the risks and drawbacks. Will the gain in learning justify the valuable class time and effort involved? Could the same learning outcomes be attained as richly and efficiently by staying in the classroom? A field experience should be chosen only if important benefits are realized that could not be achieved in the classroom. Clear communication is helpful in assuring parents, students, and school (and school board) administration that a field experience is the best way to meet specific curriculum goals.

CHOOSING THE SITE

The key criterion in choosing a field-trip site is that it advances curricular objectives by extending and enriching areas of investigation that are being (or will be) pursued in the classroom. Field experiences should be seen as one more data source to be accessed in a unit, albeit a more intriguing one.

We need not limit our choices of field site to destination settings such as museums, local historical sites, or other typical attractions. A field experience might be as simple as a walk through the neighbourhood to record the range of home types, or a trip to the shopping mall to observe product marketing, if these will help attain curriculum objectives. One of the most successful field experiences I am aware of took place at a construction site of new government offices, which was around the corner from the school. Several grade 2 students had observed the beginning of construction on the way to school one morning and reported this event to the class. The teacher, eager to capitalize on this serendipitous lesson on community change, took students to the site almost every day during construction. Students observed construction plans, materials, and methods, and interviewed construction workers. After the building opened, and government workers had moved in, students interviewed them to find out how well their new offices met their needs. What made this experience so successful was the uniting of keen student interest with the achievement of social studies objectives. (See Schuler [2002] for a delightful account of her grade 2 class's rewarding exploration of their community.)

In considering alternatives, a site should not be rejected out-of-hand merely because most students may have been there before. I remember my surprise when I learned that a little boy in my grade 4 class in a suburb of Vancouver had never visited Stanley Park. In the nine years of his life, his family had never climbed into a car or onto a bus and travelled there to spend the day at the zoo or aquarium, or simply exploring the seaside. We cannot assume that all students will have had these seemingly common experiences. As well, a family excursion can and should be quite a different experience than a structured field trip. During a field experience, students observe with particular purposes in mind, which guide their information gathering. Also, field trips offer opportunities for in-depth activities. For instance, it is always enjoyable to visit an aquarium, but it is a much richer experience when students are invited behind the scenes to observe feeding routines or attendants caring for a sick animal.

Table 26.1, "Range of Field Sites," outlines various possibilities available in many communities, and suggests questions or tasks to focus these experiences. There has been no attempt to assign sites according to grade level. Many sites visited in the primary years for one purpose may well be revisited in later grades for other purposes.

PREPARATORY ACTIVITIES WITH STUDENTS

Prior activities set the context for the experience, and help students participate with an inquiring attitude. First and foremost, students need to be aware of field-trip objectives. For instance, the reason for a trip to a local branch of the public library might be to discover the special services offered to particular community groups (for example, children, seniors, visually impaired) and how these services are delivered. A second objective might be to explore how these services or their delivery might better meet people's needs. Such a trip could be part of a larger unit on community services. Do not assume that students will automatically make the connections between their experiences on the trip and other learning activities. The objectives to be addressed should be discussed explicitly.

Provide students with site-related pamphlets, posters, websites, kits of sample items, or video programs that preview the field experience. Students can use these materials to generate questions to guide their observations at the site. The teacher can also give key questions to the students.

Prior to the trip, a permission form providing basic facts about the trip, such as the one shown in Figure 26.1, should be sent home. Considerable preparation is required if interviews or surveys are to be conducted at the site. The highlighted text "Advice on Conducting Interviews" offers suggestions for carrying out interviews and surveys.

TABLE 26.1   RANGE OF FIELD SITES

FIELD SITES	FOCUS QUESTIONS OR TASKS
School • physical layout • roles of various staff members	• What types of rooms are in our school (for example, classrooms, offices, gym)? How is each one used? • What types of occupations are there in our school? What tasks do people do? How are these tasks important? • How could the physical layout be altered to better meet the needs of the people who use the school?
Local neighbourhood • modes of transportation • safety measures (for example, crosswalks, sidewalks, signs, fire hydrants)	• How do people get to work and to school? What do people in the neighbourhood think of the transportation services? How could they be improved to better meet people's needs? • What safety features are in our neighbourhood? What is the function of each? Are other safety features needed? How could we go about getting them?
Public services • fire station • police station • public library • public health unit	• What places in our community provide services? Which services does the government provide? Which services are special to our community and which are provided in most communities? • Are other services needed in our community? How could we go about getting them?
Retail businesses • grocery store • bakery • shopping mall	• Which places sell goods? Are there enough goods and services available in our community? Do all communities need goods and services from other communities?
Manufacturing or commercial sites • assembly line • newspaper plant • warehouse • advertising agency	• What is the product(s) here? Where does the facility fit in terms of the product's production, distribution, marketing, or sale? What happens at this site? What happened to the product before it arrived at this site? What happens next? • Is it safe working here? Why or why not?
Community celebrations • multicultural festivals • Remembrance Day ceremonies • heritage days	• What things do people in our community choose to celebrate? • What is the history of this event? • Why are these celebrations important to people in this community?
Historical sites • restored homes, forts, and villages • graveyards and monuments • museums (local and provincial)	• What can we learn about the past at this site? Is it important to maintain sites like this one? Why or why not? • What might life have been like when people lived and worked here?
Resource development sites • mines • lumber mills • farms • refineries	• What resource is being developed? Give a step-by-step description of the process used to develop this resource. • What are the environmental effects of development of this resource? What environmental protection measures are used here? Are these measures sufficient? • Where does the product(s) go? How are transportation systems used to transport the product from this site?

TABLE 26.1 RANGE OF FIELD SITES (CONT.)

FIELD SITES	FOCUS QUESTIONS OR TASKS
Environmental preservation sites • fish hatchery • water-treatment plant • landfill facility	• What happens at this facility? • How does it contribute to environmental preservation? • Does this site create any pollution?
Government operations • all-candidates meeting • provincial legislature in session • city council in session • ratepayer meeting on a local issue • mock trial in a courtroom	• All-candidates meeting: Choose two election issues. What is each candidate's stance on these issues? Which issues seem to be of most concern to the audience? Who are the strongest candidates? Why? • Simulated city council meeting: What strategies did you use to try to win others over to your point of view? How successful were you? Did you change your position in any way based on what others said? • Actual city council meeting: Describe the decision-making process used by the city council. Were points in favour of each argument taken into consideration? Did some opinions seem to carry more weight than others? What recommendations would you offer to city councils about the process of making decisions?
Transportation and communication venues • railway station • bus depot • port facilities • television station • post office • airport	• How are things organized so that employees work together to keep things running smoothly? Draw a flow chart. • Describe what it would be like to work at a job at one of these sites. • What are some examples of the technology used at this facility?

FIGURE 26.1 SAMPLE FIELD TRIP PERMISSION FORM

In conjunction with their local history study, our class will be visiting McAdam Heritage Home. Volunteers at the home will involve students in activities that people living in the home would have engaged in the late 1800s.

Date of trip _____

Destination _____

Duration _____

Transportation _____

Time leaving school _____ Time of return _____ Cost to student _____

Items to bring _____

Teacher's name _____ Phone _____

- -

Please return this section

I give my permission for _____ to participate in the trip to the McAdam Heritage Home on October 3, 2006.

Signature _____ (parent/guardian)

Phone number: Home _____ Work _____

Emergency contact _____

ADVICE ON CONDUCTING INTERVIEWS AND SURVEYS

Preparation

- Decide what information is needed to meet the research objectives.
- Consider whether survey or interview is the better format to obtain the required information. Use surveys when a minimal amount of common information is needed from a fairly large number of people. An interview works best when smaller numbers are involved and the answers may be lengthy or need to be clarified.
- Research background information before the interview or survey. The more information you have, the more pertinent your questions are likely to be.
- Decide on the type of questions to ask: questions where people can indicate YES/NO or AGREE/DISAGREE, or the type where people explain their answers. Generally with interviews it is preferable to avoid questions that could be answered with a simple "yes" or "no" because these may not be particularly enlightening. Long answers on surveys involve more work from the respondents and may be more difficult to interpret and categorize.
- Generate a list of possible questions and select those questions that most clearly and directly address the desired information.
- Decide on the "sample" (the group who will answer the questions). Check with possible respondents beforehand that they are comfortable sharing information on the research topic.
- Discuss as a class the guidelines for effective interviewing.
- Provide an opportunity for students to practise interviews with peers, parents, or other familiar individuals.

Survey guidelines

- Decide whether each respondent will be asked questions or if they will fill out the form on their own. Response rates are lower when respondents fill out their own forms because some will not do so.
- Decide whether responses will be anonymous. This will depend on the type of questions and respondents' wishes.
- Provide information on the survey in an accompanying letter. The information should include why the survey is being conducted, who is conducting it, and how the person can find out the results of the survey.

Interview guidelines

- Clearly state who you are, your purpose, how the information will be used, and how long the interview is expected to take.
- Visit with the interviewee for a few minutes before and after the interview. This will help you to see the interviewee as a person and to make the interviewee feel comfortable.
- Allow the interviewee time to think about the question before responding.
- Clarify ambiguous responses. Restate the question using other words. Or say, "Is this what you meant?" and restate the intended meaning of the response.
- Ask new questions that grow out of the interviewee's comments. By sticking to the prepared questions, valuable opportunities to delve deeper and explore ideas may be missed.
- Use a tape recorder (with the interviewee's permission) or notes to record the interview. Use the interviewee's exact words in the notes. Choice of words may be an important indicator of feelings.
- Summarize the main points for the interviewee at the end of the interview. Don't offer comments that could be interpreted by the interviewee as critical of their responses.
- Thank the interviewee at the end of the interview.

Follow-up

- Send a thank-you note to all interviewees.
- Summarize impressions in writing as soon as possible after the interview. Tabulate survey results by adding up the totals of similar answers and clustering common themes contained in open-ended answers.
- Prepare an oral and/or written report of the results.
- Send a copy of the report to all those who wish to have it.

ACTIVITIES AT THE SITE

An ideal field experience is structured and purposeful. Students observe and record their observations in an organized manner. Here are some approaches to recording information at the site:

- **Tally sheets.** Students may find tally sheets useful if they are looking for specific information that can be counted. The following example shows how students might calculate on a tally sheet how much traffic goes over the school crosswalk during a specific period of time. Students could also use a tally sheet to solicit opinions for a survey.

TRAFFIC OVER A CROSSWALK

TIME PERIODS	NUMBER OF PEOPLE
8:00–8:15	///
8:15–8:30	////
8:30–8:45	
8:45–9:00	////
...	

- **Maps.** A simple street map of the community can be used to record the location of community features such as housing types (for example, apartments, single-family dwellings, duplexes).
- **Note-taking sheets.** Encourage students to record responses during the field experience on sheets with teacher- or student-made questions. The questions should direct students to the features of the site that relate to the intended understanding, especially those that students may not notice otherwise.
- **Photographs/video.** One or more students could record important aspects of the trip by means of photographs or video. These visual records assist in making detailed observations following the trip and in preparing PowerPoint presentations, bulletin boards, class booklets, or websites.
- **Sketches.** Drawings are a useful way to record information because students can focus on particular details rather than record everything as a camera would.
- **Journals.** Students could record impressions in a journal, perhaps writing in the role of someone working at a site or living in a particular historic time.
- **Interviews.** It may be appropriate for students to conduct interviews at the site. Primary students could use a chart, such as the one in Figure 26.2, to record interview information obtained from members of the school or the local community.

> Think of a particular site that would enhance the study of a topic in the social studies curriculum. Develop an activity sheet based on one of the ideas discussed above that would structure students' experiences while at this site. Focus the activity so that the field experience provides students with insights that they could not achieve from a classroom-based study.

FOLLOW-UP ACTIVITIES

After a field experience three kinds of activities are helpful:

- Students organize and interpret the data they have gathered.
- Students share their findings with others.
- Students review and assess the experience itself, including its preparatory and follow-up activities.

In preparation for interpreting data, students should review their notes, diagrams, photographs, drawings, or other records and then select and organize this information. (The pre-visit questions or the recording charts provide an organized format for the data.) Students should then interpret and draw conclusions from the information. This might include asking questions such as the following:

- Is there a particular point of view from which this information was presented?
- Is there another side to this story?
- What conclusions can I draw from this information? Does other evidence support these conclusions?
- Was I able to answer all my questions or do I need to consult other sources?
- What other questions arise now that my original questions have been answered?

Encourage students to develop effective and interesting ways of presenting their findings. Presentation formats include individual or group bulletin board displays, models, photo albums, stories, reports, letters, poems, tape recordings, journals, articles in the school newspaper, a play to be put on for other classes, and so on. Choices are as varied as for any other kind of research. (See chapter 11, "Escaping the Typical Report Trap," in this volume for other ideas.)

Finally, it may be useful to invite students, orally or in writing, to review and assess the field experience itself. Students could address the following questions:

- What were our purposes in engaging in this community experience?
- Did we achieve our purposes? Was the trip interesting?
- Are there things we could have done differently in order to achieve our purposes?
- Was the trip the best way to obtain the needed information?
- What were some of the pleasant and unpleasant surprises we encountered? How could we reduce the possibility of encountering the unpleasant surprises in another field experience?

Students could write letters reviewing the experience and send them as thank-you notes to coordinators at the site. Figure 26.3, "Note of Appreciation," provides a structure for primary students to communicate their findings and to acknowledge community members' contributions.

Local Experts

Local resource people provide students with unique learning opportunities to initiate relationships with adults they may not normally meet. Students enjoy asking their own questions, receiving first-hand responses to those questions, and drawing their own conclusions.

Bringing in a resource person can be used to dispel stereotypes. For example, in the unit on pioneer life discussed earlier in this chapter, a local senior who had lived in the

FIGURE 26.2 SAMPLE INTERVIEW FORM

Hello,

Our names are _____

Thank you for agreeing to answer our questions.

Q. What is your role or job in our community?	A.
Q. Where do you work?	A.

We have been studying how people in our community help meet each other's needs.

Q. In your role, do you help people LEARN? If yes, how?	A.
Q. In your role, do you help people be SAFE? If yes, how?	A.
Q. In your role, do you help people be HEALTHY? If yes, how?	A.
Q. In your role, do you help people have FUN? If yes, how?	A.
Q. In your role, do you help people BELONG? If yes, how?	A.
Q. In your role, do you help people GET AROUND? If yes, how?	A.
Q.	A.

Thank you for answering our questions.

FIGURE 26.3 NOTE OF APPRECIATION

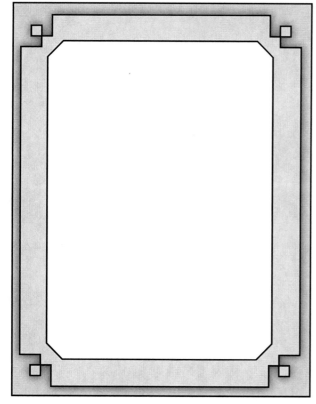

To: _____

Role: _____

Place: _____

We appreciate many things that you do to help our community meet
its needs:

1. _____

2. _____

3. _____

But we REALLY appreciate how you help the community meet its

need to _____

when you _____

_____

Thank you very, very much.

Signed _____

---

community as a child spoke to the class. For one child, a pre-dominant impression from the experience was how healthy the senior was. The guest had announced to the class that the reason she had come a day early was because she was going skiing the next day. Clearly, the child's conception of "elderly" was broadened considerably when he realized that a seventy-six-year-old woman could be so physically healthy and active (McKay 1990). A similar result occurred when a grade 6 class invited local seniors to the school for a senior citizens' tea (Sears and Bidlake 1991). The students served refreshments, provided entertainment, and interviewed their guests. Not only did students learn about local historical events, they developed empathy for seniors and interest in their life decisions and experiences.

SOURCES OF EXPERTS

If given the opportunity, many people are willing to come to the classroom and share their expertise with students:

- **Parents.** It is easy to forget this rich source that is so close at hand. Every classroom will have parents who have

travelled widely. Many parents may have come to Canada as immigrants. Parents will also have a variety of occupations and interests. It can be useful to send a form home at the beginning of the year outlining topics that the class will be exploring, and asking for parents who have some related expertise to share it.

- **Industry and commerce representatives.** Chambers of commerce, public relations departments of large firms, business lobby groups, owners of small businesses, and professional people such as doctors and lawyers are often prepared to come to schools or to arrange for interviews.

- **Interest and service groups.** Representatives from community organizations such as local historical societies, environmental lobby groups, veterans' organizations, and ethnic group associations are often prepared to meet with students. Museums sometimes provide resource people, as well as kits of materials for classroom use.

- **Government officials.** Politicians are often willing to visit schools to present their perspectives on pertinent issues and to answer student questions. Local law courts, police departments, embassies, and consulates are other possibilities.

- **Individuals with unique backgrounds.** Some people have unique life experiences to share. Such people might include Holocaust survivors, refugees from war-torn countries, and workers for humanitarian organizations in developing countries. The possibilities are limitless.

PREPARATION

Hosting a resource person is likely to be a profitable experience only if both students and guest are adequately prepared. In her article "Beyond Guest Speakers," Diana Hess (2004) discusses the futility having of guests who lecture the class for thirty minutes and answer a few vague or irrelevant student questions. A guest expert's visit is far more likely to be a meaningful experience if there is genuine interaction between the resource person and students. This may mean that the guest does not simply speak to the class but shares artifacts, documents, or issues for students to examine and discuss. The highlighted text "Checklist for Guest Experts" suggests planning ideas to ensure a meaningful experience.

FOLLOW-UP ACTIVITIES

Follow-up activities should provide students with opportunities to compare ideas provided by the expert and previously acquired information, interpret the lessons learned, draw conclusions, and develop further questions. The visit should be acknowledged with a written thank-you letter. Students might also send copies of pictures, stories, or other projects to the visitor.

Community-Developed Materials

In addition to the community resources already discussed—field experiences and resource people—community organizations offer an amazing variety of materials for teachers and students:

- **Consulates.** A vast array of materials are available from some countries (for example, Japan, Switzerland).
- **Federal agencies.** Many national government agencies (for example, Canadian International Development Agency, Library and Archives Canada, National Film Board, Canada Revenue Agency, Citizenship and Immigration Canada) are rich sources of print, electronic, and video resources.
- **Provincial and local services.** Materials are available from fire and law-enforcement services, municipal and provincial bodies, and many local agencies. Museums often have kits of materials that schools can borrow.
- **Political parties.** The websites of major political parties contain information about the party, its organization, and its position on key issues.

CHECKLIST FOR GUEST EXPERTS

Students
- ☐ Discuss the objectives of the visit with students.
- ☐ Emphasize that the guest is volunteering valuable time, therefore students should be on their best behaviour.
- ☐ Help students formulate questions ahead of time. The questions should be in keeping with previously established objectives. They could be listed on the blackboard and then students could choose the most appropriate questions. These questions could be recorded on chart paper.
- ☐ Appoint recorders to record the guest's responses.
- ☐ Involve the class in choosing students to introduce and thank the guest.
- ☐ Allow unstructured time at the end of the session for casual interaction between students and the resource person.

Resource person
- ☐ Consider whether the guest is the best resource for students about this particular topic. Consider alternatives such as audiovisual materials, library resources, and so on.
- ☐ Consider timing. Scheduling the guest's visit for the end of a unit of study rather than at the beginning means that students will have greater background knowledge. This may make the session more rewarding for both students and guest.

- ☐ Discuss with the guest the purpose of the talk, how it fits into the theme of the unit of study, and what the individual can offer to students. Point out aspects that are of particular interest to students. Encourage the guest to do more than simply talk at students; perhaps the guest can bring in materials for the students to examine or develop a topic for students to discuss.
- ☐ Discuss the length of the session. The guest may not be used to being with students at this grade level. Alert the guest to questions that the students may ask.
- ☐ Help the guest prepare content and visuals. Point out the value of interactive learning and the use of visual aids to increase student interest.
- ☐ Determine whether the guest requires specific directions to the school or if transportation arrangements need to be made.
- ☐ Determine audiovisual equipment needs and arrange for necessary equipment to be available.
- ☐ Arrange to meet the guest in advance of the scheduled time.
- ☐ Send the guest a written note of appreciation.

- **Resource industries.** Industry associations often work with teachers to develop teaching materials (for example, provincial mining or forestry associations).
- **Environment and development organizations.** Non-governmental groups (for example, Greenpeace, Western Canada Wilderness Committee) can provide materials.

Community-developed resources may be particularly useful in providing information that presents an alternative, more current perspective than that found in textbooks. Because these materials may not have been originally intended for use in classrooms, the information and views contained in them must be scrutinized carefully. The following questions may help teachers critically examine these materials:

- What are the aims of the organization? Are these acceptable in a public education system?
- How are these aims reflected in the materials available to teachers and students?
- Does the organization have any formal ties to education or the production of educational materials?
- How suitable are the materials for classroom use and what levels might they be appropriate for? Can they be adapted for use?
- Which curricular objectives can these materials be used to help attain?
- If the organization provides human resources for classroom or professional purposes, how can these resources be used to enhance social studies?

Select a topic in the social studies curriculum and brainstorm the range of field experiences, resource people, and community-developed resources that might be used to supplement or even replace the traditional educational resources used to address this topic.

Conclusion

A rich social studies program requires access to a wide array of resources, including those in the community. Community resources offer important experiences and insights that can deepen student understanding of social studies. Careful preparation is the key to making the most of such resources. Preparation includes carefully choosing a field-trip site or resource person, making students aware of the purposes for using the resource, and helping students develop questions to guide their discovery. Most importantly, unlike the teacher cited at the opening of this chapter, let us not ignore the exciting possibilities all around us. The rewards are immense.

GOVERNMENT-RELATED RESOURCES

The Library of Parliament website has two very helpful compilations of annually updated resources and programs about parliamentary democracy and citizenship education.

- "Background Resources for Educators" lists resources produced by parliamentary groups, organized under three headings:
    - Parliament
    - Senate
    - House of Commons

    This document can be found online at www.parl.gc.ca/information/about/education/resources/index-e.htm.
- "Links to External Organizations" lists contact information and educational resources available from numerous federal and provincial departments and educational organizations organized under six headings:
    - Information about Parliament
    - Parliamentary history
    - Multimedia
    - Professional development
    - Youth programs and contests
    - Provincial and territorial assemblies

    View this document at www.parl.gc.ca/information/about/education/resources/related/index.asp?Language=E.

ACKNOWLEDGMENT

Thanks to Marg Franklin, retired elementary school principal and University of British Columbia sessional instructor in elementary social studies, for her helpful comments on this chapter.

ENDNOTE

1   I would like to thank Marjorie Redbourn, a student in a Simon Fraser University social studies methods class, for reminding me of this episode of *The Wonder Years* and its applicability to field experiences.

REFERENCES

Galloway, G. 2004. The adventures of Flat Mark and Paul Martin. *Globe and Mail,* January 21.

Hess, D. 2004. Beyond guest speakers. *Social Education* 68 (5): 347–348.

McDiarmid, G.L. 1970. The value of on-site learning. *Orbit* 1 (3): 4–7.

McKay, R. 1990. Children's construction of meaning in a thematic unit. Unpublished doctoral dissertation, University of Alberta, Edmonton.

Oliver, H. 1970. Philadelphia's Parkway Program. *Orbit* 1 (3): 22–23.

Schuler, D. 2002. Studying the community. *Social Education* 66 (5): 320–324.

Sears, A. and G. Bidlake. 1991. The senior citizens' tea: A connecting point for oral history in the elementary school. *Social Studies* 82 (4): 133–135.

Taber, J. 2003. Flat Mark has the next prime minister's ear. *Globe and Mail.* December 10.

ADDITIONAL READINGS

Globe-trotting teddies provide geography lesson for students. 1998. *Vancouver Sun.* May 5.

27 Using Artifacts to Foster Historical Inquiry

Linda Farr Darling

The Importance of Historical Inquiry

Developing historical understanding is a central goal for social studies education, but it presents challenges for elementary teachers who wonder about children's readiness to engage in historical investigation. Many teachers are concerned that young children are disconnected psychologically, lack sufficient background knowledge about the past, and are missing concepts dealing with chronology that are required for any understanding of history.

These challenges are important considerations but they are not insurmountable. Various researchers have shown how engaging students in historical inquiry—turning the study of history into an interpretive practice—can be accessible and exciting even to young students. Children continually strive to make "human sense" of the world (Donaldson 1978), and historical inquiries can bring to life stories about people, places, and times that enhance this sense-making. Although children may feel disconnected from broad historical discussions of political movements, wars, revolutions, and so on, they rarely feel disconnected from discovering what life was like for their teachers, parents, and grandparents when they were children. From constructing personal timelines and learning to divide the past into recognizable eras based on family photographs, young students can build chronological sense using narratives found in their own homes and communities. These stories from the past provide starting places for acquiring and refining the concepts necessary for historical understanding.

Paramount in this enterprise is the teacher's role in engaging students in what might be called "disciplined inquiry" by harnessing and shaping the natural curiosity that bubbles up in the form of children's spontaneous questions. The authors of *Doing History* define disciplined inquiry as "purposeful investigations that take place within a community that establishes the goals, standards and procedures of study" (Levstik and Barton 1997, 13). The rich potential embedded in historical inquiry is lost without a teacher framing and guiding the questions that students ask. Too often, questions encountered in the elementary social studies curriculum remain at very concrete and literal levels. Attention stays on gathering information and detail, sometimes at the expense of analysis or synthesis, and without sufficient regard for the "human sense" behind the facts. Unlike fact-finding questions that tend to shut down inquiry, the focus should be on questions that open up inquiry, go beyond recall, deepen understanding, and expand curiosity. Students can engage in sustained inquiries, even without considerable prior knowledge of history. In fact, as the authors of *Doing History* suggest, the inquiry can become the process through which students construct their understanding of historical themes. However, these authors caution that "authentic, disciplined inquiry is not easy; teachers must guide and support students at every step of the process—stimulating their interest, helping them develop questions, modelling procedures for collecting information and so on" (77). Despite these requirements, the rewards of inquiry are worth the effort.

The Role of Artifacts in Inquiry

Before introducing an extended scenario about a primary classroom inquiry, I want to comment on the value of artifacts as starting points for purposeful historical investigation. Levstik and Barton write that "although young children who are still developing their reading skills will have trouble using some kind of written primary sources—particularly from more remote time periods—analyzing photographs and artifacts allows them to use important historical materials in an authentic way" (77). There are several reasons why study of a single historical artifact presents an imaginative entry into larger investigations of the past. Children are attracted to the details about people's everyday lives; physical objects make these lives seem more real and accessible. The opportunity to handle and use physical artifacts stimulates curiosity about "things that work," and engages children's natural inclinations to be active and involved in their learning. Manipulation of hand drills, old egg beaters, and other implements from various eras is absorbing and fun, and importantly adds to children's first-hand knowledge of tools and technologies.

In my own work with young students, I have found that investigations of historical artifacts introduce the past to students in a way that is rooted in something concrete and easy to grasp, but can easily grow to something more. For example, the examination of a glass inkwell or a slate chalkboard can lead to important historical questions about continuity and change in society as reflected in schoolrooms over the last hundred years. I now want to illustrate this potential by describing the inquiry that evolved when I brought a historic artifact to a grade 3 class.

A Classroom Inquiry

As students are getting settled, I look around and see that inquiry is clearly valued in this classroom. There's a large hand-printed letter to author Robert Munsch asking, among other things, "How do you think up your stories?" and "Who do you tell your stories to before you write them down?" On the windowsill are a dozen bean plants of various heights, each with a graph attached and questions about conditions for healthy growth. It's a pleasant jumble of a room, a mixture of works-in-progress and remnants of last week's literary performances and yesterday's science experiment. Stretching towards the door is a blue rug and on it twenty children are now gathering after a stretch. They are more or less sitting in a semicircle of barely contained energy.

First I introduce the term "artifact," then "historic artifact," and write both on the board with a brief definition. The artifact I have brought is a curious object, a solid wooden sphere the size of a tennis ball with a turned handle protruding two inches from one side (see photograph). I hold up the sphere for students to see and I invite them to raise their hands to ask me what they are curious about. I explain I won't answer right away because there will be so many kinds of questions, and I will need to think about them. Students begin posing their questions:

"Is it really old?"
"Why does it have a handle?"
"Who gave it to you?"
"Is it a toy?"
"Do you have any more of them?"
"Is it breakable?"
"Is it worth a lot of money?"
"Is there something inside it?"

I stop them after the eighth question and say, "You have asked so many questions that I am getting confused. How can we keep track of them?" Someone volunteers that we could make a list and we are off and running with the first stage of our inquiry lesson. I begin recording the questions on the board, but one student notices that some questions are "like other ones kids already asked." Soon it is obvious to some stu-

Photo by author.

dents that there are different sorts of questions and we should find a way to organize them.

We decide to make three columns. We label them, "Questions about what the artifact is like," "Questions about where it came from," and finally, "Questions about what it is for." Our purpose in creating these categories is to frame the questions and eventually the hypotheses that students will generate about the artifact. More questions are asked and students help me decide where to place them in our categories. Then I ask the class to think of how we might find answers to their questions. "We can ask you!"

"What makes you think I will know the right answers?" I reply.

"It belongs to you, so you know." With this response noted, I ask them to imagine that this historical artifact just appeared on their windowsill. How would we learn about it then? They suggest the following methods:

- look in a book;
- ask a grown-up;
- go to a museum or a place with old stuff.

At this stage I want students to understand that we will start building our knowledge of the artifact so we can discover not only what it is, and how it is used, but also how it fits into a historical context. "What do you know about it before you look in a book or find an expert?" I ask. I encourage children to pass the artifact around so that everyone has a chance to touch it, sniff it, and roll it around in their palm. We talk about careful and respectful treatment of artifacts and establish a few rules for handling—no throwing, no hitting it against something, and no dropping.

Next, students work in groups of four to write down everything they already know about the artifact. Collaborative effort is productive in building understanding. Students learn that by observing carefully and putting their observations together they know quite a lot. The object is round, hard, smooth, heavy but not too heavy to hold, somebody made it because it wouldn't grow like that, it's made out of wood, you're probably supposed to hold it by the handle, it probably won't bounce, it is darker in some places than others, and it probably floats. Direct observation has led to additional knowledge and new questions that we add to our three lists.

I invite students to ask me any of the questions we have generated, but I tell them I can answer only "yes" or "no," and I will not answer the same question twice so they will have to keep track. This means that they will have to rethink the form of some of the questions on the board and listen carefully to make sense of my replies. If they get stuck, I may offer another piece of information. They will hear many clues and then they will be asked to form hypotheses about the identity of the artifact.

Through questioning me, students eliminate possibilities and collect further information: No, it was not carved. Yes, the sphere and handle were both created using a special carpenter's tool (a lathe). Yes, it is older than me and my mother and even my grandmother. No, it is not part of a spinning wheel. No, it has no other parts. No, the artifact is not a toy, nor is it furniture. Yes, it is useful, but no, not for cooking or in the kitchen. Yes, more women than men used it, but men travelling on their own (such as gold miners and cowboys) would have found it helpful. Yes, it was used to fix or mend something. Yes, it fixed something most people needed. Yes, other things, most notably burned-out light bulbs once electricity was in wide use, served the same purpose.

There are a few tentative hypotheses offered: it's something for weaving, a tool for knitting. I assure them they are very close and that they have done wonderful work. It is time to demonstrate the artifact in use. I take out a hand-knitted wool sock with a hole in the heel, a thick blunt needle, and some strong white thread. Even those children who have never seen someone darning know exactly what I am trying to do. They can see that the round ball provides the right curve to support mending a hole in the heel. What a useful tool! They are delighted with their efforts as investigators (even though they were not completely successful) and they are eager to hear the story of my artifact, which I can now share.

The artifact is a late nineteenth-century darning ball that came from the family of a friend in the Maritimes. It is made of eastern white oak (a common hardwood in the forests of Nova Scotia and New Brunswick). The wooden ball and handle were turned on a lathe, probably by an amateur woodworker who gave it to his wife, my friend's great-grandmother. The decorative handle bears a strong resemblance to details on country furniture built in the 1870s and 1880s. I hadn't previously seen one like it and it surprises me that darning balls are not more common in attics, antique stores, or at flea markets. Presumably most nineteenth-century European Canadians wore hand-knitted socks that developed holes in their heels. The darning ball is a household object that was at one time rather commonplace. In later decades, burned-out light bulbs were used for the same purpose. There are countless other examples of functional objects that were once familiar in North American homes: hand-held irons, primitive toasting racks, copper bed warmers, wooden butter paddles, carved butter presses, and metal thimbles. Any of these artifacts can lead to "disciplined inquiry" beginning with questions such as, "What are some household inventions that have changed family life since your great-grandparents' day?" This in turn could be linked to other historical questions such as, "What are some ways in which our society has adapted to changing conditions and demands?" Related ideas and topics include:

- obsolescence
- technological innovation
- consumables
- household inventions
- the Industrial Revolution
- textile mills

This time, the darning ball proves to be a catalyst for a social studies unit on recycling and reusing. Part of the study is an investigation of changing societal values. Once socks were mass-produced in knitting mills, people generally attached much less value to them. (See Ulrich 2001, especially chapter 11, "An Unfinished Stocking.") Instead of owning only two or three pairs of socks as people did in the eighteenth and nineteenth centuries, today many people own lots of relatively inexpensive machine-made socks. However, if a favourite aunt or other relative had spent the time it takes to knit a pair of socks, the recipient would likely treasure these socks.

We read *Ox-Cart Man* (Hall and Cooney 1979), the story of a farm family who makes almost everything it uses. Students draw elaborate illustrations of the way that members of this family grew food, collected goose down for stuffing quilts, built furniture from trees on the property, and so on. On one page of the book, the mother sits by the fire mending torn clothing. The children search Barbara Cooney's illustration for evidence of a darning ball and conclude it must be in the basket of mending at her feet.

The next day, I bring in a colourful pair of warm, hand-made Peruvian socks. They prompt stories of special socks, shoes, and other favourite pieces of clothing that we save even after we outgrow them. This exchange naturally leads to a rich discussion of what we mean when we say we value something. We read Pablo Neruda's poem about a favourite pair of hand-knit stockings called "Ode to my Socks" (1968). I read each line first in Spanish and then the translation. The poet thinks the socks are too beautiful for his old, tired feet. He calls the socks twin parrots and later in the ode he refers to them as two woven flames. The students look at their feet. They might throw away socks when they get holes (or perhaps turn them into puppets), but it wasn't always this way.

I recite a short poem that my grandmother had cross-stitched on a sampler because it speaks of an important domestic value common to families even two generations ago:

Use it up,
Wear it out,
Make it do,
Or do without.

The darning ball has done its job—it has stimulated powerful questions that guide our inquiry.

Lessons Learned

Through this inquiry, students were introduced to the kinds of standards and procedures that are integral to historical study (for example, we must have reasons or evidence for our conclusions; we have to think for ourselves, the teacher won't always give us the answers; we can tell a lot by looking for clues; we can pool our individual observations). Students worked together to generate both questions and knowledge claims about the artifact. By working as a community of inquirers, the children entered into the practice of actually doing history. Concepts relevant to understanding the contexts in which the artifact might have been used were introduced naturally and informally as questions arose from the students themselves. The students were given opportunities to make sense of important historical themes (for example, technological obsolescence, shifting values, and change and continuity). Throughout the inquiry, the teacher's role was to stimulate children's thinking, help students focus and organize their inquiry, prompt students to think for themselves, help students learn from each other, and, most importantly, raise for consideration the bigger issues embedded in the particulars of their inquiry. In our inquiry, the important point was not the specific fact that we no longer darn our socks. Instead, the broader point was made that things that once had value in our society may no longer be appreciated. A related theme concerned losses and gains associated with technological advances. Certain technologies have qualitatively changed how we live our lives.

> Identify a topic in the curriculum dealing with a past event, period, or person. Think of possible artifacts that might be used as an entry point to raise important themes connected with the historical topic you have identified. List several questions you might ask of students to guide them to the bigger issues raised by the artifact.

Clearly, there are countless humble artifacts that could be enlisted as tools to help young students make sense of history. Items need not be expensive or rare to be useful for historical inquiries. Even objects that were commonplace in your own childhood can present wonderful mysteries to young students. The primary criterion for selection is the potential for an artifact to raise important historical ideas (for example, self-sufficiency, changing values, enduring traditions). The artifact is simply the vehicle for grounding and drawing students into a historical inquiry. Other criteria to remember when selecting artifacts include the following. Artifacts should:

- have the potential to excite children's imagination and to personalize history;
- not be too fragile for young children to handle;
- not be dangerous or cause damage (for example, stain clothing); and
- be easily displayed in a classroom (not too big or too small).

The highlighted text, "Using Artifacts to Support Historical Inquiry," includes suggestions for other activities that support historical inquiry using artifacts as the entry point.

Although it is desirable, especially with younger children, to have physical objects to share with students, this is not always feasible—some objects are too big, impossible to find, or are otherwise unavailable. Photographs of artifacts can be useful substitutes for the "real" thing. Many museums have developed virtual collections of artifacts. For example, the Archives Society of Alberta has produced a virtual train station filled with artifacts from Canadian immigrant experiences (www.archivesalberta.org, click on "Letters from the Trunk"). Similarly, the McCord Museum of Canadian history, in partnership with seven museums, has produced "Keys to History" (www.mccord-museum.qc.ca/en/keys), a searchable database of nearly 110,000 images (dating from 1840–1945), of which 2,000 are fully documented.

The example of a slide presentation described in the highlighted text "Same or Different" illustrates how photographic representations of objects from ancient Roman times stimulated a grade 7 class's historical inquiry into the differences between Roman and contemporary societies.

USING ARTIFACTS TO SUPPORT HISTORICAL INQUIRY

- **Artifact study sheet.** Develop a chart, such as the one illustrated on the next page, to accompany artifact investigation that students conduct either in groups, on their own at home (if interviewing family members), or in other settings, such as on a field trip to a museum. Emphasize that students are to offer reasons or evidence for their answers: What clues can we point to that suggest an answer?
- **Old Main Street treasure hunt.** Most towns and cities have a neighbourhood that is full of antique shops, junk stores, second-hand clothing stores, pawnshops, auction houses, consignment stores, or thrift shops. These can be treasure troves for artifact collectors. Sometimes sources for historical artifacts are scattered throughout a wider geographical area. If it seems workable in your situation, consider a field trip for students and arrange for them to have a small amount of money to purchase an artifact or an old newspaper, catalogue, or calendar. If a field trip is not feasible, consider collecting artifacts in a treasure chest of your own. Among the items I have discovered on my own city's Main Street include: biscuit tins, military uniform buttons, initialled handkerchiefs, roller-skate keys, eight-track cassettes, long-playing records, player piano music rolls, apple corers, meat grinders, embroidery hoops, decorative hair combs, stocking garters, hand-forged nails, and inkwells. Each of these offers an imaginative entry into studying how people lived in the past.
- **"Then and now" charts.** Many important questions about societal change and continuity over time can be raised by inviting students to sort artifacts (or representations of objects) into "then" and "now" categories. Primary students can be introduced to Venn diagrams to represent tools, toys, and implements that have changed over the years between the childhoods of their parents, their grandparents, and their own lives. Students can draw pictures of objects that fit into the circle labelled "then" or the circle labelled "now." Certain items may have stayed the same over time and would be placed in the space where the circles overlap. Varying diagrams might be devoted to different themes (for example, kitchen tools, games and toys, women's clothing).
- **Artifact timelines.** A good activity for building understanding of chronology is for young children to arrange artifacts in chronological sequence. Using investigative methods discussed in class, students find out as much as they can about objects brought from home or found in the teacher's treasure chest. In small groups or as a whole class, students use the information gathered to decide where to place artifacts on a timeline. Beforehand, the teacher might write in significant dates, decades, historical periods, or personal time frames (for example, My grandma's childhood, My parents' teen years, When I was a baby). Using clothespins, hang drawings of the objects along a clothesline stretched across a corner of the classroom. Alternatively, arrange the actual objects on a windowsill or counter that has been organized into a timeline.
- **Invent the artifact's story.** Invite older elementary students to write their own stories from the point of view of particular artifacts. Based on the knowledge acquired about an artifact and their own abilities to judge the plausibility of various hypotheses, students write a story which explains the following:
  - Who invented me? Why?
  - Who made me? Where?
  - Who has owned me?
  - Where have I lived? Where have I travelled?
  - What have I been used for? Have I been misused or neglected?
  - Does anyone use me now? Has a newer invention taken my place?

continued on next page

	CLUES	CONCLUSIONS
Where did it come from?		
Who made it?		
How old is it?		
Who used it?		
For what purpose?		
Is there a modern counterpart?		

SAME OR DIFFERENT?

The lesson was introduced using a photograph (shown opposite) of a clay model of a sheep's liver. Explained in a manner intended to make the practice seem odd, students were told that in ancient times, fortune tellers or soothsayers would sacrifice an animal, slice open its belly, and pull out its organs, which were then "read" for any clues they offered about the future. This clay model was a teaching tool used in Mesopotamia to train would-be fortune tellers about what to look for when reading animal entrails. Each of the squares outlined on the clay model represented a different prediction. For example, a scar or blemish appearing in one part of the grid might indicate five years of good luck or suggest that the person would have many children. A mark in another area of the liver would signal poor health or great financial misfortune. After hearing this explanation, students were asked to indicate whether ancient soothsaying is very similar to or completely different from what happens today. The most common and predictable reaction was reflected in remarks such as "totally weird" and "strange."

The teacher then asked students to more directly consider contemporary fortune-telling. The teacher and students discussed various modern forms (for example, horoscopes, tea leaves, tarot cards, and palm reading) and the basis for predicting used by each (for example, the position of stars and planets, the configuration of leaves in the cup, the symbols on cards, and the length and intensity of lines on the palm). The teacher then observed that instead of the location of the scars on the liver, modern fortune tellers consult the location of the stars in the sky or the lines on the hand. Students were asked to reconsider how different this is from past practices. For many students, what was once a bizarre practice now seemed much less foreign.

The lens guiding their inquiry was now in place—students would look beyond the obvious differences between present and past practices to uncover more basic commonalities and differences. Students were then shown clusters of pictures of Roman objects on a common theme—pictures about entertainment showed the coliseum, gladiators, and chariot races. The stories behind each of these pictures were shared by the teacher. In small groups, students identified what they saw as the contemporary parallels for each practice—the parallels for entertainment included football stadiums, kick-boxing, and demolition derbies. They then considered whether or not the differences between then and now were significant. This routine was repeated several times with other aspects of Roman civilization (for example, water systems, architecture, transportation, politics). In each case, students looked at photographs of artifacts from Roman times and identified parallels in their own society. The fact that statues of famous Romans often had their noses and ears broken off was of particular interest to students. One reason for this originated in the time when Christianity took hold in Rome. In the eyes of some Christians, these statues encouraged idolatry and had to be destroyed. Because there were so many marble statues and they were difficult to remove or destroy completely, a common strategy was to mar the face of the statues by breaking off the noses and ears. Students were amused to realize that we still "deface" property—although now more frequently by graffiti than by knocking off appendages.

The culminating activity invited students to offer an overall assessment of the extent to which life in ancient Rome was similar to or different from contemporary society. As they debated their conclusions and shared their evidence, students understood that they were not simply talking about old relics but were engaged in an inquiry into the roots of Western civilization. As one student remarked, "I know why we study ancient Rome. Everything we do now, well, they did something just like it."

Photo by Susan Duncan. Courtesy of the photographer.

Assemble several objects (or photographs of objects) that have historical significance. Design a lesson involving the use of these items to help students learn about some aspect of the curriculum.

Conclusion

In this chapter I have tried to show how the use of artifacts, or images of them, can be an exciting and effective approach to developing historical understanding, especially in younger children. Historical objects offer accessible opportunities to involve students in historical investigation. The main challenges to effective use are to select objects that can connect with key themes in the curriculum, to engage students' curiosity through strategic questioning, and to support students in drawing out the bigger lessons from their inquiry into the artifact.

REFERENCES

Donaldson, M. 1978. *Children's minds.* New York: Norton.

Hall, D. and B. Cooney. 1979. *Ox-cart man.* New York: Random House.

Levstik, L. and K. Barton. 1997. *Doing history: Investigating with children in elementary and middle schools.* Mahwah, NJ: Lawrence Erlbaum Associates.

Neruda, P. 1968. Ode to my socks. Reprinted and translated in 1994 in *Rethinking schools: Teaching social justice in classrooms.* Milwaukee, WI: Rethinking Schools, Ltd.

Ulrich, L.T. 2001. *The age of homespun: Objects and stories in the creation of an American myth.* New York: Random House.

28

Training the Eye of the Beholder
Using Visual Resources with Elementary Students

Penney Clark

The statement "a picture is worth a thousand words" is a truism. Photographs, paintings, films, and other visual resources can convey immense detail at a glance—detail that would take pages of print to describe. They can depict nuances of colour, texture, and facial expression that are difficult to convey in words. They may also be artifacts that provide rich historical insights. Certain photographs are so powerful that they come to represent an era, such as the poignant image of John Kennedy, Jr. saluting his father's coffin, Pierre Elliott Trudeau pirouetting behind the queen, or the sole Chinese student in front of sixteen tanks in Tiananmen Square. Much of Canada's early history (and that of other countries, too, for that matter) was recorded for posterity by painters, before photography came into common use. For example, Paul Kane produced more than a hundred oil paintings of aboriginal people based on sketches done in his travels from the Great Lakes to Vancouver Island between 1845 and 1848. We are indebted to Frances Ann Hopkins, whose husband was the secretary to George Simpson, governor of the Hudson's Bay Company, for her detailed paintings of the voyageurs on several canoe journeys that she took with them between 1858 and 1870.

Given their importance, visual resources should be a key part of a social studies program. If students are to make effective use of visual resources, they first need to see them as an important part of the variety of information sources available to them. Yet, visuals are often overlooked. For instance, pictures in textbooks are ignored while students scour the print segments for information. Students need to learn to examine pictures from a critical perspective. They are not only a rich source of information and insights, but deliberate constructions, rather than mere reflections, of reality; and as constructions, they represent their creators' purposes and perspectives. Coupled with this is the need to examine visuals actively to uncover the meanings that lie under their surface images. In order to make them yield all that they have to offer, students must spend time studying them and learn to ask compelling questions about them.

This chapter discusses the thoughtful classroom use of photographs and paintings, as well as visual resources with an audio component, such as videos, films, and CD-ROMs.

Paintings and Photographs

The most abundant and accessible visual resources are photographs and paintings. Most authorized textbooks are full of them. Other sources include:

- travel brochures
- calendars
- newspapers
- magazines
- government publications
- discarded textbooks
- store advertising displays
- CD-ROM encyclopedias
- archives and museums
- the internet
- art books
- family albums
- public relations material
- art galleries

In this section I look at concerns about interpreting paintings and photographs at face value and offer a few strategies for "interrogating" these visual resources.

PAINTINGS

Paintings (and other art forms) can give students a powerful sense of how the world was viewed in the time and place in which they were produced. However, students need to be aware that paintings are not necessarily intended to represent events as they actually happened. For instance, a famous painting showing the death of French commander the Marquis de Montcalm, at the Siege of Quebec, shows him dying on the battlefield. In fact, he died the next morning in Quebec. An equally famous painting of the death of General Wolfe, the British commander, depicts people who weren't actually present, and some who were there are not shown.

Students should discuss why artists do not always represent events as they actually happened. One of the reasons for altering the details is to represent the artist's social and political purposes. Students can see the influence of national perspective on the depiction of events by comparing paintings by different artists on a particular incident. For example, American artist John Trumbull's painting of the death of the American commander Richard Montgomery during the 1775–76 American invasion of Quebec shows Montgomery as the centre of attention. The painting by British artist Johan Frederick Clemens shows a chaotic battle scene with many more things happening at once. It is interesting to note that neither painting is authentic in that Montgomery died on the battlefield on December 31, but his frozen body was not found until the next day.[1]

Students can use historical paintings to construct a written account of life in a particular place at a particular time in the past. For instance, Peter Rindisbacher, a Swiss settler who lived at Red River from 1821 to 1826, created numerous drawings and paintings depicting the activities of aboriginal people in the area. (*Life at Red River: 1830–1860*, a text in the Ginn "Studies in Canadian History" series, contains reproductions of several Rindisbacher paintings.) Students could examine these paintings and then write a few paragraphs describing what they see. They might also compare the information extracted from the drawings and paintings to information extracted from written sources and attempt to account for any differences.

PHOTOGRAPHS

"While photographs may not lie, liars may photograph" (Lewis Hine, quoted in Everett-Green 1996, E1). Students (and many others) tend to take photographs at face value, while they are ready to accept that drawings and paintings represent the perspectives of their creators (Gabella 1994). It is difficult to repudiate the visual evidence of a photograph because it is a record of a particular moment in time. Students may not stop to consider that even photographs are not always what they seem and that the person behind the camera will likely have constructed the picture to suit particular purposes. Photographic evidence may be unreliable in four ways:

- Photographers or subjects may stage photographs in order to deliver a particular message.
- Photographs may depict an atypical situation or event, one that is not representative of the people or circumstances shown.
- Photographs may be deliberately altered.
- Photographs may exclude important aspects of a situation.

STAGED PHOTOGRAPHS

Photographers may arrange subjects or objects in a photo in order to deliver a particular message. For example, a famous photo by Alfred Eisenstaedt shows a sailor and a nurse kissing in the middle of a crowd on VJ Day (official end of the fighting between the Allies and Japan in World War II). The photographer had two people pose for the shot. He did not happen upon a spontaneous eruption of joy, as most people who see the photograph imagine. Such photos are clever and capture the imagination, but they are not "real," in that they would not have happened without the photographer's intervention.

Photographs can be "created" in much less dramatic ways than the VJ Day example. It was common practice for nineteenth-century photographers, intent on preserving traditional images of Native people for posterity, to stage their photographs. For instance, Edward S. Curtis, who photographed Native peoples from Alaska to the American Southwest, used wigs and costumes, as well as other props, so his subjects would appear as he imagined First Nations people would have looked before being affected by European culture.

In other cases, it is not so much that the photos have been deliberately staged, but rather that the reality they are intended to convey has been slightly altered to suit the momentous occasion of the photograph itself. For instance, the photograph on the following page shows children dressed in ragged and dirty clothing, yet with freshly scrubbed faces. Someone has prepared the children for this photograph. Students have to be aware of such anomalies so that they do not take such photographs at face value (no pun intended). It is interesting to speculate about the photographer's motives and the effect on the audience of seeing poorly dressed children with fresh faces.

A photograph may also, in some sense, be staged by its subjects. Joy Kogawa, in *Obasan*, a novel about a Japanese family that was transported first to an internment camp and then to an Alberta beet field, says of a photograph of another Japanese family taken at the time: "'Grinning and happy' and all smiles standing around a pile of beets? That is one telling. It's not how it was" (1981, 197). The photo did not reflect the

GRAFLEX CAMERA PHOTOGRAPH

THE SHAME OF THE CITY—CAN WE GIVE OUR CHILDREN NO BETTER PLAYING SPACE?

"The shame of the city: Can we give our children no better playing space?" —*Winnipeg, 1912*
Library and Archives Canada (C-030947)

reality of the lives of the subjects of the photo. The camera can create its own reality.

Students need to learn to look beyond distortions created by photographers or subjects to examine other evidence that photographs may offer. J. Robert Davison (1981–82) describes a photograph labelled "Indians, Fraser River," taken about 1868 by photographer Frederick Dally. The photograph, which appears on the following page, shows a group of Native people "praying." However, the photographer contradicts the evidence of the photograph by writing underneath, "Indians shamming to be at prayer for the sake of photography." Above the photo is written, "At the priests [sic] request all the Indians kneel down and assume an attitude of devotion. Amen." Even without the help of the caption, close examination of the photograph reveals that it is a sham:

> The two priests have set a fine, holy example, but their spiritual and physical distance from the group is palpable; they are easily picked out standing (here kneeling) apart—curiously not aloof, for in this case it is the Native group that is aloof. They have gone along with the play, but there is little conviction.

Some emulate the priests, but only tentatively, as if they were unsure of what exactly constitutes an "attitude of devotion." A few others seem to have thought it barely worth the effort. They have pulled their dignity and their pride around them like their blankets, refusing the pious assault on their spirit (Davison 1981–82, 2).

Much can be ascertained from such a photograph and its captions. It can be used to demonstrate to students that critical examination of a visual resource can reveal messages that are not evident at first glance. Students could discuss why it might be in the best interests of the priests to have such a photograph taken and how it might be used. Also, it would be interesting to consider why the photographer, in writing his captions, refused to go along with the sham. Students could examine other photographs and their captions to determine how a caption can alter the message conveyed by a photograph.

"Indians shamming to be at prayer for the sake of photography. Fraser River." —*Frederick Daly*
British Columbia Archives (E-04419)

UNREPRESENTATIVE IMAGES

A second way photographs lead viewers to draw unwarranted conclusions occurs when they are highly unrepresentative of the reality of the person or the situation. The famous photograph showing candidate Robert Stanfield fumbling a football kickoff during a national election campaign is an example of this. The photograph, which was widely reprinted, left the impression that Stanfield was an incompetent bungler. Other evidence does not support this impression. Students could be shown such a photograph and asked to locate additional evidence that supports or refutes the impression conveyed by the picture. They could then be asked to draw a conclusion about the person or event based on the wider array of evidence, which they now have at hand. They should also consider the power of such impressions, where connections can be made which are not warranted. In this case, competence in football is not related to competence in politics or, for that matter, governing, but these connections were made.

Daniel Francis (1996) points out that early photography technology was instrumental in developing an image of nineteenth-century aboriginal people that was less than accurate. Francis says:

> A mask-like quality was particularly pronounced in early photographs, because exposure times were prolonged and subjects had to keep themselves and their expressions immobile for up to half a minute. Since photographs were often the only glimpse most non-natives got of native people, this simple technological imperative may have contributed to the stereotype of the grim, stoical, cigar-store Indian (2).

Here, the camera has created rather than captured unrepresentative images. The result is the same—a misleading impression is created.

To help students appreciate that photographs may lead viewers to draw unwarranted conclusions, students could role-play particular historical events while another student takes photographs at dramatic moments. Invite students to examine the photographs and discuss what they convey about the event and what is misleading. Students might also speculate about the conclusions historians using family photo albums as evidence might draw about contemporary family life. Using their own family albums as an example, students may conclude that a historian would judge the family to be avid travellers and partygoers, without realizing that these were the types of events that family members recorded by means of photographs. Such albums often do not record the more typical routines of a family.

ALTERED PHOTOGRAPHS

With the advent of digital technology, photographs are "as malleable as clay" (Grady 1997, A23). People can be moved from one location to another, objects can be placed in the photograph, unwanted people can be removed, and so on. However, these sorts of alterations did not suddenly appear with the advent of the computer. They have occurred since photography was invented. Stephen Jay Gould describes his unearthing of "conscious skulduggery" (1981, 171) in the work of psychologist H.H. Goddard. Goddard maintained that the "feeble-minded" could be recognized by their facial characteristics and "proved" this point by means of photographs of poor families. Seventy years after publication of the photographs, examination by experts revealed that facial features had been altered to make the people appear mentally disabled. Communist regimes have rather routinely altered historical evidence, including photographs, to suit current political thinking. For instance, in *The Book of Laughter and Forgetting*, Milan Kundera (1980) describes a scene on the balcony of a palace in Prague in 1948, where Communist leader Klement Gottwald was addressing hundreds of thousands of Czechoslovakian people. Photographs of the group on the balcony were reproduced widely in posters and textbooks. However, after Vladimir Clementis, who was on the balcony and in the photographs, was executed for treason in 1952, his image was removed from the photographs—which, once doctored, showed a bare palace wall where he had stood.

More commonly, a photograph intended for publication will be cropped before printing in order to suit layout requirements sometimes radically altering its meaning in the process. Students can apply two L-shaped frames to photographs from magazines and newspapers in various ways in order to see for themselves how the meaning can be altered by the practice of cropping.

SELECTIVE FOCUS

Photographs can also exclude; that is, they may only represent "part" of a story. An example of this is the famous photo, which has appeared in many textbooks, of Donald Smith and other dignitaries at the Last Spike ceremony to mark the completion of the Canadian Pacific Railway at Craigellachie, British Columbia. It is important in such a case to ask who is included and who excluded. Another, less famous photo shows the labourers who had built the railway holding their own Last Spike ceremony while they waited for the train that would take them back east. A comparison of these two photographs, which appear on the next page, can be used to show that the historical record is selective. However, it is not only the first photo that excludes. Encourage students to note who is missing from the photograph of the labourers as well. Even

"Hon. Donald A. Smith driving the last spike to complete the Canadian Pacific Railway"
—*November 7, 1885, Alexander Ross, Ross, Best & Co., Winnipeg*
Alexander Ross/Library and Archives Canada (C-003693)

"Hon. Donald A. Smith driving the last spike to complete the Canadian Pacific Railway"
—*November 7, 1885, Alexander Ross, Ross, Best & Co., Winnipeg*
Library and Archives Canada (C-014115)

though there was a large contingent of Chinese workers on the railway, they are not represented in the second picture. This, too, tells students something about historical perspectives. Many textbooks dwell on the activities and achievements of prominent Caucasian men, while ignoring those of working-class people, people of other races, and women.

In the highlighted text is a question sequence that could be used with the two Last Spike photographs. Similar questions aimed at helping students consider who is excluded, as well as who is included in the photos, could be posed about many historical pictures. For instance, there is a photo showing the Fathers of Confederation at the Charlottetown Conference. Since historians (Cuthbert Brandt 1992) have acknowledged that the social aspects of the Conference were key to its success, it seems fair to ask why the politicians' wives, who organized these social events, do not appear in official photographs.

Students can also take their own photographs as a way of helping them understand that photographs offer selective views of the world. Primary students can be assigned a word that describes a quality of their community (for example, cooperation, safety, peace). Then they can take a photograph within the school grounds or in the neighbouring community that captures that particular quality. It might also be interesting to ask students to take pictures that capture the opposite attributes (for example, isolation, danger, discord). Photographs and captions can then be separately taped to the board and class members guess which caption belongs with each picture and explain why they think it fits. The students who take each photograph are expected to provide an adequate explanation as to why it is an appropriate photograph for their caption. Finally, students may create a neighbourhood montage with magazine photographs representing the original captions.[2]

STRATEGIES FOR INTERROGATING PHOTOGRAPHS AND PAINTINGS

There are many different kinds of questions that we might use with students to help them examine photographs and paintings (as well as other visual resources) critically. We might ask students to:

- attend carefully to detail;
- consider geographic data (for example, climate, landscape);
- consider historical data (for example, type of clothing, hairstyles, furniture);
- consider sociological data (for example, social class, relationships);
- consider emotional context (for example, feelings of people depicted);
- consider aesthetic qualities (for example, general appeal, use of colour, light, texture); and
- consider photographer's or artist's perspective and purpose (for example, intended audience, messages conveyed).

Questions that fit within one category may not necessarily be asked all at once. It may be helpful to follow a sequence that stems logically from students' responses. Two examples of the use of these questions to interrogate visuals are shown in the highlighted areas. The first example, intended for upper elementary students, uses the painting "Canoe Manned by Voyageurs Passing a Waterfall" by Frances Ann Hopkins. The second example is intended for primary students and uses a contemporary photograph of a grandfather and his granddaughter.

In the following highlighted text (adapted from Scott, Falk, and Kierstead, 2002), students are asked to decipher the drawing of a scene set in ancient Egypt by developing plausible hypotheses and then using the hypotheses to form conclusions about life at this time.

The following framework (adapted from the Ontario

INTERROGATING A PAINTING: AN EXAMPLE FOR UPPER ELEMENTARY STUDENTS

"Canoe Manned by Voyageurs Passing a Waterfall"—1869, Frances Ann Hopkins
Library and Archives Canada (C-002771)

Attend carefully to detail
- Describe the people you see in this painting. Note the clothing and various types of headgear.
- What are the people doing?
- What objects do you see? Describe them.

Geographic data
- What is in the foreground of the painting? The background?
- Where do you think these people are?

Historical data
- What can you learn about the voyageurs from this painting?
- What questions would you like to ask the artist about the lives of the voyageurs?

Sociological data
- Who are the woman and man in the centre of the canoe? What clues suggest this?

- Why do you think they are not paddling? Is this explanation supported by anything in the painting?

Emotional context
- How do you think the voyageurs felt about having the well-dressed man and woman in the canoe with them? How might their presence affect the behaviour of the voyageurs?
- What aspects of this painting convey a sense of tranquility?

Aesthetic qualities
- How is light used in this painting? What is the purpose of this use?
- What are some of the ways the artist has made the painting artistically pleasing?

Photographer's or artist's perspective and purpose
- Why do you think the artist chose to paint a journey by voyageurs?
- Why might the artist have chosen to convey the voyageurs amid such a tranquil scene?
- Do you think the artist has a positive feeling for voyageurs?

Ministry of Education, 1989, 137–138) supports students in examining the aesthetic features of photographs and paintings by focussing on techniques (for example, use of light, focus, and frame) that highlight or subdue various aspects of a picture. These questions can be used with any of the visuals discussed in this chapter.

- **Subject.** What is the photograph or painting about? Does the photographer or painter wish us to think about an object, a place, a person, an event, or an idea? Is the subject unusual or revealing? Does the subject have an impact on the viewer? Is the subject representational or universal?

- **Frame.** In what way has the subject been isolated from its

INTERROGATING A PHOTOGRAPH: AN EXAMPLE FOR PRIMARY STUDENTS

"Grandparent and Child"—*Penney Clark*

Attend carefully to detail

- What do you see here?
- What or who do you see in this picture? What do you see in the background?
- What do you think the people are doing?

Geographic data

- What natural objects do you see? What is the land like?
- What do you think the weather was like on the day the photo was taken? What clues help you to answer this question?
- Where do you think the man and the little girl are?

Sociological data

- What can you tell about the people by the way they are dressed?
- Do you think the man and the little girl are related? How do you think they might be related? Why do you think this?

Emotional context

- What words could be used to describe how these people are feeling? Are they in a hurry? Relaxed? Comfortable? Anxious?

Aesthetic qualities

- What are some things that the photographer has done to make this photo one that you enjoy looking at?

Photographer's or artist's perspective and purpose

- Who do you think might have taken the photograph? Why do you think it was taken?
- Do you think the people in the photo knew it was being taken? Why or why not? If not, why would the photographer choose to take the photo when the people weren't aware it was being taken?

surroundings? Are there particular objects that become more interesting to us as a result of the frame established by the photographer or painter? What new meaning between objects or people is created within the frame? What comparisons, contrasts, or tensions are created by the framing? What effects has the point of view had on the meaning of the subject?

- **Light.** Students should examine the use of light in terms of its quality (for example, sunlight or artificial light), quantity (for example, under- or overexposure), and angle (for example, how the subject is lit, whether a flare was used). Guide their discussion with questions such as the following: How has light been used creatively to create the overall effect? Is the subject lit from a specific angle? Do lines of light and shadow create or enhance the

meaning? What reasons do you think the artist had for using light the way he or she did?

- **Focus.** How much detail is in focus in the picture? Did the artist isolate certain elements and leave the rest fuzzy? Has the artist used "sharp" or "soft" focussing to create a specific mood? Did the artist make the best choice in the details emphasized in the photographs? Is the picture too "busy" with sharply focussed details?

Select three or four pictures pertaining to a particular topic in the curriculum (for example, a specific community, historical event, or time period). Develop a lesson where you teach students to read the pictures and notice the similar and contrasting information contained in them.

DECIPHER THE DRAWING

Explain that much of what we know about ancient Egypt is a result of the work of archaeologists, who have examined murals/pictures that the Egyptians painted on walls and paper. The archaeologists have to make educated guesses because often there is no written explanation. Tell students that their challenge will be to act as archaeologists in trying to explain what is going on in a drawing about ancient Egypt that they have found.

Ask students to interpret the following drawing of ancient Egypt using the 5Ws (who, what, where, when, and why). Alternatively, if students are new to interpreting drawings, you might provide a possible explanation of the scene in the picture. For example, ask students to find evidence to support or refute this explanation:

Groups of farmers are working their fields near a river or a summer day in order to grow food to eat.

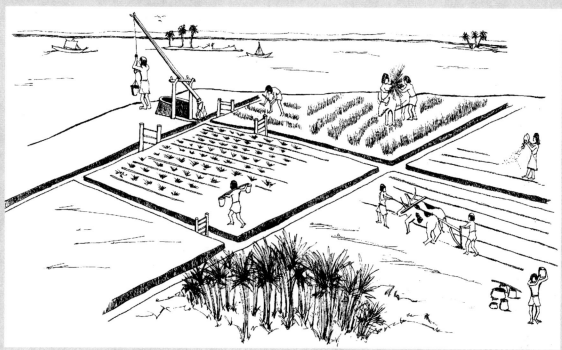

Illustration by Danna deGroot. Courtesy of the publisher.

	HYPOTHESIS	EVIDENCE
Who are the people in the drawing?		
What are the people doing?		
Where does the drawing take place?		
When did the action in the drawing take place?		
Why is the action happening?		

Audiovisuals

Audiovisual resources—CD-ROMs, videos, films—have many positive features that make them useful in teaching social studies. Students with different learning styles may benefit from their use because they deliver information through both auditory and visual means. They provide alternative ways to gather information for less capable readers. In some cases, they can be more useful for data gathering than field trips because they focus on the most important aspects of the experience and eliminate extraneous details. They can convey a great deal of information in a relatively brief span of class time. Through such methods as animation, slow motion, time-lapse photography, and microphotography, they allow students to view scenes they would otherwise not have an opportunity to observe. Those that use motion have their own advantages. For instance, processes that can be difficult to visualize when described in print can be seen in action. Motion can also add to student interest. Finally, they can be more motivating than many other resources; they are usually less intimidating than textbooks, as well as being colourful and appealing.

Historian Graeme Decarie has warned us to "beware of technologies standing under streetlights, calling, 'Hi, sailor'" (1988, 98). He was referring to the production and indiscriminate classroom use of poor-quality (both technically and in terms of meeting curriculum objectives) audiovisual aids of various kinds. He urged teachers to choose such resources carefully and use them selectively. With the advent of computer technology, there are many more audiovisual materials available now than there were a decade ago. Therefore, it is more important than ever that they be chosen carefully and used selectively.

The type of audiovisual technology chosen will depend on its accessibility and the purpose for which it is being used. Specific audiovisual resources should be selected for classroom use based on criteria such as interest, accuracy and currency of content, conceptual level, whether content fits intended purposes, quality of photography and sound, and the way in which information is organized for presentation.

HELPING STUDENTS BECOME CRITICAL VIEWERS

As with other visual resources, it is important to help students see that these resources have been created by human developers with particular perspectives and for particular purposes. Like the other resources, these must be actively investigated in an effort to reveal the messages that lie underneath the surface. Below are sample questions (adapted from Cates 1990) for deconstructing an audiovisual resource:

- **Dialogue.** Notice consistent use of words that have positive or negative connotations. What is the effect of using the word "cheap" instead of "inexpensive," or "conceited" in place of "high self-esteem," or "forthright" instead of "domineering"?
- **Actors.** Is there any relationship between the type of character played and the physical appearance of the actor? For instance, do homely actors play "bad guys," while attractive people play the "upstanding characters"? Are people of a particular race overrepresented among the evil characters?
- **Character development.** Are characters stereotypical (for example, are Native people presented as uniformly good or uniformly bad, or are attractive blonde women presented as unintelligent)?
- **Colour and lighting.** Is the depiction light and airy, dark and brooding, or some variation of this? Are some scenes lighter and brighter than others? What is the content of these scenes? What about the darker scenes? Are any scenes in black and white? Why do you think this is the case?
- **Music.** Can you find examples where the choice of music or its volume influences the way you view particular characters or events?
- **Camera angle and choice of shot.** Is the action ever shown from the viewpoint of a character? If so, in what cases and for what purposes?
- **Selection and arrangement of scenes.** Does the film alternate among different viewpoints, places, or people? Are different viewpoints given equal time and emphasis?
- **Overall impression.** What is the developer of this resource attempting to convey through use of some of the devices presented here?

Use of audiovisual resources need not be limited to those developed specifically for classrooms. Popular films, for example, can be used to help students learn to analyze a medium to which they receive constant exposure in their daily lives. This is important to do for the following reasons: many people are predominantly visual learners; films present details graphically that may not necessarily be communicated through writing; their dramatic telling can amplify and illuminate themes and ideas from history; they are an important art form in their own right because of their pervasiveness in our culture; and they are a gauge of the tastes and ideologies prevalent in North American culture (Johnson and Vargus 1994).

Peter Seixas (1994) has used the 1989 Kevin Costner film *Dances with Wolves*, in conjunction with the 1956 John Ford film *The Searchers*, to determine how students' ideas about a currently popular historic film are challenged by viewing an older film with differing perspectives on Native-white interactions. Students endorsed segments in *Dances with Wolves* as "true" windows on the past because they were congruent with their own views. The moral stance of the movie, with its critical view of the US army and westward expansion and the Sioux as their victims, was in keeping with revisionist popular culture. *The Searchers,* on the other hand, with its depiction of Native people as violent and vengeful, represents an earlier view of Native-white interaction during the period of settlement of North America. The contrasting historical interpretations posed a moral dilemma for most of the students. While Seixas used the two films for research purposes, contrasting film clips can be used to develop students' sense of the problematic relationships between historical evidence and historical interpretation. The use of popular film is an engaging way to help students develop such understandings.

IDEAS FOR USING AUDIOVISUAL RESOURCES

This section discusses previewing, viewing, and follow-up activities for use with audiovisual resources. It is, generally speaking, not sufficient merely to turn on the video machine and let students sit back and watch the show. These following activities are helpful in turning what may simply be an entertaining interlude into an educational experience.

PREVIEWING ACTIVITIES

Previewing activities should arouse interest, build background knowledge, clarify purposes for viewing, and reveal what students already know about a topic. In order to arouse interest and build background knowledge, teachers might briefly describe the topics to be explored in the audiovisual resource and ask students to bring pertinent newspaper and magazine pictures and articles to class. These materials could form part of a bulletin board display that would evolve throughout the unit of study. In order to clarify purposes for viewing, students can be given key questions that identify main ideas, establish relationships among different aspects of a topic, or help students examine the material for accuracy, authenticity, or bias. These questions need not be numerous; one general question may be quite sufficient. The important point is that students have the questions prior to, rather than following, the viewing to provide a focus or purpose for their viewing. Students can be assigned different questions and therefore have different purposes. They pool their information following the viewing. A previewing activity might also consist of a discussion of students' prior knowledge of the topics dealt with in the audiovisual. They could record what they already know in a retrieval chart (such as Figure 28.1, which is intended for use with an audiovisual resource on an assigned Canadian region).

After viewing, students can refer back to their charts to add to and confirm the accuracy of the information they recorded prior to viewing.

Previewing activities signal to students that the viewing is to be an educational rather than a recreational experience. Because videotapes in particular, and also CD-ROMs, are accessible in many homes, students develop a mindset that such materials are for pleasure use only. Unless reminded by means of such previewing activities, students may not view them with the same intensity that they might read a textbook or other "serious" information source.

VIEWING ACTIVITIES

The purpose of viewing activities is to give students a focus while encountering the resource. It is preferable that students not take detailed notes during the viewing because there is a danger that the recording task will occupy their attention to such an extent that they will miss important points. Audiovisuals can be stopped frequently in order to check on student comprehension and to discuss and clarify points made. The entire audiovisual need not be viewed if only a portion is appropriate to curricular intents. If the entire audiovisual is pertinent, one viewing can be insufficient to allow students to cope well with the information. It may be best to view it in its entirety once and then show selected portions a second time, or as many times as necessary.

FOLLOW-UP ACTIVITIES

Following the viewing, students might record and then compare their responses to questions asked during the previewing phase. If there are discrepancies, pertinent sections of the audiovisual can be viewed again to determine why. If students have recorded hypotheses prior to viewing, they might confirm their accuracy. Other follow-up activities might relate the material in the audiovisual to the ongoing unit of instruction in which they are engaged. For example, students might use an audiovisual resource as one of a set of information sources to prepare for a talk or a report that they will prepare.

The example in Figure 28.2 (adapted from Clark 1991) of an approach to previewing, viewing, and follow-up activities is an adaptation of the well-known SQ3R (Survey, Question, Read, Record, Review) strategy for dealing with print material. Its purpose is to provide students with a structured format that gives them purposes for viewing, ways to record information, and ways to summarize the information once recorded. Students can then proceed to more sophisticated strategies involving probing underneath the surface discourse for the author's purpose, and so on. They may also wish to view the resource a second time.

FIGURE 28.1 DATA KNOWLEDGE CHART

Region of Canada _____

	PRIOR KNOWLEDGE	ADDITIONAL KNOWLEDGE
Topography		
Climate		
Vegetation		
Natural resources		
Industries		
Major cities		
Transportation and communication		
Wilderness preserves		

Conclusion

Visual resources should be a key part of a social studies program. They add interest and variety. Their use teaches students that the print medium is not the only means by which information is attainable. However, visual resources, like other learning resources, represent the perspectives of their creators. Visual resources are particularly seductive sources of misleading information because of the powerful effect they can have on the viewer. Therefore, students need systematic strategies for interrogating this source of information and they should view these resources with the same healthy scepticism with which we would want them to view any other resource.

Select a video resource that has been recommended for use in a particular grade level. Identify specific outcomes in the curriculum that might be addressed using this resource. Design an activity and student support material to achieve these outcomes using the selected resource.

FIGURE 28.2 VIEWING GUIDE

SURVEY. Listen to your teacher read you a brief summary of the video. List five topics you think will be addressed in this video.

1. _____

2. _____

3. _____

4. _____

5. _____

QUESTION. Create a question about an important aspect for each of the above topics. Write your questions on the lines below.

1. _____

2. _____

3. _____

4. _____

5. _____

VIEW AND RECORD. View the video to find the answers to your questions. Record your answers below. All of your questions may not be answered in the video. You may want to check other sources for those answers.

1. _____

2. _____

3. _____

4. _____

5. _____

REVIEW. Review your answers above. Use this information to write a summary of the video.

_____

_____

_____

_____

ACKNOWLEDGMENT

The author is grateful to Marg Franklin, retired elementary school principal and sessional instructor in elementary social studies curriculum and instruction at the University of British Columbia, for her helpful comments in the preparation of this chapter.

ENDNOTES

1   Trumbull's painting of the death of Montgomery can be found at http://en.wikipedia.org/wiki/Invasion_of_Canada_(1775); Clemens's painting can be found at http://explorer.monticello.org/?s1=0ls4=4_42.

2   This activity is described in greater detail in McDiarmid, Manzo, and Musselle (2007, 5–6.)

REFERENCES

Cates, W.M. 1990. Helping students learn to think critically: Detecting and analyzing bias in films. *Social Studies* 81: 15–18.

Clark, P. 1991. *Government in Canada: Citizenship in action.* Montreal: National Film Board of Canada.

Cuthbert Brandt, G. 1992. National unity and the politics of political history. *Journal of the Canadian Historical Association* 3: 2–11.

Davison, J.R. 1981–82. Turning a blind eye: The historian's use of photographs. *BC Studies* 52: 16–35.

Decarie, G. 1988. Audio-visual aids: Historians in Blunderland. *Canadian Social Studies* 23 (2): 95–98.

Everett-Green, R. 1996. Photography's white lies. *Globe and Mail*, November 9.

Francis, D. 1996. *Copying people, 1860–1940.* Saskatoon, SK: Fifth House.

Gabella, M.S. 1994. Beyond the looking glass: Bringing students into the conversation of historical inquiry. *Theory and Research in Social Education* 22 (3): 340–363.

Gould, S.J. 1981. *The mismeasure of man.* New York: Norton.

Grady, M. 1997. Photography as "monster." *Vancouver Sun.* May 17.

Johnson, J. and C. Vargus. 1994. The smell of celluloid in the classroom: Five great movies that teach. *Social Education* 58 (2): 109–113.

Kogawa, J. 1981. *Obasan.* Boston: David R. Godine.

Kundera, M. 1980. *The book of laughter and forgetting.* New York: Knopf.

McDiarmid, T., R. Manzo, and T. Musselle. 2007. *Critical challenges for primary students.* Rev. ed. Vancouver, BC: The Critical Thinking Consortium.

Ontario Ministry of Education. 1989. *Media literacy resource guide.* Toronto: Queen's Printer.

Scott, D., C. Falk, and J. Kierstead. 2002. *Legacies of ancient Egypt.* Richmond, BC: The Critical Thinking Consortium.

Seixas, P. 1994. Confronting the moral frames of popular film: Young people respond to historical revisionism. *American Journal of Education* 102 (3): 261–285.

Wilson, K. 1970. *Life at Red River: 1830–1860.* Toronto: Ginn.

SUPPLEMENTARY READINGS

Allen, R. 1994. Posters as historical documents: A resource for the teaching of twentieth-century history. *Social Studies* 85 (2): 52–61.

Allen, R.F. and L.E.S. Molina. 1993. Snapshot geography: Using travel photographs to learn geography in upper elementary schools. *Canadian Social Studies* 27: 62–66.

Braun, J.A. and D. Corbin. 1991. Helping students use videos to make cross-cultural comparisons. *Social Studies and the Young Learner* 4 (2): 28–29.

Burke, P. 2001. *Eyewitnessing: Uses of images as historical evidence.* Ithaca, NY: Cornell University Press.

Considine, D.M. 1989. The video boom's impact on social studies: Implications, applications, and resources. *Social Studies* 80 (6): 229–234.

Downey, M.T. 1980. Pictures as teaching aids: Using the pictures in history textbooks. *Social Education* 44 (2): 92–99.

Felton, R.G. and R.F. Allen. 1990. Using visual materials as historical sources: A model for studying state and local history. *Social Studies* 81 (2): 84–87.

Hennigar-Shuh, J. 1988. Learn to look. *History and Social Science Teacher* 23 (3): 141–146.

Jackson, D. 1995. A note on photo CDs: A valuable resource for the classroom. *Canadian Social Studies* 30 (1): 28–29.

Morris, S. 1989. *A teacher's guide to using portraits.* London: English Heritage Education Service.

Nelson, M. 1997. An alternative medium of social education—The "horrors of war" picture cards. *Social Studies* 88 (3): 100–107.

Osborne, K. 1990. Using Canada's visual history in the classroom. In *Canada's visual history,* 4–19. Ottawa and Montreal: National Museum of Civilization and National Film Board of Canada.

Pazienza, J., and G. Clarke. 1997. Integrating text and image: Teaching art and history. In *Trends and issues in Canadian social studies,* ed. I. Wright and A. Sears, 175–940. Vancouver, BC: Pacific Educational Press.

Segall, A. 1997. "De-transparent-izing" media texts in the social studies classroom: Media education as historical/social inquiry. In *Trends and Issues in Canadian social studies,* ed. I. Wright and A. Sears, 328–349. Vancouver, BC: Pacific Educational Press.

Seixas, P. 1987. Lewis Hine: From "social" to "interpretive" photographer. *American Quarterly* 39 (3): 381–409.

Sunal, C.S. and B.A. Hatcher. 1986. How to do it: Studying history through art. *Social Education,* 50 (4): 1–8.

Werner, W. 2000. Reading authorship into texts. *Theory and Research in Social Education* 28 (2): 193–219.

———. 2002. Reading visual texts. *Theory and Research in Social Education* 30 (3): 401–428.

———. 2004. Towards visual literacy. In *Challenges and Prospects for Canadian Social Studies,* ed. I. Wright and A. Sears, 202–215. Vancouver, BC: Pacific Educational Press.

OTHER RESOURCES

Internet resources

Canadian Heritage Gallery: http://www.canadianheritage.org

Canadian Museum of Civilization: http://www.civilization.ca

CanPix Canadian Gallery: http://northernblue.ca/canchan/canpix/gallimag.php

McCord Museum "Keys to History": http://www.mccord-museum.qc.ca/en/keys/

National Archives of Canada: http://www.archives.ca

Royal BC Museum "Amazing Time Machine": http://www.bcarchives.gov.bc.ca/exhibits/timemach/index.htm

Royal Ontario Museum: http://www.rom.on.ca

A Scattering of Seeds: http://www.whitepinepictures.com/seeds

United States Holocaust Memorial Museum: http://www.ushmm.org

WebMuseum, Paris (also known as LeWebLouvre): http://www.ibiblio.org/wm

Films using paintings

National Film Board of Canada. 1972. *Paul Kane goes west.* Montreal: Author. A source of Paul Kane paintings depicting Canada's early history.

———. 1977. *Pictures from the 1930s.* Montreal: Author. Juxtaposes paintings produced during the Depression with newsreel footage about both domestic and international events. Features female artists such as Emily Carr and Paraskeva Clark.

———. 1980. *A visit from Captain Cook.* Montreal: Author. Illustrates how European artists projected their own ethnocentric perspectives on what they observed and recorded.

CD-ROM on Canadian history

National Film Board of Canada. 1997. *Canada's visual history.* CD-ROM. Montreal: National Museum of Civilization and National Film Board of Canada. This rich source of visual information deals with Canada's social and economic history. Includes visuals from pre-European contact to the recent past. Includes articles by Canadian historians and suggestions for further reading.

Videos on Canada

National Film Board of Canada. *Postcards from Canada.* Montreal: Author. Includes stunning postcard-like images from coast to coast.

————. *Transit series.* Montreal: Author. Individual titles are:

AIR: Climate

WATER: Reserves and Networks

LAND: Territory and Resources

FIRE: Energy

LIFE: People, Fauna and Flora

These documentaries examine Canada's geography from five different themes. The cinematography is stunning.

National Film Board (NFB) resources contact:
National Film Board of Canada
P.O. Box 6100, Station Centre-Ville
Montreal, Quebec H3C 3H5
NFB website: http://www.nfb.ca/store

29 Promoting the Aesthetic Experience
Responding to Literature in Social Studies

Roberta McKay

The idea of incorporating fictional and non-fictional literature into a social studies program is not a new one. Young people enjoy stories and poems that relate to social studies and many teachers have long known that literature can be use to directly teach content directly. In this chapter, I address a different role for literature, arguing that literature has an essential place in social studies because of its aesthetic qualities—qualities that educate the heart and complement a subject area that cannot be mere facts, but includes human feelings and emotions.

I begin by considering what literature is and the importance of an aesthetic experience in social studies. I then discuss specifically how literature as an aesthetic experience contributes to the major knowledge, skill, and attitude dimensions of social studies. I discuss general considerations in choosing literature for aesthetic purposes in social studies and sources of annual lists of high-quality literature. As well, I identify characteristics and criteria for selecting particularly relevant categories of literature, including contemporary realistic fiction, historical fiction and biography, and folk tales. In the final section, I suggest an approach to encouraging students' aesthetic responses to literature. The chapter concludes with lists of references on dealing with various kinds of literature.

The Power of Literature

Charlotte Huck and Barbara Kiefer, noted experts in children's literature, define literature as "the imaginative shaping of life and thought into the forms and structures of language" (Huck and Kiefer 2004, 3). In literature for children, language works with pictures to evoke what Huck and Kiefer describe as an inner experience of art, an aesthetic experience, which enables the reader to perceive patterns, relationships, and feelings. The subject matter of literature is the human condition and the experience of literature is the coming together of text and reader. While literature for children and young people exhibits similar qualities to adult literature, it is important that literature for children appropriately reflects their emotions and experiences.

The power of literature rests in its ability to engage simultaneously with the feelings and thoughts of the reader or listener. Young people need to be introduced to literature as a source of wonder, delight, joy, and sorrow—as a window on the human condition. Literature engages us at an affective and aesthetic level, connecting us with our own experiences and the experiences of others. Literature helps us to shape and understand our human experience on affective and cognitive dimensions simultaneously. Literature connects us to the human community through time and space—it provides a doorway to other worlds. Imagination and curiosity are fuelled by literature. As young people enter other possible worlds, they encounter new perspectives on people, events, places, times, and ideas. The realms of possibility are widened and deepened on every dimension as children engage with literature. "Literature enables us to live many lives, good and bad, and to begin to see the universality of human experience" (Huck and Kiefer 2004, 9).

The Role of Literature in Social Studies

Textbooks are written primarily to transmit information. Although literature can enhance social studies knowledge and attitudes, its primary purpose is to engage us aesthetically. We must not violate this purpose by utilizing literature as a textbook to "teach" social studies (McKay 1995). Literature should be used in social studies for literature's sake—to provoke an aesthetic response, to stir a feeling of affinity with the human condition, to capture our hearts and imaginations as well as our minds, and to connect us to ourselves and others. These qualities of literature can make a lasting contribution to the social studies program. In light of their different purposes, literature requires different teaching and learning responses than those needed to teach from a textbook. While literature often includes considerable information about the world both past and present, it should not be used as a textbook, or, as Huck and Kiefer assert, "literature should never be distorted to fulfill the purposes of a lesson" (2004, 552).

Louise Rosenblatt (1991) distinguishes a reading continuum which streched from the "efferent" stance—reading for information—to the "aesthetic" stance—reading for the aesthetic experience. Rosenblatt asserts that all readings are a mix of efferent and aesthetic stances. For example, we may read the story *Sadako and the Thousand Paper Cranes* (Coerr 1977), which deals with the aftermath of war, and experience the poignancy in the death of Sadako while acquiring some information about World War II. Because readings have this mix of efferent and aesthetic stances, it is essential to be clear on the purpose for which we are having students read. Because children's literature is written predominantly from an aesthetic stance, young readers should first experience the piece, then recapture and reflect upon it, followed perhaps by further aesthetic responses (for example, talking, drawing, singing, writing, or engaging in dramatic forms such as tableaux, mime, reader's theatre, or role plays). Rosenblatt suggests that secondarily to the aesthetic responses, the text may be discussed for informational purposes, but, she states, "first, if it is indeed to be 'literature' for these students, it must be experienced" (1991, 447). For example, when studying Canadian history, a novel about prairie settlement is valuable primarily as a way of experiencing what it would have been like to live at that time. Factual information contained in the literature may be recalled at a later time as a starting place for further research or to enrich prior information.

There is one exception to my belief that the role of literature in social studies should first be to evoke aesthetic response. Non-fiction is a category of literature for children that is slightly different: while non-fiction books are not textbooks, they are also not fiction. These books characteristically have aesthetic value as a result of being finely written and illustrated and thereby evoke reader satisfaction and delight. But such non-fiction books also fulfill a specific teaching function in that their primary purpose is to provide information, usually on a single topic. These non-fiction books often provide depth and a richness of detail about a topic that is unlikely in a textbook. These books are written with a predominantly efferent stance and while they may also have some aesthetic value as noted above, they certainly may be utilized primarily for information gathering purposes. The pairing of non-fiction and fiction books in dealing with a social studies topic or theme is a powerful way to introduce children to the value of using a variety of sources.

Literature and Social Studies Objectives

Incorporating literature into the social studies as aesthetic experiences enriches the curriculum both directly and indirectly. The knowledge, skill, and attitude dimensions of social studies all benefit from immersing young people in related literature.

- **Personalizes and contextualizes people, events, and situations.** Knowledge outcomes are enhanced as people, events, and situations are personalized and contextualized. Factual information and concepts are developed through the familiar format of story. Literature enables young people to relate facts, concepts, and generalizations to their own lives, thereby facilitating individual construction of meaning. Literature offers entry into many possible worlds and provides vicarious experience that enables young people to gain insight into people, places, events, situations, and times far removed from their immediate experience. Their world view is expanded. Literature often acts as a springboard for research as inquiries generated from a story motivate a quest for further information.

- **Develops language.** In addition to engaging children at a profoundly aesthetic level, literature simultaneously develops language on several crucial dimensions. Oral language is enhanced by listening to stories and poetry and engaging in conversation about them. Literature provides experience with abstract language patterns and structures that are similar to those encountered in school. A sense of story is developed and there is exposure to a vast vocabulary. Reading fluency is increased by reading many and varied books and the content, structure, vocabulary, and conventions in young people's writing reflects the amount and type of reading to which they are exposed. Reading as an enjoyable and thoughtful experience is promoted in the context of the content area. Young people get further exposure to language structures and vocabulary present in literature and become acquainted with additional authors and memorable characters, plots, and moods. Because of a definite link between language and thought, literature plays a role in developing thinking abilities.

- **Develops multiple skills.** Many skills outcomes of social studies can be realized through literature. Creative thinking and problem solving are stimulated in a variety of contexts. Reading is an individual meaning-making activity, providing opportunity to draw conclusions, speculate and imagine, and make self-initiated discoveries. Comparing, contrasting, analyzing, synthesizing, and evaluating are all required when listening to and reading stories and poetry. Communication and participation skills are meaningfully utilized as young people respond to literature individually and collectively through talking, writing, drawing, and dramatizing.

- **Nurtures empathy, sensitivity, and other social values.** It is perhaps in the area of the value and attitude outcomes that literature makes its most profound and powerful contribution to the social studies. Literature evokes feeling, stimulates emotion, and helps shape our human experience. Values and attitudes are personalized in literature and are treated as living forces that motivate human behaviour and are embedded in complex situations. Conflict, change, and ethical dilemmas are presented as part of what it means to be human. Through aesthetic engagement with literature, young people can come to understand their own lives more fully by seeing that they share areas of conflict in their lives with other human beings who, for better or for worse, have responded to these conflicts in their lives. Empathy and the ability to view life from different perspectives are promoted. Through literature, young people identify and analyze the values and attitudes of characters in literature and often relate these to their own experiences, past, present, or future. This can develop positive attitudes towards themselves and others in their immediate as well as the global environment.

- **Addresses delicate topics sensitively.** Literature can be a vehicle for considering many sensitive social issues. Authors currently writing for young people deal with a wide range of contemporary topics including sibling and peer relationships, divorce, death, adoption, sex roles, and discrimination. Reading or listening to stories and poetry that concern the feelings and responses of other young people in similar situations can be very beneficial to young people in the classroom who are facing these situations as real-life experiences. Literature can provide models of alternative behaviours that are removed from an individual and personal context. Folk tales and fairy tales also provide a rich array of value-laden dilemmas and conflicts to stimulate reflection and discussion.

- **Builds community.** Literature can also contribute to a sense of classroom community and other citizenship goals by focussing on the qualities required for living with others (Orr 1995). Literature often celebrates uniqueness, considers friendship and acceptance, and deals with concepts related to sharing and caring for others. These aspects of human relationships can be catalysts for young people to reflect individually and collectively upon the meaning they have in their own classroom community. For instance, literature that reflects themes of caring for and about others may encourage young people to examine their own behaviour towards one another in the classroom. Providing opportunities for listening to, reflecting upon, and responding to literature may help young people develop a sense of what a classroom community could be.

- **Celebrates diversity.** Literature can form the heart of multicultural education by celebrating and building upon the diversity in young people's backgrounds and experiences. Rosenblatt has argued that aesthetic responses evoked by literature, such as heightened sensitivity to the needs and problems of others and greater imaginative capacity, are "part of the indispensable equipment of the citizen in a democracy" (cited in Pradl 1991, 274). It is currently popular to promote multicultural education through literature, and many professional resources are available (Ramirez and Ramirez 1994, Zarrillo 1994, Bieger 1996, Finazzo 1997, Harris 1997, Cai 2002).

The four-level model proposed by James Banks (1989) is helpful when integrating ethnic and cultural content into the curriculum because it reduces the likelihood of superficial treatment of multicultural concepts. Banks' model for integrating ethnic and cultural content into the curriculum is hierarchical, based on the degree to which multicultural issues are central to the curriculum, the extent to which changes occur in the traditional curriculum, and the extent of teacher and student commitment to diversity and social justice. Banks' model provides a theoretical framework for incorporating literature into multicultural education. Making use of literature at the transformative and decision-making/social action levels can assist young people to understand and value cultures and experiences different from their own.

Choosing Literature

Choosing literature for social studies is both challenging and rewarding. Our opportunities to find high-quality material for young people are better now than ever before, but our need to select wisely is also heightened. I offer three general considerations when choosing literature for our students: literary value, curriculum fit, and student suitability. I introduce other criteria, particular to various literary genres, when I discuss specific categories of literature.

TABLE 29.1   INCORPORATING LITERATURE INTO MULTICULTURAL EDUCATION

BANKS' LEVEL OF INTEGRATION OF ETHNIC/CULTURAL CONTENT IN THE CURRICULUM	USE OF LITERATURE	NATURE OF COMMITMENT TO DIVERSITY AND SOCIAL JUSTICE
Contributions Cultural concepts and content are "separate" from the curriculum and are introduced as a result of special ethnic/cultural holidays, heroes, customs, or contributions.	• In February, reading literature about Chinese New Year.	• Eurocentric perspective is used as the basis for selection of elements to be studied. • May reinforce stereotypes and mistaken beliefs. • A focus on visible aspects of a culture may lead to superficial understanding.
Additive Cultural concepts and content from a Eurocentric perspective are "added" to social studies curriculum.	• During a Canadian history unit, reading about European immigration.	• Diverse views of events and issues are presented.
Transformative Cultural concepts and content "alter" the structure of the curriculum as perspectives of various ethnic/cultural groups are included.	• During a Canadian history unit, reading literature (including historical fiction and biography) about immigration that incorporates perspectives of diverse cultural groups (for example, Native, Ukrainian, Chinese, German).	• Diverse cultures are recognized and presented in the curriculum.
Decision making and social action Cultural concepts and content "alter" the structure of curriculum by including diverse perspectives and related social issues.	• During a Canadian history unit, reading literature about immigration that identifies and deals with social issues (for example, discrimination). • Social issues are discussed in relation to students' own school or community leading to social actions.	• Diverse views and social issues are recognized and explored through problem solving, decision making, and social action.

LITERARY VALUE

Because of my emphasis on literature as an aesthetic experience, the first criterion for choosing literature in social studies is literary or aesthetic qualities. These qualities in fiction are traditionally judged by the elements of plot, setting, theme, characterization, style, point of view, and format. According to Huck and Kiefer, high-quality fiction for children includes "a well-constructed and well-paced plot, a significant theme, an authentic setting, a credible point of view, convincing characterization, appropriate style and an attractive format" (2004, 24). They provide an excellent expanded explanation of these elements, useful guidelines for evaluating literature for children (14), and specific guidelines for evaluating the literary merit of poetry (368). Young people evaluate literature by their responses to it and as teachers we need to value their interpretations and judgments while also acquainting them with the qualities in a story or a poem that make it acclaimed for its literary and aesthetic merit. Professional organizations such as the International Reading Association (IRA) and the National Council for the Social Studies (NCSS) publish annual annotated bibliographies of exemplary children's books. In addition to these annual listings, the journals *Social Education*, *Social Studies and the Young Learner*, *Language Arts*, and *The Reading Teacher* often publish excellent practical articles for teachers on ways to incorporate literature into social studies. (See the resource list at the end of this chapter.[1])

CURRICULUM FIT

A second criterion to consider when choosing literature for social studies is "curriculum fit"—the suitability of a work to the specific content and issues in the social studies curriculum. Selecting appropriate books is a serious responsibility because the best books can enhance social studies understandings while poor selections may reinforce misconceptions and stereotypes. Sullivan (1996) offers four criteria to guide literature selection to enhance global understanding:

- shows our common humanity;
- provides sound geographic, social, historical, political, economic, and/or religious information;
- shows that other people have different but valid approaches to our common human concerns and needs; and
- increases understanding, empathy, and the ability to learn from other peoples and cultures.

As previously discussed, stories and poetry may present only one perspective on an event, issue, or topic and several selections may be chosen to represent varying points of view.

STUDENT SUITABILITY

While suitability to the age and reading level of the students is a third consideration, student interest is often the more important criterion. Many stories and poems that young people express interest in, enjoy, and understand may be too difficult for individual reading, but can be read out loud by the teacher. Quality picture books that may appear to be suitable for a younger audience can stimulate discussion and writing, and art and drama projects with older students.

> Locate one or two pieces of children's literature that have been used or recommended for students in a grade level of your choice. Assess how well this resource(s) meets each of the three criteria mentioned by the author. Would you "Highly recommend," "Recommend," or "Not recommend" this book(s)? Explain the reasons for your rating.

Categories of Literature

Four categories of literature for children are particularly powerful in promoting the aesthetic dimension in social studies. These are contemporary realistic fiction, historical fiction and biography, folk literature, and poetry. The nature and criteria for selecting suitable titles of each for use in the classroom are explored separately.

CONTEMPORARY REALISTIC FICTION

Contemporary realistic fiction can make a powerful contribution to a social studies program because of the nature of the story and the topics explored. Contemporary realistic fiction is imaginative writing that accurately reflects life as it could be lived today, including its opportunities, challenges, and values (Huck and Kiefer 2004). Through contemporary realistic fic-

ANNUAL LISTINGS OF EXEMPLARY LITERATURE FOR CHILDREN

The NCSS annual listing, "Notable Children's Trade Books in the Field of Social Studies," appears in their journal, *Social Education*. The books are grouped in subject categories such as biography, memoir and diary, contemporary issues, folk tales, legends and myths, geography, people, place, social interactions and relationships, world history, and culture. While many of the titles could be placed under more than one category, the review panel of teachers and other professionals from both NCSS and the Children's Book Council have categorized the books in ways they see as most useful in social studies education. The criteria for selecting the literature on this yearly list reflect literary and aesthetic qualities and social studies concerns. Their criteria for selection include: written primarily for children in grades K–8; emphasize human relations; represent a diversity of groups and are sensitive to a broad range of cultural experiences; present an original theme or a fresh slant on a traditional topic; are easily readable and of high literary quality; and have a pleasing format and, where appropriate, illustrations that enrich the text (*Social Education* 2004). IRA annual listings appear in their publication, *The Reading Teacher*, and the books are selected for literary and aesthetic qualities, as well as for the potential for use across the curriculum.

tion, young people may experience the social issues of our times in relation to growing up, coping with the problems of the human condition, and living in a diverse world. Through such literature, young people experience models, both good and bad, that may assist them in making sense of their own life experiences and, ultimately, of the human condition. Contemporary realistic fiction has changed dramatically in the last thirty years in its depiction of life. Studies of young people's preferences consistently show it to be the most popular category of story (Huck and Kiefer 2004). This category of book is often controversial and is closely scrutinized for bias and stereotyping because its realistic content addresses issues such as family and peer relationships and changes, developing sexuality, physical and mental disabilities, aging and death, and ethnic and racial diversity.

Multicultural literature is one type of contemporary realistic fiction and deserves particular attention in social studies. There continues to be debate surrounding the definition of the term multicultural literature (Cai and Bishop 1994). Bainbridge and Pantaleo suggest that "literature can be considered multicultural today when it contains a central character, plot, theme, setting, or style that is culturally or socially diverse in nature" (1999, 114). Contemporary multicultural literature provides young people with opportunities to enhance their self-concepts and to understand and develop pride in their own cultural heritage. It also provides opportunities for experiencing cultures other than their own in ways that foster respect, appreciation, and sensitivity.

Multicultural literature should meet the previously discussed general criteria for literary and aesthetic value, as well as specific criteria for both text and illustrations. Cultural accuracy is a major criterion in selection. Since no single book can portray the full range of experience in a culture, it is important to provide a collection that portrays members of a culture in a wide spectrum of occupations, educational backgrounds, living conditions, and lifestyles. Young people need to understand that within any culture there is diversity. Illustrations should reveal differences in individual appearances while portraying distinctive characteristics of a group or race. Stereotyping of appearance, artifacts, and occupations in the text and illustrations should be avoided. Huck and Kiefer (2004, 23) offer a set of guidelines for evaluating multicultural literature and suggest that the term "literature of diversity" might provide an alternative to the term multicultural literature that would help us broaden our understanding of the term culture. Authors of contemporary realistic fiction are increasingly sensitive to such stereotyping and the number of books that positively and fairly depict our diverse population is increasing. Historical realistic fiction and traditional literature such as folk tales present cultures and ethnic groups from views and values of times past and are considered biased and stereotypical when evaluated by criteria for selection of contemporary multicultural fiction. However, these forms should not be eliminated from classrooms when they may actually be historically authentic or true to a traditional genre. Issues related to historical fiction and folk tales are discussed separately in this chapter.

HISTORICAL FICTION AND BIOGRAPHY

Historical fiction and biography are categories of literature for children that are in particular demand in social studies. Although neither of these are as popular with young readers as contemporary realistic fiction is, there are many outstanding books available that not only enhance social studies but also expand young people's experiences with a category of literature that they may not choose on their own. Historical fiction and biography draw upon both fact and imagination. Historical fiction encompasses "all realistic stories that are set in the past" (Huck and Kiefer 2004, 484) and depends on the author's ability to present the facts of the past accurately while also being able to speculate imaginatively on what it was like to live during that time. Biography is a life story that reads like fiction but centres on facts and events that can be docu-

mented. Huck and Kiefer suggest that the best biographies "combine accurate information and fine writing in a context that children enjoy—the story that really happened" (588). Both historical fiction and biography embed the facts that young people encounter in social studies textbooks within the context of human emotions. As discussed previously, this elicits an aesthetic response that enables the content to be experienced on a more personal dimension.

Historical fiction helps young people develop a sense of what history is and a feeling of continuity as they realize through story that their lives and times are linked individually and collectively to past lives and times. This linking of past to present helps young people see themselves as part of a continuum of human experience; the current way of life is a result of the past, and will have an impact on our way of life in the future. Historical fiction offers vicarious experience of past conflicts, accomplishments, tragedies, and high points along the journey of what it means to be human. Comparisons with the present are inevitably created, and conflicting points of view on issues are presented. Through the aesthetic experience of historical fiction, young people learn that while change is inevitable there are certain aspects of being human that remain constant through time. Our interconnectedness as a human community is reinforced.

In selecting historical fiction, the first consideration, as discussed previously, is aesthetic quality—that it engages us in story. There are several other considerations and issues in the selection and use of historical fiction. While the factual details should be accurate and authentic, they should be background to the story, blended with the fiction. At the same time, contradictions and distortions of the actual record of history must be avoided. In addition to accurate and authentic portrayal of the facts, the story must also reflect the values and spirit of the times as accurately as possible. Huck and Kiefer state, "historical fiction can't be made to conform to today's more enlightened point of view concerning women or minorities or knowledge of medicine" (2004, 485). Teachers have a rich opportunity to help students examine the values and attitudes of today in light of those reflected in historical fiction. The language of the times also reflects values and attitudes. While authenticity of language is important in historical fiction, some vocabulary used in previous times is offensive by today's standards. Derogatory and demeaning labels for particular people and cultural groups are examples of language that may have been used in the past but is unacceptable today. The use of these labels in historical fiction is helpful in understanding characters and events of the past provided they accurately and authentically reflect the values and attitudes of the times. Young people should be taught to respond to these labels in the context of the past and make links to the present, while appreciating the hurt and damage that derogatory and demeaning labels inflict. In this way, another essential feature of good historical fiction is realized—insight into the problems of today, as well as those of the past, is stimulated.

A final consideration when including historical fiction in social studies relates to recognizing that there are many and varied points of view on the issues and events of the past as well as the present. The use of different pieces of historical fiction on a particular topic or event can assist young people in recognizing that there is never only one point of view on any historical event. Events such as the Riel Rebellion need to be understood from the perspectives of the Métis and other Native peoples, as well as from the perspectives of the Canadian government and European settlers. The perspectives of women have often been ignored in Canadian history, as well as the perspectives of Native peoples, Asian Canadians, and other cultural groups. As discussed previously in this chapter in relation to Banks' hierarchical model, in order for literature to make a meaningful contribution to social studies, it must be incorporated at the transformative and social action levels. In terms of historical fiction, this may require using multiple pieces of literature on any historical event in order to present the event from the points of view of the various peoples and cultures involved.

FOLK LITERATURE

Folk literature, also termed traditional literature, is another category of literature that can have a profound impact on social studies because it is "literature derived from the human imagination to explain the human condition" (Huck and Kiefer 2004, 237). Folk tales, fables, myths, epics, and legends are included in this category of literature, which many consider the foundation of the understandings about the human condition that are reflected in modern literature. Folk literature derives from oral tradition as human beings sought to explain themselves and their world—in short, it is oral history. Bruno Bettelheim (1976), noted child psychologist, suggests in his book *The Uses of Enchantment: The Meaning and Importance of Folktales* that there is more to be learned from this literature about our inner problems and possible solutions to our predicaments than from any other type of story that a child can comprehend. Folk literature can provide insights into inherent cultural values and beliefs, as well as into human motivations and inner feelings. It can have a profound impact in social studies because it engages young people with universal patterns of experience.

Folk literature is popular with young people because the engaging stories demand full use of the imagination. They tend to be short, fast-moving, concrete, and deal with the imponderables of life such as truth, beauty, good, evil, and justice. They often include inspirational concepts such as courage,

nobility of character, accomplishment, tenderness, and optimism. Folk literature is a compelling resource because it deals with universal issues and problems of daily life that have embedded within them ethical and moral dimensions.

Every culture has folk literature that can provide insights into the beliefs, values, jokes, lifestyles, and histories of that culture. In this way, folk literature can help young people understand other cultures. Because similar types of stories can be traced from country to country and continent to continent, a cross-cultural study of folk literature can help young people see universal patterns that show the similarities in our experiences of being human. Cinderella-type stories are a good example of folk literature that appears in many versions across many cultures. Huck and Kiefer (2004) list a number of cross-cultural folk tale versions as well as cross-cultural motifs, for example, the motif of magical powers that appears in folk literature from many cultures.

Folk literature has been criticized for being violent, sexist, and even ageist (sorcerers and witches are often portrayed as old men and women). But, as previously suggested, experts in the area of literature for young people maintain that folk literature should not be eliminated for being true to its genre. As with historical fiction that is authentic for the historical period, folk literature must be introduced as stories that present cultures, views, and values from times long past.

POETRY

Poetry is a category of literature that can enrich the social studies program because the use of language is particularly vivid, intense, and aesthetically evocative. Contemporary poetry for young people often reflects experiences of hurt, fear, and sadness, as well as experiences of happiness, satisfaction, and expectation. In social studies, poetry can be introduced in conjunction with prose. Huck and Kiefer provide one listing of thematically arranged poetry/prose connections that include themes such as family, death/loss, sibling rivalry, relationships, courage, and holocaust/war (2004, 394–396). Poetry in social studies must be presented as an aesthetic experience. Poetry that is too difficult, sentimental, or abstract is to be avoided as are required memorization and detailed analysis (391). Social studies teachers can deepen learning and foster delight in poetry by selecting contemporary poems that reflect familiar experiences and humour and that employ poetic forms such as narrative verse, limericks, and rhymes.

Responding to Literature from an Aesthetic Stance

Throughout this chapter, I have stressed that literature should be incorporated into a social studies program to evoke an aesthetic response—to stir a feeling of affinity with the human condition, to capture our hearts and imaginations as well as our minds, and to connect us to ourselves and others. In this section, I outline an approach to responding aesthetically to literature. In language arts, engaging young people with literature in this way is called a reader-response perspective. In reader-response, the major focus is on reading the literature for its own sake. This stance encourages engagement, personal involvement, and connection with the literature, and the use of personal response to build further interpretive response (Tompkins and McGee 1993). Although not widely held by social studies educators, this stance towards literature has receiving increased recognition and attention within social studies (Lamme 1994, Kornfeld 1994, Koeller 1996, Mathis 2001).

We can support students' aesthetic response to literature in social studies by creating three kinds of opportunities:

- experiencing the literature aesthetically;
- responding personally;
- revisiting the piece in ways that enable personal response to be connected to broader concepts, issues, and values.

EXPERIENCING THE LITERATURE AESTHETICALLY

Whether young people personally read the stories, poems, and novels, or listen to them, literature related to social studies topics and issues should first be encountered whole, not in parts or in fragments reproduced in textbooks. That is, literature should be engaged in aesthetically—its flow and complexity should not be interrupted by predetermined questions, probes, and activities. In this way, young people can experience and respond to literature for the sheer joy and pleasure it evokes.

RESPONDING PERSONALLY

Responding to literature aesthetically means acknowledging and valuing the personal connections, meanings, and questions young people construct as they read and listen to stories and poems. Students will respond differently to the same piece of literature depending on age, life experience, and literary and reading experience. Answering other people's questions, taking someone else's perspective, and aiming for someone else's purposes do not facilitate aesthetic response. Our role as teachers is to enable young people to express their responses

and then to revisit the literature with a range of activities that deepen and enrich personal meanings by connecting them to understandings about other people and the world. Tompkins and McGee (1993, 137) suggest that aesthetic reading is stimulated by questions that focus on personal meaning:

- What did the story or poem remind you of?
- What images came to mind as you read?
- What were your feelings as you read?
- What do you think?

Questions such as these provide opportunities to express personal responses in conversations and in expressive writing such as journal writing. Although the sharing of personal responses should never be forced, individual meaning is enriched by hearing the range and diversity of responses evoked by a piece of literature. Where young people feel that their personal responses are valued by the teacher and classmates, most of them, over time, will want to share personal meanings and connections.

REVISITING THE PIECE

After young people express their personal responses to literature, it is important to "revisit" the piece. Revisiting experiences are defined by their relevance to students' interests and questions. This means allowing for student choices in how to engage with the piece. Revisiting experiences are characterized by active learning and open-endedness and by their ability to reflect that "inner experience of art" evoked by the piece. While the possibilities for this type of experience are almost endless, they include art and media, writing and reading, collecting and constructing, drama and talk, and singing and movement.[2]

The highlighted text illustrates the three phases of an aesthetic response for primary and intermediate level literature.

Conclusion

Social studies is about the human condition in all its complexity, and literature enables young people to access that complexity. Literature should not be used as a social studies textbook. "In social studies classes, literature is a work of art enabling the study of character issues and relationships between persons sharing contexts or ideas" (Koeller 1996, 102). The role of literature in social studies is to evoke the aesthetic response—to illuminate, inspire, inform perspective, and educate the heart as well as the mind. Promoting the aesthetic experience through the use of literature in social studies is necessary for the full development of humane and responsible citizens.

SAMPLE AESTHETIC RESPONSE (K–3)
THE NEW LAND: A FIRST YEAR ON THE PRAIRIE

This beautiful Canadian piece of historical fiction, written by Marilynn Reynolds and illustrated by Stephen McCallum (1997), details a family's journey by boat, train, and wagon to their new home on the prairies and describes their first year there. The story begins in the springtime as the family leaves the old country. It takes us along with them through their long voyage, and we accompany them as the locate their homestead's iron stake, find water, build a house, and survive their first winter. As spring comes to the prairies the family plants apple trees "that would bloom every spring, just like the trees they had left behind."

Purpose

- To experience what it might have been like for one family who moved to the western prairies from the old country.

Experiencing the story

- Prior to reading the book, read the title to students and show them the cover of the book (an illustration of the family on their ox-drawn wagon). Ask them what they think this story might be about and how the title and picture makes them think this.
- Ask if any of them has ever moved to another country or province and how they felt. Alternatively, they could be asked to speculate on how they might feel if they did move. Ask students to listen to the story and imagine what it would have been like for the children in the story.
- Read the book through once without interrupting the flow of the text, even to show the pictures. Read the book a second time and show students the stunning pictures that complement the text on each page, giving them ample time to enjoy and comment on the details.

Responding personally

- Personal response to the book will have begun in the form of questions and comments students have as they listen to the story and look at the illustrations. Questions that facilitate personal response may include:
    - Did the story remind you of anything that has happened to you or that has happened in another story that you know?
    - What was the most significant or important part of the story for you and why?
    - What feelings did you have as you listened to the story? Why?
- Alternatively, students could be asked to write in their journals in response to one of these questions or more generally on what they liked about or learned from the story.

Revisiting the story

- Invite students to recreate the sequence of the story in a series of tableaux representing:
    - the voyage by sea
    - the ox-cart journey across the prairie
    - finding the iron stake on their homestead
    - finding water
    - building a house
    - surviving the winter
    - the arrival of spring

Divide students into seven groups and assign each group the task of creating a "frozen picture" or tableau of one of the scenes. Students may use facial expressions, placement of body, gestures, and stances to convey the scene. Give students enough time to discuss the aspect of the story their tableau will represent and how they will achieve this, and to prepare their expression, placement, and stance. When they are ready each group "freezes" in their picture (that is, no talking, no movement) and the rest of the groups observe. The teacher may ask the observing students to comment on what the scene shows and how this is conveyed.

- Have students choose from the following revisiting possibilities:
    - Write an "I" poem from the viewpoint of the father, mother, the boy, John, or the little girl, Annie. For example:

        I am Annie, a little girl.
        I am scared to leave my friends.
        I am only six years old.
        I was sick for fourteen days on the boat.
        I loved the train ride to the prairie.

    - Draw a picture that interprets the story or some aspect of it.
    - Create a collage of words and/or pictures that represents the experiences of the pioneer family in the story.
    - Construct a "soddie" like the first home of the family.
    - Read another book, informational story, or poem about pioneer family life.

SAMPLE AESTHETIC RESPONSE (GRADES 4–8)
GHOST TRAIN

This award-winning Canadian piece of historical fiction, written by Paul Yee and illustrated by Harvey Chan, won the Governor General's Literary Award in 1996 and the Amelia Frances Howard-Gibbon Illustrator's Award in 1997. Through the story of the love between a daughter and her father, readers get a glimpse of the building of the Canadian railway from the perspective of the Chinese labourers, many of whom lost their lives during the construction of the railway through the mountains of British Columbia. The author and illustrator, both Chinese Canadians, provide an insider perspective on Chinese-Canadian history and culture. In the story, Choon-yi comes to Canada to join her father, who has been working on building the railroad. When she arrives, she learns that her father has been killed in a railway accident. Choon-yi, a gifted artist, attempts to paint a train as a memorial to her father. The night before she is to return to China, her father appears before her in a dream and Choon-yi then begins a fantastical journey through which she glimpses the hardships of the Chinese railroad workers. The faces of the many dead workers become part of Choon-yi's painting, which her father instructs her to take home to China and burn so that the souls of the men may "sail on the four winds" and find their way home. This is a complex story and the teacher will need to preview the book and be alert for issues that might be sensitive in his or her particular classroom.

Purpose
- To experience what the building of the Canadian railway might have been like from the perspective of one Chinese labourer and his daughter.

Experiencing the story
- Prior to reading the book, read the title to students and show them the front and back covers of the book (on the front, an illustration of a Chinese girl on a railroad track holding a stick of burning incense and on the back, an illustration of a train engine and two figures, the same girl and a man). Ask them what they think this story might be about and what in the title and pictures make them think this.
- Ask students if any have a parent who has ever gone to a different city, province, or country to work while the rest of the family stayed home. Some students may wish to share how they felt and what this experience was like for them and their family. Ask the students to listen to the story of Choon-yi, the young girl in the story, and her father who decided to leave his home in China and come to Canada to work on the building of the railway and imagine how this decision changed their lives.
- Read the book through once without interrupting the flow of the text. Read the book a second time and give the students ample time to look at, savour, and comment upon the stunning illustrations that complement the text.

Responding personally
- Personal response to the book will have begun in the form of questions and comments students have as they listen to the story and look at the illustrations. Questions that facilitate personal response may include:
  - Did the story remind you of anything that has happened to you or that has happened in another story that you know?
  - What was the most significant or important part of the story for you and why?
  - What feelings did you have as you listened to the story? Why?
- Alternatively, students could be asked to write in their journals in response to one of these questions or more generally on what they liked or learned from the story. Students who wish to could be given the opportunity to share some of what they wrote with class members or a smaller group.

Revisiting the story
Following are a number of revisiting possibilities from which to choose. Tableaux and readers' theatre are powerful whole-class strategies that are very motivating to many students in this age group.
- Recreate the sequence of the story in a series of tableau such as these or others that the students may choose:
  - the father's decision to leave China for work in Canada building the railroad
  - Choon-yi arriving in Canada and learning of her father's death
  - Choon-yi painting the train
  - the ghost train journey
  - the painting arriving home in China

Divide the students into the same number of groups as there are scenes. Each group must create a "frozen picture" or tableau of one of the scenes. Students may use facial expressions, placement of body, gestures, and stances to convey the scenes. Give the students enough time to discuss the aspect of the story their tableau will represent and how they will achieve this, and to prepare their expressions, placements, and stances. When they are ready each group "freezes" in their picture (that is, no talking, no movement) and the rest of the groups observe. The teacher may ask the observing students to comment on what the scene shows and how this is conveyed. A "thoughts in the head" strategy may also be used. While students are in their tableau, the teacher touches a character in the scene on the shoulder. At this time, the student, in the role of the character, says the thoughts that are going through his or her mind. The student may remain silent if he or she does not wish to speak. For example, in the scene where Choon-yi's father leaves China, one of the characters might be Choon-yi. During the "thoughts in the head" strategy, the student

continued on next page

who is Choon-yi might say, "Oh, how I will miss my father. I am scared that he is going so far away. What will happen to him? What will happen to our family?"

- Assist the students to prepare a readers' theatre script from part or all of the story. In the readers' theatre format, the emphasis is on oral reading of the script, not memorization of it. The script is based on the story and can be a combination of wording from the actual story, as well as rewritten portions of the original text. In a readers' theatre script for *Ghost Train,* there would be two main characters who speak (Choon-yi and her father) and a narrator. More dialogue could be scripted, for example, for the mother and railroad official, as well as dialogue created for some of the Chinese railroad workers on the ghost train. In the readers' theatre, students practise and then read their parts. Voice, gesture, and facial expressions are used to communicate the story as it is read.

- Draw scenes, characters, or interpretations from the story. The style of the illustrator could be examined for technique.
- Retell the story or a portion of the story by writing a personal journal, with various entries, from the point of view of Choon-yi or her father.
- Find a "factual" account of the building of the Canadian railway. For example, consult the *Canadian Encyclopedia* (www.histori.ca). Compare the information on the Chinese workers in the factual account with that presented in *Ghost Train.* Students may also wish to examine the photograph of the Last Spike, which celebrated the completion of the railway, and discuss who is in the photograph and who is absent.
- Read another piece of historical fiction, an informational book, or a poem about the building of the Canadian railway.

The aesthetic value of children's literature depends in part on its ability to bring students inside the lives of others and to reflect on this experience. Select a piece of children's literature that you already know and describe a few activities that you might plan for students that would help them powerfully engage in this experience.

ENDNOTES

1 Although these listings and articles originate in the United States, many of the titles and ideas are applicable to Canadian social studies. Teacher librarians, public librarians, and school district and professional associations can provide local and provincial listings of available literature for use in social studies. The April, 1992 issue of *The Reading Teacher* featured a column exclusively on Canadian literature for children and young people and cited organizations such as the Canadian Children's Book Centre which publishes an annual listing of the best Canadian books published for children. Bainbridge and Pantaleo (1999), in their text on using literature in the Canadian elementary classroom, highlight Canadian authors, illustrators, and award-winning Canadian books, many of which have a place in the social studies program.

2 Huck and Kiefer (2004), Hoyt (1992), and Tompkins and McGee (1993) provide outstanding descriptions of a wide range of specific revisiting experiences to engage young people. Lamme (1994), Kornfeld (1994), and Koeller (1996) provide examples of personal response and revisiting experiences related to various social studies topics.

REFERENCES

Bainbridge, J. and S. Pantaleo. 1999. *Learning with literature in the Canadian elementary classroom.* Edmonton, AB: University of Alberta Press and Duval House Publishing.

Banks, J.A. 1989. Integrating the curriculum with ethnic content: Approaches and guidelines. In *Multicultural education: Issues and perspectives,* ed. J.A. Banks and C.A.M. Banks, 189–207. Boston: Allyn and Bacon.

Bettelheim, B. 1976. *The uses of enchantment.* New York: Knopf.

Bieger, E.M. 1996. Promoting multicultural education through a literature-based approach. *Reading Teacher* 49 (4): 308–311.

Cai, M. 2002. *Multicultural literature for children and young adults: Reflections on critical issues.* Westport, CT: Greenwood Press.

Cai, M. and R. Bishop. 1994. Multicultural literature for children: Towards a clarification of the concept. In *The need for story: Cultural diversity in classroom and community,* ed. A. Haas Dyson and C. Genishi, 57–71. Urbana, IL: National Council of Teachers of English.

Coerr, Eleanor. 1977. *Sadako and the Thousand Paper Cranes.* New York: G.P. Putnam's Sons.

Finazzo, D. 1997. *All for the children: Multicultural essentials of literature.* Albany, NY: Delmar Publishing (ITP).

Harris, V., ed. 1997. *Using multiethnic literature in the K–8 classroom.* Norwood, MA: Christopher Gordon Publishers.

Hoyt, L. 1992. Many ways of knowing: Using drama, oral interactions, and the visual arts to enhance reading comprehension. *Reading Teacher* 45 (8): 580–584.

Huck, C. and B. Kiefer, with S. Hepler and J. Hickman. 2004. *Children's literature in the elementary school,* 8th ed. New York: McGraw-Hill.

Koeller, S. 1996. Multicultural understanding through literature. *Social Education* 60 (2): 99–103.

Kornfeld, J. 1994. Using fiction to teach history: Multicultural and global perspectives of World War II. *Social Education* 58 (5): 281–286.

Lamme, L.L. 1994. Stories from our past: Making history come alive for children. *Social Education* 58 (3): 159–164.

Mathis, J. 2001. Respond to stories with stories: Teachers discuss multicultural literature. *Social Studies* 92 (4): 155–160.

McKay, R. 1995. Using literature in social studies: A caution. *Canadian Social Studies* 29 (3): 95–96.

Orr, J. 1995. *Classroom as community.* Unpublished doctoral dissertation, University of Alberta, Edmonton.

Pradl, G.M. 1991. Reading literature in a democracy: The challenge of Louise Rosenblatt. In *The experience of reading: Louise Rosenblatt and reader-response theory*, ed. J. Clifford, 23–46. Portsmouth, NH: Boynton/Cook.

Ramirez, G. and J.L. Ramirez. 1994. *Multiethnic children's literature.* Albany, NY: Delmar.

Reynolds, M. and S. McCallum, illus. 1997. *The new land: A first year on the prairie.* Victoria, BC: Orca.

Rosenblatt, L. 1991. Literature—S.O.S.! *Language Arts* 68 (6): 444–448.

Sullivan, J. 1996. Real people, common themes: Using trade books to counter stereotypes. *Social Education* 60 (7): 399–401.

Tompkins, G. and L. McGee. 1993. *Teaching reading with literature.* New York: Macmillan.

Yee, P. and H. Chan, illus. 1996. *Ghost train.* Toronto, ON: Groundwood Books.

Zarillo, J. 1994. *Multicultural literature, multicultural teaching.* Orlando, FL: Harcourt Brace Jovanovich.

SUPPLEMENTAL READINGS

Literature in social studies (general)

Alter, G., ed. 1995. Varieties of literature and elementary social studies. Special issue, *Social Studies and the Young Learner* 8 (2).

Billig, E. 1977. Children's literature as a springboard to content areas. *Reading Teacher* 30 (8): 855–859.

Combs, M. and J.D. Beach. 1994. Stories and storytelling: Personalizing the social studies. *Reading Teacher* 47 (6): 464–471.

Cullinan, B.E., M.C. Scala, and V.A. Schroder. 1995. *Three voices: An invitation to poetry across the curriculum.* York, ME: Stenhouse.

Eeds, M. and D. Wells. 1991. Talking, thinking, and cooperative learning: Lessons learned from listening to children talk about books. *Social Education* 55 (2): 134–137.

Farris, P.J. and D.J. Fuhler. 1994. Developing social studies concepts through picture books. *Reading Teacher* 47 (5): 380–386.

Fredericks, A.D. 1991. *Social studies through children's literature: An integrated approach.* Englewood, CO: Teacher Ideas Press.

———. 2000. *More social studies through children's literature: An integrated approach.* Englewood, CO: Libraries Unlimited.

Friedman, A.A. and C.A. Cataldo. 2002. Characters at crossroads: Reflective decision makers in contemporary Newbery books. *Reading Teacher* 56 (2): 102–112.

Gramlich, K. and J. Bainbridge. 2001. Listening to children learning: Discovering Canada through picture storybooks. *Teacher-Librarian Today* 7 (2): 32–38.

Hennings, D.G. 1982. Reading picture storybooks in the social studies. *Reading Teacher* 36 (3): 284–289.

Krey, D.M. 1998. *Children's literature in social studies: Teaching to the standards.* Washington, DC: National Council for the Social Studies.

Kurkjian, C., N. Livingston, and Y. Siu-Runyan. 2003/4. Building text sets from the Notable Books for a Global Society Lists. *Reading Teacher* 57 (4): 390–398.

Long, T.W. and M.K. Gove. 2003/4. How engagement strategies and literature circles promote critical response in a fourth-grade, urban classroom. *Reading Teacher* 57 (4): 350–361.

McGowan, M.J. and J.H. Powell. 1996. An annotated bibliography of resources for literature-based instruction. *Social Education* 60 (4): 231–232.

McGowan, T., guest ed. 1996. Telling the story of citizenship. Theme issue. *Social Education* 60 (4).

National Council for the Social Studies. 1998. Children's literature and social studies. Theme issue. *Social Education* 62 (4).

Needham, R.L. and C. Sage. 1991. Intermediate children and notable social studies picture books. *Social Studies and the Young Learner* 4 (2): 11–12.

Pantaleo, S. 2000. Canadian picture books in social studies instruction. *Canadian Social Studies*, 34 (3), 48–52.

Rosen, H. 1986. The importance of story. *Language Arts* 63 (3): 226–237.

Roser, N.L. and S. Keehn. 2002. Fostering thought, talk, and inquiry: Linking literature and social studies. *Reading Teacher* 55 (5): 416–26.

Waters, S.D. 1999. Children's literature: A valuable resource for the social studies classroom. *Canadian Social Studies* 33 (3): 80–83.

Woll, C.B. 1991. Support resources for whole language lovers. *Social Studies and the Young Learner* 4 (2): 26–27.

Zarnowski, M. and A.F. Gallagher. eds. 1993. *Children's literature and social studies: Selecting and using notable books in the classroom.* Washington, DC: National Council for the Social Studies.

Contemporary realistic fiction (general)

Banaszak, R.A. and M.K. Banaszak. 1997. Trade books for reducing violence. *Social Education* 61 (5): 270–271.

Barnes, B.R. 1991. Using children's literature in the early anthropology curriculum. *Social Education* 55 (1): 17–18.

Gallagher, A.F. 1991. Peace (and war) in children's literature. *Social Studies and the Young Learner* 4 (2): 22–23.

Hoffbauer, D. and Prenn, M. 1996. A place to call one's own: Choosing books about homelessness. *Social Education* 60 (3): 167–169.

Houser, N.O. 1999. Critical literature for the social studies: Challenges and opportunities for the elementary classroom. *Social Education* 63 (4): 212–215.

McCall, A.L. and M.P. Ford. 1998. Why not do something? Literature as a catalyst for social action. *Childhood Education* 74 (3): 130–136.

McGowan, T., M. McGowan, and R. Lombard. 1994a. Children's literature: Empowering young citizens for social action. *Social Studies and the Young Learner* 7 (1): 30–33.

———. 1994b. Children's literature: Social education as the curriculum integrator: The case of the environment. *Social Studies and the Young Learner* 6 (3): 20–22.

Owens, W.T. and L.S. Nowell. 2001. More than just pictures: Using picture story books to broaden young learners' social consciousness. *Social Studies* 92 (1): 33–40.

Rule, A. and J. Atkinson. 1994. Choosing picture books about ecology. *Reading Teacher* 47 (7): 586–91.

Reed, C.A. 1992. Children's literature and antiracist education: A language-planning project. *Alberta Teachers' Association Multicultural Education Journal* 10 (2): 12–19.

Social Education. 2004. Notable children's trade books in the field of social studies. May/June. 1–15.

Yenika-Agbaw, V. 1997. Taking children's literature seriously: Reading for pleasure and social change. *Language Arts* 74 (6): 446–53.

Contemporary realistic fiction (multicultural)

Au, K.H. 1993. *Literacy instruction in multicultural settings.* Orlando, FL: Harcourt Brace Jovanovich.

Bainbridge, J., S. Pantaleo, and M. Ellis. 1999. Multicultural picture books: Perspectives from Canada. *Social Studies* 90 (4): 183–189.

Bieger, E.M. 1996. Promoting multicultural education through a literature-based approach. *Reading Teacher* 49 (4): 308–311.

Finazzo, D. 1997. *All for the children: Multicultural essentials of literature.* Albany, NY: Delmar.

Galda, L. 1992. Exploring cultural diversity. *Reading Teacher* 45 (6): 452–460.

Gillespie, C., J. Powell, N. Clements, and R. Swearingen. 1994. A look at the Newbery Medal books from a multicultural perspective. *Reading Teacher* 48 (1): 40–50.

Hillard, L.L. 1995. Defining the "multi-" in "multicultural" through children's literature. *Reading Teacher* 48 (8): 728–729.

Koeller, S. 1996. Multicultural understanding through literature. *Social Education* 60 (2): 99–103.

Madigan, D. 1993. The politics of multicultural literature for children and adolescents: Combining perspectives and conversations. *Language Arts* 70 (3): 168–176.

Mathis, J.B. 1999. Multicultural literature: Mirror and window on experience. *Social Studies and the Young Learner* 11 (3): 27–30.

Mikkelsen, N. 1984. A place to go to: International fiction for children. *Canadian Children's Literature,* 35/36, 64–68.

Pang, V.O., C. Colvin, M. Tran, and R.H. Barba. 1992. Beyond chopsticks and dragons: Selecting Asian-American literature for children. *Reading Teacher* 46 (3): 216–224.

Ramirez, G. and J.L. Ramirez. 1994. *Multiethnic children's literature.* Albany, NY: Delmar.

Rasiniski, T.V. and N.V. Padak. 1990. Multicultural learning through children's literature. *Language Arts* 67 (6): 576–580.

Stewig, J.W. 1992. Using children's books as a bridge to other cultures. *Social Studies* 83 (1): 36–40.

Taylor, S.V. 2000. Multicultural is who we are: Literature as a reflection of ourselves. *Teaching Exceptional Children* 32 (3): 24–30.

Yokota, J. 1993. Issues in selecting multicultural children's literature. *Language Arts* 70 (3): 156–167.

Yokota, J. and the Committee to Revise the Multicultural Booklist. 2001. *Kaleidoscope: A multicultural booklist for grades K–3,* 3rd ed. Urbana, IL: National Council of Teachers of English.

Zarillo, J. 1994. *Multicultural literature, multicultural teaching.* Orlando, FL: Harcourt Brace Jovanovich.

Historical fiction

Caldwell, J.J. 1988. Historical fiction as a modern tool. *Canadian Journal of English Language Arts* 11 (1): 24–32.

Collins, F.M. and J. Graham, ed. 2001. *Historical fiction for children: Capturing the past.* London: David Fulton Publishers.

Danielson, K.E. 1989. Helping history come alive with literature. *Social Studies* 80 (2): 65–68.

Drew, M.A. 1991. Merging history and literature in teaching about genocide. *Social Education* 55 (2): 128–129.

———. 1995. Incorporating literature into a study of the Holocaust: Some advice, some cautions. *Social Education* 59 (6): 354–356.

Erlandson, B. and J. Bainbridge. 2000. Living history through Canadian time-slip fantasy. *Language and Literacy: A Canadian E-journal.* Available at http://educ.queensu.ca/~landl/archives/vol32papers/timeslip.htm.

Freeman, E.B. and L. Levstik. 1988. Recreating the past: Historical fiction in the social studies curriculum. *Elementary School Journal* 88 (4): 330–337.

Galda, L. 1993. Stories of our past: Books for the social studies. *Reading Teacher* 46 (4): 330–338.

Handley, L.M. 1991. Sarah, plain and tall: A model for thematic inquiry. *Social Studies and the Young Learner* 4 (2): 24–25.

Harms, J.M. and L.L. Lettow. 1993. Bridging time and space: Picture books with historical settings. *Social Education* 57 (7): 363–367.

———. 1994. Criteria for selecting picture books with historical settings. *Social Education* 58 (3): 152–154.

Johnson, N.M. and M.J. Ebert. 1992. Time travel is possible: Historical fiction and biography—Passport to the past. *Reading Teacher.* 45 (7): 488–495.

Kazemek, F.E. 1994. Two handfuls of bone and ash: Teaching our children about Hiroshima. *Phi Delta Kappan* 75 (7): 531–534.

Kornfeld, J. 1994. Using fiction to teach history: Multicultural and global perspectives of World War II. *Social Education* 58 (5): 281–286.

Lamme, L.L. 1994. Stories from our past: Making history come alive for children. *Social Education* 58 (3): 159–164.

Levstik, L.S. and K.C. Barton. 2001. *Doing history: Investigating with children in the elementary and middle schools.* Mahwah, NJ: Erlbaum.

Tunnell, M.O. and R. Ammon. 1996. The story of ourselves: Fostering multiple historical perspectives. *Social Education* 60 (4): 212–215.

Folk literature

Hickey, M.G. 1995. Focus on folk tales. *Social Studies and the Young Learner* 8 (2): 13–14.

Spagnoli, C. 1995. These tricks belong in your classroom: Telling Asian trickster tales. *Social Studies and the Young Learner* 8 (2): 15–17.

Taub, D.K. 1984. The endearing, enduring folktale. *Instructor* 94 (4): 61–70.

Wason-Ellam, L. 1988. Making literacy connections: Trickster tales in Canadian literature. *Canadian Journal of English Language Arts* 11 (1): 47–54.

Young, T.A., J. Bruchac, K. Livingston, and C. Kurkjian. 2004. Folk literature: Preserving the storytellers' magic. *Reading Teacher* 57 (8): 782–792.

30 Four Principles of Authentic Assessment

Roland Case

There is a common saying in educational circles: "What is counted counts." This expression implies that the truly important learning objectives are those we assess. Student sensitivity to this maxim is implied by their common refrains: "Is this on the test?" and "Will it be for marks?" Consequently, if we value critical thinking or the ability to apply knowledge in new contexts, then we should be concerned that our assessment practices reflect these goals. Unfortunately, most assignments and tests emphasize recall of information. The effect of this is to signal to students that what really matters is remembering facts.

This shortcoming will not be redressed simply by devoting more attention to assessing other goals. Ironically, many ways in which thinking abilities are currently assessed are self-defeating. The "timed" nature of tests and the "once-over and one-time nature" of many assignments do not invite thoughtful student reflection. Advocates of "higher" standards typically call for raised expectations of student performance and for expanded testing. It is not obvious that these steps enhance student learning. High-achieving students who are motivated by grades may already be trying their best, and may be distracted from genuine learning by heightened fears of not doing well on the test. Lesser-motivated students may be doubly discouraged by raising the "educational bar" even further out of their reach and by constantly reminding them of their inferior performance (Assessment Reform Group 2002, 4). In addition, many important educational goals—such as student responsibility, real-life problem solving, reflection, and empathy—are rarely measured. In the rush to "teach to the test," less time may be devoted to these goals. Numerous research studies suggest that many of our system-wide and classroom-based assessment practices inhibit genuine learning.

Overcoming what many regard as the negative effects of common assessment practices is the driving motive for what is referred to as "authentic assessment." The term "authentic" refers to measuring the real, actual, or genuine thing as opposed to measuring a poor substitute. The aim is to supplement traditional assessment practices with "alternative" approaches that offer more meaningful and productive ways of assessing students (Gronlund and Cameron 2004, 10). Although writers describe authentic assessment in varying ways, three interrelated purposes underlie this movement:

- **Greater "authenticity."** Advocates of assessment reform seek a closer fit between the attributes and abilities actually measured by an assessment device and the educational goals that we most value. Too often we assess what is easiest to measure (for example, whether or not students can remember information) and neglect what is more difficult to assess yet nonetheless important (for example, students' ability to think critically and to use their knowledge to solve realistic problems).

- **Supporting learning.** Advocates of assessment reform are committed to using evaluation to help students learn. Often assessment interrupts or discourages learning. We can enhance learning by making assessment tasks more meaningful, by demystifying the process, and by involving students in assessing their efforts and those of fellow students.

- **Fairness to all students.** Advocates of alternative assessment are concerned that some students are penalized by current assessment practices, not because these students know less, but because of the methods and the conditions under which assessment occurs. For example, some students struggle to communicate what they know under the pressure of a single, timed written examination.

In this chapter, I explore four principles for guiding our assessment practices in more authentic ways:

- Focus assessment on what really matters;
- Ensure that assessments are valid indications of student competence;
- Use assessment to support student learning; and
- Develop assessment practices that use the teacher's time efficiently.

In the two follow-up chapters, I discuss ways of nurturing

student ownership of assessment and suggest how to develop and use assessment strategies to further these principles. Before proceeding with these principles, I invite you to assess an assessment device that I used in my own teaching.

Assessing my Assessment

Years ago, after graduating with my teaching certificate, I proudly developed a marking sheet for a research project my students had just completed. Towards the end of a unit on India, I asked students to select an aspect of India (for example, climate, religion, geography, customs) they wished to pursue though independent research. I instructed them to consult several library resources on the basis of which they were to prepare a written report. The report was to include several visuals (for example, charts, graphs, maps) and, unlike previous efforts, these visuals were to clearly connect to ideas in the text. To discourage mere copying of reports from published sources, students were to submit research notes with their final report. When the project was completed, I evaluated and returned their work with a Research Report Assessment sheet (Figure 30.1) attached to the front of each assignment.

Make a written list of the strengths and weaknesses of my marking sheet. Imagine that I am a student teacher and you are supervising my teaching practicum. Decide the grade you would assign to my assessment practices based on the following scale:

outstanding	A+/A
very good	A-/B+
good	B/B-
satisfactory	C+/C
poor	C-/D
very poor	F

Since developing this assessment device I have asked several hundred pre-service and practising teachers to assess my early effort at assessment. The grades assigned to my marking sheet have ranged the entire spectrum from "outstanding" to "very poor" with the vast majority (approximately 90 per cent of responses) dividing fairly evenly between "good," "satisfactory," and "poor." This variance is cause for some concern. As professionals, how can we have confidence in our assessment practices if there is such latitude in our conclusions about the quality of my marking scheme? This lack of agreement is especially disturbing since our assessments have potentially profound effects on our students. For example, if I was a secondary student and if this assessment was typical of my evaluations, it would have the following consequences:

FIGURE 30.1   RESEARCH REPORT ASSESSMENT

1. Bibliography (1 mark for each book)   /4

2. Notes
       very good (3)
       good (2)
       satisfactory (1)
       poor (0)   /3

3. Charts, maps, drawings, etc.
                      #1   #2   #3
       a) neat:
       b) accurate:
       c) relevant: /9

4. Text
       a) neatness: /2
       b) spelling, grammar, punctuation:
          (1/2 mark off per error)   /5
       c) coverage of major points:
          all (5)
          almost all (4)
          most (3)
          some (2)
          few (1)   /5
       d) well written:
          good (2)
          satisfactory (1)
          poor (0)   /2
                                                /14

5. Comments:

TOTAL   /30

- "Outstanding" would qualify me for university scholarships.
- "Very good" would enable me to attend the university of my choice, but not on scholarship.
- "Good" would allow me to get into a university, but perhaps not my first choice.
- "Satisfactory" would mean I would be lucky to get into a community college.
- "Poor" would prevent me from directly continuing post-secondary studies.
- "Very poor" would require that I repeat the grade.

Although I do not wish to infer too much from my informal survey, it suggests considerable inconsistency in our understanding of what counts as good assessment. As indicated earlier, I believe there are four principles, which if better understood and implemented, would improve this predicament. My present purpose is to explain the implications and importance of the four principles. Although there are other principles and other ways of expressing the ones I suggest, the four principles offer a reasonably comprehensive set of considerations for improving our assessment practices.

At the close of the chapter, I will ask you to revisit your initial assessment of my assessment in light of what I hope will be a clearer, more thorough grasp of these key principles. Just as we should use criteria to assess our students' work, so too should we use the principles of authentic assessment as the basis for judging our assessments. The implicit message in my chapter is that we should neither be satisfied with, nor confident in, our assessments of students' work until we have seriously scrutinized our own assessment practices. Let us now look in turn at the four principles that I recommend as a basis for this assessment.

Focus on What Really Matters

The most significant question to ask ourselves when judging our assessment practices is whether or not we are assessing what really matters. Are the criteria we are using—consciously or not—to judge students' work reflective of the most important educational objectives? As suggested above, what teachers assess has important implications for what students consider important and ultimately what they learn. Do our assessment practices do justice to the breadth and complexity of the goals of social studies? Assessments that are skewed towards a limited range of desired outcomes, for example, outcomes related exclusively to factual knowledge, fail to assess and possibly inadvertently discourage student growth along other desired dimensions. This concern is at the root of much of the criticism of standardized testing. Many standardized tests used to evaluate students, teachers, and schools focus on those curriculum outcomes that are easily measured by machine-scoreable questions. This leaves a considerable gap between the outcomes that schools are expected to promote and the outcomes used to measure school performance. In a study from the University of Wisconsin, the overlap between the curriculum and the test for one subject was just 5 per cent (cited in Simmons 2004, 37). The author suggests that the effect is to undervalue some of the most important life skills such as critical thinking and problem solving.

The most shocking realization when I first had occasion to look back at my marking sheet was the imbalance in my assessment. One-third of the total mark for the project (10 marks out of 30) dealt with mechanics (that is, neatness, spelling, and punctuation). Although these are appropriate criteria to use, it now strikes me as mistaken that I would weigh these

twice as much as I did the content of the report (the extent to which the report addressed the main ideas accounted for only 5 out of 30 marks). Notice the consequences of this kind of weighting: students who knew a lot about their topic, but who did not write in standard English, might fail the assignment. On the positive side, the fact that I placed some value on information gathering (the use of multiple references and on the taking of competent notes) and on content knowledge (that is, the need for students to cover the main points of the topic) showed some sensitivity to the importance of these goals. Regrettably I did not appear to attach any special importance to the students' ability to think about the material they were researching.

Over the course of a unit or term (not necessarily on any given assignment), we should assess for all relevant goals, and the emphasis assigned these goals should reflect their relative importance. Completing what is called a "table of specifications" is one strategy for checking that each goal is weighted appropriately in one's overall assessment plan. At the end of a reporting period, list all the graded assignments and tests. Record in a table similar to Table 30.1 the amount of marks devoted to each goal. In Table 30.1, the five main goals are indicated in the left-hand column, and the different assessment strategies appear across the top of the chart. The column on the far right reports the percentage of marks assigned to each goal: for example, understanding of key concepts is worth 40 per cent of the total marks (160/400). Be prepared for a surprise when you discover the importance you actually attached to the various goals. The actual weighting of marks should be matched against the importance these goals deserve according to the curriculum and your own professional sense of what really matters, given the students you teach. Although not always possible, setting up a table of specifications beforehand, or partway through a term, allows you to make adjustments for any imbalances in the weighting of certain goals.

Provide Valid Indications

A second consideration in authentic assessment is validity. Although validity has a long history as a complex technical term, in the context of authentic assessment it can be defined as a close fit between the kinds of attributes actually measured by an assessment device and the intended educational goals. In simplest terms, an assessment strategy is valid if it actually assesses the outcomes it claims to assess.

My intention with the marking sheet on the research project was to assess students' ability to identify and use multiple sources of information. I now doubt that assigning a mark for each reference in the bibliography measures this ability. Students could score very well on this part of the assignment even if they did not actually use more than one of

TABLE 30.1 SPECIFICATION OF GOALS ASSESSED

UNIT GOALS	ASSESSMENT STRATEGIES						
	Quizzes	Activity sheets	Group project	In-class observation	Research report	TOTAL MARKS	% OF TOTAL MARK
Critical thinking about issues	15	–	–	20	25	60	15
Information gathering	15	–	20	–	25	60	15
Recall of factual information	50	30	–	–	–	80	20
Understanding of key concepts	20	20	70	–	50	160	40
Co-operation with others	–	–	30	10	–	40	10
TOTAL	100	50	120	30	100	400	100

the books listed in their bibliography. For that matter, I could not be sure that students knew how to find books on their topic—perhaps someone had obtained the books for them. My reliance on the number of references in the bibliography was not a valid indicator of students' research abilities. If I wanted to assess the students' ability to locate and find appropriate sources, I should have created a task in the library where students would be expected to retrieve and assess relevant sources. I could have measured their ability to make use of multiple sources by assigning marks to students who cited several sources of relevant information in their final report. The outcome measured in the "coverage of the main points" section of my marking scheme is equally problematic. Students may have written on all the main points without really understanding what they had put down. If I was serious about finding out if they had gained any understanding of the topic, I would have been better advised to ask students to tell me orally in their own words what they had found out.

The importance of validity was first brought home to me when I was preparing my grade 6 students for a day-long field trip. Several weeks before beginning to plan for a picnic lunch on our field trip, we practised answering word problems like the following:

If there are thirty students in the class and students want on average two sandwiches each, how many slices of bread will be required? How many loaves of bread will we need if there are twenty slices of bread in each loaf? What will be the total cost if bread sells for $1.25 per loaf? How much must each student contribute to cover the cost of the bread?

Despite their ability to successfully solve these kinds of word problems (as determined by a quiz), my students were incapable of determining how much money each would have

to bring for lunch on our field trip. They made no connection between the arithmetic we had been doing and the challenge before them. Even after the connection was explained, they were unable to solve the problem. In the word problems I had provided, all of the mathematical "ingredients" had been supplied to them. Not only did they not know the answers to the real-life questions (that is, the number of sandwiches we would want, the number of slices in a loaf, and the actual cost of bread), beyond getting an adult to tell them, they had no idea how they could come up with the answers. This is one of the dangers when assessment is based largely on isolated assignments and quizzes.

Although I had taught my students to solve word problems on costing lunches, I had not taught them how to cost the lunch. As Grant Wiggins suggests, "school tests make the complex simple by dividing it into isolated and simplistic chores—as if the students need not practise the true test of performance, the test of putting all elements together" (1989, 706). My students' mastery of all the requisite competencies involved in this task and their ability to integrate them successfully were tested only when they were charged with planning the actual lunch. Significantly, I would never have realized the gaps in their abilities, and subsequently addressed them, unless I had assigned this "real-life" assessment task. If we do not assess beyond isolated competencies in artificial situations, we are unlikely to know whether students are able to use their knowledge in significant ways.

Another factor affecting validity is the conditions under which the assessment occurs. The use of "surprise" tests and a failure to make clear to students the basis upon which they will be judged may impair students' abilities to show what they actually know. Instead, students may be rewarded for anticipating what the teacher wants. As well, traditional timed tests reward students who perform well in on-the-spot situations and may discriminate against students who are equally knowledgeable but are unable to perform under contrived conditions. A very common concern for validity, especially acute with students whose first language is not English, is that students' answers may be a function of their written fluency and not their understanding of the content. Although this obstacle cannot be completely overcome, there may be ways to mitigate its effects:

- Assignments and questions should be explained orally to students, and perhaps have someone translate the instructions and make frequent use of visual aids and other low vocabulary prompts.
- Whenever feasible, allow students to represent their answers in graphic form, orally, in written point form, or perhaps even in their native tongue.
- Whenever appropriate, offer alternative assignments, reduced expectations, or additional assistance to offset any language impediment.

Besides being careful when developing measures to devise questions or tasks that capture what we intended, validity may also be enhanced by using several devices of different sorts to gather information about student achievement. The point of considering a variety of approaches is to increase the likelihood of finding a valid way to assess the desired outcomes. If, for example, the ability to solve real-life problems is an important goal then, at some point, we should assess the students' ability to act on a real problem and not be satisfied by asking students to list the factors they would consider in a hypothetical context. An observation checklist or rating scale may be particularly effective in assessing student performance in group projects and class presentations. Having students keep a journal while participating in a project or a simulation activity may provide rich information about student attitudes towards themselves and others. For example, while preparing for a class discussion or debate, students might comment on their reflections about expressing and defending their positions, or about working with others.

Use Assessment to Support Learning

Advocates of assessment reform are emphatic about using assessment to enhance learning. The enhanced emphasis on using assessment to support learning is reflected in the distinction between the traditional phrase "assessment of learning" and the more recently introduced notion of "assessment for learning" (Assessment Reform Group 1999, 2). In their review of numerous studies, this group concludes that students would be better motivated and learn more if assessment

practices focussed more on supporting learning than on measuring learning (Assessment Reform Group 2002, 10). More recently, educators are talking about assessment as learning to heighten awareness of the potential to use assessment tasks as opportunities for learning, not simply to provide formative feedback (British Columbia Ministry of Education 2005, 23-24). Self-assessment is an example of an assessment task that is also a learning task as students examine their own work and think through its strengths and shortcomings.

Greater validity of assessment measures is in itself an attempt to use assessment to support learning. As suggested by the example about planning for the field trip lunch, if an assessment does not capture what it is we really value, then we are less likely to know when we have succeeded (or have failed to succeed) in reaching our objective. Only after the real-life task did I realize that my students could not calculate the cost of our lunch. Assessment practices can support learning in at least four other important ways:

- clearly communicate expectations;
- involve students in the assessment process;
- provide helpful feedback on learning; and
- provide opportunities and incentives for students to improve.

COMMUNICATE EXPECTATIONS

If students know clearly what is expected of them they are more likely to succeed at the task. One of the most obvious ways in which I could have used my assessment practices to support learning was by presenting students with the marking sheet before they embarked on the research assignment. As it was, they saw the criteria only after they had completed their report. If my measure had had validity and had focussed on the important goals, I would have been signalling to students what was important and what they were required to do to demonstrate their learning. But because of its flaws, had I distributed my original marking sheet beforehand, unwittingly I would have been encouraging students to attend to the technical dimensions more than the content. The fact that I instructed students to select graphs, charts, and maps that related to their text and that I assessed for this, encouraged students to attend to this feature in their reports.

Students may be even clearer about expectations if they are informed specifically about the "criteria" upon which they will be marked and the importance of those criteria (that is, the number of marks assigned to each criterion) and the "standards" for achievement of these criteria. Because the concepts of criteria and standards are often used interchangeably, let me explain the distinction drawn between these two terms.

Criteria are the features or attributes that provide the grounds for judging quality. Sample criteria include:

- historical accuracy
- originality of ideas
- use of several sources
- clarity of presentation
- depth of answer
- active participation in project
- openness to new ideas
- flow/structure of the paper
- neatness
- spelling accuracy

Standards are the benchmarks, performance levels, or degrees of achievement of a given criterion (that is, "high" and "low" standards). Standards can be binary (for example, correct/incorrect, pass/fail, satisfactory/unsatisfactory) or have multiple levels (for example, A+ to F, outstanding to very weak, well above expectations to not yet meeting expectations). Sample standards for three criteria are listed in Table 30.2.

My grade 6 students might have been better able to succeed had I clearly indicated all the criteria and standards for assessment. When assessing their notes I merely indicated whether they were "very good," "good," and so on, without indicating the basis for this assessment. What criteria was I using? Was it the neatness of the notes? Conciseness? Amount of notes? Or, perhaps all of these? Furthermore, even if students knew the criteria, they may still not know what distinguished a "good" from a "satisfactory" standard of note-taking. And yet, if I wanted them to improve, this is precisely the understanding they require. I did a slightly better job of communicating the criteria and standards for the "main points": my criterion was the amount of coverage and my standards were distinguished by the number of main points covered (for example, all, most, a few). Besides supporting learning, another powerful reason for clearly articulating standards is that it reduces inconsistency and arbitrariness in assessments. I now wonder when I look at the standards I offered for "coverage of main points" if there is any real difference between "almost all" and "most" points and between "some" and a "few" points. If there is no clear distinction between these performance levels, how can I have reliably distinguished among them?

In the spirit of living the principles I preach, I offer in Figure 30.2 detailed descriptions of performance levels or standards for each of the four principles that I offer as the criteria for judging authentic assessments. After you have finished reading about all four of these principles, and have a clear understanding of what each involves, I will ask you to use this assessment rubric to reassess your original judgment of my marking sheet. For the time being, I offer this as an example of a way in which we can support learning by clearly articulating the standards for our assessment criteria. Read my descriptions of each standard and decide if you would recognize what each involves.

TABLE 30.2 SAMPLE STANDARDS

CRITERION	STANDARDS	DESCRIPTIONS OF PERFORMANCE LEVELS
Historical accuracy	excellent	no factual inaccuracies
	good	at most, a few minor factual inaccuracies that do not affect the conclusion
	satisfactory	one major inaccuracy and several minor factual inaccuracies
	unsatisfactory	several or more major factual inaccuracies that completely undermine the conclusion
Depth of answer	in-depth	all main topics are analyzed in a probing and careful manner
	modest depth	although there is evidence of careful analysis, some aspects are not addressed in much depth
	superficial	for the most part, topics are not addressed superficially
Spelling accuracy	excellent	zero errors
	very good	at most 2 errors
	good	between 3 and 5 errors
	satisfactory	between 6 and 9 errors
	poor	10 or more errors

FIGURE 30.2   ASSESSING THE ASSESSMENT

	HIGHLY EVIDENT	MOSTLY EVIDENT	PARTIALLY EVIDENT	COMPLETELY ABSENT
Focusses on the important goals	6 The weighting of marks closely matches the important objectives of the assignment.	4 The weighting of marks generally matches with the important objectives of the assignment.	2 The weighting of marks is out of balance with important objectives of the assignment.	0 The weighting of marks misses or seriously under-represents all the important objectives of the assignment.
Provides valid indications of student ability	6 The assignment and the marking scheme directly measure student ability on all intended outcomes.	4 The assignment and the marking scheme measure in a fairly direct way student ability on important intended outcomes.	2 The assignment and the marking scheme are unlikely to measure student ability on some of the key intended outcomes.	0 The assignment and the marking scheme measure student ability in a superficial, contrived, or distorted manner.
Supports student learning	6 The device very clearly identifies the criteria and standards and provides very helpful feedback for improvement. Has significant potential to reinforce and encourage important student learning.	4 The device is generally clear about the criteria and standards and provides some helpful feedback for improvement. Has some potential to reinforce and encourage student learning in some major areas.	2 The device contains significant gaps or ambiguities in communicating the criteria and standards and offers little helpful feedback for improvement. Key aspects of the assessment fail to reinforce and encourage student learning.	0 The device is very vague or confused about the criteria and standards, and offers no helpful feedback for improvement. Offers nothing to support, and may discourage, significant learning.
Uses teacher time efficiently	3 The assessment and feedback method very efficiently uses teacher time in providing significant information to students.	2 The assessment and feedback method is somewhat efficient in its demands on teacher time relative to the rewards.	1 The assessment and feedback method is somewhat inefficient in its demands on teacher time.	0 The assessment and feedback method requires very extensive teacher time relative to what it communicates.

Outstanding (A⁺/A):	19–21
Very Good (A⁻/B⁺):	16–18
Good (B/B⁻):	12–15
Satisfactory (C⁺/C):	9–11
Poor (C⁻/D):	5–8

Total: /21

Grade:

INVOLVE STUDENTS IN ASSESSMENT

Involving students directly in the assessment process is another way to support learning. The next chapter in this collection, "Building Student Ownership of Assessment," has more to say on each of the following areas for student involvement:

- **Setting criteria and standards.** Joint teacher and student negotiation of the criteria upon which students are to be judged increases student understanding of what is expected and ultimately of their performance in light of these expectations. Students can also be involved in deciding upon standards—by articulating what might be required in order for the work to be regarded as excellent, good, and so on.
- **Creating assessment tasks.** Another way to involve students is by inviting them to assist in developing the tasks upon which they will be assessed.
- **Self- and peer assessment.** Involving students in self- and peer assessment can greatly enhance their learning. The very exercise of assessing their peers on the specific criteria related to the lesson would likely reinforce the students' own understandings of what is expected of them. Furthermore, involving students in assessment encourages students to take greater ownership of their learning. An important dimension of self-assessment is communicating the results to others—either to the teacher, their peers, or parents.

PROVIDE FEEDBACK ON LEARNING

We can enhance learning by helping students see how they might improve. Providing students with useful feedback must go beyond assigning a mark or offering a brief summative comment. For example, in my marking scheme, I provided students, albeit after the fact, with a detailed breakdown of how well they did on each aspect, with a place for general comments. This helped them understand what they did well and where more attention was needed.

Although some students may be concerned exclusively with their mark on an assignment, Paul Black and Dylan Wiliam (1998) have found that this leads to no improvement in student achievement—marks are entirely about assessment of learning, not assessment for learning. In fact, they conclude that grading and other forms of comparative feedback actually get in the way of learning and are especially demotivating for less accomplished students. Because of the negative effects of repeated failure, some educators recommend providing scores only at the end of the grading period when it is necessary to prepare an evaluation report. According to the Assessment Reform Group (2002, 10), ideally teachers should assign marks only if students have a good chance of succeeding. In the interim, students should be provided with abundant feedback and encouragement.

If we want students to improve, our feedback must clearly communicate what has been successfully done, where improvement is needed, and how to do this. A carefully prepared rubric can go a long way in providing this feedback, both in terms of indicating how students have done and what might be done to improve their performance. In my own experience, students benefit most from the use of rubrics when marks are not indicated. The lack of a summative judgment requires them to read the descriptors more carefully and encourages them to believe that it is not too late to improve. Other methods of providing effective feedback include:

- very specific written teacher comments;
- teacher conferences;
- comments by fellow students explaining areas for improvement;
- large and small group discussion of answers; and
- exemplars—samples of high-quality performance—of student work, so long as improvement requires more than simply copying the ideas in the exemplar.

PROVIDE OPPORTUNITIES AND INCENTIVES TO IMPROVE

Where feasible, use assessment to encourage students to learn on their own and to revise and rethink their work. Possible strategies include establishing a habit of assessing key objectives in subsequent units, and making it clear to students that certain abilities will be assessed routinely. Some students may be motivated by supplemental tests or makeup assignments for those who make some effort to improve their understanding. One of my most counter-productive assessment habits as a public school teacher was my penchant for "one-shot" efforts. Rarely did I ask students to seriously revise their work—if work was revisited it was only to tidy up typos or add a missing sentence or two. Now, in my university teaching, I no longer have one-time assignments. In my graduate class, for example, instead of writing three different papers, my students write the same paper three times. The first and second drafts are distributed to everyone in the class for critique. In the first draft, students show largely what they could do before the course. The significant improvement—the deeper, more insightful learning—occurs with the two subsequent revisions where students work through the ideas raised by their colleagues and by me.

Before inviting students to undertake serious revision, we should ensure that they have meaningful input as to how they did initially and what they might do to improve. Since elementary and secondary students may be less motivated to engage in subsequent revisions than are students in graduate school, we must encourage them in this regard:

- Ask students to redo only a part of the original assignment (for example, the two worst [or preferred] answers, or the opening and closing paragraphs of an essay).
- Create additional incentives for revising a draft (for example, revised assignments might be exhibited in a fair, submitted to the newspaper, published in a book, or otherwise shared with adults or other students).
- Comment on but do not mark the initial mandatory draft. Establish that only the revised draft "counts" for marks.
- Ask students weeks or months later to revisit an earlier work to see how much they have progressed in the intervening time.

When encouraging students to learn from feedback, it is not simply a matter of them redoing completed assignments, but also formulating plans to use the lessons learned to improve upcoming projects. For example, we might ask students to identify a learning goal, anticipate an obstacle they might face, and suggest how they might overcome it.

Using Teachers' Time Efficiently

The final, perhaps one might say the bottom-line, criterion of good assessment is efficient use of teacher time. Although efficiency has no direct relationship to authentic assessment, the incredible press on teachers' time means that changes, however desirable, are unlikely to occur if they are more time-consuming. Generally speaking, marking sheets, including the one I developed for the independent research project, are efficient assessment tools. Once familiar with the layout it is easy to complete the sheet quickly because it keeps the assessor focussed and saves having to repeatedly write out the same comments. Rubrics are great savers of marking time, but they require considerable up-front development time. For this reason, I am inclined to develop rubrics for major projects during the year—starting with the one that causes the biggest marking headache—and when I want students to undertake peer or self-assessment.

Clearly articulated criteria and standards, communicated beforehand, increase the likelihood of students providing what the teacher is looking for, and help focus the teacher's attention when marking assignments. Clear expectations reduce the likelihood of protracted discussions with students who complain that they did not know what was required of them.

Student peer and self-assessment can save teacher time provided students are adequately trained in the practice. It

saves time because it means that students are giving each other feedback that otherwise the teacher would have to give. Developing students' abilities to assess their own work and their peers' work may be one of the more efficient "learning" strategies. In my university teaching, I marvel at how much graduate students learn about (and improve upon) their own writing from frequent opportunities to critique the work of fellow students. They are better able to appraise their own writing after noting the similar strengths and weaknesses in others' writing and they benefit considerably from other students' critiques of their own work. But perhaps the biggest efficiency arising from self-assessment comes from a shift in the perceived ownership of learning. When students truly realize that they, and not the teacher, have primary responsibility for the grade they receive, the relationship between student and teacher changes. There is less need for the teacher to chase after the students and drum the information into them. Students acquire more independence, self-reliance, and commitment—and, and as a result, more is learned.

A Final Reflection

Return to your initial assessment of my marking sheet. While reviewing any notes you took, consider the merits and oversights in your earlier thoughts about my device. Use the assessment rubric presented earlier to reassess my marking sheet. What grade do you now think that it is worth? Even if your assessment is largely unchanged, do you now have greater confidence in the grade you assigned? Is it a fairer, more valid assessment? Are you clearer about how you might help me improve my assessment practices? I hope the answer is yes to all these questions, and to one further question: Do you have a better understanding of principles to follow in making your assessment practices more authentic?

Select an assessment device (for example, a quiz, end-of-unit project, an observation checklist) that you have developed or that is included in a teaching resource. Use the rubric "Assessing the Assessment" to evaluate this device. Based on what you have learned about the four principles discussed in this chapter, suggest ways to make the device more authentic.

ACKNOWLEDGMENT

I am grateful to Rosemary Evans of Branksome Hall School for her helpful suggestions when revising this chapter.

REFERENCES

Assessment Reform Group. 1999. *Assessment for learning: Beyond the black box.* Cambridge, UK: University of Cambridge. Available at http://arg.educ.cam.ac.uk/publications.html.

———. 2002. *Testing, motivation and learning.* Cambridge, UK: University of Cambridge. Available at http://arg .educ.cam.ac.uk/publications.html.

Black P. and D. William. 1998. Inside the Black Box: Raising Standards Through Classroom Assessment. *Phi Delta Kappan* 80 (2): 139–148. Available at http://www.pdkintl.org/kappan/kbla9810.htm.

British Columbia Ministry of Education. 2005. *Social Studies 10: Integrated Resource Package 2005* (Response Draft). Victoria, BC: Author.

Gronlund, N.E. and I.J. Cameron. 2004. *Assessment of student achievement* (Canadian edition). Toronto: Pearson Education Canada.

Simmons, N.E. 2004. (De)grading the standardized test. *Education Canada* 44 (3): 37–39.

Wiggins, G. 1989. A true test: Toward more authentic and equitable assessment. *Phi Delta Kappan* 70: 703–713.

31 Building Student Ownership of Assessment

Roland Case

Years ago, I read an article entitled "So, What Did I Get on my Muffin?" The author, a home economics teacher, suggested that this was a common student response to returned assignments (Emblem 1994). The upsetting element of this comment is the student's apparent lack of recognition that marks are earned. Rather it seems the student views teachers as random dispensers of marks. Consequently, assessment is like gift-giving at holiday time. Students present the teacher with a product and hope the teacher reciprocates by "giving" them good marks. If students are lucky and the teacher is in a favourable mood, they get a good mark; if the teacher doesn't like how students chose to do the assignment, they get a lousy grade.

Since reading this article, whenever my university students' comments revealed an absence of personal responsibility for the mark I had awarded them, I would think to myself, "Oh, you don't like what I gave you for your muffin." Naturally, I was disappointed by these incidents because they signalled my failure to promote student ownership for learning. I began to explore ways of communicating the evaluation criteria (criteria are the qualities we look for in student assignments) and eventually by making more transparent the standards for evaluation (standards specify the extent to which the criteria are met). These were improvements, but I continued to own all the assessment cards—I was simply being more explicit in communicating to students what the rules were. Gradually I learned to share responsibility for assessment with my students by negotiating the criteria, jointly articulating the standards, and eventually involving students in peer and self-evaluation.

After several years of trial and error, I recall a student commenting that in previous university courses he would regularly ask what he had to do to get an "A." If he thought the instructor's requirements were too onerous, he would ask what was needed for a "B." In these classes, the standards were external to the student. Fortunately, the student felt differently about my course. Because he had participated in setting the criteria and standards, he didn't feel that they were simply my priorities, and he didn't have to worry or guess what mark I would give him because the assessment rubrics were there for him to apply. He saw my job as corroborating his assessments; I was no longer the dispenser of marks. At the end of the course, he remarked that for the first time in his university career he hadn't done the bare minimum to get an acceptable grade. Instead, he wanted to do his best—the marks weren't a factor, because he knew they would come. He knew what his "muffin" was worth because he had contributed to setting the rules for evaluating his achievement.

In this chapter, I discuss the challenges to and strategies for building student ownership of assessment. In particular, I explore four areas:

- creating meaningful assessment tasks;
- setting criteria;
- establishing standards; and
- supporting peer and self-assessment.

Creating Meaningful Tasks

I want to start by making a somewhat obvious point about the relationship between assessment and learning activities. We will be hard pressed to build student ownership in assessment if students are turned off by the tasks and assignments that are being assessed. Students are less likely to take ownership for how well they do if they don't care about the work they are doing. We would be well advised to keep three principles in mind when thinking of assessment tasks:

- **Less is more.** Students are more likely to be drawn into their work if they have more time to do it and if there is less of it—both in terms of the size of the individual tasks and the frequency of assignments. For example, instead of posing a dozen test questions, reduce the number by half and encourage students to do a more thorough job of the questions that are asked. We might learn as much about students' knowledge of a topic by asking them to

329

provide a detailed labelled diagram than we can by requiring an extended written explanation. Rather than grading homework assignments every week or research projects every second month, reduce their frequency and devote more time to helping students learn to better complete these tasks.

- **Students can contribute.** Another way of increasing the likelihood of students buying into an assessment task is to involve them in creating the task.
    - Ask students to draft examination questions and sample answers that are actually used as the basis of an end-of-unit test.
    - Provide students with a list of specific outcomes you wish to assess and invite them to propose projects or activities that are feasible to accomplish and would enable students to demonstrate their understanding of the intended outcomes.
    - Invite students to develop "source materials" for use in an assessment. For example, students might prepare accounts of various events containing four or five deliberately placed errors that other students would be expected to detect, or students might construct profiles of mystery famous people or historical events that other students would identify based upon the clues provided.
- **Assessments don't have to be boring.** We can go a long way towards increasing student "buy-in" by making our assessment tasks more interesting and relevant. Here are a few examples.
    - Game-show-type contests can be use to replace multiple-choice written quizzes.
    - Instead of a research essay on immigration, students might draft and send a formal brief to the minister responsible for immigration, or prepare and present an application for permanent residency in Canada to a mock immigration tribunal.
    - A biography of a famous person can be made more interesting by converting it into a request for a candid letter of reference or for responses to a census or attitude questionnaire completed from that person's point of view.

The opportunities to develop engaging assessments are limited only by our imagination.

Setting Criteria

Inevitably, when we assess something we rely on criteria. For example, if I announce that a particular movie is wonderful, I will have reasons for this assessment such as it had an exciting plot, breathtaking cinematography, and engaging actors.

These reasons reveal the implicit criteria forming the basis for my assessment of the movie. Unless we are explicit about our criteria, our assessments may be misleading since different people may employ different criteria. For example, someone else might judge the movie unfavourably because of the trivial message, implausibility, and lack of originality. Neither of us will be able to reconcile our assessments until we recognize the different criteria we used. This problem is even more acute if our assessments are based on narrow or inappropriate considerations. The problems of differing and, in some cases, dubious criteria may explain why some students have such vague ideas about what their work is worth.

Thus, the first challenge in building student ownership is to ensure that our assessments are based on a *relevant, representative,* and *manageable* set of criteria that are *clear* to students. These four considerations are, in effect, the criteria for identifying and justifying assessment criteria. Understanding these criteria for good assessment will help to ensure that the criteria we set on our own or in consultation with students are sound. Certainly, if we want students to set their own assessment criteria, we will want them to recognize when these four considerations are present.

RELEVANT CRITERIA

How do I know whether the criteria I select (or those that students generate) are good criteria for assessment? This is essentially a question about the relevance of the criteria, and relevance depends largely on the purpose of the assignment. For the most part, the objectives or curriculum outcomes for the activity should direct what we look for when assessing students' work. In social studies, it would not be relevant to evaluate a report or other piece of extended writing largely on the basis of grammar and punctuation. An emphasis on this set of assessment criteria is more appropriate in language arts or English composition because one of the main goals of these subjects, unlike in social studies, is mastery of the technical aspects of written expression. Rather, a piece of extended writing in social studies should focus (for the most part) on criteria such as clarity of communication, ability to use information to support a position, accuracy of information, and depth of analysis. These are the kinds of outcomes that social studies seeks to promote. On any individual assignment, the criteria should relate to the particular objectives for that assignment, which in turn should be connected to the more general goals or intended outcomes of social studies. Two strategies to help identify relevant criteria are as follows:

- **Consider the purpose.** One way to determine the relevance of a criterion is to consider the curricular intent or purpose of the learning activity. For example, two common purposes for writing a paragraph are to communicate ideas and to persuade people to accept a position. Any criteria that affect these purposes will be potentially relevant considerations (for example, clarity of expression, use of examples, organization of ideas, number and quality of arguments, amount and quality of supporting evidence). Conversely, it would be largely irrelevant whether the paragraph was written in the first or third person, unless the purpose of the paragraph was to make the reader feel as though the writer actually experienced the event being described.

- **Think of specific sample responses.** Thinking of very good and very poor sample answers is also effective in identifying criteria. For example, share with students a poorly written paragraph and an especially well-written paragraph. Ask them to identify what makes the outstanding paragraph so good and the inferior one so poor.

Interestingly, the poor examples are often more useful in identifying criteria. In Figure 31.1, "Sample Notes," students consider three sets of notes summarizing a short passage about the Inuit's use of the seal and the caribou. By considering the strengths and weaknesses of each set of notes, students learn to identify the relevant criteria for good notes.

REPRESENTATIVE CRITERIA

Assessment criteria should include a representative range of the important considerations. For example, when deciding on the merits of a proposed solution to a social problem, it would not be sufficient to consider only whether the solution was likely to be effective in addressing the problem. Other important considerations include fairness to all sides and feasibility. Articulating a representative range of criteria helps

FIGURE 31.1 SAMPLE NOTES

Below is a short passage on the Inuit's use of the seal and the caribou and three sets of notes summarizing this text. Identify the strengths and weaknesses of each set of notes.

RESEARCH TOPIC: Inuit use of seal and caribou

TEXT: In the fall, the Inuit hunt caribou with bows and arrows. The caribou have spent the summer grazing and are now fat. As well, their coats are getting thicker to protect them during the long winter. Caribou are also hunted in the late spring as they migrate north for the summer. The caribou are very important to the Inuit. The Inuit kill many caribou because much food and many skins are needed.

SAMPLE NOTES

#1	#2	#3
• bows and arrows • fall • coats • migrate north • important • kill • hides	• kill caribou in fall when they are fat • thick coats • also hunt in late spring • important for food and hides • many caribou needed	• Inuit hunt caribou with bows and arrows in fall • caribou have spent summer grazing • now they are fat • their coats are getting thicker • thick coats protect them during the long winter • Inuit also hunt caribou in late spring when caribou migrate north for summer • caribou very important to the Inuit • they kill many because much food and many skins are needed
Strengths:	Strengths:	Strengths:
Weaknesses:	Weaknesses:	Weaknesses:

students recognize the full set of requirements for a particular curriculum expectation. Table 31.1 gives some of the relevant criteria that may be applied to a sampling of social studies assignments.

MANAGEABLE NUMBER OF CRITERIA

Another factor to consider is the number of criteria for any given assignment. Obviously, younger students will be able to deal with fewer criteria than older students. Very young students may be able to handle only one or two criteria. Even with older students, it may be overwhelming to introduce many criteria at any one time. Although no one assignment need address the full range of criteria for a particular curriculum outcome, the broader range of relevant criteria can be assessed over the unit or term. One way to avoid overburdening students with too many criteria is to frame them in broader, more general terms that subsume several specific criteria. For example, "effective presentation manner" may be used in lieu of specifying several more detailed criteria, such as clarity and audibility of voice, posture, and eye contact. However, if the presentation is a major part of the assignment, then it may be unwise to lump these more specific criteria under the broader heading.

CLEAR TO STUDENTS

A final consideration is the need for clearly articulated criteria. Obviously, students will better understand both what is wanted of them and how well they have succeeded in completing their assignment if the basis for assessment is clearly specified. One of the most confusing tendencies is to identify criteria in vague terms such as "active listener" or "creative." Students must understand more precisely what we mean by them in order for criterion-based assessment to be effective. We are better off substituting more specific terms for ambiguous concepts such as "creativity" (for example, offers ideas not mentioned in class or that is not a very obvious possibility) and "active listening" (for example, attends carefully to what others say, refers to other students' ideas during discussions).

Assessment criteria can be articulated in two ways—in *descriptive* or *qualitative* terms. The type of terms used to specify criteria has implications for the quality of direction we provide students:

- **Descriptive criteria** specify the desired features entirely in directly observable or immediately identifiable terms that describe what is required. For example, descriptive criteria for assessing a paragraph may include:
  - Opens with a statement of position.
  - The body must contain three reasons for the position.
  - Closes with a summary statement.
- **Qualitative criteria** specify the desired features in evaluative terms—in terms of attributes or qualities that characterize the effectiveness of each constituent part. For example, qualitative criteria for assessing a paragraph may include:
  - Opens with a *clear* and *accurate* statement of position.
  - The body of the paragraph contains *plausible* and *relevant* reasons for the position.

TABLE 31.1 SAMPLE CRITERIA FOR ASSESSING SAMPLE ACTIVITIES	
Justification for a conclusion	• Is the information factually accurate? • Does the answer reveal depth of understanding? • Are the reasons supported with evidence?
Oral presentation	• Is the presentation thoughtfully structured? • Is it presented in a clear manner? • Does the presentation engage the audience?
Plan to solve a problem	• Is the solution doable? • Is it fair to all parties? • Will the solution solve the problem? • Is the solution safe to implement?
Co-operative group work	• Did students apply themselves to the task? • Were students willing to take turns? • Did students show sensitivity to the feelings of others?

- ◆ Closes with a *concise* and *powerful* summary statement.

Articulating criteria in descriptive terms has the advantage of being easier for students and teachers to recognize—for example, we simply look for the required number of sentences and reasons, and check that the closing sentence offers a summary. With younger students and generally in the early stages of students' work on a topic, it *may* be appropriate to specify criteria largely in descriptive terms—simply expecting students to come up with three reasons (for that matter, even one reason) for their position. The use of descriptive criteria makes most sense if our sole concern is that students understand the concept (for example, that they know what a reason or a topic sentence is).

The disadvantage of descriptive criteria is that they may not allow us to distinguish when the desired feature has been competently completed. For example, the three "reasons" provided may be largely irrelevant to the position taken, or the opening sentence may be confusing. With descriptive criteria, students may simply include the identified component without any attention to its quality. For this reason, we may be better advised to assess knowledge of concepts such as reason or topic sentence prior to asking students to use them in a paragraph. We might do this by asking students to provide a definition, recognize examples and non-examples, and offer a sample of each. Once students show their understanding, we will want to teach them what is required for effective application of these concepts. After all, it is not just any three reasons that we seek, but three "plausible" and "relevant" reasons.

Qualitative criteria identify those qualities that indicate effective application of the concept. In applying qualitative criteria we must judge the extent to which the requirements have been met (for example, how "clear" is the synthesis or how "plausible" are the reasons). Of course, we will need to help students recognize what is involved in satisfying these qualitative requirements.

There are various ways to foster students' understanding of assessment criteria.

- • Provide students with clear indicators of what may be involved in satisfying the criterion: "I know I am being *friendly* when I …
  - ◆ compliment others on their work,
  - ◆ offer to help others before they ask me to,
  - ◆ use friendly words and smile, and
  - ◆ am willing to share my supplies and my ideas."
- • Ask students to provide concrete indicators of each criterion: What does it look like? Sound like? Feel like? As suggested in the highlighted text, "Generating Criteria," students can be aided in making the transition from de-

scriptive to qualitative criteria by adding an additional question: "What are the underlying qualities that make these actions and words effective?"

- • Invite students to restate in their own words the criteria for an assignment.
- • Provide student samples that meet and do not meet the assigned criteria and ask them to compare these samples (for example, Which of the three examples of notes on Inuit use of seal and caribou meet the criteria for clear, comprehensive, and concise note-taking?).

DECIDING UPON CRITERIA

Before leaving the discussion of criteria, it is worth considering the question: "Who should set the criteria?" As is the case with virtually all educational decisions, the answer depends on the circumstances. While, generally speaking, it may be desirable to involve students in establishing assessment criteria, there are times when this is not feasible or worth the effort required. For example, if students lack knowledge of the topic, they may be able to offer little to the discussion about criteria. In these situations, students would need to learn more about the topic before discussing criteria. For major assignments or assignments in which student ownership is especially important, it may be worthwhile to devote the time needed to jointly set criteria; on other occasions, it may be sufficient simply to invite students to comment on or suggest additions to the criteria you propose. In most occasions, the class as a whole should be able to agree on the criteria; however, it may sometimes be useful to allow individual students to add unique criteria of their own. Sharing samples of exemplary and non-exemplary performance, as was suggested with the three versions of notes described earlier, provides a valuable focus for class discussions of criteria.

> Imagine you have just asked students to create an information drawing or poster about a particular community or country. Identify, in terms that would be clear to students, three or four relevant and representative criteria drawn from the curriculum outcomes for a particular grade. Explain how you would ensure that all students understood the learning objectives for this task.

Establishing Standards

Identifying assessment criteria is only the first step in building student ownership of assessment; we must then decide what counts as meeting these objectives. As suggested earlier, this is a matter of articulating the levels of achievement or standards

GENERATING CRITERIA[1]

As a first step in generating criteria, ask students to brainstorm what success on a task looks and sounds like. The focus in the following example is harmonious group work. In two columns as indicated below, record student suggestions about what harmonious groups look and sound like (typically these will be identified in terms of descriptive criteria). Ask students to look for the qualities underlying or implicit in these sights and sounds—these are likely to be qualitative criteria. For example, students nodding at each other or saying, "that's a good idea" are examples of supportive behaviour. After identifying the underlying qualities for all the suggested actions and words, ask students to review their list of criteria:

- Are all the suggestions relevant? (For example, it might have been suggested that the "look" of a harmonious group requires that everyone be sitting down.)
- Is the list representative of the important features of a harmonious group?
- Should some criteria be eliminated or combined to make the list a more manageable number?
- Is each criterion clearly stated (that is, does everyone know what each means)?

HARMONIOUS GROUP WORK	
Looks like	**Sounds like**
students smile at each other students look at each other students nod to each other	"What do you think about this?" "That's an interesting idea." "Are you okay?"
Underlying qualities	
are supportive/encouraging of each other are interested in the ideas of others are sensitive to each other's feelings	

for each criterion. The task of specifying standards is a matter of deciding the degree to which each criterion has been met (for example, What would a "clear" position statement look like? How would this differ from a "very clear" position statement?). Articulating standards is important for three reasons:

- **Supports student learning.** There is immense educational value in helping students recognize when their work meets or fails to meet certain standards. Students may know that their report will be assessed on criteria, such as clarity and organization, but it is another matter for them to appreciate what a very clear or moderately well-organized paragraph looks like. Standards communicate to students what is required to succeed (partially or completely) in meeting these criteria. Instead of learning simply that they did well, articulating standards helps students learn what "doing well" means, and what doing even better would require.

- **Facilitates fair grading.** Articulating standards is necessary if we are to translate performance on an assignment into a grade or other summative judgment. What does "at grade level" look like and how does this differ from "above" or "below" grade level? How good is 30 out of 35? Is it "outstanding," warranting an A or an A⁺? Or is

it "very good," warranting a B or B⁺? Perhaps it warrants some other grade? Teachers and students should share a common understanding of the basis for these performance levels, which means we need to be clear about the standards we are using. This is especially true when students take part in peer and self-assessment. When a single teacher assesses a class set of assignments, there is some expectation that a common set of standards will have been applied even if the standards were not explicitly articulated. Consistent standards are unlikely when thirty different students are assessing themselves and others.

- **Builds student ownership.** Making the bases for our assessments more explicit assists in changing students' mindsets from one of "What grade did you *give* me?" to one of "Where along this scale does my work fall?" If the standards are well articulated and students are trained in making careful, fair-minded assessments of their work and that of their peers, the teacher's role in assessment becomes less prominent, relegated increasingly to checking the soundness of students' assessments.

JUSTIFYING STANDARDS

Although judgment is inevitable in justifying standards, the decision should not be arbitrary. Standards, whether in the form of letter grades or in evaluative terms such as "excellent" and "poor," can be justified on either norm-referenced or criterion-referenced bases.

- **Norm-referenced standards** are determined by how well a particular product or performance matches the work of a normal or typical population (for example, Is this a "typical" performance for a grade 6 student? Would only about thirty per cent of the class meet this level? Would this be within the top ten per cent of the province?). Norm-referenced judgments are based on the extent of students achieving a given level. For example, some universities insist that not more than twenty per cent of students in a given class receive an "A." Notice that with norm-referenced standards, it is theoretically impossible for all students to get a top score—students are rated relative to how well other students perform. To this extent, norm-referenced standards may discourage co-operation among students, because as students do better, the standard becomes higher for everyone.
- **Criterion-referenced standards** are determined by benchmarks that are not directly dependent on how well others in the population perform, but on an external reference (for example, what is needed in order to read the newspaper, be understood by an intelligent reader, successfully meet an agreed-on goal). Criterion-referenced judgments are based on expectations that are not dependent on what the average student is likely to achieve, but on an independent level of expectation. With criterion-referenced standards, it is theoretically possible for everyone to achieve a high rating.

Neither norm-referenced nor criterion-referenced standards should be arbitrary—there should be a reasonable basis for setting each level. Criterion-referenced standards may be justified in terms of what would likely be required in order to be employable, or to read and understand the newspaper, or complete a task (for example, by grade 3, students should be able to write a clear, four-sentence paragraph; after completing the unit, students should have mastered eighty per cent or more of the content on this exam; by the end of elementary school, students should be able to draw warranted inferences from newspaper articles). Norm-referenced standards may be justified in terms of the places available in the next educational level or a "normal" distribution of the population (for example, the bell curve—the top ten per cent get "excellent," the next twenty per cent get "good," and so on)—or a comparison with what "average" students have done in previous years.

Pre-established standards in certain areas are available from provincial ministries of education. For example, Table 31.2, developed by the British Columbia Ministry of Education (2001, 19, 61, 139), summarizes performance standards for three aspects of social responsibility at various grade ranges.

When setting standards for our own assignments, we should be sensitive to both norm- and criterion-referenced considerations. There is little merit in adopting a criterion-based standard that either no student could meet because it is too demanding or would challenge no one because it is too easy. In other words, we should temper this standard with norm-referenced expectations. Conversely, it seems counterproductive to decide beforehand on norm-referenced grounds that on a given assignment only the top five students will be allowed to do "very well" and at least five students must do "poorly." Rather, we should rely on published guidelines, past experience, and our own professional intuitions about what are fair and educationally realistic expectations. In justifying the standards articulated in the "thoughtful report" example appearing below, I tempered my impression of a truly masterful essay to accommodate the reasonably expected abilities of secondary students—I should not require them to operate at a level expected of graduate students. Just as with the setting of criteria, it would be appropriate to ask students to comment on the reasonableness of the proposed expectations. Or perhaps in some circumstances, we can help students set the standards for "good" and "very good" performances on an assignment.

COMMUNICATING STANDARDS

Assessment standards that are identified simply by a set of labels (for example, excellent, good, satisfactory, poor) offer little help to students. These labels identify the levels but don't explain or articulate what is required for each. The most common way of articulating standards is through an assessment rubric, which is a scale describing the criteria and standards for an assignment or test. Two types of scales are used in rubrics:

- **Holistic scales** cluster criteria so that the description of standards for all criteria are aggregated—one would make a single overall judgment about an assignment taking into consideration all the criteria. The rubric in Figure 31.2 offers a holistic scale for judging which one of five descriptions best characterizes the overall thoughtfulness of a report on a social issue.
- **Analytic scales** specify the standards for criteria separately, and one would make judgments for each criterion used to assess an assignment. The rubric in Figure

TABLE 31.2 SAMPLING OF STANDARDS FOR SOCIAL RESPONSIBILITY

ASPECT	EXCEEDS EXPECTATIONS	FULLY MEETS EXPECTATIONS	MEETS EXPECTATIONS (MINIMUM LEVEL)	NOT YET WITHIN EXPECTATIONS
Contributing to the classroom and school community (kindergarten–grade 3 expectations)	• Welcoming, friendly, kind, and helpful • Participates in and contributes to classroom and group activities; often takes on extra responsibilities	• Usually welcoming, friendly, kind, and helpful • Participates in and contributes to classroom and group activities	• Usually friendly and, if asked, will help or include others • May need prompting to participate in and contribute to classroom and group activities	• Often unfriendly or disrespectful of others • Generally reluctant to participate in and contribute to classroom and group activities
Solving problems in peaceful ways (grade 4–5 expectations)	• Considers others' views, and uses some effective strategies for resolving conflicts; takes responsibility and shows good judgment about when to get adult help • Can explain an increasing variety of problems or issues and generate and evaluate strategies	• Tries to manage anger, listen to others, and apply logical reasons to resolve conflicts; usually knows when to get adult help • Can explain simple problems or issues and generate and select simple, logical strategies	• Tries to state feelings and manage anger; often needs support to resolve conflicts, frequently overestimating or underestimating the need for adult help • Can identify simple problems or issues and generate some strategies; tends to rely on the same strategies for all problems	• Does not take responsibility or listen to another's views in a conflict situation; tends to blame and put down others • Has difficulty stating problems or issues, and may be unable to suggest or choose appropriate strategies
Valuing diversity and defending human rights (grade 8–10 expectations)	• Respectful and ethical; speaks out and takes action to support diversity and defend human rights, even when that may not be a popular stance	• Respectful and fair; increasingly willing to speak up or take action to support diversity and defend human rights	• Usually supports those who speak up or take action to support diversity and defend human rights	• Sometimes disrespectful; may stereotype or avoid those perceived as different in some way

31.3, "Self-assessment of role play," discussed later in this chapter, is an analytic scale used to self-assess students' performance in a decision-making simulation on four criteria—acting in role, contributing ideas, supporting others, and seeking a "win-win" solution.

An advantage of holistic scales is that we need make one judgment only. This often reduces the time required to assess student work. The disadvantage of holistic scales is that students may overlook particular criteria embedded in the global descriptors. On the other hand, analytic scales focus students' attention on each aspect of an assignment. When self-assessing, it may be easier to begin with analytic scales so students can attend to one criterion at a time. Having said this, the difference between analytic and holistic scales may

be a matter of degree: specific criteria can always be clustered into more general categories, thereby modifying an analytic scale so that it more closely resembles a holistic scale. The social responsibility rubric shown earlier is a modified analytic scale. The ministry has grouped several criteria within each of the three general categories of contributing to community, solving problems, and defending human rights.

Another variable in assessment rubrics is the level of detail in the descriptions of performance levels—rubrics can be fully articulated or skeletal in their detail (Mertler 2001):

• **Fully articulated rubrics.** The most elaborate rubrics richly describe each level of performance. These "fully articulated" rubrics are difficult to develop, requiring numerous revisions before balanced and precise descrip-

FIGURE 31.2 HOLISTIC RUBRIC: THOUGHTFUL REPORT

SCORE	DESCRIPTION OF REPORT
4	**Accomplished and very thoughtful.** The report clearly identifies all the main ideas of the issue. The discussion explains the important points carefully and with lots of detail. Personal opinions are well explained and supported with convincing examples and believable reasons.
3	**Competent and thoughtful.** The report is generally clear about the main ideas of the issue. The discussion explains most of the important matters in a careful manner. Personal observations are generally supported with relevant examples and believable reasons.
2	**Some thoughtfulness, but flawed.** The report identifies some of main ideas of the issue, but misses other important ones. The discussion explains some important points, but often states the obvious or overlooks basic points. Personal opinions are supported with a few reasons and examples that are not always convincing.
1	**Little or no thoughtfulness.** The report does not clearly identify any of the main ideas of the issue. The discussion does very little to explain the important points. Personal opinions are not supported with relevant examples and believable reasons.
0	**Not done.** No report submitted.

tions are produced. Unless the descriptions of standards are clear and mutually exclusive (i.e., no overlap between descriptors), the rubric is unreliable. Fully articulated rubrics may be worth the effort, especially for major projects involving student self- and peer assessment. The elaborate descriptions provide considerable guidance, clarity, and consistency, which are especially important when students adopt an assessor's role. However, because they are difficult to produce, it may be wise to use fully articulated rubrics with major projects where the time required to develop the rubric will pay off in terms of enhanced student achievement.

- **Skeletal rubrics.** On a more regular basis it may be advisable to use less elaborate rubrics in which the de-

scriptions for each level are not articulated in detail. In most of these cases, standards can be delineated using a single word or phrase describing various levels of performance—"always," "often," "occasionally," and "rarely." See the rubric in Figure 31.3 for students to use in self-assessing their efforts during a role play of a simulated town hall meeting. Where possible, use words that clearly communicate the basis for distinguishing between each level (for example, quantity of correct answers, degree of clarity, extent to which criterion is present) rather than words such as "excellent" or "poor," which are vague evaluative terms and, therefore, less specific about the differences between levels.

GUIDELINES FOR DEVELOPING FULLY ARTICULATED RUBRICS

- **Generating criteria.** Brainstorm criteria for assessing the assignment for which the rubric is being developed.
- **Prioritizing criteria.** Select the most important and relevant criteria, justified in light of curriculum expectations and your purpose for the assignment.
- **Consolidating criteria.** Cluster criteria around common themes. Consider rephrasing some criteria more generally to reduce the number of specific criteria. Make a provisional selection of a manageable number of criteria, organized into categories (for example, presentation,

content, research). Be especially careful about vague terms such as "creativity" and "critical thinking." Where possible, use precise criteria (for example, goes beyond the obvious, questions the accuracy of the author's claims, offers evidence to support position).

- **Setting levels.** Decide on the number of performance levels or standards to specify—rubrics commonly articulate between three and five levels. With younger students, three levels may be most appropriate. More than five levels may
continued on next page

be too difficult to distinguish for any students. Besides, it is always possible to assign a mark midway between two levels.

- **Selecting the variables to distinguish performance levels**. Each level of performance can be distinguished in two ways:
  - alter the extent and degree to which the criterion has been met. For example, performance levels for "clear explanations" may range from *"every important* idea has been *clearly* explained" through "the *most important* ideas are *generally clearly* explained" to "*no clear* explanations are provided".
  - add an additional condition at certain levels of performance. For example, the highest performance level for "clear explanations" may be distinguished by inclusion of an additional expectation ("every main idea has been clearly explained in the students' own words") that is not present in the other descriptors ("the main ideas are generally clearly explained" or "no clear explanations are provided").

Many rubrics are flawed in their use of variables to distinguish performance levels in two ways:
  - use of quantitative variables to distinguish entirely descriptive criteria. For example, performance levels for "provides reasons" may range from "provides *three or more* reasons" through "provides *two* reasons"" to "*no* reasons provided." The problem rests with reliance on purely descriptive features. Is a student who provides three reasons that are irrelevant and unsound actually performing at a higher level than a student who provides only one irrelevant, unsound reason?
  - use of inconsistent variables across performance levels. For example, it would be inappropriate to distinguish levels for "provides reasons" with descriptors that range from "provides several *plausible* reasons" through "provides a few *clear and relevant* reasons" to "reasons are *not supported with any examples*"). The problem arises because different *kinds* of variables (plausible, clear, relevant, supported with examples) are used at each level. Performance levels should be distinguished by varying the degree of achievement for common variables.

- **Draft polar descriptors**. Begin by describing the standards at the very top and the very bottom of the scale: What would the best performance look like? What would the worst level of performance look like? Decide whether the performance is better articulated in a single description (making it a holistic scale) or whether, for ease of preparation and clarity to students, discrete descriptions are more useful (making it an analytic scale). Because it is better to start with the best that students can achieve rather than the worst, many assessment experts recommend describing the highest performance level on the left-hand side of a rubric and the lowest level on the right-hand.

- **Draft intermediate descriptors**. The most difficult task in creating a rubric is describing the in-between standards. It may be helpful to look at existing rubrics for ideas on the kinds of words to use in distinguishing different gradations of performance. An advantage of using an odd number of performance levels (three or five levels) is that the intermediate levels can be distinguished by splitting the difference between the poles. For example, on a five-point scale, the third level would be exactly midway between the descriptions of a "one" and a "five," and the second level would then be midway between the descriptions of a "one" and a "three." With an even number of levels, it is necessary to divide the distance between the poles into equal intervals. For example, on a four-point scale, the second level is one-third of the distance between the descriptions of a "one" and a "four," and the third level is two-thirds the distance between a "one" and a "four."

- **Refine draft**. After developing an initial version of the rubric, check that the descriptors distinguish variables in mutually exclusive and precise terms, and that the intervals between the levels are "approximately equivalent" (i.e., the amount of improvement between any two levels should be roughly the same). This step is the most demanding and frustrating since it is difficult finding precise words to distinguish each performance level for each criterion. Very subtle changes in wording may make all the difference between a reliable rubric and one that provides little guidance. Be especially careful about the use of vague terms such as "good" or "successful," since the very point of articulating standards is to operationalize for students what these kinds of terms look like.

- **Finalize the performance levels**. Assign labels to each level and decide, in light of the relative importance of the criteria, the weight to be attached to each criterion. If appropriate, decide on the grade to be awarded for each range of marks by asking the following sorts of questions: "If a student received 15 out of 20 marks on this assignment, what grade does this mark deserve?" "What about a 10 out of 20?" Translating a mark to a grade requires deciding whether to use criterion- or norm-referenced standards. Will it be based on what percentage of the class will be allowed to receive an A, B, C, and so on (hence norm-referenced), or is there an independent benchmark to which we can refer (hence criterion-referenced), or should it involve a balancing of both considerations?

- **Pilot the rubric.** Before using a rubric in an actual assessment situation, score a sample of assignments to uncover any unanticipated problems or flaws. If this is not feasible, ask for critical feedback from someone who has not participated in developing the rubric (for example, Based on these descriptions, would you know what a "good" or "fair" assessment requires? Does the weighting of marks seem reasonable? Are the levels clearly distinguished?)

FIGURE 31.3   SELF-ASSESSMENT OF ROLE PLAY

During the meetings I acted in role ... ☐ almost never ☐ about half the time ☐ all of the time	Evidence to support my evaluation:
During the meetings I contributed my ideas ... ☐ almost never ☐ a few times ☐ whenever appropriate	Evidence to support my evaluation:
During the meetings I supported other people's ideas ... ☐ almost never ☐ a few times ☐ whenever appropriate	Evidence to support my evaluation:
During the meetings I worked to find a "win-win" solution ... ☐ not at all ☐ made an effort ☐ worked very hard	Evidence to support my evaluation:
I made my greatest contribution during the meetings when I ...	

Recently, educators have expressed concerns about the misuse and negative implications of rubrics. For example, Alfie Kohn reports a teacher's observation that her students appear "unable to function unless every required item is spelled out for them in a grid and assigned a point value" (2006, 13). Rather than building ownership in learning, for some students rubrics have accentuated their focus on doing things simply for the marks. These problems can be lessened by ensuring that assessment criteria reflect important curriculum outcomes and by articulating assessment standards in qualitative terms that reflect the intent of the assignment.

In addition to providing or involving students in developing rubrics, we can help students understand assessment standards in several ways:

- Provide actual samples of previous students' work at each performance level.
- Provide a set of standards and ask students to assess their own work and identify what would be required to bring it up to the next level.
- Ask students to prepare a sample answer to match each performance level on the scale. For example, students

might write a "weak," "good," and "excellent" answer to a question.

Supporting Peer and Self-Assessment

It is essential when building ownership for learning that we involve students in assessing their own work and that of their peers. This can be as simple as inviting students to informally review an assignment in light of several identified criteria or as formal as assigning a mark based on an assessment rubric.

The highlighted text, "Introducing Peer Critique," contains detailed suggestions for grooming students as self- and peer assessors. Below are a few general guidelines to consider:

- Begin by critiquing the work of those not in the class. Before asking students to put their work on the line, invite the class to critique something you have produced (for example, an essay you wrote as a student, a mock presentation you make). When it is time for peer critique, start with group assignments so the responsibility is shared among several students. Ensure that the early instances of critique are low-risk, relatively easy to perform, and have an obvious benefit (for example, bonus marks).

- Emphasize peer and self-assessment as critique—seeing the positives, not just the negatives. In the early days of peer critique, do not allow negative comments—only allow positive remarks. A good indication of when to allow comments about concerns/weaknesses is when students start asking each other for what is "wrong" with their work.

- Establish and model a few simple guidelines for giving peer critique: perhaps students should (1) start with two (or more) positive comments before offering a (single) concern, and (2) phrase negative comments in the form of a query (for example, I'm not sure I understand why you did it this way. Could you help me see what you had in mind?).

- Make sure students understand the criteria and standards they are to use in assessing their work and the work of others. Because of the inconsistent standards that different students will apply, it may be best to limit peer or self-assessment to informal critique unless there is a rubric for students to use.

- Until students demonstrate the ability and commitment to assess conscientiously and fairly, it is ill-advised to use their assessments for awarding marks. Because teachers have the ethical and legal responsibility for assigning grades, reserve the right to veto any student-assigned mark that is clearly unwarranted.

- Provide feedback to students about the quality of their assessment judgments. In order to signal to students that peer and self-assessment are important, you may want to assess their assessments. The rubric in Figure 31.4 might be used to assess students' self-evaluation of the role play illustrated earlier.

FIGURE 31.4   ASSESSING STUDENTS' SELF-ASSESSMENT OF THEIR ROLE PLAY PERFORMANCE

	WELL DEVELOPED	COMPETENT	UNDERDEVELOPED
Justification for self-assessments	Offers clear and specific evidence to support each self-assessment and the evidence is highly consistent with the assigned rating.	Offers some evidence to support each self-assessment and the evidence is generally consistent with the assigned rating.	Offers no evidence to support any of the self-assessments or the evidence is clearly inconsistent with the assigned rating.
Reasonableness of personal ratings	Every one of the ratings seems completely deserved given the student's performance in the role play.	The ratings seem generally deserved given the student's performance in the role play.	The ratings seem completely undeserved given the student's performance in the role play.

INTRODUCING PEER CRITIQUE

When introducing students to peer critique, it is advisable to model the procedure initially in a whole class setting, with an assignment volunteered by a student(s) willing to undergo public scrutiny (alternatively, use a former student's assignment). Afterwards, students can repeat the process with their own assignments in small groups.

Review the criteria

Begin by reviewing two sets of criteria with students—the criteria related to the assignment being critiqued and the criteria for peer critique.

- *Criteria for judging the assignment.* Review with students, perhaps with an overhead transparency or a checklist distributed to each student, a handful of criteria that students are to consider when commenting on the selected assignment. Limit the number of criteria to four or five, especially if students are new to the enterprise. You might also ask students to look for specific strategies that contributed or did not contribute to achievement of the criteria (strategies for achieving clarity include using specific examples, supplementing oral comments with visual aids, limiting the number of points made).

- *Criteria for peer critiques.* Explain to students that just as there are criteria for judging the merits of an assignment, so too there are criteria for successful critiques. Explain the following criteria:
  - *respectful*: comments should not be mean-spirited,

insulting, or condescending (stress the importance of this criterion)

- *relevant*: comments—whether positive or negative—should not be trivial or off-topic but connected to the criteria for a successful assignment
- *specific*: comments should identify particular aspects rather than very vague remarks (using an example, illustrate the value of specific compared to vague comments)
- *constructive*: draw attention to the fact that the primary purpose of critique is to improve performance—not to belittle or to criticize; therefore advice on how to improve is preferable to comments that merely note areas of strength and weakness

Examine the assignment

While examining the assignment to be critiqued, invite students to make written notes in light of the criteria discussed. It may be sufficient for students to record comments in two columns—"Positive Features" and "Areas for Improvement." A more sophisticated approach is to subdivide the columns into rows, one for each criteria that students are to consider. Students would then explicitly look for "positive features" and "areas for improvement" for each criteria. In the following chart, students would indicate the criteria they are considering for both strengths and "Areas to think about."

Set the terms of the critique

Once the assignment has been reviewed, structure the sharing of the critique in the following manner:

- *Lead with the positives*. I firmly believe that critiques should always begin with "unqualified" comments on the "strengths" of the assignment. This reduces the considerable anxiety that all of us feel when we subject our work to scrutiny. Even when reminded about starting with the positives, students have a tendency to slip into qualified (partly negative) comments. Politely interrupt whenever

apparently positive comments begin to take on an implied criticism. As well, students will often have difficulty coming up with positive comments—not because they are not there in the assignment but because we are prone to notice what is wrong. Beforehand, prepare a list of positive comments to infuse into the discussion in the event that student-generated comments are not forthcoming. Remind students that the point is not to show off or to make others feel inadequate, but to help fellow students produce the best possible product.

- *Suggest areas for improvement*. Only after abundant expression of the strengths should concerns or areas of improvement be expressed. Encourage students to provide specific suggestions about how the assignment might be improved.

Coach the recipient of the critique

Just prior to the critique, encourage the student (or group of students) receiving the critique to assume an active listening role—limiting comments to asking for clarification or elaboration, checking for understanding and whether or not ideas offered by individual commentators are shared by others in the class. Encourage recipients not to be defensive, and not to feel that they should defend what they have done. Their role is to hear what others have to say, and after the critique is over, to decide for themselves which, if any, of the comments are worth acting upon. Praise students for agreeing to subject their work to public scrutiny.

Debrief the critique

Close the activity by asking for student observations, beginning with the recipient(s) of the critique. The teacher's role throughout should be to acknowledge how difficult peer critique can be, especially for recipients, but to stress that the experience can be very fruitful when the criteria of peer critique are well met. Encourage students to integrate the comments from the critique of their assignment into their final draft.

STRENGTHS

CRITERIA	NOTES

AREAS TO THINK ABOUT

CRITERIA	NOTES

Conclusion

There are, of course, many other factors to consider and issues to explore in learning to build student ownership of assessment. As well, there are many practical hurdles to overcome as we unpack the "black box" of assessment for our students. My own experiences have convinced me of the importance, for educational and ethical reasons, of ensuring that students clearly understand and have some ownership of assessment of their work. In fact, class discussions about previously vague criteria and unarticulated standards have led to fruitful examination by me and my students about what it is that students need to learn. Being clear and committed to the criteria and standards for assessment can only lead to improved teaching and learning.

ACKNOWLEDGMENT

I am grateful to Robert Hogg of the Alberta Assessment Consortium and Rosemary Evans of Branksome Hall School for their helpful suggestions in preparing this chapter.

ENDNOTE

1   This example was suggested by Tom Morton, a secondary school teacher in Vancouver.

REFERENCES

British Columbia Ministry of Education. 2001. *BC performance standards: Social responsibility—A framework*. Victoria, BC: Ministry of Education, Student Assessment and Program Evaluation Branch, Province of British Columbia. http://www.bced.gov.bc.ca/perf_stands/social_resp.htm.

Emblem, S. 1994. So, what did I get on my muffin? *SnapShots 4* (2): 4–5.

Kohn, A. 2006. The trouble with rubrics. *English Journal* 95 (4): 12–15. http://alfiekohn.org/teaching/rubrics/htm.

Mertler, C. 2001. Designing scoring rubrics for your classroom. *Practical Assessment, Research and Evaluation* 7 (25). http://pareonline.net/getvn.asp?v=7&n=25

Nicol, J. and R. Case, eds. 2003. *The resourcefulness of the Inuit*. Richmond, BC: The Critical Thinking Consortium.

Northey, D., J. Nicol, and R. Case, eds. 2003. *Brazilian rainforest*. Richmond, BC: The Critical Thinking Consortium.

32 Assessment Strategies for Elementary Classrooms

Roland Case, Stefan Stipp, and Ray Appel

In this chapter we explore six common strategies for student assessment:

- regular written assignments;
- quizzes and tests;
- in-class observations;
- essays and research reports;
- projects or culminating tasks; and
- portfolios.

The principles to guide teachers in their assessment practices were discussed in an earlier chapter, "Four Principles of Authentic Assessment":

- Focus assessment on *what really matters.*
- Assessments must provide *valid indications* of student competence.
- Use assessment to *encourage student learning.*
- Assessment practices must *use teachers' time efficiently.*

The first two of these principles focus on developing assessment strategies that are valid measures of the important goals we have set for our teaching. Distinguishing between an assessment *target* and an assessment *strategy* helps to explain the nature of this requirement. An assessment target is the learning outcome we hope to assess (for example, understand key concepts, ability to think critically, ability to read maps). The assessment strategy is the means by which we will find out how well students have met the target. For example, we might assess students' ability to read a map using any number of strategies including in-class assignments, map-related questions on a quiz, in-class observations of group work, or a culminating project involving map reading. There is no single best assessment method. Each strategy has its merits and shortcomings depending on the target and context of the assessment. The ultimate decision about which strategy (or strategies) to use for a particular assessment target depends on the validity of the measures, how best to support student learning, and the most efficient use of teacher time.

Before looking at how to select and develop assessment strategies consistent with these principles, we begin by considering the advantages and disadvantages of six common strategies, and what can be done to maximize their effectiveness. In Table 32.1 is a thumbnail sketch comparing the main kinds of assessment strategies used in elementary grades. As we will see, these strategies overlap in many respects, but it is useful to distinguish them for discussion purposes.

Regular Written Assignments

The most frequent sources of evidence of student achievement are the activity sheets and written tasks completed by students as they learn each day. In some respects these are ideal assessment opportunities—they are frequent, provide tangible evidence of learning, and are a seamless part of instruction. Despite these advantages, there are concerns associated with the use of written assignments. The most obvious issue is the impediment presented by early primary students and second-language learners who cannot write. Another concern is the implications of regularly attaching marks to written assignments for students who need more time to learn.

FRAMING ASSIGNMENTS FOR NON-WRITERS

Written assignments can be framed for use with non-writers. One approach is to arrange for parent volunteers or older students to record non-writers' answers. Another approach is to use images. As suggested by the example in Figure 32.1, students can communicate their answers by sorting cards into piles. In this case, the teacher would read the description of each incident and students would paste each event on a sheet of paper under the appropriate column—"memory" or "not a memory."

In the next example in Figure 32.2, students might circle their desired answer that they would recognize after considering various clues. The teacher would read the clues one at

TABLE 32.1 STRENGTHS AND SHORTCOMINGS OF COMMON ASSESSMENT STRATEGIES

	STRENGTHS	SHORTCOMINGS
Regular Written Assignments	<ul><li>allow for ongoing feedback</li><li>involve no extra work to prepare since they are part of the instructional plan</li><li>can provide for in-depth work</li></ul>	<ul><li>present difficulties for students who have difficulty writing or who are unable to write</li><li>may not build from one assignment to the next</li><li>penalizes students who need practice time before they are ready to be assessed</li><li>may involve considerable marking on an ongoing basis</li></ul>
Quizzes and Tests	<ul><li>may be quick to mark, especially if they involve multiple-choice questions</li><li>provide a summary snapshot of student learning</li><li>can assess for a breadth of information</li></ul>	<ul><li>may focus largely on recall of factual information</li><li>often don't address a broad spectrum of curriculum outcomes</li><li>may cause stress for some students</li><li>tend to focus on short-term learning</li></ul>
In-class Observation	<ul><li>may reveal insights that would not otherwise be identified by other types of assessment</li><li>can assess abilities that are difficult to capture on paper</li><li>allow for immediate feedback</li><li>require no after-school marking</li></ul>	<ul><li>hard to manage given the real time demands of teaching a class</li><li>difficult to observe every student equally</li><li>one-time efforts may not present a true picture of students' abilities</li></ul>
Essays and Research Reports	<ul><li>allow for ongoing feedback</li><li>can provide for in-depth study of a topic</li></ul>	<ul><li>may involve a lot of student homework</li><li>are typically time-consuming for teachers to mark</li></ul>
Projects and Culminating Tasks	<ul><li>can be more fun, engaging, and worthwhile than other assessment tasks</li><li>can draw together learning over a unit</li><li>can assess for a breadth of knowledge and abilities</li><li>often further students' learning while they complete the task</li></ul>	<ul><li>may require considerable in-class and out-of-class time relative to the educational benefits</li><li>students can become bored if tasks drag on or are seen as "make work"</li><li>may be difficult to use common criteria when assessing different student projects</li></ul>
Portfolios	<ul><li>build student ownership in learning and assessment</li><li>are effective at tracking growth over time</li><li>encourage student goal-setting and self-monitoring</li></ul>	<ul><li>can become the mere accumulation of "stuff"</li><li>may require a lot of time to review and evaluate</li></ul>

a time and students would circle all the objects identified by each clue. In the upcoming example in Figure 32.4, the teacher would read out the question stem and students would respond by circling one of the faces (happy, sad, or neutral) to indicate their agreement or disagreement with the statement.

MARKING REGULAR ASSIGNMENTS

There is little disagreement about the value of providing qual-

ity feedback (whether from the teacher or from fellow students) on virtually every assignment students complete. It is another matter whether each of these assignments should be graded for reporting purposes. For years it was commonly recommended that teachers assess students on a large number of assignments to ensure that students would not be penalized significantly for an occasional poor performance. This practice has begun to be questioned because of the unfairness of assessing students before they have had ample opportu-

FIGURE 32.1   SORTING MEMORIES

I had such a great time at the beach this summer.

My birthday is next week.

I am sitting on the floor.

When I was little I ate dog food once.

FIGURE 32.2   SOLVING THE MYSTERY

It is something to eat.

It comes warm.

It is long and skinny.

nity to learn what is expected of them. More recent thinking recommends that only students' best work be assessed. Since the primary purpose of classroom assignments is to help students learn, holding students accountable for their performance while they are still learning is considered unfair. This is analogous to a theatre critic reviewing a play midway into the rehearsal period. No doubt some of the actors will have their roles in good shape but many others, including those who may deliver the finest performances on opening night, may still be exploring their character.

A parallel concern arises over the penalizing effect on students who end up mastering the material but do not do so as quickly as other students. Imagine a situation where three assignments are focussed on the same outcome (for example, understanding how to read maps). Suppose the following results are recorded for two students over the course of a unit:

	Assign-ment #1	Assign-ment #2	Assign-ment #3	Average mark	Best result
Mindy	8	8	8	8 or B⁺	8 or B⁺
Chan	4	6	10	6.7 or B⁻	10 or A

When reporting on student achievement, it would be misleading and unfair to assign Mindy a "B⁺" and Chan "B⁻" since it is arguable that Chan's understanding of the curricular outcome is superior to Mindy's understanding. The averaging of marks on a particular outcome can have a discouraging effect, since students who struggle to learn a topic will realize that even if they do very well on the final opportunity their mark will be averaged down because of earlier poor performances. The problems with not allowing opportunities for students to learn without penalty are the reasons behind a popular adage that suggests: assess often and mark rarely.

Ensuring that we assign marks to students' *best* efforts does not necessarily mean that only the *final* effort should be graded. On any given day, students may do poorly for reasons unrelated to their knowledge of the topic. It would be unfair to penalize students who did well all term simply because they were distracted when the final assignment was completed. Another concern in relying exclusively on a final assignment is that the assignments over a term may not assess identical outcomes. If the three assignments in the above example did not assess the same topic, then the last assignment should not be the sole basis on the mark for the unit. The solution is to provide opportunities to learn without being graded and to grade students only under conditions that allow them to show what they have learned.

Quizzes and Tests

Another common assessment strategy is the use of quizzes at the end of a unit of study to test how well students have mastered the content. This approach allows students to show what they have learned after they have had opportunities to study the material. Research suggests that student learning may be better served by frequent short tests rather than infrequent long ones (Boston 2002, 3), and by providing quality feedback and not simply assigning a mark (Black and Williams 1998, 144). The most significant factor in determining the value of a test is the quality of the questions.

For ease of student completion and teacher marking, quizzes tend to consist of two kinds of short-answer questions: either *closed-ended* questions such as multiple choice, true or false, labelling, and matching columns, or *open-ended* questions that can be answered in a few words or sentences. Although there is much that could be said about developing quality text items, we want to make two points only:

- use short-answer questions to assess beyond mere recall of information;
- ensure the validity of questions in quizzes and tests.

ASSESSING BEYOND RECALL

A common criticism of test questions is that they are often used to assess recall of information. This need not be so. Short-answer questions can be used to assess depth of understanding, critical thinking, social responsibility, and other important goals in social studies. Certainly, there are limits to what short-answer test questions can assess. For example, because of their format, multiple-choice questions can only measure students' abilities to select correctly from a set of supplied answers. In addition, multiple-choice questions reduce complex learning outcomes to individual test items, whereas we may be concerned with students' abilities to integrate what they know in realistic situations. While these limitations provide powerful reasons for using "alternative" strategies, there is a role for tests beyond measuring information recall. For instance, open-ended short-answer questions can be used to assess student reflection by inviting students to revisit initial ideas or opinions after they have had a chance to study and think more about the matter. Figure 32.3 outlines students' pre- and post-unit reflections on a famous person. Responses can be marked by assessing post-unit responses in terms of the accuracy of their answers, the insightfulness of their reflections, and their open-mindedness.

As the example in Figure 32.4 illustrates, closed-ended questions can also be used to gather information about student attitudes. Margaret Chapman, a British Columbia primary teacher, developed this device to assess her children's empathy for people in other countries (1991, 69). Before and after studying the needs of people in Chile, Margaret read the questions to her grade 1 students and they circled the appropriate face depending on whether they agreed (the "happy face"), were not sure (the "so-so face"), or disagreed (the "sad face") with each statement.

WATCHING FOR VALIDITY

In using short-answer questions, we may be misled into thinking we are measuring something that we are not. Consequently, it is important to check that we actually measure the outcomes we have targeted. A common oversight with short-answer questions is that of presuming to assess students' *understanding* of a concept by asking students to offer a definition of the word. Understanding a concept is a much broader notion than recalling the definition. For example, a

---

FIGURE 32.3 HERO OR CELEBRITY?

After studying about famous people, students might consider whether a particular personality (for example, a rock star, athlete, politician) is a genuine hero. Students might offer a preliminary assessment at the beginning of a unit and, based on further deliberations, reconsider their conclusions at the end of the unit.

My first opinion was that _____ was a ☐ genuine hero
                                                  ☐ not a genuine hero

because _____

_____

_____

I have ☐ changed
        ☐ not changed

my opinion because _____

_____

_____

FIGURE 32.4 ASSESSING FOR EMPATHY

1. We want all my friends to be like me.	😊	😐	☹
2. We should help other, poorer countries even if it means we have to give up things.	😊	😐	☹
3. We like learning about people who live in other countries.	😊	😐	☹
4. It is only important to me what happens to other people we know.	😊	😐	☹

discussion about "fairness" may lead some children to believe that fairness means everyone receives the same thing in an equal amount. To some extent, we have taught students this when we say that everyone in the class will receive the same object such as a snack. Yet, we know that some students may be allergic to nuts, or require another kind of snack due to dietary concerns. Under these circumstances, it would not be fair to give these students the same food.

Assessing conceptual understanding requires more than asking for a definition that students may have memorized. Students need to provide fresh examples of the concept or explain why certain situations are not examples of the concept. For example, when assessing younger children's understanding of the concept of "fairness," we might ask them to explain whether or not it is fair to give everyone the same food in the dietary examples discussed above.

In-Class Observations

Another assessment strategy is to observe students' classroom behaviour and listen to their talk. This approach, sometimes referred to as "naturalistic assessment," involves the teacher as a participant-observer—collecting information about student learning while engaged in the normal duties of teaching. In some respects, teachers are involved in naturalistic assessment every time they confirm that students have understood a lesson, or check to see whether students have done their work, or ask students to indicate any difficulties they are having. The difference between these ad hoc assessment strate-gies and naturalistic assessment lies in the extent of systematic collection of information and whether records are kept for use in student reporting.

In-class observations are particularly appropriate for assessing student abilities and attitudes not measured by traditional pen-and-paper assignments or by isolated assessment tasks. In addition, extended observation is more likely to provide rich accounts of student learning and insightful indications of factors that may influence learning, than are one-shot tests. Formal in-class observations make use of various information-gathering strategies:

- anecdotal "field notes" about significant comments or incidents—for example, by noting the strategies that a particular student uses to solve a problem, or by watching over several months for indications of students' growth in self-esteem or attitudes towards school work;
- student-teacher conferences as a means of gathering information about students while helping them learn;
- checklists or other devices to record the incidence of particular behaviour—such as completion of work, the number of books read, or students' co-operative participation in group assignments. The checklist in Figure 32.5 records how well students can use various aids to locating information.

Often, like an anthropologist, the teacher will seek to "triangulate" evidence, using several sources of information to corroborate judgments about students. For example, in drawing conclusions about students' critical-thinking abili-

FIGURE 32.5   LOCATING INFORMATION CHECKLIST

Uses information-locating aids: 0 = not at all / = somewhat ✓ = adeptly	STUDENTS					
	SAUL	PAM	CHAN	NIAM		
locate section in table of contents	/	0	✓	✓		
locate page in index	✓	0	✓	✓		
find word in glossary	✓	/	✓	✓		
find word in dictionary	✓	/	✓	✓		
skim paragraph to locate information						
use headings to locate information	0	/	✓	✓		
...						

ties, a teacher may use information obtained from peer and self-assessment of students' willingness to entertain alternative opinions, analyses of selected products for the quality of reasoning, and suggestive anecdotal comments about attitudes towards "thinking things through."

In-class observation by students is a means of inviting them to reflect on their own learning as they work. Not only does peer observation and self-monitoring save teacher time, but it is an important learning opportunity for students. As well, students may have access to information that would not be readily available to the teacher. For example, the classroom observation device in Figure 32.6 can be used by students (or by teachers) to peer assess co-operative group work.

> Identify one or two outcomes from the curriculum that would usefully be assessed by the three assessment strategies discussed thus far in this chapter (regular written assignments, quizzes, and in-class observations). Briefly outline what each strategy might look like if you were to use them to assess the selected outcome(s).

Essays and Research Reports

The use of extended-answer questions such as essays, reports, and position papers is a common assessment strategy with upper elementary and secondary students. These are generally a more holistic measure of learning than short-answer questions. There are, however, several limitations:

- essays are heavily dependent on students' writing fluency;
- students may be overwhelmed by the demands of large writing projects, particularly if used in earlier grades; and
- essays are time-consuming to mark.

For these reasons it is worth considering whether the traditional research report merits the prominence it has in some social studies classes.

Many students dislike writing reports and often do little more than transcribe ideas drawn directly from reference books. The suggestions contained in chapter 11, "Escaping the Typical Report Trap," will help greatly in reducing the im-

---

FIGURE 32.6   CO-OPERATIVE DECISION MAKING

Your name: _____   Group member's name:_____

1. For each criterion listed below, circle the number that most accurately reflects each person's behaviour while carrying out the project.
2. Wherever possible, describe an actual situation or identify a typical behaviour that is supporting evidence for your assessment.
3. Use a separate sheet for each person. Do not show your assessment to, or discuss it with, anyone else.

	Rarely or never in evidence	In evidence about half the time	Consistently in evidence	Not enough information to decide
1. Willingness to reconsider position	1 2	3	4 5	no information
Supporting evidence:				
2. Willingness to defend personal opinion	1 2	3	4 5	no information
Supporting evidence:				
3. Respectful of persons who disagree	1 2	3	4 5	no information
Supporting evidence:				
4. Challenges in responsible ways	1 2	3	4 5	no information
Supporting evidence:				
5. Works towards establishing consensus	1 2	3	4 5	no information
Supporting evidence:				

pediments to extended written reports. Even then, students might learn more effectively from smaller, less daunting assignments that place greater emphasis on multiple revisions of their ideas. Certainly we should expect students to think for themselves and not simply assemble ideas from other sources.

The merits of any given extended-answer assignment depend on the quality of the question or task. At the very least this requires providing students with explicit, unambiguous directions. We think it also helps to provide (or to help students generate) a structure for organizing their report. For example, the question "Research and defend your personal position on establishing a world government" could be made to focus more clearly on thinking critically about the ideas (rather than rehashing undigested arguments found in books). To do this, the assignment might be described as follows:

Present and defend your personal position on establishing a world government using the following structure:

1. explain in your own words what this would involve;
2. identify and explain the major reasons to support your position;
3. identify and explain the major reasons that opponents might offer against your position; and
4. justify your position by arguing why the supporting reasons are more convincing than the reasons against your position.

Projects or Culminating Tasks

A relatively recent alternative approach to assessment, often referred to as performance assessment, focusses on students' completing realistic tasks that a person would typically face as a citizen, writer, businessperson, scientist, community leader, historian, and so on. These tasks may involve performing a feat or producing a product.

Performing a feat
- perform a dramatic scene depicting a historical event
- hold a formal parliamentary debate on a controversial piece of legislation
- teach fellow students about family traditions
- organize and run a school fundraising event
- conduct a trial around a historical incident
- adjudicate between nominees for an award
- make a presentation to city council on a proposed change to local laws

Producing a product
- build a model of a logging site or of an ancient village
- make a film about promoting racial harmony
- create a set of exam questions and sample answers for an end-of-unit test
- prepare a "consultant's report" on a local pollution problem
- develop a foreign-language script for a radio play
- create "museum" displays depicting local history
- create a web page on the history of the school
- publish a (contemporary or historical) class newspaper or journal

Because they typically involve realistic tasks, performance assessments are more likely than traditional methods to measure students' ability to apply a complex set of "real-life" abilities and understandings. The emphasis in performance tasks is on knowledge-in-use, as opposed to regurgitation of "school" knowledge. Also important is their potential as a learning opportunity and not exclusively as an assessment tool: the working-through of the tasks should enhance—not simply measure—student understanding. A performance task to plan a summer vacation (described in Heckley Kon and Martin-Kniep 1992) illustrates these features. In this assessment, pairs of students are given a map of California and a list of state parks with camping facilities, and asked to plan the details of a family camping trip from the San Francisco area to any state camping facility in northern California. Students must measure distances, calculate travelling time, describe particulars of the travel route, and develop a contingency plan in the event of a strike by workers on the Golden Gate and Bay bridges. As well, they have to negotiate with a partner the destination and route that best accommodates the interests of family members.

As this example suggests, performance assessments can be engaging. It is suspected that some students do poorly on evaluations because they are unmotivated. The perceived irrelevance and drudgery of, for example, an extended written report may discourage some students from trying to do well. If we want to assess what students are *capable* of doing, it is only fair that we provide opportunities where students are likely to want to do well.

Because performance tasks are complex, they provide opportunities to assess a variety of outcomes using many methods, including:

- interviewing students about their experiences during the project and about their conclusions;
- analyzing students' preparatory materials for quality of research;

- analyzing group discussions for evidence of thoughtfulness in preparing reports/products and in justifying group decisions;
- assessing students' written or oral reports for quality of language use and presentation, and for content knowledge;
- scoring classroom discussions or debates for evidence of students' ability to engage in thoughtful dialogue.

Key features in developing performance assessments are choosing the task, setting the context, providing appropriate direction, and, when possible, creating an audience for students to present their work. A performance task should allow students to integrate what they have been studying into a culminating performance or product. It would be unfair to assess students on matters they have not been working with; the novel dimension of performance assessment is the drawing together of the various elements they have studied in order to solve a realistic problem. Setting a realistic context for the task provides a rich opportunity for students to think through their options. Students also require appropriate direction about the nature and requirements of the task.

In a unit on family members, the culminating project involved primary students in creating and presenting a memory box to celebrate family members. Throughout the unit, students had recalled memories associated with various relatives and then decided on the most powerful positive memory for each member. Students identified various objects associated with each powerful memory and then selected the best memorable object for each memory. These selected items were placed in each child's memory box which was shared at a celebrating families event. The rubric in Figure 32.7 was used to assess students' understanding of the concept of memory, their ability to identify memories and memorable objects, and their ability to judge the most powerful memory and memorable object for each family member.

Portfolios

The final assessment strategy we consider involves students in compiling a collection or portfolio of work they have completed over a period of time. Portfolio assessment draws heavily on the practices of artists and designers, who carefully assemble samples that represent key characteristics of their work for use in demonstrating particular competencies to others. Assessment portfolios are characterized in a similar vein, as "a purposeful collection of student work that exhibits the student's efforts, progress, and achievements in one or more areas" (Paulson, Paulson, and Meyer 1991, 60).

Because portfolios are based on cross-sections of student work completed over time, they offer a richer portrait

SUGGESTIONS FOR DEVELOPING CULMINATING PROJECTS

- Identify the important outcomes for a unit.
- Think of "real-life" feats or products that, if completed successfully, would represent exemplary achievement of several key outcomes.
- Determine more precisely the details of the performance assessment, including:
    - the realistic nature and the context of each task;
    - the amount of direction to provide students regarding what they need to consider to complete the task and how they might proceed.
- Orally or in writing, provide students with a clear articulation of the requirements and parameters of the task.
- Consider what students must know in order to successfully complete the task. Ensure sufficient prior instruction to allow students a reasonable chance of competently undertaking the task. Assessment tasks can be made easier by providing detailed direction or additional instruction.
- For each of the desired outcomes, determine the criteria to be used in assessing students' feats or products. Share the criteria with students prior to their completing the task.
- Determine how information about the criteria will be collected (for example, through observation, conferencing, analysis of written products). Where appropriate, devise rubrics, checklists, or other marking sheets.
- After using the performance assessment, consider how it may be improved for next time. Asking students for their comments may be helpful in this regard.

of a wider range of student achievements than, say, a single end-of-unit test. Also, unlike traditional forms of assessment, where assignments are marked and then forgotten, portfolios encourage both teacher and students to monitor growth over time. Typically, students are involved to varying degrees in selecting, analyzing, assessing, and reporting on the products that make up their portfolio. This involvement often results in significantly greater personal ownership of their learning. These benefits are particularly likely when portfolios are used as the focus for conferences where students explain to their parents or teacher what the portfolios show about their progress and levels of achievement. In fact, it has been suggested that portfolios be seen primarily as "a reason for talking" (Murphy and Smith 1990, 1)—that is, the collection of products is essentially a means to engage students, teachers, and parents in informed dialogue about learning.

Portfolios may be general in focus, covering many subjects, be subject-specific (for example, a social studies portfolio), or even topic-specific (for example, My Inuit Portfolio). Asking students to focus on one area can help them see that

FIGURE 32.7 ASSESSING FAMILY MEMORIES

	SOPHISTICATED UNDERSTANDING	EXTENDED UNDERSTANDING	BASIC UNDERSTANDING	PARTIAL RECOGNITION	PRE-RECOGNITION
Understands concept of memory	Correctly distinguishes memories from non-memories when given simple examples, and correctly states in own words the difference between the two terms.	Correctly distinguishes memories from non-memories when given simple examples, and provides own example of both terms.	Correctly distinguishes memories from non-memories when given simple examples.	When provided with simple examples of memories and non-memories, can correctly identify some of them.	When provided with a simple example of a memory, cannot identify it as a "memory."
Recalls family memories	Recalls many family memories with considerable detail, including the feelings evoked.	Recalls three or four family memories with some detail, including the feelings evoked.	Recalls with modest detail one or two of the most obvious family memories.	Understands what is asked, but can just barely identify a family memory.	Does not understand what is asked when invited to identify or recall a family memory.
Identifies powerful memory	Offers a powerful memory and explains the feelings evoked.	Offers a powerful memory with a simple explanation.	Offers a rather predictable powerful memory without much explanation.	Offers a powerful memory that is not very "powerful."	Unable to identify a powerful memory.
Identifies memorable objects	Identifies several memorable objects associated with a story about a family member.	Identifies two memorable objects associated with a story about a family member.	Identifies the most obvious memorable object associated with a story about a family member.	Understands what is asked, but identifies an object that is unconnected to the memory or the family member.	Does not understand what is asked when invited to identify a memorable object.
Chooses a best memorable object	Chooses a best memorable object and explains the feelings evoked.	Chooses a best memorable object with a simple explanation.	Chooses a predictable best memorable object without offering any explanation.	Chooses a best object that is not very memorable.	Unable to choose a best memorable object.

learning can be represented in different ways within the one area. When collecting samples of learning in social studies, students could web, list, write, videotape, draw, or brainstorm their understanding of specific concepts.

Portfolio assessment has five phases.

- **Accumulation of products.** At the beginning of the unit when portfolios are to be used, establish procedures for collecting and storing all student work. The date when work is completed should be indicated on every assignment. If a specific set of outcomes has been identified as

the theme for the portfolio, then ensure that students have varied opportunities during the term to produce work in these areas. The range of student materials produced during a unit, term, or year may include the following:

- annotated bibliographies of books or documents read
- artwork (preliminary sketches and final products)
- audiotapes
- book reports
- charts and graphs
- drawings

- essays (drafts and final copies)
- evaluations of self and peers
- group reports
- interview results
- journals or diaries
- maps
- notes (classroom, laboratory, or field)
- peer evaluations
- photographs of projects, models, displays, or murals
- reading inventories
- tests and quizzes
- videotapes of presentations, debates, interviews, or simulations
- worksheets

- **Selection of portfolio pieces.** From the total array of products, direct students to select a sampling for inclusion in a portfolio. Near the end of a unit, discuss with students how they are to select those work samples. Students should have some discretion in selecting portfolio contents. The selected products may represent the student's best efforts, or be indicative of typical performance. They may focus on a particular theme such as growth as a critical thinker, development of a global perspective, or appreciation of culture. It may be important to limit the *number* of pieces to include in a portfolio, since thoughtful analysis becomes unwieldy if many pieces are examined. A summary or checklist (possibly a table of contents) may be helpful.

- **Reflection.** Alone or in collaboration with peers, each student reviews the portfolio contents as a vehicle for assessing achievement or progress over the term. These reflections might involve identifying criteria and standards, analyzing patterns or key features, diagnosing strengths and problem areas, and setting personal plans and targets. Providing samples of other students' work at various performance levels may assist students in assessing their own work.

- **Reporting.** Students should be expected to report (orally or in writing) on what they observe about their learning and to recommend a plan of action. Student-led conferences with the teacher, and often with parents, are common ways of student reporting. Alternatively, students might prepare audiotaped analyses of their portfolios. It may be helpful for students to prepare and practise their oral reports with fellow students. For younger students the reporting might be as simple as the following:

The topic for my portfolio is _____

The two pieces we selected that show my learning are:
1. _____
2. _____

Things we did well:
1. _____
2. _____

Things we might improve upon:
1. _____
2. _____

My plan for next time is _____
_____

- **Feedback.** Feedback from the teacher (and parents) may occur on two fronts: (1) on student achievement or progress over the term, as evidenced in the portfolio; and (2) on the quality of student analysis and reporting since the portfolio is itself a product representing students' capacity for critical self-assessment and personal accountability. For young students the feedback might be a simple as "two stars and a wish"—noting two positive aspects and an area for improvement.

Portfolio creator _____

Two stars:
★ _____
★ _____

One wish:
→ _____

Conclusion

In this discussion we have explored various issues and techniques that deserve consideration when developing assessment strategies consistent with the principles of authentic assessment for elementary students. Our overarching objective in presenting the six strategies described here is to encourage assessment practices that are valid, fair, and that richly support student learning.

Identify four or five complementary outcomes from the curriculum. Using the three strategies discussed in the second half of this chapter (essays, culminating projects, and portfolios), briefly outline what each might look like if you were to assess the selected curriculum outcomes.

ACKNOWLEDGMENT

We wish to thank Robert Hogg of the Alberta Assessment Consortium for his helpful suggestions when revising this chapter.

REFERENCES

Abbott, M., C. Ford, and R. Case. 2003. *Celebrating families*. Richmond, BC: The Critical Thinking Consortium.

Black, P. and D. Williams. 1998. Inside the black box: Raising standards though classroom assessment. *Phi Delta Kappan* 80 (2): 139–148. Available online at http://www.pdkintl.org/kappan/kbla9810.htm.

Boston, C. 2002. The concept of formative assessment. *Practical Assessment, Research and Evaluation* 8 (9): 1–5. Available online at http://PAREonline.net/getvn.asp?v=8&n=9.

Chapman, M. 1991. *Nurturing a global perspective among primary students, using Chilean arpilleras*. Unpublished Master of Education project, Simon Fraser University, Burnaby, BC.

Heckley Kon, J. and G. Martin-Kniep. 1992. Students' geographic knowledge and skills in different kinds of tests: Multiple-choice versus performance assessment. *Social Education* 56 (2): 95–98.

Murphy, S. and M.A. Smith. 1990. Talking about portfolios. *The Quarterly* 12 (2): 1–3, 24–27.

Paulson, F.L., P.R. Paulson, and C.A. Meyer. 1991. What makes a portfolio a portfolio? *Educational Leadership* 48 (5): 60–63.

Appendix
Comparing the Elementary and Secondary Volumes

The following chart shows the congruence between chapters in the *The Anthology of Social Studies Volume 1, Issues and Strategies for Elementary Teachers,* and *Volume 2, Issues and Strategies for Secondary Teachers.* This may be of use to instructors who are teaching a combined elementary and secondary class. Chapters that closely match each other are shown on the same line in the chart. In thirteen cases, the chapters are identical.

Ten other chapters are very similar except that different examples have been used to reflect the grade-level focus. These chapters will have identical titles with the exception of an elementary or secondary designation. In seven cases, different chapters are paired because they offer a parallel discussion. For two elementary and four secondary chapters, there is no corresponding match in the other volume.

	VOLUME 1: ELEMENTARY	VOLUME 2: SECONDARY
Part One: Foundations	1 Challenges and choices facing elementary social studies teachers *Neil Smith*	1 The teaching of history and democratic citizenship *Ken Osborne*
	2 Purposeful teaching in elementary social studies *Roland Case and Mary Abbott*	2 Purposeful teaching in secondary social studies *Roland Case and Mary Abbott*
	3 Four defining purposes of citizenship education *Penney Clark and Roland Case*	3 Four defining purposes of citizenship education *Penney Clark and Roland Case*
Part Two: Ends and Means	4 Beyond inert facts: Teaching for understanding in elementary social studies *Roland Case*	4 Beyond inert facts: Teaching for understanding in secondary social studies *Roland Case*
Content knowledge	5 Beyond mere definition: Teaching for conceptual understanding in elementary classrooms *John Myers and Roland Case*	5 Beyond mere definition: Teaching for conceptual understanding in secondary classrooms *John Myers and Roland Case*
	6 Children's conceptions of space and time *Dennis Milburn*	
	7 Enriched by teaching aboriginal content *Lynn Newbery, Cathy Morgan, and Christine Eadie*	6 Enriched by teaching aboriginal content *Lynn Newbery, Cathy Morgan, and Christine Eadie*
	8 Teaching the tools to think critically *Roland Case and LeRoi Daniels*	7 Teaching the tools to think critically *Roland Case and LeRoi Daniels*
	9 Supporting a community of critical thinkers *Roland Case and Philip Balcaen*	8 Supporting a community of critical thinkers *Roland Case and Philip Balcaen*
Critical thinking	10 Historical thinking in the elementary years *Amy von Heyking*	9 Portals to understanding: Embedding historical thinking in the curriculum *Mike Denos*
		10 Portals to geographic thinking *Kamilla Bahbahani and Roland Case*
		11 Teaching a "critical" history *Avner Segall*

Acknowledgments

CHAPTER 2   "Social Studies is… A Poem" by Donna Robinson was originally cited in "Social Studies Poems," ed. John J. Chiodo, *Social Education* 54 no. 7 (November/December 1990): 467–468. © National Council of the Social Studies. Reprinted by permission.

Cartoon © John Anfin. Used by permission.

CHAPTER 4   "The 'Suburb of Happy Homes'" illustration by Fraser Wilson. First published in 1942 in the *Vancouver Sun* on the occasion of the fiftieth anniversary of Burnaby's incorporation.

CHAPTER 6   "Children's Conceptions of Space and Time" is an abridged and edited version of an article published in 1985 as "Children in Time and Space" in Jim Parsons, Geoffrey Milburn, and Max van Manen, eds., *A Canadian Social Studies*, 2nd ed. Edmonton: University of Alberta. 120–141. Used by permission.

CHAPTER 7   "The Road Less Travelled" cartoon is by Erica Ball, a librarian at Hazelton Secondary School, Hazelton, BC. Used by permission.

CHAPTER 8   Figure 8.1, Promoting Critical Thinking, is adapted by permission of the publisher from Mike Denos and Roland Case, *Teaching about Historical Thinking* (Vancouver, BC: The Critical Thinking Consortium, 2006), 75. © 2006 by The Critical Thinking Consortium.

Table 8.1, Thinking Critically About Logging Old-Growth Forests, is used by permission of the authors from Sharon Balin, Roland Case, Jerrold R. Coombs, and LeRoi Daniels, "Conceptualizing Critical Thinking," *Journal of Curriculum Studies* 31 (3): 285–302.

CHAPTER 10   Ancient Egypt illustration by Danna deGroot. Reprinted by permission of the publisher from David Scott, Cliff Falk, and Jenny Kierstead, *Legacies of Ancient Egypt* (Richmond, BC: The Critical Thinking Consortium, 2002), 75. © 2002 Ministry of Education, Province of British Columbia.

CHAPTER 11   Figure 11.2, Evaluating Resources on Canadian Explorers, is adapted by permission of the publisher from John Harrison, Neil Smith, and Ian Wright, eds., *Selected Critical Challenges in Social Studies—Intermediate/Middle School* (Richmond, BC: The Critical Thinking Consortium, 2004), 81. © 2004 The Critical Thinking Consortium.

Figure 11.3, Assessing Students' Notes, is adapted by permission of the publisher from Jan Nicol and Roland Case, eds., *The Resourcefulness of the Inuit.* (Richmond, BC: The Critical Thinking Consortium), 116. © 2002 Ministry of Education, Province of British Columbia.

"Summary of Emily's Talk" by Laura Brown is printed by permission of the author and that of her teacher, Vivian Brighten, and her mother, Wendy Pitt-Brooke.

CHAPTER 14   Figure 14.1, Documenting the Details, is adapted by permission of the publisher from David Scott et al., *Legacies of Ancient Egypt.* (Richmond, BC: The Critical Thinking Consortium). © 2002 Ministry of Education, Province of British Columbia.

CHAPTER 15   "The Eporuvians Come to Call": The Eporuvian role play was developed by Anne Hill, an elementary teacher in Terrace, BC. Used by permission.

CHAPTER 16   "Believe it or Not" is reprinted by permission of the publisher from Jan Nicol and Roland Case, eds., *The Resourcefulness of the Inuit.* (Richmond, BC: The Critical Thinking Consortium), 95. © 2002 Ministry of Education, Province of British Columbia.

CHAPTER 17   This chapter is reprinted by permission of the authors from Robert Fowler and Ian Wright, eds., *Thinking Globally about Social Studies Education.* (Vancouver, BC: Research and Development in Global Studies, University of British Columbia), 51–60. © 1995.

CHAPTER 18   Figure 18.1, Who Has a Responsibility, is adapted by permission of the publisher from Maureen McDermid, Mary Abbott, and Roland Case, eds., *Rights, Roles, and Responsibilities at School* (Richmond, BC: The Critical Thinking Consortium), 88–89. © 2003 Ministry of Education, Province of British Columbia.

Figure 18.2, Drawing the Line on Our Right to Food is adapted by permission of the publisher from Jan Nicol and Dan Kirk, *Caring for Young People's Rights.* (Richmond, BC: The Critical Thinking Consortium), 79. © 2004 The Critical Thinking Consortium.

CHAPTER 19   The articles in this chapter, which are reprinted by permission of the publisher, appeared originally in *Canadian Social Studies* volumes 26 (1), 23–26 (1991) and 27 (1), 28–29 and 30 (1992). © 1991, 1992 *Canadian Social Studies*, www.quasar.ualberta.ca/css. Minor alterations to the original articles have been made for stylistic and format purposes.

CHAPTER 20   Figure 20.1, Consequences for Stakeholders, is adapted by permission of the publisher from Roland Case, Cliff Falk, Neil Smith, and Walt Werner, *Active Citizenship: Student Action Projects.* (Richmond, BC: The Critical Thinking Consortium), 55. © 2004 The Critical Thinking Consortium.

Figure 20.2, Action Plan, is adapted by permission of the publisher from Roland Case et al., *Active Citizenship: Student Action Projects.* (Richmond, BC: The Critical Thinking Consortium), 57. © 2004 The Critical Thinking Consortium.

Figure 20.3, Reflecting on Our Project, is adapted by permission of the publisher from Roland Case et al., *Active Citizenship: Student Action Projects.* (Richmond, BC: The Critical Thinking Consortium), 69. © 2004 The Critical Thinking Consortium.

CHAPTER 22   Figure 22.6, Sample Unit Plan, is adapted by permission from a unit by primary teachers Janis Chappell, Robin Johnson, Kerrin McLeod, and Danielle Doucette.

"The Descent of the Fraser River" is a shortened version of "The Descent of the Fraser River" in M.G. Parks and C.W. Jefferys, illus. *Discoverers and Explorers in Canada—1763–1911* Portfolio II #4. (Imperial Oil Ltd., n.d.) Reprinted by permission.

CHAPTER 23   This chapter is used by permission of the author. An earlier edition appeared online in *Canadian Social Studies* 39 (2). © 2005 *Canadian Social Studies*, www.quasar.ualberta.ca/css.

CHAPTER 24   The lesson plan presented in this chapter is adapted from Mary Abbott, Roland Case, and Jan Nicol, *I Can Make a Difference.* (Richmond, BC: The Critical Thinking Consortium), 101–118. © 2002 Ministry of Education, Province of British Columbia.

CHAPTER 25   The lesson plan presented in this chapter is adapted from Jan Nicol and Roland Case, eds., *The Resourcefulness of the Inuit.* (Richmond, BC: The Critical Thinking Consortium), 61–65, 150–154. © 2002 Ministry of Education, Province of British Columbia.

CHAPTER 26   "Globe-Trotting Teddies" is adapted by permission of the author from Penney Clark, "Listening to the ambulance sirens: Is this any way to teach?" *Canadian Social Studies* 34 (3): 38. © 2000 *Canadian Social Studies*, www.quasar.ualberta.ca/css.

Figure 26.2, Sample Interview Form, is adapted by permission from Mary Abbott, Carole Ford, and Roland Case, eds., *Contributing to Family and Community,* (Richmond, BC: The Critical Thinking Consortium), 119–120. © 2003 Ministry of Education, Province of British Columbia.

Figure 26.3, Note of Appreciation, is adapted with permission from Mary Abbott et al., eds., *Contributing to Family and Community,* (Richmond, BC: The Critical Thinking Consortium), 121. © 2003 Ministry of Education, Province of British Columbia.

CHAPTER 27   Clay liver picture is used courtesy of Susan Duncan.

CHAPTER 28   The photo "The shame of the city: Can we give our children no better playing space?" courtesy Library and Archives Canada (C-030947). Used by permission.

The photo "Indians shamming to be at prayer for the sake of photography. Fraser River" courtesy British Columbia Archives (E-04419). Used by permission.

The photo "Hon. Donald A. Smith driving the last spike to complete the Canadian Pacific Railway" by Alexander Ross courtesy Library and Archives Canada (C-003693). Used by permission.

The photo "Hon. Donald A. Smith driving the last spike to complete the Canadian Pacific Railway" by Alexander Ross courtesy Library and Archives Canada (C-014115). Used by permission.

The photo "Canoe manned by voyageurs passing a waterfall" courtesy Library and Archives Canada (C-002771). Used by permission.

"Decipher the Drawing" is adapted by permission from David Scott et al., *Legacies of Ancient Egypt,* (Richmond, BC: The Critical Thinking Consortium), 3–5. © 2002 Ministry of Education, Province of British Columbia.

Ancient Egypt illustration by Danna deGroot. Reprinted by permission from David Scott et al., *Legacies of Ancient Egypt,* (Richmond: The Critical Thinking Consortium), 75. © 2002 Ministry of Education, Province of British Columbia.

CHAPTER 31   Figure 31.1, Sample Notes, is adapted from Jan Nicol and Roland Case, eds., *The Resourcefulness of the Inuit,* (Richmond: The Critical Thinking Consortium), 110. © 2002 Ministry of Education, Province of British Columbia.

Figure 31.3, Self-Assessment of Role Play, is adapted by permission from Don Northey, Jan Nicol, and Roland Case, eds. *Brazilian Rain Forest,* (Richmond, BC: The Critical Thinking Consortium), 106. © 2003 Ministry of Education, Province of British Columbia.

Figure 31.4, Assessing Students' Self-Assessment of their Role Play Performance, is adapted with permission from Don Northey et al., eds., *Brazilian Rain Forest,* (Richmond, BC: The Critical Thinking Consortium), 113. © 2003 Ministry of Education, Province of British Columbia.

CHAPTER 32   Figure 32.1, Sorting Memories, is adapted by permission from Mary Abbott et al., eds., *Contributing to Family and Community,* (Richmond, BC: The Critical Thinking Consortium), 95. © 2003 Ministry of Education, Province of British Columbia.

Figure 32.2, Solving the Mystery, is adapted by permission from Mary Abbott et al., eds., *Contributing to Family and Community,* (Richmond, BC: The Critical Thinking Consortium), 83. © 2003 Ministry of Education, Province of British Columbia.

Figure 32.7, Assessing Family Memories, is adapted by permission from Mary Abbott et al., eds., *Contributing to Family and Community,* (Richmond, BC: The Critical Thinking Consortium), 98. © 2003 Ministry of Education, Province of British Columbia.

Contributors

EDITORS

ROLAND CASE is the co-founder of and senior editor at The Critical Thinking Consortium. Prior to this he was professor of social studies education at Simon Fraser University. Roland has edited or authored over one hundred published works. In addition to teaching elementary school and at four Canadian universities as a professor, Roland has worked with fifteen thousand classroom teachers across Canada, and in the United States, England, Israel, Russia, India, Finland, and Hong Kong to support the infusion of critical thinking into classrooms. Roland is the 2006 recipient of the Distinguished Academics Career Achievement Award sponsored by the Confederation of University Faculty Associations of British Columbia.

PENNEY CLARK is an associate professor in the Department of Curriculum Studies at the University of British Columbia and the director of The History Education Network/Histoire et Éducation en Réseau (THEN/HiER). She teaches social studies curriculum and instruction courses to pre-service teachers and history of curriculum and politics of curriculum development courses to graduate students. She is a co-author of three Canadian history textbooks, which are authorized in several provinces. She has contributed articles to *The History of the Book in Canada* volumes I and II, *Canadian Journal of Education, American Journal of Education, Canadian Social Studies,* and *Theory and Research in Social Education.*

AUTHORS

MARY ABBOTT began her career as a primary teacher and subsequently taught all elementary grades, library, and special education. She currently works in teacher education at Malaspina University-College and she has also worked with pre-service teachers and practising teachers at Simon Fraser University. Her teaching areas have included social studies methods, language arts methods, and literacy development and assessment. As a member of The Critical Thinking Consortium, Mary was involved in the creation and editing of the primary level social studies resources and has been facilitating critical thinking workshops for several years.

RAY APPEL has used the critical thinking model in the classroom, and finds the students to be very engaged when their ability to think is valued. Ray has taught grades 2 to 7, and has been a faculty associate at Simon Fraser University, working with pre-service teachers in the Fraser Valley. He has also been a school district math/science coordinator, working extensively with teachers, students, and administrators. Ray is a contributing writer to Pearson Education Canada's *Math Makes Sense* (grades 4–7). He enjoys facilitating workshops, interacting with teachers.

PHILIP BALCAEN is a faculty member at the University of British Columbia–Okanagan in Kelowna where he teaches methods courses in mathematics and science education and graduate courses in curriculum studies, and facilitates the Learning Communities Seminars for pre-service secondary teachers. Previously, he taught at Simon Fraser University and in the public secondary school system in British Columbia. Philip is senior editor for The Critical Thinking Consortium's series of Science and Mathematics resources. His research interests include school-university collaboration, critical thinking, environmental studies, and computer-supported learning communities.

WANDA CASSIDY is an associate professor of education, and director of the Centre for Education, Law, and Society at Simon Fraser University. She is the author of several books, articles, and curriculum resources on law-related education. Her most recent book is *Once Upon a Crime: Using Stories, Simulations and Mock Trials to Explore Justice and Citizenship in Elementary School*. A former classroom teacher, Wanda is interested in fostering school environments that are rooted in the ethics of care and social justice.

CHUCK CHAMBERLIN was at the time of his death a professor emeritus in the Department of Elementary Education, University of Alberta. He was passionate in his commitment to social activism.

LEROI DANIELS is a professor emeritus in the Faculty of Education at the University of British Columbia. He is a founding member of The Critical Thinking Consortium and an author of the model of critical thinking that forms the conceptual foundation of the consortium's work. LeRoi has written various articles on critical thinking and was co-editor of Critical Challenges Across the Curriculum, a series of teaching resources for critical thinking.

LINDA FARR DARLING is a member of the Faculty of Education at the University of British Columbia. She is an associate professor of curriculum studies specializing in elementary social studies and in curriculum for early childhood education. She has received recogniton for her work with pre-service and in-service teachers, including the University's Killam Teaching Award in 2000. Her research interests are the ethical dimensions of teaching and the moral and social development of young children, topics that have made her a popular speaker for community and parent groups as well as at schools.

CHRISTINE EADIE emigrated from Holland to northern British Columbia when she twelve years old. At age fifteen she found a job working in a Hudson's Bay trading post. After university, Christine taught in a number of communities spanning a range of grade levels. More recently, she was a faculty associate in Simon Fraser University's teacher education program in northwestern British Columbia.

MARGARET FERGUSON is a teacher in northern British Columbia. She has a law degree from the University of Alberta. She was school reorganizing coordinator for the Legal Resource Centre, Faculty of Extension, University of Alberta for thirteen years, and has published numerous articles on law-related education.

JOHN FIELDING has retired from teaching Canadian and World History Curriculum at the Faculty of Education of Queen's University after 13 years. Previous to Queen's, John taught secondary school history for twenty-four years. John was the project manager for Ontario's Canadian and World Studies Curriculum. He continues to write textbooks (four in print), design learning resources, and consult on the teaching of Canadian history and global issues.

SUSAN GIBSON is a professor of social studies education in the Department of Elementary Education at the University of Alberta. She has spent the last ten years examining how technology can be used effectively to enhance learning and how best to prepare pre-service teachers for the integration of technology into the teaching of social studies.

GARFIELD GINI-NEWMAN is an instructor at OISE/University of Toronto. Previously he was a curriculum consultant with the York Region District School Board. During that time, he led teams in the development of history and philosophy curriculum for at-risk learners in grades 10, 11, and 12. He has spoken widely at conferences on critical thinking, brain research, curriculum design, and assessment. Garfield has also authored six textbooks and has taught in the faculties of education at York University and the University of British Columbia. Garfield taught high school history for many years.

LAURA GINI-NEWMAN is currently the instructional coordinator for Canada and World Studies and the social sciences with the Peel District School Board. Prior to entering education, she did doctoral studies in economics, attended law school, and was employed as a chartered accountant. She taught eleven years in the public education system and is an instructor for advanced qualification history courses at OISE/University of Toronto. Laura is a senior author of *Philosophy: Questions and Theories*, the text for the grade 12 philosophy course in Ontario.

LARRY GLASSFORD is a professor in the Faculty of Education, University of Windsor, where he teaches history and social studies curriculum and methods. He has also taught history and politics at the secondary school level. He is the author of *Reaction and Reform: The Politics of the Conservative Party under R.B. Bennett, 1927–1938* (University of Toronto Press 1992) and co-author of *Challenge of Democracy: Ideals and Realities in Canada* (Nelson 1984).

MICHAEL LING is a senior lecturer in the Faculty of Education at Simon Fraser University. He works primarily with in-service teachers in graduate diploma and degree programs. He is interested in what occurs at the intersection of culture, education, and the arts, in the ways they contribute to our collective and individual pursuit of meaning in the world, and to a meaningful life.

ROBERTA A. MCKAY is a professor in the Department of Elementary Education at the University of Alberta. She has authored social studies textbooks for use in elementary and secondary school. With her colleague Susan Gibson, she recently authored *Social Studies for the Twenty-First Century: A Review of the Current Literature and Research* (Edwin Mellen Press).

DENNIS MILBURN was a professor in the Faculty of Education at the University of British Columbia. His areas of interest included geography and early childhood education.

CATHY MORGAN began teaching primary grades in a small northern community in British Columbia in 1971. She has taught at the elementary and secondary levels. For several years, Cathy was a faculty associate in Simon Fraser University's professional development program, where she worked with aboriginal and non-aboriginal student teachers.

TOM MORTON is one of the founders of the British Columbia Co-operative Learning Association and is the author of *Co-operative Learning and Social Studies: Towards Excellence and Equity* (Kagan Cooperative Learning). In 1996, the BC Social Studies Teachers' Association named him teacher of the year and in 1998 he was awarded the Governor-General's Award for Excellence in Teaching Canadian History.

JOHN MYERS is currently a curriculum instructor in both elementary and secondary pre-service programs at OISE/University of Toronto. He has taught in elementary, secondary, and university classes in three provinces and three countries. His teaching and research interests include assessment and teaching strategies in differentiated instruction.

PAUL NEUFELD is an assistant professor of reading and learning disabilities at Simon Fraser University. His research interests are in the areas of reading development and instruction for students who struggle with learning to read.

LYNN NEWBERY graduated from the University of Toronto in the mid-sixties. She moved to a coastal community in British Columbia where she first discovered the excitement of teaching about First Nations history and culture. She has held teaching or administrative positions in secondary and elementary schools and been active in the communities in which she has lived. After retiring from the public school system, Lynn became a Faculty Associate at Simon Fraser University, working with student teachers.

ÖZLEM SENSOY is an assistant professor in the Faculty of Education at Simon Fraser University, where she teaches courses in social education, critical media literacy, and anti-oppression education. She is a contributing editor to the textbook *Who Are the Turks?* (American Forum for Global Education) and is a recent contributor to the journal *Radical Pedagogy.* Her current research examines the relationship between school-derived and media-derived knowledge about social groups.

NEIL SMITH is an instructor of social studies curriculum and instruction courses at Malaspina University College in Nanaimo, British Columbia. His particular area of interest is global education.

STEFAN STIPP has taught secondary humanities in Surrey, BC, for ten years. He has been a faculty associate in Simon Fraser University's teacher education program. Additional background about his work with portfolio assessment can be found in his master's thesis, "Tilling the Soil: Making Portfolio Assessment Work in an Integrated High School Humanities Setting."

AMY VON HEYKING is an associate professor in the Faculty of Education at the University of Lethbridge. Her areas of research include history teaching and learning and the history of school curricula in Canada. She is author of the teaching resource *Teaching with Dear Canada* (Scholastic Canada, 3 vols.), head author of the Teaching Social Studies Through Literature series (Scholastic Canada), and author of *Creating Citizens: History and Identity in Alberta's Schools* (University of Calgary Press).

WALT WERNER is a former social studies teacher who works in the Department of Curriculum Studies at the University of British Columbia. His current work focusses on visual literacy across the curriculum.

Index

Italicized page numbers indicate figures, tables, and highlighted text. Endnotes are indicated by "n" after the page number.

contemporary realistic literature, 310–11

folk literature, 311–12

historical fiction and biography, 311–12

law-related titles, 6, 181–82, 184

non-fiction, 307

objectives and curriculum fit, 307–8, 309–10

poetry, 312

resource lists, 317–18

local experts, 277–80

follow-up activities, 279, 280

interviews and surveys, 111, 276, 277, 278

planning and preparation, 280, 280

in unit plans, 235–36

logic and fallacies, 78, 79, 80, 83

M

maps

cognitive maps, 65, 164

as indicators of global perceptions, 162

mind maps, 55, 58n1, 247

spatial cognitive development, 61–64, 62, 63, 64, 65

McCord Museum of Canadian History, 135, 287

McDiarmid, Tami (teacher case study), 85

Media Awareness Network, 131

metacognition, 124

See also reflection

mind maps, 55, 58n1, 247

mock trials

in citizenship and law-related education, 180–81, 275

"neighbourhood conflict" example, 181

procedures for, 182, 183

required skills, 6, 6

Montgomery, Richard, 291

moral awareness, 84, 104, 159n1, 301

See also values education

Morgan, Cathy (teacher case study), 71

motivation, 42

assessment and, 319, 323, 326–27

from audiovisuals, 300

computer-based resources, 133, 134

for critical thinking and inquiry, 86, 120

for history learners, 245–50

from lesson introductions, 236–37

from readers' theatre and role-playing, 248, 315

research projects, 109

stories and narrative, 5, 306–7

multicultural awareness and education. See global/multicultural education

multimedia presentations, 131, 133, 281

museums, 72, 132, 135, 287

N

naming, of concepts, 50, 56, 57

National Council for the Social Studies (NCSS), children's literature listing, 310

nationalism, 155, 168

Newberry, Lynn (teacher case study), 69

New Land: A First Year on the Prairie (M. Reynolds), 314

Newmann, F., on citizenship education, 189

no call-out rule, 54

note-taking

assessment of, 118, 331, 333

collaborative, 124–25, 126

for field trips, 277

for others' presentations, 116

for research projects, 113, 114

See also information management (gathering, organizing, sharing)

O

"Obituary or Eulogy" history activity, 250

objectives, curricular. See outcomes and objectives, specific

Oldenberger, Steve (teacher case study), 202

Ontario social studies curricula

co-operative learning in, 16

goals, themes, and strands, 13, 14, 15, 17n1

overall expectations, 12

rationale, 14

specific outcomes, 9, 10

open-mindedness and flexibility

in course planning, 225

in critical thinking, 78, 83–84

in global/multicultural education, 164–65, 168, 170, 170n1

in values education, 151

optimism, in current events teaching, 171–74

organizing themes, 13, 14, 15, 231

outcomes, general. See goals, of course or unit

outcomes and objectives, specific

as assessment targets, 321, 330, 343

in course planning, 224, 230, 232

in critical challenges, 45

curricular purpose as context, 9–10, 10, 11

and general outcomes, compared, 12

identifying and sequencing, 232

in lesson plans, 236, 240

for literature activities, 307–8

in unit plans, 235, 237–38

See also expectations; provincial curricula

overall expectations. See goals, of course or unit

P

paintings, 290–91, 296–98, 297

Parker, Walter, 34, 35, 77

"Passing Along Kindness" lesson plan, 251–61

Paul, Richard, 77

peer assessment and feedback, 97, 326, 327, 339–41, 339, 340–41

See also assessment: student involvement and ownership

peer mediation, 184, 184

perception

concepts and, 48

of current events, 171–74

choice of values, 149–51
in citizenship education, *27*, *149*, 150, 189, 193–94, 195
in community classrooms, *92*, 93
controversial values, 150
in co-operative learning, 210–11
in course plans and vision, *227*, 228, *229*, *233*
as curriculum goal, *12*
direct experiences of, 152–53
historical artifacts and, 286
"Honouring Individual" example, *45*
"Immigration Quotas" example, *157–59*
in literature studies, 308, 311
nurturing values, 151–57
"Personal Coat of Arms" example, *155–56*
reinforcing environments for, 151–52
in social action projects, 199
universal values, 163
values analysis, 154, 156–57, *157–59*
values clarification, 154, *157–59*
Venn diagrams, 58n1, 125, *126*, 142, *287*
vision, in course planning, 173, 224, 225–28

visual resources, 290–303
    See also audiovisual resources
visual tools and graphic organizers
    graphic webs, *105*, 106
    mind maps, 55, 58n1, 247
    timelines, *10*, 116, *233*, 247, *287–88*
    Venn diagrams, 58n1, 125, *126*, 142, *287*
vocabulary
    for "Arctic Survival" lesson (needs vs. wants), 262
    in critical thinking, 79, *81*, 82, 83, *83*, 95
    in literature studies, 307
    See also conceptual knowledge

W

"War of 1812" example, *72*
webbing, 109, *110*, 258–59
WebQuest, 134–35, *135*, 137
Wesley, Edgar, 25, 33
Where the Spirit Lives (film), 152
Whitehead, Alfred North, 34, 35
Wrong, George, 33–34